WAR CRIMES IN INTERNAL ARMED CONFLICTS

Does international law make individuals responsible for perpetrating war crimes during internal armed conflicts?

Eve La Haye explores the content of international criminal law applicable in such conflicts and questions the 1995 finding of the Appeals Chamber of the International Criminal Tribunal for the Former Yugoslavia that responsibility could be enforced on the basis of customary international law. This finding is evaluated with regard to state practice and the practice of international organisations.

The means to enforce individual criminal responsibility for such crimes are also investigated. The states on whose territory the crimes took place have sometimes tried such perpetrators, but can other states prosecute perpetrators of war crimes under the principle of universal jurisdiction? The applicability of universal jurisdiction to war crimes committed in civil wars and the practice of domestic courts are examined, alongside the role and achievements of prosecutions carried out by international courts and tribunals.

EVE LA HAYE is a former Associate Legal Officer of the Appeals Chamber of the ICTY and is now Legal Advisor at the International Committee of the Red Cross, Geneva.

WAR CRIMES IN INTERNAL ARMED CONFLICTS

EVE LA HAYE

CAMBRIDGE
UNIVERSITY PRESS

CAMBRIDGE UNIVERSITY PRESS

Cambridge, New York, Melbourne, Madrid, Cape Town, Singapore,
São Paulo, Delhi, Dubai, Tokyo

Cambridge University Press
The Edinburgh Building, Cambridge CB2 8RU, UK

Published in the United States of America by Cambridge University Press, New York

www.cambridge.org
Information on this title: www.cambridge.org/9780521860734

First published 2008
Reprinted 2008
First paperback Edition 2010

Printed in the United Kingdom at the University Press, Cambridge

A catalogue record for this publication is available from the British Library

ISBN 978-0-521-86073-4 hardback
ISBN 978-0-521-13227-5 paperback

A mes parents

CONTENTS

vii

ACKNOWLEDGEMENTS

This book grew from many personal and professional experiences, researching and teaching at the London School of Economics and Political Science, working at the International Criminal Tribunal for the former Yugoslavia (ICTY) and taking part in the negotiations of the International Criminal Court (ICC) statute and the elements of crimes, and from stimulating discussions with many friends and colleagues along the journey.

Like any thesis, it would not have been possible without the help and support which I received from many people and institutions. First, I am particularly indebted to Christopher Greenwood, CMG QC and Professor of International Law at the London School of Economics (LSE) for his stimulating advice, critical suggestions and unrelenting support. I am most grateful for the financial support provided by the Art and Humanities Research Board, the Morris Finer Memorial Scholarship and the LSE law department.

I am immensely indebted to the Advisory Service on International Humanitarian Law of the International Committee of the Red Cross for giving me unrestricted access to their database and information sources. Particular thanks go to Monica Cometti, Knut Doermann, Thomas Graditsky, Anne-Marie La Rosa and Jean Perrenoud. I also benefited greatly from stimulating discussions and debates about my work with a number of friends or colleagues. Many thanks are due to His Excellency Judge Mohamed Shahabuddeen, Professor Luigi Condorelli, Colonel Charles Garraway (Ministry of Defence, UK), Herman von Hebel, Pierre Galinier, Catherine Marchi-Uhel and Darryl Mundis (ICTY), Niccolo Figa Talamanca (No Peace Without Justice), Reinhold Gallmetzer (ICC), Maria Kelt (Ministry of Justice of Sweden), Gérard Dive (Ministry of Justice of Belgium), J. F. R. Boddens Hosang (Ministry of Defence of the Netherlands) and Catarina de Albuquerque (Procuradoria-Geral da Republica – Portugal). Special thanks also go the library of the Graduate Institute of International Studies in Geneva, where I updated my work and to Gill Marchment for polishing the language.

A Ph.D. existence can be a solitary one, and so many thanks are due to my friends at the LSE between 1997 and 2000 as well as my colleagues and friends at the ICTY and International Criminal Tribunal for Rwanda (ICTR) in The Hague, in particular Katie Gallagher, Mélanie Deshaies, Daniela Kravetz, Elena Martin-Salgado, Claudia Hoefer and Inneke Onsea for their friendship and encouragement and for having made my time there so rewarding. Lastly, in the last sixteen months, during which I attempted to improve this manuscript, Sophie and Miranda provided me with much-needed moral support and two dear friends made many precious comments on various parts of this book. I am most indebted to Dr Salvatore Zappala and Guénaël Mettraux for their unfailing support and their challenging criticism of some parts of this work. Any errors or omissions which may unwittingly remain are mine.

Thanks are also due to Cambridge University Press and in particular to Finola O'Sullivan, Richard Woodham and Jane Belford for their patience and their help in the production of this manuscript. I would also like to thank Major-General A. P. V. Rogers for having been an insightful Ph.D. examiner providing me with constructive criticisms and suggestions.

My warmest gratitude goes to my parents-in-law, Ann and Tom Low-Beer, for their relentless review of my use of the English language throughout this book and for having provided me with invaluable emotional and intellectual support at every stage of the project.

I am indebted beyond expression to my parents for their unfailing love and support throughout my studies, and to my wonderful husband, Daniel, for his emotional support and his patience during the years. This book is dedicated to them.

The book contains information up to 1 January 2007.

ABBREVIATIONS AND ACRONYMS

AFDI	Annuaire français de droit international
AJIL	American Journal of International Law
Akayesu trial	*Prosecutor v. Akayesu*, ICTR-96-4-T, trial judgment, 2 September 1998
Akayesu appeal	*Prosecutor v. Akayesu*, ICTR- 96-4-A, appeal judgment, 1 June 2001
Aleksovski trial	*Prosecutor v. Aleksovski*, IT-95-14/1-T, trial judgment, 25 June 1999
Aleksovski appeal	*Prosecutor v. Aleksovski*, IT-95-14/1-A, appeal judgment, 24 March 2000
Bagilishema trial	*Prosecutor v. Bagilishema*, ICTR-95-1A-T, trial judgment, 7 June 2001
Bagilishema appeal	*Prosecutor v. Bagilishema*, ICTR-95-1A-A, appeal judgment, 3 July 2002 with reasons issued 13 December 2002
Blagojević trial	*Prosecutor v. Blagojević & Jokić*, IT-02-60-T, trial judgment, 17 January 2005
Blaškić trial	*Prosecutor v. Blaškić*, IT-95-14-T, trial judgment, 3 March 2000
Blaškić appeal	*Prosecutor v. Blaškić*, IT-95-14-A, appeal judgment, 29 July 2004
Brdjanin trial	*Prosecutor v. Brdjanin*, IT-99-36-T, trial judgment, 1 September 2004
BYIL	British Yearbook of International Law
Čelebići trial	*Prosecutor v. Delalić et al.*, IT-96-21-T, trial judgment, 16 November 1998
Čelebići appeal	*Prosecutor v. Delalić et al.*, IT-96-21-A, appeal judgment, 20 February 2001
common Article 3	Common Article 3 to the 1949 Geneva Conventions
Criminalise	To render a conduct criminal

Cyangugu trial	*Prosecutor v. Ntagurera et al.*, ICTR-99-46-T, trial judgment, 25 February 2004
DRC	Democratic Republic of Congo
ECHR	European Convention on Human Rights
EJIL	European Journal of International Law
Erdemović trial	*Prosecutor v. Erdemović*, IT-96-22-T, trial sentencing judgment, 29 November 1996
Erdemović appeal	*Prosecutor v. Erdemović*, IT-96-22-A, appeal judgment, 7 October 1997
EUFOR	European Union Forces in Bosnia and Herzegovina
1949 Final Record	Final Record of the diplomatic conference of Geneva of 1949 (Berne, 1951)
Furundžija trial	*Prosecutor v. Furundžija*, IT-95-17/1-T, trial judgment, 10 December 1998
Furundžija appeal	*Prosecutor v. Furundžija*, IT-95-17/1-A, appeal judgment, 21 July 2000
GA	United Nations General Assembly
Galić trial	*Prosecutor v. Galić*, IT-98-29-T, trial judgment, 5 December 2003
Galić appeal	*Prosecutor v. Galić*, IT-98-29-A, appeal judgment, 30 November 2006
Hadžihasanović trial	*Prosecutor v. Hadžihasanović et al.*, IT-01-47-T, trial judgment, 15 March 2006
Hadžihasanović command responsibility appeal decision	*Prosecutor v. Hadžihasanović et al.*, IT-01-47-AR72, decision on interlocutory appeal challenging jurisdiction in relation to command responsibility, 16 July 2003
Halilović trial	*Prosecutor v. Halilović*, IT-01-48-T, trial judgment, 16 November 2005
ICC	International Criminal Court
ICCPR	International Covenant on Civil and Political Rights
ICJ	International Court of Justice
ICLQ	International Comparative Law Quarterly
ICRC	International Committee of the Red Cross
ICTR	International Criminal Tribunal for Rwanda
ICTY	International Criminal Tribunal for the former Yugoslavia

ILC	International Law Commission
ILM	International Legal Materials
ILR	International Law Report
ILSA	International Law Student Association
IMT	International Military Tribunal
Internal conflict	Internal armed conflict or conflict of a non-international character
IRRC	International Review of the Red Cross
Jelisić trial	*Prosecutor v. Jelišić*, IT-95-10-T, trial judgment, 14 December 1999
Jelisić appeal	*Prosecutor v. Jelišić*, IT-95-10-A, appeal judgment, 5 July 2001
JICJ	Journal of International Criminal Justice
Kajelijeli trial	*Prosecutor v. Kajelijeli*, ICTR-98-44A-T, trial judgment, 1 December 2003
Kajelijeli appeal	*Prosecutor v. Kajelijeli*, ICTR-98-44A-A, appeal judgment, 23 May 2005
Kamuhanda trial	*Prosecutor v. Kamuhanda*, ICTR-95-54A-T, trial judgment, 22 January 2004
Kamuhanda appeal	*Prosecutor v. Kamuhanda*, ICTR-95-54A-A, appeal judgment, 19 September 2005
Kayishema trial	*Prosecutor v. Kayishema and Ruzindana*, ICTR-95-1-T, trial judgment, 21 May 1999
Kayishema appeal	*Prosecutor v. Kayishema and Ruzindana*, ICTR-95-1-A, appeal judgment, 1 June 2001
KLA	Kosova Liberation Army
Kordić trial	*Prosecutor v. Kordić & Čerkez*, IT-95-14/2-T, trial judgment, 26 February 2001
Kordić appeal	*Prosecutor v. Kordić & Čerkez*, IT-95-14/2-A, appeal judgment, 17 December 2004
Krnojelac trial	*Prosecutor v. Krnojelac*, IT-97-25-T, trial judgment, 15 March 2002
Krnojelac appeal	*Prosecutor v. Krnojelac*, IT-97-25-A, appeal judgment, 17 September 2003
Krstić trial	*Prosecutor v. Krstić*, IT-98-33-T, trial judgment, 2 August 2001
Krstić appeal	*Prosecutor v. Krstić*, IT-98-33-A, appeal judgment, 19 April 2004

Kunarac trial	*Prosecutor v. Kunarac et al.*, IT-96-23-T, trial judgment, 22 February 2001
Kunarac appeal	*Prosecutor v. Kunarac et al.*, IT-96-23-A, appeal judgment, 12 June 2002
Kupreškić trial	*Prosecutor v. Kupreškić et al.*, IT-95-16-T, trial judgment, 14 January 2000
Kupreškić appeal	*Prosecutor v. Kupreškić et al.*, IT-95-16-A, appeal judgment, 23 October 2001
Kvočka trial	*Prosecutor v. Kvočka et al.*, IT-98-30/1-T, trial judgment, 2 November 2001
Kvočka appeal	*Prosecutor v. Kvočka et al.*, IT-98-30/1-A, appeal judgment, 28 February 2005
Laws of war	Laws and customs of war – Laws of armed conflicts
Limaj trial	*Prosecutor v. Limaj*, IT-03-66-T, trial judgment, 30 November 2005
LRA	Lord's Resistance Army
Milošević rule 98*bis* decision	*Prosecutor v. Milošević*, IT-02-54-T, decision on motion for judgment of acquittal, 16 June 2004
Musema trial	*Prosecutor v. Musema*, ICTR-96-13-T, trial judgment, 27 January 2000
Musema appeal	*Prosecutor v. Musema*, ICTR-96-13-A, appeal judgment, 16 November 2001
Naletilić trial	*Prosecutor v. Naletilić et al.*, IT-98-34-T, trial judgment, 31 March 2003
Naletilić appeal	*Prosecutor v. Naletilić et al.*, IT-98-34-A, appeal judgment, 3 May 2006
Nicaragua case	*Military and Paramilitary Activities in and against Nicaragua* (Nicaragua v. USA) (Merits) 76 ILR 5
NGO	Non-governmental Organisation
NILR	Netherlands International Law Review
Ntakirutimana trial	*Prosecutor v. Ntakirutimana E. and G.*, ICTR-96-10/17-T, trial judgment, 21 February 2003
Orić trial	*Prosecutor v. Orić*, IT-03-68-T, trial judgment, 30 July 2006

OSCE	Organisation for Security and Co-operation in Europe
Para(s).	Paragraph(s)
PCIJ	Permanent Court of International Justice
Protocol II	1977 Additional Protocol II to the 1949 Geneva Conventions
Recueil des cours	Recueil des cours de l'Académie de droit international de La Haye
RGDIP	Revue générale de droit international public
Rome statute	1998 Rome statute for the International Criminal Court
RPF	Rwandan Patriotic Front
RUF	Revolutionary United Front
Rutaganda trial	*Prosecutor v. Rutaganda*, ICTR-96-3-T, trial judgment, 6 December 1999
Rutaganda appeal	*Prosecutor v. Rutaganda*, ICTR-96-3-A, appeal judgment, 26 May 2003
SADEC	South African Development Community
SC	United Nations Security Council
SC Res.	United Nations Security Council Resolution
Semanza trial	*Prosecutor v. Semanza*, ICTR-97-20-T, trial judgment, 15 May 2003
Semanza appeal	*Prosecutor v. Semanza*, ICTR-97-20-A, appeal judgment, 20 May 2005
SFOR	Stabilisation Force in Bosnia and Herzegovina
SFRY	Socialist Federal Republic of Yugoslavia
SG	Secretary-General of the United Nations
SG Report	Report of the UN Secretary-General
Simić trial	*Prosecutor v. Simić*, IT-95-9-T, trial judgment, 17 October 2003
Stakić trial	*Prosecutor v. Stakić*, IT-97-24-T, trial judgment, 31 July 2003
Stakić appeal	*Prosecutor v. Stakić*, IT-97-24-A, appeal judgment, 22 March 2006
Stat.	United States Statutes at large

Strugar trial	*Prosecutor v. Strugar*, IT-01-42-T, trial judgment, 31 January 2005
Tadić jurisdiction decision	Decision on the defence motion for interlocutory appeal on jurisdiction, IT-94-1-AR72, 2 October 1995
Tadić trial	*Prosecutor v. Tadić*, IT-94-1-T, trial judgment, 7 May 1997
Tadić appeal	*Prosecutor v. Tadić*, IT-94-1-A, appeal judgment, 15 July 1999
Third state	a state other than the state where the internal armed conflict is taking place
UAE	United Arab Emirates
UNMIK	United Nations Interim Administration Mission in Kosova
UNPROFOR	United Nations Protection Force
UNTAET	United Nations Transitional Administration in East Timor
UNTS	United Nations Treaty Series
Vasiljević trial	*Prosecutor v. Vasiljević*, IT-98-32-T, trial judgment, 29 November 2002
Vasiljević appeal	*Prosecutor v. Vasiljević*, IT-98-32-A, appeal judgment, 25 February 2004
YbIHL	Yearbook of International Humanitarian Law

Introduction

For the second year running, all the major armed conflicts in the world in 2004 and 2005 fell within the category of internal armed conflicts.[1] The UN Secretary-General remarked that 'as internal armed conflicts proliferate, civilians have become the principal victims. It is now conventional to say that, in recent decades, the proportion of war victims who are civilians has leaped dramatically to an estimated 75 per cent and in some cases even more . . . Furthermore, and particularly in conflicts with an element of ethnic or religious hatred, the affected civilians tend not to be the incidental victims of these new irregular forces: they are their principal object.'[2] Since 1949, a growing body of international norms has become applicable in internal armed conflicts, but at the same time actual observance of these rules by belligerents has been limited. An example of this phenomenon is the agreement reached between the parties to the conflict in Bosnia-Herzegovina on 22 May 1992 whereby all belligerents recognised the applicability of substantive principles of the laws and customs of war[3] to the conflicts in Bosnia.[4] The four following years of conflicts and the fall of Srbrenica are tragic evidence of the extent to which this agreement was disregarded in practice.

Bert Röling noted that 'the laws of war derive their authority, during a war, from the threat of reprisals, prosecution and punishment after the war'.[5] Until the adoption of the statute of the International Criminal Tribunal for Rwanda, conventional law applicable in internal armed conflicts did not establish individual criminal responsibility for war crimes committed in these conflicts and did not contain any enforcement mechanism. States coming out of an internal armed conflict often granted unconditional amnesties to individuals who had violated the laws of war during the conflict.[6] With no real risk of prosecutions for war crimes, there were therefore few incentives for belligerents to respect the laws of war in internal armed conflicts.

In the 1990s, the Security Council recognised the direct link between justice and peace when it established the International Criminal

Tribunals for the former Yugoslavia and Rwanda.[7] It also sent the clear message that amnesties for war crimes were not acceptable whatever the nature of the armed conflict.[8] The Government of Rwanda affirmed in 1994: 'it is impossible to build a state of law and arrive at true national reconciliation' without eradicating 'the culture of impunity'.[9] The Secretary-General affirmed recently that 'amnesty cannot be granted in respect of international crimes such as genocide, crimes against humanity or other serious violations of international humanitarian law'.[10] Even if some doubt the wisdom of criminal prosecutions,[11] justice allows for the exposure of the truth and enables a society to move beyond the pain and horror of the past.[12] Furthermore, prosecutions establish the responsibility of individuals, rather than having whole groups shouldering the burden of collective guilt. They bring public and official acknowledgement to the victims and are an important step in their healing process.[13] It is submitted that prosecutions of war crimes committed in internal armed conflicts are a necessary ingredient to secure enduring peace in the aftermath of a civil conflict.[14]

This book shows the extraordinary change that the law of internal armed conflict underwent in the last fifteen years. It aims to assess whether individuals can be held individually responsible for war crimes committed in internal armed conflicts and if so, how that responsibility can be enforced.

The state of the laws of war today will be explored in order to establish the existence of an international law norm creating individual criminal responsibility for serious violations of the laws of war or war crimes committed in internal armed conflicts. Chapter 1 defines the contours of the concept of internal armed conflict and adopts a working definition of it for the purpose of this book. The laws of war, both conventional and customary norms applicable in internal armed conflicts, are then studied in turn in chapter 2 before sketching the regime of war crimes in chapter 3. Chapter 4 assesses the quantum leap which took place in the 1990s when a number of treaties extended the principle of individual criminal responsibility to war crimes committed in internal armed conflicts. Particular attention is paid in the second part of chapter 4 to the state of customary international law. The practice and *opinio juris* of states and international organisations are studied in detail to find out if this principle is reflected in customary law today.

The second objective of this book is to study the means of enforcement of individual criminal responsibility for war crimes when committed in internal armed conflicts. First, domestic prosecutions on the basis of either the territoriality principle or universal jurisdiction are evaluated. The strengths and weaknesses of both types of prosecutions are assessed, with special emphasis placed on the concept of universal jurisdiction. The state of customary law is explored again in chapter 5 to find out whether there is a right enshrined in customary law for states to extend universal jurisdiction over war crimes committed in internal armed conflicts.

Secondly, the 1990s have seen the establishment of international criminal tribunals set up to prosecute individuals for international crimes, including war crimes committed in internal armed conflicts. Individuals have been successfully prosecuted for war crimes committed in internal armed conflicts for the first time in history. The achievements and the legacy of the ad hoc tribunals are studied before turning to the potential role that the International Criminal Court could play in the fight against impunity. War criminals now need to think twice about their actions in internal armed conflicts.

Notes

1. See *SIPRI Yearbook, armaments, disarmament and international security* (Oxford: Oxford University Press, 2005 and 2006) p. 83 and p. 108. Nineteen major armed conflicts were recorded in 2004 and seventeen in 2005. This research shows that 2004 is the first year that no interstate conflict has been reported (p. 83). This research uses the terminology of 'intra-state conflict', which covers the concept of internal armed conflict, as defined in this book.
2. Report of the Secretary-General to the Security Council on the protection of civilians in armed conflict, UN.Doc.S/2001/331 (30 March 2001) para. 3.
3. For convenience hereafter referred to as 'the laws of war'.
4. Reported in the *Tadić* jurisdiction decision, para. 73.
5. B. Röling, 'Criminal responsibility for violations of the laws of war' (1976) *Revue belge de droit international* 10.
6. Up to the First World War, amnesties were regarded as an essential element of the establishment of peace and were included in most international peace treaties.
7. On this point, see R. Goldstone, 'Justice as a tool for peace-making: truth commissions and international criminal tribunals' (1996) 28 *International law and politics* 486–87.
8. Article 6.5 of Protocol II provides that 'at the end of hostilities, the authorities in power shall endeavour to grant the broadest possible amnesty to persons who have participated in the armed conflict'. This provision was understood by some commentators and courts to support amnesties of serious violations of the laws of war in internal conflicts. The ICRC is, however, clear that this article is

inapplicable to amnesties that extinguish penal responsibility for persons who have violated international law. It only encourages amnesties for those detained or punished for the mere fact of having participated in hostilities, see N. Roht-Arriaza and L. Gibson, 'The developing jurisprudence on amnesty' (1998) 20 *Human rights quarterly* 865. See also the whole vol. 59 of *Law and contemporary problems* entitled 'Accountability for international crime and serious violations of fundamental human rights'. In particular, M. Scharf, 'The letter of the law: the scope of international legal obligation to prosecute human rights crime' (1996) 59 *Law and contemporary problems* 41; K. Ambos, 'Impunity and international criminal law, a case study on Colombia, Peru, Bolivia, Chile and Argentina' (1997) 18 *Human rights law journal* 1; T. Farer, 'Restraining the barbarians: can international criminal law help?' (2000) 22 *Human rights quarterly* 90–117; M. Freeman Harris *et al.*, 'Bringing war criminals to justice: obligations, options, recommendations' in D. Orentlicher *et al.* (ed.), *Making justice work: the report of the Century Foundation* (New York: Century Foundation Press, 1998) pp. 27–32; L. Olson, 'Provoking the dragon on the patio. Matters of transitional justice: penal repression vs. amnesties' (2006) 88 *IRRC* 275–94.

9. See UN.Doc.S/PV.3453 (1994) p. 14.

10. Report of the Secretary-General on the establishment of a Special Court of Sierra Leone, S/2000/915 (4 October 2000) para. 22.

11. For an overview of the major objections raised to criminal prosecution, see M. Osiel, 'Why prosecute? Critics of punishment of mass atrocities' (2000) 22 *Human rights quarterly* 118.

12. Truth can be established in a variety of ways other than criminal prosecutions. They include fact-finding commissions, prosecutions of a few leaders or truth and reconciliation commissions. These methods, however, fall outside the scope of this book.

13. On these points, see A. Cassese, 'Reflections on international criminal justice' (1998) 61 *The modern law review* 1–10 and Goldstone 'Justice as a tool for peacemaking' 488–90.

14. This book will concentrate on criminal prosecutions only and does not cover civil liability actions that could be open to victims before domestic courts.

1

Towards a workable definition
of internal armed conflicts

Internal armed conflict can be defined as the use of armed force within the boundary of one state between one or more armed groups and the acting government, or between such groups.[1] Different terms can cover such situations: rebellion, revolution, internal disturbances, violence, terrorism, guerrilla warfare, resistance, internal uprising, civil war, war of self-determination . . . These terms depict the scale, the various levels of intensity of a conflict, or express for some of them the method of combat, such as guerrilla warfare, or the goal of the conflict, such as war of self-determination. They all carry a certain political weight and some fall within the legal category of internal armed conflict.[2] Whereas certain scholars have studied the concept of internal armed conflict by looking at the causes of such conflicts,[3] international lawyers have started to define the concept of internal armed conflict when international law was deemed to regulate some aspects of such conflicts. The 1949 Geneva Diplomatic Conference on the laws of war established the modern distinction between international armed conflicts, replacing the old concept of war, and internal armed conflicts, defined as a conflict of a non-international character. Prior to that date, it had been generally agreed that it was the sovereign right of each government in power to maintain internal order and 'to punish the insurgents in accordance with its penal laws'.[4] When a specific treaty provision was adopted to regulate certain aspects of internal armed conflicts, it became important to define the contours of this category of conflict and to determine in which cases international law was applicable.[5] This exercise proved to be, and remains, a very controversial issue, which is at the heart of the enforcement of the laws of armed conflicts.

An internal armed conflict has the characteristics of a chameleon: it is an evolving situation, which gathers under the title of internal armed conflict many successive levels of conflict, each of them being dependant on contextual evidence and therefore not easily apprehensible by the law. There is always some type of violence within a state. The early stages of armed violence may fall short of an armed conflict, whereas later stages will fall within the general category of internal armed conflicts. The approach chosen here is to examine the characteristics of an internal conflict, by differentiating such conflict from internal disturbances on the one hand, and from international conflicts on the other. In determining the lower threshold between internal violence and an armed conflict, the various definitions of internal armed conflicts found in treaties and international case law will be discussed.

Next, the higher threshold which separates internal conflict from international conflict will be considered, looking especially at the circumstances in which an internal armed conflict is considered in international law to amount to an international armed conflict. This can happen through recognition of belligerency, a third-state intervention or a UN armed forces intervention in the internal armed conflict. These categories of internationalised conflicts, together with so-called wars of self-determination, will be dealt with briefly, for they are not central to the subject at hand.[6]

1. Establishment of an armed conflict

The first attempt to define the characteristics of a civil war came with the institution of the recognition of belligerency during the eighteenth and nineteenth centuries. It gradually became acceptable to apply the rules of war to certain large-scale civil wars, in instances where the rebels' side was recognised as being belligerents by the legitimate government or a third party. The recognition of belligerency was a discretionary and purely subjective recognition by a state of the factual existence of a war providing certain specific conditions were fulfilled. Four conditions had to be satisfied before a state of belligerency could be recognised:[7]

i) an armed conflict within the state concerned, of a general, as opposed to a local character;
ii) the insurgents must occupy and administer a substantial part of the state territory;
iii) they must conduct their hostilities in accordance with the laws of war, through organised armed forces under a responsible command;
iv) circumstances exist that make it necessary for third states to make clear their attitude to those circumstances by recognition of belligerency.[8]

The category of civil war regulated by international law at that time consisted only of armed conflicts of a general character where the rebels were an organised force under a responsible command and occupying a substantial part of state territory. These criteria were the first defined characteristics of large-scale civil wars. If the conflict in question was not seen as fulfilling these criteria, its regulation would be considered to fall within the reserved domain of the state.[9]

1.1 Definition of armed conflicts in international treaties

There are three distinct definitions of internal armed conflict given in international treaties. Common Article 3 of the 1949 Geneva Conventions[10] and 1977 Protocol II additional to the Geneva Conventions[11] are the two main instruments regulating the conduct of hostilities in internal armed conflicts. Each instrument has a different definition of this concept, resulting in the fragmentation of the legal regimes regulating internal armed conflicts. More recently, the Rome statute of the International Criminal Court[12] also gives a definition of the general category of internal armed conflicts.

The 1949 Diplomatic Conference was the first opportunity for states both to consider the issue of internal armed conflict and to adopt substantive law applicable in such conflicts. In 1949, a majority of states agreed on the necessity of adopting some rules for internal armed conflicts; however, it became clear that the future conventions themselves could not be applied irrespective of the nature of the conflict.[13] For most of the participants, it was necessary to define precisely the context in which states would have to apply these rules. In fact, it was not acceptable for the great majority of states seriously to erode their capacity to maintain internal order. The study of the *travaux préparatoires* shows that there was a consensus to have certain internal situations excluded from the scope of common Article 3,[14] i.e. 'forms of disorder, anarchy or brigandage'[15] or 'mere riot or disturbances'.[16] This interpretation[17] was specifically included in the final version of Protocol II in its Article 1.2. Protocol II is not deemed to apply to situations which are not armed conflicts: 'internal disturbances and tensions, such as riots, isolated and sporadic acts of violence and other acts of a similar nature'. Protocol II 'develops and supplements Article 3 without modifying its existing conditions of application'.[18] The exclusion of internal disturbances and tensions from the scope of application of Protocol II is, however, an accepted principle for the general category of internal conflict falling under common Article 3.[19] It can therefore be concluded that an armed conflict presupposes the existence of hostilities of a certain scale or duration, as they cannot be either isolated or sporadic acts.[20]

The threshold between internal disturbances and an armed conflict is however difficult to determine in practice, if one does not specify the character or the intensity of these hostilities. During the 1949 Diplomatic Conference, several criteria were proposed: the organised character of the rebels groups, their control over part of the territory, the use of regular military forces against them, or the duration and intensity of the conflict.[21] None of these criteria appears in the final version of common Article 3, as the conference could not agree on an acceptable definition of internal conflict.[22] They finally adopted an article listing a few provisions applicable to a wide and vague category of conflicts, qualified as not of an international character.[23] At present, however, it is reasonable to believe that an armed conflict, as defined in common Article 3, presupposes the existence of armed hostilities in the territory of one of the high contracting parties, between the regular military forces and some organised armed groups, or between these groups; moreover these hostilities need to be regarded as being sufficiently serious and prolonged. There is no established formula or test furthering the level of seriousness or the length of the hostilities. Concerning the extent of organisation of the rebel groups, it is generally agreed that 'rebels should be organised to such a degree as to be able to carry out those obligations and assume responsibility for their implementation'.[24]

The absence of a precise definition of internal armed conflict, coupled with the absence of any mechanism for the monitoring and enforcement of its application in common Article 3, enabled states on whose territory such a conflict was taking place to argue that the hostilities encountered did not amount to an armed conflict. In the few decades which followed the adoption of common Article 3, the record of application and respect of common Article 3 turned out to be poor.[25] The 1974–77 Geneva Diplomatic Conference tried to tackle these lacunae as well as to adopt more substantive rules of the laws of war applicable in internal armed conflicts.

The scope of application of Protocol II is more restricted than the scope of common Article 3, creating two types of internal armed conflict governed by different treaty provisions. Negotiators agreed on a more precise definition of internal armed conflict but their definition only governed Protocol II without modifying the conditions under which common Article 3 is applicable. This instrument defines internal armed conflict as a conflict which 'takes place in the territory of a High Contracting Party between its armed forces and dissident armed forces or other organised armed groups, which under responsible command exercise such control over a part of its territory as to enable them to carry out sustained and concerted military operations and to implement this protocol'.[26] There are evident similarities between these conditions and the classic conditions of the recognition of belligerency, as well as with the definition of internal armed conflict proposed by the French during the 1949 Diplomatic Conference.[27] The Protocol only applies to conflict between governmental forces and dissident armed groups, and not to conflicts between two or more dissident groups.[28] Furthermore, these dissident armed groups must be organised under a responsible command and control a sufficiently great part of the territory to enable them to carry out sustained and concerted military operations. Nothing is stated concerning the amount of territory they must control, or for how long, nor who will ultimately judge whether the applicable conditions are fulfilled.[29] Furthermore, by requiring dissident groups to be able to implement the Protocol, this condition recalls the principle of reciprocity[30] and seems to make the link between the organisation of the group and their ability to implement the Protocol more obvious.[31] The definition in Protocol II, while being more precise about the character of internal armed conflicts, seems only to cover a small category of internal armed conflicts of high intensity within the larger category of internal armed conflicts governed by common Article 3. Interestingly, when the Rome conference for the creation of a permanent International Criminal Court faced the question of the definition of internal armed conflict, the delegations deliberately and substantially deviated from the definition appearing in Protocol II.[32] The ICC statute contains a definition inspired by the case law of the International Criminal Tribunal for the Former Yugoslavia (ICTY) and creates a much lower threshold than the one appearing in Protocol II. According to Article 8.2.f) of the statute, the court will have jurisdiction over serious violations of the laws and customs of war committed in armed conflicts that take place in the territory of a state when there is protracted armed conflict between governmental authorities and organised armed groups or between such groups.[33]

1.2 Definition of armed conflicts in international case law

International tribunals have rarely dealt with the definition of internal armed conflict. The few cases at hand, however, are good illustrations of the complexities of applying the criteria spelled out in treaties to factual circumstances.

Some judgments and decisions of the ICTY[34] throw some light on the definition of internal armed conflict. The appeal decision on jurisdiction in the *Tadić* case clarifies first that 'the temporal and geographical scope of both internal and international conflicts extends beyond the exact time and place of hostilities'.[35] The rules contained in common Article 3 will therefore apply outside the actual theatre of combat operations 'in the whole territory under control of a party whether or not actual combat takes place'.[36] The Appeals Chamber went on to define the existence of an armed conflict 'whenever there is a resort to armed force between states or protracted armed violence between governmental authorities and organised armed groups or between such groups within a state'.[37] The Appeals Chamber in this case took the view that 'different conflicts of different nature took place in the former Yugoslavia and that it would be for each Trial Chamber, depending on the circumstances of the case to make its own determination of the nature of the armed conflict upon the specific evidence presented to it'.[38] Since that first ruling, each judgment of the Tribunal has taken as a starting point the definition of armed conflict appearing in the *Tadić* case.[39] On the one hand they looked particularly at the organised nature of the rebel groups, and on the other the duration or intensity of the armed violence between such groups or between governmental authorities and a rebel group.[40] In assessing the intensity of the conflict, Trial Chambers have looked at various factors such as the seriousness of attacks and their recurrence,[41] the spread of these armed clashes over territory and time,[42] whether various parties were able to operate from a territory under their control,[43] an increase in the number of government forces, the mobilisation of volunteers and the distribution of weapons among both parties to the conflict,[44] as well as whether the conflict had attracted the attention of the UN Security Council and whether any resolutions on that matter had been passed.[45] In order to assess the organisation of the parties to the conflict, Trial Chambers took into account such factors as the existence of headquarters, designated zones of operation and the ability to procure, transport and distribute arms.[46]

In total, the existence of an international conflict in the place and time where the crimes were committed was found in seven ITCY cases, the *Tadić, Blaškić, Aleksovski, Kordić, Naletilić*[47], *Brdjanin*[48] and *Čelebići* cases. In sixteen other cases, the Prosecutor chose to prove only the existence of an armed conflict.[49] In most instances, Trial Chambers did not need to go into a great deal of detail to appreciate the factual circumstances of the case, as the existence of protracted armed hostilities was often admitted by all parties to the conflict.

Of particular interest is the recent ICTY judgment rendered in the *Limaj* case.[50] The Trial Chamber had to determine whether the conflict in Kosovo in 1998 between the Kosova Liberation Army (KLA) and the governmental forces amounted to an armed conflict capable of falling within the ambit of Article 3 of the ICTY statute. The defence in this case submitted *inter alia* that, in order to determine the existence of an armed conflict, the Chamber should consider 'the insurgents' status as belligerents and whether the insurgents have a state-like organisation and authority to observe the rules of war'.[51] The Trial Chamber rejected this submission by stating that such criteria, drawn from the commentary to common Article 3, are only convenient criteria to distinguish a genuine armed conflict from an act of banditry or an unauthorised or short lived insurrection; they are by no means 'obligatory'.[52] The defence further argued that in order to be bound by the laws of armed conflicts, 'a party to the conflict must be able to implement international humanitarian law and, at the bare minimum, must possess: a basic understanding of the principles laid down in common Article 3, a capacity to disseminate the rules and a method of sanctioning the breaches'.[53] Referring to Protocol II, the defence also submitted that it must be established that the KLA 'was sufficiently organised to carry out continuous and persistent military operations and to impose discipline on its troops'.[54] The Trial Chamber rejected these arguments and took the view that 'some degree of organisation by the parties will suffice to establish the existence of an armed conflict'.[55] The Chamber then went on to analyse whether the KLA possessed the characteristics of an organised armed group and whether the acts of violence that occurred in Kosovo reached the level of intensity required to establish the existence of an armed conflict.[56]

The Trial Chamber in this case reviewed meticulously all the evidence establishing that the KLA constituted an organised armed group able to engage in an internal armed conflict. In doing so, it considered *inter alia* the following factors: the organisation and structure of the KLA with a general staff and the creation of eleven zones with one commander for each zone,[57] the adoption of internal regulations,[58] the nomination of a spokesperson,[59] the issuance of orders,[60] political statements and communiqués,[61] the establishment of headquarters,[62] the capacity to launch co-ordinated actions between KLA units,[63] the establishment of a military police and disciplinary rules,[64] the ability of the KLA to recruit new members[65] and its capacity to provide military training,[66] the weapons distribution channels,[67] the use of uniforms and various other equipment,[68] and the participation by the KLA in political negotiations to resolve the Kosovo crisis.[69]

In reviewing the intensity of the armed conflict to determine whether the armed conflict in Kosovo in 1998 amounted to 'protracted armed violence', the Trial Chamber looked at the following factors: the various acts of violence and military operations carried out over the entire territory throughout 1997 and 1998,[70] the increased involvement of governmental forces,[71] the types of weapons used,[72] the fact that the conflict led to a large displacement of people,[73] and the amount of territory under the control of the KLA.[74] The Chamber concluded[75] that the conflict could be described as 'periodic armed clashes occurring virtually continuously at intervals averaging three to seven days over a widespread and expanding geographic area'.[76] The *Limaj* case provides a very detailed and thorough analysis of the definition of armed conflict and gives an excellent illustration of the factors that a tribunal takes into account before it can conclude that an internal armed conflict is taking place within a state.

The International Criminal Tribunal for Rwanda[77] uses the same test as the ICTY to 'evaluate both the intensity and organisation of the parties to the conflict' for each of their cases.[78] This Tribunal took the view that assessing whether the hostilities are of sufficient intensity 'does not depend on the subjective judgment of the parties to the conflicts', but rather on the objective level of violence taking place between the various armed groups.[79]

The recent *Tablada* case before the Inter-American Commission on Human Rights[80] offers, together with the *Limaj* case, the most detailed jurisprudential discussion of the characteristics of an armed conflict. The Commission needed to determine whether the 30-hour-long armed confrontation at the *Tablada* base between attackers and Argentine armed forces was 'merely an example of internal disturbances or tensions or whether it constituted a non-international armed conflict within the meaning of common Article 3'.[81] Looking at the International Committee of the Red Cross (ICRC) 1973 commentary on the draft additional protocols to the Geneva Conventions, the Commission gives further examples of what constitute internal disturbances and tensions: riots, isolated and sporadic acts of violence or other acts of a similar nature which incur in particular mass arrest of persons.[82] According to the Commission, the level of violence is the main distinguishing feature between serious tensions and internal disturbances. The Commission believes that an armed conflict requires: 'the existence of organised armed groups that are capable of and actually do engage in combat and other military actions against each other'.[83] Article 3 armed conflicts do not 'require the existence of large-scale and generalised hostilities or a situation comparable to a civil war in which dissident armed groups exercise control over parts of national territory'.[84] Looking at the factual circumstances of the case, and despite the brief duration of the incidents, they conclude that the events at the *Tablada* base can be differentiated from internal disturbances by 'the concerted nature of the hostile acts undertaken by the attackers, the direct involvement of governmental armed forces and the nature and level of violence attending the events'.[85] To qualify as a situation of internal conflict, the Commission emphasises that the parties to the conflict must be organised and that the open armed confrontations are characterised by a high level of violence. It concluded that the armed confrontation at the *Tablada* base which lasted for about 30 hours amounted to an armed conflict, as an armed conflict could be short but very intense.[86] It seems therefore to put more weight on the level of violence than on the duration of such hostilities.

There does not seem to be a unique and universally accepted definition of internal armed conflict in the laws of armed conflicts. However, both the various treaties and the international case law give us the main characteristics and the ways one can distinguish internal disturbances from an armed conflict. The condition of control by the armed groups over part of the territory, specified in Additional Protocol II, describes the character of high intensity conflicts, but does not form part of the common accepted criteria defining an armed conflict in customary international law. It is submitted that the level of organisation of armed groups as well as the intensity of armed hostilities seem to be the common accepted criteria differentiating armed conflict from internal disturbances in current international law.

2. International and internal armed conflicts

After considering the lower threshold between internal armed conflicts and internal disturbances, we can now turn to the higher threshold between internal and international conflicts. At first sight, the distinction seems clear: an international armed conflict opposes two or more states, whereas an internal armed conflict generally opposes the governmental forces to rebel groups and takes place within the internal boundaries of a single state. It would follow from this premise that all armed conflicts between armed groups taking place within the boundaries of a state should qualify as internal armed conflict. For the purposes of the law of armed conflicts, however, some of these conflicts are considered to be international armed conflicts, which trigger the application of the law of armed conflicts applicable in international armed conflicts. Such conflicts do not fall within the category of internal armed conflicts and are therefore not within the scope of this book.

2.1 Recognition of belligerency

The first kind of internationalised conflicts are conflicts where either the government in place or a third state formally recognises the rebels as belligerents. As discussed in the first section of this chapter, recognition of belligerency is a recognition of the factual existence of a war if the rebels have fulfilled a number of conditions. In these now very rare situations,[87] the laws of war applicable in international conflicts shall apply between both belligerents in what will be considered to be an international conflict.

2.2 Wars of self-determination

Similarly, there is an established kind of internal armed conflict, wars of self-determination, that has gradually come to be considered as being governed by the laws of war applicable in international armed conflicts.[88] This evolution started in the 1960s when the UN General Assembly called for the application of the 1949 Geneva Conventions in internal armed conflicts such as in Southern Rhodesia,[89] Angola and Mozambique,[90] South Africa[91] or Namibia.[92] In 1973, the General Assembly resolution 3103 recognised explicitly that the Geneva Conventions should apply to wars of self-determination, as such conflicts should be considered international.[93] This view, greatly supported by the non-aligned movement during the 1974–77 Geneva Diplomatic Conference, was adopted during the negotiations, and Article 1.4 of Protocol I explicitly includes armed conflicts in which peoples are fighting against colonial domination, alien occupation and against racist regimes in the exercise of their right of self-determination, within the realm of international conflicts.[94] Other conflicts fought against oppressive regimes on political, social or religious grounds are not able to fall within Article 1.4 of Protocol I.[95]

2.3 *Foreign intervention in internal armed conflicts*

A third type of internal armed conflict to be considered is the difficult situation where there is foreign intervention in an internal armed conflict. Notwithstanding the condemnation of foreign intervention in internal armed conflicts,[96] foreign interventions have been frequent occurrences during the past sixty years. Such foreign intervention can range from bringing economic or logistic aid, to delivery of arms or to the sending of foreign troops to help either the legitimate government or the rebels. Do any of these situations change the character of the conflict? When is the threshold between internal and international conflict crossed? The doctrine is divided as to whether and when a foreign intervention turns an internal armed conflict into an international one.[97] Some authors have advocated that a foreign intervention, which decisively influences an internal armed conflict, internationalises the whole conflict.[98] There have been situations where the government in power responded positively to the ICRC call for respect of the Geneva Conventions such as in the Congo in 1961, in Yemen or in Cambodia.[99] Whereas in others cases, such as in the Spanish Civil War or in Afghanistan, there was a refusal to apply the Geneva Conventions, notwithstanding clear foreign interventions in these conflicts.[100]

Others have argued that one should divide such internal armed conflict into different bilateral relations between the various parties to the internal conflict.[101] The International Court of Justice (ICJ) in the *Nicaragua* case explicitly used this theory by distinguishing the conflict between the USA and Nicaragua, classified as an international armed conflict, from the conflict between the contras and Nicaragua, which remained an internal armed conflict.[102]

The case law of the ICTY has thrown some more light on these difficult issues, both on the consequence of a third-state intervention in internal armed conflict, as well as on the level of intervention necessary to pass from an internal to an international conflict.[103] First, there seems to be a general trend in the case law of the Tribunal not to apply the 'theory of pairings' and divide the conflicts into bilateral relationships as indicated above. It is for the Trial Chamber in each case to decide whether the acts of the accused were committed in an international or an internal armed conflict.[104] Each Trial Chamber looks at the conflict in the area where the crimes were committed in its entirety as internal or international. In this regard, the reasoning taken by the ICJ in the *Nicaragua* case does not seem upheld, and when the conflict is deemed international, the law applicable in international conflicts will apply between all parties to the conflict. In the Bosnian conflicts however, foreign states (i.e. Serbia or Croatia) intervened on the side of an organised armed group against the 'central government'. It remains open to debate whether the case law of the ICTY has changed the previously held view that, where foreign troops support the established government against the rebels, the conflict remains an internal armed conflict between the government and the rebel group.[105] The help provided by the foreign state to the government in place does not internationalise the conflict.[106]

Secondly, the question when an internal armed conflict becomes international as a consequence of a foreign intervention has been dealt with at great length in a few cases of the Tribunal. The Trial Chamber in the *Rajic* case had to look at the consequences of the Croatian involvement in the conflict between the forces of Bosnia-Herzegovina and the Croatian community of Bosnia. The Chamber found that the significant and continuous intervention of the Croatian Army in support of the Bosnian Croats sufficed to transform the internal conflict into an international one.[107] The Chamber went further to look at the relationship between the Croatian Army and the Bosnian Croat forces. It ruled that the Bosnian Croats were agents of Croatia, as Croatia was exercising a general political and military control over them.[108] The Chamber chose to apply the rules of state responsibility, as illustrated in the Nicaragua case, but did not find it necessary to prove that Croatia had specific operational control over the Bosnian Croat forces.

The Trial Chamber in the *Tadić* trial judgment used similar reasoning when looking at the protected persons status of Bosnian Muslims in the hands of Bosnian Serbs. Were the Bosnian Serb forces de facto organs of the Republic of Serbia, therefore rendering the conflict international and the victims protected persons under the Geneva Conventions? The Trial Chamber probably influenced by the *Rajic* decision, used the general framework of the law of state responsibility and the Nicaragua case in order to determine the nature of the conflict in question. On the basis of Article 8.1 of the International Law Commission Draft on state responsibility, for a non-official person or group of persons to engage the responsibility of a state, one must prove that this person or group was in fact acting on behalf of that state. The Trial Chamber in the *Tadić* trial judgment, concluded that there was a 'general level of co-ordination' between the Republic of Serbia and the Bosnian Serbs' military units as mere allies, but that the Prosecutor did not prove an effective control of these units by the neighbouring state.[109] It concluded therefore that the

Bosnian Serb forces were not de facto organs of Serbia and the conflict was of an internal character.[110]

The use of the *Nicaragua* case in the *Tadić* trial judgment has been criticised by commentators.[111] The ICJ addresses two distinct principles in the *Nicaragua* case relevant to the issue under study here. In dealing with the question of the law applicable, the ICJ determines the character of the conflict in Nicaragua, and uses the theory of pairings,[112] as indicated above. Secondly, the court looks at the attribution of responsibility to the USA for violations of the laws of armed conflicts committed by the contras.[113] The alleged violations by the contras were not imputable to the USA, as the contras were not acting as a de facto organ of the USA and did not commit these acts on instruction from the USA. These two issues were dealt with separately and the court never made the nexus, used in *Tadić*, between the imputability of the acts of the contras and the nature of the conflict. T. Meron proposed not to apply the test of imputability, borrowed from state responsibility, to determine whether a foreign intervention leads to the internationalisation of a conflict.[114] He seems to suggest that the crucial factors should include the 'dimensions, scope and duration of a foreign military intervention, the foreign state's direct participation in the hostilities, the nature of the states and political entities involved in the conflict'[115] and that 'the provisions of the Fourth Geneva Convention on termination of the application of the Convention, including article 6 are relevant, not the legal tests of imputability and state responsibility'.[116] In the absence of direct participation of a foreign state in an armed conflict, it is unclear what degree of indirect participation of a foreign state internationalises an internal armed conflict. If at first, the laws on state responsibility do not seem to be the adequate tool to determine the nature of an armed conflict, they nonetheless allow for a determination of the international status of the entities party to an armed conflict. If the acts of an armed group can be imputed to a foreign state, the latter should surely be seen as a de facto organ of that foreign state and the conflict would therefore be an international one. The international legal status of each party to the conflict, state officials, de facto organ of a state or armed group acting independently of the orders of a state for example, constitutes the correct criteria establishing the character of an armed conflict.

The Appeals Chamber, in its judgment of 15 July 1999, reversed the conclusion reached by the Trial Chamber concerning the character of the conflict, but did use both the laws of armed conflicts and the laws on state responsibility in order to determine whether the acts of individuals or organised armed groups could be attributed to a foreign state.[117] The Chamber tried first to establish the nature of the conflict, and believed that there are two ways by which an internal conflict may become international:

1) if another state intervenes in that conflict through its troops or
2) if some of the participants in the internal armed conflict act on behalf of that other state.[118]

In trying to establish that some participants to an armed conflict act on behalf of another state, the Appeals Chamber draws a distinction between the situation where an individual acts as a de facto organ of a state and the case where an armed and organised group acts as a de facto organ of an intervening state. It went on to determine the criteria for the legal imputability to a state of acts performed by individuals and a group not having the status of state officials.[119] According to the Appeals Chamber, a state will be internationally responsible for acts in breach of international law committed by 'individuals who make up organised groups subject to the state's control and regardless of whether or not the state has issued specific instructions to those individuals'.[120] Therefore, imputability of acts of an organised group to the state can be proved if 'the state wields overall control over the group, not only by equipping and financing the group, but also by co-ordinating or helping in the general planning of its military activity'.[121] Regarding 'individuals or groups not organised into military structure', the Chamber believes that an overall level of control is not sufficient and one needs to prove that the individual acted upon specific instructions or directives from the state.[122]

In conclusion, the Appeals Chamber believes therefore that 'international rules do not always require the same degree of control over armed groups or private individuals for the purpose of determining whether an individual not having the status of a state official, can be regarded as a de facto organ of the state.'[123] In the *Tadić* case, the Appeals Chamber goes on applying this legal test and concludes that the Republic of Serbia has an overall control over the Bosnian Serb military groups, which seem therefore to act as de facto organs or agents of Serbia. The apparent internal conflict is therefore rendered international in character, if one can prove that the intervening state exercises *overall control* of the rebel group, as opposed to *effective control* as the Trial Chamber first established.[124]

The Appeals Chamber judgment in *Tadić* seems in this respect to be the most clearly articulated and relevant case which clarifies the circumstances in which an internal conflict becomes internationalised as a consequence of a foreign intervention in such conflict. The Appeals Chamber seems not ready to accept the proposal that a foreign intervention, which decisively influences an internal conflict, could internationalise the latter. It upholds the relevance of the link between the imputability of the acts of rebels to the intervening state, and the nature of the conflict. Mere financial or logistical support to an organised armed group will not internationalise the conflict, unless the foreign state has an overall control over such group. This 'overall control' test is less difficult to establish than 'effective control'; it is not necessary to show that a well-structured rebel group, such as some armed groups in Bosnia-Herzegovina, receives all its orders from a foreign state for it to be considered a de facto organ of the latter.[125] The 'overall control' test can be seen as an adequate tool to grasp the intricacies of foreign state intervention in internal armed conflicts. Finally, one must welcome the fact that the Chamber did not uphold the theory of pairings used by the ICJ in Nicaragua, which would have created two different bodies of applicable law, rendering the tasks of Trial Chambers, as well as soldiers on the ground, unworkable. This theory of 'overall control' has been consistently upheld in successive ICTY trial judgments such as in the *Aleksovski*,[126] *Blaškić*,[127] *Naletilić* trials[128] and the *Kordić* and *Čerkez* cases[129] and the appeal judgments in *Čelebići*,[130] *Aleksovski*[131] and *Kordić* and *Čerkez*.[132] From an evidentiary point of view, the complexity of proving the existence of overall control by a foreign state of an organised armed group has led the ICTY Prosecutor either not to include or even to withdraw Article 2 (grave breaches) charges from some indictments.[133]

2.4 UN intervention in internal armed conflicts

In a study of the threshold between internal and international conflict, it may be necessary to add a few words on the consequences of the intervention of UN troops in an internal armed conflict. As this complex issue is not the subject of this book, a few preliminary remarks will suffice.[134] In the case of peace-keeping interventions by UN forces or UN authorised forces in an internal armed conflict, the UN troops do not become party to the conflict and are often allowed to use force only in restricted cases of self-defence.[135] It is therefore possible to think that the involvement of such peace-keeping forces in an internal armed conflict will not change the nature of the conflict. In those cases, the UN troops strive to remain neutral and the very occasional use of force in self-defence should not decisively affect the nature of the armed conflict.

If the character of UN forces is not peace-keeping but peace-enforcing or peace-restoring, the forces' mandate, most often established under chapter 7 of the UN Charter, may allow them to use force to restore peace and security in the country.[136] In those circumstances, it seems that the UN forces can therefore become party to the internal armed conflict and the nature of the conflict will be changed to an international conflict, at least between the UN forces and the other parties to the conflict.[137] Examples of such internationalised conflicts are the UN-led actions against North Korea, and to a certain extent the conflict in Somalia, where the conflict between the UN troops and a rebel group must be seen as an international conflict, as long as the rebel group is sufficiently organised.[138] The doctrine remains divided as to whether the intervention by UN troops will automatically affect the nature of the conflict between the warring factions themselves.[139]

Defining what constitutes an internal conflict is a complex question, as there is no universally accepted definition in international law. For the purpose of this book, internal armed conflict will be defined as serious and prolonged armed hostilities in the territory of a state between the regular military forces and one or more organised armed groups, or between these groups. The first section of this chapter attempted to distinguish internal disturbances or violence from an armed conflict. The second section aimed to exclude certain types of internal armed conflicts from the scope of this study: wars of self-determination, situations when a third state exercises an overall control of a rebel group and certain cases of UN intervention in civil conflicts, all governed by the law applicable in international conflicts. The recent case law of the international criminal tribunals has shed new light on both of these issues. From a purely subjective and discretionary decision in case of recognition of belligerency, the existence of an internal armed conflict can now be objectively assessed by the states concerned and other actors in the international community. The applicability of international law to internal armed conflicts is now based on an objective assessment of the armed conflict on a case-by-case basis. Does the armed violence between the government and organised armed groups or between such groups amount to prolonged and serious armed hostilities? However, there is ultimately no independent body assessing on a case-by-case basis whether the internal situation in a state amounts to an armed conflict and what type of conflict it amounts to.[140] The weakest link in the enforcement of the laws of armed conflicts in internal conflicts remains the fact that it will be for the states themselves to assess each situation. It will be open for them to claim that the criteria or factors highlighted by the recent case law of the tribunals are not met in practice and to negate the existence of an armed conflict and the application of the laws of armed conflicts to it.[141]

Notes

1. See among the various definitions of internal armed conflict given in the literature L. Oppenheim and H. Lauterpacht, *International law– a treatise* (London: Longman, Green and Co., 1952) vol. II, p. 209: 'A civil war exists when two opposing parties within a state have recourse to arms for the purpose of obtaining power in the state, or when a large portion of the population of a state rises in arms against the legitimate government'. L. C. Green, *The contemporary law of armed conflicts* (Manchester, New York: Manchester University Press, 1993) p. 303: 'A non international armed conflict is one in which the governmental authorities of a state are opposed by groups within that state seeking to overthrow those authorities by force of arms.' See also the definition of civil war given by the Institute of International Law in its Wiesbaden session (1975) 56 *Annuaire de l'Institut de Droit International* 545–47.
2. As to terrorism, it can be argued that isolated acts of violence could amount to terrorism and fall short of internal armed conflicts. Repetitive acts or sustained use of force by organised armed groups however might be reported to be terrorism by the central government but nonetheless be regulated by the laws of armed conflicts applicable in internal armed conflicts.
3. See for example, E. Luard, 'Civil conflicts in modern international relations' in E. Luard (ed.), *The international regulation of civil wars* (London: Thames and Hudson, 1972) pp. 7–25, as well as K. Rupesinghe, *Civil wars, civil peace, an introduction to conflict resolution* (London: Pluto Press, 1998) pp. 25–58.
4. The USA representative at the 1949 Diplomatic Conference in Geneva, *Final record of the diplomatic conference of Geneva of 1949* (Berne, 1951), vol. II, section B, p. 42 (hereafter '1949 Final Record').
5. For an historical overview see R. Abi-Saab, *L'article 3 commun aux Conventions de Genève* (Geneva: Institute Henri Dunant, Pedone, 1986) as well as R. Abi-Saab, 'Les conflits internes aujourd'hui' in V. Y Ghebali, D. Kappeler (eds.), *Les multiples aspects de relations internationales: études à la mémoire du professeur Jean Siotis* (Brussels: Bruylant, 1995) pp. 313–25.
6. See, in particular, L. Moir, *The law of internal armed conflict* (Cambridge: Cambridge University Press, 2002).
7. G. I. A. D. Draper, 'Humanitarian law and internal armed conflicts' (1983) 13 *Georgian journal of international and comparative law* 257.
8. See H. Lauterpacht, *Recognition in international law* (Cambridge: Cambridge University Press, 1947) p. 176.

9. For a thorough study of the concept and practice of recognition of belligerency, see Moir, *The law of internal armed conflict*, pp. 4–18.

10. Hereafter referred to as 'common Article 3'.

11. 1977 Protocol Additional to the Geneva Conventions of 12 August 1949, and Relating to the Protection of Victims of Non-international Armed Conflicts, UN.Doc.A.32/144 (1977); (1977) 16 *ILM* 1391. Hereafter referred to as 'Protocol II'.

12. Hereafter referred to as 'the Rome statute' or the 'ICC statute'.

13. The draft proposal, which came before the 1949 Diplomatic Conference, extended the application of the entire conventions to non-international armed conflicts on the basis of reciprocity. See T. Farer, 'The humanitarian laws of war in civil strife: towards a definition of international armed conflict', (1971) 7 *Revue belge du droit international* 20–55 at 31.

14. For example, the French representative stated: 'It was impossible to carry the protection of individuals to the point of sacrificing the rights of states', see 1949 Final Record, p. 10. Similarly, the Mexican delegate said: 'In any case, the rights of states should not be placed above all humanitarian considerations', *ibid.*, p. 11.

15. See the statement of the French representative, *ibid.*, p. 10, as well as the statement of the Rumanian delegate, *ibid.*, p. 11.

16. See 1949 Final Record, p. 129, as well as pp. 99, 121, 333 and 335.

17. Such an interpretation also appears in the ICRC commentary of common Article 3, in J. Pictet and others (eds.), *Commentary on the Geneva Conventions of 12 August 1949* (Geneva: ICRC, 1960) vol. II, pp. 52–54.

18. Article 1.1 of Protocol II.

19. It is interesting to note that the Rome statute has included Article 1.4 of Protocol II in Article 8.2(d). The court will not have jurisdiction over acts committed in internal disturbances or tensions.

20. The Secretary-General's report on respect for human rights in conflicts observed as well that 'the suggested attempts at defining armed conflicts tended in most cases to exclude situations of internal disturbance or internal tensions'. See UN.Doc.A.8052, 18 September 1970, pp. 65–66, cited in D. Ciobanu, 'The concept and determination of the existence of armed conflicts not of an international character' (1975) 58 *Rivista di diritto internazionale* 48–79 at 54. See also R. J. Dupuy and A. Leonetti, 'La notion de conflit armé à caractère non international' in A. Cassese (ed.), *The new humanitarian law of armed conflict* (Naples: Editoriale Scientifica, 1979) pp. 258–76 at p. 260. In general, see also, D. Momtaz, 'Le droit international humanitaire applicable aux conflits armés non internationaux' (2001) 292 *Recueil des cours* 49–55.

21. The French proposed that the 'rebels forces must be an organised military force belonging to a responsible authority capable of respecting or enforcing respect for the convention in a given territory'. Spain believed that the sign of an armed conflict was the use by the acting government of regular military forces against the insurgents. On the contrary, the USA, China, Canada, Australia and the UK believed that common Article 3 could only apply in conflicts fulfilling the

characteristics of a recognition of belligerency. See 1949 Final Record, pp. 10–15. For an overview of all the amendments proposed to define internal armed conflict, see 1949 Final Record, pp. 120–27.

22. Some of these criteria are included in the ICRC commentary to common Article 3 and are presented by the ICRC as 'convenient criteria' to determine the existence of an internal armed conflict. See J. Pictet, *The Geneva Conventions of 12 August 1949– commentary on the IV Geneva Convention relative to the protection of civilian persons in times of war* (Geneva: ICRC, 1958) pp. 35–36.

23. The commentary by the ICRC on the notion of conflict not of an international character sends us back to the criteria proposed during the negotiations as useful ones to distinguish internal violence from armed conflicts. See Pictet, *Commentary on the Geneva Conventions of 12 August 1949*, pp. 52–54.

24. See G. Draper, 'The Geneva Conventions of 1949' (1965/I) 114 *Recueil des cours* 90–91. See also Commission of Experts report on the question of aid to the victims of internal conflicts (Geneva, 25–30 October 1962) (1963) *IRRC* 81, which provides guidelines on this matter: 'the existence of an armed conflict, within the meaning of article 3, cannot be denied if the hostile action, directed against the legal government, is of a collective character and consists of a minimum amount of organisation'.

25. Practice of states in relation to common Article 3 will be looked at in more detail in chapter 2 of this book. An American delegate during the 1974–77 diplomatic conference said blankly: 'The non-observation of Article 3 was an almost universal phenomenon', see *Official records of the diplomatic conference on the reaffirmation and development of international humanitarian law applicable in armed conflicts, Geneva (1974–77)* (Berne, 1978) CDDH/III/SR.32, p. 9.

26. Article 1.1 of Protocol II.

27. See 1949 Final Record, vol. II, section B, p. 10.

28. This excludes from the scope of application of Protocol II, conflicts such as those which took place in Lebanon or in Somalia.

29. During the diplomatic conference of 1974–77, an independent UN body, the ICRC, the ICJ or an ad hoc arbitral tribunal were all envisaged as institutions able to determine the existence of an armed conflict. All proposals were rejected, see Ciobanu, 'The concept and determination of the existence of armed conflicts not of an international character' 73.

30. This seems therefore to contradict one of the purposes of international humanitarian law. See Dupuy and Leonetti, 'La notion de conflit armé à caractère non international' 270.

31. See S. Cho, 'Applicability of international humanitarian law to internal armed conflicts', Ph.D. thesis, University of Cambridge (1996) p. 49.

32. The definition of internal armed conflict contained in Protocol II was not included in the draft statute at the start of the negotiations in Rome or within the first 'bureau discussion paper' (UN.Doc.A/CONF.183/C.1/L.53, 6 July 1998). It was introduced, most probably at the request of some countries from the Arab

group, in the second discussion paper (UN.Doc.A/CONF.183/C.1/L.59, 10 July 1998). An important number of countries reacted against this inclusion and the package deal, which was then presented to all delegations on 16 July 1998 (UN.Doc.A/CONF.183/C.1/L.76.Add.2, 16 July 1998) did not include it.

33. See Rome statute, Article 8.2(f). It is interesting to note that the only difference between the text in the Rome statute and the case law of the ICTY is the word 'violence', which has been changed for the word 'conflict' (protracted armed conflict, instead of protracted armed violence). The word 'violence' was seen as too low a threshold. This definition was proposed by the delegation of Sierra Leone, see UN.Doc.A./CONF.183/C.1/L.62 (13 July 1998).

34. Hereafter referred to as ICTY.

35. *Prosecutor v. Tadić*, case No. IT-94-1-AR72, decision on the defence motion for interlocutory appeal on jurisdiction, 2 October 1995, para. 67. Hereafter referred to as 'the *Tadić* jurisdiction decision' (available online on www.un.org/icty (1996) 35 *ILM* 32).

36. *Ibid.*, para. 70.

37. *Ibid.*, para. 70.

38. *Ibid.* See for an application, *Prosecutor v. Simić and others*, case No. IT-95-9-PT, decision on the pre-trial motion by the prosecution requesting the Trial Chamber to take judicial notice of the international character of the conflict in Bosnia-Herzegovina, 25 March 1999.

39. This definition was also used by the Court of Appeals of Amsterdam in the *Bouterse* case of 20 November 2000; see in particular para. 5.3.2, available online on www.rechtspraak.nl as well as in (2000) 3 *YbIHL* 677.

40. For the application of such test to the factual circumstances of each case, see for example *Tadić* trial, paras. 561–68, *Aleksovski* trial, paras. 43–44, *Jelisić* trial, paras. 29–31, *Furundžija* trial, para. 59, *Kordić* trial, paras. 22–31 and 160, *Kunarac* trial, paras. 402 and 567–69, *Čelebići* trial, paras. 183–92, *Stakić* trial, paras. 566–74 and *Limaj* trial, paras. 83–174.

41. See *Tadić* trial, para. 565, *Kordić* trial, para. 29, *Čelebići* trial, paras. 186–89.

42. See *Tadić* trial, paras. 566 and 568, *Kordić* trial, para. 30, *Kunarac* trial, para. 567, *Čelebići* trial, para. 186, *Stakić* trial, para. 572.

43. See *Čelebići* trial, para. 187.

44. See *Čelebići* trial, para. 188, *Milošević* rule 98*bis* decision, paras. 30–31.

45. See *Tadić* trial, para. 567 and *Čelebići* trial, para. 190.

46. See *Milošević* rule 98*bis* decision paras. 23–24.

47. See paras. 177–202.

48. See paras. 122–25 and 144–54 (appeal pending).

49. These cases are the *Simić* trial (para. 978), *Krstić* trial (paras. 481–83), *Kvočka* trial (paras. 123–26), *Krnojelac* trial (paras. 51 and 61), *Kunarac* (trial judgment, paras. 402 and 567–69, appeal judgment, paras. 55–65), *Erdemović* appeal (para. 3), *Furundžija* trial (para. 59), *Kupreškić* trial (para. 760), *Stakić* trial

(paras. 566–74), *Vasiljević* trial (paras. 24–27 and 57), *Galić* trial (paras. 9–12), *Jelisić* trial (paras. 29–31), *Halilović* trial (paras. 23–29), *Blagojević* trial (paras. 536 and 549), *Strugar* trial (paras. 215–17) and *Limaj* trial (paras. 83–174) cases.

50. *Limaj* trial, paras. 83–174.
51. *Limaj* trial, para. 85.
52. *Limaj* trial, para. 85.
53. *Limaj* trial, para. 88.
54. *Ibid.*
55. *Limaj* trial, para. 89.
56. See *Limaj* trial, paras. 93–134.
57. See *Limaj* trial, paras. 94–97.
58. *Limaj* trial, paras. 98 and 110–12.
59. *Limaj* trial, paras. 99 and 102.
60. *Limaj* trial, paras. 100, 105, 109.
61. *Limaj* trial, paras. 101–3.
62. *Limaj* trial, para. 104.
63. *Limaj* trial, para. 108.
64. *Limaj* trial, paras. 113–17.
65. *Limaj* trial, para. 118.
66. *Limaj* trial, paras. 119–20.
67. *Limaj* trial, paras. 121–22.
68. *Limaj* trial, paras. 123–24.
69. *Limaj* trial, paras. 125–29.
70. *Limaj* trial, paras. 135–63.
71. *Limaj* trial, paras. 146, 159 and 164–65.
72. *Limaj* trial, paras. 136, 138, 156, 159, 161, 164–66.
73. *Limaj* trial, para. 167.
74. *Limaj* trial, paras. 146, 158, 159.
75. See the conclusions of the Chamber appearing in *Limaj* trial, paras. 171–73.
76. *Limaj* trial, para. 168.
77. Hereafter referred to as 'ICTR'.
78. See *Akayesu* trial, paras. 619–26, *Kayishema* trial, para. 170, *Musema* trial, para. 250, *Rutaganda* trial, paras. 92–93, *Cyangugu* trial, para. 767 (judicial notice of the state of internal armed conflict had been taken in this case), *Semanza* trial, paras. 355 and 514, *Bagilishema* trial, paras. 99–101 or *Kamuhanda* trial, paras. 721–24. In Rwanda, the Rwandan Patriotic Front (RPF) told the ICRC that it considers itself bound by the Geneva Conventions and their Additional Protocols; see Report of the UN High Commissioner for Human Rights on his mission to Rwanda of 11–12 May 1994, Doc.E/C.N4/S-3/3, 19 May 1994.
79. See *Akayesu* trial, para. 603. For a commentary, see H. Speiker, 'The International Criminal Court and non-international armed conflicts' (2000) 13 *Leiden journal of international law* 408–9.

80. *Abella v. Argentina*, Inter-American Commission on Human Rights, Report No. 55/97, Case No. 11.137: Argentina, OEA.Ser/L/V.II.97, Doc. 38, 18 November 1997. Extracts reprinted in M. Sassoli and A. Bouvier (eds.), *How does law protect in war* (Geneva: ICRC, 1999) pp. 1042–53 (referred hereafter as '*Tablada* case').

81. *Tablada* case, para. 148. See the relevant extracts on this point, paras. 147–56.

82. *Tablada* case, para. 149. See also ICRC, Draft Additional Protocols to the Geneva Conventions, Commentary, Geneva, October 1973, CDDH/3.

83. *Tablada* case, para. 150, and see also ICRC, *Protection and assistance activities in situations not covered by international humanitarian law* (1985) IRRC 13.

84. *Tablada* case, para. 153. The Commission goes on to say that 'common article 3 is generally understood to apply to low intensity and open armed confrontations between relatively organised armed forces or groups that take place within the territory of a particular state', para. 152.

85. *Tablada* case, para. 155.

86. On this point, see also Dupuy and Leonetti, 'La notion de conflit armé à caractère non international', p. 270.

87. The last formal recognition of belligerency was during the Boer War 1899–1902. For a thorough study of this concept, see Moir, *The law of internal armed conflict*, pp. 4–18.

88. For a good overview of this topic see R. Provost, *International human rights and humanitarian law* (Cambridge: Cambridge University Press, 2002) pp. 253–60.

89. See UN General Assembly resolutions UN.Doc.A/2383 (7 November 1968), UN.Doc.A/2508 (21 November 1969) and UN.Doc. A/2547 (11 December 1969).

90. See UN General Assembly resolutions UN.Doc.A/2395 (29 November 1968), UN.Doc.A/2547 (11 December 1969) and UN.Doc.A/2707 (14 December 1970).

91. See UN General Assembly resolution UN.Doc.A/2396 (2 December 1968).

92. See UN General Assembly resolutions UN.Doc.A/2547 (11 December 1969) and UN.Doc.A/2678 (9 December 1970).

93. See UN General Assembly resolution UN.Doc.A/3103 (12 December 1973) adopted with eighty-three votes in favour, thirteen against and nineteen abstentions. See E. David, *Précis de droit des conflits armés* (Brussels: Bruylant, 1994) p. 64.

94. Protocol I will apply to such conflicts only if the authority representing the people engaged in an armed conflict against a state makes a special declaration undertaking to apply the 1949 Geneva Conventions and Protocol I in relation to that conflict pursuant to Article 96.3 of the said Protocol.

95. See Provost, *International human rights and humanitarian law*, p. 255, which states that 'there is no absolute identity between the notions of self-determination as understood in general international law and national liberation armed conflicts under humanitarian law'.

96. See Article 3.2 of Protocol II on non-intervention which states: 'nothing in this Protocol shall be invoked as a justification for intervening, directly or indirectly,

for any reason whatever, in the armed conflict or in the internal or external affairs of the High Contracting Party in the territory of which that conflict occurs.'

97. In general on this point, see D. Schindler, 'Le droit international humanitaire et les conflits armés internationalisés' (1982) *IRRC* 263, R. Kolb, *Ius in bello, le droit international des conflit armés, précis* (Basle: Helbing and Lichtenham, 2003) pp. 85–93, R. Pinto, 'Les règles du droit international concernant la guerre civile' (1965/I) 114 *Recueil des cours* 482, and H. Wehberg, 'La guerre civile et le droit international' (1938/I) 63 *Recueil des cours* 63. See also R. Bierzanek, 'Quelques remarques sur l'applicabilité du droit international humanitaire des conflits armés aux conflits internes internationalisés' in C. Swinarski (ed.), *Studies and essays on international humanitarian law and Red Cross principles in honour of J. Pictet* (Geneva: ICRC, Martinus Njihoff Publishers, 1984) pp. 281–90.

98. See David, *Précis de droit des conflicts armés*, pp. 61–63 and Kolb, *Ius in bello*, p. 88.

99. ICRC, Reports of activities, 1961, pp. 48–49, 1963, p. 15 and 1970, pp. 29–32. See on this point David, *Précis de droit des conflicts armés*, p. 61.

100. A German court has considered that the Spanish conflict remained a civil war notwithstanding the direct involvement of German troops in the conflict. See *Spanish Civil War pension entitlement case*, F. R. G., Fe.Social Court, 14 December 1978, 80 *ILR* 672. For the refusal by the Afghan authorities to consider the offer of service by the ICRC, see ICRC Report of Activities, 1981, pp. 37–38. It is interesting to note that the UN General Assembly resolutions UN.Doc.41/158 (4 December 1986) and 42/135 (7 December 1987) were asking the belligerents to respect the Geneva Conventions of 1949 and the 1977 Protocols.

101. See, for example, Meyrowitz, 'Le droit de la guerre dans le conflict vietnamien' (1967) *AFDI* 156, E. David, *Précis de droit des conflicts armés*, pp. 58–60 and Schindler, 'The different types of armed conflicts according to the Geneva Conventions and Protocols' (1979/II) 163 *Recueil des cours* 150. See also Ciobanu, 'The concept and determination of the existence of armed conflicts not of an international character' 55.

102. 'Military and paramilitary activities in and against Nicaragua (*Nicaragua v. USA*) (merits)' 76 *ILR* 5, para. 219. In this case, the USA was helping the contras in Nicaragua. In other cases, where the third state was helping the legitimate government, certain authors have argued that this did not change the character of the conflict and that the combats between this intervening state and the rebels were regulated by the law of internal armed conflicts, see Bierzanek, *Quelques remarques*, p. 285.

103. See in general, G. Mettraux, *International crimes and the ad hoc tribunals*, (Oxford: Oxford University Press, 2005) pp. 55–59 and L. Moir, *The law of internal armed conflict*, pp. 46–52.

104. The Chamber concluded that in each case under analysis, it will be necessary for the Trial Chamber to determine the character of the conflict, notwithstanding the

conclusions reached earlier by the Committee of Experts set up by SC resolution 780, 1992, which stated: 'The character and complexity of the armed conflicts concerned, combined with the web of agreements on humanitarian issues the parties have concluded among themselves, justify an approach whereby it applies the law applicable in international armed conflicts to the entirety of the armed conflicts in the territory of the former Yugoslavia.' UN.Doc.S/1994/674, para. 44.

105. The *Tadić* appeal judgment seems to suggest that the direct intervention of a state in an internal armed conflict through his troops internationalises the entire conflict, *Tadić* appeal, para. 84. The Appeals Chamber does not mention the side that a foreign state must take in the conflict for it to be seen as an international armed conflict.

106. See Y. Dinstein, *War, aggression and self-defense* (Cambridge: Cambridge University Press, 4th edn, 2005) pp. 6–7 or Kolb, *Ius in bello*, pp. 88–92.

107. *Prosecutor v. Rajić*, Case No. IT-95-12-R61, Review of the indictment pursuant to Rule 61 (13 September 1996), para. 21.

108. *Ibid.*, paras. 25–26. See also T. Meron, 'Classification of armed conflict in the former Yugoslavia: Nicaragua's fallout' (1998) 92 *AJIL* 240.

109. *Tadić* trial, paras. 605–6.

110. *Ibid.*, para. 607. Judge McDonald in her dissenting opinion, believed that 'the appropriate test of agency from Nicaragua is one of dependency and control and a showing of effective control is not required', para. 4 of her dissenting opinion.

111. See Meron, 'Classification of armed conflict' 236–42, and James Stewart, 'Towards a single definition of armed conflict in international humanitarian law: a critique of internationalized armed conflict' (2003) 85 *IRRC* 313–49 at 326, which states: 'the application of the three-pronged test remains complex, convoluted and the subject of considerable confusion, even among Appeals Chamber Judges themselves'. See also M. Momtaz, 'Le droit international humanitaire applicable aux conflits armés non internationaux' (2001) 292 *Recueil des cours* 59–66.

112. *Nicaragua* case, paras. 446–49.

113. *Ibid.*, paras. 463–64.

114. Meron argues: 'I suggest the Appeals Chamber reject the Nicaragua imputability test and return to the simple, common sense and time-tested approaches of public international law.' He believes that the Tribunal is concerned with individual criminal responsibility and therefore should not use a test borrowed from the law of state responsibility, Meron, 'Classification of armed conflict' 241.

115. Meron, 'Classification of armed conflict' 241.

116. Meron, 'Classification of armed conflict' 242.

117. The Appeals Chamber first looks at the laws of armed conflicts and the principles regulating the status of lawful combatants. It finds that for irregular armed groups to be qualified as lawful combatants, it must be shown that a party to the conflict has control over them (paras. 88–97). In order to determine the degree of control

necessary, the Appeals Chamber looks at general international law and the laws on state responsibility, which set out the legal criteria for attributing acts performed by individuals or armed groups to a foreign state (para. 98). It states in para. 105: 'international humanitarian law does not include legal criteria regarding imputability specific to this body of law. Reliance must therefore be had upon the criteria established by general rules on state responsibility.'

118. *Tadić* appeal, para. 84.

119. *Ibid.*, para. 104.

120. *Ibid.*, para. 123.

121. *Ibid.*, para. 131.

122. *Ibid.*, para. 132.

123. *Ibid.*, para. 137.

124. See also, the *Aleksovski* trial, where Judge Vohrah and Judge Nieto-Navia stated that 'there must be some evidence of the control, direction or command of the state that is sufficiently strong to impute the rebel forces' acts to it', and concluded that the Prosecutor had failed to prove that the 'HVO was in fact acting under the overall control of the HV in carrying out the armed conflict against Bosnia'. See paras. 14 and 27 of the Joint Opinion of the majority, Judge Vohrah and Judge Nieto-Navia, on the applicability of Article 2 of the statute pursuant to para. 46 of the judgment, *Aleksovski* trial.

125. See M. Momtaz, 'Le droit international humanitaire applicable aux conflits armés non internationaux' (2001) 292 *Recueil des cours* 65.

126. *Ibid.*

127. See the *Blaškić* trial where the Chamber concluded that the conflict in question was of an international character. It was proved that Croatia directly intervened in Bosnia-Herzegovina by sending its own military forces (para. 94), and that Croatia exercised an overall control over the Bosnian Croats and HVO forces (para. 122). This finding was not overturned on appeal, see *Blaškić* appeal, paras. 167–89.

128. *Naletilić* trial, paras. 183–88.

129. See *Kordić* trial where the Chamber concludes that Croatia exercised overall control over the HVO through its provision of financial and training assistance, military equipment and operational support, and by its participation in the organisation, co-ordination and planning of military operations with the HVO, see para. 145. This finding was not overturned on appeal, see *Kordić* appeal, paras. 299–313.

130. See *Čelibići* appeals, where the Appeals Chamber confirms the international character of the conflict found by the Trial Chamber and upheld the 'overall control' test identified in *Tadić* appeal, see para. 26.

131. *Aleksovski* appeal, paras. 120–36.

132. *Kordić* appeal, paras. 307, 310 and 313.

133. See Mettraux, *International crimes and the ad hoc tribunals*, p. 59, giving the examples of the *Krnojelac* and *Hadžihasanović* cases.

134. For an excellent review of this topic, see R. Kolb, G. Porretto and S. Vité, *L'application du droit international humanitaire et des droits de l'homme aux organisations internationale, Forces de paix et administrations civiles transitoires* (Brussels: Bruylant, 2005) pp. 175–93.

135. On the issue of the respect by UN forces of international humanitarian law, see the administrative circular issued by the UN Secretary-General entitled 'Observance by UN forces of international humanitarian law', UN.Doc.ST/SGB/1999/13.

136. Such intervention has been possible thanks to a broadening by the Security Council of its own jurisdiction to include internal armed conflicts within the ambit of the collective security system of the UN Charter. A great number of internal conflicts presenting gross humanitarian violations have been interpreted as constituting threats to international peace and security. For a good overview of this evolution, see G. Fox, 'International law and civil wars' (1994) 26 *International law and politics* 633–54.

137. See C. Emmanuelli, 'Les forces des Nations Unies et le droit international humanitaire' in L. Condorelli (ed.), *The United Nations and international humanitarian law* (Paris: Pedone, 1996) pp. 345–70 at p. 358; D. Shraga, 'The United Nations as an actor bound by international humanitarian law' in L. Condorelli (ed.), *The United Nations and international humanitarian law* (Paris: Pedone, 1996) pp. 317–38 and Kolb, Porretto and Vité, *L'application du droit international humanitaire et des droits de l'homme aux organisations internationales*, pp. 184–86.

138. In respect of the conflict in Somalia, note the surprising decision from the Military Court of Belgium, 17 December 1997 (1998) *Journaux des tribunaux* 286, which refuses to acknowledge even the applicability of common Article 3 to the Somali conflict. In determining the conditions of applicability of common Article 3, the court applies the conditions of applicability of Protocol II, and believes that they are not fulfilled by the parties to the conflict in Somalia. The court took the view that the warring factions *'n'appartenaient pas à une quelconque structure étatique et n'opéraient pas d'une manière permanente et coordonnée mais plutôt d'une manière anarchique . . . éparse et désordonnée'* ((2003) *Revue belge de droit international* 631). For a good critique of this decision see, A. Weyembergh 'La notion de conflit armé, le droit international humanitaire et les forces des Nations Unies en Somalie' (1999) *Revue de droit pénal et de criminologie* 177–201. Weyembergh believes that the conflict between factions in Somalia was governed by common Article 3, and that the active participation in the conflict of UN forces rendered the whole conflict international.

139. See, in particular, F. Hampson, 'States' military operations authorized by the United Nations and international humanitarian law' in L. Condorelli (ed.), *The United Nations and international humanitarian law* (Paris: Pedone, 1996) pp. 371–426 at p. 391 and Kolb, Porretto and Vité, *L'application du droit*

international humanitaire et des droits de l'homme aux organisations inter-
nationales, pp. 184–90.

140. During the negotiations of Additional Protocol II, Italy put forward the proposal
that the ICRC could be vested with the task of verifying whether the situation at
hand called for the application of Additional Protocol II. This was rejected. See
A. Cassese (ed.), *The new humanitarian law of armed conflict, proceedings of the
1976 and 1977 conferences* (Naples: Ed. Scientifica, 1980) p. 109.

141. For a recent illustration of this problem, see the position of the Russian
Government towards the events in Chechnya, and see N. Quénivet, 'The Moscow
hostage crisis in the light of the armed conflict in Chechnya' (2001) *YbIHL* 348–72.

2

The laws of war applicable in internal armed conflicts

'Attached to force are certain imperceptible limitations hardly worth mentioning, known as international law and custom, but they scarcely weaken it.'

Clausewitz, *On war*, 1832.[1]

Clausewitz was probably commenting on the use of force between independent states on the battlefield and did not have civil conflicts in mind. Time seems to have proved Clausewitz wrong. The nineteenth century saw the adoption of the first international conventions regulating the conduct of warfare between states, and the twentieth century witnessed the slow genesis of the need for international law to regulate internal armed conflicts. Whilst the trend in conventional international law since 1832 has gone against Clausewitz, his comment is still valid for the actual practice of war in internal armed conflicts throughout the centuries and up to the present day. From the French revolution where General Westerman declared in 1793, 'Il n'y a plus de Vendée, elle est morte sous notre sabre libre avec ses femmes et ses enfants',[2] to the genocide in Rwanda in 1994, internal armed conflicts remain inhumane and destructive.

The acceptance of the principle that international law could regulate some aspects of internal armed conflict was a long and slow process. Civil conflicts were generally thought to fall within the reserved domain of each state. The state was free to decide on the means to restore peace and order. Taking up arms against your state was in itself a crime under the law of the state concerned and insurgents were usually tried for treason. The idea of limiting the sovereignty of the state in this domain was a real challenge to the laws of war. Slowly, the application of a few basic principles of humanity towards rebels became acceptable. The laws applicable in internal armed conflicts stem from the law applicable in international conflicts. It is now possible to draw a parallel between the two bodies of law, even if this parallelism is far from being complete.

Before looking at the principle of individual responsibility for war crimes, the content of the law binding on individuals in internal armed conflicts will be assessed. This chapter will present an overview of the conventional law applicable in such conflicts, introduced by a short historical section on the laws of war up to 1949. This is followed by a study of the two main treaty provisions in force today: common Article 3 and Protocol II to these conventions.[3] The third section of this chapter then looks more closely at the content of customary law applicable in internal armed conflicts.

1. The laws of war applicable in internal armed conflicts before 1949

The purpose of this section is to sketch the origins of the laws of war and their evolution over the centuries from antiquity to the Spanish Civil War.[4] Was there any law deemed applicable in civil conflicts? When did international law start to regulate the way belligerents fought each other in civil conflicts?

1.1 The laws of war and internal armed conflicts prior to the twentieth century

In many ancient civilisations, ruthless behaviour in war seems to have co-existed with the application of basic principles of humanitarian law.[5] The Chinese adopted pragmatic views on the means and methods of warfare,[6] as did the religious literature of India, which laid down fundamental principles of the laws of warfare. The distinction between combatants and non-combatants, as well as the category of protected persons and those 'hors de combat', were recognised by the ancient Hindus.[7] Furthermore, certain weapons deemed to cause indiscriminate loss of life like poisoned or barbed weapons were prohibited.[8] Places of religious worship and houses belonging to persons who were not participating in the war or property that was not in the possession of armed forces could not be attacked or destroyed in accordance with recognised custom and spiritual texts.[9] A great number of these principles are surprisingly similar to the provisions of the Geneva Conventions of 1949 and Additional Protocol I, making ancient India a civilisation with the highest humane ideals of warfare.[10]

Similar rules of warfare were used by the Greeks and the Romans when fighting other 'civilised States properly organised, and enjoying a regular constitution, and not conglomerations of individuals living together in an irregular and precarious association'.[11] Even if these rules of warfare were unevenly respected and applied mainly for pragmatic reasons, these ancient civilisations developed many fundamental principles of the laws of warfare. The dichotomy between international and internal conflicts did not exist at that time; respect for the rules of warfare grew from recognition of the nature of the enemy as a civilised and organised group.[12]

In the Middle Ages, chivalry was a normative code of conduct for knights and soldiers. Meron describes it as a 'way of life intimately linked to the pursuit of war, effectively serving as a social mystique associated with the conduct of war'.[13]

This precise code of conduct contrasts sharply with attitudes towards what was considered to be rebellion. Recent research into the work of Shakespeare has highlighted the content of the rules of chivalry in the Middle Ages as well as their conditions of applicability.[14] L. Rosensweig Blank suggests that in the Middle Ages, the common law distinguished between international and internal wars through the notion of allegiance. A war between the sovereign and foreign armies, who owed no allegiance to this king, was 'international', and a conflict between sovereign and subjects, who owed allegiance to him, was a domestic conflict. The study of Shakespeare's plays shows clearly that the norms and obligations of chivalry did not apply in domestic conflicts.[15] Rebellion against the sovereign was seen as destroying the kingdom from within[16] and amounted to treason. Shakespeare emphasised that such conflict was wholly within the king's domain and that rebels, whom one 'beats down, rather than fights',[17] will be 'brought to the correction of the king's law'.[18]

The rise of the 'nation state' in the seventeenth century reinforced both the dichotomies between national and international conflicts and the application of the principles of chivalry in conflicts between states. Classical writers detailed the fundamental principles of the laws of war inherited from both ancient civilisations and the code of chivalry.[19] They shared the view that, these principles regulating the conduct of belligerents were only applicable in conflicts between states and that internal uprisings remained solely within the domestic sovereignty of the state.

The great classical writer of the eighteenth century, Vattel, reinforced these concepts but called, however, for the applicability of the 'common laws of war, those maxims of humanity, moderation and probity' between the parties to a civil conflict of a magnitude similar to international conflicts.[20] He was one of the earliest writers to advocate such principle for reasons of convenience, but also on the basis of humanitarian principles.[21]

The question of potential restraint during civil conflicts only came within the purview of international law during the nineteenth century. Gradually, it became acceptable to distinguish between civil conflicts on the basis of their scale and magnitude. Rebellion or internal uprisings, notwithstanding that they could be dealt with quickly by the central government, remained a purely domestic matter. No laws or customs of war were thought to be applicable, and municipal law was applied against the traitors.

A more organised rebellion amounting to a credible threat to the government was defined as insurgency.[22] Recognition of insurgency by third states amounted to the acknowledgement of a civil conflict of a certain magnitude, leaving the third party free to determine the consequences of such recognition.[23]

The legal status of a civil war was changed when the conflict reached the scale and magnitude of an inter-state conflict and the belligerents were treating each other as if they were in a war between recognised states. The recognition of belligerency was the first attempt to apply the laws and customs of war to civil conflicts.[24] As indicated in chapter 1, the factual existence of war was recognised if certain specific conditions were fulfilled.[25] The acting government needed to be faced with a conflict of a general character, where the insurgents under responsible command were occupying a part of the territory and conducting the hostilities in accordance with the laws of war.

This recognition could come on the initiative of the government fighting the rebels, or from a third state. It was a purely discretionary move from the government, which usually would recognise the status of belligerency for reasons of convenience, self-interest, or humanitarian considerations.[26] The government was therefore putting the belligerents under an obligation to respect the customs of war against its own forces, and at the same time freeing itself from any responsibility for acts committed by the recognised belligerents.[27]

More frequently, recognition of belligerency has come from one or more third states usually for political motives.[28] A third state may support the struggle of the insurgents politically or may want to protect its own nationals or property in the territory controlled by the insurgents.[29]

The direct consequence of recognition of belligerency was to make the laws of war applicable between the parties. It also rendered the international law of neutrality applicable between the recognising third state

and the parties to the conflicts.[30] Recognition of belligerency was beneficial to the insurgents,[31] but was often implicit, by granting the status
of prisoners of war to rebels for example. Such recognition was granted
in a limited number of cases and generally was accompanied by a fair
amount of respect for the laws of war.[32]

The American Civil War provides an example of a civil conflict where
recognition of belligerency introduced an early respect for the customs
of war. President Lincoln published in 1863 the 'Instructions for the
Government of Armies of the US in the field', the famous Lieber Code.[33]
It represented the first attempt to codify the laws and customs of war and
covered a wide range of issues from the treatment of prisoners of wars,
the principle of military necessity, the protection of civilians and civilian
property, to the prohibition of rape, or the use of poison in modern
warfare.[34] Ironically, the Lieber Code having been established to apply
in a civil war became the basis of further codification of the laws of war
in international conflicts.[35] Lieber argued that the Union could accord
the privileges of belligerency to the South without implying recognition
of the belligerents,[36] or the legitimacy of their government.[37] It is interesting to note that they applied the laws of war to a civil conflict, which
had the characteristics of an inter-state conflict, while keeping a specific
section of the code, section 10, for 'Insurrection-Civil war-Rebellion'.[38]
According to Meron, Lieber added this section as he 'wanted to avoid the
impression that the Code was applicable to civil rather than to international wars'.[39] The dichotomy between international and civil conflicts
seems to be reaffirmed in the Lieber Code. It should not be seen as
enacting rules applicable in civil wars, where only municipal law applied
in the nineteenth century, but rather codifying for the first time, the law
applicable in international conflicts and large-scale civil wars.[40]

There were also a number of cases where the recognition of belligerency by third states had no effect on the violence and bloodiness of the
conflicts and where very few customs of war were applied between
belligerents. The US and the UK had recognised at an early stage the
nature of belligerents of most Spanish Colonies in South America.[41]
This recognition at first had no effect on the violent way the rebellion
was quashed by Ferdinand of Spain between 1810 and 1824.[42]

Finally, state practice in the nineteenth century shows that where no
recognition of belligerency was granted either by a third state or by
the government in place, the laws of war were rarely thought to be
applicable or respected.[43] The various European revolutions in Portugal,
Poland, Italy, Austria, Prussia and France between 1830 to 1849 as well as

the Paris Commune in 1871 were violently repressed by the governments in power.[44]

We can therefore conclude that in the nineteenth century, the extension of the laws of war to civil conflicts remained purely discretionary on the basis of the recognition of belligerency. Despite a few voices calling for a humanisation of civil conflicts,[45] they remained primarily regulated by municipal law. State practice reveals as well that states did not feel under any *obligation* to extend the rules of war to civil conflicts. The sovereignty-orientated approach was therefore still predominant, even if many events throughout the century certainly highlighted the issue of the laws applicable in civil wars.

1.2 The laws of war and internal armed conflicts at the beginning of the twentieth century

The codification of the laws of war in international conflicts began in 1856 with the Paris declaration on aspects of maritime law and the Lieber Code. It was followed by many conventions on both the treatments of sick or wounded, prisoners of war and civilians (Geneva Conventions of 1864, 1906 and 1929) and on the means and methods of warfare (Declaration of St Petersburg 1868, Hague Conventions 1899 and 1907). These conventions were purely applicable between parties to an international conflict and civil conflicts were not mentioned in these instruments.

The Martens Clause, appearing in the preamble of the 1907 Hague Convention IV respecting the laws and customs of war on land,[46] speaks about the application of the principles of the law of nations in cases not covered by the instrument in question. Therefore, one wonders if this clause was meant to cover cases of internal armed conflicts. The *travaux préparatoires*, however, reveal that this clause was introduced in order to resolve the contentious issue of the status of civilians who took up arms against an occupying force.[47] Should they be treated as *franc-tireurs* or should the occupying power treat them as legitimate combatants? Unable to agree on this question, the parties adopted the Martens Clause. Civilians and combatants remain 'under the protection and the rule of the principles of the laws of nations, as they result from the usages established among civilised nations, from the laws of humanity, and the dictates of public conscience'.[48] The Martens Clause seems to refer therefore to the importance of customary principles in the laws of war, to the laws of humanity which have been interpreted as 'prohibiting means and methods of war which are not necessary for the attainment of a definite military advantage'[49] and to the dictates of public conscience,[50] a concept 'too vague to really be used as the basis for a separate rule of law'.[51]

Nowadays, the Martens Clause can be found in Article 1.2 of the 1977 Additional Protocol I, and in the preamble of Protocol II.[52] In conclusion, it seems clear that from 1907 onwards, this clause could not be interpreted as being applicable in internal armed conflicts and states did not feel under any obligation at the beginning of the century to apply any substantive rules in civil conflicts.

Nonetheless, the beginning of the twentieth century also saw efforts by the International Committee of the Red Cross (ICRC) for some international regulation to be applicable in civil conflicts.[53] In 1921,[54] the International Red Cross Conference adopted a resolution establishing for the first time the rights of all victims of civil wars to receive aid and relief from Red Cross Societies and in default the ICRC.[55] In the midst of the Spanish Civil War, the ICRC obtained the adoption of a more substantial resolution on 'the role and activity of the National Red Cross in time of civil war'[56] during the 1938 Conference of the Red Cross Societies. This resolution requested the ICRC or the National Red Cross Societies to obtain from the belligerents:

> The application of the humanitarian principles ... in the Geneva Conventions of 1929, the Tenth Hague Convention of 1907 ...; humane treatment for all political prisoners, their exchange, and as far as possible, their release; respect of the life and liberty of non-combatants, facilities for the transmission of news of a personal nature; and effective measures for the protection of children.[57]

This resolution seems to be the first of its kind to extend the application of the main principles of the laws of war to civil conflicts.[58]

The Spanish Civil War represents a turning point in the international regulation of civil wars in many respects. First, as has been seen, when faced with the daily atrocities of the Spanish Civil War, states recognised plainly the role of the ICRC and Red Cross Societies in 1938, and they called for civil conflicts to be made more humane.[59]

Secondly, the institution of the recognition of belligerency really showed its limits and its desuetude in relation to civil conflicts.[60] The Spanish Civil War had the characteristics of a large-scale civil war where the insurgents controlled a portion of the territory, and had a governmental organisation and a regular army abiding by the laws of war.[61] The Spanish Government exchanged prisoners with the insurgents and declared a blockade on those harbours under the control of the insurgents.[62] In 1936, third states even signed an agreement of non-intervention in the Spanish conflict. Notwithstanding these facts, the acting government never undertook formal recognition of belligerency and massive violations of the laws of war were perpetrated by both sides.[63]

Thirdly, the scale of these violations and the killing of civilians showed clearly that limits needed to be imposed by international law on the means and methods of warfare used in civil conflicts.[64] Cassese shows in his detailed study that many states called consistently for both sides to respect the fundamental principles of the laws of war: the prohibition on intentional bombing of civilians,[65] of attacks on non-military objectives[66] and respect for the rule concerning the precautions that must be taken when attacking objectives.[67] The magnitude and the duration of the conflict, as well as the use of aerial bombardment, created the view that 'certain human values must be proclaimed and protected at all times, regardless of whether the conflict is internal or international'.[68]

The end of the 1930s saw a real evolution in the laws applicable in civil conflicts. It became much more widely accepted amongst states that the fundamental principles of the laws of war should apply in large-scale civil wars, regardless of any recognition of belligerency.[69] The Spanish Civil War witnessed therefore the birth of a core of customary law principles applicable in internal conflicts,[70] and created the impetus necessary for the adoption of some treaty norms applicable in internal conflicts.

2. Treaty law applicable in internal armed conflicts after 1949

The Spanish Civil War and its catalogue of violations made states aware of the necessity to adopt some treaty norms dealing with means and methods of warfare in civil wars, but real developments were not possible until after the Second World War. The minimum humanitarian requirements contained in common Article 3 will be examined, before looking at Protocol II and some more recent treaty norms said to be applicable in internal armed conflicts.

2.1 Adoption and content of common Article 3[71]
of the 1949 Geneva Conventions[72]

The discussions around common Article 3 were some of the most lengthy and disputed of the Geneva diplomatic conference. Views formed during the Spanish Civil War were mainly applicable to large-scale civil wars, so when it came to agreement on treaty norms for internal armed conflicts at large, a more conservative and sovereignty-orientated approach emerged from the diplomatic conference.

Shortly after the end of the Second World War, the ICRC launched a campaign for the codification of the laws applicable in internal armed conflicts. Several proposals were discussed during the 1946[73] and the 1948 Conferences of the National Red Cross Societies. The draft proposal which came before the diplomatic conference, extended to armed conflict not of an international character, the whole provisions of the convention on the basis of reciprocity.

Two main topics of division among negotiating states were quickly discernible: first, the opportunity to have such an article was contested notably by the delegation from Burma, which took the view that under no circumstances could the laws of war be applied to rebels.[74] Furthermore, a group of states, among which were the UK, Canada, Greece and the USA, were afraid that such an article could cover all forms of insurrection or civil disorder, thereby obliging governments to grant belligerent status to all rebels and limiting states in their legitimate measures of repression.[75] Opposing these points of view were a small group of states advocating the humanisation of civil conflicts and favouring the Stockholm text of 1948.[76]

Secondly, the main area of discord remained up to the very end the conditions of applicability of common Article 3. The USA and Greece wanted to make the applicability of Article 3 conditional on a prior recognition of belligerency by the government in place, or by the Security Council.[77] The French proposed instead to lay down some conditions for the applicability of Article 3. They suggested it should apply only when the rebels exhibited some of the characteristics of a state, such as possession of an organised military force under the control of a responsible civilian authority, and the capacity to ensure respect for the provisions of the conventions.[78] Neither of these proposals was agreed by the representatives, the more progressive states arguing that they would render Article 3 entirely inapplicable.[79]

It soon become clear that the conference needed either to choose to limit the type of conflicts covered by the protection of Article 3, or to limit the extent of the provisions contained in Article 3. The first alternative would result in most of the conventions applicable in international conflicts also applying to large-scale civil conflicts. In the second alternative, only minimal provisions would be applicable to larger types of civil conflicts. As efforts to define what was meant by a civil war were inconclusive, the conference decided to establish the minimum humanitarian principles which governments could apply to conflicts not of an international character, independently of any recognition of belligerency. After numerous proposals, amendments and rejections, the plenary meeting adopted common Article 3 by thirty-four votes to twelve, with one abstention.[80]

This compromise, now appearing in common Article 3, spells out in a series of specific prohibitions the convention's most basic humanitarian principles.[81] The benefactors of the protection, under paragraph 1 of Article 3, are the wounded and sick of armed forces in the field or at sea, captured combatants, and the civilian population. The article was considered to apply to 'all persons of the state in which the internal armed conflict was unfolding, except combatants at the time engaged in fighting'.[82] These categories of people should be treated humanely[83] in all circumstances and be spared violence to life and person, in particular murder, mutilation, cruel treatment and torture. Similarly prohibited are the taking of hostages, and outrages upon personal dignity, particularly humiliating and degrading treatment. Expressly prohibited are the passing of sentences and the carrying out of executions without judgment of a regularly constituted court, affording all the judicial guarantees recognised as indispensable by civilised people.[84] It does not however seem that states are required to subject rebels to treatment different from that of common criminals.[85]

Finally, there is a general duty to collect and care for the wounded and the sick.[86] The protection given to captured combatants does not, however, amount to the status of prisoners of war. Furthermore, Article 3 neither deals with the problem of access to captured combatants or civilians, nor with the treatment of those engaged in hostilities.

On the basis of Article 3, both parties to an internal armed conflict, the government in place and the insurgents, become bound by this 'miniature convention'.[87] The ICRC has a right of initiative but on the basis of Article 3, states are under no obligation to accept the offer of service.[88] Finally, the article itself states that it does not affect the legal status of the rebels.[89] It is however the first time that insurgents or rebels are given some rights and obligations under international law automatically on the basis of the nature of the conflict.[90]

The last issue is to determine when the content of Article 3 becomes operative. The scope of application of Article 3 is negatively defined: it applies in conflicts not of an international character. The contours of the category 'internal armed conflict' were outlined in chapter 1. An armed conflict consists of armed hostilities, in the territory of one of the High Contracting Parties, between regular forces and organised armed groups, or between these groups, when these hostilities are sufficiently serious and prolonged.

The application of such criteria demands a close scrutiny of the circumstances of the conflict in question and inevitably, the next question is who will do this? Article 3 is silent on this issue. The ICRC in its commentary suggests that Article 3 applies 'automatically'[91] in an armed conflict occurring within the territory of a state which is party to the conventions. The absence of any precise definition of an internal armed conflict, as well as the silence on any procedural qualification of the conflict, has enabled states to deny the existence of armed conflict on their territory or to minimise the scale and the effect of the violence. This practice is often based on political considerations. States see the repression of what they call 'internal violence' as their sovereign prerogative and wish to choose the means and methods of re-establishing law and order. Similarly, they fear that acknowledgement of the applicability of Article 3 could give the rebels some form of legitimacy. The absence of any conventional procedure to decide on the application of common Article 3[92] leaves recognition of the existence of an armed conflict to individual governments.[93]

Practice has shown that the application of Article 3 is far from automatic.[94] The UK in Kenya, Cyprus and Northern Ireland,[95] refused to admit that Article 3 was applicable in these cases. Portugal never admitted any obligation to apply Article 3 to rebel forces in Mozambique and Angola.[96] Similarly, Pakistan, Sri Lanka, or Russia, during the conflicts in Chechnya, never publicly recognised any obligations under Article 3.

A few countries have recognised the applicability of Article 3 to the fighting occurring on their territory between their governmental forces and rebels. Express recognition by both parties to a conflict was made in Guatemala in 1955, Cuba in 1958, Algeria in 1956, Lebanon in 1958, the Congo in 1961, the Dominican Republic in 1965, and in the Nigerian civil war of 1967.[97] In certain cases, the parties have used Article 3.3. and agreed to render applicable to an internal armed conflict a large part of the principles of international armed conflicts. This was the case of Yemen in 1962[98] or in ex-Yugoslavia in 1992.[99] But these cases remain a minority and it should be remembered that such recognition does not guarantee the effective application of Article 3.[100]

The last major drawback of Article 3 is the absence of any enforcement or supervisory mechanism. Individual criminal responsibility is not provided for and there are no means at the disposal of the state or the international community to force rebel groups to respect Article 3. If an offer of services by the ICRC is accepted, then this institution will in effect, act as a supervisory agent. This role is, however, a limited one, as any public denunciation of violations could impair the work of the ICRC for the victims of the conflict. Furthermore, the presence of the ICRC in a conflict cannot guarantee effective observance of Article 3.

Notwithstanding the lacuna illustrated above, as well as the difficulties of application, Article 3 must be recognised as the first major encroachment on the sovereignty of states in 1949. For a long time it was the only provision giving some minimum humanitarian protection in an internal conflict to the civilian population, sick and wounded or detained persons.[101] One may regret, however, the absence of any provisions concerning the conduct of hostilities and the means and methods of warfare. The application of Article 3 is not based on reciprocity by the other party, but certainly represents the limits to which states were prepared to go in 1949, in dealing with internal armed conflict. One can only agree with Draper when he states: 'The establishment of a legal norm may precede its regular enforcement, but the existence of such a norm is a value in itself.'[102]

2.2 Adoption and content of Additional Protocol II to the 1949 Geneva Conventions[103]

During the period between 1949 and the adoption of Protocol II to the Geneva Conventions, internal armed conflicts increased both in frequency and intensity. The distinction between international and internal armed conflicts became much more blurred: many third-world countries wanted wars of decolonisation to be recognised as international armed conflicts. Similarly, some type of intervention by third states, through logistical, financial or political support to one party in the conflict was recurrent. These factors did not change the nature of civil conflicts in practice, as many legitimate governments denied even the application of Article 3, nor did it render these conflicts less cruel. It was reported that 'eighty percent of the victims of armed conflict since World War II have been created in non-international armed conflict'.[104]

The numerous lacunae in Article 3 and the bloody nature of post-Second World War conflicts[105] called therefore for the adoption of a comprehensive instrument regulating internal armed conflicts. Between 1974 and 1977, a diplomatic conference met in Geneva and took as

the basis of their discussion an ICRC draft.[106] The conference soon
split into three distinct groups:[107] certain western states, Austria, Italy
or Switzerland, favoured an extensive additional protocol; other western
states such as the USA, France and Germany and some socialist countries wished to extend the protection afforded by the new protocol, but
only to well-defined types of internal armed conflicts. A third group of
third-world states canvassed for wars of decolonisation to be included in
the category of international armed conflicts. They obtained in 1974 the
inclusion of 'armed conflicts in which peoples are fighting against
colonial domination and alien occupation and against racist regimes
in the exercise of their right of self-determination', within the ambit of
Protocol I dealing with international armed conflicts.[108] This success
secured, they did not see any need to extend the protection given to
insurgents in other civil conflicts beyond Article 3. Afraid of foreign
intervention in domestic affairs of states, they wanted to reduce as much
as possible the regulation of other types of internal armed conflicts by
international law.

Third-world states did not prevent the adoption of a substantive draft
of 49 articles by consensus during the first phase of debates.[109] However,
in 1977 Pakistan, dissatisfied with the first draft and supported by states
such as China, India, Indonesia, Iraq or Ghana, presented a shorter
version of Protocol II intended as a compromise between maximalists
and minimalists.[110] In fact, the proposal brought major changes to the
first draft protocol by adding two heavy parameters to the conditions of
applicability. Protocol II will apply in:

> an armed conflict which takes place in the territory of a high contracting
> party between its armed forces and dissident armed forces or other
> organised groups which, under responsible command, exercises such
> control over a part of its territory as to enable them to carry out sustained
> and concerted military operations and to implement this Protocol.[111]

The interpretation given to this threshold and the consequences of such
an instrument for the laws of armed conflicts were studied in chapter 1.
The conditions of application of Protocol II resemble the classical conditions for recognition of belligerency. The applicable rules for each type
of conflict are radically different though: in the latter, the entire law of
armed conflict will apply while in the former, a bare skeleton of these
rules will become operative.

Furthermore, the direct consequence of having different thresholds of
applicability between Article 3 and Protocol II is to create two categories

of internal armed conflicts and two legal regimes: in large-scale conflicts between governmental forces and organised dissident groups, both instruments will be applicable. In conflicts not fulfilling the conditions of Protocol II, only Article 3 remains applicable.

With regard to the content of Protocol II, a few contributions must be noted. First, the content of the humanitarian protection of Article 3 is developed in part two on humane treatment. This part details the fundamental guarantees afforded to each person,[112] as well as the guarantees of protection afforded to the persons whose liberty has been restricted[113] and finally judicial guarantees which are positively developed from Article 3.[114] This part extends considerably the content of Article 3; it is inspired by Articles 6, 7 and 8 of the International Covenant on Civil and Political Rights, and has the advantage, contrary to the covenant, of being inderogable rights.

Secondly, the protection and care of the wounded, sick, and the shipwrecked is developed in part three of the protocol which spells out the duty of protection of medical and religious personnel as well as medical units and transports.[115]

Thirdly, another breakthrough of the protocol is the inclusion of specific provisions dealing with the protection of the civilian population from attacks, the protection of objects indispensable to the survival of the civilian population, and of cultural objects.[116]

However, the absence of any provisions on means of combat and on the prohibition of certain weapons is regrettable. The provisions borrowed from Hague law and included in the first draft were dropped in the Pakistani proposal. It therefore seems that a state cannot use napalm, dum dum bullets or gas on foreign states but can use them on their own citizens.[117] Furthermore, any mention of the ICRC is omitted in the final version of the protocol,[118] and according to Article 18.2 relief actions for the civilian population which is suffering undue hardship owing to a lack of the supplies essential to its survival, are subject to the consent of the High Contracting Party.[119]

Finally, provisions on the supervision and enforcement of Protocol II included in the first draft, were entirely abandoned in the final simplified version of the protocol.[120] These omissions can be explained by the general fear in third-world countries of foreign intervention on humanitarian grounds, in what they saw as internal affairs of states.[121] States agreed neither on a procedure for the determination of the applicability of Protocol II,[122] nor on any supervisory mechanism for the enforcement of the instrument. Just like Article 3, Protocol II is silent on the consequences of violations of its provisions. It neither provides for state responsibility nor for individual criminal responsibility. These factors, coupled with the difficulty of applying in practice the high threshold of the instrument, will greatly hamper the usefulness of Protocol II as an international instrument regulating civil conflicts.

Practice since 1977 shows that in the instances where Protocol II could be deemed to apply, legitimate governments have had a tendency not to recognise its applicability. In the conflict in El Salvador, for example, the government never expressly acknowledged the applicability of Protocol II in the conflict with the Farabundo Marti National Liberation Front (FMNL).[123] In other cases, like the Ethiopian–Eritrean conflict, or in Yemen, the legitimate government refused the application of Protocol II in their respective internal armed conflicts, though both such conflicts fulfilled the formal conditions of applicability of Protocol II.[124] In the recent conflict in Chechnya, and contrary to the admission of Russia during the first conflict in that region,[125] the central government believes that this armed conflict only amounts to an anti-terrorist operation.[126] The importance of respect for Protocol II has, however, often been recalled by bodies like the ICRC[127] and the UN General Assembly.[128] In a few instances, such as the conflict in ex-Yugoslavia, parties went beyond the application of Protocol II and concluded separate agreements on the application of the Geneva Conventions and Protocol I.[129]

The last-minute fix, adopted by consensus in 1977, is today the most detailed conventional instrument to regulate certain types of civil conflicts. Protocol II helps in clarifying and developing the protection embodied in Article 3, but does leave open a number of questions concerning its scope of applicability and its relevance as a universal instrument. Like Article 3, Protocol II does not mention any provisions on means of warfare and no supervisory or enforcement mechanism was provided.

There are today 159 states party to Protocol II. In section 3 of this chapter, we will look at the body of customary law applicable in internal armed conflicts to discover how much of Protocol II reflects customary international law. As seen in chapter 1, when faced with the recurrent question of a definition of internal armed conflict, states clearly rejected the threshold provided in Article 1.1 of Protocol II during the 1998 Rome conference, but used the content of Protocol II to define war crimes in internal armed conflicts.[130] States showed a clear willingness to break away from the restrictive threshold adopted in Protocol II. With the emergence of customary law principles, the importance of Protocol II as a conventional instrument with such a restricted scope of application has certainly decreased.[131]

2.3 Other relevant treaties[132]

It is a human-rights approach, which has been chiefly developed in Article 3 and Protocol II, leaving out any provision dealing with means of warfare. Treaties on weaponry did not traditionally include internal armed conflicts in their scope of application. Article 1 of the 1980 Convention, on prohibition or restrictions on the use of certain conventional weapons which may be deemed to be excessively injurious or to have indiscriminate effects, applies only to international conflicts, and to wars of national liberation as defined in Article 1.4 of Additional Protocol I.[133] There is, however, a new trend developing, whereby internal armed conflicts are included in conventional instruments dealing with outlawed weapons.[134]

A first review conference refused to extend the scope of the 1980 Convention to internal armed conflicts.[135] However, during the second review conference on 21 December 2001, an amendment to Article 1 of the 1980 Convention on prohibition or restrictions on the use of certain conventional weapons was adopted.[136] The 1980 Convention and its annexed protocols 'shall also apply to situations referred to in Article 3 common to the 1949 Geneva Conventions'. This amendment has entered into force and, as of 1 December 2006, fifty states are party to it.[137] All existing protocols are therefore applicable in internal armed conflict,[138] but the amendment of Article 1 will not automatically apply to additional protocols adopted after 1 January 2002.[139]

Protocol II to the 1980 Convention, on prohibitions or restrictions on the use of mines, booby-traps and other devices as amended on 3 May 1996,[140] includes in its scope of application situations referred to in Article 3.[141] This protocol represents a stricter regime of restrictions on the use of land mines and therefore increases the protection of the civilian population, notably in internal armed conflicts.[142] This protocol counts eighty-seven states parties and entered into force on 3 December 1998.[143]

The 1995 Protocol IV to the 1980 Convention,[144] on blinding laser weapons, seems at first sight to be governed by the general scope of application of the 1980 Convention, and therefore restricted to international armed conflicts. It has been argued, however, that it was the intention of the negotiating parties to make it applicable in internal armed conflicts as well. The ICRC supports this view, and believes that it was not specified in the text, as the negotiations on the land mines protocol did not reach an agreement on this issue at the time of the adoption of the laser protocol.[145] This additional protocol bans the use of 'laser weapons specifically designed, as their sole combat function or as one of their combat functions, to cause permanent blindness to unenhanced vision, that is to the naked eye or to the eye with corrective eyesight devices'.[146] It remains lawful to use other types of laser weapons which are not designed to cause permanent blindness. This protocol has today eighty-five states parties and entered into force on 30 July 1998.[147] Protocol V to the 1980 Convention on explosive remnants of war was adopted on 28 November 2003 and includes both international and internal armed conflicts in its scope of application.[148]

In the area of chemical weapons, the 1993 Convention prohibits all use of chemical weapons in warfare *under any circumstances.*[149] This has been interpreted as being also applicable in internal armed conflicts.[150] This convention also outlaws the manufacture, acquisition, stock-piling and transfer of chemical weapons and establishes a far more extensive prohibition than the 1925 Protocol.[151]

One may also note the 1994 Convention on the Safety of UN and Associated Personnel which applies to any UN operations other than enforcement action under Chapter VII of the Charter, to which the law of international armed conflict applies.[152] It provides for a comprehensive regime of protection of UN operations and personnel, which will apply in internal armed conflicts when UN troops carry out peace-keeping and not peace-enforcing operations.

Another breakthrough in this area has been the adoption of the 1997 UN Convention on the Prohibition of the Use, Stockpiling, Production and Transfer of Anti-personnel Mines and on their Destruction.[153] It will be prohibited for the parties to this convention to use anti-personnel mines under any circumstances.[154] This comprehensive instrument calling for a complete ban on the use and transfer of land mines is therefore applicable in internal armed conflicts, but excludes mines 'designed to be detonated by the presence, proximity or contact of a vehicle as opposed to a person'.[155] This convention entered into force on 1 March 1999 and has 152 states parties to it.[156]

One can also note the 1954 Hague Convention for the Protection of Cultural Property in the Event of Armed Conflict and its Protocol II of 26 March 1999. The 1954 Convention is applicable to internal armed conflicts and the second protocol provides for measures to reinforce, respect and implement this instrument. This regime is applicable explicitly in internal armed conflicts.[157]

Finally, mention must be made of the 2000 Optional Protocol to the Convention on the Rights of the Child on Involvement of Children in Armed Conflict. It enjoins states to take all feasible measures to ensure that members of their armed forces who have not attained the age of eighteen do not take direct part in hostilities and that children under eighteen are not compulsorily recruited into their armed forces. Article 4 of this protocol prohibits armed groups, that are distinct from the armed forces of a state, to recruit or use in hostilities persons under the age of eighteen.

The 1990s have seen successful campaigns by the ICRC, non-governmental organisations and various activists for a concrete ban on the use and production of the most deadly weapons used in armed conflicts. Some of these conventions have the merit of extending their scope of applicability to the most numerous conflicts that the world knows today: internal armed conflicts. It is, however, regrettable that no provision on the use of weapons has been included in the list of war crimes applicable in internal armed conflicts in the International Criminal Court (ICC) statute.

3. Customary laws of war applicable in internal armed conflicts in the twenty-first century

3.1 Introduction

International custom is defined in Article 38 of the statute of the International Court of Justice (ICJ), as evidence of a general practice accepted as law. This general practice has 'to be both extensive and virtually uniform',[158] and coupled with a psychological or subjective belief by states that such behaviour is required by law. A customary norm can reflect an existing treaty provision or represents a distinct source of obligations for all states. Identification of customary international norms seems therefore essential for reaching non-states parties, such as states not yet party to Protocol II, or the United Nations.[159] Described by some as a dynamic source of law for its flexibility and adaptability to the needs of the international community,[160] the determination of the existence and the content of a customary norm is in practice a delicate process often left to academic debates. The conventional provisions applicable in internal armed conflicts do not refer to customary law and the preamble of Protocol II includes part of the famous De Martens Clause, omitting specifically the reference to 'the usages established among civilised peoples'. Further, in internal armed conflicts especially, compliance with treaty provisions is often scarce. One is therefore tempted to ask whether there are any customary principles applicable in internal armed conflicts, and whether there is any hope that a rebel group could be aware of these principles and respect them.[161]

International and national case law seem, however, to have high-lighted the existence and the importance of customary principles in the laws of war. The International Military Tribunal for the Trial of German Major War Criminals believed that by 1939 the Hague Conventions were 'recognised by all civilised nations' and were regarded as being 'declaratory of the laws and customs of war',[162] therefore binding parties and non-parties alike.[163] Further, the ICJ in the *Nicaragua* case identified some customary principles of the laws of war applicable in all conflicts.[164] More recently, customary international law was found to be of special relevance in the determination of the subject matter jurisdiction of the International Criminal Tribunal for the former Yugoslavia (ICTY). The report of the Secretary-General to the UN pursuant to resolution 808 establishing the ICTY, declared that international humanitarian law exists 'in the form of both conventional law and customary law'.[165] In order to respect the principle *nullum crimen sine lege*, the Tribunal 'should apply rules of international humanitarian law which are beyond any doubt part of customary law'.[166] This Tribunal, entrusted to apply 'existing inter-national humanitarian law',[167] recalled the vital importance of customary law especially in internal armed conflict in its landmark decision in the *Tadić* jurisdiction decision.[168] In interpreting Article 3 of its statute, the Appeals Chamber reviewed the content of the customary rules of the laws of war governing internal armed conflicts, and showed that some basic principles of the laws of war applicable in international armed conflicts have been extended to apply in internal armed conflicts.[169]

Customary international law can also be taken into account by national courts and applied by them. The recent *Pinochet* litigation represents a landmark in the use by English courts of customary inter-national law. Their Lordships made extensive use of the concept of customary law throughout their judgment.[170] Lord Millett considered that torture was already in 1973 an international crime governed by universal jurisdiction, and therefore English courts 'have and always have had extra-territorial criminal jurisdiction in respect of crimes of universal jurisdiction under customary international law'.[171] The majority of their Lordships refused, however, to consider as extraditable the crimes committed prior to 1988, because English courts had no jurisdiction over these crimes between 1973 and 1988. Lord Browne-Wilkinson found that torture was 'an international crime long before the Torture Convention', but universal jurisdiction attached to this crime was not established in customary international law.[172] Similarly, Lord Hope found that 'none of the offences, if committed prior to the coming into force of section 134 of the Criminal Justice Act 1988, could be said to be extra-territorial offences against the law of the UK ... *as there is no basis* upon which they could have been tried extra-territoriality in this country'[173] (emphasis added), apparently rejecting therefore customary law as a possible basis for the jurisdiction of English courts over the crime of torture prior to 1988.

On a smaller scale, some civil law jurisdictions have recently referred to customary international law. On the basis of Article 55 of the French Constitution, customary law is not directly applicable in French law. The French Conseil d'Etat has recently admitted, however, in the absence of conflict between international customary norms and domestic legislation, that customary norms should be respected, opening up the possibility for a claimant to rely on a customary norm before French jurisdictions in the future.[174]

Recent practice by national and international tribunals seems therefore to have revived the importance of customary law. This section proposes to determine how customary law complements the treaty provisions applicable in internal armed conflicts. An exhaustive study of the customary principles applicable in internal armed conflict is beyond the scope of this book.[175] We will only outline the customary norms applicable in internal armed conflicts and study the threshold of applicability of such customary principles. The status of Article 3 and Protocol II as customary norms will be looked at briefly, before studying other customary principles of the laws of war applicable in internal armed conflicts: the protection of civilians from hostilities and the means of warfare prohibited in internal armed conflicts.

3.2 Common Article 3 and Additional Protocol II as customary international law

Debates about the customary nature of Article 3 might appear futile, as the 1949 Geneva Conventions have attained universal ratification.

The ICJ has, however, noted in its *Nicaragua* judgment that even if a customary norm covers the same ground as a treaty provision, the customary norm retains its separate existence.[176] In the case of Article 3, it is widely accepted nowadays that it largely reflects customary international law applicable in internal armed conflicts.[177]

In the *Nicaragua* judgment, the ICJ assessing the legality of the US distribution of military manuals to the contras, found that:

> Article 3 which is common to all four Geneva Conventions of 12 August 1949 defines certain rules to be applied in the armed conflicts of a non-international character. There is no doubt that, in the event of international armed conflicts, these rules also constitute a minimum yardstick, in addition to the more elaborate rules which are also to apply to international conflicts; and they are rules which, in the court's opinion, reflect what the court in 1949 called 'elementary considerations of humanity'.[178]

These principles were later qualified as 'customary international law' in the operative part of the judgment,[179] even if the court never really examined in detail the practice or *opinio juris* of states.[180]

In the *Tadić* jurisdiction decision, the ICTY looked at the content of customary law applicable in internal armed conflicts and declared that Article 3 became part of customary law.[181] Similarly, this view has been upheld by the International Criminal Tribunal for Rwanda (ICTR) in the *Akayesu* judgment:

> It is today clear that the norms of common Article 3 have acquired the status of customary law in that most states, by their domestic penal codes, have criminalized acts which if committed during internal armed conflict, would constitute violations of common Article 3.[182]

Further, some national cases, such as the litigation against *Karadzic* in the USA, acknowledged the customary nature of the obligations contained in Article 3. This case was a civil action based on the Alien Tort Act whereby the US courts can have jurisdiction in any civil action by an alien for a tort only committed in violation of the law of nations or a treaty of the USA. The district court found itself competent to look at Karadzic's liability for war crimes, qualifying the violations of Article 3 of 'most fundamental norms of the laws of war, which bind parties to internal conflicts regardless of whether they are recognised nations or roving hordes of insurgents'.[183] Even if a thorough study of state practice and *opinio juris* has never really been undertaken, the ICJ, both international criminal tribunals, some national courts, and many authors have found the provisions of Article 3 to reflect customary international law.[184]

The customary nature of the normative provisions of Protocol II is, however, much more debatable.[185] The Protocol was adopted 30 years ago and today accounts for 159 states parties.[186] As seen in section 2 of this chapter, the Protocol was not declarative of customary international law at the time of its adoption.[187] Looking at the list of parties to the Protocol today, one may notice that some major states recently implicated or still embroiled in an internal armed conflict, e.g. Morocco, Sudan, Angola, Iraq, Israel, Syria, Turkey, Afghanistan, India, Indonesia and Sri Lanka, have not taken any steps to ratify the Protocol. This factor 'makes the transformation of the Protocol's provisions into customary law more difficult',[188] even if a significant number of other states which are or have been involved in an internal armed conflict have recently become party to Protocol II.[189] The significant increase of states parties in the 1990s cannot hide entirely the poor record of compliance with Protocol II shown by belligerents in internal armed conflicts.[190] That led the Secretary-General of the UN in his report pursuant to the creation of the ICTR, to express what is still the prevalent view on Protocol II:

> The Security Council has included within the subject matter jurisdiction of the Rwanda Tribunal international instruments regardless whether they were considered part of customary international ... Article 4 of the Statute, accordingly includes violations of Additional Protocol II which, *as a whole*, has not yet been universally recognised as part of customary international law (emphasis added).[191]

As a whole, Protocol II cannot be said to reflect customary international law;[192] however, both Criminal Tribunals and most commentators agree today that 'the core of Protocol II' forms part of customary international law.[193] Looking at the content of customary international law in internal armed conflict, the Appeals Chamber in the *Tadić* jurisdiction decision stated:

> Many provisions of this Protocol can now be regarded as declaratory of existing rules or as having crystallised emerging rules of customary law or else as having been strongly instrumental in their evolution as general principles.[194]

Similarly, the ICTR in its *Akayesu* judgment upheld the views taken in *Tadić* and further explained that:

> All the guarantees as enumerated in article 4 (of Protocol II) reaffirm and
> supplement common Article 3 . . . As discussed above common Article 3
> being customary in nature, the Chamber is of the opinion that these
> guarantees did also at the time of the events alleged in the Indictment
> form part of existing international customary law.[195]

Next to Article 4 of the Protocol, the core of customary norms may well include the customary human rights borrowed from the Convenant on Civil and Political Rights[196] and appearing in Articles 5 and 6 of Protocol II. At the time of the conflict in Iraq between the central government and the Kurds, the Special Rapporteur of the Commission of Human Rights on the situation of human rights in Iraq stated:

> It is evident that the conflicts were of such a nature as to have reached the
> threshold of applicability of common Article 3. In addition to these stan-
> dards, and though Iraq is not a party to the 1977 Protocol II . . . there are
> standards expressed in this Protocol which are generally the same as those
> expressed in the instruments of international human rights law . . . Indeed,
> it should be noted that many of these most fundamental protections may be
> said to be reflecting the customary law of human rights.[197]

It seems therefore that the core of Protocol II, which reflects customary law, includes at least the provisions of Articles 4–6, 9 and 13[198] of this instrument.[199] The transformation of treaty provisions into customary law binding non-states parties does not, however, prevent the creation and the development of other general principles applicable in internal armed conflicts, as the Appeals Chamber said in the *Tadić* case 'there exists a corpus of general principles and norms in internal conflicts embracing common Article 3 but having a much greater scope'.[200] Part of this corpus of general principles and norms stems from Protocol II, as we have just seen, but we now turn to other customary principles on the protection of civilians and on means and methods of warfare in internal armed conflicts.

3.3 Customary international law and the particularities of the laws of armed conflicts[201]

The *Tadić* jurisdiction decision revived the importance of customary international law in the laws of war and represents one of the most detailed judicial discussions on the formation of customary law applic-able in internal armed conflicts.[202] It would, however, be interesting to find more evidence of state practice and *opinio juris* underlying some customary principles applicable in internal armed conflicts, next to the core of Protocol II and Article 3. A detailed study of all humanitarian principles capable of being extended to internal armed conflicts is beyond the scope of this book.[203] We will therefore only concentrate on the prohibition of attacking civilians and of using certain means of warfare in internal armed conflicts. A few remarks on customary law and the particularities of the laws of armed conflicts will be made first with the view to answering two questions: How does one prove the existence of a customary norm? And what elements will have to be considered in ascertaining the existence of a customary norm?

Under the traditional definition of customary law,[204] the norm in question, as for example the prohibition of attacking the civilian population during internal armed conflicts, must be a practice adopted by states over a certain amount of time in 'a both extensive and virtually uniform' manner.[205] This element of repetition over a certain time must be coupled with the belief by states that this principle is legally obligatory or in other words 'states must therefore feel that they are conforming to what amounts to a legal obligation'. As the ICJ puts it in the *North Sea Continental Shelf* case:

> An indispensable requirement would be that within the period in question, short though it might be, state practice, including that of states whose interests are specially affected, should have been both extensive and virtually uniform in the sense of the provision involved and should moreover have occurred in such a way as to show a general recognition that a rule of law or legal obligation is involved.[206]

Another important indication brought out by the ICJ in the *Nicaragua* case is that this practice does not need to conform absolutely with the rule in question. The court affirmed:

> It is sufficient that the conduct of states should in general be consistent with such rules and that instances of state conduct inconsistent with a given rule should generally have been treated as breaches of that rule not as indications of the recognition of a new rule.[207]

This passage is of particular importance for the laws of armed conflicts. In internal armed conflicts especially, where instances of breaches of the law are recurrent and quickly made public, is it possible really to pinpoint a practice in general consistent with the rule in question? The manner in which the breaches to the rules are justified will be of special importance in the laws of armed conflicts. Similarly, how much weight can be given to unilateral statements by states or rebels that they will respect basic humanitarian principles? Does a custom generally arise from acts of conduct or from promises of such acts? Some commentators have indicated that the 'very essence of every kind of custom has been based upon material deeds and not words . . . or to put it in other words, customs arise from acts of conduct and not from promises of such acts'.[208] This opinion can be compared with the view taken by the ICTY Appeals Chamber in the *Tadić* jurisdiction decision:

> When attempting to ascertain state practice with a view to establishing the existence of a customary rule or a general principle, it is difficult, if not impossible, to pinpoint the actual behaviour of the troops in the field for the purpose of establishing whether they in fact comply with or disregard, certain standards of behaviour . . . In appraising the formation of customary rules or general principles one should therefore be aware that, on account of the inherent nature of this subject-matter, reliance must primarily be placed on such elements as official pronouncements of states, military manuals and judicial decisions.[209]

In armed conflicts, it is indeed difficult to have access to the battlefields and to check the exact behaviour of belligerents. It is also good to bear in mind that generally the only aspect of conflicts often rendered public are the many violations of international humanitarian law, while compliance to the rules usually goes unnoticed. It seems therefore that in considering the laws of armed conflicts, more weight needs to be placed on the 'indirect conducts' of states,[210] i.e. their legislation, the instructions they issue in military manuals, military codes, criminal codes or judicial decisions rather than their 'direct conduct' on the battlefields.[211] Furthermore, an important part of state practice and *opinio juris* will be 'their promises' to adhere to the laws of armed conflicts and their statements on the state of the laws of armed conflicts, with special emphasis on their justifications of a breach or the condemnation by third states of breaches.

Keeping the particularities of the laws of war in mind, the customary nature of the prohibition of attacks against the civilian population and the prohibition of certain means of warfare in internal armed conflicts will be proven by looking first at the practice of belligerents in internal armed conflicts, the states whose interests are specially affected. The record of adherence, violations and explanations of these violations especially for conflicts which took place during the 1990s will be studied to see if they extended by agreement any other provisions of the Geneva Conventions to the conflict in question. Similarly, did they make any unilateral statements about respecting international humanitarian law, and did the rebels take any position in this regard?[212] Finally, the military manuals of these belligerents as well as some of their national legislation will be covered.

Further, the declarations made by third states either individually or collectively in the United Nations or other international forum as well as the adoption of resolutions by these international organisations will be looked at as they also amount to state practice. As the ICJ highlighted in the *Nicaragua* case and more recently in the *Nuclear Weapons* advisory opinion,[213] General Assembly (GA) or Security Council resolutions 'can provide evidence important for establishing the existence of a rule of the emergence of an *opinio juris*'.[214] All the UN Security Council resolutions since 1970, the UN Secretary-General reports mainly in the 1990s, some GA resolutions, some reports of the Human Rights Commission, of the ICRC and individual statements made by states will be studied.[215]

It will be necessary to weigh the indirect practice and *opinio juris* of states with the record of direct state practice on the battlefields, but generally one can agree with R. Baxter when he states:

> The firm statement by the state of what it considers to be the rules is far better evidence of its position than what can be pieced together from the actions of that country at different times and in a variety of contexts.[216]

Finally, one might also note that it is often difficult to separate evidence of state practice from *opinio juris*, as the same act can be evidence of both state practice and *opinio juris*.[217] While the International Criminal Tribunals have mainly relied on *opinio juris* in order to identify the existence of customary norms,[218] the International Court of Justice recalled that the existence of a customary norm is established 'by induction based on the analysis of a sufficiently extensive and convincing state practice and not by deduction based on preconceived ideas' as to what the law should be.[219]

3.4 The protection of civilians from the effects of hostilities

Civilian populations are usually the first victims and have gradually become the targets of belligerents during internal armed conflicts. This section proposes to look at the existence, as customary principles, of the rules prohibiting attacks against the civilian population, including the prohibition of intentionally bombing civilians and the prohibition of attacks on non-military objectives.

3.4.1 Practice of belligerents during internal armed conflicts

One of the first large-scale civil wars of last century saw great civilian casualties due to the use of new methods of warfare such as aerial bombardments. During the Spanish Civil War, both sides launched indiscriminate attacks against the civilian population. Similarly, civil conflicts in the 1960s and 1970s witnessed the great sufferings of civilian populations in the Congo, Yemen, Nigeria, Cambodia and Vietnam.[220] The attacks on the Palestinian population of Beirut in 1982 are still alive in people's minds and prompted the Security Council to call for the respect of the rights of civilians and for the parties to restrain from all acts of violence against these populations.[221] Further, civilians have not been spared during the many civil conflicts of the 1990s, e.g. ex-Yugoslavia, Rwanda, Liberia, Sierra Leone, Kosovo, Chechnya and more recently in the Darfur region of Sudan. Belligerents have often used the civilian population as deliberate targets of their policies with the notable examples of 'ethnic cleansing' and mass rape campaigns in ex-Yugoslavia. The records of violence towards the civilian population during recent civil conflicts make it difficult to believe that the rule, which prohibits attacks on civilian population, is respected in a consistent and virtually uniform manner by belligerents.

As underlined by the ICJ in the *Nicaragua* case, the way in which belligerents explain these violations is of particular importance when ascertaining the *opinio juris* of states. A number of authors have shown, for example, that both parties in the Spanish Civil War, when directly accused of such violations, would deny the facts of which they were accused.[222] Insurgents, when accused of having attacked non-military objectives for example, claimed that the targets of their bombings were only military objectives.[223] Similarly, in the Nigerian conflict, when faced with allegations of attacking civilian villages, the Federal Government denied the attacks and later issued instructions to the troops to abstain from such bombing.[224] The insurgents in Biafra rejected suggestions of violations and claimed adherence to the Geneva Conventions.[225] Further, in the last conflict in Chechnya, Russian forces were claiming to be 'fight[ing] a war against terrorism' and have continuously issued 'blanket denials' about all the abuses committed by Russian forces.[226] These are only a few examples of a widespread practice by governments of denying the existence of an armed conflict on their territory, or the occurrence of violations of the laws of war. Generally, belligerents have not taken the view that attacks on a civilian population were permissible behaviour during armed conflicts and they have not challenged the legal validity of the rule. The reactions of states to these breaches seem therefore to reinforce the compulsory character of the rule rather than to weaken it.

It is also interesting to look at the official pronouncements of belligerents about respect for international humanitarian law and the law applicable during the internal armed conflict they are facing. The Spanish Civil War is a good example of the contradictory aspect of the laws of war whereby both sides committed serious violations of the laws of war but both consistently undertook to apply the 1929 Geneva Convention on Prisoners of War for example.[227] The ICRC has played an important role in many conflicts in obtaining an undertaking by the parties to respect common Article 3 and Protocol II, if applicable, as we have seen in section 2 of this chapter.[228] In the Nigerian civil war for example, both parties recognised the character of full war to the hostilities and accepted the observance of the Geneva Conventions.[229] During civil conflicts in Hungary and Iraq, only the rebels called for a respect of common Article 3, and in El Salvador rebels undertook to respect both Article 3 and Protocol II.[230] A good example of a unilateral undertaking is the public statement of the Congolese Prime Minister in 1964 undertaking 'to limit action to military objectives' and respect the Geneva Conventions.[231]

In the recent conflicts in Bosnia-Herzegovina, parties agreed on the basis of Article 3 to bring into force some core provisions from the Geneva Conventions including the provisions protecting the civilian population borrowed from the Fourth Geneva Convention.[232] There is therefore a sharp contrast between the actual practice of belligerents in the midst of hostilities and their own undertakings to respect conventional norms and other principles like the protection of civilians applicable in internal conflicts. These undertakings show, however, that states do feel bound to respect basic humanitarian principles in internal armed conflicts, including the protection of civilians from hostilities and do not question their legal validity.

Another important part of state practice and *opinio juris* can be found in national legislation and the military manuals of belligerents. The prohibition of bombing civilians and targeting non-military objectives appears in a number of military manuals or military codes of belligerents. At the beginning of the civil war, the Nigerian Government issued an operational code of conduct for Nigerian armed forces integrating the basic principles of the Geneva Conventions, including the sparing of civilians and civilian objects, from the effects of hostilities.[233] The code of conduct was enforced by commanders and found by independent observers for the most part to be followed by federal troops,[234] even if a federal official proclaimed that starvation was a legitimate weapon of warfare.[235] The Nigerian Air Force code of operations stated that 'non-military targets were not to be bombed and that any gathering of the civilian population was to be spared from bombing'.[236] Similarly, the code of conduct for the Uganda National Resistance Army deals with discipline between soldiers as well as behaviour towards the civilian population: never to abuse, insult, or beat any member of the public, never kill any civilian or captured prisoner.[237] Furthermore, Article 214 of the Colombian military manual prohibits any attacks on civilians in internal and international conflicts.[238] The recent Russian manual on the application of the rules of international humanitarian law by the armed forces is a good illustration of the growing inclusion by a number of states, of rules of humanitarian law within their military manuals. The Russian manual adopted in 1990 includes the rules to be found in the Geneva Conventions and Additional Protocols and details the prohibited methods and means of warfare and prohibited conduct in respect of war victims to 'be applied to all cases of declared war or any other armed conflict'. The manual cites Article 3 and prohibits attacks on civilian objects and the practice of terrorising a local population.[239] One may cite lastly, the interesting order of the commander and head of the department of the interior troops of the Ministry of Internal Affairs of the Republic of Tadjikistan issued in 1996. 'Taking into consideration the actual conduct of hostilities of a non-international character by the Republic of Tadjikistan against illegal armed units', it orders the governmental troops to 'be strictly guided by the standards and principles of IHL contained in Geneva Conventions of 1949, and both Additional Protocols'.[240]

Cases have also arisen where rebels or the legitimate governments have refused to respect the Geneva Conventions. Robert Mugabe of Zimbabwe refused to accept a code of conduct based on the Geneva Conventions for the Patriotic Front Fighters under his command; similarly, in ex-Zaire, the Mobutu Government rejected the applicability of Article 3 in the Shaba province.[241] Generally, however, military manuals of belligerents include clauses prohibiting attacks on civilians and represent the best illustration that states do feel under an obligation to respect this principle and other basic humanitarian provisions and order their forces to do so.

Furthermore, some national legislation of those states 'whose interests are mostly affected', such as the new military criminal code of

Yemen, include a provision on attacks against civilians and protected objects which are qualified as war crimes in international and internal armed conflicts.[242] Similarly, Article 472 of the code of military justice of the Democratic Republic of the Congo (DRC) provides for the death penalty for any soldiers who commit serious violations against civilian populations during an armed conflict.[243] These examples are taken from legislation of recent belligerents embroiled in internal armed conflicts, but the great majority of implementing legislation of the Geneva Conventions and various criminal codes recognise that basic humanitarian provisions have to be respected in internal armed conflicts, including protection of civilians from the effect of hostilities.[244] A recent military manual must also be cited here. The 2004 *Manual of the Law of Armed Conflict* published by the UK Ministry of Defence includes, in the section dealing with the law applicable in internal armed conflicts, such principles as the immunity of civilians from direct attack and from the incidental effects of military operations as well as the prohibition of indiscriminate attacks.[245]

The first part of this chapter covered mainly the practice and *opinio juris* of some states 'whose interests are specially affected'. From their military manuals, their unilateral undertakings to respect these rules, together with some of their national legislation and their reactions to accusations of violations, it appears that even if violations were committed systematically or sometimes on a large scale in certain internal armed conflicts, this behaviour has clearly been interpreted as breaches of the rules protecting the civilian population by the belligerents themselves.

3.4.2 Practice of third states and international organisations

Having dealt with the practice and *opinio juris* of belligerents, the next stage is to investigate positions taken by third states either individually, how they react to allegations of serious violations of humanitarian law by belligerents, or collectively, by the UN Security Council, the General Assembly or the European Union. Finally, some reports of the UN Secretary-General and some resolutions of the ICRC and Red Cross conferences will also be considered, as they can be instrumental in the creation of customary law.

States have sometimes taken individual positions against violations of the principle of protection of civilians from the effects of hostilities committed by third parties. As early as 1938, one can find strong condemnation by the British Prime Minister of the continuous bombing of civilians. He affirmed:

> The one definite rule of international law is that the direct and deliberate bombing of non-combatants is in all circumstances illegal.[246]

Similarly, the US Secretary of State took the view that:

> any general bombing of an extensive area wherein there resided a large population engaged in peaceful pursuits is contrary to every principle of law and of humanity.[247]

The positions expressed by third states during the Spanish Civil War showed that already at that time deliberate attacks on a civilian population as well as bombing civilian objectives were thought to be principles of international conflicts applicable in internal armed conflicts of a certain scale.

More recently in the course of the conflicts in ex-Yugoslavia, the British Government took numerous positions to condemn the 'abhorrent practice of ethnic cleansing which constitutes a grave breach of the Geneva Convention',[248] and qualified the deliberate targeting of the civilian population as a grave breach of international humanitarian law.[249] Similarly, the French Administration continuously condemned attacks against the civilian population and the practice of ethnic cleansing during this conflict.[250] It is interesting to note as well that the resolution, authorising NATO bombing around Sarajevo, reiterated the indignation of the NATO Council after repetitive and indiscriminate attacks on the civilian population in Sarajevo.[251]

During the first conflict in Chechnya, one may note a comment from the French Minister of Defence about the conduct of hostilities by the Russian forces:

> L'importance des pertes civiles montre que les méthodes et les moyens militaires employées vont bien au-delà des règles générales fixées pour l'usage des forces armées dans les conflits internes.[252]

Similarly, the German Minister of Foreign Affairs took the view that Russia had a 'legitimate right to maintain its territorial integrity' but that at the same time the use of military force against the civilian population was 'unacceptable and not compatible with European and international norms'.[253]

In relation to the internal armed conflict in the Darfur region of Sudan, a British Parliamentary Under Secretary of State at the Foreign and Commonwealth Office stated on 17 January 2002: 'we have made it absolutely clear to the Government of Sudan that the bombing of civilians and aid workers is unacceptable.'[254]

The resolutions adopted by the UN Security Council from 1970 to the present are of particular interest in revealing the practice of this body towards armed conflicts and international humanitarian law. They participate in the creation of customary international law as they reflect the practice of the UN and can provide evidence of the existence of custom. They can also be seen as collective state practice, as the fifteen members of the Security Council discuss and vote on each of the resolutions adopted by this body. Since 1989, the Security Council has been deeply involved in many conflict situations, especially in internal armed conflicts. At the beginning of such conflicts, the Security Council starts by a general condemnation of the outbreak of violence and the killings. A second step is taken by the Council when the situation amounts to an armed conflict and, without defining the character of such conflict, it calls for the respect of human rights and humanitarian law.[255] A third step consists of Security Council condemnations of specific acts qualified first as serious humanitarian violations and then as international crimes becoming the responsibility of perpetrators.

Between 1970 and 1989, the Security Council called for the parties to respect international humanitarian law only in one instance, the Lebanese conflict, where it specifically called 'upon all parties to respect the rights of the civilian population without any discrimination and repudiates all acts of violence against those population'.[256] Since 1989, the Security Council has repeatedly called for parties to many internal armed conflicts to respect the principles of humanitarian law and has condemned certain acts that it qualified as serious violations of international humanitarian law:

– The indiscriminate attacks against the civilian population[257]
– Mass forcible expulsion and deportation of civilians and the practice of 'ethnic cleansing'[258]
– Rape and detention of women[259]
– Attacks on UN personnel, as non-military objectives[260]
– Attacks on 'safe areas' and undefended towns[261]

The practice of the Security Council during the armed conflicts of the 1990s onwards of ex-Yugoslavia, Rwanda, Somalia, Liberia, Angola, Georgia, Kosovo, Burundi, Democratic Republic of the Congo, Afghanistan, Azerbaidjan, Yemen, Tadjikistan, Sierra Leone, Guinea-Bissau, East Timor and Darfur is therefore extensive and virtually uniform *in condemning* the attacks against civilian populations, safe areas, undefended towns and the UN peace-keeping personnel as well as acts of ethnic cleansing and rape, once the armed conflict has reached a certain stage. Similarly, this practice is extensive and virtually uniform *in qualifying* these conducts as serious violations of humanitarian law entailing individual criminal responsibility. The Security Council treats international and internal armed conflicts alike. It has recently adopted resolutions 1265, 1296 and 1314 on the protection of civilians in armed conflicts reiterating the principles outlined above and 'strongly condemning the deliberate targeting of civilians in situations of armed conflicts as well as attacks on objects protected under international law'.[262] Such consistent and general Security Council affirmation proves the definite application of such rules in internal armed conflicts and may imply the customary character of such principles.

Similar principles also appear in certain League of Nations and General Assembly resolutions. In 1938, the Assembly of the League of Nations adopted unanimously a resolution about the regulation of hostilities during the Spanish conflict and the Chinese-Japanese war. This resolution affirmed clearly that:

1) The intentional bombing of civilian populations is illegal
2) Objectives aimed at from the air must be legitimate military objectives and must be identifiable
3) Any attack on legitimate military objectives must be carried out in such a way that civilian populations in the neighbourhood are not bombed through negligence[263]

In 1968 and 1970, the General Assembly adopted two famous resolutions entitled respectively 'Respect of human rights in armed conflict' and 'Basic principles for the protection of civilian population in armed conflicts',[264] which affirmed the application of various humanitarian principles in 'armed conflict of all types', such as: the prohibition of attacks launched against the civilian population, and the principle to make at all times a distinction in the conduct of military operations between persons actively taking part in the hostilities and civilian populations. In internal armed conflicts, the latter principle is sometimes difficult to implement if armed groups do not carry their arms openly. The US Department of Defence found as far back as 1972 that these principles were 'declaratory of existing customary law'.[265] Both resolutions were adopted unanimously, but it can seem a bit premature to consider that they were reflecting customary law, as they appear to be much more a desire by socialists and third-world countries to extend greater protection to civilians in internal armed conflicts including conflicts of self-determination.[266]

More recently, the General Assembly adopted resolutions on the dire situations in Sudan and the Democratic Republic of Congo and condemned clearly the indiscriminate attacks against the civilian population as well as the incidence of rape, arbitrary executions or the use of child soldiers.[267]

Furthermore, the European Union has frequently stated its support for the respect of international humanitarian principles during internal armed conflicts and particularly of the prohibition of attacks against civilian population. During the conflict in ex-Yugoslavia, the European Union condemned the following conduct:

> All policies of ethnic cleansing and forced expulsions. Attacks on unarmed civilians, such as those by Serb forces at Sarajevo and Gorazde, are wholly contrary to the basic precepts of international humanitarian law.[268]

Similarly during both conflicts in Chechnya, the European Union deplored:

> The renewed escalation of violence and the appalling loss of civilian lives in connection with recent fighting in Chechnya. Reports of unprovoked attacks by Russian forces on civil targets . . . is a matter of deep concern.[269]

Recently, the Presidency, on behalf of the European Union, again condemned attacks on civilian populations qualified as breaches of international humanitarian law, in Burundi and Colombia,[270] and welcomed the cessation by the Sudanese air force of the bombing of civilian targets in South Sudan.[271]

Lastly, this review would not be complete without reference to UN Secretary-General reports on these issues and some resolutions adopted by the international conferences of the Red Cross and Red Crescent. They cannot amount to state practice but rather to the practice of international bodies. Even if the latter is not binding, it will be able to influence the positions of states on these issues or might already be evidence of custom. The reports from the Secretary-General often prelude the adoption of Security Council resolutions studied above. In the case of the conflict in Bosnia-Herzegovina, a conflict of mixed character, reports of the Secretary-General gave a list of violations of international humanitarian law committed in Srebrenica, Zepa, Banja Luka and Sanski Most and concluded that:

> The reports provide undeniable evidence of a consistent pattern of summary executions, rape, mass expulsions, arbitrary detentions, forced labour and large-scale disappearance.[272]

When creating the concept of 'safe areas', the Secretary-General defined these zones as 'areas free from armed attacks and from any other hostile acts that would endanger the well-being and the safety of their inhabitants'[273] and the mission of the United Nations Protection Force (UNPROFOR) at that time was 'to protect the civilian populations against armed attacks and other hostile acts'.[274] The protection of civilian populations from attacks and the effects of hostilities does therefore seem to be an undeniable right in international humanitarian law and the UN intended by creating these 'safe areas' to force parties to respect it. The Special Rapporteur of the Commission on Human Rights in ex-Yugoslavia reached similar conclusions and affirmed in its final report about the fall of Srebrenica:

> In the context of the armed conflict, civilians were targeted by shelling and other forms of military activity resulting in death and injury and prisoners of war were badly mistreated and in all likelihood executed in flagrant violation of international humanitarian law.[275]

Similarly, during conflicts in Rwanda,[276] Kosovo,[277] Sierra Leone[278] and the Darfur region in Sudan,[279] the Secretary-General has condemned many times the serious violations of humanitarian law perpetrated against the civilian population, leaving no doubt as to the applicability of these principles and the importance of their respect in internal armed conflict.

The need to respect principles of proportionality and the condemnation of indiscriminate attacks against civilians was also reaffirmed by the Human Rights Commission in a number of instances, notably in the conflict in Chechnya.[280] Finally, one may recall the consistent affirmation by the International Committee of the Red Cross of the applicability of certain principles of protection of civilians from the effects of hostilities. These appear both in the resolution adopted by the twentieth international conference of the Red Cross and Red Crescent in 1965 and the one of 1993 on the protection of war victims.[281]

In practice, violations of this principle, including instances where the civilians are not incidental victims but the principal object of the attacks, appear to be the rule much more than the exception during internal armed conflicts. This can be partly explained by the difficulty in some internal armed conflicts to distinguish between combatants who do not carry their arms openly and the civilian population. However, such violations are usually denied by the side which commits them and numerous military manuals and national legislation of belligerents call for such a principle to be respected. Furthermore, the principle prohibiting attacks against the civilian population and other non-military objectives seems consistently affirmed by UN Security Council resolutions, General Assembly resolutions, numerous statements by the European Union and many third states. Lastly, the inclusion of this principle within the ICC statute is yet another illustration of the *opinio juris* of states and reinforces the customary nature of the prohibition of attacking civilians in internal armed conflicts.[282] There is little doubt that the amount of state practice and *opinio juris* highlighted here fulfils the criteria of an extensive and virtually uniform practice coupled with the belief that this principle is legally obligatory.

This conclusion was reached by the ICTY Appeals Chamber in its seminal *Tadić* jurisdiction decision[283] and has been constantly reaffirmed by Trial Chambers ever since.[284] The ICRC, in its work on customary international humanitarian law published in 2005,[285] has identified twenty-four rules, all derived from the obligations to distinguish between civilians and combatants, which amount to customary rules applicable in internal armed conflicts. Extensive state practice is cited to support these findings.[286]

3.5 The means of warfare prohibited in internal armed conflicts

International conflicts are regulated by a solid body of customary rules on the means and methods of warfare dating back to 1899 and 1907. A proposal to extend such principles in internal armed conflict was put forward during the diplomatic conference of 1949 by the US representative who stated:

> In cases of non-international armed conflicts, all combatants should be entitled to protection as stated by the humanitarian principles of the convention ... The use of poison or gas for instance was prohibited by international law; but international law only applied to wars between states and the prohibition should be extended to cover civil wars also.[287]

This proposal was rejected by the diplomatic conference of 1949. Twenty-eight years later, a similar fate was encountered by the proposal, contained in the first draft of Additional Protocol II, to prohibit the use of means and methods of warfare which are of a nature to cause superfluous injury or unnecessary suffering.[288] In July 1998, without prejudging the illegality of the use of poison or gas in internal armed conflicts, the Rome conference declined to include these acts as crimes falling within the jurisdiction of the ICC during internal armed conflict. The extension to internal armed conflicts of principles limiting the use of certain weapons by treaty provisions is only a very recent phenomenon, and we will therefore look at the possible existence in customary law of principles prohibiting the use of certain weapons in internal armed conflicts.

3.5.1 Practice of belligerents during internal armed conflicts

Fortunately, there does not seem to have been much use of gas, poison or chemical weapons during internal armed conflicts. During the Iran-Iraq war, chemical weapons were used by both sides and especially against the Iranian civilian population.[289] Iraq was later accused of having used chemical weapons against its Kurdish population. Such use was denied by Iraq, who reaffirmed its adherence to the 1925 Geneva Protocol on chemical weapons.[290] More recently, in December 1999, Russian troops admitted having used incendiary weapons to destroy 'terrorist camps in poorly dense areas of the south of Chechnya'.[291] The protocol on prohibitions or restrictions on the use of incendiary weapons, additional to the 1980 Convention on Conventional Weapons, explicitly prohibits in all circumstances making any military objective located within a concentration of civilians, the object of attack by air-delivered incendiary weapons.[292] This protocol was only applicable, however, in international conflicts at the time Russian forces used it.[293] Are any of these prohibitions applicable in internal armed conflict as a norm of customary law? It is interesting to look at the answer given by belligerents or their statements concerning the use of weapons in internal armed conflicts.

Iraq denied using chemical weapons against its civilian population and reiterated the importance of the 1925 Geneva Protocol. The Russians, however, did seem to acknowledge the use of such weapons in Chechnya. They are party to Protocol III on incendiary weapons additional to the 1980 Convention since 1982, but seem to believe that this set of prohibitions of certain conventional weapons as well as the general prohibition of using weapons of a nature to cause unnecessary suffering, are not applicable in internal armed conflicts. During the Spanish Civil War, the Spanish lawful government made a reference to the prohibition on using toxic gases during the Civil War.[294] The agreement concluded by the parties in the conflicts of Bosnia-Herzegovina on the basis of Article 3 extend to what the parties believed at the time was mainly an internal armed conflict, the provisions on conduct of hostilities, in particular the prohibition to employ weapons, projectiles and material and methods of warfare of a nature to cause superfluous injury or unnecessary suffering.[295] Military manuals of recent belligerents do not generally contain provisions dealing with weapons prohibited in internal armed conflicts.[296] This can be explained by the absence of any provisions on the prohibitions of the use of certain weapons in common Article 3 or Protocol II, and the slow inclusion of recent conventions like the new Protocol II on land mines of 1996, or the Protocol on laser weapons, in their national legislation or military manuals.

Extensive practice and *opinio juris* of belligerents concerning the means of warfare prohibited in internal armed conflicts are therefore difficult to pinpoint. There have only been a few instances of the use of gas or chemical weapons in internal armed conflicts. This may imply that in general belligerents feel bound not to use in internal conflicts, weapons which are outlawed in international conflicts. Furthermore, they usually deny having used such weapons, as in the case of Iraq in 1988. These factors have to be tempered, however, by the absence in much national legislation or military manuals of specific provisions outlawing their use in internal armed conflicts.

3.5.2 Practice of third states and international organisations

In this search for state practice and *opinio juris*, it is now interesting to turn to the practice of international organisations and third states. Some states have individually expressed their condemnation of the use of chemical weapons in internal armed conflicts. The British Government 'condemned the use of chemical weapons anywhere and called for the complete cessation of the use of any such weapons'. It qualified the use of chemical weapons by Iraq against the civilian population as 'a serious and grave violation of the 1925 Geneva Protocol and international humanitarian law'.[297] Similarly, the French Government strongly condemned the use of chemical weapons during the conflict between Iran and Iraq, as well as the alleged used of chemical weapons by Russian forces in Afghanistan and the use of such weapons by Iraq against its own population.[298] Lastly, one can find similar statements made by the German Parliament[299] and the US State Department, which stated:

> It is clear that such use against the civilian population would be contrary to the customary international law that is applicable to internal armed conflicts, as well as other international agreements.[300]

As far as the practice of international organisations is concerned, the Security Council has so far never adopted a resolution dealing with the use of gas or chemical weapons in internal armed conflict.[301] In 1938, the Assembly of the League of Nations in its resolution about the regulation of hostilities during the Spanish conflict and the Chinese-Japanese war, affirmed that the 'use of chemical or bacteriological weapons during armed conflict is contrary to international law'.[302] The General Assembly adopted a few resolutions especially in the 1970s calling for the respect of certain principles during internal armed conflicts. Resolution 2444 on the respect of human rights during armed conflicts confirmed resolution XXVIII adopted in 1965 by the Red Cross Conference. It affirmed that all parties should respect the principle according to which 'the right of the parties to a conflict to adopt any means of injury on the enemy is not unlimited'.[303] Similarly, resolution 2677 adopted on 9 December 1970 called on 'all parties to any armed conflict to respect the rules contained in the Hague Conventions of 1899 and 1907 as well as the 1925 Geneva Protocol'.[304] These resolutions illustrate the wishes of the international community to limit the use of certain weapons in internal armed conflict, but do not seem to reflect existing customary law at the time of their adoption. Interestingly though, the General Assembly condemned Portugal in 1971 for the attacks on civilian populations and the use of chemical weapons in the conflicts in Angola, Mozambique and Guinea Bissau.[305] The General Assembly does not seem, however, to have adopted any resolution condemning the use of chemical weapons by Iraq against its civilian population in 1988, or more recently to have taken any position concerning the use of incendiary weapons during the conflict in Chechnya. However, in relation to the events in Sudan, the General Assembly adopted resolution 56/173, which *inter alia* urges all parties:

> To stop immediately the use of weapons, including landmines and indiscriminate artillery shelling, against the civilian population, which runs counter to principles of international humanitarian law.[306]

The Human Rights Commission as well as the Conference on Security and Co-operation in Europe have recently adopted a declaration of minimum humanitarian standards first elaborated by a group of experts. This declaration aims to lay down principles of human rights and humanitarian norms applicable in situations of internal violence, ethnic, religious and national conflicts, disturbances, tensions and public emergency and provides in Article 5.3:

> Weapons or other material or methods prohibited in international armed conflicts must not be employed in any circumstances.[307]

Endorsed by the Organisation for Security and Co-operation in Europe (OSCE) and adopted by the Commission on Human Rights, this declaration appears to reflect *opinio juris* of states in this area, but such a declaration is not binding and falls into the category of 'soft law'. Furthermore, it seems to overlook the fact that certain chemical weapons are only prohibited in armed conflicts but can be used by countries for policing purposes as riot-control agents.[308]

It is also interesting to look at the reactions from a group of states, the European Union, to the alleged use of chemical weapons in internal armed conflicts. In 1988, the twelve member states declared:

> Their concern at reports of the alleged use of chemical weapons against the Kurds by the Iraqi authorities. They confirmed their previous positions condemning any use of these weapons and called for respect of international humanitarian law including the Geneva Protocol of 1925.[309]

More recently, the European Union did not condemn the use of incendiary weapons in Chechnya but just 'urged the Russian Government to fulfil its obligations under international humanitarian law'.

In conclusion, state practice and *opinio juris* cannot be said to be really extensive in this area but there has been a consistent pattern of condemnations of the use of gas and chemical weapons by third states. Such use in internal armed conflicts has been widely recognised to be a violation of international humanitarian law. Similarly, belligerents did not seem to question the validity of the rule, rather they argued that they did not use these weapons. These factors and the rarity of such use in internal armed conflicts seem to support the conclusion reached by the ICTY Appeals Chamber in 1995 when it said that:

> There undisputedly emerged a general consensus in the international community on the principle that the use of those weapons is also prohibited in internal armed conflict.[310]

Can one extend to internal armed conflicts the prohibitions of weapons other than gas or chemical weapons, whose use is outlawed in international conflict especially in light of the paucity of state practice in internal armed conflicts? The ICRC, in its customary law research published in 2005, believed that the prohibitions to use poison, biological weapons, chemical weapons, expanding bullets, exploding bullets, weapons primarily injuring by non-detectable fragments and blinding laser weapons are customary law principles applicable in internal armed conflicts. Similarly, the two general prohibitions, of using means and methods of warfare which are of a nature to cause superfluous injury or unnecessary suffering and of using weapons which are by nature indiscriminate, are also customary principles applicable in internal armed conflicts. The ICRC takes the view that generally 'states do not have a different set of military weapons for international and non-international armed conflicts' and that 'practice shows that parties to a conflict abstain from using in non-international armed conflicts weapons prohibited in international armed conflicts'.[311] A number of military manuals and national legislation are cited in support of these findings. Some of the military manuals that specifically include the prohibitions of certain weapons in internal armed conflicts were adopted in the late 1990s only. Furthermore a lot of the others do not make specific reference to internal armed conflicts in the section dealing with weapons and contain a distinct chapter dealing with internal armed conflicts, which do not mention the outlawed weapons.[312] This can be explained by the novelty in various treaties on weaponry to include internal armed conflicts within their scope of application. With the ratification of these treaties and the Rome statute on the ICC, more states will change their military manuals and internal legislation. It is, however, permitted to think that it was rather premature for the ICTY Appeals Chamber in 1995 to conclude that 'what is inhumane and consequently proscribed, in international wars, cannot but be inhumane and inadmissible in civil strife'.[313]

The conclusions reached by the ICTY and the ICRC on weaponry must also be put in perspective with the fact that the Rome statute on the ICC contains no provision on weapons applicable in internal armed conflicts. The draft statute for the International Criminal Court contained a provision dealing with weapons. Its inclusion in the statute and the exact wording were linked to the outcome of the discussions on weapons applicable in international armed conflicts.[314] The list of weapons applicable in international armed conflicts to be included within the jurisdiction of the court was one of the most contentious issues in the Rome conference. A majority of states favoured a list of weapons, which would include chemical and biological weapons as well as nuclear weapons.[315] The inclusion of the latter crime was obviously unacceptable for the permanent members of the Security Council. At the end of the diplomatic conference, the only option left to resolve the deadlock was the deletion from the draft statute of all weapons of mass destruction.[316]

Debates did very much concentrate on the question of which weapons to include in the war crimes section applicable in international armed conflicts leaving out any sort of debate on which weapons to include in internal armed conflicts. A draft provision on weapons applicable in internal armed conflicts was, however, included in the draft statute as well as the first 'bureau proposal'. That provision was mysteriously deleted between the first 'bureau proposal' dated 6 July 1998 and the second 'bureau proposal' dated 10 July 1998.[317] The Rome statute was the occasion for states to remedy the lacunae of Article 3 and Protocol II and to include within the law applicable in internal armed conflicts means and methods of warfare, including some provisions on outlawed weapons. A number of key provisions applicable in internal armed conflicts, such as the prohibitions of using starvation as a means of warfare or certain weapons, were left out of the package deal submitted to a vote in Rome. This might be explained by the fact that some countries were strong opponents of the inclusion of any crime applicable in internal armed conflicts.[318] The bureau might have thought that the package deal could be more acceptable to states without any weapons provisions in the section dealing with internal armed conflicts. Furthermore, an influential delegation also expressed the view that it would be difficult to include, within the list of war crimes in internal armed conflicts, a prohibition to use certain weapons, because some weapons, such as expanding handgun bullets are used for law enforcement. It would as a result be very difficult for soldiers on the ground to assess whether they face internal disturbances or an internal armed conflict and to decide which weapons to use.[319] It was therefore safer not to include any provision dealing with weapons in internal armed conflicts. Such a provision was sacrificed for the sake of political compromise in the absence of a clear *opinio juris* on this issue. The absence of reactions from states to the deletion of the weapons provision in internal armed conflicts therefore cast a doubt on the customary nature of these prohibitions in internal armed conflicts.

4. Conclusion

The peculiarity of the laws of war consists in the gap that exists between the violations of basic rules of humanity on the battlefields and the content of military manuals or public statements made by states. Albeit rendering the process slower, this gap does not, however, prevent the creation of customary rules in internal armed conflicts. At the beginning of the twenty-first century, it is possible to conclude that the customary laws of war applicable in internal armed conflicts form a distinct and significant part of the law applicable in internal armed conflicts. The acceleration of state practice, particularly during the 1990s, has enabled the creation of this solid body of principles containing at least common Article 3, the core of Protocol II, and the rules prohibiting attacks against the civilian population and civilian objects as well as the prohibition of using gas or other chemical weapons. The threshold of applicability of these principles in internal armed conflicts is similar to common Article 3. If the core of Protocol II forms part of customary law today, the threshold of applicability of the instrument has not passed into customary law.

The view taken by the Appeals Chamber in the *Tadić* case that the 'general essence' of the rules applicable in international conflicts has become applicable in internal armed conflict seems therefore reflected in law today.[320] As far as the customary principles applicable in internal armed conflicts are concerned, the parallel between internal and international conflict is not complete, as this core of customary principles does not contain some of the means and methods of warfare prohibited in international armed conflicts. Even if recent military manuals and national legislation contain provisions applicable in armed conflicts of both types, the Rome conference decided not to have a single list of war crimes applicable in both internal and international armed conflicts. The ICTY Appeals Chamber decision in the *Tadić* case, often qualified as revolutionary or seminal,[321] might have been over inclusive,[322] it nonetheless had an immense impact on the law applicable in internal armed conflicts. Without it, states would not have been persuaded of the need to include within the jurisdiction of the ICC war crimes committed in internal armed conflicts.

Next to the conventional and customary laws of war applicable in internal armed conflicts highlighted in this chapter, a few words must also be said about the complementarity of the laws of war and human rights in internal armed conflicts.[323] Human rights complement the protection afforded by Article 3 and Protocol II in internal conflicts.[324] For internal armed conflicts, international humanitarian law can be seen as *jus specialis*, whereas human rights can be considered as *jus generalis*. Human rights conventions apply in times of peace and armed conflicts, being international or internal. However, most treaties permit states to derogate from certain human rights obligations in circumstances of public emergency. In such a situation, a small number of non-derogable rights will go on applying to internal armed conflicts. The great advantage of the European Convention on Human Rights (ECHR) and the International

Covenant on Civil and Political Rights (ICCPR) over international humanitarian law is that these non-derogable rights would apply notwithstanding a refusal by the state concerned of the existence of an armed conflict on its territory. Similarly, Article 3 lacks any enforcement mechanism, whereas human rights conventions contain a developed supervisory mechanism. The overlap between these two branches of the law is also evident especially in Articles 4 and 6 of Protocol II.

There is therefore a real convergence between the provisions of the laws of war and the content of human rights conventions. Human rights have a significant role to play in internal armed conflicts, in particular when the government refuses to recognise the applicability of common Article 3 as well as in the area of enforcement and supervision embodied in human rights treaties.[325]

Notes

1. C. von Clausewitz, *On war* (Princeton NJ: Princeton University Press, 1989) book 1, chapter 1, para. 2 cited in L. Green, 'What is – why is there – the law of war?' in M. Schmitt and L. Green (eds.), *The law of armed conflicts into the next millennium* (Newport, Rhode Island: Naval War College, 1998) vol. 71, pp. 141–83 at p. 141.

2. 'There is no more Vendée, it died by our free swords with its women and children ...'

3. For a thorough study of common Article 3 and Additional Protocol II, see L. Moir, *The law of internal armed conflict* (Cambridge: Cambridge University Press, 2002) pp. 30–132.

4. For a detailed analysis of this topic, see L. Perna, *The formation of the treaty law of non-international armed conflicts* (Leiden, Boston: Martinus Nijhoff Publishers, 2006), in particular her chapters 1 and 2.

5. For a good overview of ancient civilisations, see Green, 'What is – why is there – the law of war?', pp. 141–83.

6. Around the sixth century BC, Sun Tzu commented: 'Generally in war the best policy is to take a state intact; to ruin it is inferior to this. To capture the enemy's army is better than to destroy it, to take intact a battalion, a company or a five-man squad is better than to destroy them ... to subdue the enemy without fighting is the acme of skill ... The worst policy is to attack cities. Attack cities only when there is no alternative.' Sun Tzu, *The art of war* (Oxford: Clarendon Press, 1963) pp. 78–79 cited in Green, 'What is – why is there – the law of war?', p. 147.

7. See P. V. Kane, *History of Dharmasastra* (vol. 3, 1973), p. 210, as well as, *Sacred Books of the East*, vol. 14, 1882, I.10.18, 11 cited in L. Penna, 'Written and customary provisions relating to the conduct of hostilities and treatment of victims of armed conflicts in ancient India' (1989) *IRRC* 340–41.

8. Penna, 'Written and customary provisions in ancient India' 339–40 as well as Green, 'What is – why is there – the law of war?', p. 147.

9. Penna, 'Written and customary provisions in ancient India' 338.

10. In this respect see the comments made by A. Bashma reproduced in Penna, 'Written and customary provisions in ancient India' 337.

11. C. Phillipson, *The international law and custom of ancient Greece and Rome* (London: Macmillan and Co., 1911) pp. 207–12, cited in Green, 'What is–why is there– the law of war?', p. 149.

12. Philipson goes on saying that 'barbarians, savage tribes, bands of robbers and pirates, and the like were debarred from the benefits and relaxation established by international law and custom', *ibid.*

13. T. Meron, *Henry's wars and Shakespeare's laws: perspectives on the law of war in the later Middle Ages* (Oxford: Clarendon Press, 1993) pp. 7–8, cited in L. Rosensweig Blank, 'The laws of war in Shakespeare: international vs. internal armed conflict' (1997–1998) 30 *International law and politics* 251–90. A few fundamental precepts of the code of chivalry were: granting of quarter between knights, respect for churches and the clergy, and fair treatment of prisoners where once a soldier is made prisoner, mercy needed to be shown and a ransom would generally be demanded. See also M. H. Keen, *The laws of war in the late Middle Ages* (London: Routledge and K. Paul, 1965).

14. See both Meron and Rosensweig Blank on this issue, *ibid.*

15. Rosensweig Blank, *ibid.*, 254.

16. *Ibid.*, 257.

17. *Ibid.*, 259.

18. 2 Henry IV, IV iii. 85, cited by Rosensweig Blank, *ibid.*, 268.

19. Grotius in *De jure belli ac pacis* stated that 'one should not destroy that whose loss does not strengthen him or weaken the enemy'. See also Gentili who wrote about means and methods of warfare: 'Our only precaution must be not to allow every kind of craft and every kind of cunning device; for evil is not lawful, but an enemy should be dealt with according to law ... but the laws of war are not observed toward one who does not observe them.' Gentili, *De jure belli*, Lib. II, cap. III, VI, XXIII, pp. 142–44, 159 and 172, cited in Green, 'What is – why is there – the law of war?', p. 154.

20. E. De Vattel, *The law of nations*, (London: Newbery, Richardson, Crowder, Caslon, Longman, Law, Fuller, Coote and Kearsly, 1760) book 3, pp. 109–11 argued that: 'A civil war breaks the bonds of society and government, or at least it suspends their force and effect; it produces in the nation two independent parties, considering each other enemies, and acknowledging no common judge ... Thus they are in the case of two nations, who having a dispute which they cannot adjust, are compelled to decide it by force or arms. Things being thus situated, it is very evident that the common laws of war, those maxims of humanity, moderation and probity ... are in civil wars to be observed by both sides.'

21. On this point, see G. I. A. D. Draper, 'Humanitarian law and internal armed conflicts' (1983) 13 *Georgian journal of international and comparative law* 253–77 at 257. Draper believes that 'Vattel's work had considerable influence. It preceded the two revolutions of 1776 and 1789. As has been pointed out by Professor Albert de Lapradelle, Grotius had written the international law of absolutism, Vattel has written the international law of political liberty.' For a detailed study of Vattel's work, see Siotis, *Le droit de la guerre et les conflits armés d'un caractère non international* (Paris: Librairie de droit et de jurisprudence, 1958) pp. 55–59.

22. See L. Moir, 'The historical development of the application of humanitarian law in non-international armed conflict to 1949' (1998) 47 *International and comparative law quarterly* 337–61 at 338, citing R. P. Dhokalia, 'Civil wars and international law' (1971) 11 *Indian journal of international law* 225.

23. See H. Lauterpacht, *Recognition in international law* (Cambridge: Cambridge University Press, 1947) pp. 276–77 and Moir, *The law of internal armed conflict*, pp. 4–5.

24. For a detailed study of the concept of recognition of belligerency, see Moir, *The law of internal armed conflict*, pp. 4–21.

25. In the *Prize* case (1862), a US court put it in legal terms: 'When the party in rebellion occupy and hold in a hostile manner certain portions of territory; have declared their independence; have cast off their allegiance; have organised armies; have commenced hostilities against their former sovereign, the world acknowledges them as belligerents, and the contest a war', cited by Draper, 'Humanitarian law and internal armed conflicts' 260.

26. It came as well as a clear recognition that this same government was unable to put down the resistance quickly and effectively.

27. On this latter point, see Moir, 'The historical development of the application of humanitarian law in non-international armed conflict to 1949' 344.

28. *Ibid.*, 342.

29. Economic interests were specially taken into account when the conflict extended to the seas, see *ibid.*, 343.

30. See A. Möller, *International law in peace and war* (Copenhagen: Levin and Munksgaard, 1935) part 2, p. 157; J. Brierly, *The law of nations*, 6th edn, edited by H. Waldock (Oxford: Clarendon Press, 1963) p. 141 and Moir, 'The historical development of the application of humanitarian law in non-international armed conflict to 1949' 341.

31. See Moir *ibid.*, citing H. Wheaton, *Elements of international law*, 8th edn edited by R. Dana (London: Sampson Low, Son & Co., 1866) p. 37, n. 15: 'They gained the great advantage of a recognised status and the opportunity to employ commissioned cruisers at sea, and to exert all the powers known to maritime warfare, with the sanction of foreign nationals. They could obtain abroad loans, military and naval materials, and enlist men, as against everything but neutrality laws; their

flag and commissions were acknowledged, their revenue laws ... respected, and they acquired a quasi-political recognition.'

32. The American War of Independence is a first example where belligerency was recognised early and both belligerents showed good respect for the laws and customs of war. The British even declared themselves ready to respect the laws of war and to punish any violations of the laws and customs of war. See Siotis, *Le droit de la guerre et les conflits armés d'un caractère non international*, p. 60.

33. Instructions for the Government of Armies of the United States in the Field, General Orders No. 100, 24 April 1863. Reprinted in D. Schindler and J. Toman (eds.), *The laws of armed conflict. A collection of conventions, resolutions and other documents* (Dordrecht: Martinus Nijhoff, 1996) p. 3.

34. See M. H. Hoffman, 'The customary law of non-international armed conflict: evidence from the US Civil War' (1990) *IRRC* 322–43 and T. Meron, 'Francis Lieber's code and principles of humanity' (1997) 36 *Columbia journal of transnational law* 271–81.

35. The code was also the basis of the Brussels Declaration of 1874 and it was adapted as guidance for the Prussian army during the Franco-Prussian war. It is well recognised to have influenced greatly the Hague regulations on the laws and customs of war of 1899 and 1907. On these points, see B. Carnahan, 'Lincoln, Lieber and the laws of war: the origins and limits of the principle of military necessity' (1998) 92 *AJIL* 213–31 at 215.

36. On this point, see Siotis, *Le droit de la guerre et les conflits armés d'un caractère non international*, pp. 58–62. Britain recognised the insurgents at a very early stage of the conflict; France, Spain, Brazil and the Netherlands declared their neutrality later. See also para. 152 of the Lieber Code.

37. See on this point, Carnahan, 'Lincoln, Lieber and the laws of war: the origins and limits of the principle of military necessity' 214.

38. See Articles 149–57 of the Lieber Code.

39. Meron, 'Francis Lieber's Code and principles of humanity' 277, see also Hoffman, 'The customary law of non-international armed conflict: evidence from the US Civil War' 326.

40. Article 154 of the Lieber Code, affirming the right of the legitimate government to try leaders of rebellion, and Article 157 treating armed or unarmed resistance movements as traitors, illustrate the way armed resistance was treated, in the absence of any recognition of belligerency.

41. See Siotis on this point, *Le droit de la guerre et les conflits armés d'un caractère non international*, p. 68.

42. At the very end, the Spanish did sign an agreement with Bolivar and the rebels which applied some principles of the laws of war such as caring for wounded soldiers and the status of prisoners of war. See Siotis on this point, *ibid.*, pp. 65–68 and D. Momtaz, 'Le droit international humanitaire applicable aux conflits armés non internationaux' (2001) 292 *Recueil des cours* 24.

43. One exception is maybe the short civil war that took place in Switzerland in 1847–1848, in which the general heading the governmental forces enjoined his troops to respect the local population and the enemy combatants when they were captured or wounded. See 'Recommendations sur la conduite à tenir envers les habitants et les troupes', issued by General Dufour in November 1847, reproduced in O. Reverdin, 'Le Général Guillaume-Henri Dufour, précurseur d'Henri Dunant' in C. Swinarski (ed.), *Studies and essays on international humanitarian law and Red Cross principles in honour of J. Pictet*, (Geneva: ICRC, Martinus Njihoff Publishers, 1984) pp. 951–58 at p. 956.

44. The Commune is said to have been one of the bloodiest conflicts of the nineteenth century with 30–35,000 dead during the 70 days of conflict and 20–25,000 more rebels executed at the end of the hostilities. See Siotis, *ibid.*, pp. 91–95.

45. The majority of the doctrine took the view that the laws of war could not be applicable in civil conflicts in the absence of recognition of belligerency; one could find, however, certain scholars who advocated the application of the laws of war in all civil conflicts of a certain scale on an automatic basis. See T. Woolsey, *Introduction to the study of international law*, 4th edn, (London: Sampson Low, Marston, Low and Searle, 1875) p. 168, cited in Moir, 'The historical development of the application of humanitarian law in non-international armed conflict to 1949' 344–45.

46. Reprinted in A. Roberts and R. Guelf (eds.), *Documents on the laws of war* (Oxford: Clarendon Press, 1989) p. 45.

47. See F. Karlshoven, *Constraints on the waging of war* (Geneva: ICRC, 1991) p. 14, as well as R. Ticehurst, 'The Martens Clause and the laws of armed conflict' (1997) *IRRC* 125–34.

48. The drafters explained that 'it was not their intention that unforeseen cases should in the absence of a written undertaking, be left to the arbitrary judgment of military commanders'. Cited in Karlshoven, *ibid.*, p. 14.

49. E. Kwakwa, *The international law of armed conflict: personal and material fields of application* (Dordrecht: Kluwer, 1992) p. 36, cited in Ticehurst, 'The Martens Clause and the laws of armed conflict' 129. The expression 'laws of humanity' can be traced in the preamble of the 1868 Declaration of St Petersburg directed against the use of lightweight explosive bullets: 'the employment of such arms would therefore, be contrary to the laws of humanity'. See Green, 'What is – why is there – the law of war?', p. 161.

50. This last element has been used by states in the advisory opinion on the legality of the threat or use of nuclear weapons, in order to support the view that the use of nuclear weapons is no longer compatible with the dictates of public conscience. See, for example, Australia oral statement before the ICJ, p. 57, cited in Ticehurst, 'The Martens Clause and the laws of armed conflict' 130. Generally, the ICJ did not clarify the meaning of the Martens Clause when it stated: 'it has proved to be an effective means of addressing the rapid evolution of military technology'. See

Advisory opinion on the legality of the threat or use of nuclear weapons [8 July 1996] (1996) *International Court of Justice Report* 226, para. 78.

51. C. Greenwood, 'Historical development and legal basis' in D. Fleck (ed.), *The handbook of humanitarian law in armed conflicts* (Oxford: Oxford University Press, 1995) p. 28. The opposite view has been expressed in the *US v. Krupp* case where the court stated that the Martens Clause 'is much more than a pious declaration. It is a general clause, making the usages established among civilised nations, the laws of humanity, and the dictates of public conscience into the legal yardstick to be applied if and when the specific provisions on the Hague Convention and the regulations annexed to it do not cover specific cases occurring in warfare, or concomitant to warfare.' *US v. Krupp*, US Military Tribunal sitting at Nuremberg, judgment of 30 July 1948, Trials War Criminals, vol. 9, 1341.

52. It is interesting to note that the Martens Clause remains placed in the preamble of the Protocol applicable in internal conflicts and that reference to 'established custom' has been omitted. See Green, 'What is–why is there– the law of war?', p. 168.

53. On this point see Momtaz, 'Le droit international humanitaire applicable aux conflits armés non internationaux', 24–27 as well as Moir, *The law of internal armed conflict*, pp. 21–22.

54. In 1912, the ICRC had sought to have a resolution adopted by the International Conference of the Red Cross and Red Crescent to allow the ICRC to provide aid on both sides during civil conflicts. This was refused by a majority of states as an interference in domestic affairs of states. See Siotis, *Le droit de la guerre et les conflits armés d'un caractère non international*, pp. 135–36, and Moir, 'The historical development of the application of humanitarian law in non-international armed conflict to 1949' 354, citing A. Schlögel, 'Civil war' (1970) 108 *IRRC* 123–34 at 125.

55. Moir, 'The historical development of the application of humanitarian law in non-international armed conflict to 1949' 354. See resolution XIV of the 10th International Red Cross and Red Crescent Conference, Geneva 1921. This resolution enabled the ICRC to offer its service in the Upper Silesia conflict, as the German and the Polish National Red Crosses could not intervene. See Siotis, *ibid.*, pp. 144–45.

56. See Draper, 'Humanitarian law and internal armed conflicts' 261.

57. *Ibid.*, 261–62.

58. Resolution XIV of the 16th International Red Cross and Red Crescent Conference, London 1938, see also Schlögel, 'Civil war' 126–27.

59. Both belligerents accepted the intervention of the ICRC, the exchange of prisoners, visits of camps and prisons, and they respected the special protection given to medical personnel and to the Red Cross emblem. See Siotis, *Le droit de la guerre et les conflits armés d'un caractère non international*, pp. 160–69.

60. See N. Padelford, 'International law and the Spanish Civil War' (1937) 31 *AJIL* 226–43.

61. General Franco asked third states to award his troops the status of belligerents and he stressed that they did fulfil all the above-mentioned conditions. See A. Cassese,

'The Spanish Civil War and the development of customary law concerning internal armed conflict' in A. Cassese (ed.), *Current problems of international law: essays on UN law and on the laws of armed conflict* (Milan: A. Giuffre, 1975) p. 288.

62. In contrast with the views of Cassese or Siotis, Padelford believed: 'that the announcement regarding the treatment of prisoners, taken in conjunction with that regarding blockades, constituted recognition of belligerency by Madrid regardless of the failure to abide by the government'. Padelford, 'International law and the Spanish Civil War' 230.

63. See H. J. Taubenfeld, 'The applicability of the laws of war in civil war' in J. Moore (ed.), *Law and civil war in the modern world* (Baltimore: John Hopkins University Press, 1974) pp. 499–517. Both sides had agreed, however, in formal declarations to the ICRC to apply the 1929 Geneva Convention concerning the Wounded and Sick. See Cassese, 'The Spanish Civil War and the development of customary law concerning internal armed conflict', p. 294.

64. Cassese comments: 'the UK, France and the US realised that compelling humanitarian demands required that the most strikingly inhumane aspects of the conduct of hostilities should be taken out of the domestic sphere and be governed by international rules'. Cassese, *ibid.*, p. 293.

65. See Cassese, *ibid.*, pp. 298–301: the prohibition of the bombardment of the civilian population, especially for the purpose of terrorising or demoralising them, appears clearly from the many positions taken by third states, the contending parties and the League of Nations. This body adopted a number of resolutions, including the one of 30 September 1938, stating in general terms that the intentional bombing of civilian population is illegal. This resolution was referring to the Sino-Japanese war as well as to the Spanish Civil War; many delegates took the view that such attacks were breaching an existing rule of international law. See extract in Cassese, *ibid.*, p. 300.

66. In June 1938, Chamberlain stated in the House of Commons: 'a rule which undoubtedly applied to the Spanish Civil War was that whereby targets which are aimed at from the air must be legitimate military objectives and must be capable of identification', cited by Cassese, *ibid.*, p. 301. Similar views were held by representatives of the Soviet Union, China and France in the League of Nations, *ibid.*, pp. 301–3. The Council of the League of Nations adopted a resolution stating that 'profoundly moved by the horrors resulting form the use of certain methods of warfare, the Council condemns the employment, in the Spanish struggle, of methods contrary to international law and the bombing of open towns', *ibid.*, p. 305.

67. Similarly, the Assembly of the League of Nations adopted a resolution stating that 'any attack on legitimate military objectives must be carried out in such a way that civilian populations in the neighbourhood are not bombed through negligence'. See Cassese, *ibid.*, pp. 310–11.

68. *Ibid.*, p. 314.

69. Interestingly, Cassese notes that the contending parties in the Spanish Civil War, even when they were not complying with the principle for the protection of civilians, were formally upholding them and only denied the facts of which they were accused. *Ibid.*, p. 313.

70. Cassese believes that these principles developed above had attained the status of customary norms applicable in civil wars bearing the characteristics of the Spanish Civil War. *Ibid.*, p. 316.

71. The expressions 'common Article 3 of the 1949 Geneva Conventions', 'common Article 3' and 'Article 3' are used interchangeably in this section.

72. For a thorough study of the adoption and content of common Article 3, see Moir, *The law of internal armed conflict*, pp. 23–88. See also, R. Provost, *International human rights and humanitarian law*, (Cambridge: Cambridge University Press, 2002) pp. 264–69; Momtaz, *'Le droit international humanitaire applicable aux conflits armés non internationaux'*, pp. 28–30; L. Zegveld, *Accountability of armed opposition groups in international law* (Cambridge: Cambridge University Press, 2002) pp. 9–18.

73. The 1946 International Conference of Red Cross and Red Crescent adopted a text which would have rendered the whole Convention applicable to internal conflicts, 'unless one of the parties declares its refusal to conform thereto'. See Siotis, *Le droit de la guerre et les conflits armés d'un caractère non international*, pp. 187–89. The 1947 Conference of governments' experts voiced concern about the adequacy of extending the entire convention to internal conflicts and recommended to apply only the principles of the conventions in internal conflicts. For full details of the historical background of common Article 3, see D. Elder, 'The historical background of common Article 3 of the Geneva Convention of 1949' (1979) 11 *Case Western Reserve journal of international law* 37–69, as well as Moir, 'The historical development of the application of humanitarian law in non-international armed conflict to 1949' 354–55 and Siotis, *Le droit de la guerre et les conflits armés d'un caractère non international*, pp. 189–91.

74. *Final Record of the Geneva Diplomatic Conference of 1949* (Federal Political Department Bern, 1951) vol. 2, p. 322 (hereafter 1949 Final Record).

75. See, for example, the Canadian position, in 1949 Final Record, vol. 2–B, p. 13: 'It would be inconceivable to suggest that even in a large-scale civil war supporters of the rebels could justifiably demand from the lawful government that they be treated as protected persons under the civilian convention, although they were not living in the part of the country controlled by rebels. No lawful government would be able to quell a rebellion under these circumstances.' Cited in Moir, 'The historical development of the application of humanitarian law in non-international armed conflict to 1949' 356.

76. The delegations of Norway, Mexico, Denmark, Romania and Hungary shared this point of view. See Siotis, *Le droit de la guerre et les conflits armés d'un caractère non international*, p. 197.

77. See Siotis, *ibid.*, p. 198.

78. Moir, 'The historical development of the application of humanitarian law in non-international armed conflict to 1949' 357. For the first and second French proposals see 1949 Final Record, vol. 3, p. 27 annex 12, and vol. 2, p. 45.

79. See the Italian reaction to this proposal, cited in Siotis, *Le droit de la guerre et les conflits armés d'un caractère non international*, pp. 199–200.

80. For a comprehensive explanation of the negotiation process, see Elder, 'The historical background of common Article 3 of the Geneva Convention of 1949' 43–52, as well as Moir, 'The historical development of the application of humanitarian law in non-international armed conflict to 1949' 355–60.

81. For a more detailed study of the content of common Article 3, see Moir, *The law of internal armed conflict*, pp. 58–67.

82. Elder, 'The historical background of common Article 3 of the Geneva Convention of 1949' 58, citing 1949 Final Records, vol. 2–B, p. 84. So, an individual soldier falling into the hands of the adversary will benefit from Article 3, notwithstanding the status of the rest of his armed group.

83. Elder notes that the *travaux préparatoires* provide little assistance in reporting debates about the content of this humane treatment. The Soviet representative criticised the last draft as failing to apply all the humanitarian provisions of the Conventions to civil conflicts. He noted that the immunity of civilian hospitals from attack, unrestricted transportation and distribution of medicines and medical equipment, as well as special protection of women and minor children were not included in common Article 3. See Elder, 'The historical background of common Article 3 of the Geneva Convention of 1949' 59–60.

84. For a detailed commentary on this provision, see Elder, *ibid.*, 63–65.

85. See J. Pictet and others (eds.), *Commentary to the Geneva Conventions I of 12 August 1949* (Geneva: ICRC, 1960) p. 40.

86. This protection must be afforded 'without any adverse distinction founded on race, colour, religion or faith, sex, birth or wealth, or any other similar criteria'. The question of discrimination on the basis of nationality is left hanging: this criterion was not included in the listing and the US and the French delegates mentioned that it was 'perfectly legal' to treat insurgents of another nationality differently from nationals. Elder concludes that 'in light of the affirmative obligation of humane treatment and any other similar criteria, this provision must be interpreted to mean that nationality could allow the imposition of more or less severe humane punishment on foreign nationals who participate in the conflict', Elder, 'The historical background of common Article 3 of the Geneva Convention of 1949' 62. It is interesting to note that Article 2 of Protocol II mentions national or social origin as a possible prohibited distinction.

87. It is in these terms that the Soviet representative, Morozov, depicted quite critically Article 3. The Soviet Union would have liked to see a more substantive content given to Article 3.

88. The presence of the ICRC in the fields does not guarantee any compliance by the parties with Article 3; by accepting the offer of the ICRC, states seem to 'promote the appearance of compliance, while enjoying the putative benefits of violations'. See S. Cho, 'Applicability of international humanitarian law to internal armed conflicts', Ph.D. thesis, University of Cambridge (1996) p. 13.

89. Without this disposition, Article 3 would not have been accepted. The protection given to rebels should therefore not be interpreted as recognition of the insurgents neither should it limit states in their right to punish the rebels in accordance to their legislation.

90. In this respect, Abi-Saab argued that common Article 3 'confers a certain objective legal status on rebels', in G. Abi-Saab, 'Wars of national liberation and the laws of war' (1972) 3 *Annales d'études internationales* 96. The issue of imposing obligations on and of giving rights to rebels as non-state party to the treaty itself, is dealt with in chapter 3 of this book.

91. A number of delegations took this view during the 1949 diplomatic conference. See 1949 Final Records, vol. 2–B, p. 79 for the Soviet delegate, p. 82 for the French delegation and p. 335 for the Swiss delegation views.

92. The ICRC usually raises the issue of applicability of Article 3 with the parties. It is not an institution, however, empowered to make any legal or binding qualification of the conflict. It will merely recall the applicability of the minimum humanitarian principles in situations amounting to internal armed conflict.

93. Even if states have great latitude of appreciation of the conflict, the question of applicability of common Article 3 is of a legal nature, which should be undertaken by the state facing an internal conflict in an objective manner. It is generally admitted that the application of international humanitarian law cannot be made dependent on the view of the government concerned. See Cho, 'Applicability of international humanitarian law to internal armed conflicts', pp. 25–29.

94. For a detailed study of Article 3 and state practice, see Moir, *The law of internal armed conflict*, pp. 67–88.

95. See M. Veuthey, 'Les conflits armés de caractère non international et le droit humanitaire' in Cassese (ed.), *Current problems of international law: essays on UN law and on the laws of armed conflict* (Milan: Giuffre, 1975) p. 246. In the case of Northern Ireland, the UK has given the benefit of Article 3 rights to those who were taken prisoner. It rejected, however, the argument that it has any legal obligation to do so.

96. See J. E. Bond, *The rules of riot: internal conflicts and the laws of war* (Princeton: Princeton University Press, 1974) pp. 58–61. Contrary to the view held by the ICRC, Bond believes that: 'though there has been no lack of opportunities for the applications of Article 3 in the twenty-five years of its adoption, states have generally ignored it', p. 58.

97. See the ICRC *Annual reports* (Geneva: ICRC) on their activities in Guatemala, 1955, p. 36; Cuba, 1959, p. 18; Lebanon, 1958, pp. 13–17; Congo, 1960, pp. 7–15;

1961, pp. 48–50; Dominican Republic, 1965, p. 41; and Nigeria, 1967, p. 37. On Algeria, see Moir, *The law of internal armed conflict*, pp. 68–74. Next to these cases, where both parties recognised the applicability of common Article 3, there were two cases where only the insurgents recognised its application: in Hungary in 1956, see ICRC *Annual report* (1956) p. 6 as well as Iraq in 1962, see ICRC *Annual report* (1962) pp. 28–29. See Veuthey for a complete review of these conflicts, 'Les conflits armés de caractère non international et le droit humanitaire', pp. 236–48. See also T. Farer, 'The humanitarian laws of war in civil strife: towards a definition of international armed conflict' (1971) *Revue belge de droit international* 35–43.

98. See ICRC, *Le CICR et le conflit du Yémen*, p. 6. See Veuthey, *ibid.*, p. 240.

99. See Agreements signed between belligerents in the conflict in Bosnia-Herzegovina on 22 May 1992. See ICRC *Annual report* (1992) p. 91.

100. The ICRC argues that in the cases of Indochina, Costa Rica, Laos, Angola, Guinea-Bissau and Mozambique, the parties have implicitly accepted the application of common Article 3. For a good overview of states' practice and Article 3, see Cho, 'Applicability of international humanitarian law to internal armed conflicts' pp. 39–41, D. Forsythe, 'Legal management of internal war: the 1977 Protocol on non-international armed conflicts' (1978) 72 *AJIL* 275 and Moir, *The law of internal armed conflict*, pp. 67–88.

101. One needs also to add in the list of lacunae of Article 3, the absence of any provision related to the means and methods of warfare. Similarly, the protection of the civilian population from indiscriminate attacks is not dealt with by Article 3. See the comments of G. Abi-Saab, 'Non international armed conflicts' in UNESCO, *International dimensions of humanitarian law* (Dordrect: Martinus Nijhoff, UNESCO, Henri Dunant Institute, 1988) pp. 217–39.

102. G. Draper, 'The Geneva Conventions of 1949' (1965–I) 114 *Recueil des cours* 100.

103. For a detailed study of the adoption and content of Additional Protocol II, see Moir, *The law of internal armed conflict*, pp. 89–132. See also, H. Spieker, 'Twenty-five years after the adoption of additional Protocol II: breakthrough or failure of humanitarian legal protection' (2001) 4 *YbIHL* 129–66, Momtaz, 'Le droit international humanitaire applicable aux conflits armés non internationaux', pp. 30–33, Provost, *International human rights and humanitarian law*, pp. 260–64, Zegveld, *Accountability of armed opposition groups in international law*, pp. 9–18 and Perna, *The formation of the treaty law of non-international armed conflicts*, pp. 99–106.

104. Statement of the German delegate during the diplomatic conference on humanitarian law held in Geneva 1974–1977, quoting Red Cross sources, see CDDH/I/SR.23, p. 10. Cited in Forsythe, 'Legal management of internal war: the 1977 Protocol on non-international armed conflicts' 272.

105. Some commentators have taken strong views on the adequacy and the impact of common Article 3. Taubenfeld concludes: 'Despite the existence of Article 3 in each of the 1949 Conventions, internal war has lost little of its savagery in the

observed conflicts in the post-1949 period', Taubenfeld, 'The applicability of the laws of war in civil war' in Moore (ed.), *Law and civil war in the modern world* (Baltimore: John Hopkins University Press, 1974) p. 499. Similarly, a US delegate at the 1975 session of the Geneva Conference said: 'The non-observance of Article 3 common to the Geneva Conventions of 1949 . . . was an almost universal phenomenon', CDDH/III/SR.32, p. 9, cited in Forsythe, 'Legal management of internal war: the 1977 Protocol on non-international armed conflicts' 274.

106. The ICRC prepared a series of drafts on additional Protocol II which had been submitted to government experts' meetings in 1971 and 1972. A proposal to internationalise internal conflict of a large scale or the ones which saw a foreign intervention was rejected. The ICRC concentrated its efforts therefore on defining the conditions of application of the Protocol as well as the content of the protection given. For a precise account of diverse proposals and the negotiation process, see Abi-Saab, 'Non international armed conflicts', pp. 261–64.

107. See M. Bothe, 'Conflits armés internes et droit international humanitaire' (1978) 82 *RGDIP* 82–102 at 86.

108. Article 1.4 of Additional Protocol I.

109. See Forsythe, 'Legal management of internal war: the 1977 Protocol on non-international armed conflicts' 277–79.

110. I.e. the maximalists hoping to adopt an extensive Protocol, and the minimalists who gave the 'priority to states sovereignty and domestic jurisdiction at the expense of humanitarianism', Forsythe, *ibid.*, 281.

111. Article 1.1 of Protocol II.

112. See Article 4 of Protocol II. For a detailed analysis of this article, see Abi-Saab, 'Non international armed conflicts', p. 272, Bothe, 'Conflits armés internes et droit international humanitaire' 94–96, and Forsythe, 'Legal management of internal war: the 1977 Protocol on non-international armed conflicts' 282. One may notice the explicit mention in Protocol II of collective punishments, acts of terrorism, rape, enforced prostitution and any indecent assault, slavery, pillage and a specific right concerning children, in the list of fundamental guarantees of Article 4.

113. Article 5 of Protocol II. This article is seen as a real expansion of common Article 3 and provides for specific rights of persons whose liberty has been restricted.

114. Article 6 of Protocol II. This article gives a precise and long list of essential judicial guarantees of independence and impartiality. Article 6.4 provides for the non-pronouncement of the death penalty against children and pregnant women.

115. Articles 7–12 of Protocol II.

116. Articles 13–17 of Protocol II.

117. See A. Cassese, 'La guerre civile et le droit international' (1986) 90 *RGDIP* 571–73.

118. Relief societies located in the territory of the High Contracting Party such as the Red Cross organisations may offer their service according to Article 18.1.

119. See Cassese on these points, 'La guerre civile et le droit international' 572.

120. Article 39 of the first draft enabled organisations such as the ICRC to help in the observance of the protocol.

121. Finally, one can observe that all references to 'parties to the conflicts' have been omitted in the final version of Protocol II. As Abi-Saab points out, it seems that the provisions of Protocol II are only directed towards the legitimate government. Abi-Saab argues, however, that Article 3 continues to apply alongside Protocol II and therefore, some of the lacunae or setback of the protocol are covered by the provisions of common Article 3. See Abi-Saab, 'Non international armed conflicts', pp. 268–69.

122. An amendment to insert a clause that the determination of the applicability should be left for the state in which the conflict occurs, was rejected during the negotiations of Protocol II. See Cho, 'Applicability of international humanitarian law to internal armed conflicts', p. 54.

123. ICRC *Annual report* (1983) p. 29. Later on in 1988, the FLMN confirmed the application of both Protocol II and Article 3 in the conflict. See *Tadić* jurisdiction decision, para. 107. In 1987, the government, while declaring that Protocol II was not formally applicable to the conflict, undertook to comply with it. For a good overview of state practice and Protocol II, see Cho, 'Applicability of international humanitarian law to internal armed conflicts'.

124. Cited in Cho, *ibid.*, pp. 53 and 56. For Ethiopia, see Forsythe, 'Human rights and internal conflicts: trends and recent developments' (1982) 12 *California western international law journal* 301. For the Yemenite conflict, see the letter by Yemen to the Security Council, UN.Doc.S/1994/685 and S/1994/692.

125. During the first Chechen conflict, the Constitutional Court of Russia admitted the applicability of Protocol II on 31 July 1995. See Momtaz, 'Le droit international humanitaire applicable aux conflits armés non internationaux', p. 68.

126. See (2000) 3 *YbIHL* 565. This interpretation was specifically refuted by the Parliamentary Assembly of the Council of Europe, which took the view that the conflict could not be qualified of internal disturbances. On this point, see Momtaz, 'Le droit international humanitaire applicable aux conflits armés internationaux', p. 68, who cites recommendation 1444 of the Council of Europe dated 27 January 2000.

127. For the conflict in El Salvador, see ICRC *Annual report* (1989) p. 39, and (1987) p. 39.

128. For the conflict in El Salvador, see UN General Assembly resolution 39/119, 14 December 1984.

129. On 27 November 1991, the Federal Republic of Yugoslavia, Croatia and Serbia made such an agreement, see (1991) 31 *IRRC* 610. See also, *Tadić* jurisdiction decision, para. 73. Similarly, the parties in the conflicts in Bosnia-Herzegovina also entered into such an agreement on 22 and 23 May 1992, ICRC *Annual report* (1992) p. 91.

130. As seen in chapter 1, it is the recent definition of internal armed conflict, appearing in the *Tadić* jurisdiction decision, which has been included in the statute.
131. Already in 1978, a commentator remarked: 'It is difficult to be optimistic about the short term importance of this legal instrument', Forsythe, 'Legal management of internal war: the 1977 Protocol on non-international armed conflicts' 294.
132. For a detailed study of some of these treaties, see Perna, *The formation of the treaty law of non-international conflicts*, pp. 113–34.
133. Article 1 specifies that the Convention and its annexed protocols shall apply in these two situations only. See (1342) *UNTS* 137.
134. On this issue, see D. Turns, 'At the vanishing point of international humanitarian law: methods and means of warfare in non-international armed conflicts' (2002) 45 *German yearbook of international law* 115–48 at 122–26.
135. On the first review conference, see P. Herby, 'First session of the review conference of states parties to the 1980 UN Convention on Certain Conventional Weapons (CCW)' (1996) 312 *IRRC* 361.
136. See L. Maresca, 'Second review conference of the Convention on Certain Conventional Weapons' (2002) 845 *IRRC* 255.
137. 44 out of 100 states parties to the 1980 Convention.
138. Additional Protocol I on non-detectable fragments and Protocol III on prohibitions or restrictions on the use of incendiary weapons are therefore applicable in non-international conflicts if the state in question has ratified the amendment to Article 1 of the 1980 Convention.
139. See (2001) 4 *YbIHL* 411.
140. Reprinted in (1996) 35 *ILM* 1206.
141. See Article 1 of this Protocol. It is also specified that the Protocol shall not apply to situations of internal disturbances and tensions, such as riots, isolated and sporadic acts of violence.
142. For a detailed analysis of this amended Protocol, see C. Greenwood, 'The law of weaponry at the start of the new millennium' in M. Schmitt and L. Green (eds.), *The law of armed conflicts into the next millennium* (Newport, Rhode Island: Naval War College, 1998) vol. 71, pp. 185–231 at p. 208.
143. As of 1 December 2006, source: ICRC website, www.icrc.org.
144. Reprinted in (1996) 35 *ILM* 1218.
145. See L. Doswald-Beck, 'New protocol on blinding laser weapons (1996) *IRRC* 272–98 at 287. Doswald-Beck explains that 'seven states indicated their preference for the Protocol to be applicable in all circumstances and three preferred it to apply to international and non-international armed conflicts'. She also points out the resolution adopted by the 26th International Conference of the Red Cross and Red Crescent which 'welcomes the general agreement achieved at the review conference that the scope of application of this Protocol should cover not only international armed conflicts'. 26th International Conference, 1995, resolution 2, Section H, paragraph f), (1996) *IRRC* 68.

146. Article 1 of the Protocol on Blinding Laser Weapons, Protocol IV to the 1980 Conventions.

147. As of 1 December 2006, source: ICRC website, www.icrc.org.

148. As of 1 December 2006, this Protocol counts twenty-nine states parties and entered into force on 12 November 2006.

149. Article 1.1 of the 1993 Chemical Weapons Conventions. As of 1 December 2006, there are 181 states parties to this Convention. Reprinted in (1993) 32 *ILM* 804.

150. A similar reasoning is also applicable to the 1972 Convention on Bacteriological and Toxin Weapons, 10 April 1972, 1015 *UNTS* 164. The use of the phrase 'never under any circumstances' allows us to believe that this treaty is applicable in internal armed conflicts.

151. *Ibid.* Similarly, states are required to destroy their existing stock of chemical weapons. For a detailed analysis on this question, see Greenwood, 'The law of weaponry at the start of the new millennium', pp. 211–13.

152. See Article 2 of the Convention on the Safety of UN and Associated Personnel, reprinted in (1995) *ILM* 482.

153. Reprinted in (1997) 36 *ILM* 1507.

154. See Article 1.a) of the Convention. The first Austrian draft of this article contained the phrase 'including armed conflict and times of peace'. It was finally deemed superfluous during the negotiations as the agreement bans the use of land mines in every circumstance. See S. Maslen and P. Herby, 'An international ban on anti-personnel mines, history and negotiation of the Ottawa treaty' (1998) *IRRC* 693–713 at 698.

155. Article 2 of the 1997 Convention on Land Mines. For a detailed commentary, see *ibid.*, as well as C. Greenwood, 'The law of weaponry at the start of the new millennium', pp. 208–11.

156. As of 1 December 2006, source: ICRC website, www.icrc.org.

157. See Article 22 of the Second Protocol to the Hague Convention of 1954, 26 March 1999.

158. *North Sea Continental Shelf* case (*FRG v. Denmark; FRG v. Netherlands*), [1969] *International Court of Justice Reports* 43 (hereafter *ICJ Reports*).

159. See on this point T. Meron, 'The continuing role of custom in the formation of international humanitarian law' (1996) 90 *AJIL* 246.

160. See M. Shaw, *International law*, 3rd edn (Cambridge: Cambridge University Press, 1997) pp. 60–79.

161. The issue of determining how a non-state entity can be bound by treaty provisions or customary norms will be dealt with in chapter 3 of this book.

162. 'Trial of German major war criminals' [1946] *CMD* 6964, MISC No. 12, 65 cited in T. Meron, 'The Geneva Conventions as customary law' (1987) 81 *AJIL* 359.

163. See also on this point, G. Abi-Saab, 'The 1977 Protocols and general international law: some preliminary reflexions' in A. Delissen and G. Tanja (eds.),

Humanitarian law of armed conflicts, challenges ahead: essays in honour of Fritz Kalshoven (Dordrecht: Martinus Nijhoff Publisher, 1991) pp. 115–26 at p. 116.

164. *Military and paramilitary activities in and against Nicaragua (Merits) (Nicaragua v. US)* [1986] *ICJ Reports* 14. Hereafter referred to as the '*Nicaragua case*'.

165. Report of the Secretary-General pursuant to paragraph 2 of the Security Council resolution 808, 1993, UN.Doc.S/25704, para. 33. The Secretary-General continues saying that 'while there is international customary law which is not laid down in conventions, some of the major conventional humanitarian law has become part of customary international law', para. 33.

166. *Ibid.*, para. 34.

167. *Ibid.*, para. 29.

168. *Prosecutor v. D. Tadić*, IT-94-1AR72, decision on the defence motion for interlocutory appeal on jurisdiction of 2 October 1995 (1996) 35 *ILM* 32. Hereafter referred to as the *Tadić* jurisdiction decision.

169. *Tadić* jurisdiction decision, paras. 96–127.

170. Customary international law was heavily relied on by the Lords for the issue of state immunity where they looked at the state of customary international law to determine the extent of the immunity of a former head of state. Similarly, customary international law was looked at to determine the regime of jurisdiction of the crime of torture before the entry into force of the international convention against torture.

171. Opinion of Lord Millett, in *Regina v. Bow Street Stipendiary Magistrate and others ex parte Pinochet*, House of Lords, judgment of 24 March 1999 [1999] 2 *All ER* 102.

172. Lord Browne-Wilkinson stated: 'The Torture Convention was agreed not in order to create an international crime which had not previously existed but to provide an international system under which the international criminal – the torturer – could find no safe heaven', *ibid.*, 13–14.

173. Opinion of Lord Hope of Craighead, *ibid.*, 56.

174. The French conseil d'etat had first refused to declare illegal an administrative decision contrary to an international customary norm on the basis of the absence of direct applicability of such norms in the French legal order (conseil d'etat, 18 April 1986, *Société des mines de potasse d'Alsace*). The *Aquarone* decision, 6 June 1997, opens the door for a larger applicability and respect of international customary norms by French courts. See (1999) *RGDIP* 1054–67. Recently, however, the court of cassation has refuted the possibility of trying a person for crimes against humanity of torture committed in 1955 and 1957 on the sole basis of the existence of such crime in customary international law. The absence in the French legal order of the concept of crimes against humanity prevents any prosecutions for such crimes to take place in France for acts committed before 1994. See court of cassation, decision of 17 June 2003, reported in (2004) *RGDIP* 754–62.

175. See the research recently undertaken by the ICRC. J. M. Henckaerts, L. Doswald-Beck (eds.), *Customary international humanitarian law*, 2 vols. (Cambridge: Cambridge University Press, 2005).

176. *Nicaragua* case, para. 178.

177. The overlap between the treaty norm and the customary norm is not complete. Paragraph 3 of common Article 3 which states: 'the parties to the conflict should further endeavour to bring into force by means of special agreements all or part of the other provisions of the present convention' does not seem to reflect customary international law for example.

178. *Nicaragua* case, paras. 218–20.

179. *Ibid.*, para. 292(8).

180. For a detailed comment of this part of the judgment, see Meron, 'The Geneva Conventions as customary law' 355–58.

181. *Tadić* jurisdiction decision, paras. 89–98. See also *Tadić* trial, paras. 65, 67, 71 and 72.

182. *Akayesu* trial, paras. 603–5. See also *Rutaganda* trial, paras. 84–88.

183. *Kadić v. Karadzić*, 70 F.3d 232 (2nd Cir., 1995).

184. In the doctrine, see M. Momtaz, 'Le droit international humanitaire applicable aux conflits armés non internationaux', p. 29; D. Schindler, 'The different types of armed conflicts according to the Geneva Conventions and Protocols' (1963) 163 *Recueil des cours* 151.

185. See on this point, R. Myren, 'Applying international laws of war to non international armed conflicts: past attempts and future strategies' (1990) 37 *NILR* 367.

186. It is also interesting to note that a small number of ratifications were accompanied by reservations.

187. Ten years after its adoption, the International Court of Justice did not refer to Protocol II when it looked at the customary principles applicable in internal armed conflicts in the *Nicaragua* case.

188. T. Meron, *Human rights and humanitarian norms as customary law* (Oxford: Clarendon, 1989) pp. 75–76.

189. Algeria (1989), Chad (1997), Egypt (1992), Ethiopia (1994), Nigeria (1988), South Africa (1995), Uganda (1991), Zimbabwe (1992), Lebanon (1997), Cambodia (1998), Colombia (1995), Peru (1989) and Mozambique (2002) are now party to Protocol II.

190. On this point, see section 2.2 in this chapter.

191. Report of the Secretary-General pursuant to para. 5 of Security Council resolution 955, S/1995/134 (13 February 1995) para. 12.

192. Some national tribunals have, however, taken the opposite view. The constitutional court of Columbia held that the Geneva Conventions and Additional Protocols have passed into customary international law in their entirety (judgment C-574/92, section V, B2c, 28 October 1992 and judgment C-225/95, Section VD, 18 May 1995, both unpublished and cited in Moir, *The law of internal armed conflict*, p. 141, footnote 33).

193. *Tadić* jurisdiction decision, paras. 98 and 117, where the Appeals Chamber cites the deputy legal adviser of the US State Department, M. J. Matheson, who had declared in 1987: 'The basic core of Protocol II is, of course, reflected in common Article 3 of the 1949 Geneva Conventions and therefore is, and should be, a part of generally accepted customary law' (1987) 2 *American University journal of international law and policy* 430–31. See also, Meron, *Human rights and humanitarian norms as customary law*, pp. 71–74; Meron, 'The continuing role of custom in the formation of international humanitarian law' 247; C. Greenwood, 'Customary law status of the 1977 Geneva Protocols', A. Delissen and G. Tanja (eds.), *Humanitarian law of armed conflicts, challenges ahead: essays in honour of Fritz Karlshoven* (Dordrecht: Martinus Nijhoff, 1991) pp. 112–13; Sandoz, Swinarski and Zimmermann (eds.), *Commentary on the Additional Protocols of 1977 to the Geneva Conventions of 1949* (Geneva: ICRC/Martinus Nijhoff, 1987) pp. 1408, 1443, 1448; L. Zegveld, *Accountability of armed opposition groups in international law*, pp. 20–21 and Moir, *The law of internal armed conflict*, pp. 143–44.

194. *Tadić* jurisdiction decision, para. 117.

195. *Akayesu* trial, para. 610. See also *Rutaganda* trial, paras. 86–90.

196. See Meron, *Human rights and humanitarian norms as customary law*, p. 73, as well as the ICRC Commentary of Protocol II, p. 1340.

197. Report on the situation of human rights in Iraq, prepared by Mr M. van der Stoel, Special Rapporteur of the Commission on Human Rights, UN.Doc.E/CN./1992/31 (18 February 1992) para. 27. The rapporteur gives a list of customary principles borrowed from human rights: protection of the right to life, from torture, against arbitrary punishments, pillage, etc.

198. As to Article 13 of Protocol II, the ICTY Appeals Chamber stated that 'the principles prohibiting attacks on civilians and unlawful attacks on civilian objects stated in Articles 51 and 52 of Additional Protocol I and Article 13 of Additional Protocol II are principles of customary international law'. See *Prosecutor v. Pavle Strugar*, IT-01-42-AR72, decision on interlocutory appeal (22 November 2002) para. 10. See also *Prosecutor v. Dario Kordić*, IT-95-14/2-PT, decision on the joint defence motion to dismiss the amended indictment for lack of jurisdiction based on the limited jurisdictional reach of Articles 2 and 3 (2 March 1999) para. 31.

199. See G. Mettraux, *International crimes and the ad hoc tribunals* (Oxford: Oxford University Press, 2005) pp. 138–40 and Zegveld, *Accountability of armed opposition groups in international law*, pp. 20–21. Zegveld also makes reference to the work of the Inter-American Commission, which found that the prohibitions on recruiting children under the age of 15, of starvation of civilians as a method of combat, of attacks against cultural objects and places of worship and the forced movement of population amount to customary rules. These prohibitions are laid down in Articles 4(3), 4, 16 and 17 of Protocol II respectively. See Inter-American Commission on Human Rights, *Third Report on the Situation of*

Human Rights in Colombia, OEA/Ser.L/V/II.102, Doc. 9 Rev. 1, at 83 para. 42 and at 94–95 para. 82.

200. *Tadić* jurisdiction decision, para. 116.

201. See in general, D. Fleck, 'The protocols additional to the Geneva Conventions and customary international law' (1990) 29 *Revue de droit pénal militaire* 497–505, as well as A. Borrowdale, 'The future of the law of war: the place of the Additional Protocols of 1977 in customary international law' (1981) 14 *Comparative and international law journal of Southern Africa* 79–91.

202. For an analysis of this part of the decision, see Meron, 'The continuing role of custom in the formation of international humanitarian law' 238–44.

203. Such a study has been undertaken by the ICRC and is now available. See J. M. Henckaerts, L. Doswald-Beck, *Customary international humanitarian law*.

204. Much has been written recently on customary international law and there is considerable disagreement amongst international lawyers as to the scope and formation of a customary norm. See, for example, A. Roberts, 'Traditional and modern approaches to customary international law: a reconciliation' (2001) 95 *AJIL* 757–91; J. Kammerhofer, 'Uncertainty in the formal sources of international law: customary international law and some of its problems' (2004) 15 *EJIL* 523–53; R. Kolb, 'Selected problems in the theory of customary international law' (2003) *NILR* 119–50. See also K. Zemanek, 'The legal foundations of the international system' (1997) 226 *Recueil des cours* 157–67, who takes the view that: 'if the term [custom] proves immutable it would nevertheless be high time to recognize that what it really denotes is not custom in the ordinary meaning of the term, but the current and regular conduct of states which corresponds to the current consensus of opinion on what the law requires', at 167.

205. *North Sea Continental Shelf* case, p. 43. Prior to this case, the court had found in the *Asylum* case (1950), that the customary rule must be in accordance with a constant and uniform practice by the states in question. Similarly, the court found in the *Anglo Norwegian Fisheries* case that some degree of uniformity amongst state practice was essential before a custom could be created. For a short overview of the ICJ practice, see M. Shaw, *International law*, pp. 60–79.

206. *Ibid.*, pp. 43–44.

207. *Nicaragua* case, p. 98.

208. K. Wolfke, *Custom in present international law* (Dordrecht, Boston: Martinus Nijhoff, 1993) p. 41. See also, F. Bravo, 'Méthodes de recherche de la coutume internationale dans la pratique des Etats' (1985) 192 *Recueil des cours* 237–316 and K. Zemanek, 'The legal foundations of the international system', pp. 157–67.

209. *Tadić* jurisdiction decision, para. 99.

210. These conducts have also been coined 'verbal acts of states' as opposed to physical acts of states, such as their battlefield behaviour. See J. M. Henckaerts, 'Study on customary international humanitarian law: a contribution to the understanding and respect for the rule of law in armed conflict' (2005) 87 *IRRC* 175–212.

211. *Ibid.* For a list of types of relevant practice, see 'Report on the follow up to the International Conference for the Protection of War Victims, 26th International Conference of the Red Cross and Red Crescent', Commission I, Item 2, Doc.95. C.1/2/2,1995, pp. 7–8, cited in Meron 'The continuing role of custom in the formation of international humanitarian law' 248. On the importance of military manuals and national legislation, see Meron, 'The Geneva Conventions as customary law' 360–61 where he states: 'Manuals of military law and legislation of States providing for the implementation of humanitarian law norms as internal law should be considered as among the best types of evidence of such practice and sometimes perhaps, as a statement of *opinio juris* as well.' See also, Wolfke, *Custom in present international law*, p. 77, and Bravo, 'Méthodes de recherche de la coutume internationale dans la pratique des Etats', p. 280.

212. Taking into account the practice of armed groups could be questionable, as in general custom it is said to arise only from state practice.

213. *Nicaragua* case, para. 188, *Legality of the threat or use of nuclear weapons*, Advisory Opinion [1996] *ICJ Report* para. 70.

214. *Ibid.*, para. 70.

215. As Meron points out when reflecting on the *Tadić* decision, the study of pronouncements by states put the emphasis on *opinio juris* and compensates therefore for the scarcity of supporting state practice. See Meron, 'The continuing role of custom in the formation of international humanitarian law' 240.

216. R. Baxter, 'Multilateral treaties as evidence of customary international law' (1965–66) 41 *BYIL* 300.

217. See Henckaerts, 'Study on customary international humanitarian law' 182.

218. In this regard, Kolb takes the view that: 'It is thus specially in the field of human rights and humanitarian law that custom is defined more readily according to an *opinio juris* than to practice. This is easily understood; the actual practice of states is characterized by too many violations to serve as a sound basis of induction'. Kolb, 'Selected problems in the theory of customary international law' 124. Kolb also believes that in certain areas, such as international criminal law, the requirement of practice is softened in the face of quite urgent social needs, such as combating impunity, Kolb, 'Selected problems in the theory of customary international law' 129. See also Mettraux, *International crimes and the ad hoc Tribunals*, pp. 13–18.

219. See Delimitation of the Maritime Boundary in the Gulf of Maine Area, judgment [1984] *ICJ Reports* para. 111.

220. See M. Veuthey, 'Les conflicts armés de caractère non international et le droit humanitaire' in A. Cassese (ed.), *Current problems of international law, essays on UN law and on the law of armed conflicts* (Milan: Giuffre, 1975) pp. 179–266.

221. The Lebanese conflict is the only instance between 1970 and 1989 where the Security Council adopted a series of resolutions condemning 'the criminal massacres of Palestinian civilians in Beirut' and calling on parties to respect the

Geneva Conventions. See Security Council resolutions 512 (19 June 1982) 513 (4 July 1982) and 521 (19 September 1982).

222. See Cassese, 'The Spanish Civil War and the development of customary law concerning internal armed conflict', pp. 287–318.

223. *Ibid.*, p. 303.

224. See M. Bothe, 'Article 2 and Protocol II: case studies of Nigeria and El Salvador' (1982) 31 *American University law review* 902–3, cited in Myren, 'Applying international laws of war to non-international armed conflicts: past attempts and future strategies' 354.

225. See U. O. Umozurike, 'The application of international humanitarian law to civil conflicts' (1992) 4 *African journal of international and comparative law* 500.

226. See Human Watch Reports, 'War crimes in Chechnya and the response of the West' on www.hrw.org/campaigns/russia/chechnya.

227. Cassese, 'The Spanish Civil War and the development of customary law concerning internal armed conflict', p. 294. See also *Tadić* jurisdiction decision, para. 100.

228. Such insurances were obtained by both parties in Algeria, Cuba, Guatemala, Lebanon, Congo, and the Dominican Republic. See Veuthey, 'Les conflits armés de caractère non international et le droit humanitaire', pp. 236–45.

229. E. I. V. Nwogugu, 'The Nigerian civil war: a case study in the law of war' (1974) 14 *Indian journal of international law* 13–53. Similarly, both parties in the conflict in Yemen in 1962 agreed to abide by the Geneva Conventions. See Veuthey, 'Les conflits armés de caractère non international et le droit humanitaire', p. 240 and *Tadić* jurisdiction decision, para. 103.

230. As mentioned in section 2 of this work, the government of El Salvador was not ready to apply Protocol II but the rebels took this unilateral undertaking, see *Tadić* jurisdiction decision, para. 107.

231. Public statement of the Prime Minister of the Democratic Republic of the Congo, 21 October 1964, reprinted in (1964) *AJIL* 616, cited in *Tadić* jurisdiction decision, para. 105.

232. See Agreement of 22 May 1992 concerning Bosnia-Herzegovina at the invitation of the ICRC, see *Tadić* jurisdiction decision, para. 103.

233. See Nwogugu, 'The Nigerian civil war: a case study in the law of war' 29–30, Umozurike, 'The application of international humanitarian law to civil conflicts' 498–500 as well as *Tadić* jurisdiction decision, para. 106.

234. See on this point, Nwogugu, *ibid.*, 45. In 1968, the Federal Government of Nigeria invited a team of military observers to report on its conduct of the war. The team found that there was no evidence of genocidal intent by Federal troops. Final report of the observer team to Nigeria Federal Government, Publication NN.PG/ 279/68/50.

235. See Umozurike, 'The application of international humanitarian law' 500.

236. Nigerian Air Force code of operations, 14 January 1968, cited in 'Evaluation/ assessment of the level of implementation of IHL in Nigeria', paper presented by

Professor Sagay at the national seminar on the implementation of international humanitarian law in Nigeria (on file with the author).

237. Code of conduct for the National Resistance Army, Legal Notice No. 1of 1986, 7 April 1987.

238. Derecho internacional humanitario, manual basico para personerias y fuerzas armadas de Colombia, Article 214.

239. See Manual on the application of the rules of international humanitarian law by armed forces of the USSR, Appendix to the USSR Defence Minister order, No. 75, 1990.

240. Order of the Commander and Head of the Department of the Interior Troops of the Ministry of Internal Affairs of the Republic of Tajikistan, No. 26, 23 April 1996.

241. See Myren, 'Applying international laws of war to non-international armed conflicts: past attempts and future strategies' 355.

242. See the new military criminal code of 25 July 1998.

243. Zairian code of military justice, 1972, Article 472.

244. See also the 'Instructions on safety of innocent civilians and treatment of the wounded and dead' issued in 1989 by the Ministry of National Defence of the Republic of the Phillipines; the 'Disciplinary regulations for the armed forces' of Burkina Fasso, in particular Article 35; Article 34 of Decret 90–1159 du 12 octobre 1990 portant règlement de discipline dans les forces armées of Senegal (all available on the ICRC webiste). National legislation and criminal codes will be studied in greater detail in chapter 4 of this book.

245. *Manual of the law of armed conflict*, UK Ministry of Defence (Oxford: Oxford University Press, 2004) pp. 386–98 and in particular paras. 15.8, 15.15, 15.16.

246. House of Commons Debates, vol. 333, col. 1177, 23 March 1938. See *Tadić* jurisdiction decision, para. 100, as well as Cassese, 'The Spanish Civil War and the development of customary law concerning internal armed conflicts' pp. 298–312.

247. Cited in Cassese, *ibid.*, p. 308.

248. House of Lords Debates, vol. 541, col. 810, 19 January 1993, cited in UK materials on international law (1993) *BYIL* 722.

249. UK representative statement to the UN Security Council, 22 February 1993, S/PV.3175, p. 24, cited in UK materials on international law (1993) *BYIL* 722–23. See also the statement of the Minister of State, Foreign and Commonwealth Office on 12 August 1992: 'The forcible removal of civil population is wholly contrary to accepted tenets of international humanitarian law', reprinted in UK materials on international law (1992) *BYIL* 814 as well as his statement concerning the Chechen attack in a theatre in Moscow: 'they have perpetrated such attacks on civilians targets before; they have also used land mines indiscriminately; and they have maltreated Russian prisoners. Of course, allegations have also been made about the conduct of Russian forces. We believe that any such operations have to be proportionate and in accordance with the rule of law', reprinted in UK materials on international law (2003) *BYIL* 909.

250. See practice of the French administration in (1993) *AFDI* 1022–024, as well as (1995) *AFDI* 936–44.

251. See OTAN, Conseil de l'Atlantique Nord, Decision autorisant le recours à des frappes aériennes pour soutenir l'action de la FORPRONU à Sarajevo, 9 Février 1994, reprinted in (1994) 98 *RGDIP* 567.

252. (1995) *AFDI* 911–12.

253. Cited in (2002) 5 *YbIHL* 508. In 1999, during the second conflict in Chechnya, the German Minister of Foreign Affairs also condemned the Russian ultimatum against the population of Grozny in Chechnya. He said that the threat of the use of force against an entire town was unacceptable. Cited in (2000) 3 *YbIHL* 507.

254. Reprinted in UK materials on international law (2002) *BYIL* 953, see also a similar statement made on 8 July 2002 and 20 May 2002, reproduced on pp. 955 and 958 respectively.

255. It is interesting to note in this respect that in the conflicts in ex-Yugoslavia, the Security Council passed its first resolution on 25 September 1991, but recalled the obligations under the Geneva Conventions for the first time only on 13 July 1992.

256. See UN SC resolutions 512 (19 June 1982) 513 (4 July 1982) and 521(19 September 1982).

257. For a condemnation of the repression of the Iraqi civilian population in Iraq, see UN SC resolution 688 (5 April 1991). During the conflict in ex-Yugoslavia, the SC has condemned attacks on civilians in many instances, see SC resolutions 769 (7 August 1992), 770 (13 August 1992), 771(13 August 1992), 802 (25 January 1993), 819 (16 April 1993), 824 (6 May 1993), 900 (4 March 1994), 913 (22 April 1994), 998 (16 June 1995), 1004 (12 July 1995), 1009 (10 August 1995), 1010 (10 August 1995). Similarly for Rwanda, see SC resolutions 912 (21 April 1994), 918 (17 May 1994), 925 (8 June 1994), 929 (22 June 1994), 935 (1 July 1994). For Somalia, see SC resolution 794 (3 December 1992). For Liberia see SC resolutions 950 (21 April 1994), 1001 (30 June 1995). For Angola, see SC resolutions 804 (29 January 1993), 1237 (7 May 1999). For Georgia, see SC resolution 993 (12 May 1995). For Kosovo, see SC resolutions 1199 (23 September 1998), 1203 (24 October 1998), 1244 (10 June 1999). For Burundi, see SC resolutions 1012 (28 August 1995), 1049 (5 March 1996), 1072 (30 August 1996), 1286 (19 January 2000) and 1375 (29 October 2001). For Democratic Republic of Congo, see SC resolutions 1208 (19 November 1998), 1291 (24 February 2000), 1304 (16 June 2000), 1332 (14 December 2000), 1341 (22 February 2001), 1355 (15 June 2001), 1468 (20 March 2003). For Afghanistan, see SC resolutions 1193 (28 August 1998), 1214 (8 December 1998). For Azerbaijan, see SC resolution 884 (12 November 1993). For Sierra Leone see SC resolutions 1181 (13 July 1998), 1231 (11 March 1999) and 1370 (18 September 2001). For East Timor see SC resolutions 1264 (15 September 1999) and 1272 (25 October 1999). For Sudan, see SC resolutions 1547 (11 June 2004), 1556 (30 July 2004), 1564 (18 September 2004), 1590 (24 March 2005), 1591 (29 March 2005).

258. See SC resolutions adopted during the conflicts in ex-Yugoslavia: 771 (13 August 1992), 779 (6 October 1992), 780 (6 October 1992), 787 (16 November 1992), 808 (22 February 1993), 819 (16 April 1993), 820 (17 April 1993), 824 (6 May 1993), 827 (25 May 1993), 836 (4 June 1993), 941 (23 September 1994), 1019 (9 November 1995), 1034 (21 December 1995). For Georgia, see SC resolution 876 (19 October 1993). For Sudan, see SC resolutions 1547 (11 June 2004), 1556 (30 July 2004).

259. See SC resolutions adopted during the conflicts in ex-Yugoslavia 798 (18 December 1992), 820 (17 April 1993), 827 (25 May 1993), 1019 (9 November 1995), 1034 (21 December 1995). For Sierra Leone, see SC resolution 1400 (28 March 2002). For the Democratic Republic of Congo, see SC resolution 1468 (20 March 2003). For Sudan, see SC resolutions 1547 (11 June 2004), 1556 (30 July 2004), 1590 (24 March 2005), 1591 (29 March 2005).

260. See SC resolutions adopted during the conflicts in ex-Yugoslavia 802 (25 January 1993), 819 (26 April 1993), 820 (17 April 1993), 998 (16 June 1995), 1009 (10 August 1995). For Rwanda, see SC resolution 912 (21 April 1994). For Somalia, see SC resolutions 837 (6 June 1993), 865 (22 September 1993), 897 (4 February 1994). For Liberia, see SC resolutions 788 (19 November 1992), 813 (26 March 1993), 950 (21 October 1994), 972 (13 January 1995), 1059 (31 May 1996), 1083 (27 November 1996). For Angola, see SC resolutions 804 (29 January 1993), 811 (12 March 1993), 823 (30 April 1993). For Burundi, see SC resolutions 1049 (5 March 1996) and 1072 (30 August 1996). For East Timor, see SC resolutions 1264 (11 June 1999) and 1272 (15 October 1999). For the RDC, see SC resolution 1355 (15 June 2001). See also SC resolution 1502 (26 August 2003) which says that 'there are existing prohibitions under international law against attacks knowingly and intentionally directed against personnel involved in a humanitarian assistance or peacekeeping mission'.

261. See SC resolutions adopted during the conflicts in ex-Yugoslavia 819 (26 April 1993), 824 (6 May 1993), 836 (4 June 1993), 913 (22 April 1994), 941 (23 September 1994), 959 (19 November 1994), 998 (16 June 1995), 1004 (12 July 1995), 1010 (10 August 1995), 1034 (21 December 1995).

262. SC resolutions 1265 (17 September 1999), 1296 (19 April 2000) and 1314 (11 August 2000). Resolution 1296 includes a statement by the Security Council that 'the deliberate targeting of civilian population or other protected persons and the committing of systematic, flagrant and widespread violations of international humanitarian law and human rights in situations of armed conflict may constitute a threat to international peace and security' (para. 5). See also similar terms used in SC resolution 1325 (31 October 2000). The SC often condemns also the impact of armed conflict on children, see SC resolutions 1379 (20 November 2001) and 1314 (11 August 2000).

263. League of Nations, *Official Journal Spec. Supp.* 183, 1938, pp. 135–36, cited in *Tadić* jurisdiction decision, para. 101.

264. GA resolution 2444, UN.Doc.A/7218 (1968) and GA resolution 2675, UN.Doc.A/ 8028 (1970). For a detailed study of their content, see *Tadić* jurisdiction decision, paras. 110–111.

265. See (1973) 27 *AJIL* 124 cited in *Tadić* jurisdiction decision, para. 110.

266. It is difficult to accept that these resolutions were declaratory of customary law at the time of their adoption, as they were more an injunction addressed to parties to respect most of the rules applicable in international armed conflicts in internal conflicts. See E. David, *Précis de droit des conflicts armés*, (Brussels: Bruyant, 1994) pp. 81–83. For an opposite view, see *Tadić* jurisdiction decision, para. 112.

267. For the RDC, see GA resolutions UN.Doc.56/173 (2002), 57/233 (2003) and 58/ 196 (2004). For Sudan, see GA resolutions UN.Doc.56/175 (2002) and 57/230 (2003).

268. EPC 3/92 and 73/92, cited in UK materials on international law (1992) *BYIL* 813.

269. Declaration by the European Union on the situation in Chechnya, press release 6055/96 (25 March 1996). For examples, see also press release 4215/95 (17 January 1995), press release 4385/95 (23 January 1995), press release 9563/96 (23 August 1996) and the statement by the Presidency on behalf of the European Union urging 'the Russian government to fulfil its obligations under international humanitarian law' in Chechnya, press release 14309/99 (30 December 1999). See finally, UK materials on international law (1995) *BYIL* 712.

270. See declaration by the Presidency on behalf of the EU on the killings of civilians in Burundi, press releases 10613/99 (3 September 1999) and 11285/99 (8 October 1999). Declaration by the Presidency on the human rights and humanitarian situation in Colombia, press release 8737/00 (23 May 2000).

271. Declaration by the Presidency on behalf of the EU on the bombing of civilian targets by the Sudanese air force, press release 7705/00 (5 May 2000). The use of the words 'civilian targets' by the European Union should be condemned. See also the EU Presidency statement issued on 18 August 2000 reproduced in UK materials on international law (2000) *BYIL* 581 as well as the declaration by the Presidency of the EU on the situation in Southern Sudan, press release 10349/02 (25 June 2002), where 'The EU recalls the universal humanitarian principle, that civilian populations must be protected from the consequences of military operations'.

272. See UN Secretary-General reports UN.Doc.S/1995/755 (30 August 1995) and S/1995/988 (27 November 1995).

273. See para. 2 of report of the Secretary-General pursuant to SC resolution 844 (1993), UN.Doc.S/1994/555 (9 May 1994).

274. *Ibid.*, para. 16. See also UN. Doc.S/1994/291 (11 March 1994), S/1994/600 (19 May 1994) and S/1994/1389 (1 December 1994).

275. Para. 53 of the final report on the situation of human rights in the territory of the former Yugoslavia submitted by Mr T. Masowiecki, UN.Doc.E/CN.4/1996/9 (22 August 1995).

276. See SG report UN.Doc.S/1994/640 (31 May 1994) and S/1994/1125 (4 October 1994), which include the report from the commission of experts established in accordance with SC resolution 935 (1994). See also the statement by the President of the Security Council on the situation in Rwanda UN.Doc.S/PRST/1994/21 (30 April 1994) and the report on the situation of human rights in Rwanda, UN.Doc.E/CN.4/1995/7 (28 June 1994).

277. Attacks on civilians were mainly qualified as grave human rights violations by the Secretary-General in his many reports, see, for example, para. 10 in UN.Doc.S/1998/834 (4 September 1998) and paras. 7 and 28 in UN.Doc.S/1998/912 (3 October 1998). In another report, the Secretary-General qualified such violations as war crimes, see para. 66 in UN.Doc.S/1999/779 (12 July 1999).

278. See the seventh report of the Secretary-General on the UN observer mission in Sierra Leone, UN.Doc.S/1998/836 (30 July 1999).

279. See, in particular, SG reports UN. Doc.S/2004/947 (3 December 2004), para. 7 and S/2005/140 (4 March 2005) paras. 2, 14 and 15. See also the report of the SG on the protection of civilians in armed conflict UN.Doc.S/2004/431 (28 May 2004).

280. See, in particular, E/CN.4/Res/2000/58, where the Commission on Human Rights underlined the need to respect the principle of proportionality and condemned the disproportionate and indiscriminate use of Russian military force, including attacks against civilians.

281. See (1965) *IRRC* 570 as well as (1994) 33 *ILM* 297.

282. The principle to include war crimes committed in internal armed conflicts within the jurisdiction of the ICC was opposed by a few states. The great majority of states, however, wanted the ICC to have jurisdiction over war crimes in internal armed conflicts and the inclusion of the prohibition to attack civilians was not opposed by any of these states.

283. *Tadić* jurisdiction decision, paras. 96–127.

284. See, for example, *Galić* trial, para. 19.

285. For the prohibition to attack civilians and the obligation to distinguish between civilians and combatants, see Henckaerts and Doswald-Beck, *Customary international humanitarian law*, vol. I, pp. 5–8.

286. *Ibid.*, pp. 3–76.

287. See 1949 Final Records, vol. II, section B, p. 90, cited in F. Karlshoven, 'Applicability of customary international law in non-international armed conflicts' in A. Cassese (eds.), *Current problems of international law: essays on UN law and on the laws of armed conflict* (Milan: Giuffre, 1975) p. 276.

288. See CDDH, *Official records*, vol. VII, CDDH/SR.51, 3 June 1977, p. 114.

289. The Security Council strongly condemned such practices in its resolution 612 (9 May 1988).

290. See *New York Times* (16 September 1988) cited in *Tadić* jurisdiction decision, para. 123.

291. See *Le Monde* (29 December 1999) p. 4. Human Rights Watch reported on 18 February 2000 that a Russian military official acknowledged Russia's intention to use fuel air explosives in Chechnya. See Human Rights Watch website, www.hrw.org/hrw/press/2000.

292. Article 2.2 of the Protocol on Prohibitions or Restrictions on the Use of Incendiary Weapons 1980.

293. Article 1 of the Convention on Prohibitions or Restrictions on the Use of Certain Conventional Weapons, which may be deemed to be excessively injurious or to have indiscriminate effects. However, on 21 December 2001, Article 1 of this convention was amended to be applicable also 'to situations referred to in Article 3 common to the Geneva Conventions'.

294. See Cassese, 'The Spanish Civil War and the development of customary law concerning internal armed conflicts', p. 297.

295. Agreement of 22 May 1992 between the different parties to the conflict in Bosnia-Herzegovina, para. 2.5. See (1992) ICRC *Annual report* 91.

296. The Russian military manual refers to humanitarian law instruments which shall apply to all cases of declared war or any other armed conflict, and gives a detailed list of prohibited weapons. However, this list does not mention any instruments applicable in internal armed conflicts.

297. Cited in UK materials on international law (1988) *BYIL* 579–80. See also (1986) *BYIL* 632–33, as well as (1990) *BYIL* 625.

298. See (1988) *AFDI* 899–900, (1984) *AFDI* 997–99; as well as (1989) *AFDI* 889.

299. Cited in *Tadić* jurisdiction decision, para. 121.

300. US Department of State, press guidance, 9 September 1988, cited in *Tadić* jurisdiction decision, para. 122.

301. SC resolution 1296 (19 April 2000) on the protection of civilians in armed conflicts does mention, in its para. 20, the entry into force of the 1997 Mine Ban Convention, and notes the beneficial impact of its implementation on the safety of civilians.

302. League of Nations, *Official Journal Spec. Supp.* 183, 1938, pp. 135–36.

303. GA resolution 2444, UN.Doc.A/7218 (1968).

304. See GA resolution 2677, UN.Doc.A/8178 (1970).

305. See GA resolution 2795 UN.Doc.A/8549 (1971) paras. 4 and 6, and resolution 2707 UN.Doc.A/8187 (1970) para. 9.

306. See GA resolution UN.Doc.56/175 (2002).

307. Declaration of minimum humanitarian standards reprinted in UN.Doc.E/C.N.4/1995/116 (1995). See also *Tadić* jurisdiction decision, para. 119, as well as Eide, Rosas and Meron, 'Combating lawlessness in gray zone conflicts through minimum humanitarian standards' (1995) 89 *AJIL* 215.

308. The use of riot-control agents also known as 'irritant agents' is only prohibited as a method of warfare according to the 1993 Chemical Weapons Convention, Article 1.5.

309. (1988) 4 *European political co-operation documentation bulletin* 92, cited in *Tadić* jurisdiction decision, para. 120.

310. *Ibid.*, para. 124.

311. Henckaerts and Doswald-Beck, *Customary international humanitarian law*, vol. 1, p. 240.

312. Only a few military manuals contain references to means of warfare applicable in internal armed conflicts. The French, Canadian, Australian, New Zealand military manuals do not include any provisions on the prohibition of the use of certain weapons in internal armed conflicts. One might cite, however, the new British military manual of 2004 (para. 5.28), as well as the German military manual of 1992 (para. 401) which do. On this issue, see also D. Turns, 'At the vanishing point of international humanitarian law: methods and means of warfare in non-international armed conflicts' (2002) 45 *German yearbook of international law* 115–48, especially 138–42.

313. *Tadić* jurisdiction decision, para. 127, see also Meron, 'Criminalisation of internal atrocities' (1995) 89 *AJIL* 561.

314. See UN.Doc.A/CONF.183/2/Add.1 (14 April 1998) p. 24. The actual Article 8.2.e) contained another war crime labelled l) in the draft statute. It contained two options. Option 1: no provision on prohibited weapons; option 2: a reference to arms, in the light of the discussions on para. B) o). The ICRC suggested, during the work of the Preparatory Committee on the Establishment of an International Criminal Court, the inclusion of one generic crime dealing with weapons in internal armed conflict: the prohibition 'to employ weapons, projectiles and material and methods of warfare of a nature to cause superfluous injury or unnecessary suffering, or inherently indiscriminate'. See ICRC, *Commentary, definition of war crimes*, working paper prepared by the ICRC for the Preparatory Committee for the Establishment of an International Criminal Court, New York, 14 February 1997.

315. The Non-Aligned Movement as well as the Arab League were strong supporters of the inclusion of nuclear weapons within the jurisdiction of the ICC. See UN.Doc.A/CONF.183/C.1/L.26 (29 June 1998) (proposal from Iraq); UN.Doc.A/CONF.183/C.1/L.33 (30 June 1998) (from the Ukraine); UN.Doc.A/183/C.1/L.72 (14 July 1998) and UN.Doc.A/CONF.183/C.1/L.94 (17 July 1998) (both proposals put forward by India).

316. On this point see H. von Hebel and D. Robinson, 'Crimes within the jurisdiction of the court' in Roy S. Lee (ed.), *The International Criminal Court, the making of the Rome statute, issues, negotiations, results* (The Hague: Kluwer Law International, 1999) pp. 79–141, in particular pp. 113–16.

317. See UN.Doc.A/CONF.183/C.1/L.53 (6 July 1998) p. 10 and UN.Doc.A/CONF.183/C.1/L/59 (10 July 1998) p. 9.

318. These states included India, China, Indonesia, Nigeria and most countries from the Arab League.

319. View held during informal consultations between states that took place on 26 June 1998 at the Rome conference.

320. *Tadić* jurisdiction decision, para. 126.

321. D. Turns 'At the vanishing point of international humanitarian law' 118 and 127.

322. Among the criticism addressed to the *Tadić* jurisdiction decision, see in particular, P. Rowe, 'The International Criminal Tribunal for Yugoslavia: the decision of the Appeals Chamber on the interlocutory appeal on jurisdiction in the *Tadić* case' (1996) 45 *ICLQ* 691. Meron characterised the *Tadic* decision of a 'legislative' judicial process and took the view in 1987 that: 'tribunals have been guided, and are likely to continue to be guided, by the degree of offensiveness of certain acts to human dignity; the more heinous the act, the more the tribunal will assume that it violates not only a moral principle of humanity, but also a positive norm of customary law'. T. Meron, 'Geneva Conventions as customary law' (1987) 81 *AJIL* 361.

323. On the relationship between human rights and humanitarian law, see R. Provost, *International human rights and humanitarian law* (Cambridge: Cambridge University Press, 2002); A. Robertson, 'Humanitarian law and human rights' in C. Swinarski (ed.), *Studies and essays on international humanitarian law and Red Cross principles, in honour of J. Pictet,* (Geneva: ICRC, Martinus Njihoff Publishers, 1984) p. 793; R. Kolb, 'The relationship between international law and human rights: a brief history of the 1948 Universal Declaration of Human Rights and the 1949 Geneva Conventions' (1998) *IRRC* 409; H. Burgos 'The application of international humanitarian law as compared to human rights law in situations qualified as internal armed conflict' in F. Karlshoven and Y. Sandoz (eds.), *Implementation of international humanitarian law* (Dordrecht: Martinus Nijhoff Publishers, 1989) p. 1 and W. Abresch, 'A human rights law of internal armed conflict: the European Court of Human Rights in Chechnya' (2005) 16 *EJIL* 741–67.

324. See A. Reidy, 'The approach of the European Commission and Court of Human Rights to international humanitarian law' (1998) *IRRC* 513; L. Zegveld, 'The Inter-American Commission on Human Rights and international humanitarian law: a comment on the *Tablada* case' (1998) *IRRC* 505.

325. See, in particular, D. O'Donnell, 'Trends in the application of international humanitarian law by UN human rights mechanisms' (1998) *IRRC* 481.

3

The regime of war crimes

A classical definition of war crimes was given by Manfred Lachs in 1945:

> A war crime is any act of violence qualified as crime, committed during and in connection with a war under specially favourable conditions, created by the war and facilitating its commission, the act being directed against the other belligerent state, its interests, or its citizens, against a neutral state, its interest, its citizens as well as against stateless civilians, unless it is justified under the law of warfare.[1]

The punishment of individuals for war crimes is as old as the rules regulating warfare.[2] Sanctions for violating the laws and customs of war have been an integral part of the laws of warfare and probably an essential trigger to assure some compliance with this body of law by soldiers. Prosecutions could naturally be undertaken by the enemy into whose hands the alleged offender had fallen, or alternatively by the military authorities of the alleged offender. The principle of individual criminal responsibility slowly found its way into international instruments codifying the laws and customs of war. In the twentieth century, an essential ingredient of the regime of war crimes was added with the creation of international tribunals able to prosecute war criminals for what had become international crimes. This chapter will give a brief historical overview of the regime of war crimes as well as a study of the regime of war crimes regulating international armed conflicts. The last section will discuss in detail each element of Manfred Lachs' definition of war crimes in order to determine whether the concept of war crimes can be extended to internal armed conflicts.

1. The customary right to try belligerents for violations of the laws of war: brief historical survey[3]

Violations of the laws of war entailed individual responsibility in many ancient civilisations such as in China, India or in Asia, where, for example, according to the code of Bushido 'every soldier must report to the commander about prisoners of war ... He shall be guilty of manslaughter if he kills them with his own hands.'[4] Similar principles formed part of the law of arms in the Middle Ages.[5] The right for belligerents to try enemy personnel who fell into their hands and against whom evidence was available that they had committed violations of the laws of war, was unequivocally recognised.[6] In 1268 in Naples, Conrandin von Hohenstafen was tried and sentenced to death for having initiated an unjust war.[7] In 1474, the trial of Peter von Hagenbach is one example of a quasi-international tribunal,[8] which convicted von Hagenbach of murder, rape, perjury and other crimes 'against the laws of man and of God' committed in the village of Breisach.

In the following centuries, little documentation on war crimes trials per se can be found,[9] even if classical writers constantly reaffirmed the right of the belligerents to punish enemies guilty of serious violations of the laws of war. In 1625, Grotius, shadowing the concept of inter-national crime or offences against mankind, wrote:

> The fact must be recognised that kings, and those who possess rights equal to those kings, have the right of demanding punishment not only on account of injuries committed against themselves or their subjects, but also on account of injuries which do not directly affect them but exces-sively violate the law of nature or of nations in regard to any persons whatsoever.[10]

Similar views were expressed by, for example, F. de Vitoria in 1532, C. Wolf in 1764, J. Moser,[11] the Institute of International Law in 1882[12] or Holland writing in 1908:

> Individuals offending against the laws of war are liable to such punish-ment as is prescribed by the military code of the belligerent into whose hands they fall, or in default of such code, then to such punishment as may be ordered in accordance with the laws and usages of war by military court.[13]

This rapid overview clearly shows that individuals could always be held criminally responsible if they breached the laws of war. They could either be tried by their own authorities or by the enemies in the hands of whom they had fallen.[14] This principle was applicable in what we would call today, international armed conflicts. In civil war, offenders would be tried for offences committed during the conflict in accordance with the particular country's criminal law, with emphasis being paid to the law of treason.[15] The principle applicable in international conflicts and largely shared by many domestic legal systems over the centuries was included in some early instruments of codification of the laws of war.

Early instruments of codification of the laws of war contained some injunctions on states to disseminate the content of these instruments to the armies and a call to enact national legislation in order to repress certain violations in time of war.[16] The Hague Conventions of 1899 and 1907, however, failed specifically to establish the international criminal responsibility of individuals as well as a universal right for other states to try perpetrators for violations of the laws of war.[17] They only provided for the responsibility of states to pay damages in case of violations of the conventions,[18] and generally states had a tendency to try individuals responsible for violations of the laws of war domestically.[19]

A number of atrocities committed by Germany in the early years of the First World War, as well as the genocide committed by the Turkish authorities against the Armenian people,[20] prompted European governments to acknowledge the criminality of certain behaviours and the individual responsibility of perpetrators in international law for such acts. The Versailles Treaty was the first to include specific provisions dealing with individual criminal responsibility for violations of the laws of war. Article 227 of the Versailles Treaty provided for the trial of the former Emperor of Germany, and Articles 228 and 229 recognised the 'right of the Allied and Associated Powers to bring before military tribunals Germans accused of having committed acts in violation of the laws and customs of war'. The German Emperor was, however, never tried as the German authorities refused to hand their nationals to the allied powers to be tried by foreign military tribunals.[21] As a result, only a few Germans accused of serious violations of the laws of war were tried by the Allies in Europe during or after the First World War.[22] The Allies were on the other hand under no obligation by the Versailles Treaty to try their own soldiers for violations of the laws of war. The prosecution of war criminals, or its absence, was therefore characterised by the one-sidedness of an international justice invoked by the Allies and the failure to establish an international tribunal to try perpetrators, as proposed by the Commission on the Responsibility of the Authors of the War and on Enforcement of Penalties in 1919.[23]

During the Second World War, numerous statements about the individual responsibility of perpetrators who violated the laws of war were made by the Allies.[24] In 1942, the Allies decided to set up the UN War Crimes Commission for the investigation of war crimes and affirmed:

the UN commission should proceed upon the footing that international law recognises the principle that a war crime is a violation of the laws and customs of war, and that no question can be raised as to the right of the United Nations to put on trial as a war criminal in respect of such violations any hostile offender who may fall into their hands.[25]

At the end of the Second World War, these undertakings were fulfilled at the national level with 2,116 known military tribunal hearings conducted by the USA, Great Britain, Australia, France, the Netherlands, Poland, Norway, Canada, China and Greece up to 1949[26] and at the international level with the creation of two International Military Tribunals. On 8 August 1945, the USA, Great Britain, France and the USSR established by the London Charter the International Military Tribunal of Nuremberg (IMT).[27] The Nuremberg Tribunal tried twenty-four accused whose crimes had no specific location for crimes against peace, war crimes[28] or crimes against humanity.[29] Furthermore, the Nuremberg Tribunal recognised a number of principles which form the basis of modern international criminal law.[30] In relation to war crimes, this tribunal took the view that the laws of war contained in the Hague Conventions of 1907 reflected customary international law,[31] and it affirmed that the violations of the Hague Conventions of 1907 'constituted crimes for which the guilty individuals were punishable is too well settled to admit of argument'.[32] In 1946, the International Tribunal for the Far East was established and prosecuted those superior officers, Japanese and German, whose crimes had not been limited to a specific location.[33]

2. The current regime of war crimes committed in international armed conflicts

Nuremberg and Tokyo remain to a great extent the symbol of international justice imposed by the victors on the vanquished. The Allies themselves did not instigate many prosecutions against their own soldiers who had committed what we would consider today war crimes, and usually considered that their actions were never as evil as the conduct of the Axis Power.[34] The selectivity of the prosecutions after the Second World War coupled with the necessity to create an effective mechanism to enforce individual responsibility for war crimes, as well as the need to update the old-fashioned content of the laws of war, encouraged states to negotiate and adopt four conventions on the laws of war, the so-called 1949 Geneva Conventions. Together with the rules contained in Protocol I, they form a modern and complex set of norms regulating mainly international armed conflicts. The 1949 Geneva Conventions clearly affirm the individual criminal responsibility of perpetrators for serious violations of these instruments and contain an elaborate regime of repression of such violations. It is largely admitted that any violation of the laws of war does not amount to a war crime.[35] Some are too minor to attract international criminal responsibility. In international law, war crimes represent only the most serious violations of the laws of war. In the Geneva Conventions regime, these most serious violations are called grave breaches,[36] and are contained in Articles 50, 51, 130 and 147 of the four 1949 Geneva Conventions respectively, as well as Articles 11 and 85 of Protocol I. The grave breaches of the Geneva Conventions deal primarily with the protection and humane treatment of persons who are in the hands of the enemy, prisoners, sick or wounded, or civilians, whereas the grave breaches of Protocol I include some 'battle crimes'. Any prohibited conduct listed in these provisions, if committed against a protected person or protected property under the 1949 Geneva Conventions,[37] will entail criminal responsibility of the individual perpetrator in international law. The Geneva Conventions provide for the responsibility of those who have committed or who have ordered the grave breaches to be committed.[38]

Under the 1949 Geneva Conventions, states are under several obligations with regards to grave breaches: first to legislate and provide effective penal sanctions for grave breaches, secondly to extradite the perpetrators to a requesting state or alternatively to search for, and bring to trial before its own courts the perpetrators of such violations. The regime of grave breaches does not only entitle states parties to try or extradite offenders but creates a direct obligation on any states' party either to try or to extradite the offenders if they are found on their territory. This advanced jurisdictional regime often called *aut judicare, aut dedere*, is meant to oblige states, belligerents or neutrals, to implement the conventions domestically and to give the means to their judiciary to try or extradite individuals who might have committed a grave breach of the conventions. The Geneva Conventions have been almost universally ratified[39] and have therefore established a potentially strong enforcement mechanism of individual responsibility for grave breaches. This regime has not, however, been successful at apprehending and trying war criminals since 1949. Many states have implemented the Geneva Conventions internally but have felt under no compulsion to arrest, extradite or try suspected war criminals at least up to the 1990s.[40]

Next to the most serious violations subjected to *aut judicare, aut dedere* regime, the Geneva Conventions call on states to 'suppress all acts contrary to the provisions of the convention other than grave breaches'.[41] This leaves a choice of means to suppress these violations; for example, states can attach criminal penalties to any violation of the conventions or take administrative action against them. Criminal responsibility can therefore be attached to these violations, but there does not seem to be any internationally recognised criminal responsibility.[42] In most national legislation implementing the Geneva Conventions, individual criminal responsibility is only attached to the grave breaches provisions.

The 1949 Geneva Conventions provided the first conventional regime establishing individual responsibility for the violations of the laws of war and the means to enforce this responsibility. However, the 1949 Geneva Conventions and Protocol I do not contain an exhaustive list of war crimes. There are other serious violations of the laws of war falling within the generic category of war crimes, which are not covered by the conventions and protocols. The Commission of Jurists in 1919 found that the use of deleterious and asphyxiating gases, of explosive or expanding bullets as well the poisoning of wells amount to war crimes.[43] Similarly the Nuremberg Tribunal emphasised that the employment of poisoned weapons was considered traditionally as a war crime.[44] The jurisdictional regime of this wider category of war crimes differs from the regime of grave breaches in that international law only provides for a right, and not an obligation, for any state to exercise jurisdiction over the perpetrators of war crimes.

The recent negotiations of the Rome statute on the establishment of an International Criminal Court (ICC) offered the opportunity for states to compile a more exhaustive list of war crimes, on the eve of the twenty-first century.[45] Article 8.2.a) of the ICC statute reproduces the grave breaches of the Geneva Conventions and Article 8.2.b) contains twenty-six other serious violations of the laws of war, based on a mixture of provisions from Protocol I and from the Hague regulations. It is interesting to note that one crime in this list, Article 8.2.b)iii), war crime of intentionally directing attacks against humanitarian workers and peace-keeping missions, is for the first time recognised as criminal in the Rome statute as it appears neither in the Hague regulation nor in Protocol I.[46] Moreover, some of the provisions under Article 8.2b), such as the sexual violence crimes, the crimes of pillaging, of declaring that no quarter will be given or of using children to participate in the hostilities, were previously considered to be violations of the laws of war but are treated as war crimes per se for the first time in the Rome statute.[47] Notwithstanding these advances, some violations often considered to be war crimes by a majority of countries, such as the use of weapons of mass destruction, could not be included in the final version of the statute.[48]

From a traditional practice between belligerents, the right to try individuals who violated the laws of war in international armed conflict, has been transformed into an obligation for all states under the 'grave breaches' regime. The individual criminal responsibility for war crimes committed in international armed conflicts is therefore firmly established in customary international law, as well as in treaty law; this culminated with the establishment of the ICC.

3. The extension of the concept of war crimes to internal armed conflicts: some conceptual issues

If the individual criminal responsibility for serious violations of the laws of war, or war crimes, is clearly established in international armed conflict, is a similar principle enshrined in internal armed conflict? Can the characteristics of war crimes be applicable in internal armed conflicts, notwithstanding the particularities of such conflicts? In this section, we shall see whether the concept of war crimes can be transposed into the context of internal armed conflicts, whether or not there are conceptual problems to the application of the former in the latter. In order to do so, we shall discuss in turn each element of the definition of war crimes given by Manfred Lachs.[49]

3.1 Nexus between the crime and the armed conflict

A war crime is commonly defined as a serious violation of the laws of war, 'qualified as a crime', and committed in an international armed conflict. As seen earlier in chapter 2, a fair amount of international humanitarian law provisions, both conventional and customary, apply in internal armed conflicts and serious violations of this corpus of norms are regularly committed. According to Judge Lachs, a war crime is committed 'during and in connection with an armed conflict under specially favourable conditions, created by the war and facilitating its commission'. In the context of an internal armed conflict, the necessity of the connection between the conduct in question and the ongoing conflict – often called nexus – is crucial in order to determine if one faces a violation of domestic law or a war crime.

3.1.1 The nexus in the case law of the ad hoc tribunals

The International Criminal Tribunal for the former Yugoslavia (ICTY) has explored in more detail the intricacies linked to the establishment of this nexus between the conduct of the perpetrator and the armed conflict.[50] In the *Tadić* case, the Trial Chamber found that:

> There must be an obvious link between the criminal act and the armed conflict ... It is sufficient that the alleged crimes were closely related to the hostilities occurring in other parts of the territories controlled by the parties to the conflict.[51]

In the *Delalić* case, the same Trial Chamber stressed the fact that a war crime can be perpetrated even if 'substantial clashes were not occurring in the region at the time and place' where the crimes were allegedly committed.[52] More detailed pronouncements on this issue were made by the ICTY Appeals Chamber in the *Kunarac* case:[53]

> 58. What ultimately distinguishes a war crime from a purely domestic offence is that a war crime is shaped by or dependent upon the environment – the armed conflict – in which it is committed. It need not have been planned or supported by some form of plan or policy. The armed conflict need not have been causal to the commission of the crime, but the existence of an armed conflict must, at a minimum, have played a substantial part in the perpetrator's ability to commit it, his decision to commit it, the manner in which it was committed or the purpose for which it was committed. Hence, if it can be established, as in the present case, that the perpetrator acted in furtherance of or under the guise of the armed conflict, it would be sufficient to conclude that his acts were closely related to the armed conflict ...
>
> 59. In determining whether or not the act in question is sufficiently related to the armed conflict, the Trial Chamber may take into account, *inter alia* the following factors: the fact that the perpetrator is a combatant; the fact that the victim is non-combatant; the fact that the victim is a member of the opposing party; the fact that the act may be said to serve the ultimate goal of a military campaign; and the fact that the crime is committed as part of or in the context of the perpetrator's official duties.

As a result, an example such as rape committed between soldiers in a military camp during a conflict, would be a crime committed in the context of an armed conflict but not connected to it. It would therefore not amount to a violation of the laws of war, but to a violation of domestic criminal legislation. In the words of one commentator, 'parasitical criminality that opportunistically uses the cover of the armed conflict does not, in principle, satisfy the requirement of the nexus'.[54]

The ICTR Trial Chambers seem to be more restrictive by requiring the acts of the perpetrator 'to be committed in conjunction with the armed conflict'[55] or the existence of a 'direct link between the crimes committed and the hostilities'.[56] These requirements, however, reflect the real nature of war crimes, especially when they are committed during an internal armed conflict. The ICTR Appeals Chamber reaffirmed the findings of the *Kunarac* case and made two further comments on this issue. It recalled the necessity of considering a whole number of factors when determining the relationship between the offence and an armed conflict and warned that 'particular care is needed when the accused is a non-combatant'.[57] In the *Rutaganda* case, the Appeals Chamber took into account the following factors: the fact that the perpetrator participated in attacks against the civilian population alongside soldiers of the presidential guard, the fact that he exercised de facto influence and authority over a paramilitary group, which committed the massacres, and the fact that the victims were persons protected under common Article 3 and Protocol II.[58]

Up to very recently, both International Criminal Tribunals have not required proof of any knowledge by the perpetrator of the nexus requirement. The ICTY seemed to treat the contextual element as a jurisdictional one and did not attach any mental element to it.[59] In 2006, the Appeals Chamber reversed this long-standing practice and found that both the existence and the international character of an armed conflict are jurisdictional prerequisites as well as substantive elements of crimes pursuant to Article 2 of the ICTY statute. According to this new case law, the accused must be aware of the factual circumstances establishing the existence and the nature of the armed hostilities.[60]

3.1.2 The nexus in the statute of the International Criminal Court

The elements of crimes for war crimes adopted by the Preparatory Commission for the ICC took due account of the case law of both Tribunals. In the war crimes section, it contains a contextual element, which reads: 'the conduct took place in the context of and was associated with an international armed conflict'.[61] The drafters chose to use both expressions cumulatively, on the understanding that the words 'in the context of' refer to the existence of an armed conflict in the country/area where the conduct was committed,[62] and that the expression 'was associated with' refers to the necessary nexus between the armed conflict and the conduct of the perpetrator.[63] The words 'associated with' also indicate that conduct which takes place after the cessation of active hostilities, but are still associated with the conflict, can amount to war crimes.

During the negotiations of the elements of crimes for war crimes, the mental element attached to this nexus became a controversial issue. Article 30.3 of the ICC statute requires the perpetrator to have knowledge of or awareness that a circumstance exists. Applied literally, it could mean that the perpetrator had to be aware of the existence and the nature of the conflict in which his conduct took place. As there were diverging views of delegations on this issue, it was agreed that the general introduction of war crimes should specify the common interpretation reached by the drafters on the adopted contextual element.

First, the general introduction to the section on war crimes makes clear that the perpetrator need neither make a legal evaluation as to the character of the conflict as international or non-international, nor legally assess the existence of an armed conflict. Secondly, this mental element attached to the nexus requirement must not be understood as requiring the perpetrator to be aware of the facts that established the character of the conflict. In other words, the perpetrator does not need to be aware of the nature or character of the conflict, i.e. whether the conflict is internal or international.[64] But does the perpetrator need to know the facts that established the character of the violence, i.e. does he need to know that he committed his crime in an internal armed conflict and not during internal disturbances? The answer is not spelt out specifically in the general introduction but the common understanding of the text would certainly tend towards answering in the negative. If he does not need to be aware of the facts establishing the character as international or internal, it logically follows that he does not need to know the facts establishing the character of the violence, i.e. internal armed conflict or internal disturbances. In the specific context of a distinction between an armed conflict and internal disturbances, this distinction is important, as requiring the perpetrator to be aware of the facts establishing the character of the conflict, would come dangerously close to making a legal evaluation of the character of the conflict itself.

Delegations could agree on these two points but there were more heated discussions on the issue of whether the perpetrator needed to be aware of the existence of an armed conflict.[65] For the majority of delegations, the perpetrator needed to be aware of some factual circumstances establishing the existence of an armed conflict, in order to distinguish between a war crime and an ordinary crime. It was stressed that some conduct, such as the use of certain weapons, could be illegal during an armed conflict but legal in other situations not amounting to an armed conflict. It would therefore be unfair to convict a person who was not aware of the existence of the armed conflict, for having used this weapon during an armed conflict. They argued further that in most situations, it would be so obvious that there was an armed conflict going on and that the perpetrator knew it, that no particular proof as to a mental coverage would be required. A few others argued that the proof of the existence of the conflict and the proof of the nexus between the act of the perpetrator and the armed conflict, represent an objective test and in fact amount to a jurisdictional threshold for the court to satisfy. Following the case law of the ICTY up to 2006, no mental element needed be attached to this contextual element. These delegations were particularly concerned about the consequences of having to prove that the perpetrator knew the circumstances establishing the existence of a conflict in the context of an internal armed conflict. The line between the character of the conflict and the existence of a conflict is blurred in internal armed conflict. In determining the lower threshold between internal disturbances and internal conflicts, establishing the existence of an armed conflict is a similar process to determining the legal nature of such a situation, i.e. internal armed conflict or internal disturbances. Moreover, the factual circumstances establishing the existence of the conflict are used both to determine the character and the existence of an armed conflict. Even in the legal doctrine, the determination of these factual circumstances establishing the existence of an internal armed conflict is open to controversy. For these delegations, requiring the perpetrator to be aware of factual circumstances establishing the existence of an armed conflict, could require him to make a legal evaluation of the existence and the character of the conflict itself: internal conflict or internal disturbances.

The compromise between these two views appears now in the elements of crimes and in the introduction to Article 8. First, a mental element has been added to the contextual element in each set of crimes and requires the perpetrator to be 'aware of factual circumstances that established the existence of an armed conflict'. It is important to note that this mental element uses the expression 'aware of factual circumstances' and not 'aware of *the* factual circumstances'. It was understood by the drafters that the absence of the word 'the' highlights the fact that the awareness of the perpetrator does not need to relate to the whole complexity of facts determining the existence of an armed conflict, but rather that only some facts should be known by the perpetrator, sufficient for him to be aware of the existence of some sort of armed conflict. Secondly, this mental element attached to the context is further explained in the third clarification included in the introduction and reads:

> there is only a requirement for the awareness of the factual circumstances that established the existence of an armed conflict that is implicit in the terms 'took place in the context of and was associated with'.

By this compromise, it is understood that if the prosecutor provides the necessary proof to establish the existence of the armed conflict and the nexus between the armed conflict and the acts of the perpetrator, he would not normally have to provide additional proof of the knowledge of the perpetrator of some factual circumstances that establish the existence of an armed conflict.

It is submitted that in the context of an international armed conflict, it is conceivable that some factual circumstances, which establish the existence of an armed conflict, could be identified. For example, the presence of foreign uniforms and foreign troops on the territory could be one of these factual circumstances. A similar process in the context of an internal armed conflict is more difficult. The compromise does not seem to resolve all the difficulties highlighted above or clarify what, if anything, the perpetrator is meant to know under the ICC statute.

3.2 Potential perpetrators of war crimes

The most obvious potential perpetrators of war crimes are individual soldiers. Judge Lachs in his monograph on war crimes in 1945 defined potential perpetrators as 'any members of the armed forces, government, administrative police, and any person entrusted with political, legal or economic function connected with the war'.[66] It is widely accepted that not only soldiers but civilians can commit war crimes.[67] The Charter of the International Tribunal at Nuremberg provided that the tribunal had:

> the power to try and punish persons who, acting in the interest of the European Axis countries, whether as individuals or as members of organisations, committed any of the following crimes . . .

Individuals not belonging to the armed forces were thus seen as potential war criminals, even if, for jurisdictional purposes, they needed to have acted in the interest of the European Axis countries to be tried by this tribunal.[68] Numerous tribunals after the Second World War, convicted civilians for war crimes who were 'accessory to a violation of the laws and customs of war'.[69] In the *Zyklon B* case for example, a British military court took the view that:

> the provisions of the laws and customs of war are addressed not only to combatants and to members of state and other public authorities, but to anybody who is in a position to assist in their violation.[70]

In the *Hadamar* trial, doctors working in a sanatorium were found guilty of war crimes for the murder of about 400 patients, notwithstanding any connection between doctors and the Nazi state.[71] In this trial, the US military commission held that:

> the provisions of the laws and customs of war are addressed not only to combatants but also to civilians and that civilians, by committing illegal acts against nationals of the opponent, may become guilty of war crimes.

In the *Flick* trial, the US Military Tribunal, rebutting the argument that international law is 'a matter wholly outside the work, interest and knowledge of private individuals', stated:

> International law as such binds every citizen just as does ordinary municipal law. Acts adjudged criminal when done by an officer of the Government are criminal also when done by a private individual.[72]

The ICTY has not dealt specifically with this question, as in most instances, indictees were either members of the armed forces or various armed groups directly participating in the conflict. The elements of crimes for war crimes under the ICC regime do not contain a specific mention of the category of perpetrators, as it was agreed during the negotiations that soldiers and civilians alike can commit war crimes. They only require proof that the acts of the accused took place in the context of and were associated with the armed conflict.

The International Criminal Tribunal for Rwanda (ICTR), however, analyses in detail whether the perpetrator in question forms part of the class of potential perpetrators of serious violations of common Article 3 or Protocol II. The Trial Chamber in the *Akayesu* judgment affirmed:

> the categories of persons covered by these terms (members of armed forces) should not be limited to individuals of all ranks belonging to

the armed forces under the military command of either belligerent parties but should be interpreted in their broadest sense, to include individuals who are legitimately mandated and expected as public officials or agents or persons otherwise holding public authority de facto representing the Government to support or fulfil the war efforts.[73]

The Trial Chamber seems in this extract to restrict unnecessarily the categories of perpetrators, rather than taking into account the necessary limitations of war crimes by imposing the proof of a close relationship between the acts of the perpetrators and the armed conflict.[74] The ruling of this Trial Chamber was overturned by the Appeals Chamber in the *Akayesu* case when it declared:

The Appeals Chamber is therefore of the opinion that international humanitarian law would be lessened and called into question if it were to be admitted that certain persons be exonerated from individual criminal responsibility for a violation of common Article 3 under the pretext that they did not belong to a specific category.[75]

This nexus between violations and the armed conflict implies that, in most cases, the perpetrator of the crime will probably have a special relationship with one party to the conflict. However, such a special relationship is not a condition precedent to the application of common Article 3 and, hence of article 4 of the statute. In the opinion of the Appeals Chamber, the Trial Chamber erred in requiring that a special relationship should be a separate condition for triggering criminal responsibility for a violation of article 4 of the statute.[76]

The post-Second World War trials unequivocally support the imposition of individual criminal liability for war crimes on belligerent soldiers and civilians alike and recent case law from both international criminal tribunals confirms it. The majority of the doctrine and recent international case law require the acts of the perpetrator to be associated with the armed conflict rather than requiring the perpetrator himself to have a close relationship with one party to the armed conflict. In internal armed conflicts, soldiers of armed opposition groups and civilians could therefore be found responsible for war crimes, if the nexus between their acts and the armed conflict can be established.

3.3 Categories of victims of war crimes

Combatants and civilians alike may be potential victims of war crimes. Under the 1949 Geneva Conventions, certain categories of persons or property are specifically protected against serious violations of the laws of war. In internal armed conflicts, common Article 3 provides for the protection of 'persons not taking active part in the hostilities, including members of armed forces who have laid down their arms and those placed *hors de combat* by sickness, wounds, detention, or any other cause'. Protocol II does not contain a generic article dealing with the potential victims of violations of the protocol, however, Article 4 affords fundamental guarantees to 'all persons who do not take a direct part or who have ceased to take part in hostilities'.

The ICTY Trial Chambers find out if the victim was protected under common Article 3 by:

> asking whether at the time of the alleged offence, the alleged victim of the proscribed acts was directly taking part in hostilities, being those hostilities in the context of which the alleged offences are said to have been committed. If the answer to that question is negative, the victim will enjoy the protection of the proscriptions contained in common Article 3.[77]

According to the ICTR case law, a civilian will be considered to be 'directly taking part in hostilities' and will loose the protection of common Article 3 if he was involved in 'acts of war which by their nature or purpose were likely to cause actual harm to the personnel and equipment of the enemy armed forces'.[78] This interpretation might not be seen as an accurate interpretation of the expression 'directly taking part in hostilities'. The study of the final record of the 1949 Geneva Diplomatic Conference reveals that the drafters believed common Article 3 to apply to all persons 'except combatants at the time engaged in fighting'.[79]

In the finalised draft of the elements of crimes for war crimes, negotiators wanted to define more specifically who were these persons not taking active part in the hostilities. The element defining the categories of victims in this document under common Article 3 now reads: 'such person or persons were either *hors de combat*, or were civilians, medical personnel or religious personnel taking no active part in the hostilities'.[80]

As highlighted by Judge Lachs in his definition of war crimes, a particularity of the classical definition of war crimes is the fact that they are committed against 'the other belligerent state, its interest or its citizens'. In other words, war crimes are committed against individuals of a different nationality than that of the perpetrators. In international armed conflicts, the laws of war only bind members of the armed forces vis-à-vis foreign belligerents, or 'the other side' and not vis-à-vis their own nationals. In the context of internal armed conflicts, it is submitted that such particularity does not prevent the application of the concept of war crime. The laws of war applicable in internal armed conflicts bind members of armed forces and armed groups vis-à-vis their opponents who share the same nationality. If the laws of war are applicable between belligerents of the same nationality, a war crime could also be committed against another belligerent in internal armed conflict. Therefore, a war crime is not only committed against individuals of a different nationality to that of the perpetrators.

The ICTY had to resolve a similar issue of nationality when it applied the concept of grave breaches to internationalised conflicts, where both belligerents share the same nationality. The Appeals Chamber affirmed:

> While previously wars were primarily between well-established states, in modern inter-ethnic armed conflicts such as that in the former Yugoslavia, new states are often created during the conflict and ethnicity rather than nationality may become the grounds for allegiance ... allegiance to a party to the conflict and, correspondingly, control by this party over persons in a given territory may be regarded as the crucial test.[81]

3.4 How can rebel forces be bound by the laws of war in internal armed conflicts?

The last issue to look at is the question of attribution of the violations of the laws of war to individuals, who are members of rebel forces or individuals linked with such rebel forces. One wonders in fact how a rebel group can be bound by treaties it would not have signed and how it could therefore be found responsible for breaches of those norms.[82] In other words, how can a non-state entity, the rebel group, be bound by the 1949 Geneva Conventions to which it has never agreed and to which it has no capacity to become a party?[83]

The ICRC commentary on common Article 3 suggests that as a responsible authority heading the insurgents and exercising effective sovereignty, the rebels claim to represent the state and therefore are bound by the treaties to which the state is a party.[84] This argument can only apply to those groups, which exercise de facto authority and effective sovereignty over some persons or territory and do claim to represent the state.[85] A more convincing approach, often referred to as the doctrine of legislative jurisdiction, was advanced during the 1949 Geneva Conference by the Greek delegate who took the view that each legally constituted government can legislate for all of the nationals of that state, and therefore each national, including the rebels, would be bound by common Article 3.[86] This, however, implies that the rebels would be bound by common Article 3 as domestic law, and their responsibility could be engaged only for breaches of domestic law and not for war crimes per se. It is also difficult to see how insurgents will feel bound to respect domestic law as they might even declare domestic law null and void in the territory they control.[87]

A third and more satisfactory approach is that international humanitarian law instruments and customary law not only put obligations on states but also create rights and obligations under international law for individuals.[88] Treaty norms applicable in internal armed conflicts create rights and obligations for rebels, as for any other citizen of the states which have ratified international humanitarian law treaties. Similarly, customary norms in the field of international criminal law are addressed to individuals. Individuals will be directly bound by these customary and treaty norms and therefore there is no obstacle to concluding that violations of these norms can be attributed to a rebel, whose responsibility could be engaged on the international plane if he commits a serious violation of the laws of war. This reasoning, also applicable to civilians linked to a party to a conflict and therefore potential perpetrators of war crimes in international conflicts as we have seen above, seems equally valid in the case of serious violations of the laws of war committed in internal conflicts. This third approach seems the one followed by human rights institutions and UN organs. The UN Commission on Human Rights[89] and the Inter-American Commission on Human Rights took the view that, in internal armed conflicts, paramilitary groups were bound by humanitarian law by effect of their participation in the armed conflicts and that both common Article 3 and Protocol II bind all parties to the conflict.[90] The Secretary-General confirmed this reasoning in a recent report on the protection of civilians in armed conflict when he affirmed:

> I would like to recall the prohibition against targeting civilians, enshrined in customary international law, which is binding not only on states and their governments but equally and directly so on armed groups that are parties to the conflict. The practise of the two ad hoc tribunals and the ICC statute have underlined the principle of direct responsibility of armed groups for violations of international humanitarian law.[91]

Similarly, the Security Council stresses that armed opposition groups in internal armed conflicts are 'obliged to respect international humanitarian law' and that they must take 'all necessary steps to respect international humanitarian and human rights law'.[92]

3.5 Conclusion

There does not seem to be any serious obstacle against the application of the concept of war crimes in the context of internal armed conflicts. The definition of war crimes, as defined by Judge Lachs in 1945, seems in all its aspects to find possible application in internal armed conflicts. But is it desirable that such a concept finds application in these conflicts? Are not violations of the laws of war such as murder or rape already criminal under the domestic law of the country itself? What can be the advantage of applying the concept of war crimes in internal armed conflicts?

The legal regime under common Article 3 and Protocol II is flawed, as it does not provide for any enforcement mechanism. The prevailing view for a long time has been that murder or rape committed against civilians during an internal armed conflict should be treated as domestic crime and perpetrators of such crimes should be tried by domestic courts. Reality has shown, however, that serious violations of these instruments were plentiful and often committed on a widespread scale. The end of hostilities would often witness the absence of any criminal trials of offenders and the granting of a broad amnesty to all parties in a conflict. The very serious character of the violations of the laws of war committed during internal armed conflicts coupled with the ineffectiveness of domestic jurisdictions to deal with these crimes, call for the application of the concept of war crimes in internal armed conflicts.

It is not only desirable, but also crucial to curb the phenomenon of impunity attached to serious violations of the laws of war in internal armed conflicts. From a domain regulated purely by domestic law, internal armed conflicts have gradually been subject to the law of armed conflicts, as seen in chapter 2. The logical consequence of the regulation by international law of this domain is to attach to the violations of the laws of war the criminal responsibility of the perpetrators in international law. The advantages of this principle are not only to fight against impunity in internal armed conflicts, but to recognise greater stigma and gravity to these crimes in such conflicts. As a result, amnesty laws should not be seen as covering these types of offences and no statute of limitations should apply to war crimes committed in internal armed conflicts. Furthermore, the recognition of the status of war crimes to these serious violations might trigger the use of universal jurisdiction by states. Perpetrators of such crimes could be prosecuted by international tribunals or possibly by courts of third states on the basis of universal jurisdiction.[93]

Notes

1. M. Lachs, *War crimes, an attempt to define the issues* (London: Stevens, 1945) p. 100.
2. For an extensive historical background, see L. C. Green, 'Enforcement of the law in international and non-international conflicts, the way ahead' (1996) 24 *Denver journal of international law and policy* 285–320; R. Cryer, *Prosecuting international crimes, selectivity and the international criminal law regime* (Cambridge: Cambridge University Press, 2005), pp. 9–48 and T. McCormack, 'From Sun Tzu to the sixth committee: the evolution of an international criminal law regime' in G. Simpson and T. McCormack (eds.), *The law of war crimes, national and international approaches* (The Hague, London, Boston: Kluwer Law International, 1997) pp. 31–64.
3. Many historical books or articles have covered this issue. See in particular, G. Draper, 'The modern pattern of war criminality' (1976) *Israel yearbook of human rights* 9–48; L. Green, *The contemporary law of armed conflict* (Manchester and New York: Manchester University Press, 1996); D. Wells, *War crimes and the laws of war*, 2nd edn (Lanham: University Press of America, 1991) especially chapter 6 entitled 'The prosecution for war crimes in history', p. 65; H. Lauterpacht, 'The law of nations and the punishment of war crimes' (1944) *BYIL* 58–95; T. McCormack, 'Selective reaction to atrocity: war crimes and the development of international criminal law' (1997) 60 *Albany law review* 681–731; H. Levie, 'War crimes' in M. Schmitt (ed.), *The law of military operations: lieber amicorum Jack Grunawalt* (Newport, Rhode Island: Naval War College, 1998) pp. 95–112; E. Greppi, 'The evolution of individual criminal responsibility under international law' (1999) 835 *IRRC* 531 and L. Penna, *The formation of the law of non-international armed conflicts* (Leiden, Boston: Martinus Nijhoff Publishers, 2006) pp. 135–38.
4. Sixteenth century, C. Samio Adachi, 'The Asian concept' in UNESCO, *International dimensions of humanitarian law* (Dordrecht: Henry Dunant Institute, UNESCO, Martinus Nijhoff, 1988) p. 13 cited in Green, *The contemporary law of armed conflict*, pp. 276–80 at p. 277 and McCormack, 'Selective reaction to atrocity' 684.
5. Green, *The contemporary law of armed conflict*, p. 278, see also M. H. Keen, *The laws of war in the late Middle Ages* (London: Routledge and K. Paul, 1965) p. 3 and T. Meron, 'Crimes and accountability in Shakespeare' (1998) 92 *AJIL* 1–40.
6. On this issue see Draper, 'The modern pattern of war criminality' 10.
7. McCormack, 'Selective reaction to atrocity' 689 citing C. Bassiouni, *Crimes against humanity in international law* (The Hague: Martinus Nijhoff, 1992) p. 196.
8. Twenty-eight judges drawn from the allied states of the Holy Roman Empire formed the tribunal which found von Hagenbach guilty and condemned him to

death. See Levie, 'War crimes', p. 96, McCormack, 'Selective reaction to atrocity' 689–91 and Cryer, *Prosecuting international crimes*, pp. 17–21.

9. For an overview of various war crimes trials over the Middle Ages, see Wells, *War crimes and the laws of war*, p. 65.

10. H. Grotius, *De jure belli ac pacis libri tres (1625)* vol. II, chap. XX, section XL (Carnegie, *Classics of international law*, F. Kelsey trans., 1925) p. 504.

11. For an overview of these writers, see H. Lauterpacht, 'The law of nations and the punishment of war crimes' 62–64.

12. *Annuaire de l'institut de droit international* vol. 5 (1881–1882) p. 174.

13. Holland, *The laws of war on land*, paras. 117–18, cited in Lauterpacht, 'The law of nations and the punishment of war crimes' 62.

14. At that point, there was not as such a universal right for any state to try the perpetrators. The issue of universal jurisdiction is dealt with in more detail in chapter 5, section 1 of this book.

15. See L. Green, 'Criminal responsibility of individuals in non-international armed conflicts' (2002) 45 *German yearbook of international law* 82–114 at 85.

16. The Geneva Convention of 1864 and the Declaration of St Petersburg do not contain any provision dealing with the repression of violations. The Lieber Code, however, contained several references to individual criminal responsibility for breaches of its provisions (see Articles 44 and 71). The 1906 Geneva Convention is the first international treaty to contain a chapter dealing with repression of abuses and infractions (see Articles 27 and 28). Within the framework of the Institute of International Law, the 'Oxford manual' was adopted to serve as a model for national military codes and provides in its Article 84: 'offenders against the laws of war are liable to the punishments specified in the penal law'. For a full review of early instruments dealing with the laws of war, see C. Bassiouni and E. Wise, *Aut dedere, aut judicare– the duty to extradite or prosecute in international law* (Dordrecht: Martinus Nijhoff, 1995) p. 86; Y. Sandoz, 'Penal aspects of international humanitarian law' in Bassiouni (ed.), *International criminal law* (Dobbs Ferry: International Publishers, 1986) vol. I, pp. 209–32 or G. Abi-Saab, 'The concept of war crimes' in S. Yee and W. Tieya (eds.), *International law in the post-cold war world: essays in memory of Li Haopei* (London: Routledge, 2001) pp. 99–118. On these issues, see also Levie, 'War crimes' p. 96; L. Green 'The law of armed conflict and the enforcement of international criminal law' (1984) *Canadian yearbook of international law* 3–25, as well as Wells, *War crimes and the laws of war*, p. 68.

17. Article 56 of the Hague regulations respecting the laws and customs of war on land is an exception in this regard. Article 56 suggests that individuals who destroy or intentionally damage historical monuments, works of art or science should be made the subject of proceedings.

18. The Hague Convention IV contains a general provision dealing with responsibility of states in its Article 3: 'a belligerent party, which violates the provisions of

the said regulation, shall if the case demands, be liable to pay compensation. It shall be responsible for all acts committed by persons forming part of its armed forces.'

19. There are several cases where states ascertained their right to punish individuals for violations of the laws of war. For example, in 1902, a private commission in the USA investigated the atrocities committed by US troops during the Philippine insurrection of 1899–1902. A number of soldiers were tried by US courts martial. See McCormack, 'Selective reaction to atrocity' 696 and G. Mettraux, 'US courts-martial and the armed conflict in the Philippines (1899–1902): their contribution to national case law on war crimes' (2003) 1 *JICJ* 135.

20. On the allied attempts to prosecute the alleged perpetrators of genocide against the Armenian people, see V. Dadrian, *The history of the Armenian genocide* (Providence and Oxford: Berghahn Books, 1995) pp. 303–13 and on the national criminal prosecutions that took place in 1919 and 1920 in Turkey, see pp. 317–36.

21. Pursuant to Article 228 of the Versailles Treaty, a list of 896 alleged war criminals was submitted by the Allies to the German authorities. The latter refused to turn them over and finally, the German supreme court of the Reich of Leipzig tried only twelve individuals. Nine were acquitted and three were found guilty (the so-called 'Leipzig trials'). See McCormack, 'Selective reaction to atrocity' 705–70; Levie, 'War crimes', pp. 97–98; Wells, *War crimes and the laws of war*, p. 70; Cryer, *Prosecuting international crimes*, pp. 33–35 and J. Maogoto, *War crimes and realpolitik, international justice from World War I to the twenty-first century* (London: Lynne Rienner Publishers, 2004) pp. 37–64.

22. During the conduct of the conflict, there are accounts of war crimes' trials conducted by individual Allied states against German soldiers convicted for violations of the laws of war such as pillage, robbery or assassination of wounded soldiers on the field of battle. See McCormack, 'From Sun Tzu to the sixth committee', p. 44.

23. The Allied Governments established this commission whose mandate involved the investigation of responsibility for breaches of the laws of war and the drafting of proposals for the establishment of a tribunal. Despite the proposals of the commission, a 'high tribunal' was never constituted. See McCormack, 'From Sun Tzu to the sixth committee' pp. 45–48; Cryer, *Prosecuting international crimes*, pp. 31–33 and Maogoto, *War Crimes and realpolitik*, pp. 47–50.

24. In 1942, nine countries at war with Germany published the Inter-Allied Declaration on Punishment for War Crimes, establishing the United Nations War Crimes Commission (the so-called 'Declaration of St James'). This declaration is reproduced in United Nations War Crimes Commission, *The history of the UN war crimes commission and the development of the laws of war* (London: HMSO, 1948) p. 90. In 1943, the main four Allied powers issued the so-called Moscow Declaration, reproduced in *The history of the UN War Crimes Commission*, pp. 107–8. On this issue, see Green, *The contemporary law of*

armed Conflict, p. 14; Cryer, *Prosecuting international crimes*, pp. 36–37 and Maogoto, *War crimes and realpolitik*, pp. 87–97.

25. *The history of the UN War Crimes Commission*, p. 171.

26. Wells, *War crimes and the laws of war*, p. 74. The details for prosecuting Germans whose offences had taken place in a specific country were specified in Control Council Law No. 10. Under Control Council Law No. 10, the Americans, for example, set up 6 tribunals in the official zone controlled by the USA in West Germany, and tried 177 persons out of 2,116 mentioned above.

27. Many legal or historical books have been written about the IMT at Nuremberg, see, for example, E. Davidson, *The trials of the Germans, an account of the twenty-two defendants before the IMT at Nuremberg* (New York: the Macmillan Company, 1966); B. Smith, *Reaching judgment at Nuremberg* (London: Andre Deutsch Ltd, 1977); W. Bosch, *Judgment on Nuremberg, American attitudes toward the major German war-crime trials* (Chapel Hill: The University of California Press, 1970); A. Wieviorka (ed.), *Les procès de Nuremberg et de Tokyo* (Brussels: Editions Complexe, 1996); Maogoto, *War crimes and realpolitik*, pp. 98–100; A. and J. Tusa, *The Nuremberg trial* (New York: Cooper Square Press, 2003); G. Ginsburgs and V. Kudriavtsev (eds.), *The Nuremberg trial and international law* (Dordrecht: Martinus Nijhoff Publishers, 1990). See also T. Meron, 'Reflections on the prosecutions of war crimes by international tribunals' (2006) 100 *AJIL* 551–79.

28. Article 6 b) of the London Charter defined war crimes as: 'namely violations of the laws or customs of war. Such violations shall include, but not be limited to, murder, ill treatment or deportation to slave labour or for any other purpose of civilian population of or in occupied territory, murder or ill treatment of prisoners of war or persons on the seas, killing of hostages, plunder of public or private property, wanton destruction of cities, towns or villages, or devastation not justified by military necessity.'

29. See Article 6 of the London Charter.

30. See the report of the International Law Commission, which formulated the Nuremberg principles (1950) 2 *Yearbook of the International Law Commission* 374.

31. *Judgment of the International Military Tribunal for the trial of German major war criminals*, Nuremberg, 30 September–1 October 1946 (London: Stationery Office, 1946) p. 65.

32. *Ibid.*, p. 64.

33. Twenty-five Japanese were tried along with eight Germans. Additional trials of persons, whose crimes had been located in a specific country, were conducted at national level. See Wells, *War crimes and the laws of war*, pp. 74–77; Cryer, *Prosecuting international crimes*, pp. 42–48; Maogoto, *War crimes and realpolitik*, pp. 100–6; R. H. Minear, *Victors' justice, the Tokyo war crimes trial* (Princeton: Princeton University Press, 1971) and C. Hosoya, N. Ando, Y. Omuma and R. Minear (eds.), *The Tokyo war crimes trial, an international symposium* (New York, Tokyo: Kodansha International Ltd, 1986).

34. See McCormack, 'Selective reaction to atrocity' 719. For a constructive criticism of both Nuremberg and Tokyo, see Maogoto, *War crimes and realpolitik*, pp. 98–109.

35. See, for example, B. Röling, 'Criminal responsibility for violations of the laws of war' (1976) 12 *Revue belge de droit international* 13; Draper, 'The modern pattern of war criminality' 23; Y. Dinstein, 'The distinctions between war crimes and crimes against peace' in Y. Dinstein, M. Tabory (eds.), *War crimes in international law* (The Hague, Boston: Martinus Nijhoff, 1996) p. 3 and Lauterpacht, 'The law of nations and the punishment of war crimes' 77.

36. The expression 'war crimes' was not chosen by delegates during the negotiations of the 1949 Geneva Conventions, as 'crimes' can have different meanings in the various legislation. The generic category of war crimes contains the so-called 'grave breaches'.

37. Article 4 of Geneva Convention IV defines a protected person as a 'person who at a given moment and in any manner whatsoever, finds himself in case of conflict or occupation, in the hands of a party to the conflict or occupying power of which he is not a national'.

38. Furthermore, Article 86 of Protocol I renders criminal the failure to act when the individual is under a duty to do so.

39. As of 1 December 2006, 194 states are party to the 1949 Geneva Conventions, which have attained universal acceptance.

40. On the use of universal jurisdiction and grave breaches, see chapter 5 of this book for more detail.

41. See Articles 49, 50, 129 and 146 of the four Geneva Conventions respectively. Under common Article 1 of the four Geneva Conventions, states have to respect and ensure respect of the conventions under all circumstances. It has been argued by some commentators that states can take action in order to stop violations of the conventions, including initiating criminal proceedings against wrongdoers on the basis of common Article 1. See L. Boisson de Chazournes and L. Condorelli, 'Quelques remarques à propos de l'obligation des Etats de "respecter et faire respecter" le droit international humanitaire "en toutes circonstances"' in C. Zwinarski (ed.), *Etudes et essais sur le droit international humanitaire et sur les principes de la Croix-Rouge en l'honneur de Jean Pictet* (Geneva, Dordrecht: ICRC, Martinus Nijhoff Publishers, 1984) p. 17 as well as B. Kessler, 'The duty to ensure respect under common Article 1 of the Geneva Conventions: its implications on international and non-international armed conflicts' (2001) 44 *German yearbook of international law* 498–516.

42. In this respect, a Trial Chamber of the ICTY affirmed: 'Assuming *arguendo* that there is no clear obligation to punish or extradite violators of non-grave breach provisions of the Geneva Conventions, such as common Article 3, all states have the right to punish those violators.' *Tadić* trial, para. 71.

43. See Y. Sandoz, 'Penal aspects of international humanitarian law' in C. Bassiouni (ed.), *International criminal law*, pp. 226–28.

44. See *Judgment of the International Military Tribunal for the trial of German major war criminals*, Nuremberg, 30 September–1 October 1946 (London: Stationery Office, 1946) p. 40. See also Dinstein, 'The distinctions between war crimes and crimes against peace' p. 3.

45. For an explanation of the negotiating history of Article 8 of the ICC statute, see H. v. Hebel and D. Robinson, 'Crimes within the jurisdiction of the Court' in R. Lee (ed.), *The International Criminal Court: the making of the Rome statute, issues, negotiations and results* (The Hague, Boston: Kluwer Law International, 1999) pp. 79–141.

46. *Ibid.*, p. 110.

47. For Article 8.2.b)xii) declaring that no quarter will be given, see Article 23 d) of the Hague regulation and Article 40 of Protocol I. For b)xvi) pillaging, see Article 28 of the Hague regulation. The war crime of pillaging, notwithstanding its very old status, is not even included in Additional Protocol I. For Article 8.2.b)xi) killing or wounding treacherously individuals belonging to the adverse party, see Article 23 b) of the Hague regulation and Article 37 of Protocol I. These instruments did not provide for the criminal responsibility of individuals who might violate these principles.

48. See Hebel and Robinson, 'Crimes within the jurisdiction of the court' pp. 109–18.

49. This definition was given in the introduction to chapter 3: 'A war crime is any act of violence qualified as crime, committed during and in connection with a war under specially favorable conditions, created by the war and facilitating its commission, the act being directed against the other belligerent state, its interests, or its citizens, against a neutral state, its interest, its citizens as well as against stateless civilians, unless it is justified under the law of warfare.'

50. For a thorough commentary of the law of the tribunals on this issue, see G. Mettraux, *International crimes and the ad hoc tribunals* (Oxford: Oxford University Press, 2005) pp. 38–47.

51. *Tadić* trial, para. 572.

52. *Čelibići* trial, paras. 196–97. This was reaffirmed by the Appeals Chamber in the *Kunarac* appeal, para. 57.

53. *Kunarac* appeal, paras. 58–59.

54. Mettraux, *International crimes and the ad hoc tribunals*, p. 44.

55. *Akayesu* trial, para. 643.

56. *Kayishema/Ruzindana* trial, paras. 603 and 623.

57. *Akayesu* appeal, para. 570.

58. See *Rutaganda* appeal, para. 577, see also para. 579.

59. See *Tadić* trial, para. 572. When dealing with the requirement of the existence of an armed conflict in the context of crimes against humanity, the Appeals Chamber stated: 'The prosecution is moreover correct in asserting that the armed conflict requirement is a *jurisdictional* element, not a substantive element of the *mens rea* of crimes against humanity (i.e. not a legal ingredient of the subjective element of the crime).' See *Tadić* appeal, para. 249.

60. See *Kordić* appeal, para. 311 and *Naletilić* appeal, paras. 109–22. For a criticism of this finding and its consequences in internal armed conflicts, see the discussion below on the commentaries to the elements of crimes of the ICC.

61. See report of the Preparatory Commission for the International Criminal Court, PCNICC/2000/1/Add.2.

62. In that respect, the Appeals Chamber in the *Tadić* case, held that 'some of the provisions of the Geneva Conventions apply to the entire territory of the Parties to the conflict, not just the vicinity of actual hostilities. Certainly, some of the provisions are clearly bound up with the hostilities and the geographical scope of those provisions should be so limited. Others particularly those relating to the protection of prisoners of war and civilians are not so limited.' *Tadić* decision on jurisdiction, para. 68.

63. For more details on these negotiations, see E. La Haye, 'The elaboration of elements for war crimes' in F. Lattanzi and W. Schabas (eds.), *Essays on the Rome statute of the International Criminal Court*, vol. II (Ripa di Fagnano Alto: Il Sirente, 2004) pp. 305–31 at p. 309. See also C. Kress, 'War crimes committed in non-international armed conflict and the emerging system of international criminal justice' (2000) 30 *Israel yearbook on human rights* pp. 103–78 at pp. 125–27 as well as K. Dörmann, *Elements of war crimes under the Rome statute of the International Criminal Court, sources and commentary* (Cambridge: Cambridge University Press, 2002) pp. 18–28.

64. This finding presupposes that the nature of the armed conflict has no incidence on the legality or illegality of the conduct of the accused. This finding might be problematic in the case of a weapon whose use is allowed in internal armed conflict but prohibited in international armed conflict. In this unlikely event, a commander might be found guilty of a war crime, even if he did not know the international character of the armed conflict and believed he was facing an internal armed conflict, in which he could legally use that weapon.

65. For more details, see La Haye, 'The elaboration of the elements of war crimes' pp. 311–14.

66. Lachs, *War crimes*, p. 100.

67. See, for example, H. Lauterpacht writing in 1952: 'such hostile or other acts of soldiers or other individuals as may be punished by the enemy on capture of the offender'. L. Oppenheim, *International law* H. Lauterpacht (ed.) 7th edn (London: Longman, 1952) p. 566. See Draper, 'The modern pattern of war criminality' 23, as well as Dinstein, 'The distinction between war crimes and crimes against humanity', p. 4.

68. For more details, see Provost, *International human rights and humanitarian law*, pp. 79–83.

69. See the *Zyklon B* case, reported in United Nations War Crimes Commission, *Law reports of trials of war criminals*, vol. I (London: Stationery Office, 1947) p. 103.

70. *Ibid.*, p. 103. Similar conclusions were reached in the *Essen Lynching* case and the *Hadamar* trial, see, United Nations War Crimes Commission, *Law reports of trials of war criminals*, vol. I (London: Stationery Office, 1947) p. 88 and pp. 46–55.

71. *US. v. Klein and six others* (Hadamar trial), *ibid.*, p. 46.
72. *US. v. F. Flick and five others* (Flick trial), United Nations War Crimes Commission, *Law reports of trials of war criminals*, vol. 9 (London: Stationery Office, 1947) p. 18. For a thorough overview of this question, see Provost, *International human rights and humanitarian law*, pp. 79–88.
73. *Akayesu* trial, paras. 630–34. This jurisprudence was upheld in the subsequent trial cases: *Rutuganda* trial (paras. 96–98), *Musema* trial (paras. 264–75) and *Kayishema/Ruzindana* trial (paras. 173–76). For a commentary and critique of the *Akayesu* judgment, see D. M. Amann, 'Prosecutor v. Akayesu, case ICTR-96-4-T, 2 September 1998' (1999) 93 *AJIL* 195–99 at 199.
74. Some authors disagree with this view. R. Arnold believes that one needs to prove the link between the perpetrator and one of the party to the armed conflict, rather than only a link between the acts of the perpetrator and the armed conflict. A civilian needs to be linked to a party to the conflict if he is to be found responsible for war crimes. See R. Arnold, 'The liability of civilians under international humanitarian law's war crimes provisions' (2002) 5 *YbIHL* 344–59.
75. *Akayesu* appeal, para. 443.
76. *Ibid.*, para. 444.
77. *Tadić* trial, para. 615. See also *Akayesu* appeal, para. 438, which defines this category as 'persons who are not taking any active part in the hostilities'; *Naletilić* trial, para. 229; *Čelebići* appeal, para. 420; *Semanza* trial, para. 365 or *Musema* trial, para. 280.
78. *Musema* trial, para. 279. A civilian taking up arms on behalf of one of the belligerents will be considered a combatant.
79. See the comments on the text of the working group made by the French delegate in *Final Record of the Diplomatic Conference of Geneva of 1949* (Berne, 1951) vol. II–B, p. 84. (hereafter referred to as '1949 Final Records').
80. For the negotiating history of this provision, see E. La Haye and others, 'War crimes', in R. Lee (ed.), *The International Criminal Court: elements of crimes and rules of procedure and evidence* (Ardsley: Transnational Publishers, 2001) p. 118.
81. *Tadić* appeal, para. 166.
82. It goes without saying that special agreements pursuant to common Article 3 or ad hoc declarations by rebel groups can be a means by which they expressly agree to be bound by the laws of war applicable in internal armed conflict.
83. On this issue see Zegveld, *Accountability of armed opposition groups*, pp. 14–20 and Moir, *The law of internal armed conflict*, pp. 52–58.
84. See J. Pictet (and others), *Commentary to Convention I* (Geneva: ICRC, 1952) p. 51 and R. Baxter, 'Jus in bello interno: the present and future law' in J. Moore (ed.), *Law and civil war in the modern world* (Baltimore: Johns Hopkins University Press, 1974) p. 518. See also Elder, 'The historical background of common Article 3 of the Geneva Conventions of 1949' (1979) 11 *Case western reserve journal of international law* 55. Pinto concurs with the ICRC view, in 'L'article 3 des

Conventions de Genève de 1949' (1965) 114 *Recueil des cours* 528, as well as D. Schindler, 'The different types of armed conflict according to the Geneva Conventions and Protocols' (1979) 163 *Recueil des cours* 151, who affirms: 'A second reason emanates from the fact that treaties into which a state has entered are binding for all authorities exercising effective power in that state.'

85. See Zegveld, *Accountability of armed opposition groups*, p. 15 and Moir, *The law of internal armed conflicts*, pp. 55–56.

86. 1949 Final Records, vol. II–B, p. 94. See also, Elder, 'The historical background of common Article 3 of the Geneva Conventions of 1949' 55 who comments that this approach is known in American law as the principle of legislative jurisdiction. Draper concurs with the analysis. See G. Draper, 'The Geneva Conventions of 1949' (1965) 114 *Recueil des cours* 95–96. Cassese disagrees with this view as being based 'on a misconception of the relationship between international and domestic law', see A. Cassese 'The status of rebels under the 1977 Geneva Protocol on non-international armed conflicts' (1981) 30 *ICLQ* 423.

87. See Moir, *The law of internal armed conflicts*, p. 54.

88. Cassese believes that common Article 3 does confer rights and obligations on both sides. See A. Cassese, 'La guerre civile et le droit international' (1986) 90 *RGDIP* 553–78 at 567. See also, Schindler, 'The different types of armed conflict according to the Geneva Conventions and Protocols', p. 151 and P. Rowe, 'Liability for war crimes during a non-international armed conflict' (1996) *The military law and laws of war review* 152.

89. See, for example, UN Commission on Human Rights, E/CN.4/1985/18, p. 37, Final report of the Special Representative on El Salvador; cited in Zegveld, *Accountability of armed opposition groups*, p. 11.

90. See Inter-American Commission on Human Rights, 'Third report on the situation of human rights in Columbia', OAS Doc.OEA/Ser.L/V/II, doc.102 (1999), chapter IV, paras. 13 and 85, cited in Provost, *International human rights and humanitarian law*, p. 94. See also the view taken by the Inter-American Commission on Human Rights in the *Tablada* case, when it stated: 'common Article 3's mandatory provisions expressly bind and apply equally to both parties to internal conflicts, i.e. government and dissident forces. Moreover, the obligation to apply common Article 3 is absolute for both parties and independent of the obligation of the other'. Report No. 55/97, Case No. 11.137 (Argentina) para. 174 (30 October 1997), cited in Zegveld, *Accountability of armed opposition groups*, p. 10.

91. Report of the Secretary-General, UN.Doc.S/2001/331 (30 March 2001) para. 48. See also UN.Doc.S/2004/431 paras. 41–42.

92. See, for example, in relation to the conflict in the region of Darfur, SC resolutions 1564 (18 September 2004) and 1574 (19 November 2004).

93. The issue of jurisdiction will be dealt with in chapter 5 of this book.

4

Individual criminal responsibility for war crimes committed in internal armed conflicts

'There is no moral justification, and no truly persuasive legal reason for treating perpetrators of atrocities in internal conflicts more leniently than those engaged in international wars.'[1] If moral principles have always called for atrocities committed in internal armed conflicts to be criminalised, state sovereignty has resisted the application of the concept of war crimes to internal armed conflicts for a very long time.[2] The view expressed by the International Committee of the Red Cross (ICRC) in 1993, reflected very well a widely held view when it commented on the establishment of the International Criminal Tribunal for the former Yugoslavia (ICTY): 'according to international humanitarian law as it stands today, the notion of war crimes is limited to situations of international armed conflict'.[3] In 1993, the Commission of Experts on Yugoslavia adopted a similar conservative approach by concluding that the scope and the content of customary international law applicable to internal armed conflict was 'debatable' and did not incorporate individual criminality. Common Article 3, for example, was found to be part of customary law but according to this commission, violations of common Article 3 do not amount to war crimes.[4] The Secretary-General followed some of these conclusions, stressing that the ICTY shall apply 'rules of international humanitarian law which are beyond any doubt part of customary law' but failed to include Article 3 or Protocol II within the lists of instruments which have beyond doubt become part of international customary law.[5] Similarly, in 1994 the Secretary-General took the view that the International Criminal Tribunal for Rwanda (ICTR) statute included within its subject matter jurisdiction 'international instruments regardless of whether they were considered part of customary international law or whether they have customarily entailed the individual criminal responsibility of the perpetrator of the crime' and admitted that the ICTR statute 'for the first time criminalises common Article 3 of the four Geneva Conventions'.[6]

In contrast, the Appeals Chamber of the ICTY in its *Tadić* jurisdiction decision concluded in October 1995:

> Customary international law imposes criminal liability for serious viola-
> tions of common Article 3, as supplemented by other general principles
> and rules on the protection of victims of internal conflict, and for
> breaching certain fundamental principles and rules regarding means
> and methods of combat in civil strife.[7]

In 1998, an ICTR Trial Chamber in the *Akayesu* case concurred with the findings in *Tadić*: 'the Chamber considers this finding of the ICTY Appeals Chamber convincing and dispositive of this issue, both with respect to serious violations of common Article 3 and of additional Protocol II.'[8] Were these Tribunals correct to conclude that, by the early 1990s, the concept of individual criminal responsibility for war crimes in internal armed conflicts was established in customary international law?

The 1995 *Tadić* jurisdiction decision has been the main catalyst in the evolution of the applicable law and the concept of criminality in internal armed conflicts. The 1990s saw states increasingly relying on international criminal justice, primarily in the context of internal armed conflicts. State sovereignty has gradually been eroded even in the area of criminal jurisdiction, traditionally well-rooted in the reserved domain of states. Since 1993, the evolution of the law in this area has been exponential with the adoption of a few international instruments establishing individual criminal responsibility for war crimes in internal armed conflicts. This chapter will study these two phenomena. First, the evolution of the content of international treaties in respect of the principle of individual criminal responsibility for war crimes in internal armed conflicts will be examined. Secondly, the conclusion reached by the Appeals Chamber in the *Tadić* case in 1995 will be scrutinised. Was the principle of individual criminal responsibility for war crimes committed in internal armed conflicts reflected in customary law in the early 1990s? Finally, section three of this chapter shall attempt to draw up a list of war crimes applicable in internal armed conflicts.

1. International treaties and the principle of individual criminal responsibility for war crimes committed in internal armed conflicts

Treaty law applicable in internal armed conflicts consists chiefly of common Article 3 and Protocol II. Neither of these instruments, however, provides for the international criminal responsibility of individuals who may have breached them. The *travaux préparatoires* of the 1949 Geneva Diplomatic Conference show that the question of responsibility for violations of common Article 3 was discussed only superficially. A few states wished for common Article 3 to include the possibility for states to consider violations of this article as war crimes.[9] These states were mainly those which supported the application of most principles of the 1949 Conventions in the case of internal armed conflicts. However, at the time, most states clearly rejected this proposal. The majority view was that, except for Article 3, the provisions of the four Geneva Conventions, as well as the grave breaches regime, were not applicable in internal armed conflicts.[10] Similarly, the study of the negotiation process of the grave breaches provisions during the 1949 Conference shows that their application in internal armed conflicts was not even envisaged.[11]

During the negotiation of Protocol II, the ICRC concentrated on obtaining protection and guaranteeing rights for individuals prosecuted for criminal offences related to the armed conflict.[12] According to the ICRC, Article 6 of Protocol II did not affect the right of authorities to try individuals who might have committed violations of the Protocol during the armed conflict.[13] International criminal responsibility for violations of the Protocol was, however, never discussed or admitted as such. Prosecution of individuals who might have violated provisions of the Protocol seems to be left to the discretion of the state on the basis of domestic criminal codes.

Since 1949, some authors have discussed whether the violations of common Article 3 or Protocol II in internal armed conflict were war crimes but this was never clearly established.[14] In the absence of any explicit treaty provision, the opportunity to prosecute internal atrocities has remained the reserved domain of states until the 1990s.[15] The end of the Cold War, however, and the reaction of public opinion to the scale and brutality of atrocities committed in internal armed conflicts, created the necessary impetus for the UN Security Council to establish ad hoc international criminal tribunals, each of which was given jurisdiction to try individuals for serious violations of the laws of war, genocide and crimes against humanity.

1.1 The statutes of the two ad hoc International Criminal Tribunals

1.1.1 The statute of the International Criminal Tribunal for the former Yugoslavia[16]

The most significant development in the law applicable in internal armed conflict has arisen from the statute of the ICTY, when paradoxically a literal reading of this statute seems to exclude the violations of the laws of war committed in internal armed conflicts from the jurisdiction of the Tribunal. The ICTY, established by Security Council resolution 827, has the power to prosecute persons responsible for genocide, crimes against humanity in international and internal conflicts, grave breaches of the Geneva Conventions of 1949 as well as violations of the laws of war committed in the territory of the former Yugoslavia since January 1991.[17] As far as the violations of international humanitarian law are concerned, the scope of application of both Article 2, grave breaches of the Geneva Conventions, and Article 3, serious violations of the laws of war, seem to be confined to international armed conflicts.

From 1991 onwards, the Security Council consistently called for *all* parties to respect their obligations under international humanitarian law and in particular the Geneva Conventions of 12 August 1949 (emphasis added).[18] It stated in numerous resolutions that those who 'commit, order or have ordered the commission of such violations will be held individually responsible in respect of such acts,'[19] without, however, determining explicitly the nature of the conflict in question.[20] Similarly, the Secretary-General's report on the establishment of the International Tribunal did not determine the nature of the armed conflict. The report reiterated that 'the international tribunal should apply rules of international humanitarian law which are beyond any doubt part of the customary law,'[21] but mentioned neither common Article 3, nor Protocol II in the list of conventional humanitarian law instruments which have beyond doubt become part of international customary law.[22]

The absence of qualification by the Security Council is understandable, as between 1991 and 1996 there were several conflicts between various parties in those states, which then made up the Federal Republic of Yugoslavia. A single qualification of the conflict as international or internal seemed, therefore, impossible as the Council dealt with different situations: the conflict between the armed forces of Croatia against the Federal Army of Belgrade, the conflict between Croatia and Bosnia, and the various conflicts within Bosnia Herzegovina between different armed groups. If some situations could without question be qualified as international conflicts, others seemed to be of a mixed nature; the issue of qualification seemed best left to the Tribunal rather than to a political organ such as the UN Security Council.[23]

Even though the Security Council and the Secretary-General remained extremely cautious about the nature of the armed conflicts, and therefore on the explicit application of the principle of war crimes in internal armed conflicts, nevertheless a number of members of the Security Council at the time the ICTY statute was adopted understood Article 3 of the statute, violations of the laws of war, to include:

> all obligations under humanitarian law agreements in force in the territory of the former Yugoslavia at the time the acts were committed, including common Article 3 of the 1949 Geneva Conventions, and the 1977 Additional Protocols to these Conventions.[24]

This view was later upheld by the Tribunal itself in the *Tadić* jurisdiction decision. The Appeals Chamber noted that the many Security Council statements and resolutions revealed the Council's awareness of the mixed character of conflict, and that the Security Council was not only calling for the perpetrators of grave breaches to be called to justice, but that equally the perpetrators of other violations of international humanitarian law, including potential war crimes in internal armed conflicts, should be held individually responsible for their conduct. The Chamber concluded that:

> the conflicts in the former Yugoslavia have both internal and international aspects, that the members of the Security Council clearly had both aspects of the conflicts in mind and that they intended to empower the International Tribunal to adjudicate violations of humanitarian law that occurred in either context.[25]

The Appeals Chamber held that Article 2, grave breaches of the 1949 Geneva Conventions, was limited to international conflicts,[26] whereas Article 3, violations of the laws of war, should cover 'all violations of international humanitarian law other than the grave breaches of the four Geneva Conventions'.[27] Article 3 is interpreted by the Tribunal as a 'general clause covering all violations of humanitarian law' and therefore specifically includes the violations of common Article 3 and other customary rules in internal armed conflicts.[28] As shown in chapter 2, this interpretation in the *Tadić* jurisdiction decision has allowed the Tribunal to elaborate on the customary law principles applicable in internal armed conflicts as well as on the criminality of violations of these principles in such conflict. The Appeals Chamber looked specifically at the *opinio juris* and practice of states in this area and concluded that:

> customary international law imposes criminal liability for serious violations of common Article 3, as supplemented by other general principles and rules on the protection of victims of internal conflict and for breaching certain fundamental principles and rules regarding means and methods of combat in civil strife.[29]

The Tribunal can therefore extend its jurisdiction over all conduct in internal armed conflict, which is a violation of common Article 3 or of any other customary rule applicable in such conflicts. From an institution, which did not seem to encompass internal armed conflict clearly within its jurisdiction, the statute of the ICTY, as applied by the Tribunal, has become the instrument with the widest subject matter jurisdiction in internal armed conflict, when compared to the statute of the ICTR or the International Criminal Court (ICC). The establishment by the *Tadić* jurisdiction decision of the applicability in customary international law of the principle of individual criminal responsibility for serious violations of the law of war in internal armed conflicts, could have seemed premature in 1995. However, it is now seen as a crucial stepping stone in the evolution of the law in this area of international law.[30]

1.1.2 The statute of the International Criminal Tribunal for Rwanda[31]

Faced with large-scale massacres of innocent people in Rwanda during 1994, the Security Council condemned:

> all breaches of international humanitarian law in Rwanda, particularly those perpetrated against the civilian population, and recalled that persons who instigate or participate in such acts are individually responsible and should be brought to justice.[32]

The Commission of Experts set up by the Security Council qualified the armed conflict which took place between 6 April 1994 and 15 July 1994 as a non-international conflict and found both common Article 3 and Protocol II to be applicable.[33] The Commission concluded that both instruments were violated on a systematic, widespread and flagrant basis and that overwhelming evidence existed to prove that acts of genocide had been committed. It further registered its strong support for the creation of an international criminal tribunal to undertake prosecutions of individuals on the basis of international law, without, however, explicitly covering the issue of the applicability of the principle of individual responsibility for war crimes in internal armed conflicts.[34]

The Security Council created the ICTR by resolution 955 and gave it the power to prosecute individuals who might have committed genocide, crimes against humanity or serious violations of the laws of war, in Rwanda between January and December 1994.[35] The Secretary-General's report stated clearly that the choice of the subject matter jurisdiction of the Tribunal was guided by 'the nature of the conflict as non-international in character'.[36] The Secretary-General took the view that Article 4 'includes violations of Additional Protocol II, which, as a whole, has not yet been universally recognised as part of customary international law and for the first time criminalises common Article 3 of the four Geneva Conventions'.[37] He admitted that the Security Council took:

> a more expansive approach to the choice of the law applicable than the one underlying the statute of the Yugoslav Tribunal, and included within the subject-matter jurisdiction of the Rwanda Tribunal international instruments regardless of whether they were considered part of customary law or whether they have customarily entailed the individual criminal responsibility of the perpetrator of the crime.[38]

This statement might appear awkward as it seems to imply that the criminality of the conduct listed in Article 4 of the statute was not established in treaty or customary international law at the time of the commission of the acts and therefore could be seen as violating the maxim *nullum crimen sine lege*.[39]

It is interesting to note that at the same time as the adoption of the ICTR statute, the Special Rapporteur of the Commission on Human Rights in Rwanda reported that:

> many of the acts alleged, such as murder, political assassination, execution of hostages and other inhuman acts committed against the civilian population or unarmed soldiers by the armed forces of the two parties to the conflict, constitute war crimes in direct violation of the four Geneva Conventions of 12 August 1949, which have been ratified by Rwanda and their common Article 3.[40]

Similarly, the Appeals Chamber affirmed about a year later in the *Tadić* jurisdiction decision that the violations of common Article 3, and various other customary principles stemming from Protocol II, entail the criminal responsibility of the perpetrators as a matter of customary international law. Finally, the first judgment given by the ICTR in the *Akayesu* case did not share the doubts of the Secretary-General and Security Council, and embraced the conclusions given in the *Tadić* jurisdiction decision[41] considering that:

> it is clear that the authors of such egregious violations must incur individual criminal responsibility for their deeds. The Chamber, therefore, concludes the violation of these norms entails, as a matter of customary international law, individual responsibility for the perpetrator.[42]

1.2 *The statute of the International Criminal Court*

The establishment of both ad hoc Criminal Tribunals gave a new impetus to the campaign for the creation of a permanent international criminal court. The International Law Commission adopted in 1994 a draft statute for an international criminal court, which proposed giving the future court jurisdiction over genocide, aggression, serious violations of the laws of war applicable in armed conflict, crimes against humanity and other crimes, established under or pursuant to the treaty provisions listed in the annex, which having regard to the conduct alleged, constitute exceptionally serious crimes of international concern.[43] This annexed list did not contain Protocol II or common Article 3. According to the commentary given by the International Law Commission, the category of 'serious violations of the laws and customs applicable in armed conflicts' is meant to cover provisions such as the ones contained in Article 3 of the ICTY statute and Article 22 of the draft code of crimes against peace and security of mankind.[44] The question whether the expression 'armed conflicts' is meant to include both international and internal conflicts was not clearly settled by the International Law Commission in 1994.[45]

In 1995, the General Assembly established an Ad Hoc Committee on the Establishment of an International Criminal Court by resolution 49/53 and a Preparatory Committee on the Establishment of an International Criminal Court in 1996 by resolution 50/46, which had the mandate to prepare a draft statute for an ICC. During numerous debates in these committees, states were able to give their views on the choice of crimes falling within the subject matter jurisdiction of the future court. Such debates were particularly interesting in revealing whether states believed that the concept of war crimes was applicable in internal armed conflicts and whether such crimes were serious enough to fall within the jurisdiction of the future court. The negotiators wanted to include within the jurisdiction of the court only those norms, which were considered serious enough to be included and were established principles of customary law.[46] Furthermore, these norms needed to give rise to individual criminal responsibility under customary international law.[47]

In relation to crimes committed in internal armed conflicts, the debates triggered a battle between two camps, which lasted up to the very last day of the Rome conference. On the one hand, a large majority of states was persuaded that the jurisdiction of the court should extend to internal armed conflicts and include violations of common Article 3 and Protocol II.[48] These delegations drew attention to the increasing frequency in recent years of such conflicts and argued that 'national criminal justice systems were less likely to be able to adequately address such violations'.[49] They noted that individuals could be held 'criminally responsible for such violations as a matter of international law', and referred to the ICTR statute and the *Tadić* jurisdiction decision.[50] On the other hand, a minority stressed that Protocol II 'had not achieved the status of customary law' and did not contain any criminal offence or enforcement provisions, noting that 'customary law had not changed in this respect since the Rwanda Tribunal Statute'.[51] They argued further that 'individual criminal responsibility for such violations was not clearly established as a matter of existing law'.[52] Despite the resentment of this group of states,[53] proposals were included in the draft statute to give jurisdiction to the court over serious violations of common Article 3 as well as violations of some provisions derived from Protocol II, and from the Hague regulations or the Geneva Conventions.[54]

The ICC statute was adopted on 17 July 1998, 120 out of 162 states voting in favour.[55] It is the second international instrument, after the ICTR statute, expressly to include a great number of war crimes committed in internal armed conflicts.[56] The court will have jurisdiction according to Article 8.2.c) over serious violations of common Article 3,[57] as well as other serious violations of the laws of war applicable in armed conflicts not of an international character.[58] Article 8.2.e) contains this list of other serious violations of the laws of war in internal conflict, which for a great part mirrors the content of Article 8.2.b) which deals with serious violations of the laws of war applicable in international conflicts. The drafters have been greatly influenced by the conclusions reached by the Appeals Chamber in its *Tadić* jurisdiction decision, notably that 'what is inhumane and consequently proscribed in international wars, cannot but be inhumane and inadmissible in civil strife,'[59] as well as the finding that there has been a 'gradual extension to internal armed conflicts of rules and principles concerning international wars'.[60] They undertook to find out which violations of the law of war entail individual criminal responsibility in customary international law, if committed during internal armed conflicts.[61] The final version of the statute contains twelve provisions mainly borrowed from Protocol II and the Hague regulations.[62] The ICC statute is the first instrument to recognise explicitly the international criminality of most of these acts if committed in internal armed conflicts.

Out of these twelve norms, nine are closely related to provisions contained in Protocol II:

- Intentionally directing attacks against the civilian population (Article 13 of Protocol II)
- Intentionally directing attacks against buildings, material, medical units and transport, and personnel using the distinctive emblems of the Geneva Conventions (Articles 9, 11 and 12 of Protocol II)
- Intentionally directing attacks against buildings dedicated to religion, education, art, science or charitable purposes, historic monuments, hospitals and places where the sick and wounded are collected, provided they are not military objectives (Articles 11 and 16 of Protocol II)
- Pillaging a town or place, even when taken by assault (Article 4.2.g of Protocol II – Article 28 of the Hague regulations)
- Committing rape, sexual slavery, enforced prostitution, forced pregnancy, enforced sterilisation, and any other form of sexual violence (Article 4.2.f of Protocol II prohibits slavery and slave trade in all their forms and Article 4.2.e of Protocol II prohibits rape, enforced prostitution and any form of indecent assault)
- Ordering the displacement of the civilian population for reasons related to the conflict (Article 17.1 of Protocol II)
- Declaring that no quarter will be given (Article 4.1 of Protocol II – Article 23.d) of the Hague regulations)
- Subjecting persons in the power of another party to the conflict to mutilation or medical or scientific experiments (Articles 4.2.a), 5.2.e) of Protocol II) and

- Conscripting or enlisting children under the age of fifteen years into armed forces or groups or using them to participate actively in hostilities (the recruitment of children below the age of fifteen is prohibited in Article 4.3.c. of Protocol II, as well as in Article 38.3 of the 1989 Convention on the Rights of the Child)[63]

Two more war crimes committed in internal armed conflicts are closely related to similar provisions from the Hague regulations and are recognised for the first time as war crimes in internal armed conflicts:

- Killing or wounding treacherously a combatant adversary (Article 23.b)
- Destroying or seizing the property of an adversary unless such destruction or seizure be imperatively demanded by the necessities of the conflict (Article 23. g.)

Robinson and von Hebel report that:

> Although the Hague Regulations were drafted for the purpose of international conflict, these provisions have long been recognised as customary international law and were considered so well established as to give rise to criminal responsibility even in internal conflicts.[64]

The last war crime in internal armed conflict falling within the jurisdiction of the ICC can be found only in the 1994 Convention on the Safety of UN and Associated Personnel as an explicit violation of international humanitarian law.[65] Article 8.2.e).iii) prohibits:

> intentionally directing attacks against personnel, installations, material, units or vehicles involved in a humanitarian assistance or peacekeeping mission in accordance with the Charter of the UN, as long as they are entitled to the protection given to civilians or civilian objects under the international law of armed conflicts.

This provision is recognised as a war crime for the first time in the ICC statute but emerges as an extension of the first two prohibitions appearing in this statute: attacks against civilians and persons *hors de combat*. The UN peace-keeping mission will only be protected as long as it is entitled to the protection afforded to civilians or civilian objects and as such this provision does not represent a new crime per se. The drafters believed that this provision had a:

> symbolic importance as a clear signal by the world community that it attaches great importance to the work and protection of such personnel and considers attacks against them as a serious crime of international concern.[66]

These negotiations leading to the adoption of a substantive list of war
crimes in internal armed conflicts have revealed the *opinio juris* of
states on the existence of a principle of individual criminal responsibility for war crimes in internal armed conflicts, as well as the determination of which provisions entail criminal responsibility for war
crimes in international law today and should therefore fall within the
court's jurisdiction.[67] Interestingly enough, these negotiations have
also revived discussions over the scope of application of Article 8.2.e)
and therefore indirectly of the definition of an internal armed conflict.
A proposal to include a threshold equivalent to Article 1.1. of Protocol
II was strongly rejected by a majority of delegations as being far too
restrictive.[68] As seen in chapter 1, Article 8.2.f) was included instead
and is inspired by paragraph 70 of the *Tadić* jurisdiction decision.[69]
It reads:

> Paragraph 2.e) applies to armed conflicts that take place in the territory of
> a State when there is protracted armed conflict between governmental
> authorities and organised armed groups or between such groups.

The inclusion of this definition was not meant to create two sorts of
internal armed conflicts, one regulated by common Article 3 and reproduced in Article 8.2.c) and d) and another covered by Article 8.2.e).[70]
This definition was included as a reaction to the suggestion to adopt the
threshold of additional Protocol II within the statute and to reassure
countries that internal disturbances or unrest do not amount to an
internal armed conflict. The prolonged nature of hostilities and the
organised character of armed groups are the two criteria necessarily
defining any internal armed conflict.[71] It is submitted that conflicts
falling within this definition form the greatest part of internal armed
conflicts and are regulated by common Article 3 as well as other customary law principles applicable in internal armed conflicts.

   In the ICC statute, a more restricted list of war crimes is applicable to
internal conflict than to international conflicts. Even if a close parallel
can be established between the two lists, certain provisions which were
considered by a number of states to amount to war crimes in internal
armed conflict, were not included in the final version of the statute.[72]
Four provisions appearing in the draft statute were ultimately not
included in the adopted statute.[73] First, there is regrettably no provision
on prohibited weapons applicable in internal armed conflicts. The inclusion of some provisions on weaponry applicable in international armed
conflict was one of the most contentious issues of the diplomatic

conference.[74] Minimalist provisions were ultimately included in the statute in the section dealing with international conflicts: using poisoned weapons, asphyxiating, poisonous or other gases and bullets, which expand or flatten easily in the human body. Anti-personnel mines, chemical, bacteriological, blinding laser and nuclear weapons were excluded from the list of prohibited weapons applicable in international conflicts. States, which were members of the non-aligned movement, were the main advocates for the inclusion of nuclear weapons in the statute.[75] The permanent members of the Security Council vehemently rejected this proposal. They were equally against the inclusion of the other mentioned weapons on the basis of the absence of their clear ban in customary international law.[76] As far as internal armed conflicts were concerned, lack of time and interest by the states to fight for the inclusion of at least the former provisions in internal conflicts, partially explain their absence in the ICC statute.[77] Furthermore, in order for some provisions on weapons to be included in international conflicts and to allow the inclusion of some war crimes in internal armed conflict altogether, it was probably safer to abandon the proposal to include certain weapons in internal armed conflicts.[78] The absence of prohibition on the use of weapons in internal armed conflicts is therefore more the fruit of political bargaining than an affirmation by states that employing expanding bullets or poisoned weapons in internal armed conflicts can be seen as lawful conduct.

Secondly, a number of provisions inspired by Protocol II were included in the draft statute at a late stage in 1997 but did not receive enough support during the Rome conference to be included in the final version. Regrettably, the crimes of (a) using starvation as a method of warfare inspired by Article 14 of Protocol II, (b) intentionally launching an attack in the knowledge that such attack will cause incidental loss of life to civilians, damage to civilian objects, or widespread, long-term and severe damage to the natural environment and (c) intentionally launching an attack against works or installations containing dangerous forces in the knowledge that such attack will cause excessive loss of life, injury to civilians or damage to civilian objects inspired by Article 15 of Protocol II, were not included in the statute. There again, even if the majority of states wanted to see these provisions included, a handful of countries did not want any provisions applicable in internal armed conflicts to be included in the statute. Their absence is therefore the fruit of political compromises and the price to pay in order to get the other twelve provisions appearing under Article 8.2.e).

Thirdly, one might also notice that the ICC statute does not include the prohibitions of attacks against civilian objects and attacks which cause disproportionate incidental civilian damage within Article 8.2.e). The latter was included in the draft statute but was, as mentioned above, ultimately sacrificed together with starvation and other provisions inspired by Article 15 of Protocol II. As to the former, the drafters did not go beyond the text of Protocol II, which does not include a general prohibition of attacks against civilian objects, notwithstanding the position taken by the ICTY Appeals Chamber in the *Tadić* case and the established customary law nature of this war crime. The absence of a war crime prohibiting attacks against civilian objects appears to be even more awkward in light of the inclusion of Articles 8.2.e) iii) and iv). Article 8.2.e)iii) prohibits attacks against personnel, installations, material, units or vehicles of peace-keeping missions as long as 'they are entitled to the protection given to civilians or *civilian objects* under the international law of armed conflicts' (emphasis added). Similarly, Article 8.2.e)iv) recalls the content of Articles 11 and 16 of Protocol II but goes beyond it[79] and provides for the prohibitions of attacks against certain installations provided they are not military objectives.

The inordinate list appearing in Article 8.2.e) is the result of compromises and amounts to a patchwork of norms in which the inclusion of certain crimes, pushed by some states, amounts to a novelty in international law[80] while the absence of others, such as a prohibition to attack civilian objects, begs for correction.[81] This has lead commentators to conclude that 'article 8, far from being a faithful snapshot, is but a mere artist's sketch of war crimes in general international law'.[82] Notwithstanding these lacunae, the statute of the ICC has the merit of affirming explicitly that violations of the law of war in internal armed conflicts are war crimes and of providing for a mechanism for their prosecution at an international level. Furthermore, the statute is the instrument containing the widest list of war crimes in internal armed conflicts.[83] This achievement remains one of the most fundamental breakthroughs of the Rome statute.

1.3 The statute of the Special Court for Sierra Leone[84]

Some of the most horrific atrocities committed against a civilian population in the 1990s took place in Sierra Leone over a decade-long internal armed conflict between the Revolutionary United Front and the Government of Sierra Leone. After regaining control of most of the country in 2000, the Sierra Leone Government called on the Security Council to assist in 'establishing a strong and credible court that will meet the objectives of bringing justice and ensuring lasting peace' in Sierra Leone.[85] Recognising the need to end impunity and to help in the restoration and maintenance of peace, the Security Council, by resolution 1315, requested the Secretary-General of the UN to negotiate an agreement with the Government of Sierra Leone to create an independent court.[86]

The statute of the Special Court for Sierra Leone is established as 'a treaty based *sui generis* Court of mixed jurisdiction and composition'.[87] This Special Court has:

> the power to prosecute persons who bear the greatest responsibility for serious violations of international humanitarian law and Sierra Leonian law committed in the territory of Sierra Leone since 30 November 1996.[88]

It tries persons for crimes against humanity, violations of common Article 3 to the Geneva Conventions and of Protocol II, other serious violations of international humanitarian law[89] and some offences under Sierra Leonean law.[90] It is interesting to note that the crime of genocide does not fall within the subject matter jurisdiction of the Special Court.[91] The Special Court has jurisdiction over persons who were fifteen years and more at the time of the alleged commission of the crimes, extending for the first time the jurisdiction of an international judicial institution over juvenile offenders between fifteen and eighteen years of age.[92] This court has primacy over the national courts of Sierra Leone, but this primacy does not extend to courts of third states and it lacks the power to request the surrender of an accused from any third state. Similarly, the court cannot force third states' tribunals to comply with the subpoena of witnesses and arrest warrants issued by the Special Court or production of testimony or other evidence. Finally, the statute provides that an amnesty granted to any person falling within the jurisdiction of the Special Court in respect of the crimes referred to in Articles 2–4 of the statute, shall not be a bar to prosecution.[93]

This new hybrid institution applying international and national law has a subject matter jurisdiction inspired by the statutes of both the ICTR and the ICC, but at the same time addresses the specificities of the Sierra Leonean conflict.[94] Recognising the internal nature of the conflict which entangled Sierra Leone in the 1990s, the judges are able to try individuals for violations of common Article 3 and Protocol II,[95] as well as three other offences, characterised as other serious violations of international humanitarian law and largely inspired by the ICC statute. The three other offences are: committing an attack against a civilian population, against peace-keeping personnel and the abduction and forced recruitment of children under the age of fifteen into armed forces or groups for the purpose of using them to participate actively in the hostilities.[96] It is interesting to note that the Secretary-General is of the view that 'the international crimes enumerated are crimes considered to have had the character of customary international law at the time of the alleged commission of the crime'.[97] However, for the crime of recruiting children, the statute of the Special Court contains a different definition than the one appearing in the ICC statute. The latter renders criminal the conscription or the enlistment of children under the age of fifteen, or their use for active participation in the hostilities, whereas the statute for the Special Court in Sierra Leone defined the offence as the abduction and forced recruitment of children in order to transform them and use them as 'child combatant'. The report of the Secretary-General explains this choice because the customary nature of the ICC statutory crime is said to be doubtful.[98] In relation to the crime of child recruitment, it is interesting to note the findings made by the Appeals Chamber of the Special Court in a recent interlocutory appeal decision.[99] It held that the prohibition of recruiting children had crystallised into customary international law prior to 1996 and that such an act was already a crime recognised in customary international law by the time-frame relevant to the indictments.[100] The definition of this offence in Article 4 of the statute has been criticised by commentators for at least two reasons. First, those who recruited child soldiers whose ages were between fifteen and eighteen could not be prosecuted by the Special Court. The age of fifteen was chosen in the ICC statute, as many states allow conscription from the age of fifteen or sixteen. The 2000 Additional Protocol to the Convention on the Rights of the Child or the Involvement of Children in Armed Conflicts provides, however, for the prohibition of recruiting children under the age of eighteen.[101] The specific nature of the Sierra Leonean conflict should have called for the age of eighteen to be chosen, allowing therefore for the prosecution of persons who had recruited children between the ages of fifteen and eighteen into the armed forces. Secondly, the statute seems to restrict prosecutions of people who have abducted or recruited by force children under the age of fifteen years, whereas other international instruments, such as the ICC statute, make all recruitment, by force or voluntary, of children under the age of fifteen, a crime.[102]

The choice of crimes falling within the jurisdiction of this Special Court seems to have been guided by the specific nature of the Sierra Leonean conflict. The subject matter jurisdiction of this court appears to be not as great as the future ICC but wider than the ICTR's, as some of the crimes appearing in the ICC statute are included within the jurisdiction of this Special Court. This seems to indicate once again that more principles and crimes apply in internal armed conflicts than those stemming from common Article 3 or Protocol II.

1.4 Other treaties

Serious violations of the laws of war committed in internal armed conflicts are clearly considered by these international instruments to entail individual criminal responsibility for war crimes in international law. The ICC expressly recognises the criminality of violations of common Article 3, as well as the main violations of Protocol II and some Hague provisions. This list of war crimes in internal armed conflicts is bound to have a great impact on international law but does not necessarily amount to an exhaustive list of all war crimes in internal armed conflicts.[103]

First, is there any illegal weapon whose use entails individual criminal responsibility in internal armed conflicts? A number of conventions which apply both in internal and international conflicts, do not explicitly establish international criminal responsibility of the individual who might use the outlawed weapons, but put the obligation on ratifying states to ensure the imposition of penal sanctions on these individuals. This is the case in the 1993 Chemical Weapons Conventions,[104] the 1996 Amended Protocol II to the 1980 Convention on Prohibitions or Restrictions on the Use of Mines, Booby-traps and other Devices,[105] as well as the 1997 Convention on the Prohibition of the Use, Stockpiling, Production, and Transfer of Anti-personnel Mines and on their Destruction.[106] Article 9 of the latter provides:

> Each party shall take all appropriate legal, administrative and other measures, including the imposition of penal sanctions, to prevent and suppress any activity prohibited to a state party under this convention undertaken by persons or on territory under its jurisdiction or control.[107]

These instruments establish per se neither the character of war crimes to these violations, nor the application of universal jurisdiction. However, they impose a duty on states parties to enact penal sanctions, a new and welcome trend in weaponry conventions.

Secondly, in two other international instruments certain conduct has been recognised to amount to war crimes when committed in internal armed conflicts. The 1994 Convention on the Safety of UN and Associated Personnel enjoins states parties to 'make the crimes set out in paragraph 1 punishable by appropriate penalties which shall take into account their grave nature'.[108] Furthermore, the Second Protocol to the Hague Convention of 1954 for the Protection of Cultural Property in the Event of Armed Conflict of 26 March 1999 establishes the criminal responsibility of persons who violate the Protocol. Article 22 of this instrument provides for its application in the event of an armed conflict not of an international character.[109]

Thirdly, the list of war crimes appearing in the ICC statute might not be an exhaustive list of war crimes in internal armed conflicts. The Rome conference had to reconcile concerns of humanity with concerns of state sovereignty and the crimes falling within the jurisdiction of the court can be seen as the most serious offences only.[110] Some humanitarian law violations might not have been included in the statute of the ICC but could be recognised as war crimes in customary international law. It is now necessary to look at state practice and *opinio juris* in order to find out whether the principle of individual criminal responsibility in internal armed conflicts is established in customary law and furthermore for which crimes this could be the case.

2. Customary international law and the principle of individual criminal responsibility for war crimes in internal armed conflicts

In order to establish the criminal responsibility of individuals who violate the laws of war, the Nuremberg Tribunal looked at a number of factors: the clear and unequivocal recognition of these norms, the establishment of state practice indicating an intention to criminalise these norms, the gravity of the acts and the interests of the international community in their prohibition.[111] Chapter 2 of this book aimed to establish the treaty law and customary law applicable in internal armed conflict and came to a conclusion that there exists a clear and unequivocal recognition of a substantive body of principles applicable in internal armed conflicts. Have these principles been criminalised in customary international law?

In the *Tadić* case, the ICTY Appeals Chamber answered this question positively but put forward a surprisingly small amount of state practice to support its conclusion. It first cited the International Criminal Tribunal of Nuremberg, affirming that 'a finding of individual criminal responsibility is not barred by the absence of treaty provisions on punishment of breaches'.[112] The Chamber then went over state practice by citing four military manuals, two domestic criminal codes, two Security Council resolutions, and the case law of Nigerian rebels and members of the Federal Army taken to court for violations of international humanitarian law,[113] before concluding that 'all of these factors confirm that customary international law imposes criminal liability for serious violations committed in internal armed conflicts'. It is questionable whether the Appeals Chamber was wise to address these issues *obiter* and it is surprising to see it satisfied that the concept of war crimes in internal armed conflicts is reflected in customary international law on such a paucity of state practice.[114] Judge Li, in his dissenting opinion, commented that it amounted to 'an unwarranted assumption of legislative power'[115] and others have cautioned:

> The efforts of the Tribunal to expand the scope of the law applicable to internal armed conflict may give the impression that criminal convictions are being made for acts committed in a non-international armed conflict on the basis of crimes that would generally have been thought actionable only in international conflicts.[116]

Generally, however, the *Tadić* jurisdiction decision was welcomed as 'a carefully reasoned and innovative judgment, which is likely to have a profound effect upon the development of international humanitarian law'.[117]

Was it premature to conclude that the principle of individual criminal responsibility for war crimes was customarily applicable in internal armed conflicts in 1995? Has the content of customary law evolved since then and is such a principle now reflected in customary international law? Practice and *opinio juris* of states and international organisations will be examined to determine whether there is sufficient evidence of a general practice accepted as law, establishing the applicability of war criminality in internal armed conflicts. This will be done by looking at the direct practice of states through their various national legislation dealing with the law of war, their criminal codes, military manuals,[118] as well as their statements and unilateral declarations.[119] The practice of international organisations such as the UN, through General Assembly resolutions, Security Council resolutions and Secretary-General reports,[120] as well as statements made by the European Union will then be examined. Finally, the list of material sources, where evidence of states practice can be found, often includes international and national judicial decisions, as well as a pattern of treaties in the same form.[121]

2.1 Practice of states

2.1.1 National legislation, criminal codes and military manuals[122]

Theodor Meron takes the view that:

> Manuals of military law and legislation of states providing for the implementation of humanitarian law norms as internal law, should be considered as among the best types of evidence of such practice and sometimes perhaps, as a statement of *opinio juris* as well.[123]

States parties to the Geneva Conventions and to Protocol I are under an obligation to enact legislation necessary to provide effective penal sanctions for persons committing or ordering to be committed any of the grave breaches of these conventions and Protocol I.[124] For all other violations of the 1949 Conventions, including violations of common Article 3, states shall take 'measures necessary for the suppression of all acts contrary to the provisions of the Conventions'.[125]

States can choose from various options in order to enact penal sanctions of the grave breaches provisions domestically.[126] States can take the view that the domestic offences included in their criminal codes already cover the acts mentioned under the grave breaches provisions and that there is no need to enact further legislation.[127] Alternatively, states can choose to enact specific legislation which will entirely incorporate the grave breaches provisions.[128] Furthermore, if states choose to include a provision in their criminal laws, such legislation could only be of a general character and send the reader back to the relevant provisions of the Geneva Conventions and Protocol I.[129] Alternatively, the criminalisation could be of a mixed nature with the inclusion of a chapter dealing with war crimes in the domestic criminal codes or military criminal codes. In the latter case, this chapter could incorporate some, often redrafted, provisions from the Geneva Conventions.[130] In order to highlight state practice in this area, it is therefore necessary to review the legislation implementing the 1949 Geneva Conventions and Protocols, the legislation implementing obligations under Security Council resolutions 827 and 955, and the legislation implementing the ICC statute, together with criminal codes, military criminal codes and military manuals.[131] Various piece of legislation and other documents from more than one hundred states have been reviewed,[132] in order to find out if and how states criminalise serious violations of the laws of war committed in internal armed conflicts. This was conducted to try and see whether states treat violations committed in internal armed conflicts on the same footing as grave breaches committed in international armed conflicts. While treaty obligations only enjoin states to provide for penal sanctions relating to the grave breaches provisions, the question arises whether violations of common Article 3 or Protocol II are included in the repressive regime enacted by states? Did they treat such violations as violations of their domestic criminal code, or as international crime on the basis not of a treaty provision, absent in the case of common Article 3 or Protocol II, but of a customary norm?

This research has highlighted the fact that out of 194 states parties to the 1949 Geneva Conventions, some have never enacted any type of implementing legislation of the 1949 Geneva Conventions and 1977 Protocols, some failing to do so, others believing that their domestic criminal codes already covered the conduct mentioned in these conventions. In this respect, an evolution of state practice is evident: states are gradually abandoning the idea that domestic offences, such as murder or theft, are best suited to address or cover war crimes, such as willful killing or pillaging. This is coupled with an increasing trend towards treating violations of the laws of war committed in internal armed conflicts as international crimes, attaching therefore a greater stigma and heavier penalty to what used to be criminalised purely as domestic offences.

2.1.1.1 National legislation implementing the 1949 Geneva Conventions and the 1977 Additional Protocols

Some countries have not implemented any legislation to deal specifically with violations of the laws of war. To this author's best knowledge, this remains the case for countries such as Indonesia,[133] Israel,[134] Morocco,[135] Nepal,[136] Pakistan,[137] Lesotho[138] and Tunisia among others. These countries did not implement the obligations under the grave breaches provisions of the Geneva Conventions, so *a fortiori*, they do not treat violations of the laws of war committed in internal armed conflicts as war crimes. Some other countries did not pass any specific legislation as they took the view that their domestic law, such as the existing criminal codes or military criminal codes, were adequate to provide effective criminal sanctions for those who had violated the provisions of the Geneva Conventions. Examples of such countries are Austria,[139] Cameroon,[140] China,[141] Iraq[142] and Togo.[143] This group of countries does not seem to have attached the stigma of war crimes and heavier penalties to violations of international humanitarian law, be they committed in international or internal armed conflicts.

The second and fairly large group of countries are those which implemented the Geneva Conventions within their legislation, but only criminalised the grave breaches of the Geneva Conventions and Protocol I. Violations of common Article 3 and Protocol II are not mentioned in these documents and are therefore not criminalised on the basis of a treaty or customary obligation recognised in international law. A great number of common law countries have enacted a 'Geneva Conventions Act' which usually contains a provision criminalising grave breaches in the domestic law of the land and refers back to the common articles of the Geneva Conventions for a definition of each of the offences. The UK Geneva Conventions Act of 1957 reads for example:

> any person, whatever his nationality, who, whether in or outside the United Kingdom commits, or aids, abets or procures the commission by any other person of, any such grave breach of any of the scheduled conventions as is referred to in the following articles respectively of those conventions: Articles 50, 51, 130, 147 of the Geneva Conventions, shall be guilty of felony and on conviction ... shall be sentenced to imprisonment for life.[144]

A number of common law countries enacted similar legislation, such as the Cook Islands,[145] Gambia,[146] Ghana,[147] India,[148] Kenya,[149] Malawi,[150] Malaysia,[151] Mauritius,[152] Namibia,[153] Nigeria,[154] Trinidad and Tobago[155] and Zimbabwe.[156]

Furthermore, a number of civil law countries have taken the same position and qualify as war crimes or grave breaches only the serious violations of the laws of war committed in international armed conflicts. Civil law countries have often amended their domestic criminal codes or their military criminal codes so as to include the grave breaches of the Geneva Conventions and Protocol I. This group of countries does not recognise as war crimes the violations of the laws of war in internal armed conflicts. Examples of such countries are Burkina Fasso,[157] France,[158] Greece,[159] Japan,[160] Luxembourg,[161] Mali,[162] Romania[163] and Turkey.[164]

These two groups of countries represent a substantial number of states, which either did not implement the 1949 Geneva Conventions or have traditionally implemented only the grave breaches contained in the Geneva Conventions and Protocol I. The legislation of over thirty states studied does not treat serious violations of the laws of war committed in internal armed conflicts as war crimes.

The third group consists of states which have enacted criminal provisions for the serious violations of the Geneva Conventions and Protocols, which could be interpreted as covering serious violations of the laws of war committed in internal armed conflicts. However, a number of these provisions do not have a specific or clear scope of application. Others seem restricted to conduct committed during international armed conflicts, because their scope of application is 'during combat actions', 'in times of war or in combat' or 'war or occupation'. This is the case, for example, for the criminal codes of Cuba,[165] the Czech Republic,[166] Estonia,[167] the Ivory Coast,[168] Guinea,[169] Hungary,[170] Lebanon,[171] Peru,[172] Ukraine,[173] Uzbekistan,[174] Vietnam[175] and Yemen.[176] It remains unclear whether these states are really able to prosecute violations of the laws of war committed in internal armed conflicts.

Fourthly, an important and growing number of criminal codes or domestic legislation criminalises serious violations of the laws of war committed in *armed conflicts* (emphasis added). Such provision was interpreted by the Appeals Chamber of the ICTY in the *Tadić* case to 'imply that they also apply to internal armed conflicts'.[177] In the great majority of cases, the authors of the legislation or various commentaries of the provisions make clear that the expression 'armed conflict' is intended explicitly to cover both international and internal conflicts. Such provisions can be found in the legislation of Argentina,[178] Armenia,[179] Azerbaijan,[180] Bangladesh,[181] Belarus,[182] Bosnia-Herzegovina,[183] Costa Rica,[184] Croatia,[185] Colombia,[186] Ethiopia,[187] Finland,[188] Jordan,[189] Kazakhstan,[190] Lithuania,[191] Moldova,[192] Mozambique,[193] the Netherlands,[194] Norway,[195] Paraguay,[196] Poland,[197] Russia,[198] Sweden,[199] Slovenia,[200] Spain[201] and Switzerland.[202]

Fifthly, a group of countries have alleviated any kind of doubt as to the scope of application of their legislation, by specifically mentioning that war crimes provisions apply in international and internal armed conflicts. This is the case for a growing number of countries such as Belgium,[203] Republic of Congo[204] (Brazzaville), Democratic Republic of Congo (DRC),[205] El Salvador,[206] Georgia,[207] Italy,[208] Ireland,[209] Latvia,[210] Nicaragua,[211] Niger,[212] Portugal,[213] Rwanda,[214] the USA,[215] Tajikistan[216] and Thailand.[217] These last two groups of states which clearly criminalise war crimes in internal armed conflicts represent a fairly large group of states within the international community. It must be noted, however, that only a handful of these states had decided to treat serious violations of the laws of war committed in internal armed conflicts as war crimes before 1991.[218]

2.1.1.2 Military manuals   Military manuals were equally considered by the ICTY Appeals Chamber to be good evidence of practice and *opinio juris* of states.[219] A number of military manuals present themselves as a code of conduct, enjoining troops to respect discipline and the basic principles of humanitarian law at all times. Often, however, these manuals do not contain any provisions on the responsibility or the penalties of potential offenders, such provisions being inserted in the military criminal code or in the criminal code.[220]

In some cases, they do include provisions on the repression of violations, but these provisions only provide for the repression of grave breaches of the Geneva Conventions and Protocol I. This still seems to be the case for the military manuals of Russia,[221] Australia[222] and New Zealand. The latter contains, for example, a provision dealing with breaches of Protocol II which reads:

> Although breaches of Protocol II would amount to war crimes if committed in international conflict, both the governmental and rebel authority should treat them as breaches of the national criminal law, since the law concerning war crimes relates to international conflicts.[223]

However, some recent military manuals call on soldiers to respect principles of humanitarian law in all armed conflicts, and provide explicitly for the application of the concept of war crimes to offences committed in internal armed conflicts. Some American military manuals, such as the *Annotated supplement to the commander's handbook on the law of naval operations, and the law of land warfare FM 27–10 of 1956,* treat all violations of the laws of war as war crimes.[224] Violations of Protocol II are specifically mentioned as constituting war crimes.[225] Similarly, the German military manual of 1992 enjoins 'German soldiers to comply with the rules of international humanitarian law in the conduct of military operations in all armed conflicts however such conflicts are characterised'.[226] It further qualifies as grave breaches of international humanitarian law violations of common Article 3 and many violations of Protocol II such as, for example, starvation (Protocol II Article 14), launching an attack against works or installations containing dangerous forces (Article 15) or perfidious use of recognised protective signs (Article 12).[227]

Furthermore, the 1999 Canadian *Manual on the law of armed conflict at the operational and tactical level* (B-GG-005-027/AF-021) spells out 'the basic principles and spirit of the law of armed conflict to be applied, as a minimum, by all members of the Canadian forces taking part in all

Canadian military operations other than Canadian domestic operations'.[228] Chapter 17 of the manual deals specifically with non-international conflicts and affirms:

> When Additional Protocol II was adopted, states refused to make violations of its provisions regarding criminal offences. Certain nations were reluctant to allow other states to interfere in their internal affairs by way of trials for war crimes alleged to have taken place in their national territory. Today however, many provisions of Additional Protocol II are recognised under customary international law as prohibitions that entail individual criminal responsibility when breaches are committed during internal armed conflicts. Violations of many provisions of the protocol committed by individual members of a party to an internal conflict are thus criminal offences under international law.[229]

The 2004 UK *Manual of the law of armed conflict* is a good illustration of the evolution of the law in this area. In contrast to previous official documents,[230] the recent UK military manual squarely affirms:

> Although the treaties governing internal armed conflicts contain no grave breach provisions, customary law recognises that serious violations of these treaties can amount to punishable war crimes. It is now recognised that there is a growing area of conduct that is criminal in both international and internal armed conflict.[231]

Like national legislation, some recent military manuals have gone further than the treaty obligations contained in the Geneva Conventions or Protocols and considered that serious violations of common Article 3 or Protocol II amount to war crimes. Together with the British manual, the Canadian military manual represents another good illustration of this change, as an earlier draft of the provisions cited above affirmed:

> Although breaches of Additional Protocol II would amount to war crimes if committed in international conflicts, both the governmental and rebel authority should treat them as breaches of the national criminal law, since the law concerning war crimes relates to international conflicts.[232]

This new trend can also be illustrated by looking at how states have implemented the UN Security Council resolutions establishing the ICTY and the ICTR.

2.1.1.3 National legislation implementing Security Council resolutions establishing the ICTR and the ICTY   A number of states have implemented legislation to meet their obligations

stemming from Security Council resolutions 827 and 955 in respect of co-operation with the ICTY and the ICTR. In most cases, these legislative acts only provide the framework for judicial co-operation between national jurisdictions and both International Tribunals and deal with issues such as the requests by the Tribunals for assistance, the issue of surrendering persons to the Tribunals or other forms of assistance. They generally do not establish jurisdiction of domestic courts over those offences falling within the jurisdiction of both Tribunals.[233] A handful of states has, however, decided to go further and have established the jurisdiction of their domestic courts over the offences committed in Rwanda or the ex-Yugoslavia. This seems to be the case for Finland, Denmark, Luxembourg and France. The **Finnish** Act on the jurisdiction of the ICTY and on legal assistance to the International Tribunal provides for the jurisdiction of the Finnish courts to be 'exercised in a criminal matter according to Finnish law unless the Tribunal has prior to the institution of the proceedings or subsequently, notified that it shall assume the exclusive jurisdiction'.[234] Similarly, the legislation enacted by **Denmark** appears even more explicit by providing that: 'any offence covered by the statute and the rules of procedure and evidence of the ICTY may be prosecuted in Denmark in accordance with the provisions laid down in the legislation and the said statute and rules of procedure and evidence.'[235] It seems therefore that it gives the Danish courts jurisdiction over any offences covered by the ICTY and ICTR statute that have been committed in Rwanda or the ex-Yugoslavia. Similarly, in **Luxembourg**, an act dated 19 May 1999 on co-operation with the criminal tribunals gives local courts jurisdiction over the crimes, which fall within the jurisdiction of both international criminal tribunals, if the alleged criminals are found in Luxembourg.[236]

The explicit and rather surprising legislation in this area is the **French** legislation enacted in 1995 and 1996.[237] They not only provide for co-operation between French jurisdictions and both International Criminal Tribunals, but establish the jurisdiction of French courts over the offences appearing in both statutes if the suspected authors of grave breaches, genocide or crimes against humanity are found on French soil.[238] It is the first time that French legislation has implemented the concept of grave breaches as well as war crimes committed in internal conflicts in its domestic legislation and applies the concept of universal jurisdiction in regard to these particular crimes.[239] This legislation represents a great novelty in the French judicial system,[240] but the jurisdiction of French courts would only be extended to these crimes if they took place in Rwanda in 1994 or the ex-Yugoslavia since 1991.[241]

2.1.1.4 National legislation implementing the statute of an International Criminal Court
The adoption of the ICC statute giving the court jurisdiction over war crimes committed in internal armed conflicts, has created a new impetus for states to include such crimes within their own domestic legislation. The ICC statute does not oblige states to do so, but the preamble certainly does encourage them, by affirming that:

> the most serious crimes of concern to the international community as a whole must not go unpunished and that their effective prosecution must be ensured by taking measures at the national level and by enhancing international co-operation.

The preamble recalls further that it is 'the duty of every state to exercise its criminal jurisdiction over those responsible for international crimes'. Furthermore, the ICC will complement national jurisdictions and will only be able to act where national systems do not themselves have the will or the means to investigate or prosecute.[242] If states want to take advantage of this principle of complementarity and prevent the court from exercising its jurisdiction, they might have to review their own criminal law to ensure that prosecutions can be brought in national courts for the crimes within the ICC's jurisdiction. A number of states, which have ratified the ICC statute, have chosen to check their existing legislation and to implement new domestic legislation which criminalises the offences as defined in the ICC statute.

As already indicated, Azerbaijan, Belarus and the Congo have enacted specific provisions including all the ICC offences within their new criminal codes, even before ratifying the ICC statute itself. Currently, out of the 104 states which have ratified the ICC statute,[243] at least 17 states have already adopted specific legislation which renders every offence of the ICC statute, including serious violations of the laws of war committed in internal armed conflicts, a war crime within their own domestic system. The first state to do so was **Canada**, which adopted the Crimes against Humanity and War Crimes Act on 29 June 2000.[244] Sections 4.3 and 6.3 of this Act define war crimes as:

> An act or omission committed during an armed conflict, at the time and in the place of its commission, constitutes a war crime according to

customary international law or conventional international law applicable
to armed conflicts, whether or not it constitutes a contravention of the
law in force at the time and in the place of its commission.

Sections 4.4 and 6.4 of the Act bring an interesting precision by adding:

> For greater certainty, crimes described in articles 6, 7 and paragraph 2 of
> article 8 of the Rome statute, are as of 17 July 1998, crimes according to
> customary international law, and may be crimes according to customary
> international law before that date.[245]

By these provisions, Canada did not wish to limit or prejudice the
application of existing or developing rules of international law, and
affirmed beyond any doubt that the offences contained in the Rome
statute reflect customary international law, at least as of 17 July 1998.
This legislation allows Canadian courts to prosecute individuals for war
crimes, in international and internal armed conflicts alike, when they are
defined as such by customary or conventional international law. Judges
will therefore be able to prosecute individuals for war crimes committed
in internal armed conflicts which have not been retained in the Rome
statute, and for new war crimes which may in the future become part of
customary or conventional law. As officials in Canada put it: 'it was also
the purpose of the Act to strengthen prosecutions for conduct outside
Canada, whether in the past, present or future'.[246]

The second state to adopt similar legislation was **New Zealand**, which
enacted the International Crimes and International Criminal Court Act
2000. This Act gives jurisdiction to courts in New Zealand to prosecute
individuals who in New Zealand or elsewhere have committed genocide,
crimes against humanity or war crimes, as defined in Articles 6, 7 and 8 of
the ICC statute.[247] This Act is the first one to implement the offences of
genocide, crimes against humanity and war crimes committed in internal
armed conflicts in New Zealand law.[248] The government has clearly
chosen to give New Zealand the option of instituting its own proceedings
for all the conduct described in Articles 6 – 8 of the Rome statute.

Similarly, **the UK** International Criminal Court Act 2001 incorporates in UK law the offences set out in the Rome statute, so that these
offences can be prosecuted successfully in UK domestic courts.[249]
Section 50.1 states that 'war crimes mean war crimes as defined in
Article 8.2' of the ICC statute. Another option would have been to use
existing UK offences where they corresponded to ICC offences, supple-
mented by newly created domestic offences where there were not UK

analogues. But there again, the UK Government took the view that 'if we were to prosecute them in a way which reflected their gravity, we could not simply equate say pillage with the domestic offence of theft'.[250]

In **Belgium**, the 1993 'avant-gardiste' legislation was abrogated. The laws of 23 April 2003 and 5 August 2003 amended the criminal code so as to include within the list of war crimes in armed conflicts all war crimes as defined in the Rome statute as well as other crimes, such as violations to Protocol II to the 1954 Hague Convention.[251]

The 2002 **South African** Implementation of the Rome Statute of the International Criminal Court Act includes within South African law all the crimes contained in Article 5 of the ICC statute, including therefore all the war crimes applicable in internal armed conflicts.[252] Similarly, the **Australian** International Criminal Court (Consequential Amendments) Act 2002 introduces into the Australian criminal code all the war crimes applicable in internal armed conflicts contained in Article 8 of the ICC statute.[253] Lastly, the international crimes act of **the Netherlands**[254] of 19 June 2003, the **Danish** Act No. 342 of 16 May 2001 on the International Criminal Court,[255] the law No. 1/004 dated 8 May 2004 of **Burundi**,[256] the Act on the implementation of the provisions of a legislative nature of the Rome statute of **Finland**,[257] the 2003 Law on the application of the statute of the ICC and on the prosecution of criminal acts against the international law on war and humanitarian law from **Croatia**,[258] the International Criminal Court Act 2002 of **Malta**,[259] the International Criminal Court Act 2006 of **Trinidad and Tobago**,[260] as well as the **Argentinean** and **Uruguayan** legislations of 2006 implementing the ICC statute[261] introduce all war crimes, applicable in internal armed conflicts contained in the ICC statute, into their national criminal legislation.

Germany adopted on 26 June 2002 a code of crimes against international law which domestically implements all the offences contained in the ICC statute and other international offences contained in Protocol I or in customary international law.[262] According to the commentary to the code, when the status of existing international customary law does allow international and internal armed conflicts to be treated equally, the provisions on war crimes apply to both kinds of conflict.[263] Most of the war crimes against persons, against property, against humanitarian operations and emblems, and most notably 'war crime consisting in the use of prohibited methods of warfare and in employment of prohibited means of warfare' are all also applicable in internal armed conflicts.[264] **Portugal** decided to go beyond the content of the ICC statute in amending its criminal code. The Portuguese legislation dated 22 July 2004 contains a long list of war crimes applicable in both international and internal armed conflicts including war crimes through the use of prohibited means and methods of warfare such as the use of poison, mines, chemical or incendiary weapons, for example.[265]

Some other states, such as **Brazil**,[266] **Kenya**[267] and **Italy**[268] have introduced draft implementing legislation, which incorporate all the crimes contained in the ICC statute into their legal systems.[269]

2.1.1.5 Conclusion   Out of the ninety-nine states for which information was available, fifty-four of them clearly recognise that serious violations of the law of war committed in internal armed conflicts amount to war crimes.[270] Another twelve adopted legislation, whose scope of application reflects some ambiguity but could be interpreted as covering serious violations of the laws of war in internal armed conflicts. As the great majority of states has chosen to do this in the last fifteen years, this is therefore a new but very clear trend in state practice.[271] This practice is highly significant as a number of these states have been, or are still, engaged in internal armed conflicts themselves, such as Armenia, Azerbaijan, Ethiopia, Georgia, Bosnia, Colombia, Croatia, El Salvador, Nicaragua, the Democratic Republic of Congo, Russia and Tajikistan. An important number of states have been influenced by the negotiations and adoption of the Rome statute and have decided to include the list of war crimes of the ICC statute within their own criminal legislation. But more importantly, some of these laws go even further than the content of the Rome statute, and include, for example, starvation or the use of weapons of mass destruction as war crimes in internal armed conflicts.

It must be noted, however, that there is no uniformity among states in the way serious violations of the laws of war applicable in internal armed conflicts are criminalised. If a majority of national legislation contains at least the list of war crimes from the Rome statute, in other instances, the criminalisation of internal atrocities is much more limited. The examples of France, Luxembourg or Thailand come to mind. Furthermore, the inclusion of prohibited weapons in the list of war crimes in internal armed conflicts remains rather exceptional. Finally, one might also note a certain geographical imbalance in the criminalisation of internal atrocities. If most European and North American as well as a majority of African countries have been really active in this area, Asian and Middle Eastern states lag behind in implementing war crimes into their national legislation. The entry into force of the ICC statute and the principle of complementarity contained in the statute will encourage states parties to look at their own national legislation and, where it is not yet the case, to include war crimes committed in internal armed conflicts. Indeed over the coming years an increasing number of states will give jurisdiction to their courts over war crimes committed in internal armed conflicts.[272]

2.1.2 Declaration of states

Detailed examination of national implementing legislation, criminal codes or military manuals of states brings to light the direct practice of states, what they do compared with what they say in the field of international criminal law. Debates in the UN Security Council or during the Rome conference on the establishment of the ICC provided states with good opportunities to express their views on the criminality of internal atrocities. These declarations are telling indicators of the *opinio juris* of states.

2.1.2.1 Unilateral declarations of states during debates in the Security Council   The debates during the Security Council meetings preceding the adoption of the ICTY statute, provide information on the views of states on the proper scope of application of Article 3 of the ICTY statute, violations of laws of war. Three of the permanent members of the Security Council held explicit views in this respect. The American representative commented:

> It is understood that the laws and customs of war referred to in Article 3 include all obligations under humanitarian law agreements in force in the territory of the former Yugoslavia at the time the acts were committed, including common Article 3 of the 1949 Geneva Conventions, and the 1977 Additional Protocols to these Conventions.[273]

The French representative concurred with the USA by declaring:

> The expression laws or customs of war used in Article 3 of the statute covers specifically, in the opinion of France, all the obligations that flow from the humanitarian law agreements in force on the territory of the former Yugoslavia at the time when the offences were committed.[274]

Lastly, the UK representative added:

> It is essential that those who commit such acts be in no doubt that they will be held individually responsible. It is essential that these atrocities be

investigated and the perpetrators called to account whoever, and wherever they may be.[275]

These countries clearly intended that the future tribunal should have jurisdiction over all violations of the laws of war committed by all parties during the conflict in ex-Yugoslavia, whether characterised as an international or internal armed conflict. Thus they reaffirmed indirectly that they viewed serious violations of the laws of war committed in internal armed conflicts as war crimes and individuals should be held internationally responsible for these violations.

2.1.2.2 Declarations of states during the Rome diplomatic conference on the ICC   The UN plenipotentiary treaty conference on the establishment of an International Criminal Court in Rome in June and July 1998 enabled states to express their views about, among other things, the extent of the subject matter jurisdiction of the future ICC and therefore indirectly on the subject at stake here: whether they believe that violations of the laws of war committed in internal armed conflicts are war crimes.

First, states made general statements during the first week of the conference,[276] which highlighted the concerns and views of each state on the objectives and requirements of the statute of the future ICC. These statements are strong evidence of the *opinio juris* of states. It is noteworthy that out of eighty-three speeches of states reviewed, forty-seven specifically mentioned the importance of including within the court's jurisdiction war crimes committed in internal armed conflicts.[277] To cite but a few, the representative of Armenia stated: The ICC should 'have jurisdiction over genocide, crimes against humanity, wherever they may have been committed, war crimes, serious violations of humanitarian law in international and non-international conflict, crimes of aggression and crimes of terrorism'.[278]

The representative of Bangladesh argued:

> Bangladesh strongly supports giving full effect to the common Article 3 of the Geneva Conventions of 1949. In our view the distinction between international and non-international conflicts is increasingly becoming irrelevant viewed in terms of the structure of universal peace and security.[279]

The representative of Estonia stated:

> One of the most worrying trends in our day's world is the increasing prevalence of conflicts of non-international character. Therefore Estonia

cannot accept the exclusion from the court's jurisdiction of the war crimes committed during an internal conflict.[280]

Similarly, the representative of Uganda advanced:

> We do not support any attempts at differentiating between international and internal conflicts situations when dealing with war crimes.

Forty-three other states included similar declarations in their individual statements and groups of states such as the European Union and the Southern African Development Community (SADEC) stressed this specific point.[281] The UK foreign minister declared on 15 June 1998 on behalf of the European Union:

> We wish to emphasise that most armed conflicts today are internal, not international. So the war crimes within the Court's jurisdiction should include those committed in internal as well as international armed conflicts.[282]

Finally, it is important to point out that during the conference a group of 'like-minded' states, composed of sixty-two states from all continents, pressed for six central building blocks to be incorporated into the ICC statute. Among these six building blocks was the commitment that 'the statute must stipulate that also war crimes perpetrated in internal conflicts are punishable offences subject to the jurisdiction of the Court'.[283]

This strong support for the inclusion of war crimes committed in internal armed conflicts within the jurisdiction of the ICC contrasted with the positions taken by a handful of states, which opposed such inclusion. India was the only state explicitly to rule out war crimes committed in internal armed conflicts from the jurisdiction of the court in its opening statement:

> There is no agreement about whether or not conflicts not of an international nature could be covered under the definition of such crimes (crimes against humanity and war crimes) under customary international law.[284]

During the conference itself, further debates illustrated the division between these two groups of states. On the one hand, statements made by the USA or Germany summarise the position of the great majority of delegations.[285] The US representative stated:

> The US strongly believes that serious violations of the elementary customary norms reflected in common Article 3 should be the centrepiece of the ICC's subject matter jurisdiction with regard to non-international

armed conflicts ... The USA urges also that there should be a section ... covering other rules regarding the conduct of hostilities in non-international armed conflict.[286]

The German representative argued further:

> There was general agreement that those who committed violations of the laws and customs applicable in conflicts must be pursued wherever they might be, brought to trial and punished ... War crimes committed in non-international armed conflicts must be included in view of their increasing frequency and the inadequacy of national criminal justice systems in addressing such violations.[287]

On the other hand, only eight states, namely China,[288] Syria,[289] United Arab Emirates (UAE),[290] Bahrain,[291] Jordan,[292] Sudan, India and Turkey[293] wished that war crimes committed in internal armed conflicts be excluded from the jurisdiction of the ICC. The representative of Sudan took the view that:

> Additional Protocol II did not enjoy the status of established inter-national law and it also provided a loophole for interference in the internal affairs of states.[294]

The representative of India argued:

> There could not be a homogeneous structure of treatment of international and non-international armed conflicts so long as sovereign States existed.[295]

On the closing day of the conference, the representative of Sudan took the floor on behalf of the Arab Group and explained the opposition and fears of the group[296] towards the court for a number of reasons. Among them, he stated:

> The Arab States were afraid that the inclusion of non-international conflicts within the statute would allow interference in the internal affairs of States on flimsy pretexts.[297]

The opposition of the above-mentioned states forced others to compromise and leave out some war crimes from Article 8.2.e), but it did not prevent the inclusion of war crimes committed in internal armed conflicts within the jurisdiction of the court altogether. The positions taken by states during the Rome conference not only illustrate their view on whether or not to give the court jurisdiction over internal armed conflicts, but also show that undoubtedly the majority of states take the view that these serious violations of the law of war amount to war crimes.[298]

2.1.3 The adoption of multilateral treaties
as evidence of state practice

The adoption of multilateral treaties, establishing individual criminal responsibility for serious violations of the laws of war in internal armed conflicts, can be seen as evidence of state practice itself. As discussed in section 2 of this chapter, several treaties dealing with weaponry oblige states to enact penalties and to hold criminally responsible any person who might violate these conventions. Such treaties include the 1993 Chemical Weapons Conventions,[299] the 1996 Amended Protocol II to the 1980 Convention on Prohibitions or Restrictions on the Use of Mines, Booby-traps and other Devices,[300] and the 1997 Convention on the Prohibition of the Use, Stockpiling, Production, and Transfer of Anti-personnel Mines and on their Destruction.[301] Furthermore, the 1999 Second Protocol to the 1954 Hague Convention also includes individual criminal responsibility for its violations in internal armed conflicts. The 1997 Land Mines Convention has already reached 152 states parties and both Protocol II on land mines and Protocol IV on blinding laser weapons to the 1980 Convention are in force.[302] The fact that so many states sign these treaties and become party to them is additional evidence pointing towards recognition of the principle by which serious violations of the laws of war must engage the individual criminal responsibility of offenders in international law. The recent extension of the scope of application of the 1980 Convention and all its protocols to internal armed conflicts is symptomatic of this new trend.

As to the more general question of multilateral treaties as evidence of customary international law,[303] it is difficult to assert that any of the treaties on weaponry are declaratory of pre-existing customary international law, when they establish individual criminal responsibility for the use of these weapons in internal armed conflicts. Similarly, they do not seem to crystallise a rule of customary law but can only be seen as part of progressive development.

Less than four years were needed for the ICC to reach sixty states parties. The ICC statute now has 104 states parties and has been in force since 1 July 2002. This represents strong evidence of *opinio juris*. The drafters of the ICC statute have always taken the view that the crimes which were to be included in the court's jurisdiction must reflect customary international law.[304] This latter point combined with the various declarations of states during the Rome conference carry a lot of weight and may lead one to conclude that if the ICC statute is not declaratory of pre-existing customary law when it establishes criminal responsibility for war crimes in internal armed conflicts, it might be seen as crystallising such a rule now that it has entered into force.

2.2 Practice of international organisations

2.2.1 UN Security Council resolutions

As the ICJ highlighted in the Nicaragua case and more recently in the Nuclear Weapons advisory opinion,[305] General Assembly or Security Council resolutions 'can provide evidence important for establishing the existence of a rule of the emergence of an opinio juris'.[306] The Security Council has in fact been instrumental in developing the principle of individual responsibility for serious violations of the laws of war in internal armed conflicts, not only with the creation of the ICTY but particularly through its consistent practice. Ever since 1992, the Security Council has considered that serious violations of the laws of war committed in internal armed conflict engage the criminal responsibility of perpetrators.[307]

Since 1989, the Security Council has been deeply involved in many conflict situations, especially in internal armed conflicts thanks to an extensive interpretation of the notion of threat to peace and security. Serious violations of international humanitarian law, whether committed in internal or international conflicts, have been found capable of constituting a threat to international peace and security.[308] As highlighted in chapter 2, section 3 of this book, the Security Council seems to follow a four-step approach in dealing with internal armed conflicts. At the beginning of such conflicts, the Security Council starts by a general condemnation of the outbreak of violence and the killings. A second step is taken by the Council when the situation amounts to an armed conflict and, without defining the character of such conflict, the Council calls for the respect of human rights and humanitarian law. A third step consists of condemnations by the Council of various conduct initially qualified as serious humanitarian violations. The fourth step seems to come at a later stage of the conflict, when, for example, evidence appears of multiple violations of international humanitarian law. It consists of the affirmation that such conduct engages criminal responsibility of the authors in international law. Simultaneously, the Council calls for investigation of these violations by the states concerned and for the perpetrators to be brought to justice.

Such patterns are clearly discernible in the practice of the Security Council from 1989 to this day. Before 1989, the only mention that atrocities committed in internal armed conflict could be criminal, took place in Security Council resolution 521, which condemned the criminal massacre of Palestinian civilians in Beirut in 1982.[309] Not until the events in Yugoslavia in 1992, does the Security Council both condemn violations of the laws of war and regard such conduct as engaging the criminal responsibility of their authors.[310] Yet even at the beginning of the events in Yugoslavia, the Security Council was calling for the responsibility of individuals for grave breaches of the Geneva Conventions. As the conflict evolved, the Council condemned all violations of international humanitarian law and reaffirmed that those who commit or order the commission of such acts will be held criminally responsible for such acts.[311] Without ever mentioning the character of the conflicts as internal or international,[312] the Security Council has consistently reaffirmed, in subsequent internal armed conflicts, the criminal responsibility of all individuals who commit serious violations of the laws of war and the necessity for states to bring such persons to justice. Such practice took place during the following conflicts: ex-Yugoslavia,[313] Rwanda,[314] Somalia,[315] Liberia,[316] Angola,[317] Kosovo,[318] Burundi,[319] the Democratic Republic of the Congo,[320] Afghanistan,[321] Sierra Leone,[322] Georgia,[323] Ivory Coast,[324] East Timor[325] and Sudan.[326]

In other situations of a lesser magnitude, such as Albania,[327] Haiti,[328] Azerbaijan[329] and Guinea-Bissau,[330] the Security Council condemned the widespread violations of international humanitarian law but neither mentioned the criminal responsibility of the authors nor called for the states concerned to bring the perpetrators to justice.

Finally, it is important to note that the Security Council has recently adopted a number of resolutions of a general character on the protection of civilians in armed conflicts, which reiterate the core of its policy towards atrocities committed in armed conflicts: first, the Security Council consistently stresses that the perpetrators of crimes against humanity, crimes of genocide, war crimes and other serious violations of international humanitarian law are individually responsible and should be brought to justice.[331] Secondly, the Council emphasises that it is 'the responsibility of States to end impunity and to prosecute those responsible for war crimes or serious violations of international humanitarian law'.[332] The number of resolutions from the Security Council reveals an extensive and virtually uniform practice of the organisation, which clearly treats international and internal conflicts alike and hold individuals criminally responsible for serious violations of the laws of war committed in armed conflicts.

2.2.2 UN General Assembly resolutions
and Secretary-General reports

The reports from the UN Secretary-General often instigate the adoption of Security Council resolutions studied above and form an integral part of the practice of the UN. They can be seen as evidence of the law rather than a source of the law. In the report which lays down the foundations of the ICTY, the Secretary-General did not include common Article 3 or Protocol II among the rules of international humanitarian law which are beyond any doubt part of customary law and entail individual criminal responsibility.[333] However, in the case of Rwanda, the Secretary-General espoused the conclusions reached by the commission of experts and recommended to the Security Council that individuals who have perpetrated serious violations of international humanitarian law, in particular common Article 3 and Protocol II, as well as genocide and crimes against humanity, should be brought before an independent and impartial international criminal tribunal.[334] While commenting on the statute of the ICTR, the Secretary-General explained that it recognises for the first time the international criminality of serious violations of international humanitarian law committed in internal armed conflicts.[335] From then on, however, the Secretary-General repeatedly called for the criminal responsibility of individuals who have committed serious violations of the laws of war in internal armed conflicts such as in Burundi,[336] Kosovo,[337] the Democratic Republic of Congo,[338] East Timor,[339] Sierra Leone,[340] the Ivory Coast[341] and Sudan.[342] In the case of Sierra Leone, the Secretary-General negotiated an agreement with the Government of Sierra Leone in order to establish a statute for the Special Court for Sierra Leone.[343]

Since 1994, the Secretary-General of the UN has been at the forefront of the fight against impunity, calling for the prosecution of perpetrators of war crimes during internal armed conflicts.[344] A recent report of the Secretary-General on protection for humanitarian assistance to refugees and others in conflict situations provides a good summary of the position of the office of the Secretary-General:

> All those who violate international law must be brought to justice, whether they are State or non-State actors. States have primary responsibility for ensuring that those who violate humanitarian norms are prosecuted through the national criminal justice system or where appropriate through international criminal tribunals, including the International Criminal Court.[345]

The recent work of the General Assembly is also symptomatic of the position of the UN on violations of the laws of war in internal armed conflicts. The General Assembly has been concerned with the events unfolding in the Democratic Republic of Congo and constantly stressed that the occupying forces should be held accountable for violations of human rights and humanitarian law committed in the territories under their control.[346] Similarly, the General Assembly has urged all parties in the conflict in the Sudan 'to ensure that those responsible for violations of human rights and international humanitarian law are brought to justice'.[347]

2.2.3. The practice of the European Union

The European Union has frequently affirmed its support for the respect of international humanitarian principles during internal armed conflicts and emphasised the need to bring those responsible for humanitarian law and human rights violations to justice. The European Union took such a position on the humanitarian situation in Colombia,[348] the Democratic Republic of Congo,[349] Liberia[350] and in Burundi.[351] During the conflict in Sierra Leone, the Presidency on behalf of the European Union affirmed that:

> The accountability of individual perpetrators of grave human rights violations is important in ensuring a fair and equitable justice system and ultimately reconciliation and stability in Sierra Leone.[352]

Equally, during the conflict in East Timor, the European Union called on the Government of Indonesia to bring to justice those responsible for the attacks on international personnel and refugees[353] and recalled that:

> The international community, through the United Nations system has a responsibility to ensure that such violations are investigated and the perpetrators are brought to justice.[354]

The conflict in the Darfur region of Sudan prompted clear and unequivocal condemnation by the European Union of violations of the laws of war. The European Union stressed the need to end the climate of impunity by bringing to justice those responsible.[355] Recently, the European Union representative took the following view during debates within the Security Council:

> Perpetrators [of violations] of international humanitarian and human rights law must be brought to justice at the national level or, where not

possible, to international justice. The primary responsibility to carry that
out lies with each state.[356]

The declarations of the European Union are additional evidence of the
widespread acceptance and belief by states and international organisations that the perpetrators of serious violations of the laws of war in
internal armed conflicts must be held criminally responsible and
brought to justice.[357]

2.3 Conclusion

At the outset of this section, two main questions were put forward: was it
premature for the Appeals Chamber in the *Tadić* jurisdiction decision to
conclude in 1995 that serious violations of the laws of war committed in
internal conflicts amount to war crimes in customary international law?
If the answer to that question is positive, then does the state of customary law today allow us to conclude that this principle is now reflected in
customary international law?

When looking at national legislation implementing the 1949 Geneva
Conventions and Protocols as well as the ICC statute, a new trend is
clearly discernible in state practice. Serious violations of the laws of war
committed in internal armed conflicts, instead of being regarded as
purely domestic offences, as they were before the mid-1990s, are now
being treated as war crimes and included as such in criminal codes,
military criminal codes or military manuals by a great number of states.
This practice is far from being universal today[358] and cannot have
met the test of uniformity or consistency back in the early 1990s.
Information was found on ninety-nine states. Of these ninety-nine
states, fifty-four clearly decided to criminalise as war crimes the violations of the laws of war committed in internal armed conflicts.[359]
Another twelve states have adopted legislation, which could be interpreted as including war crimes committed in internal armed conflicts.
This group of states is likely to grow over the years, as states such as
Brazil, Austria, Greece, Kenya, Honduras, Ecuador and Mexico adopt
their draft ICC implementing legislation and amend their national
legislation in order to allow prosecutions for war crimes committed in
internal armed conflicts to take place in their countries.

The criminalisation by fifty-four states of serious violations of the
laws of war in internal armed conflicts can be regarded as amounting to
widespread practice. Furthermore, the numerous unilateral statements

of states in the Security Council or during the ICC conference, show that this practice is coupled with a strong belief by most states, that such conduct should be criminalised and individuals held responsible. Finally, the extensive practice of the Security Council, the Secretary-General and the European Union, as well as the adoption of such principles in a growing number of international treaties coupled with the case law of both the ICTY and the ICTR,[360] represent additional evidence of a recent but extensive practice accepted as law. However, a small group of states clearly took the view that war crimes committed in internal conflicts should not come within the jurisdiction of the ICC. Their statements in Rome should be interpreted as a clear rejection, from their point of view, of the application of this principle in internal conflicts. Indeed, India stated during the ICC conference: 'there could not be a homogeneous structure of treatment of international and non-international armed conflicts so long as sovereign states existed'.[361] While they may continue to oppose such a principle and be considered as persistent objectors, this might not prevent the crystallisation of a customary principle.

The practice, according to which serious violations of the laws of war committed in internal armed conflict amount to war crimes and engage individual criminal responsibility of the perpetrators, has developed only in the past fifteen years. No specific duration of practice is required for the creation of a customary norm, provided that 'the consistency and generality of a practice are proved'.[362] It is submitted that in 1995 state practice could not be seen to reflect a sufficiently extensive state practice accepted as law. Before 1990 only a handful of states treated these violations as war crimes when committed in internal armed conflicts.[363] It was therefore premature for the Appeals Chamber in the *Tadić* case to conclude that such a principle was established in customary law. Ironically, most of the subsequent practice highlighted in this work, such as the adoption of the ICC statute, the majority of national legislation and the unilateral statements by states, were made possible to a great extent only by virtue of the audacity of the ICTY Appeals Chamber in the *Tadić* case.

Extensive current evidence points to the existence of a customary principle in international law according to which individuals can be held responsible for war crimes committed in internal armed conflicts. The entry into force of the ICC statute, coupled with the extensive practice of states and international organisations accumulated so far, will reinforce the customary status of this principle and enhance the real possibility of enforcing it in international law.

3. Tentative list of war crimes in internal armed conflicts

The principle of individual criminal responsibility for war crimes committed in internal armed conflicts is reflected in customary law today. The next issue is to determine a possible list of war crimes applicable in internal armed conflicts. The claim advanced by the drafters of the ICC statute that the war crimes contained in the statute are all part of customary international law will be examined. Furthermore, might there be other crimes reflected in customary international law but not contained in the ICC statute? It is often difficult to find supporting state practice in national legislation for every single crime appearing in the ICC statute, but some general considerations and remarks can be made.

The list of war crimes in internal armed conflicts under the ICC statute contains many of the serious violations of common Article 3 as well as twelve other serious violations of the laws of war mainly borrowed from Protocol II and the Hague regulations. National legislation does not often qualify serious violations of common Article 3 as war crimes per se. The 1997 USA Expanded War Crimes Act and the German military manual of 1992 were among the only legislation before the adoption of the Rome statute explicitly to cite violations of common Article 3 in the list of war crimes or grave breaches. Since the adoption of the Rome statute, around fifteen ratifying states have implemented new legislation on the ICC, which qualify serious violations of common Article 3 as war crimes.

The number of legislative acts reproducing exactly the list of war crimes of the Rome statute is currently in the minority. The study of other national legislation and military manuals shows, however, that the majority of states criminalising violations of the laws of war in internal and international armed conflicts, have chosen to include most of the provisions listed in the ICC statute. The list of war crimes appearing in these criminal codes, military manuals or other legislation apply in time of armed conflicts, irrespective of whether they are internal or international, as demonstrated earlier in this chapter. This development has led to more uniformity between the list of war crimes in international and internal conflicts. Most legislation and many military manuals discussed here encompass the violations of the rules on the protection of the civilian population in their list of war crimes, as well as some provisions dealing with illegal means and methods of warfare. This is the case for the legislation of states such as Argentina,[364] Azerbaijan,[365] Belarus,[366] Serbia,[367] Bosnia-Herzegovina,[368] Slovenia,[369] Croatia,[370] Costa Rica,[371] the Congo,[372] Colombia,[373] Estonia,[374] El Salvador,[375] Georgia,[376] Jordan,[377] Lithuania,[378]

Moldova,[379] Russia,[380] Kazakhstan,[381] Latvia,[382] Norway,[383] Portugal,[384] Mozambique,[385] Ethiopia,[386] Finland,[387] Sweden,[388] Spain,[389] Niger,[390] Belgium,[391] France,[392] Poland,[393] Paraguay,[394] the Netherlands,[395] Rwanda,[396] the USA,[397] Switzerland[398] and Tajikistan.[399]

State practice, particularly evidenced by national legislation and military manuals, seems therefore to be consistent in considering as war crimes most of the rules appearing under Article 8.2.c) and e) of the ICC statute. Unilateral declarations of states during debates in the Security Council as well as during the Rome diplomatic conference mentioned in section 2 of this chapter, represent further evidence of the *opinio juris* of states as to the criminality in customary international law of the conducts listed in the ICC statute. The ICC list, however, might not reflect all the war crimes applicable in internal armed conflicts.

The various national legislation shows a tendency to consider that the use of the means and methods of warfare, including the use of certain illegal weapons in international law, amounts to war crimes if committed in internal armed conflicts. A number of criminal codes include not only pillaging, perfidy or destroying or seizing the property of an adversary, but also the use of such means and materials or weapons of mass destruction which are prohibited by an international treaty,[400] or means or methods of warfare which may cause superfluous injury or unnecessary suffering.[401] In Rome, however, there was opposition from some states to include the latter principle or any specific weapon in the list of war crimes applicable in internal conflicts.

Furthermore, a few provisions, which appear in the ICC statute, are not usually reflected in national legislation or military manuals. These provisions are those, which are included neither in Protocol II nor in the Hague regulations and which were not recognised as war crimes per se before the adoption of the Rome statute. The provision of the ICC statute under Article 8.2.e)iii) 'intentionally directing attacks against personnel, installations, material, units or vehicles involved in a humanitarian assistance or peacekeeping mission, as long as they are entitled to the protection given to civilians or civilian objects under the international law of armed conflicts', does not appear per se in the majority of this legislation. This crime, however, can be seen as an extension of the provision prohibiting attacks on civilians and persons *hors de combat*, prohibitions largely reflected in the great majority of national legislation studied. Similarly, Article 8.2.e)xii) 'conscripting or enlisting children under the age of 15 into armed forces or groups or using them to participate actively in hostilities', as well as the gender crime provisions such as rape, sexual slavery, enforced prostitution, forced pregnancy, enforced sterilisation and any other form of sexual violence, appear in parts in Protocol II but are conducts not specifically included in the majority of national legislation.

Further evidence of state practice and *opinio juris* can be found in the practice of international organisations, such as the UN Security Council resolutions. Over the past fifteen years the Security Council consistently considered that serious violations of international humanitarian law committed in internal armed conflicts amount to war crimes and individuals should be individually accountable for conduct such as:

– The indiscriminate attacks against the civilian population
– Mass forcible expulsion and deportation of civilians and the practice of 'ethnic cleansing'
– Rape and detention of women
– Attacks on UN personnel, as non-military objectives
– Attacks on 'safe areas' and undefended towns.[402]

It is interesting to note that only some of the above-listed crimes, which are included in so many Security Council resolutions, are included in the ICC statute. The crimes of launching indiscriminate attacks, which would result in death or injury to civilians or attacks, which cause excessive incidental civilian loss, injury or damage were included in the draft ICC statute but did not receive enough support to be included in Article 8.2.e) of the statute.[403] Similarly, attacks on safe areas and undefended towns are related to the general prohibition of launching attacks against civilian objects, a crime which does not appear in the ICC statute.

Judicial decisions are considered to be subsidiary means for the determination of rules of law but clearly participate in the creation of customary norms. The case law of both International Criminal Tribunals is illustrative of the content of customary law in this area. It also greatly influenced the positions of states during the negotiations of the Rome statute, as to whether serious violations of the laws of war amount to war crimes in internal armed conflicts and as to which serious violations amount to war crimes in customary law and should therefore be included in the statute. In its seminal *Tadić* jurisdiction decision, the Appeals Chamber affirmed:

> Customary international law imposes criminal liability for serious viola-
> tions of common Article 3, as supplemented by other general principles
> or rules on the protection of victims of internal armed conflicts, and for

breaching certain fundamental principles and rules regarding means and methods of combat in civil strife.[404]

Following the footsteps of the *Tadić* jurisdiction decision, the Appeals Chamber and the Trial Chambers of both the ICTY and ICTR have established the customary law status and convicted individuals for the following war crimes in internal armed conflicts:

– Serious violations of common Article 3, in particular murder,[405] torture,[406] cruel treatment[407] and outrages upon personal dignity[408]
– Serious violations of Additional Protocol II, in particular murder, cruel treatment, torture, outrages upon personal dignity, in particular rape,[409] slavery,[410] pillage[411] and attacks against the civilian population[412]
– Wanton destruction of cities, towns or villages, or devastation not justified by military necessity, recognised under Article 3b) of the ICTY statute and Article 23g) of the Hague regulations[413]
– Attacks on civilian objects[414]
– Seizure of, destruction or wilful damage done to institutions dedicated to religion, recognised under Article 3d) of the ICTY statute and Article 27 of the Hague regulations.[415]

Both International Criminal Tribunals have reiterated on numerous occasions that violations of common Article 3 entail individual criminal responsibility in customary international law.[416] In 2001, the Appeals Chamber studied the claims of the appellants, that the 'evidence presented in the *Tadić* jurisdiction decision does not establish that common Article 3 is customary international law that creates individual criminal responsibility because there is no showing of state practice and opinio juris'.[417] After reviewing international and national practice, the Appeals Chamber found no cogent reasons to depart from the conclusions of the *Tadić* jurisdiction decision[418] and stated:

> The Appeals Chamber is in no doubt that the acts enumerated in common Article 3 were intended to be criminalised in 1949, as they were clearly intended to be illegal within the international legal order . . .[419] The Appeals Chamber is unable to find any reason of principle why, once the application of rules of international humanitarian law came to be extended (albeit in an attenuated form) to the context of internal armed conflicts, their violation in that context could not be criminally enforced at the international level.[420]

Of particular interest is the statement made by the Trial Chamber in the *Čelibići* case concerning the customary law nature of the Hague regulations:

> The Trial Chamber finds that both the substantive prohibitions in common Article 3 of the Geneva Conventions, and the provisions of the Hague Regulations, constitute rules of customary international law which may by applied by the International Tribunal to impose individual criminal responsibility for the offences alleged in the Indictment.[421]

Trial Chambers of the ICTY have established since that both Article 3b) (wanton destruction of cities) and Article 3d) of the statute (destruction of religious buildings) entail individual criminal responsibility in internal armed conflicts.[422]

Furthermore, Trial Chambers of the ICTR have taken the view that Article 4(2) of additional Protocol II was reflected in customary law and engaged individual criminal responsibility in customary international law in a number of judgments.[423] To date, only two indictees were found guilty of war crimes committed in internal armed conflicts by the ICTR.[424] One may also note that neither tribunal has so far convicted individuals for the use of prohibited weapons in internal armed conflicts.

Lastly, one might note the list of war crimes applicable in internal armed conflicts appearing in the work undertaken by the ICRC to determine the content of customary international law in the laws of armed conflicts.[425] The list produced by the ICRC contained all the war crimes included in the ICC statute together with the following other serious violations of international humanitarian law:

- The use of prohibited weapons
- Launching an indiscriminate attack resulting in death or injury to civilians
- Making non-defended localities and demilitarised zones the objects of attack
- Using human shields
- Slavery
- Collective punishments
- Using starvation of civilians as a method of warfare.

In conclusion, the practice and *opinio juris* of states as well as the practice of international organisations and judicial institutions highlighted clearly show that the principle of individual criminal responsibility for war crimes in internal armed conflicts is recognised in international customary law for most of the conduct listed in Article 8.2c) and e) of the ICC statute together with other provisions dealing with the means and methods of warfare, in particular indiscriminate attacks and attacks against civilian objects.

Notes

1. T. Meron, 'International criminalisation of internal atrocities' (1995) 89 *AJIL* 561. Similarly, C. Greenwood affirmed: 'If violations of the international laws of war have traditionally been regarded as criminal under international law, there is no reason of principle why once those laws came to be extended to the context of internal conflict, their violation in that context should not have been criminal, at least in the absence of a clear indication to the contrary'. See C. Greenwood, 'International humanitarian law and the *Tadić* case' (1996) 7 *EJIL* 280.

2. The oldest example of an individual being tried and convicted of breaches of the laws of war in 'internal armed conflicts' is certainly the case of Captain Henry Witz, for the unlawful treatment of Union prisoners of war at Andersonville during the US civil war. See R. Falk, *The international law of civil war* (Baltimore: John Hopkins Press, 1971) pp. 61 and 73.

3. Preliminary remarks of the ICRC, 25 March 1993, unpublished. Similarly, in 1990 D. Plattner affirmed: 'the rules creating individual responsibility in international law for violations of the international humanitarian law in internal armed conflicts still remained to be created'. See D. Plattner, 'The penal repression of violations of international humanitarian law applicable in non-international armed conflicts' (1990) 30 *IRRC* 424.

4. Final report of the Commission of Experts, UN.Doc.S/1994/674, paras. 12, 13, 15–16. The Commission of Experts concluded in para. 52: 'it must be observed that the violations of the law or customs of war ... are offences when committed in international, but not in internal armed conflicts'. See also the first interim report of the Commission of Experts for Yugoslavia, UN.Doc.S/25274 para. 47.

5. See UN.Doc.S/25704 (3 May 1993) paras. 33–35.

6. See UN.Doc.S/1995/134, para. 12

7. *Tadić* jurisdiction decision, para. 134.

8. *Akayesu* trial, para. 615.

9. This was the view of the Italian delegate, M. Maresca, see 1949 Final Records, vol. II, section B, p. 48.

10. See the view expressed by the *rapporteur* of the Special Committee, M. Bolla: 'Le Comité spécial a été très nettement d'avis que les dispositions des Conventions ne sont, en principe, pas applicables à la guerre civile, et que seules certaines dispositions expressément mentionnées sont applicables à de tels conflits.' 1949 Final Records, vol. II, section B, p. 36.

11. See, for example, the fourth report of the Special Committee to the mixed Commission, where it is made clear that the grave breaches regime was only applicable for the gravest violations in international conflicts. *Ibid.*, pp. 109–13.

12. See Article 5, persons whose liberty has been restricted, and Article 6, penal prosecutions of Protocol II.

13. See *Official records of the diplomatic conference on the reaffirmation and development of international humanitarian law applicable in armed conflicts, Geneva (1974–1977)* (Bern, 1978) CCDH/I/SR/33, vol. VIII, p. 376 (hereafter referred to as *1974–1977 Official Records*).

14. See B. Röling, 'Aspects of the criminal responsibility for violations of the laws of war' in A. Cassesse (ed.), *The new humanitarian law of armed conflicts* (Naples: Editoriale Scientifica, 1979) pp. 199–231; Y. Sandoz, 'Implementing international humanitarian law' in UNESCO, *International dimensions of humanitarian law* (Dordrecht: Henry Dunant Institute, UNESCO, Martinus Nijhoff, 1988) pp. 259–82, see also L. Reydams, 'Universal jurisdiction over atrocities in Rwanda' (1996) 1 *European journal of crime, criminal law and criminal justice* 18–47. For a different conclusion, see G. Draper, 'The Geneva Conventions of 1949', p. 98, who concluded: 'Individuals who violate the prohibitions (of article 3) have violated international law for which they are individually answerable in a penal forum either of the Government or of the rebel faction.'

15. For an illustration of the absence of prosecutions of war criminals in internal armed conflicts up to the 1990s, see Perna, *The formation of the treaty law of non-international armed conflicts*, pp. 139–43.

16. Numerous articles have been written about the ICTY, see in particular, A. Pellet, 'Le tribunal criminel international pour l'ex-Yougoslavie: poudre aux yeux ou avancée décisive?' (1995) *RGDIP* 7; E. David, 'Le tribunal international pénal pour l'ex-Yougoslavie' (1992) *Revue belge de droit international* 565; G. Aldrich, 'Jurisdiction of the ICTY' (1996) 90 *AJIL* 64; P. Akhavan, 'Justice in the Hague, peace in the former Yugoslavia? A commentary on the UN War Crimes Tribunal' (1998) 20 *Human rights quarterly* 737; J. Paust, 'Applicability of international criminal laws to events in the former Yugoslavia' (1994) 9 *The American University journal of international law and policy* 499; P. Weckel, 'L'institution d'un tribunal international pour la repression des crimes de droit humanitaire en Yougoslavie' (1993) 39 *AFDI* 232; J. De Hemptinne, 'La poursuite et le jugement des hauts responsables politiques et militaires par le tribunal pénal international pour l'ex-Yougoslavie' (1997) *Revue de droit penal et de criminologie* 988.

17. See Articles 2–4 and 5 of the ICTY statute. Article 2 spells out all the grave breaches of the Geneva Conventions 1949 and Article 3 contains an illustrative list of violations of the laws of war, including crimes such as: employment of poisonous weapons, wanton destruction of cities, attack of undefended towns, or plunder of public or private property.

18. See, for example, UN SC resolution 763 (13 July 1992).

19. See report of the Secretary-General pursuant to para. 2 of the SC resolution 808, UN.Doc.S/25704 (3 May 1993), para. 10.

20. For a fine analysis of the nature of the conflict and the role played by the Security Council, see C. Gray, 'Bosnia and Herzegovina: civil war or inter-state conflict? Characterization and consequences' (1996) 67 *BYIL* 171.

21. Report of the Secretary-General pursuant to para. 2 of the SC resolution 808, UN.Doc.S/25704 (3 May 1993), para. 34.

22. Similarly, when commenting on Article 3 of the statute, the Secretary-General only referred to the 1907 Hague Convention IV, as the main source of authority establishing the criminality of these violations.

23. The Secretary-General notes in his report to the Security Council that 'it is clearly intended to convey the notion that no judgment as to the international or internal character of the conflict is being exercised'. See report of the Secretary-General pursuant to para. 2 of the SC resolution 808, UN.Doc.S/25704 (3 May 1993), para. 62.

24. Statement of the US representative to the UN Security Council during debates on the adoption of the ICTY statute, see Provisional verbatim record of meeting of the Security Council, 25 May 1993, UN.Doc.S/PV.3217 p. 15. Similarly, the French representative stated that: 'the expression "laws or customs of war" used in article 3 of the statute covers specifically all the obligations that flow from the humanitarian agreements in force on the territory of the former Yugoslavia at the time when the offences were committed', *ibid.*, p. 11. See also the UK statement, p. 19 and the Hungarian statement, p. 20.

25. *Tadić* jurisdiction decision, para. 77.

26. *Tadić* jurisdiction decision, paras. 71, 80 and 84.

27. *Ibid.*, para. 87.

28. *Ibid.*, para. 89.

29. *Ibid.*, para. 134. The customary nature of this principle is studied in section 2 of this chapter.

30. See section 2 of this chapter.

31. See in general, P. Akhavan, 'The International Criminal Tribunal for Rwanda: the politics and pragmatics of punishment' (1996) 90 *AJIL* 501; L. Sunga, 'The first indictments of the ICTR' (1997) 18 *Human rights law journal* 329; M. Mubiala, 'Le tribunal international pour le Rwanda (1995) 7 *African journal of international and comparative law* 610; D. Shraga, R. Zacklin, 'The International Criminal Tribunal for Rwanda' (1996) 7 *EJIL* 501.

32. The Security Council has consistently reaffirmed this principle, see for example, UN SC resolution 935 (1 July 1994).

33. Preliminary report of the independent Commission of Experts, UN.Doc.S/1994/1125 (4 October 1994) paras. 91 and 107.

34. The question of criminality for violations of common Article 3 and Protocol II was not explicitly covered by the Commission of Experts in its report. The Commission took the view that individual responsibility for war crimes has been firmly established in international law, but was silent as to the applicability of this principle in internal conflicts. See Preliminary report of the independent Commission of Experts, UN.Doc.S/1994/1125 (4 October 1994) paras. 125–28.

35. Article 4 contains a list of violations of common Article 3 and Protocol II, which shall include but not be limited to: violence to life, health and physical or mental

well-being of persons, in particular, murder, cruel treatment such as torture, mutilation or any form of corporal punishment; collective punishment; taking of hostages; acts of terrorism; outrages upon personal dignity, in particular humiliating and degrading treatment, rape, enforced prostitution and any form of indecent assault; pillage; the passing of sentence and the carrying out of executions without pervious judgment pronounced by a regularly constituted court; threats to commit any of the foregoing acts.

36. Secretary-General report pursuant to para. 5 of SC Res.955, UN.Doc.S/1995/134 (13 February 1995) para. 11.

37. *Ibid.*, para. 12.

38. *Ibid.*

39. In a footnote to para. 12 of this report (footnote 8), the Secretary-General tries to dismiss this criticism by adding: 'although the question of whether common Article 3 entails the individual responsibility of the perpetrator of the crime is still debatable, some of the crimes included therein, when committed against the civilian population, also constituted crimes against humanity and as such are customarily recognised as entailing the criminal responsibility of the individual'.

40. See UN.Doc.E/CN.4/1995/7 (28 June 1994) para. 54.

41. *Tadić* jurisdiction decision, para. 134.

42. *Akayesu* trial, paras. 616–17. The applicability in customary international law of the principle of individual responsibility for serious violations of the laws of war in internal armed conflicts will be dealt with in section 2 of this chapter.

43. See Article 20 of the ILC draft statute for an International Criminal Court, *Report of the International Law Commission on the work of its forty-sixth session*, UN.Doc.A/49/10 (1994) pp. 29–140.

44. *Ibid.*, pp. 78–81.

45. See *ibid.*, p. 80. Meron argued that as Article 20 of the draft statute reflects Article 22 of the draft code of crimes, it should be seen as applicable both in international and internal conflicts. See Meron, 'International criminalisation of internal atrocities' 574. According to C. Greenwood, the ILC deliberately left the question open. See Greenwood, 'International humanitarian law and the *Tadić* case' 270–75. It is interesting to note that, in 1996, the ILC adopted a draft code of crimes against peace and mankind which included, as war crimes, a list of violations of international humanitarian law in internal armed conflicts: common Article 3 and Article 4 of Protocol II (Article 20). See UN.Doc.A/CN.4/L.522 (31 May 1996).

46. See D. Robinson and H. v. Hebel, 'War crimes in internal armed conflicts: article 8 of the ICC Statute' (1999) 2 *YbIHL* 193.

47. *Ibid.*, 198.

48. See 1995 Ad hoc Committee report on the establishment of an international criminal court, UN.Doc.A/50/22 (1995), para. 74 as well as 1996 Preparatory

Committee report on the establishment of an international criminal court, UN.Doc.A/51/22 (1996) para. 78.

49. UN.Doc.A/51/22 (1996) para. 78.

50. *Ibid.*

51. See 1995 Ad hoc Committee report on the establishment of an international criminal court, para. 74 and 1996 Preparatory Committee report on the establishment of an international criminal court, para. 78.

52. *Ibid.*, para. 78. These states also argued that giving competence to the ICC over internal armed conflicts would violate the principle of complementarity and would undermine the general acceptability of the statute.

53. This minority consisted of China, India, several Arab states, the Russian Federation and Turkey.

54. See the draft statute for the International Criminal Court, UN.Doc.A/CONF.183/2/Add.1 (14 April 1998). The proposals contained in the draft statute were elaborated on the basis of two proposals. The proposal from New Zealand and Switzerland reflected a working paper prepared by the ICRC and contained the violations of common Article 3 as well as other norms. See UN.Doc.A/AC.249/1997/WG.1/DP.2 The second proposal was from the USA, which only included violations of common Article 3 in internal conflicts. See UN.Doc.A/AC.249/1997/WG.1/DP.1.

55. Out of 162 states voting, 120 voted for, 7 against and 20 states abstained.

56. It is important to note that the ICC will have jurisdiction over war crimes committed in international or internal armed conflict 'in particular when committed as part of a plan or policy or as part of a large scale commission of such crimes'. See Article 8.1 ICC statute. See in general D. Robinson and H. v. Hebel, 'War crimes in internal conflicts: article 8 of the ICC statute' 193; D. Momtaz, 'War crimes in non-international armed conflicts under the statute of the International Criminal Court' (1999) 2 *YbIHL* 177; Cryer, *Prosecuting international crimes*, pp. 281–83.

57. The statute contains the exact wording of common Article 3, as it appears in the 1949 Geneva Conventions.

58. See Article 8.2.e) of the ICC statute. These provisions are applicable to 'armed conflicts that take place in the territory of a state when there is protracted armed conflict between governmental authorities and organised armed groups or between such groups.' See Article 8.2.f) of the statute.

59. *Tadić* jurisdiction decision, para. 119.

60. *Ibid.*

61. Robinson and von Hebel add: 'in selecting the norms, the approach adopted by states was to identify those provisions applicable in international conflicts which are so fundamental in character that they must be considered applicable in internal armed conflicts as well', Robinson and von Hebel, 'War crimes in internal

conflicts: article 8 of the ICC statute' 200. The issue whether the principle of individual criminal responsibility for war crimes in internal conflicts is established in customary law is studied in section 2 of this chapter.

62. In the ICC statute, every single offence which constitutes a war crime in internal armed conflict is equally a war crime in international armed conflict. The contrary is not true, the list of war crimes in international armed conflicts being more extensive (twenty-six offences instead of twelve). In 1995 and 1996, views were expressed during the negotiations that a single list of war crimes should be applicable in internal and international armed conflicts. This suggestion was soon rejected.

63. Article 8.2.e)xii excludes situations where the children are not directly engaged in the fighting but are in charge of support or logistic tasks. It is possibly the crime whose customary law status is the more dubious out of the list of crimes in the ICC statute. On this point, see the statute for the Special Court for Sierra Leone, in section 2.3.

64. Robinson and von Hebel, 'War crimes in internal armed conflicts: article 8 of the ICC statute' 202. In contrast, it is interesting to note the position of Professor Meron in 1994: 'Whether the conflicts in Yugoslavia are characterized as internal or international is critically important. The fourth Hague Convention of 1907, which codified the principal laws of war and served as the normative core for the post-World War II war crimes prosecutions, applies to international wars only.' T. Meron, 'War crimes in Yugoslavia and the development of international law' (1994) 88 *AJIL* 78 at 80.

65. See Article 9 of the 1994 Convention on the Safety of UN and Associated Personnel, reprinted in (1995) 34 *ILM* 482.

66. See H. von Hebel and D. Robinson, 'Crimes within the jurisdiction of the Court' in R. Lee (ed.), *The International Criminal Court: the making of the Rome statute; issues, negotiations and results* (The Hague: Kluwer Law International, 1999) p. 110.

67. This issue is studied in section 2 of this chapter.

68. See UN.Doc.A/CONF.183/C.1/L.59, p. 8 (10 July 1998).

69. This text was originally put forward by the delegation of Sierra Leone, see UN.Doc.A/CONF.183/C.1/L.62 (13 July 1998).

70. This has been suggested by some commentators, see for example, L. Condorelli, 'War crimes and internal armed conflicts in the statute of the ICC' in M. Politi and G. Nesi, *The Rome statute of the International Criminal Court, a challenge to impunity* (Aldershot: Ashgate, 2001) pp. 112–13, Bothe, 'War crimes' p. 423 or J. F. Queguiner, 'Dix ans après la création du tribunal pénal international pour l'ex-Yougoslavie: évaluation de l'apport de sa jurisprudence au droit international humanitaire' (2003) 85 *IRRC* 279–81.

71. This definition, having been included in reaction to the threshold of Protocol II, does not require at all the proof that an armed group exercises control over part of

the territory. The term 'protracted' refers to a certain duration of hostilities and the term 'organised armed groups' only requires that these groups have a minimum of organisation under a responsible command.

72. Certain authors qualify this state of fact as 'regressions behind the customary standard'. See Kress, 'War crimes committed in non-international armed conflict' 134–36. See also H. Spieker, 'The International Criminal Court and non-international armed conflicts' (2000) 13 *Leiden journal of international law* 395–425 at 417–23; L. Condorelli, 'War crimes and internal conflicts in the statute of the International Criminal Court' pp. 107–17; M. Bothe, 'War crimes' in Cassese, Gaeta and Jones (eds.), *The Rome statute of the International Criminal Court: a commentary*, vol. I (Oxford: Oxford University Press, 2002) pp. 379–426 at 417–21 and A. Cassese, *International criminal law* (Oxford: Oxford University Press, 2003) pp. 59–62.

73. See in general on this point, Momtaz, 'War crimes in non-international armed conflicts under the statute of the International Criminal Court', pp. 186–88. Furthermore, one may notice that not all the violations of Article 4 of Protocol II, which are part of the ICTR subject matter jurisdiction, are included in the ICC statute. Collective punishments and acts of terrorism were not selected by the drafters of the ICC statute. (Article 4.2.b) and d))

74. For more details, see section 3.5 in chapter 2 of this book.

75. See the proposals put forward, for example, by India UN.Doc.A/CONF.183/C.1/L.72 (14 July 1998) and L.94 (17 July 1998) and by the Ukraine UN.Doc.183/C.1/L.33 (30 June 1998). The members of the non-aligned movement as well as the Arab group were strongly in favour of the inclusion of nuclear weapons and other weapons of mass destruction, see debates in the Committee of the Whole, UN Diplomatic Conference on the Establishment of an ICC, 17 and 18 June 1998. UN.Doc.A/CONF.183/C.1/SR.4. Similarly, the absence of any weapons of mass destruction among those whose use was banned as a war crime was a reason put forward by India to explain its rejection of the overall statute, see UN.Doc.A/CONF.183/C.1/SR.9.

76. See, in particular, the intervention of the USA representative to the Committee of the Whole during the Rome diplomatic conference on 17 June 1998, see UN.Doc.A/CONF.183/C.1/SR.4, p. 9, para. 53; as well as the French and the Russian intervention on 18 June 1998. See UN.Doc.A/CONF.183/C.1/SR.5 paras. 28 and 36. See also the view taken by the UK Government during debates in the House of Commons on 9 July 1998: 'we support proposals for the court to be able to try war crimes which are recognised under customary law. Despite the wide ratification of the Ottawa Convention, the use of anti-personnel land mines does not at present come into that category' (1998) *BYIL* 603.

77. The view was also expressed that the difficulties for a soldier to distinguish between an internal armed conflict and internal disturbances render the inclusion of the prohibition of certain weapons in internal armed conflicts very difficult.

78. For more details on this issue, see the remarks made in section 3.5 of chapter 2.

79. One might notice the adjunction of buildings dedicated to education, science or charitable purposes in the list of buildings that shall not be subject to attacks, provided they are not military objectives.

80. This is the case for some gender crimes, such as forced pregnancy, as well as the crime appearing in Article 8.2.e)iii) of the statute and the crime of conscripting or enlisting children into armed conflicts under Article 8.2.e)vii).

81. These crimes are, in particular, the prohibition against civilian objects, the use of certain weapons and certain methods of warfare, included in international armed conflicts, but not in internal armed conflicts. The potential harmful impact that the ICC statute could have on progressive development is somewhat recognised by Article 10 of the statute, which provides: 'nothing in this part shall be interpreted or prejudicing in any way existing or developing rules of international law for purposes other than this Statute'.

82. G. Abi-Saab, 'The concept of war crimes' p. 118. C. Bassiouni described well the negotiative process which led to the adoption of the ICC statute: 'the ICC was an exercise of political feasibility, not progressive codification', see C. Bassiouni, 'The normative framework of international humanitarian law: overlaps, gaps and ambiguities' (1998) 8 *Transnational law and contemporary problems* 199.

83. This list is, however, an exhaustive one. It cannot be broadened through interpretation by the court itself, contrary to the formula contained in Article 3 of the ICTY statute which reads: 'such violations shall include but not be limited to . . .' See Condorelli, 'War crimes in internal conflicts in the statute of the ICC' p. 112.

84. The Special Court for Sierra Leone was created by an international treaty between the UN and the Government of Sierra Leone. It exists outside the Sierra Leonean judiciary system. Other internationalised or hybrid courts and tribunals, however, form an integral part of the domestic judiciary and were created by the occupying power (for the Iraqi Special Tribunal), the UN civil administration (for Kosovo and East Timor) or by national governments with the help of the UN or the international community (Special Chamber of the state court of Bosnia-Herzegovina and Extraordinary Chambers within the domestic court structure of Cambodia). Some of these institutions (the Iraqi Special Tribunals and the special panels of the district court of Dili) have jurisdiction over war crimes in internal armed conflicts, as defined in other international instruments studied such as the ICC treaty, together with domestic crimes. All of these 'internationalised' courts or tribunals are studied in chapter 4 of this book.

85. See UN.SC res.1315 (14 August 2000).

86. For a commentary on the Special Court, see A. McDonald, 'Sierra Leone's shoestring Special Court' (2002) *IRRC* 121; O. Y. Elagab, 'The Special Court for Sierra Leone: some constraints' (2004) 8 *International journal of human rights* 249–73; N. K. Stafford, 'A model war crimes court: Sierra Leone' (2003) 10 *ILSA journal of international and comparative law* 117–42; P. Pazartzis, 'Tribunaux pénaux

internationlisés: une nouvelle approche de la justice pénale (inter)nationale?', (2003) *AFDI* 641–61; Cryer, *Prosecuting international crimes*, pp. 61–65; H. B. Jallow, 'The legal framework of the Special Court for Sierra Leone' in Ambos and Othman (eds.), *New approaches in international criminal justice: Kosovo, East Timor, Sierra Leone and Cambodia* (Freiburg: Edition iuscrim, 2003) pp. 149–71.

87. See SG report UN.Doc.S/2000/915 (4 October 2000) para. 9. For the adopted text of the statute, see UN.Doc.S/2002/246. The court is of mixed composition as each Trial Chamber is composed of three judges, of whom one shall be appointed by the Government of Sierra Leone and two by the Secretary-General of the UN. The Appeals Chamber is composed of five judges, of whom two shall be appointed by the Government of Sierra Leone and three by the Secretary-General of the UN (Article 12 of the statute). One may also note that unlike the ICTY and ICTR, which are funded by assessed contributions of UN member states, the Special Court is funded by voluntary contributions of states. The Appeals Chamber rejected a preliminary motion filed by the accused Sam Hinga Norman, in which it was argued that the funding of the Special Court by voluntary contributions of interested states deprived the court of the necessary guarantees of independence and impartiality. See *Prosecutor v. Sam Hinga Norman*, case No. SCSL-2004-14-AR72(E), Decision on preliminary motion based on lack of jurisdiction (13 March 2004).

88. Article 1 of the statute of the Special Court for Sierra Leone. The temporal jurisdiction of the Special Court was a controversial issue. It is accepted that the internal armed conflict in Sierra Leone started on 23 March 1991, when the Revolutionary United Front (RUF) armed rebel group entered the country from Liberia. The Secretary-General, however, chose 30 November 1996 as the starting date for the jurisdiction of the Special Court to avoid overburdening the prose-cutor and to encompass the most serious crimes committed in Sierra Leone during the 1990s. For a criticism of this choice, see Elagab, 'The Special Court for Sierra Leone' 268–69 and Stafford, 'A model war crimes court' 126–27.

89. See Articles 2–3 and 4 of the statute.

90. Article 5 of the statute spells out some offences relating to the abuse of girls under the Prevention and Cruelty Children Act 1926 and some other offences relating to the wanton destruction of property under the Malicious Damage Act 1861. See Elagab, 'The Special Court for Sierra Leone' 267–68.

91. This choice, made by the UN Secretary-General, was criticised by commentators who take the view that sexual violence was perpetrated along ethnic lines and these acts could amount to genocide. See Elagab, 'The Special Court for Sierra Leone' 257.

92. Persons between the age of fifteen and eighteen found guilty of one or more crimes falling within the jurisdiction of the Special Court will not be subject to incarceration. See SG report UN.Doc.S/2000/915 (4 October 2000) paras. 32–38. The prosecutor of the Special Court has, however, stated that he will 'not

prosecute children over the age of 15 because they do not bear the greatest responsibility', reported in Stafford, 'A model war crimes court' 128.

93. See Article 10 of the statute. This article runs counter to the 1999 Lomé Peace Agreement which provides a general amnesty for nearly all those responsible for the atrocities committed in Sierra Leone since 1991. See the interesting decisions from the Special Court on this issue, *Prosecutor v. Morris Kallon and Brima Buzzy Kamara*, case No. SCSL-2004-15-AR72(E) and SCSL-2004-16-AR72(E), Decision on challenge to jurisdiction: Lomé accord amnesty (13 March 2004). The Appeals Chamber took the view that 'there is a crystallising international norm that a government cannot grant amnesty for serious violations of crimes under international law' and that the Lomé peace agreement cannot constitute a legal bar to the prosecution of the accused in front of the special court. For a commentary on these, see S. Meisenberg, 'Legality of amnesties in international humanitarian law: the Lomé amnesty decision of the Special Court for Sierra Leone' (2004) 86 *IRRC* 837–51.

94. In relation to crimes against humanity, the definition appearing under this statute is inspired by the ICTR statute, with the notable addition of the list of gender crimes borrowed from the ICC statute definition of crimes against humanity (with the omission of the crime of forced sterilisation).

95. Article 3 of the statute gives jurisdiction over serious violations of common Article 3 and Protocol II. The article then gives an illustrative list of such violations. Article 3 is identical to Article 4 of the ICTR statute.

96. Whereas the two first offences are borrowed directly from the ICC statute, the last of these offences, abducting and forcing recruitment of children under fifteen, is drafted differently from the ICC statute.

97. SG report UN.Doc.S/2000/915 (4 October 2000) para. 12.

98. *Ibid.*, paras. 17–18.

99. See *Prosecutor v. Sam Hinga Norman*, case No. SCSL-2004-14-AR72(E), Decision on preliminary motion based on lack of jurisdiction (31 May 2004). For a commentary on this decision, see M. Pack, 'Developments at the Special Court for Sierra Leone' (2005) 4 *Law and practice of international courts and tribunals* 171–92.

100. *Ibid.*, paras. 30–51. Justice G. Robertson filed a dissenting opinion to this decision, finding that 'the crime of non-forcible enlistment did not enter international criminal law until the Rome Treaty in July 1998'.

101. This protocol is annexed to the GA resolution 54/263, adopted on 25 May 2000.

102. See in particular Elagab, 'The Special Court for Sierra Leone' 255.

103. As seen in section 2.2, it is important to remember that certain serious violations of the laws of war were not included in the subject matter jurisdiction of the court, either for political reasons, or because they were found not serious enough to fall within the jurisdiction of the court. They could nonetheless be considered as war crimes in internal armed conflicts.

104. See Article 7 of the 1993 Convention on the Prohibition of Development, Production, Stockpiling and Use of Chemical Weapons.

105. See Article 14.2 which provides: 'The measures envisaged in paragraph 1 of this article include appropriate measures to ensure the imposition of penal sanctions against persons who, in relation to an armed conflict and contrary to the provisions of this protocol, willfully kill or cause serious injury to civilians and to bring such persons to justice.'

106. It is interesting to note that Protocol IV to the 1980 Convention on Blinding Laser Weapons does not include any enforcement provisions.

107. An example of implementation of such obligation is the UK Land Mines Act 1998, which makes it a criminal offence, punishable by up to fourteen years' imprisonment, for any person to engage in any activity prohibited by the Ottawa Convention.

108. Article 9.2 of the 1994 Convention on the Safety of UN and Associated Personnel.

109. See Articles 15, 17 and 22 of the Second Protocol to the Hague Convention of 1954 for the Protection of Cultural Property in the Event of Armed Conflict (26 March 1999), available online on www.icrc.org.

110. See Robinson and von Hebel, 'War crimes in internal armed conflicts: article 8 of the ICC Statute' 208.

111. *The trial of major war criminals: proceedings of the International Military Tribunal sitting at Nuremberg*, part 22, pp. 445–47, cited in the *Tadić* jurisdiction decision, para. 128.

112. *Tadić* jurisdiction decision, para. 128.

113. *Ibid.*, paras. 132–33.

114. On these points see M. Sassoli, 'La première décision de la chambre d'appel du Tribunal Pénal International pour l'ex-Yougoslavie' (1996) 100 *RGDIP* 129; Greenwood, 'International humanitarian law and the *Tadić* case' 278 who affirms: 'it is also doubtful whether the practice discussed in this part of the Decision really sustains some of the inferences drawn from it'; S. Ratner and J. Abrams, *Accountability for human rights atrocities in international law* (Oxford: Oxford University Press, 1997) pp. 95–99.

115. Judge Li dissenting opinion, *Tadić* jurisdiction decision, para. 13.

116. G. Aldrich, 'The laws of war on land' (2000) 94 *AJIL* 61. Others have criticised this part of the decision for different reasons: see T. Meron, 'The continuing role of custom in the formation of international humanitarian law' (1996) 90 *AJIL* 242.

117. C. Greenwood, 'International humanitarian law and the *Tadić* case' 282.

118. On the importance of military manuals and national legislation as evidence of state practice, see the *Tadić* jurisdiction decision, para. 99.

119. The importance of statements of states was highlighted by R. Baxter: 'The firm statement by the State of what it considers to be the rules is far better evidence of its position than what can be pieced together from the actions of that country at

different times and in a variety of contexts.' See Baxter, 'Multilateral treaties as evidence of customary international law' (1965–66) 41 *BYIL* 300.

120. As highlighted in the *Nicaragua* case and in the *Nuclear Weapon* advisory opinion, the International Court of Justice believes that General Assembly or Security Council resolutions 'can provide evidence important for establishing the existence of a rule or the emergence of an *opinio juris*'. See *Advisory opinion on the legality of the threat or use of nuclear weapons* [1996] *ICJ Reports* 226, para. 78.

121. I. Brownlie, *Principles of public international law* (Oxford: Oxford University Press, 1996) p. 5.

122. If no reference is provided, all subsequent documents referred to in this section are on file with the author. Some can be found online on www.icrc.org/ ihl-nat.nsf.

123. T. Meron, 'The Geneva Conventions as customary law' (1987) 81 *AJIL* 360–61. See also *Tadić* jurisdiction decision, para. 99.

124. See Articles 49 (GCI), 50 (GCII), 129 (GCIII), and 146 (GCIV) of the 1949 Geneva Conventions.

125. *Ibid.*

126. See in general, ICRC publication, *La répression nationale des violations du droit international humanitaire*, Réunion d'experts (23–25 Septembre 1997). See also W. N. Ferdinandusse, *Direct application of international criminal law in national courts* (The Hague: Asser Institute, 2006) p. 276.

127. Up to the adoption of the ICC statute, this was, for example, Germany's choice: 'According to the government position, the German Penal Code sanctions all grave breaches mentioned in the provisions of the Geneva Conventions.' See *Collection of the national reports related to the questionnaire on investigation and prosecution of violations of the law of armed conflict*, International society for military law and the law of war, XIVth International Congress, Athens (10–15 May 1997) p. 2.

128. A number of common law countries chose that option and enacted the Geneva Conventions Acts. Similarly, some civil law countries, such as Belgium, opted for a special and distinct legislation, which criminalises the entire grave breaches provisions. See Loi du 16 juin 1993 relative à la répression des infractions graves aux Conventions internationales de Genève du 12 Août 1949 et aux Protocoles I et II du 8 Juin 1977, additionnels à ces Conventions, *Moniteur belge*, 5 Août 1993. This legislation has now been abrogated and a long list of war crimes applicable in international and internal conflicts and which includes the crimes of the ICC statute is now contained in Article 136*quarter* of the criminal code of Belgium.

129. Switzerland, for example, chose to include in its military criminal code such a generic provision; see Article 109 of the Swiss military codes: 'celui qui aura contrevenu aux prescriptions de conventions internationales sur la conduite de la guerre ainsi que pour la protection de personnes et de biens, sera, sauf si des dispositions plus sévères sont applicables, puni de l'emprisonnement'.

130. This is, for example, the case of Spain, which has included both in its military criminal code and the domestic criminal code provisions dealing with violations of the laws of war.

131. It is submitted that these types of documents are direct evidence of state practice and show whether states believe that violations of the law of war in internal armed conflict amount to war crimes. Judicial decisions, where individuals are accused of war crimes committed in internal armed conflicts, will be studied only in chapter 4. The occurrence of judicial decisions in this area being much more a question of opportunity of prosecution than a direct evidence of state practice.

132. The author is indebted to the Advisory Service on International Humanitarian Law of the ICRC for having allowed her access to their resources. All the documents mentioned in this section are on file with the author.

133. **Indonesia** is in the process of preparing a draft penal code to provide for the punishment of grave breaches. See *1999 Annual report of the Advisory Service of the ICRC, national implementation of international humanitarian law* (Geneva: ICRC, 1999) p. 36 (hereafter referred to as *1999 ICRC annual report*).

134. The laws of the state of **Israel** do not seem to contain the category of war crimes or serious violations of the laws of war, see *Laws of the State of Israel, special volume penal law*, 5737–1977.

135. The 1974 'règlement de discipline militaire' does not provide for any individual responsibility for war crimes or grave breaches in **Morocco**. Morocco does not seem to have any legislation on war crimes in international or internal armed conflict.

136. **Nepal** has no specific legislation incorporating the Geneva Conventions into domestic law, *1999 ICRC annual report*, p. 48.

137. **Pakistan** has no implementing legislation of the 1949 Geneva Conventions; the 1963 Geneva Convention Act of Pakistan only deals with the Red Cross emblem.

138. **Lesotho** is party to the 1949 Geneva Conventions and both Additional Protocols, but to date has not enacted any implementing legislation. The ratification of the ICC statute on 6 September 2000 might change this situation.

139. Grave breaches are covered under the general criminal code of **Austria**, especially by provisions dealing with murder, injury or damage to property. See *Collection of the national reports related to the questionnaire on the investigation and prosecution of violations of the law of armed conflict*, International Society for Military Law and the Law of War, XIV International Congress, Athens (10–15 May 1997) p. 4 (hereafter *The questionnaire*).

140. The penal code of **Cameroon** does not contain any specific offences dealing with the law of armed conflicts.

141. **Chinese** criminal law applies both to violations of the laws of war committed in international and internal conflicts; see *The questionnaire*, p. 23.

142. The criminal code of **Iraq** dated 1967 and the military criminal code of 1940 are deemed adequate to provide effective penal sanctions for individuals who have violated the Geneva Conventions, according to the Iraqi Government.

143. **Togo** is in the process of amending its criminal code in order to provide for the punishment of war crimes; see *1999 ICRC annual report*, p. 64.

144. Section 1.1 **UK** Geneva Conventions Act 1957. Similarly, see Geneva Conventions Amendment Act 1995, which criminalises the grave breaches contained in Protocol I. The War Crimes Act 1991 allows proceedings to be brought in front of English courts for war crimes committed by individuals, irrespective of their nationality at the time of the alleged offences, only if the offence was committed between 1939 and 1945. **New Zealand, Canada and Australia** had similar legislation, but all four countries have now adopted new legislation following their ratification of the ICC statute.

145. See the Geneva Conventions and Additional Protocols Act 2002 of the **Cook Islands**.

146. See the **Gambia**'s Geneva Conventions Act 1949.

147. The Parliament is in the process of adopting a draft Geneva Conventions Act (1998 and then 2001) which criminalises the grave breaches of the Geneva Conventions and Protocol I only. See *1999 ICRC annual report*, p. 31.

148. See the Geneva Conventions Act 1960 of **India**.

149. See the Geneva Conventions Act 1968 of **Kenya**.

150. See the Geneva Conventions Act 1967 of **Malawi**.

151. See the Geneva Conventions Act 1962 of **Malaysia**.

152. See the Geneva Conventions Act 1970, as amended by the Geneva Conventions Amendment Act 2003 of **Mauritius**. This act implements primarily the grave breaches of the Geneva Conventions and additional Protocol I. One might note, however, section 3(4B), which provides for the jurisdiction of Mauritius courts to prosecute offenders who commit any breach of the Conventions or Protocols, other than grave breaches, even if the act is done or completed outside Mauritius.

153. See the **Namibian** Geneva Conventions Act 2003, No. 15, which entered into force on 18 December 2003 and only implements grave breaches of the 1949 Geneva Conventions and Additional Protocol I. See (2004) 86 *IRRC* 697.

154. See the **Nigerian** Geneva Conventions Act, chapter 162 of the 1990 Laws of the Federation.

155. See the UK Geneva Conventions Act 1957, which applies in **Trinidad and Tobago**.

156. See the Geneva Conventions Act 1981 of **Zimbabwe** which only implements grave breaches of the Geneva Conventions and Protocol I.

157. The criminal code and the military code of justice of **Burkina Fasso** provide punishment for grave breaches of the Geneva Conventions and Protocol I, see *1999 ICRC annual report*, p. 16.

158. The 1965 code of military justice and Article 9*bis* of the Règlement de discipline générale dans les armées of 1975, cover certain violations of the law of armed conflicts committed in international armed conflicts. The **French** Government

has not enacted in its criminal code any provisions dealing specifically with the grave breaches of the Geneva Conventions. See M. P. Besson de Vezac, 'Les sanctions des violations des conventions de Genève du 12 Août 1949' (1997) 3 *Droit et défense, revue générale du droit de la sécurité et de la défense* 4. The French criminal code does not make any reference to war crimes either and to date France has not enacted any legislation implementing war crimes as defined in the ICC statute within the French legal order. For more details on this issue, see P. Rowe, 'War crimes' in D. McGoldrick, P. Rowe and E. Donnelly (eds.), *The permanent International Criminal Court, legal and policy issues* (Oxford and Portland, Oregon: Hart Publishing, 2004) p. 337 at pp. 366–78.

159. For **Greece**, see *1999 ICRC annual report*, p. 32.

160. The **Japanese** Parliament adopted on 14 June 2004 a 'Law concerning the Punishment of Grave Breaches of International Humanitarian Law'. It introduces within the criminal legal system certain grave breaches of the 1949 Geneva Conventions and Additional Protocol I. See (2005) 87 *IRRC* 220.

161. See Law of **Luxembourg** of 9 January 1985 concerning the suppression of grave breaches of the Geneva Conventions.

162. The 2001 criminal code from **Mali** contains an article on war crimes, which lists the crimes appearing in Article 8.2a) and b) of the Rome statute (Article 31). War crimes applicable in internal armed conflicts have not been included in this recent criminal code and the latter represents therefore only a partial implementation of the Rome statute into its national legislation.

163. The **Romanian** criminal code contains in Articles 358 and 359 all the grave breaches provisions; see *The questionnaire*, p. 12.

164. **Turkey** is a monist state and according to Article 90 of its constitution, international agreements duly put into effect carry the force of law. Only grave breaches of the Geneva Conventions are considered to be war crimes.

165. **Cuba**'s military criminal code contains in its Articles 42–45 prohibitions of certain conduct 'committed during combat actions'.

166. The criminal code of the **Czech Republic** contains, in a chapter entitled 'crimes against humanity', various articles dealing with serious violations of the laws of war which are 'forbidden in time of war or in combat'. See Articles 262, use of forbidden weapon or an unpermitted form of combat, 263 wartime cruelty, 263a) persecution of a population and 264 plunder in a theatre of war.

167. The criminal code of **Estonia**, which entered into force on 1 September 2002, contains a section dealing with war crimes applicable 'in war time' (chapter 8, division 4). It then lists numerous serious violations of international humanitarian law including a prohibition on biological, bacteriological, chemical weapons, gas or any weapons of mass destruction or weapon rendered illegal by international agreements (paras. 94–108).

168. Articles 138–40 of the criminal code of the **Ivory Coast** apply to individuals who, *in time of war or occupation* and in violation of the rules of international law

commit violations of the law of war (emphasis added). The expression 'time of war or occupation' seems to only cover cases of international conflicts.

169. The criminal code of **Guinea** includes certain violations of the law of armed conflicts committed in 'a zone of military operations' (Articles 569–70 and 579).

170. The 1978 criminal code of **Hungary** contains a title dealing with war crimes (Articles 158–63) which criminalises, for example, violence against the civilian population (Article 158) 'in an operational or occupied area'. It remains unclear whether internal armed conflicts were intended to be covered by that provision.

171. The 1943 criminal code of **Lebanon** does not expressly mention war crimes and the 1968 military criminal code in Articles 132 and 154 prohibit certain conduct in 'zones of military operations'. Such language cannot really be interpreted as including war crimes committed in internal armed conflicts. An amendment to this code (under review) might include a new article on war crimes, but only by reference to the grave breaches of the 1949 Geneva Conventions and Protocol I.

172. **Peru**'s code of military justice provides for the punishment of some offences 'in times of war' (Articles 91–96). Even if this expression could be interpreted as covering internal armed conflicts, this code was adopted in 1980 and it is unlikely that, at that point in time, it was intended to include internal armed conflicts.

173. Chapter XX (crimes against peace, security of mankind and international legal order) of the 2001 criminal code of the **Ukraine**, criminalises breaches of laws of war and the use of weapons of mass extermination prohibited by international law or international instruments, without, however, specifying any scope of application of the said articles (Articles 438 and 439). The Ukraine is not yet a party to the ICC statute.

174. Article 152 of the 1995 criminal code of **Uzbekistan** entitled 'violation of the laws and customs of war' does not specify any scope of application.

175. Article 279 of the **Vietnamese** criminal code criminalises various violations of international humanitarian law if committed *in time of war* (emphasis added). It is not clear if that expression includes internal armed conflicts.

176. The ICRC believes that the 1998 military criminal code of **Yemen** includes acts committed both in international and internal conflicts (see (1999) 81 *IRRC* 165) but in fact a closer look at the legislation itself reveals that the war crimes detailed there apply *during war* (Article 21) (emphasis added). There is no specific mention of internal armed conflicts and it is therefore open to discussion if it really applies in such conflicts.

177. The ICTY cited the 1990 criminal code of the Socialist Republic of **Yugoslavia** as examples of legislation which 'go as far as to make it possible for national courts to try persons responsible for violations of rules concerning internal armed conflicts', *Tadić* jurisdiction decision, para. 132. In September 2004, Serbia was considering amending its criminal code and the new draft criminal code of Serbia contains war crimes applicable during 'a war or armed conflict' (Articles 372–85) and has been put in line with the content of the ICC statute.

178. The **Argentinean** draft reform of the code of military justice contains a title 'crimes against protected persons and objects in the event of an *armed conflict*' (Articles 873–80). Article 872 includes among the protected persons 'any other person having such status under Protocol II or any other international treaties to which the Argentine Republic is a party'. This reform is still awaiting adoption by Congress.

179. The **Armenian** criminal code contains in its Article 390 a long list of 'serious breaches of international humanitarian law during armed conflicts'. However, this list includes neither all the crimes contained in the ICC statute nor all the serious breaches of the laws of war applicable in armed conflicts. This new criminal code entered into force on 1 August 2003.

180. The criminal code of the Republic of **Azerbaijan** adopted on 30 December 1999 contains in its Article 116 a long list of violations of international humanitarian law if committed in time of an *armed conflict*. It is interesting to note that this provision has been largely inspired by the provisions of the Rome statute. Additional conduct, not included in the Rome statute, have been criminalised such as starvation, using methods and means of warfare which can cause serious damage to the natural environment and directing attacks against the installations containing dangerous forces. One may also note the 1995 law concerning the protection of civilians persons and the rights of prisoners of war, which is applicable 'in cases Azerbaijan is a participant of intergovernmental armed conflict or in case of internal armed conflict in its territory, between the Azerbaijan Republic and two or more parties, even if one of these parties does not confirm the existence of such a conflict'.

181. **Bangladesh**'s International Crimes (Tribunal) Act 1973 provides that individuals should be individually responsible for 'war crimes and violation of any humanitarian rules applicable in armed conflicts laid down in the Geneva Conventions of 1949' (section 3.2).

182. The new criminal code of the **Republic of Belarus** entered into force on 9 July 2000 and contains a long list of war crimes applicable in *armed conflicts*. Article 136 contains these war crimes which are largely similar to the list appearing in Article 8 of the ICC statute. Here again, some crimes not ultimately included in the Rome statute are criminalised in this criminal code if committed in armed conflicts.

183. **Bosnia-Herzegovina** has adopted the criminal code of ex-Yugoslavia and therefore criminalises serious violations of international humanitarian law committed '*in time of war, armed conflict or occupation*'. See Articles 154–70 of the 1998 criminal code of the Federation of Bosnia and Herzegovina and Articles 433–43 of the 2000 criminal code of Republik Srspka. See also Articles 173–79 of the 2003 criminal code of Bosnia-Herzegovina, which contain similar provisions.

184. Article 378 of the **Costa Rican** criminal code provides penalties for whoever commits or orders to commit, during *armed conflicts*, acts recognised as grave violations or war crimes by international treaties to which Costa Rica is party.

Individuals can therefore be prosecuted in Costa Rica for war crimes committed in internal armed conflicts as long as they are listed in Article 8 of the ICC statute, to which Costa Rica is a party.

185. The new criminal code of **Croatia** is inspired by the criminal code of ex-Yugoslavia and contains detailed articles (Articles 158–68), such as war crimes against civilians, forbidden means of combat or illicit killing and wounding of the enemy which are applicable *in time of war, armed conflict or occupation*. See also the 2003 Law on application of the ICC statute and on the prosecution of criminal acts against international law on war and humanitarian law.

186. An amendment to the criminal code of **Colombia** was adopted on 24 July 2000. The provisions dealing with war crimes in book 2, title 2, Articles 135–64 of the criminal code are applicable *in time of armed conflicts*. The ICRC believes that this code does not make any distinction between internal and international armed conflicts, see (2001) 841 *IRRC* 211. See also (2000) 3 *YbIHL* 455–56.

187. The penal code of **Ethiopia** contains a number of provisions detailing war crimes if they are committed in *time of war, armed conflict or occupation*. See Articles 282–90. It is interesting to note that this penal code was enacted in 1957. Commentators have taken the view that Ethiopia had implemented the grave breaches of the Geneva Conventions without any distinction between international and internal conflicts. See T. S. Engelschion, 'Prosecution of war crimes and violations of human rights in Ethiopia' (1994) 8 *Yearbook of African law* 50.

188. Chapter 11 of the **Finnish** penal code (578/1995) details war crimes and offences against humanity. Section 1 provides: 'a person who in an act of war uses a prohibited means of warfare or weapons, abuses an international symbol designated for the protection of the wounded or the sick, or otherwise violates the provisions of an international instrument on warfare binding on Finland or a generally acknowledged and established rule of war under public international law, shall be sentenced for a war crime to at least four months to six years imprisonment.' See (1998) 1 *YbIHL* 619–20. Commentators have interpreted these provisions and the expression 'act of war' to cover situations both of international and internal conflicts.

189. The 2002 military penal code of **Jordan** contains in its Article 41 a long list of war crimes applicable 'in armed conflicts'. Interestingly also, Article 44 of this military penal code mentions that Article 41 also applies to civilians who might commit war crimes.

190. The new criminal code of **Kazakhstan** entered into force on 1 January 1998 and contains an article, Article 159, which provides a penalty of twelve years' imprisonment for any individual who would have, for example, deported part of a civilian population, committed pillaging or used illegal methods or means of warfare *during an armed conflict*.

191. The amendment of the criminal code of the Republic of **Lithuania** introduced in 1998 a section XVIII entitled war crimes. The scope of application of this section

is somehow surprising and remains unclear. Four articles in this section (Articles 333, 334, 335 and 344) apply in 'time of war, during an international conflict or under the conditions of occupation or annexation' whereas two others (Articles 336 and 338) apply in 'time of war, an armed conflict or under the conditions of occupation or annexation'. The criminal code was adopted in September 2000 and entered into force on 1 May 2003.

192. The new penal code of the **Republic of Moldova** was adopted on 18 April 2002 and contains various provisions dealing with war crimes which apply during armed conflicts or hostilities. Article 391 provides: 'Grave violations of international humanitarian law during international or internal military conflicts entailing grave consequences shall be punishable with imprisonment for a term from 16 to 25 years or with life imprisonment.'

193. The law of military crimes 1987 of **Mozambique** defines war crime in Article 83 as the violation of internationally accepted humanitarian laws, particularly in *armed conflicts*, such as the use of illegal means of combat or its abusive use or the practice of cruel acts against the civilian population, for example.

194. The war crime criminal law Act (Wet Oorlogsstratfrecht) of July 1952 provides in its Article 1 that it applies to war crimes committed in *any armed conflict* in which **the Netherlands** is involved either directly or as part of an international force. Article 1.3 explicitly provides that the notion of war or armed conflict includes civil war. In November 1997, the Dutch supreme court (Hoge Raad) has, however, taken the view that this article does not properly implement the obligations contained in the Geneva Conventions, as the Netherlands needs to be involved in the conflict. The war crime Act is therefore going to be reviewed.

195. Para. 108 of the **Norwegian** military criminal code provides penalties for anyone who might violate any provisions of the Geneva Conventions or any of the two Protocols (unofficial translation of the Militaer Straffelov). Similarly, para. 107 provides sanctions for 'anyone who uses a weapon or means of combat which is prohibited by any international agreement which Norway has acceded to or who is accessory thereto'. Norway, being a state party to the ICC statute, will therefore have jurisdiction over those war crimes (relating to means of combat) committed in internal armed conflicts.

196. The Law No. 1160/97 criminal code of the Republic of **Paraguay** contains an article on war crimes (Article 320) providing for penalties for anyone who, in violation of international laws of war, *armed conflict or military occupation*, commits against the civilian population, the wounded, the sick or prisoners of war, homicide, deportation or looting, for example. See (1998) 1 *YbIHL* 623.

197. The new criminal code of **Poland** of 6 June 1997 contains a long list of violations of the laws of war (Articles 121–26) which are applicable *during hostilities*. This expression seems to include both international and internal hostilities.

198. The new criminal code of the **Russian Federation** was adopted in 1996 and contains a number of provisions dealing with the use of banned means and

methods of warfare (Article 356). Anyone, who deports civilian population, commits pillaging or uses an illegal means or method of warfare during an *armed conflict*, shall be punishable by deprivation of liberty for a term of up to twenty years. It is unfortunate, however, that the 'Amnesty declaration with respect to persons who committed socially dangerous acts in connection with the armed conflict in the Chechen Republic' seems to cover persons who committed violations of Article 356 of the criminal code. For a commentary on these provisions, see (2000) 3 *YbIHL* 566–68.

199. The latest version of the **Swedish** criminal code (1990) contains a section 6, chapter 22, which defines 'a crime against the law of nations' as 'any serious violation of a treaty or agreement with a foreign power or of infraction of a generally recognized principle or tenet pertaining to international humanitarian law *in armed conflicts*.' This section then lists numerous violations of the laws of war, including the use of weapons prohibited by international law, the abuse of the Red Cross sign or attacks on civilians.

200. The 1994 penal code of the Republic of **Slovenia** contains detailed articles, such as war crimes against civilians, crimes linked with the use of illicit means of warfare or illicit killing and wounding of the enemy (Articles 373–91) which are applicable in *time of war, armed conflict or occupation*. In 2004, the penal code was amended in order to put it in line with the definition of war crimes contained in the ICC statute. See M. Bosnjak and D. Zagorac, 'Slovenia' in Kress, Lattanzi, Bromhall and Santori (eds.), *The Rome statute and domestic legal orders, vol. II, constitutional issues, co-operation and enforcement* (Baden-Baden, Ripa di Fagnano Alto: Nomos Verlagsgessellschaft, Il Sirente, 2005) pp. 309–30 at 310.

201. The 1995 penal code of **Spain** (Ley Organica 10/1995 9 December 1995) contains a long list of war crimes, which are applicable in time of *armed conflict* (Articles 608–14). Article 608 defines the persons protected under that part of the penal code and includes all persons who are protected under Protocol II. Commentators have also affirmed that by the expression 'armed conflict' in this new penal code, one must understand situations such as declared war, occupation, war of self-determination, UN peace enforcing action and internal conflicts. See M. P. Gonzalez, 'La repression des crimes de guerre et des crimes contre l'humanité dans le système juridique espagnole' in F. Lattanzi (ed.), *Crimini di guerra et giurisdizione nazionali* (Baden-Baden, Fagnagno Alto: Nomas Verlagsgessellschaft, Il Sirente, 1998) p. 155. The Organic Law No. 15/2003 amending the penal code was promulgated on 25 November 2003. It updates the penal code of 1995 and puts it in line with the crimes contained in the Rome statute. See (2004) 86 *IRRC* 285 and (2003) 6 *YbIHL* 609–14.

202. The **Swiss** military penal code (as amended in 1967) contains a chapter dealing with offences against the *jus gentium* in time of armed conflicts. This chapter is applicable in time 'of declared wars and other armed conflicts between two or

more states. The violations of other international agreements are also prosecuted if these instruments provide for a wider scope of application' (Article 108). This article has been widely interpreted by Swiss military tribunals to encompass situations of international and internal conflict. See chapter 5, section 2. See also A. Ziegler, 'Domestic prosecution and international co-operation with regard to violations of international humanitarian law: the case of Switzerland' (1997) 5 *Revue suisse de droit international et droit européen* 561–68.

203. **Belgium** was the first country to enact legislation specifically criminalising violations of Protocol II in 1993 (Loi relative à la répression des infractions graves aux conventions internationales de Genève du 12 août 1949 et aux protocoles I et II du 8 juin 1977). Violations of common Article 3 are not criminalised in this legislation, only violations of Protocol II which constitute grave breaches in the Geneva Conventions or Protocol I have been criminalised. For commentaries on this law, see A. Andries, C van den Wijngaert and E. David, 'Commentaire de la loi du 6 juin 1993 relative à la répression des infractions graves au droit international humanitaire' (1994) *Revue de droit pénal et de criminologie* 1114, as well as E. David, 'La loi belge sur les crimes de guerre' (1995) *Revue belge de droit international* 668. In 2003, the Belgian Government abrogated the 1993 legislation and replaced it with the law of 5 August 2003 on the punishment of grave breaches of international humanitarian law. New Articles 136*bis*–36*octies* were introduced in the criminal code, including therein all the war crimes contained in the ICC statute, without making a distinction between war crimes committed in international and internal armed conflicts.

204. Law No. 8 of 31 October 1998 on the definition and the repression of genocide, war crimes and crimes against humanity of the **Republic of Congo** (Brazzaville) includes the definition of these crimes as they appear in Articles 6, 7 and 8 of the Rome statute (see Article 4 of the Congolese Act).

205. See Loi modifiant et complétant certaines dispositions du code pénal, du code de l'organisation et de la compétence judiciaire, du code pénal militaire et du code de justice militaire en application du statut de la cour pénale internationale of September 2005. See Article 224 which incorporates all the ICC crimes in the criminal code of the **DRC** (legislation available on www.icc-cpi.int).

206. Article 68 of the code of military justice of **El Salvador** provides a penalty of fifteen to twenty years of imprisonment for anybody violating international humanitarian law *in time of international or internal war* (emphasis added). Similarly, title XIX entitled crimes against humanity, of the 1997 criminal code, contains a long list of violations of the laws of war applicable in international or internal armed conflicts.

207. The new criminal code of **Georgia** adopted in July 1999 introduced a complete list of breaches of international humanitarian law (Articles 411 and 413) committed *in an international or internal armed conflict* (emphasis added). Like the criminal code of Tajikistan, this list contains all the grave breaches of Geneva

Conventions and Protocol I made applicable in internal armed conflicts, plus a catch-all provision including war crimes such as pillaging, use of civilians to cover the troops or objects from the hostilities, or the use of means and materials or weapons of mass destruction which are prohibited by an international treaty. Before Georgia ratified the Rome statute, amendments to the criminal code were made to bring it in line with the Rome statute. The amendments do not distinguish between international and internal armed conflicts, see (2004) 86 *IRRC* 280–81. See also M. Turava, 'Georgia' in Kress, Lattanzi, Bromhall and Santori (eds.), *The Rome statute and domestic legal orders, vol. II, constitutional issues, co-operation and enforcement* (Baden-Baden, Ripa di Fagnano Alto: Nomos Verlagsgessellschaft, Il Sirente, 2005) pp. 105–29.

208. In **Italy**, the criminal military code of war (book III, Article 165) list the acts prohibited by the laws and customs of war and is applicable in all types of armed conflicts, independently of a declaration of war (amendment introduced by Law No. 6 of 31 January 2002, reported in (2003) 85 *IRRC* 209). Furthermore, para. 85 of the Italian military manual considers grave breaches of the Geneva Conventions and of both Protocols as war crimes, see *Manule di diritto umanitario*, vol. I, Usi e convenzioni di guerra, Roma (1991) p. 28.

209. See the Geneva Conventions (Amendment) Act 1998 of **Ireland**. Section 4 provides for criminal sanctions for breaches of Protocol II. See (1999) 2 *YbIHL* 380.

210. Chapter IX of the 2004 criminal code of **Latvia** is entitled crimes against humanity and peace, war crimes and genocide. It contains few provisions dealing with war crimes, defined as 'violation of provisions and practices, in regard to prohibited conduct of war, comprised in international agreements binding upon the Republic of Latvia' (section 74) but has no precision about the scope of application of these articles. However, Latvia has been a party to the ICC statute since June 2002, so Latvian courts will be able to prosecute war crimes committed in internal conflicts listed in the Rome statute.

211. Article 551 of the criminal code of **Nicaragua** provides for the prosecution of any violation of humanitarian law, whether committed in time of international war or civil war. See. T. Graditsky, 'La responsabilité pénale individuelle pour violation du droit international humanitaire applicable en situation de conflit armé non international' (1998) 829 *IRRC* 40.

212. The code of military justice of **Niger** was adopted on 11 March 2003. It relies heavily on Belgian legislation and contains an article (Article 214) which defines all grave breaches of the Geneva Conventions and both Protocols of 1977 as international crimes. The serious violations of Protocol II, which amount to a grave breach of the Geneva Conventions or Protocol I, are therefore criminalised in internal armed conflicts. Furthermore, a recent amendment of the criminal code introduces a section on war crimes, which refers to war crimes of the Geneva Conventions and their two additional Protocols. See Law No. 2003-025 of 13 June 2003 of Niger, referred to in (2004) 86 *IRRC* 698.

213. Article 241 of the 1996 criminal code of **Portugal** provided penalties for the war crimes committed against civilians committed in *time of war, armed conflicts or occupation*. This article has now been revoked and replaced by the Law No. 31/2004 of 22 July 2004 adapting Portuguese criminal legislation to the statute of the International Criminal Court, specifying conduct constituting crimes against international humanitarian law – seventeenth amendment to the criminal code. Section II, Articles 10–16 of this law list all the war crimes against persons, against property or through the use of prohibited means or methods of warfare, which are applicable in the 'context of an international armed conflict or in the context of an armed conflict of a non-international nature'.

214. The **Rwandan** law repressing the crime of genocide, crimes against humanity and war crimes was adopted on 15 July 2003. Articles 8 and 10 on war crimes apply during armed conflicts and make no distinction between situations of international and internal armed conflicts. See (2004) 86 *IRRC* 283–84.

215. The **USA** War Crimes Act 1996 amended title 18 of the US criminal code by inserting a new chapter 118, which provided for the punishment of grave breaches of the Geneva Conventions or any Protocol to which the USA is a party. This chapter was later amended by the Expended War Crimes Act 1997. Section 2441 of this chapter 118 now provides for the punishment of grave breaches, and war crimes, being defined as violations of Articles 23, 25, 27 and 28 of the Hague regulations, violations of common Article 3 and any protocol to such convention which deals with non-international conflict, and any violation to the 1996 Protocol II to the 1980 Convention on the use of mines.

216. The new criminal code of **Tajikistan** adopted on 21 May 1998, contains an extensive list of serious violations of international humanitarian law (Articles 403–5) applicable *in time of an armed conflict international or non-international* (emphasis added). These provisions include all the grave breaches of the Geneva Conventions and Protocol I plus an additional provision, which criminalises acts such as pillaging or the use during an armed conflict of weapons of mass destruction or materials rendered illegal by an international instrument.

217. The Act for the enforcement of the Geneva Convention relative to the treatment of prisoners of war of 12 August 1949 of **Thailand** provides in sections 18 and 19 for the liability of individuals who, 'in case of armed conflicts not of an international character', commit violations against prisoners of war. It is noteworthy that this legislation was enacted in 1955, but it only represents a very limited criminalisation of violations of the laws of war in internal armed conflicts.

218. 1991 is the beginning of the temporal jurisdiction of the ICTY. Before that date, less than ten states were criminalising serious violations of the laws of war when committed in internal armed conflicts: Yugoslavia (1990), Ethiopia (1957), Mozambique (1987), the Netherlands (1952), Switzerland (1967), Sweden (1990) and Thailand (1955).

219. The Appeals Chamber took the view that: 'in appraising the formation of customary rules of general principles one should therefore be aware that, on account of the inherent nature of this subject matter, reliance must primarily be based on such elements as official pronouncements of states, military manuals and judicial decisions'. *Tadić* jurisdiction decision, para. 99.

220. This is the case of many military manuals, such as the ones of **Nicaragua** (see the *Manual de comportamiento y proceder de la unidades militares y de los miembros del ejercito de Nicaragua en tiempo de paz, conflictos armados, situaciones irregulares o desastres naturales*), **Nigeria** (see *Operational code of conduct of the Nigerian armed forces*), **Cameroon** (see section 18 of the *Manuel de l'instructeur en vigueur dans les forces armées*), **Uganda** (*Code of conduct of the national resistance army 1987*), **Senegal** (article 34 du décret 90-1159 du 12 octobre 1990 portant règlement de discipline dans les forces armées), **Togo** and **Benin** (see *Le droit de la guerre, fasicules I, II and III 1996*) or **Tajikistan** (see *Order of the Commander and Head of the department of the interior troops of the ministry of internal affairs*, April 1996).

221. The manual on the application of the rules of international humanitarian law by the armed forces of **Russia**, 1990, contains a detailed list of prohibited conducts in cases of 'declared war or any other armed conflict' and cites explicitly common Article 3. The grave breaches of the Geneva Conventions are qualified as war crimes, but violations of common Article 3 were omitted from this list of war crimes.

222. The **Australian** *Law of armed conflict commander's guide* (ADFP 37 Supplement 1) defines war crimes in a generic term as 'illegal actions relating to the inception or conduct of armed conflict. They may be viewed as any violation of the law of armed conflict, either customary or treaty law, which is committed by any person' (para. 1302 of the commander's guide). This might imply that violations of common Article 3 of Protocol II could be seen as a war crimes, but when it comes to list these war crimes, only grave breaches of the Geneva Conventions and Protocol I are listed (see chapter 13 of the code, paras. 1304–5).

223. Para. 1824 of the **New Zealand** *Interim Law of Armed Conflict Manual*, DM-112, 1992. The chapter of this manual dealing with grave breaches and war crimes does not include any violations of common Article 3 or Protocol II.

224. See para.6.2.5 of the **USA** *Annotated supplement to the commanders' handbook on the law of naval operations*, 1989 as well as paras. 498 and 499 of the *Law of land warfare, FM 27-10*, July 1956, which provides: 'the term war crimes is a technical expression for a violation of the law of war by any person or persons, military or civilian'. Even if these military manuals refer to war crimes, American soldiers will not be tried for war crimes, but for breaches of military discipline. The conduct of armed conflicts and air operations, Air force pamphlet of 1976 does not mention internal armed conflicts at all. The 1996 *Law of armed conflict military manual* of **South Africa** contains a similar provision and provides in para. 35 that 'any breach of the law of armed conflict is a war crime'.

225. See para.6.2.5 of the *Handbook of naval operations, ibid.*, which specifically mentioned that the violations of Article 4.2a), Article 4.1, Article 4.2g, Articles 7.1, 8, 11 and 13.2 of Protocol II amount to war crimes.

226. Para. 211 of *Humanitarian law in armed conflicts,* **German** military manual August 1992, DSKVU 207 320067.

227. Para. 1209 of the German military manual.

228. See introduction to the *Manual on the law of armed conflict at the operational and tactical level* (scope of application, para. 7).

229. Chapter 17, paras. 42, 43 and 44.

230. The *Army code* of the **UK** (71130–1981) contains a section on internal conflicts (section 12) explaining the content of common Article 3 and Protocol II, as well as their respective scope of application, without however mentioning the consequences of the violations of these provisions.

231. *The manual of the law of armed conflict, UK Ministry of Defence* (Oxford: Oxford University Press, 2004) paras. 15.32 and 15.32.1.

232. See the second draft of the Canadian *Military manual on the law of armed conflict*, chapter 18, para. 1824.

233. Out of twenty legislative acts studied, sixteen deal with issues of co-operation only. This is the case, for example, for Australia, the UK, Belgium, Croatia, Bosnia-Herzegovina, Germany, Italy, Norway, Spain, the USA, Switzerland, Sweden and New Zealand to cite but a few.

234. Act on the jurisdiction of the ICTY and on legal assistance to the International Tribunal, 5 January 1994, section 3.

235. Article 1 of the Act on criminal proceedings before the ICTY, 21 December 1994.

236. Article 2 of the Loi du 18 mai 1999 introduisant certaines mesures visant à faciliter la coopération avec le TPY et le TPIR reproduced in *Journal officiel du Grand-Duché de Luxembourg*, A No. 66, 11 June 1999.

237. See Loi 95–1 du 2 Janvier 1995, portant adaptation de la législation française aux dispositions de la résolution 827 du Conseil de sécurité des NU instituant un tribunal international en vue de juger les personnes présumées responsables de violations graves du droit international humanitaire commises sur le territoire de l'ex-Yugoslavie depuis 1991, as well as Loi 96–432 du 22 mai 1996 portant adaptation de la législation française aux dispositions de la résolution 955 du Conseil de securité des NU instituant un tribunal international en vue de juger les personnes présumées responsables d'actes de génocide ou d'autres violations graves du droit international humanitaire, commis en 1994 sur le territore du Rwanda.

238. Article 2, chapter 1 of Loi du 2 janvier 1995, and Article 1 of Loi du 22 mai 1996 states: 'Les auteurs ou complices des infractions mentionnées à l'article 1er peuvent être pousuivis et jugés par les juridictions françaises s'ils sont trouvés en France.'

239. The French penal code does not contain any provision on grave breaches of the Geneva Conventions and did not seem to consider violations of common Article 3

or Protocol II as war crimes. Chapter 5 will return to the principle of universal jurisdiction.

240. Unfortunately, the French authorities do not envisage implementing the same type of legislation for the ICC statute.

241. For a commentary on these legislative acts, see P. Daillier, 'La répression pénale en France des crimes de guerre et des crimes contre l'humanité en ex-Yugoslavie', in F. Lattanzi (ed.), *Dai tribunali penali internationazionali ad hoc a una corte permanente* (Naples: Ed. Scientifica, 1996) p. 223, as well as M. Masse, 'Ex-Yugouslavie, Rwanda: une compétence virtuelle des juridictions française' (1997) *Revue de sciences criminelles* 893.

242. Article 17 of the Rome statute.

243. As of 31 December 2006.

244. The long title of this Act is 'An act respecting genocide, crimes against humanity and war crimes and to implement the Rome statute of the ICC, and to make consequential amendments to other Acts'.

245. Section 4.4 of the Act does not contain the second sentence mentioned above for offences committed within Canada.

246. D. Robinson, 'Implementing international crimes: the Canadian approach' in *Acts of the Berlin Conference on the Rome Statute, what's next: domestic and foreign approaches to the implementation of international criminal law in national law* (thereafter, *Acts of the Berlin Conference*) (Berlin: Reader & International Criminal Law Society, 2000) p. 26. In that respect it is interesting to note that section 6.5 reads: 'for greater certainty, the offence of crime against humanity was part of customary international law or war crimes according to the general principles of law recognised by the community of nations before the coming into force of either of the following: the agreement for the prosecution and punishment of the major war criminals of the European Axis, signed in London on August 8, 1945 and the Proclamation by the Supreme Commander for the Allied powers, dated January 19, 1946.'

247. See sections 8, 9, 10 and 11 of the New Zealand Act, which entered into force on 1 October 2000. Chapter 5 will return to the issue of jurisdiction.

248. Before that date, the offences of genocide and crimes against humanity were covered by general domestic law.

249. See part 5, sections 50 and 51 of the International Criminal Court Act 2001.

250. See J. Gilbert, 'UK approach to implementation of ICC crimes', *Acts of the Berlin Conference*, p. 6.

251. Article 136*quater* of the penal code. See (2003) 85 *IRRC* 655. Next to the ICC crimes, it is interesting to note that this new article of the penal code also includes the crimes of using starvation as a method of warfare, attacking civilian objectives as well as using poison, gas or other forbidden weapons.

252. Implementation of the Rome statute of the International Criminal Court Act 2002. Government Gazette, Republic of South Africa, vol. 445, 28 July 2002, No. 23642. For war crimes, see part 3 of schedule 1 to the Act.

253. See sections F and G of the International Criminal Court (Consequential Amendments) Act 2002, schedule 1, amendment of the Criminal Code Act 1995, available online on www.scaleplus.law.gov.au. Next to the war crimes contained in the ICC statute, the Australian Act also implements the grave breaches of Protocol I.

254. See section 6 of the international crimes act of 19 June 2003, which includes the war crimes applicable in 'the case of an armed conflict not of an international character'. For a commentary, see M. Boot-Matthijssen and R. van Elst, 'Key provisions of the International Crimes Act 2003' (2004) 35 *Netherlands yearbook of international law* 251–96.

255. Para. 1 of this act reads: 'The Statute of the International Criminal Court shall apply in this country.'

256. See Loi No. 1/004 du 8 mai 2004 portant répression du crime de génocide, des crimes contre l'humanité et des crimes de guerre.

257. Act No. 1284/2000 on the implementation of the provisions of a legislative nature of the Rome statute of the International Criminal Court and on the application of the Statute, issued on 28 December 2000. Section 1 states that the provisions of the ICC statute shall be in force as applicable law in accordance with the commitments of Finland.

258. See Article 10.1 of this act, which provides for the jurisdiction of the Croatian courts for violations committed in Croatia by citizens of Croatia or if the victims of these acts are Croatian citizens. Article 10.2 of this act provides that perpetrators of these criminal acts shall also be prosecuted in Croatia, regardless of the place of commission of the crimes, if the perpetrator has been arrested in or extradited to Croatia and provided that the ICC or the courts of another state have not conducted proceedings against these perpetrators.

259. See the International Criminal Court Act of November 2002, which includes within the domestic legal order all the crimes contained in the ICC statute, for war crimes, see part 5, paras. 13, 54D.

260. International Criminal Court Act 2006, 24 February 2006, available online on www.iccnow.org.

261. See the Ley de cooperacion con la CPI en materia de lucha contra el genocidio, crimines de guerra y crimines de lesa humanidad (No. 18.026) from Uruguay of 4 October 2006. See also Ley de implementacion del estatuto de Roma de la corte penal internacional from Argentina of 1 December 2006, both available online on www.iccnow.org.

262. See the act to introduce the code of crimes against international law of 26 June 2002, available online on www.iuscrim.mpg.de/forsch/online_pub.html as well as explanations and commentary attached.

263. See commentary attached to the Code, p. 52.

264. See part 2, chapter 2, sections 8–12 of the German code of crimes against international law.

265. Law No. 31/2004 of 22 July 2004 adapting Portuguese criminal legislation to the Statute of the International Criminal court, specifying conduct constituting crimes against international humanitarian law – seventeenth amendment to the criminal code.

266. In Brazil, a draft bill implementing the ICC statute in 2002 is under consideration. It includes in Brazilian law all the offences provided for in the ICC statute. See (2003) 6 *YbIHL* 458–59.

267. See part 2, section 6 of the International Crimes Bill 2005 of Kenya.

268. See the Progetto di legge no 2724, which contains a long list of crimes applicable in both international and internal armed conflicts and which goes beyond the list of crimes contained in the ICC statute, see title IV, chapters II and III (Articles 44–78).

269. Ecuador, Bolivia, Honduras, Ireland, Mexico, Norway, Sweden, Greece and Austria are in the process of drafting their ICC implementing legislation (information on some of these countries available online on www.iccnow.org). They have chosen to include all ICC war crimes in their national criminal code.

270. Information on ninety-nine states was found. Out of these ninety-nine states, twenty-seven states do not extend the concept of war crimes to violations of the laws of war committed in internal armed conflicts. Twelve others have implemented legislation dealing with serious violations of the laws of war but their scope of application is open to debate. Fifty-four states have clearly chosen to include in their domestic legal system war crimes committed in internal armed conflicts. Finally, six states have adopted draft ICC legislation, which include in their penal system all the ICC war crimes.

271. Before 1990, fewer than ten states were criminalising serious violations of the laws of war when committed in internal armed conflicts: Yugoslavia (1990), Ethiopia (1957), Mozambique (1987), the Netherlands (1952), Switzerland (1967), Sweden (1990), Thailand (1955) and the USA (1956 *Military manual*).

272. Ecuador, Bolivia, Honduras, Ireland, Mexico, Norway, Sweden, Greece and Austria are drafting their implementing legislation in that sense (information on some of these countries available online on www.iccnow.org). Sweden, for example, is drafting a Swedish act on international crimes, with a longer list of war crimes applicable in internal armed conflicts than the Rome statute, see (2002) 5 *YbIHL* 598–99. Similarly, the Republic of Yemen approved the accession to the ICC statute in 2003 and ordered the Minister of Justice to 'revise the system of penal legislation and other relevant legislation and suggest draft amendments required to make the legislation in conformity with the provisions of the ICC statute'. See Council of Ministers decision No. (82) of 2003 on approval of accession to the statute of the International Criminal Court available online on www.icrc.org

273. See UN.Doc.S/PV.3217 (25 May 1993) p. 15.

274. *Ibid.*, p. 11.

275. *Ibid.*, p. 18.

276. During the first few days of the conference each state had around eight to ten minutes to express their views on the future court.

277. All speeches are on file with the author and some have been published online on www.un.org/icc.

278. Statement of the Republic of Armenia to the diplomatic conference on the establishment of an ICC, Rome, 16 June 1998.

279. Statement of the Republic of Bangladesh, 18 June 1998.

280. Statement of the Republic of Estonia, 17 June 1998.

281. See the statement made by South Africa on behalf of the SADEC countries, 15 June 1998. Similarly, the representative of Tanzania affirmed: 'we believe that the customary distinction between international and non-international armed conflicts needs to be re-examined. This is particularly important so as not to justify the exclusion of serious crimes so frequently committed in internal armed conflict from the jurisdiction of the Court.'

282. See also similar statements made by the UK before or after the Rome conference, see (1998) *BYIL* 513–17.

283. See the statement of the German Foreign Minister made in Bonn on 14 June 1998.

284. See the statement of India, 16 June 1998.

285. During debates in the Committee of the Whole on 17 and 18 June 1998, on the inclusion of internal armed conflicts within the statute, a great number of states supported that view, among which were Australia, Costa Rica, Canada, Denmark, Belgium, New Zealand, the Czech Republic, Ireland, Korea, Brazil, the UK, Norway and Switzerland.

286. US statement on 23 March 1998 to the Preparatory Committee for the ICC.

287. Statement of the German representative to the Committee of the Whole on 17 June 1998, see UN.Doc.A/CONF.183. C.1/SR.4, p. 9.

288. China supported the deletion of any provisions dealing with internal armed conflicts within the statute (debates 18 June 1998, UN.Doc.A/CONF.183. C.1/ SR.5.p.14) and explained its rejection of the statute on 17 July 1998 on the basis (among others) of its opposition to include non-international conflicts in the jurisdiction of the court. See UN.Doc. A.CONF.183/C.1/SR.9 p. 6. This position can be put in perspective with the position taken by a representative of the Chinese Ministry of Foreign Affairs in 1954, when China remitted 410 Japanese military personnel who had committed various crimes during the Japanese invasion of China and the Chinese war of liberation. A recent report on the practice of China notes that this practice shows that China 'consistently holds that foreigners also shall take criminal responsibility for committing war crimes in internal armed conflicts'. Cited in J. M. Henckaerts and L. Doswald-Beck, *Customary international humanitarian law*, vol. II, part 2 (Cambridge: Cambridge University Press, 2005) p. 3663, para. 251.

289. Syria took this view during debates in the Committee of the Whole on 17 June 1998.

290. The representative of the UAE said that the sections dealing with internal armed conflicts in the draft statute should not be included. See A/CONF.183/C.1/SR.4 p. 11.

291. Bahrain concurred with the UAE, *ibid.*, p. 11.

292. During debates in the Committee of the Whole on 17 June 1998, Jordan expressed concerns over the inclusion of internal armed conflicts in the statute.

293. During debates on 18 June 1998, Turkey opposed the inclusion of any provisions dealing with internal armed conflicts in the statute and said that it was not clear how the court would decide whether there was an internal armed conflict. See A/CONF.183/C.1/SR.5 p. 13. On 17 July 1998, Turkey explained its abstention during the vote for the statute, as 'Articles 8.c) and d) were not satisfactory'. See UN.Doc.A.CONF.183/C.1/SR.9 p. 6.

294. See the statements made by Sudan to the Committee of the Whole on 17 June 1998, UN.Doc.A/CONF.183/C.1/SR.4 p. 12 and on 18 June 1998, UN.Doc.A/CONF.183/C.1/SR.5 p. 12.

295. See the statement made by India to the Committee of the Whole, on 18 June 1998, UN.Doc.A/CONF.183/C.1/SR.5, p. 13.

296. On the vote, which took place to accept the statute, the Arab group largely abstained.

297. See UN.Doc.A/CONF.183/SR.9 p. 10, some statements are also available online on www.un.org/icc.

298. Some states even admitted that they were responsible for committing war crimes during a civil war. The President of Guatemala admitted the state's institutional responsibility for war crimes committed during the thirty-six-year civil war and pledged to prosecute offenders. See (2000) 3 *YbIHL* 516.

299. See Article VII of the 1993 Convention on the Prohibition of Development, Production, Stockpiling and Use of Chemical Weapons.

300. See Article 14.2 of the Protocol II on Land Mines.

301. See Article 9 of the Ottawa Convention.

302. Protocol II entered into force on 3 December 1998, and Protocol IV entered into force on 30 July 1998.

303. See R. Baxter, 'Multilateral treaties as evidence of customary international law' 275.

304. The UK took that view during the entire negotiations which led to the adoption of the ICC statute; see (1998) *BYIL* 513. Similarly, see statement of the US representative to the Committee of the Whole on 17 June 1998, UN.Doc.A/CONF.183/C.1/SR.4 p. 8 as well as von Hebel and Robinson, 'Crimes within the jurisdiction of the court' p. 110

305. *Nicaragua* case, p. 100, para. 188 and the Nuclear Weapons advisory opinion p. 826, para. 70.

306. *Ibid.*, para. 70.

307. See D. Momtaz, 'War crimes in non-international armed conflicts under the statute of the International Criminal Court' 181.

308. See, for example, the SG report UN.Doc.S/25704 (3 May 1993) para. 10.

309. SC resolution 521 (19 September 1982). This conflict can also be qualified as international armed conflict.

310. See SC resolution 764 (13 July 1992). Furthermore, it is interesting to note that the SC took its first resolution on events in Yugoslavia on 5 September 1991 (SC resolution 713) and it took almost a year before the Council stated that individuals should be criminally responsible for these conducts.

311. See para. 7 of SC resolution 787 (16 November 1992).

312. See some recent resolutions taken by the Security Council about children in armed conflicts, where it stresses that 'the present resolution does not seek to make any legal determination as to whether situations which will be referred in the Secretary-General's report are or are not armed conflicts within the context of the Geneva Conventions and the Additional Protocols thereto, nor does it prejudge the legal status of the non-state parties involved in these situations'. See SC resolutions 1539 (22 April 2004) and 1612 (26 July 2005).

313. See SC resolutions 771 (13 August 1992), 780 (6 October 1992), 787 (16 November 1992), 808 (22 February 1993), 819 (16 April 1993), 820 (17 April 1993), 827 (25 May 1993), 859 (24 August 1993) in which the Security Council 'condemn once again all war crimes and other violations of international humanitarian law, by whomsoever committed, Bosnian Serbs or other individuals'; 913 (22 April 1994) in which the Security Council reiterates that 'any persons committing violations of international humanitarian law will be held individually responsible'; 941 (23 September 1994), 1009 (10 August 1995), 1010 (10 August 1995), 1019 (9 November 1995) and 1034 (21 December 1995).

314. See SC resolutions 918 (17 May 1994), 925 (8 June 1994), 935 (1 July 1994) where the Council recalls specifically that 'persons who instigate or participate in all breaches of international humanitarian law in Rwanda are individually responsible'; 955 (8 November 1994), 978 (27 February 1995) and 997 (9 June 1995).

315. See SC resolutions 794 (3 December 1992), 814 (26 March 1993), 837 (6 June 1993) and 865 (22 September 1993).

316. SC resolutions 950 (21 October 1994) and 972 (13 January 1995) (and all the previous ones on Liberia) only condemn the widespread violations of international humanitarian law and demand that all factions strictly abide by applicable rules of international humanitarian law. One needs to wait for SC resolution 1020 (10 November 1995) for the Council to call on Unomil to investigate and report to the Secretary-General on violations of human rights.

317. SC resolutions 804 (29 January 1993) and 811 (12 March 1993) only condemn the widespread violations of international humanitarian law. Resolutions 1064 (11 July

1996) and 1075 (11 October 1996) call for the 'investigation of the incidents of human rights abuses'. Resolution 1087 (11 December 1996) is the only one to stress 'the need to investigate alleged human rights violations and to punish those found guilty by due process of law.'

318. See SC resolutions 1160 (31 March 1998) and 1199 (23 September 1998) under-lying, for example, 'the need for the authorities of the Federal Republic of Yugoslavia to bring to justice those members of the security forces who have been involved in the mistreatment of civilians and deliberate destruction of property.' See also resolution 1203 (24 October 1998) calling for a complete investigation of all atrocities committed against civilians and 1244 (10 June 1999).

319. See SC resolutions 1012 (28 August 1995), 1072 (30 August 1996), 1577 (1 December 2004) and 1602 (31 May 2005) recalling that 'all persons who commit or authorise the commission of serious violations of international humanitarian law are individually responsible for such violations and should be held accountable.' See also SC resolution 1606 (20 June 2005) which recalls the need 'to investigate the crimes and identify and bring to justice those bearing the greatest responsibility for crimes of genocide, crimes against humanity and war crimes committed in Burundi *since independence*' (emphasis added).

320. SC resolutions 1080 (15 November 1996), 1097 (18 February 1997), 1208 (19 November 1998) and 1279 (30 November 1999) underline the obligations of all concerned to respect strictly the relevant provisions of international humanitarian law. Resolutions 1234 (9 April 1999), 1291 (24 February 2000), 1304 (16 June 2000), 1355 (15 June 2001) and 1341 (22 February 2001) call for an 'international investigation into all massacres with a view to bringing to justice those responsible.' Similarly, see also SC resolutions 1468 (20 March 2003), 1484 (30 May 2003), 1565 (1 October 2004), 1592 (30 March 2005), 1621 (6 September 2005) and 1635 (28 October 2005). It is also interesting to note the recent practice of the Security Council consisting in 'emphasising' that the UN forces in the Congo are authorised to use 'all necessary means' to deter any attempt at the use of force to threaten the political process and to ensure the protection of civilians under imminent threat of physical violence. See SC resolution 1592 (30 March 2005) para. 7.

321. SC resolutions 1193 (28 August 1998) and 1214 (8 December 1998) seem to consider the Afghan conflict to be an international conflict and affirm that all parties to the conflict are bound to comply with the Geneva Conventions and that persons who commit or order the commission of the grave breaches of the Conventions are individually responsible in respect of such breaches.

322. SC resolution 1231 (11 March 1999) urges the 'appropriate authorities to investi-gate all allegations of violations of human rights and humanitarian law with a view to bring the perpetrators to justice'. See also resolutions 1315 (14 August 2000) and 1400 (28 March 2002).

323. The SC condemned the violations of international humanitarian law and welcomed the sending of a fact-finding mission to Georgia to investigate reports of ethnic cleansing. See SC resolutions 876 (19 October 1993), 881 (4 November 1993) as well as SC resolutions 993 (12 May 1995), 1036 (12 January 1996) and 1065 (12 July 1996). Resolution 1339 (31 January 2001) calls 'upon both sides to investigate these incidents and bring to justice those responsible'.

324. See SC resolution 1479 (13 May 2003).

325. SC resolutions 1264 (15 September 1999), 1272 (25 October 1999) and 1319 (20 September 2000) which noted 'that grave violations of international humanitarian law and human rights law have been committed and those responsible for these violations should be brought to justice'.

326. See, in particular, SC resolutions 1556 (30 July 2004), 1564 (18 September 2004), 1574 (19 November 2004), 1590 (24 March 2005) and 1591 (29 March 2005).

327. SC resolution 1114 (19 June 1997).

328. See SC resolutions 933 (30 June 1994) and 940 (31 July 1994).

329. SC resolutions 822 (30 April 1993) and 884 (12 November 1993).

330. See SC resolutions 1216 (21 December 1998) and 1233 (6 April 1999).

331. See SC resolutions 1318 (7 September 2000), 1325 (31 October 2000), 1296 (19 April 2000) and 1379 (20 November 2001).

332. See SC resolutions 1265 (17 September 1999) and 1314 (11 August 2000).

333. See UN.Doc.S/25704 (3 May 1993) paras. 33–49.

334. See UN.Doc.S/1994/1125 (4 October 1994), in particular the preliminary report of the Commission of Experts annexed to this SG report, paras. 87–107. Earlier reports of the Secretary-General were already calling for the responsibility of perpetrators and their prosecutions. See UN.Doc.S/1994/879 (26 July 1994) paras. 1–2 and 10 and UN.Doc.S/1994/924 (3 August 1994) para. 27.

335. See UN.Doc.S/1995/134 (13 February 1995) para. 12.

336. The Secretary-General has consistently taken the view that the situation in Burundi amounted to an armed conflict (see para. 19 of UN.Doc.S/1996/660, 8 August 1996) and condemned the systematic human rights violations. However, in 1997, when the President of Burundi called for the 'establishment of an international criminal tribunal for Burundi, in order to try the instigators and perpetrators of acts of genocide since 1993', the Secretary-General replied: 'given the circumstances prevailing in Burundi, he was not in a position to recommend to the Security Council the establishment of such a Tribunal'. See SG report UN.Doc.S/1997/547 (15 July 1997) para. 18. See also UN.Doc.S/2002/1259 (18 November 2002) para. 45 and UN.Doc.S/2004/682 (25 August 2004) paras. 41–44.

337. See SG report UN.Doc.S/1998/834 (4 September 1998) para. 10, calling for the authorities to bring to justice all those involved in the mistreatment of civilians and destruction of property. See also SG reports UN.Doc.S/1998/912 (3 October 1998) para. 28; UN.Doc.S./1999/99 (30 January 1999) paras. 6, 12 and 32 and UN.Doc.S/1999/779 (12 July 1999) para. 66.

338. See SG report UN.Doc.S/1999/790 (15 July 1999) paras. 11, 13 and 24.
339. See SG report UN.Doc.S/1999/1024 (4 October 1999) which called for the accountability of those responsible for acts, which constitute breaches of international humanitarian law. The report of the High Commissioner for Human Rights on the human rights situation in East Timor affirms: 'It has become a widely accepted principle of contemporary international law and practice that wherever human rights are being grossly violated . . . that the perpetrators must be made accountable and justice rendered to the victims.' UN.Doc.E/CN.4/S-4/CRP.1 (17 September 1999) para. 4.
340. See SG report UN.Doc.S/1999/836 (30 July 1999) paras. 17–20, 47–48.
341. See SG report UN.Doc.S/2004/697 (27 August 2004) paras. 37–41.
342. See, for example, UN.Doc.S/2004/947 (3 December 2004) para. 16; UN.Doc.S/2005/10 (7 January 2005) paras. 17–18; UN.Doc.S/2005/68 (4 February 2005) paras. 3 and13; UN.Doc.S/2005/140 (4 March 2005) paras. 15–21; UN.Doc.S/2005/467 (18 July 2005) paras. 17–22; UN.Doc.S/2005/523 (11 August 2005) para. 6 and UN.Doc.S/2005/592 (19 September 2005) para. 5.
343. See SG report UN.Doc.S/2000/915 (4 October 2000). For more details, see section 2.3 of this chapter.
344. See some reports on the protection of civilians in armed conflicts UN.Doc.S/2001/331 (30 March 2001) and UN.Doc.S/2004/431 (28 May 2004) paras. 3, 13 and 39. On the situation of children in armed conflicts, see in particular, UN.Doc.S/2002/1299 (26 November 2002) paras. 3, 13 and 68. On women, peace and security, see, for example, UN.Doc.S/2002/1154 (16 October 2002) paras. 19, 23 and 25. See also a report on the rule of law and transitional justice in conflict and post-conflict societies UN.Doc.S/2004/616 (23 August 2004).
345. See SG report UN.Doc.S/1998/883 (22 September 1998) para. 41.
346. See, for example, GA resolution UN.Doc.A/56/173 (27 February 2002) p. 4; UN.Doc.A/57/233 (28 January 2003) pp. 4–5; UN.Doc.A/58/196 (11 March 2004) pp. 2–5; UN.Doc.A/59/207 (17 March 2005) p. 4.
347. See GA resolutions A/56/175 (28 February 2002) p. 5 and A/57/230 (27 February 2003) pp. 4–5.
348. Declaration by the Presidency on behalf of the European Union on the human rights and humanitarian situation in Colombia, press release 8737 (23 May 2000).
349. Declaration of the European Union on the Democratic Republic of Congo, press release 10396 (17 July 1998); declaration by the Presidency of the European Union on the massacres in the provinces of Ituri in the DRC, press release 13526/03 (13 October 2003); declaration by the Presidency on behalf of the European Union on the recent massacres in and around Drodro, north-eastern part of the DRC, press release 8433/03 (14 April 2003).
350. Declaration by the Presidency on behalf of the European Union concerning the situation in Liberia, press release 7449/05 Rev.2 (21 March 2005).

351. Declaration by the Presidency on behalf of the European Union on the recent killings of civilians in Burundi, press release 10612 (27 August 1999); declaration by the Presidency on behalf of the European Union on Burundi, press release 12373/1/02 Rev.1 (26 September 2002); declaration by the Presidency on behalf of the European Union on the judicial follow-up to the Itaba massacres in Burundi, press release 7108/03 (6 March 2003); declaration by the Presidency of the European Union on Burundi, press release 9124/05 (20 May 2005).

352. Declaration by the Presidency on behalf of the European Union on the Sierra Leone Peace Agreement, press release 9668 (15 July 1999). See also declaration by the Presidency on behalf of the European Union on the arrest and bringing into custody of Charles Taylor, press release 8008/06 Rev.1 (3 April 2006).

353. Declaration by the Presidency on behalf of the European Union concerning the situation in Timor, press release 11425 (20 September 2000), as well as press release 11129 (21 September 1999).

354. Declaration by the Presidency on behalf of the European Union on East Timor, press release 5833 (4 April 2000).

355. Declaration by the Presidency on behalf of the European Union on the adoption of UN SC resolution 1564 on Sudan, press release 12626/1/04 Rev 1 (23 September 2004); declaration by the Presidency on behalf of the European Union on the situation in Darfur, western Sudan, press release 9862/04 (26 May 2004); declaration by the Presidency on behalf of the European Union on the situation in Darfur (Sudan), press release 6750/1/04 (27 February 2004); declaration by the Presidency on behalf of the European Union on Darfur, press release 13176/1/05 (12 October 2005); declaration by the Presidency on behalf of the European Union on the signature, on 5 July, of the declaration of principles for the resolution of the Sudanese conflict in Darfur, press release 11022/05 (8 July 2005); declaration by the Presidency on behalf of the European Union on the report by the International Commission of Inquiry on Darfur, press release 6072/2/05 Rev.2 (7 February 2005), where the EU 'notes that the Commission also found rebel forces to be responsible for committing acts which could be classified as war crimes'.

356. See UN.Doc.S/PV.4877 (9 December 2003), cited in (2003) *BYIL* 854.

357. See also the Council of Europe common position of 11 June 2001 on the International Criminal Court (2001/443/CFSP), whose objective is 'to pursue and support an early entry into force of the Rome statute and the establishment of the Court'. The Council stated that 'the serious crimes within the jurisdiction of the Court are of concern for all member states, which are determined to cooperate for the prevention of those crimes and for putting an end to the impunity of the perpetrators thereof.'

358. In this section the legislation of ninety-nine states was reviewed, representing about half of the total number of UN members. The study therefore highlights consistent rather than universal practice among states.

359. Out of these ninety-nine states, fifty-four include serious violations of the laws of war committed in internal conflicts in their criminal codes, military manuals or other legislation. Twenty-seven states have not extended the concept of war crimes to internal armed conflicts and only criminalise violations of the laws of war in international armed conflicts. Another twelve have unclear legislation, which could be interpreted to extend the concept of war crimes in internal armed conflicts. Finally, another group of states (six) are in the process of adopting their ICC implementing legislation.

360. As mentioned in section 1 of this chapter, the *Tadić* case was the first one to establish individual criminal responsibility for war crimes in internal conflicts, but all decisions and judgments of both the ICTY and the ICTR subsequently confirmed this finding. As such, the practice of both institutions can be seen as further evidence of the existence of a customary principle in international law.

361. See the statement made by India to the Committee of the Whole on 18 June 1998, UN.Doc.A/CONF.183/C.1/SR.5, p. 13.

362. I. Brownlie, *Principles of public international law* (Oxford: Oxford University Press, 1996) p. 5.

363. Prior to that date, fewer than ten states were criminalising serious violations of the laws of war when committed in internal armed conflicts: Yugoslavia (1990), Ethiopia (1957), Mozambique (1988), the Netherlands (1952), Switzerland (1967), Sweden (1990), Thailand (1955) and the USA (1956 *Military manual*).

364. See Article 873 on the protection of civilians, and Article 874 on means of warfare of the Argentinean draft code of military justice.

365. See Article 116 of the 1999 criminal code of Azerbaijan.

366. See Article 136 of the 2000 criminal code of Belarus.

367. See Articles 372–85 of the 2004 Serbian draft criminal code.

368. See Article 154 of the 1998 criminal code of the Federation of Bosnia-Herzegovina and Articles 433–43 of the criminal code of Republika Srpska.

369. See Articles 373–91 of the 1994 criminal code of Slovenia.

370. See Articles 158–68 of the criminal code of Croatia.

371. See Article 378 of the criminal code of Costa Rica.

372. See the Law of 31 October 1998 of the Congo.

373. See Articles 135–64 of the Colombian criminal code.

374. See the 2002 penal code of Estonia, chapter 8 division 4.

375. See title XIX of the 1997 criminal code of El Salvador.

376. See Articles 411–13 of the 1999 Georgian criminal code.

377. See Article 41 of the 2002 military penal code of Jordan.

378. See Articles 336 and 338 of the criminal code of Lithuania.

379. See Articles 133 and 138 of the 2002 criminal code of Moldova.

380. See Articles 355 and 356 and the 1996 Russian criminal code.

381. See Article 159 of the 1998 criminal code of Kazakhstan.

382. See chapter IX of the 2004 criminal code of Latvia.

383. See paras. 107–8 of the military criminal code of Norway.

384. See Law No. 31/2004 of 22 July 2004 implementing the ICC statute in the criminal code of Portugal.

385. See Article 83 of the 1987 law of military crimes of Mozambique.

386. See Articles 282–90 of the 1957 criminal code of Ethiopia.

387. See chapter 11 of the 1995 Finnish criminal code.

388. See chapter 22, section 6 of the 1990 Swedish criminal code.

389. See Articles 608–14 of the 1995 Spanish criminal code.

390. See Article 214 of the code of military justice of Niger.

391. See Article 136*quarter* of the criminal code of Belgium.

392. See the French legislation on the basis of Security Council resolutions 827 and 955.

393. See Articles 121–26 of the 1997 Polish criminal code.

394. See Article 320 of the 1997 criminal code of Paraguay.

395. See the ICC Act of the Netherlands.

396. See the law of 15 July 2003 of Rwanda.

397. See section 2441, chapter 18 of the USA War Crimes Act.

398. See Article 108 of the Swiss military criminal code.

399. See Articles 403–5 of the Tadjik 1998 criminal code.

400. See, for example, Article 413.c) of the Georgian criminal code.

401. See, for example, Article 610 of the Spanish criminal code or the new German Code. Some criminal codes like the Latvian code in its Article 73 even prohibits the production, amassment, deployment or distribution of nuclear, chemical, biological, bacteriological, toxic or other weapons of mass destruction.

402. See section 3 of chapter 2 and section 2 of chapter 4 for supporting practice.

403. See UN.Doc.A/CONF.183/2/Add.1 (14 April 1998) p. 24.

404. *Tadić* jurisdiction decision, para. 134.

405. For the war crime of murder committed in internal armed conflict, see *Krstić* trial, paras. 484–89; *Tadić* trial, paras. 609–13; *Vasiljević* trial, para. 205; *Krnojelac* trial, para. 324; *Kupreškić* trial, paras. 560–61; *Jelisić* trial, para. 35; *Čelebići* trial, paras. 422 and 439; *Stakić* trial, paras. 584–87; *Rutaganda* trial, para. 79 (acquitted at trial but convicted for war crime on appeal, para. 584); *Semanza* trial, paras. 353, 535 and 551; *Blagojević* trial, para. 556 and *Strugar* trial, paras. 235–46.

406. For the war crime of torture committed in internal armed conflict, see *Furundžija* appeal, para. 11; *Kunarac* appeal, paras. 142–56; *Kvočka* appeal, para. 284; *Kunarac* trial, paras. 465–97; *Krnojelac* trial, paras. 177–88 and *Furundžija* trial, paras. 134–64.

407. For the war crime of cruel treatment committed in internal armed conflict, see *Tadić* trial, paras. 609–13 and *Strugar* trial, para. 261.

408. For the war crime of outrage upon personal dignity committed in internal armed conflict, see *Aleksovski* trial, paras. 47–57; *Kunarac* trial, paras. 498–514 and *Kunarac* appeal, paras. 161–66.

409. For the war crime of rape committed in internal armed conflict, see *Kunarac* trial, paras. 436–64; *Kunarac* appeal, paras. 127–133; *Furundžija* trial, paras. 165–89 and *Semanza* trial, para. 551.

410. For the war crime of slavery committed in internal armed conflict, see *Krnojelac* trial, para. 353. The Trial Chamber held in this case: 'the express prohibition of slavery in Additional Protocol II of 1977, which relates to internal armed conflict, confirms the conclusion that slavery is prohibited by customary international humanitarian law outside the context of a crime against humanity'.

411. For the war crime of pillage or plunder committed in internal armed conflict, see in particular, *Čelibići* trial, para. 315 and *Hadžihasanović* trial, paras. 49–56.

412. For the war crime of attacks against the civilian population committed in internal armed conflict, see *Galić* trial, paras. 56–62; *Prosecutor v. Pavle Strugar, Miodrag Jokić and others*, decision on interlocutory appeal, 22 November 2002, IT-01-42-AR72, para. 10 and *Strugar* trial, paras. 220–22.

413. For the war crime of wanton destruction of cities not justified by military necessity committed in internal armed conflicts, see *Hadžihasanović* trial, paras. 39–48; *Hadžihasanović* rule 98*bis* decision, paras. 95–107; *Strugar* trial, paras. 227–28 and 233 and *Orić* trial, paras. 579–89.

414. For the war crime of attacks on civilians objects committed in internal armed conflicts, see *Strugar* trial, paras. 223–26. The Trial Chamber in the *Strugar* case noted the absence of the prohibition of attacks against civilian objects in Additional Protocol II but affirmed that such violation triggered individual criminal responsibility in customary international law nonetheless (*Strugar* trial, para. 224).

415. For the war crime of seizure or destruction or wilful damage done to institutions dedicated to religion, see *Hadžihasanović* trial, paras. 57–64 and *Strugar* trial, paras. 229–33.

416. See, for example, *Čelibići* trial, para. 316; *Kunarac* trial, para. 408; *Galić* trial, para. 29; *Blaškić* trial, para. 176; *Krnojelac* trial, para. 64; *Furundžija* trial, para. 132; *Akayesu* trial, para. 608; *Oric* trial, para. 261; *Limaj* trial, para. 176; *Naletilić* trial, para. 228; *Blagojević* trial, para. 539; *Halilović* trial, para. 31; *Strugar* trial, para. 219.

417. *Čelibići* appeal, para. 157.

418. *Čelibići* appeal, paras. 153–74.

419. *Čelibići* appeal, para. 163.

420. *Ibid.*, para. 171.

421. *Čelibići* trial, para. 316. This statement was made by the Trial Chamber in the context of assessing the claim by the defendants that there was no customary law

principle applicable in internal armed conflicts according to which individuals could be found responsible for war crimes.

422. See, in particular, the *Orić*, *Hadžihasanović* and *Strugar* cases (references provided above).

423. See, for example, *Akayesu* trial, paras. 611–15; *Bagilishema* trial, para. 98; *Musema* trial, para. 242; *Rutaganda* trial, paras. 87–90 and *Semanza* trial, para. 353.

424. See *Rutaganda* appeal, paras. 556–85; *Semanza* appeal, paras. 370–71.

425. J. M. Henckaerts and L. Doswald-Beck, *Customary international humanitarian law* (Cambridge: Cambridge University Press, 2005) vol. I, pp. 590–603.

5

National prosecutions of war criminals and internal armed conflicts

Impunity of war criminals especially in internal armed conflicts has generally been the rule. It has often been recognised that impunity acts as a major encouragement to future offenders. It is submitted that the recognition that such conduct amounts to war crimes entailing individual criminal responsibility in internal armed conflict will strengthen the fight against impunity. Such recognition opens new avenues, as international tribunals as well as domestic courts could prosecute these international crimes. Responsibility for war crimes committed in internal armed conflicts can be enforced by three distinct but not mutually exclusive jurisdictions. Perpetrators could be prosecuted by the courts of the state on whose territory the offences were committed, the state of nationality of the victims or by the state of their own nationality. In internal armed conflicts, these three possible states will most of the time be one and the same, i.e. the territorial state. The national courts of the territorial state seem best placed to bring perpetrators to justice: they have direct access to witnesses as well as evidence, and their judgments carry a symbolic effect: the victims can see justice being done and this can act as a deterrent to future criminals. However, governments do not often pursue this solution, as those in power might protect suspected criminals, be the perpetrators of war crimes themselves or vote amnesty laws.[1] Even if willing to prosecute, governments may lack the financial, technical or human resources to carry out the prosecutions.[2]

One alternative to the failure of national courts of the territorial states to prosecute war criminals is to vest international tribunals with the power to prosecute such war crimes. Another alternative consists in allowing prosecutions by the courts of third states on the basis of universal jurisdiction. The perpetrators could therefore be tried by the country which has apprehended them, irrespective of the location of the crime or the nationality of the perpetrator or the victim. This solution presupposes the existence of a right by third states to use universal jurisdiction over perpetrators of war crimes committed in internal armed conflicts. War crimes committed in internal conflicts amount to international crimes. Some authors believe that international crimes, by definition, engender the application of the concept of universal jurisdiction: 'Internal atrocities are crimes under international law and therefore universally punishable.'[3] The qualification of 'international crime' would therefore automatically give a supplementary title of jurisdiction to every state in addition to the classical principles of jurisdiction: territoriality, nationality, passive personality and the protective principle, on which states may base their criminal jurisdiction.[4] This view is supported by positions from international tribunals[5] such as the International Criminal Tribunal for the former Yugoslavia (ICTY) Trial Chamber in the *Furundžija* case which held that:

> International crimes being universally condemned wherever they occur, every State has the right to prosecute and punish the authors of such crimes. As stated in general terms by the Supreme Court of Israel in *Eichmann*, and echoed by a USA court in *Demjanjuk*: 'It is the universal character of the crimes in question i.e. international crimes which vests in every State the authority to try and punish those who participated in their commission.'[6]

However, the *Pinochet* litigation has shown that there does not seem to be universal acceptance of the principle by which universal jurisdiction and international crimes are necessarily coterminous. Lord Goff of Chieveley concurred with the minority of the first Appellate Committee when they affirmed:

> It does not seem to me that it has been shown that there is any State practice or general consensus let alone a widely supported convention that all crimes against international law should be justiciable in national courts on the basis of the universality of jurisdiction.[7]

Similarly, Lord Phillips of Worth Matravers believed that:

> It is still an open question whether international law recognises universal jurisdiction in respect of international crimes.[8]

The majority of the Law Lords took the view that extra-territorial jurisdiction was not established for the crime of torture in English law before the entry into force of the Torture Convention.[9] They seemed therefore to suggest that customary international law did not establish universal jurisdiction for the crime of torture before the adoption of the

Torture Convention.[10] Lord Millet was the only one to take a different view and affirmed:

> Customary international law is part of the common law and accordingly I consider that the English Courts have and always have had extra-territorial criminal jurisdiction in respect of crimes of universal jurisdiction under customary international law.[11]

As mentioned earlier, a number of authors have considered that universal jurisdiction and international crimes are coterminous, but it is submitted that they do not always coincide and that an international crime can be established in international law, without automatically attracting the principle of universal jurisdiction.[12] Accordingly, one can distinguish the criminality of certain conduct in international law from the question of jurisdiction over perpetrators of such crimes.

The concept of universal jurisdiction will be explored briefly, before examining whether existing treaties which establish the principle of individual criminal responsibility for war crimes committed in internal conflicts, provide for the principle of universal jurisdiction. Failing a clear establishment of universal jurisdiction for these crimes in international treaties, the state of customary international law will be ascertained: is there a right to extend universal jurisdiction over war crimes committed in internal conflicts reflected in customary international law? Lastly, the recent national prosecutions by the territorial states for war crimes committed in internal armed conflicts will be studied in the last part of this chapter.

1. Universal jurisdiction and war crimes in international law

Jurisdiction has been defined as 'the authority of states to prescribe their law, to subject persons and things to adjudication in their courts and other tribunals, and to enforce their law, both judicially and non-judicially'.[13] International law has developed principles on the basis of which a state can extend its criminal jurisdiction over an offence and therefore reconcile the state's interest in a particular offence with other states' interests in the offence.[14] It is generally admitted that a state may be able to exercise its jurisdiction if 'there exists between the state and either the specific offence or the alleged offender a legitimate link, a link which is legitimate in the eyes of international law'.[15] Five principles currently constitute a legitimate basis of states' criminal jurisdiction in international law.[16] The first is the principle of territoriality, whereby a state exercises jurisdiction over an offender because the offence was committed in part or in full on its territory. The second is the principle of nationality, whereby the state will extend its jurisdiction over an offender who is a national of that state. The third is the passive personality principle, whereby the state claims jurisdiction over the offender on the ground that the victim of the offence is a national of the state concerned. The fourth principle is the protective principle, which permits jurisdiction to be extended to a conduct that threatens interests, which are vital to the integrity of the state concerned. Such conduct can cover acts against the national security of the state, counterfeiting its currency, fraud, perjury or forgery of official documents. Prosecutions of war criminals can be based on any of the first three mentioned principles: a state can try an alleged war criminal because the war crime was committed on its territory or because the war criminal or the victim is a national of that state.

Alongside these possible bases of jurisdiction, international law has given states 'the authority to punish certain crimes wherever and by whomsoever committed'[17] in the absence of any other accepted jurisdictional nexus at the time of the commission of the crime.[18] The universality principle is usually seen as a supplementary, optional and subsidiary basis of jurisdiction,[19] given to states over a limited category of offences, regardless of where the offence was committed, the nationality of the offender or the nationality of the victim.[20] The doctrine is divided on how best to define universal jurisdiction and on the rationale behind it.[21] However, the most predominant view is that every state has an interest in prosecuting crimes that 'threaten to undermine the very foundations of the enlightened international community as a whole'. In other words, all states 'have a stake in suppressing *delicta juris gentium*, and all are simultaneously endowed with the authority to exercise criminal jurisdiction'.[22]

Piracy was the first international crime to attract universal jurisdiction, allowing for the prosecutions of conduct committed in areas not subject to the jurisdiction of any state in particular.[23] Piracy is usually committed aboard vessels on the high seas or any place outside the state's jurisdiction and both pirates and the vessels are considered to be stateless.[24] Furthermore, the activities of pirates pose a threat to the interests of the international community such as the security of commerce on the high seas, the principle of the freedom of maritime communication and the principle of freedom of the high seas.[25] Next to piracy, most authors agree that the crime of slavery, because of its heinous nature, is a conduct recognised by customary international law to be subject to universal jurisdiction.[26]

More recently, states agreed to extend by treaty the principle of universal jurisdiction to other categories of offences, which, together with slavery, violate the interests of the international community and demand a more co-ordinated and repressive response from states. They include: aircraft hijacking and related offences,[27] crimes against protected persons,[28] apartheid,[29] hostage-taking,[30] offences against the 1980 Convention on the Physical Protection of Nuclear Material,[31] torture,[32] offences against the safety of maritime navigation,[33] drug-trafficking,[34] offences against the UN Convention against Transnational Organised Crimes,[35] use of mercenaries,[36] counterfeiters,[37] offences against the 1998 Convention on the Protection of the Environment through Criminal Law,[38] offences against the 1994 Convention on the Safety of UN and Associated Personnel[39] and corruption.[40] All these conventions provide for the use of the principle of universal jurisdiction by states, in cases where the preferred states, often the nationality or territorial state, have failed to prosecute and the offender is present on their territory.[41] Moreover, most of these conventions have the particularity of providing not only for a right to use universal jurisdiction, but putting states under an obligation either to try or to extradite the offenders when they are found on their territory.[42] One might also note that these conventions do not recognise the rights of states to exercise universal jurisdiction *in absentia* and require the presence of the offender on their territory.

For the purpose of this study, universal jurisdiction is defined as criminal prescriptive jurisdiction based on the nature of the crime.[43] States have translated this principle in various ways within their domestic system. Few countries have chosen to apply 'pure universal jurisdiction' and to start investigations without the presence of the alleged perpetrator in the country.[44] In most instances, states have implemented the principle contained in the above-mentioned treaties by requiring the presence of the offender on their territory. The presence of the offender is considered by part of the doctrine to be a necessary requirement before universal jurisdiction can be relied upon.[45] It is submitted, however, that this presence does not necessarily amount to a legal requirement[46] but can be seen as a procedural and practical requirement for the enforcement of universal jurisdiction at the state level rather than a legitimising link between the state and the offender.[47] Practice among states can diverge as to whether the presence of the offender within the jurisdiction of the state is required at the time an investigation is launched, an arrest warrant is issued or at the time of the trial itself.

Next to slavery, piracy and the offences provided for in the above-mentioned treaties, another category of international crime subject to universal jurisdiction is war crimes.

1.1 Universal jurisdiction over war crimes in international armed conflicts: historical background and contemporary applications

The right for belligerents to try enemy personnel who fell into their hands and against whom evidence was available that they had committed violations of the laws of war was already recognised unequivocally in the Middle Ages.[48] Universal jurisdiction, as defined above, was not per se established for serious violations of the laws of war. Only belligerents into whose hands the war criminals have fallen, or their own authorities, effectively prosecuted them. No example of neutral or third states prosecuting war criminals on the basis of universal jurisdiction can be found. Similarly, early instruments of codification of the laws and customs of war only contained injunctions on states to disseminate the laws of war and enact national legislation, but did not establish a universal right for states to try perpetrators of war crimes.[49] The end of the First World War saw a few prosecutions of war criminals but only by belligerents who had custody over them.[50] The Commission on Responsibility of the Authors of the War affirmed in 1919:

> Every belligerent has, according to international law, the power and authority to try the individuals alleged to be guilty of violations of the laws of war, if such persons have been taken prisoners of war or have otherwise fallen into its power (emphasis added).[51]

Furthermore, it is interesting to note that documents produced by international associations, such as the 1927 conference for the unification of penal law or the 1935 Harvard research in international law, do not include war crimes in their list of international crimes over which universal jurisdiction seems to extend at that time.[52] Universal jurisdiction for war crimes does not therefore seem to be reflected in customary law before the Second World War.[53]

The Second World War and the trials, which followed it, played an important role in the development of the customary principle of universal jurisdiction for war crimes. There exists, however, a certain amount of controversy among international lawyers as to the existence in 1945 of this principle in customary law and as to which title of jurisdiction military tribunals relied upon to prosecute alleged war criminals. The Nuremberg Tribunal took the view that 'in creating the Tribunal, the signatory powers have done together what any one of them might have done singly; for it is not to be doubted that any nation has the right thus to set up special courts to administer law'.[54] Some authors, like Draper, interpret this to mean: 'The Nuremberg 4 power tribunal was the collective exercise of a customary law jurisdiction which any one of the four States could have exercised individually *as a belligerent holding enemy personnel accused of war crimes*' (emphasis added).[55] It is submitted that the belligerents who prosecuted alleged war criminals were relying mostly on traditional titles of jurisdiction and that this right, belonging to belligerents only, does not amount to universal jurisdiction, as we understand it today.[56] Carnegie argued that most trials of war criminals, which took place after the Second World War, based their jurisdiction on the territoriality, the nationality or the passive personality principle.[57] Carnegie cited trials such as the *Justice* trial or the trial of *List and others*, where the court affirmed:

> As to the punishment of persons guilty of violating the laws and customs of war, it has always been recognised that tribunals may be established and punishment imposed by the state into whose hands the perpetrators fall. Those rules of international law were recognised as paramount and jurisdiction to enforce them by the injured belligerent government, whether within the territorial boundaries of the state or in occupied territory, has been unquestioned.[58]

Similarly, in the *Hostages* trial, the US Military Tribunal said:

> Such crimes are punishable by the country where the crime was committed or by the belligerent in whose hands the criminals have fallen, the jurisdiction being concurrent.[59]

On the other hand, other authors, such as Cowles, argued in 1945:

> Actual practice shows that the jurisdiction assumed by military courts, trying offences against the laws of war, has been personal or universal, not territorial.[60]

Similarly, the chairman of the War Crimes Commission affirmed:

> As to the jurisdiction, the traditional rule is that a military court, whether national or international, derives its jurisdiction over war crimes from the bare fact that the person charged is within the custody of the Court; his

nationality, the place where the offence was committed, the nationality of the victims are not generally material.[61]

Randall somehow resolves this controversy: 'reliance on the universality principle was not always obvious ... Relatively few judgments actually refer to the universality principle and the references are sometimes vague.'[62] The majority of war crimes trials held after the Second World War were relying on traditional titles of jurisdiction and in some instances, tribunals referred to universal jurisdiction. Randall affirms that 'the vast majority of the offences were punished under the territoriality, nationality or passive personality principles'. If the Nuremberg Tribunal did not rely explicitly on universal jurisdiction, Randall argues that the *List*, the *Almelo* trial, the *Zyklon B* case, the *Hadamar* trial and the *Eisentrager* cases provided explicit references to the principle of universal jurisdiction.[63] In the *Almelo* trial, a British military court sitting in the Netherlands declared that:

> Every independent state has an international law jurisdiction to punish pirates and war criminals in its custody regardless of the nationality of the victim or of the place where the offence was committed.[64]

Even if the principle of universality of jurisdiction for war crimes might not have been fully established in customary international law by 1945,[65] the universal ratification of the 1949 Geneva Conventions, coupled with more recent judgments, such as the *Eichmann* and *Demjajuk* cases,[66] leave no doubt today, as to the application in customary law of the principle of universal jurisdiction for war crimes committed in international conflicts.[67]

Offences defined as grave breaches of the Geneva Conventions attract not only a right for states to try war criminals under the principle of universality, but impose an obligation on belligerents or neutral states alike, either to try or extradite war criminals under the principle *aut judicare, aut dedere*.[68] It is open to debate whether this principle implies the right for states actively to investigate and issue arrest warrants when the alleged offender is not on its territory, or if it is understood only as an obligation for states parties to search for and prosecute or extradite war criminals found on their territory. The Pictet commentary to the Geneva Conventions states: 'As soon as one of them is aware that *a person on its territory* has committed such an offence, it is its duty to see that such person is arrested and prosecuted without delay' (emphasis added).[69] It might be noted, however, that Article 1 of the Geneva Conventions enjoined states to respect and ensure respect of the Geneva Conventions. Can a state ensure respect of the Geneva Conventions if it cannot start to investigate war crimes and issue an arrest warrant, even if the alleged offender is not yet present on its territory? Even if later conventions, on crimes such as torture or terrorism, only provide for universal jurisdiction when the alleged offender is present on the state's territory, one might agree with some authors that the Geneva Conventions do not prohibit states from actively pursuing investigations or issuing arrest warrants even if the offender is not present on their territory.[70]

Being universally ratified, these conventions establish a potentially strong enforcement mechanism of individual responsibility for grave breaches of the Geneva Conventions. However, the first reported prosecution by national courts of individuals for grave breaches only took place in 1994.[71] This is partly explained by the unwillingness of states to fulfil their obligations effectively under the Geneva Conventions. Furthermore, a substantial number of states did not incorporate the grave breaches and their penalties into their criminal code, rendering therefore any national prosecution on the basis of the Geneva Conventions difficult.[72]

In conclusion, the jurisdictional regime over war crimes committed in international conflicts is twofold. First, all the countries of the world are now party to the Geneva Conventions and are under the obligation either to try or to extradite an individual found on their territory suspected of having committed a grave breach of the Conventions. Secondly, under customary international law, the category of serious war crimes attracts the principle of universal jurisdiction, whereby all states have a right to exercise criminal jurisdiction over war criminals. As examined in chapter 3, this category of war crimes in international conflicts is wider than the list of grave breaches of the Geneva Conventions and includes some violations of the Hague Conventions. But does the newest type of war crimes committed in internal armed conflicts, attract the principle of universal jurisdiction?

1.2 Title of jurisdiction provided in international treaties for war crimes committed in internal armed conflicts

In treaty law, the 1949 Geneva Conventions and their Additional Protocols did not make the serious violations of common Article 3 or Protocol II crimes, nor did they envisage including these violations within the framework of the grave breaches regime. The Geneva Conventions require states to suppress 'all acts contrary to the provisions of the Conventions other than grave breaches'.[73] States can therefore impose penal sanctions on violations of common Article 3 for example, but in 1949, states clearly decided not to extend universal jurisdiction over all serious violations of the conventions, reserving this regime for the grave breaches only. It is submitted that the Geneva Conventions do not lay down per se a right for all states to exercise universal jurisdiction over these types of violations.[74] As the right to extend universal jurisdiction cannot be presumed, the Geneva Conventions cannot be seen to grant third states a right to extend universal jurisdictions over other crimes than grave breaches. More recently, the 1993 Chemical Weapons Convention, as well as the 1996 Protocol II to the 1980 Convention on Prohibitions or Restrictions on the Use of Mines, Booby-traps or Other Devices and the 1997 Convention on the Prohibition of the Use, Stockpiling, Production and Transfer of Anti-personnel Mines and on their Destruction, contain provisions requiring states parties to enact penal sanctions in order to 'prevent and suppress any activity prohibited to a state party under this convention undertaken by persons or on territory under its jurisdiction or control'.[75] States are simply enjoined to exercise jurisdiction over persons or territory under their control and no universal right of jurisdiction is granted to third states.

The Second Protocol of 26 March 1999 to the 1954 Hague Convention for the Protection of Cultural Property in the Event of Armed Conflict differs from previous treaties as it enjoins states to establish criminal jurisdiction over serious violations of the protocol when the alleged offender is also present in their territory.[76] Article 22 of this Protocol provides for its application in internal armed conflicts. The 1994 Convention on the Safety of UN and Associated Personnel and the Second Protocol to the 1954 Hague Convention are the only two humanitarian law instruments extending universal jurisdiction over some of their violations when committed in internal armed conflicts, if the offender is present on the territory of the prosecuting state.[77]

As far as treaties creating international judicial bodies are concerned, it is possible to argue that the establishment by the Security Council of both the ICTY and the Internationl Criminal Tribunal for Rwanda (ICTR), were an expression of the principle of universal jurisdiction: 'The member states of the UN have done together what each of them might have done singly.'[78] This practice can be seen as an implicit recognition that genocide, crimes against humanity and war crimes, committed both in international and internal conflicts, are governed by the principle of universal jurisdiction. Similarly, it is important to note that the international community as a whole supported the

creation of both tribunals to try war crimes committed both in international and internal conflicts, and that no one was opposed to the
Security Council establishing international tribunals having primacy of
jurisdiction over national courts.[79]

When it came to establishing a permanent International Criminal
Court (ICC), however, the international community was bitterly
divided over the question of giving the ICC universal jurisdiction over
the international crimes defined in the statute.[80] During the Rome
diplomatic conference, Germany argued that the court should be given
jurisdiction over war crimes, genocide and crimes against humanity
without the need for specific states to consent before the court could
exercise its jurisdiction.[81] The German proposal relied on the principle of
universal jurisdiction and contended that 'all states may exercise universal
criminal jurisdiction' concerning the crimes mentioned 'regardless of the
nationality of the offender, the nationality of the victims, and the place
where the crime was committed'.[82] If 'states parties can individually
exercise universal jurisdiction, they can also vest the ICC with similar
power. The ICC should be put in the same position as any state.'[83] This
proposal received a reasonable amount of support during the conference's
first discussion on jurisdiction, but failed to attract general acceptance and
was later dropped in a spirit of compromise.[84] The ICC statute therefore
does not include the principle of universal jurisdiction but instead imposes
some pre-conditions for the exercise of the court's jurisdiction.[85]

It seems that states found it premature to give the court the option to
exercise universal jurisdiction. This rejection was not specifically aimed
at war crimes committed in internal armed conflicts. It is disappointing,
however, that 50 years after establishing the obligation *aut judicare, aut
dedere* for the grave breaches of the Geneva Conventions, the international community is not willing to equip the first international criminal
court with universal jurisdiction and as a result to enforce individual
criminal responsibility for international crimes effectively. This rejection can be partly explained by the mistrust and fear of certain states vis à
vis the ICC.[86] The ICC statute shows a certain amount of contradiction:
on the one hand, there is this clear rejection of universal jurisdiction for
the court itself, while on the other hand, the preamble of the statute
affirms: 'it is the duty of every state to exercise its criminal jurisdiction
over those responsible for international crimes'. This part of the preamble exemplifies the principle of complementarity contained in the
statute and can be seen as strong evidence of the *opinio juris* of states.
This affirmation of every state's duty to exercise its criminal jurisdiction

over offenders falls short, however, of an explicit obligation for states to establish universal jurisdiction over the crimes listed in the statute.[87] This paragraph of the preamble has been left ambiguous as to whether this duty to exercise criminal jurisdiction is on the basis of universal jurisdiction, territoriality or nationality.[88]

Even if it would seem reasonable, and even coherent, that all types of war crimes, committed in internal or international conflicts, attract the same jurisdictional regime, international treaty law does not treat these offences in the same way. In practice, treaty law seems only to extend universal jurisdiction over two types of war crimes when committed in internal conflicts: crimes against UN and associated personnel and serious violations to the Second Protocol to the 1954 Hague Convention for the Protection of Cultural Property. The 1949 Geneva Conventions, Additional Protocol II and the few weaponry conventions do not include this principle. The Rome conference refused to extend this right to the ICC. One should then turn to customary international law to determine whether it fills the gap left open by treaty law and if there is a customary right to extend jurisdiction over war crimes committed in internal armed conflicts.

2. War crimes committed in internal armed conflicts and the principle of universal jurisdiction under customary law

The principle of universal jurisdiction over war crimes committed in internal armed conflicts is only provided for in two minor international treaties. Since the beginning of the 1990s, some national courts have extended their jurisdiction over war crimes committed in internal armed conflicts on the basis of universal jurisdiction. Were they relying on a customary right to do so? This section will try to determine whether customary international law gives a title to all states to extend universal jurisdiction over war crimes committed in internal armed conflicts. The right to extend universal jurisdiction over certain categories of crimes cannot be presumed. Universal jurisdiction is an exceptional title of jurisdiction which allows states having no link with the offence to extend its criminal jurisdiction over non-nationals who would have committed international crimes in another state. The exercise of this title of jurisdiction could be seen as conflicting with the principle of non-interference in internal affairs of states. If a right to extend universal jurisdiction over war crimes in internal armed conflicts cannot be established in customary law, it will be necessary to assert the existence or the absence of a prohibition in customary law to do so.

In order to explore the potential applicability in customary international law of universal jurisdiction over war crimes committed in internal armed conflicts, the practice of states and international organisations will be examined. First, in order to highlight state practice, national legislation and criminal codes will be studied to find out if they effectively provide national courts with such a right. If so, have states used this right and successfully prosecuted individuals for war crimes committed in internal conflicts? The second part of this section will analyse recent prosecutions of war criminals under universal jurisdiction.

2.1 Practice of states: national legislation and criminal codes

National legislation implementing the 1949 Geneva Conventions and Additional Protocols, domestic criminal codes and national legislation implementing the ICC statute are the subject of particular scrutiny. Two issues in particular will be looked at: does national legislation provide for universal jurisdiction over war crimes committed in internal armed conflicts? And if so, what are the preconditions, if any, for national courts to prosecute individuals before their courts?

2.1.1 National legislation implementing the 1949 Geneva Convention and Additional Protocols as well as domestic criminal codes[89]

As seen in chapter 4 of this book, a number of countries have not implemented any specific legislation dealing with the grave breaches of the Geneva Conventions or other violations of the laws and customs of war.[90] These states do not seem *a fortiori* to provide for the application of universal jurisdiction over war crimes committed in international or internal armed conflicts in their legislation. This group includes states such as China,[91] Iran,[92] Senegal,[93] Morocco, Nepal, Pakistan, Cameroon and Iraq.[94]

Other states, such as the USA, Bangladesh and Romania,[95] have enacted national legislation implementing the Geneva Conventions but have knowingly departed from their obligations under the Geneva Conventions, by not including the principle of universal jurisdiction. Chapter 118 entitled 'war crimes' of the US Code applies to anyone, whether inside or outside the USA, who commits a war crime. This is later qualified to apply only if the persons committing such a war crime or the victims of war crimes are members of the Armed Forces of the USA or are US nationals.[96] Similarly, the Bangladeshi legislation gives national courts the power to try or punish any person suspected of having committed any violation of the Geneva Conventions, including violations of common Article 3, but only if this conduct was committed in the territory of Bangladesh.[97]

A third group of states have either enacted national legislation providing for universal jurisdiction to apply in case of grave breaches of the Geneva Conventions and Protocol I only, or alternatively, their criminal codes contain a general provision providing for universal jurisdiction over offences for which international treaties require the ratifying states to do so. It is submitted that the latter formulation seems to exclude most war crimes committed in internal armed conflicts, as only two minor international instruments provide for the application of universal jurisdiction over war crimes committed in internal armed conflicts.[98] It is open to debate whether domestic courts might view the ICC statute, and in particular paragraph six of its preamble, as a sufficient basis allowing or obliging states to extend universal jurisdiction over international crimes, including war crimes committed in internal armed conflicts. This third group contains a number of common law countries such as the Cook Islands, Gambia, Ghana, India, Ireland, Kenya, Malawi, Mauritius, Nigeria and Trinidad and Tobago.[99] Some civil law countries have adopted a similar approach such as Armenia,[100] Austria,[101] Belgium,[102] Brazil,[103] Bolivia,[104] Bosnia-Herzegovina,[105] the Czech Republic,[106] Ecuador,[107] El Salvador,[108] Greece,[109] Guatemala,[110] Hungary,[111] Honduras,[112] Israel,[113] Lebanon,[114] Kazakhstan,[115] Moldova,[116] Mexico,[117] Panama,[118] Paraguay,[119] Peru,[120] Russia,[121] Turkey,[122] Uruguay,[123] Vietnam[124] and Yemen.[125]

A fourth group of states consists mainly of European states and newly independent republics of Eastern Europe, which have included war crimes committed in internal armed conflicts in their criminal codes and have also extended universal jurisdiction over such offences. These countries include Azerbaijan,[126] Belarus,[127] Burundi,[128] Colombia,[129] Costa Rica,[130] Croatia,[131] Denmark,[132] the Democratic Republic of Congo,[133] Estonia,[134] Ethiopia,[135] France,[136] Finland,[137] Georgia,[138] Lithuania,[139] the Netherlands,[140] Niger,[141] Norway,[142] Portugal,[143] the Republic of Congo,[144] Sweden,[145] Slovenia,[146] Spain,[147] Switzerland[148] and Tajikistan.[149]

This review shows that it is rather difficult to draw a precise picture of all the states which might extend universal jurisdiction over war crimes committed in internal armed conflicts. Precise information on every state studied in chapter 4 was not always available.[150] Similarly, an important number of criminal codes use a rather vague formulation such as 'when the state through international treaties has pledged to punish them' or 'when international treaties to which the state is a party, establish this jurisdiction'. These formulations seem to require that the international treaty establishes not only the criminality of the offences but also and primarily the application of universal jurisdiction over them, before national courts can extend universal jurisdiction over these crimes. The absence of a clear application of universal jurisdiction in all major international instruments dealing with war crimes in internal armed conflicts[151] will hamper the potential reliance by domestic judges upon those general formulations in order to prosecute war crimes committed in internal armed conflicts.[152]

2.1.2 National legislation implementing the Rome statute for an International Criminal Court

The ratification of the ICC statute has enabled a number of states to examine their existing legislation and to implement new provisions, which render criminal the offences defined in the ICC statute within their own domestic legislation.[153] Similarly, the ratification of the ICC statute triggered a debate over the choice of jurisdictional regime for these offences. The principle of universal jurisdiction has not been extended to the court itself and an obligation for party states to extend such a regime does not derive explicitly from the statute. The preamble merely recalls 'the duty of every state to exercise its criminal jurisdiction over those responsible for international crimes'.[154] Some states have nonetheless chosen to extend universal jurisdiction over the offences contained in the ICC statute so that their country is not a safe haven for perpetrators of atrocities committed elsewhere. A few states chose to extend universal jurisdiction over war crimes committed in internal armed conflicts, even if the alleged offender is not in their territory. The New Zealand International Crimes and International Criminal Court Act 2000 provides for prosecutions by New Zealand courts of genocide, crimes against humanity and war crimes, as defined in the ICC statute, regardless of:

  i) the nationality or citizenship of the person accused, or
  ii) whether or not any act forming part of the offence occurred in New Zealand, or
  iii) whether or not the person accused was in New Zealand at the time that the act constituting the offence occurred or at the time a decision was made to charge the person with an offence.[155]

With the written consent of the Attorney-General New Zealand courts can charge the person with an offence even if they are not in New Zealand territory.[156] The New Zealand Government decided that it 'would not wish to close off the possibility of a New Zealand prosecution for offending elsewhere. It considers this to be one way to help to fight against impunity for these crimes'.[157] New Zealand courts will be able to prosecute individuals for war crimes, as defined in Article 8 of the ICC statute, if the offence charged is alleged to have occurred on or after the commencement of the Act.[158]

Similarly, the Australian International Criminal Court Act 2002 (consequential amendment of the Criminal Code Act 1995) incorporates the list of crimes appearing in the ICC statute into Australian law[159] and extends the jurisdiction of Australian courts to genocide, crimes against humanity and war crimes 'whether or not the conduct constituting the alleged offence occurs in Australia; and whether or not the result of the conduct constituting the alleged offence occurs in Australia'.[160] There is no requirement that the alleged offender be present in Australian territory[161] but the consent of the Attorney-General must be obtained before any proceedings may commence.[162]

Furthermore, the 2006 International Criminal Court Act of Trinidad and Tobago extends the jurisdiction of local courts over war criminals irrespective of 'whether or not the person accused was in Trinidad at the time the act constituting the offence occurred or at the time a decision was made to charge that person with an offence'.[163]

A second group of countries decided to extend universal jurisdiction but requires the presence of the alleged offender in their territory. The Crimes against Humanity and War Crimes Act 2000 of Canada allows Canadian courts to prosecute individuals for war crimes in international and internal conflicts alike, when they are defined as such by customary or conventional international law, if:

a) At the time the offence is alleged to have been committed,
   i) the person was a Canadian citizen or was employed by Canada in a civilian or military capacity
   ii) the person was a citizen of a state that was engaged in an armed conflict against Canada or was employed in a civilian or military capacity by such a state
   iii) the victim of the alleged offence was a Canadian citizen, or
   iv) the victim of the alleged offence was a citizen of a state that was allied with Canada in an armed conflict, or
b) after the time the offence is alleged to have been committed, the person is present in Canada.[164]

It is interesting to note that the Canadian courts will be able to extend their jurisdiction for conduct committed outside Canada either before or after the coming into force of the Act.[165] This Act allows Canadian courts to extend their jurisdiction over war crimes committed in any foreign internal armed conflict, as long as they constituted at the time and place of their commission war crimes according to customary international law or conventional international law, and if their perpetrator is found on Canadian territory.[166]

Similarly, the International Criminal Court Act 2002 of South Africa extends the jurisdiction of South African courts over persons, who have committed any of the crimes contemplated in Article 5 of the ICC statute outside the territory of South Africa if:

a) that person is a South African citizen; or
b) that person is not a South African citizen but is ordinarily resident in the Republic; or
c) that person, after the commission of the crime, is present in the territory of the Republic; or
d) that person has committed the said crime against a South African citizen or against a person who is ordinarily resident in the Republic.[167]

The presence of alleged war criminals in South African territory will therefore be enough to trigger the jurisdiction of South African courts.[168] One might also note the two most recent instruments of ICC implementing legislation which extend the principle *aut dedere, aut judicare* to all crimes contained in the ICC statute. The ICC legislation adopted in Argentina and Uruguay in 2006 allows for the prosecutions of alleged offenders if they are found in Argentinean or Uruguayan territory and they are not extradited to a third state or the ICC.[169]

On 26 June 2002 Germany adopted its code of crimes against international law which implements all the offences contained in the ICC statute together with other international offences reflected either in Protocol I or in customary international law into German domestic law.[170] Section 1 of the Code provides that it 'shall apply to all criminal offences against international law designated under this Act ... even when the offence was committed abroad and bears no relation to Germany'. The possibility of prosecuting offences committed abroad, such as war crimes in internal conflicts, is, however, restricted by section 153f of the code of criminal procedure. This section provides that:

> The public prosecution office may dispense with prosecuting an offence punishable pursuant to sections 6 to 14 of the Code, if the accused is not present in Germany and such presence is not to be anticipated ... The

public prosecution office can, in particular, dispense with prosecuting an offence punishable pursuant to sections 6 to 14 of the Code if:

1. there is no suspicion of a German having committed such offence
2. such offence was not committed against a German
3. no suspect in respect of such offence is residing in Germany and such residence is not to be anticipated and
4. the offence is being prosecuted before an international court or by a state on whose territory the offence was committed, whose national is suspected of its commission or whose national was harmed by the offence.[171]

No particular link is necessary between the offender and Germany, but this provision seems to imply that in practice the presence of an accused in Germany is a quasi requirement for the public prosecution office to start prosecutions. The principle of complementarity is also visible, as the ICC or the territorial or nationality states will always have precedence over German courts. In the absence of such interests, German courts will be able to assert universal jurisdiction over these offences.[172]

Finally, the international crimes Act 2003 of the Netherlands implements all the substantive offences of the ICC statute as well as the 1984 Torture Convention, the 1999 Second Protocol to the 1954 Hague Convention for the Protection of Cultural Property in the Event of Armed Conflict and the Grave Breaches of Protocol I into the Dutch criminal system. Furthermore, it extends universal jurisdiction over all these crimes subject to the presence of the accused in Dutch territory.[173]

The UK by contrast, did not follow these examples. The International Criminal Court Act 2001 does not extend the principle of universal jurisdiction to war crimes. Some link with the UK is necessary before its courts can extend jurisdiction over these international offences. Sections 50 and 51 of the Act introduce into domestic legislation the offences of genocide, crimes against humanity and war crimes, as defined in the ICC statute, but this section applies only to acts committed in the UK, or to acts committed outside the UK by UK nationals, by UK residents or persons subject to UK service jurisdiction.[174] The initial draft did not include 'UK residents' and illustrated the UK Government's option to assume universal jurisdiction only where an international agreement expressly requires it. During debates on the Bill, Baroness Scotland of Asthal, argued in the House of Lords that the Rome statute does not require universal jurisdiction, and that:

> There are significant practical difficulties when our courts have to pro-
> secute crimes that have taken place elsewhere in the world . . . Rather than
> taking jurisdiction that will be difficult to enforce, we believe that those
> countries in which the offences took place should be encouraged to
> prosecute.[175]

Sections 67 and 68 of the Act define a UK resident as a person who becomes resident in the UK after the commission outside the UK of one of the crimes defined in the ICC statute.[176] Proceedings may be brought against such a person if he is a resident of the UK at the time the proceedings are brought and the acts in respect of which the proceedings are brought would have constituted that offence if they had been committed in that part of the UK. The extension of the jurisdiction of British courts over 'residents' is not a form of universal jurisdiction as this clear link between the offender and the UK must be established for a perpetrator of war crimes committed in a foreign internal armed conflict to be prosecuted in the UK.[177] This additional basis of jurisdiction should allow the UK, however, not to become a safe heaven for criminals.[178]

Finally, some countries which have ratified the ICC statute and included all the ICC offences within their criminal code have chosen not to extend universal jurisdiction over any of these crimes to their courts. This is the case for Kenya who, in its draft implementing legislation, chose to rely on the classical basis of jurisdiction, such as territoriality, as well as active and passive personality principles only.[179]

Out of the 104 states, which have so far ratified the ICC statute, Canada, Australia, New Zealand, South Africa, Germany, the Netherlands, Trinidad and Tobago, Argentina and Uruguay have amended their criminal provisions to allow for prosecutions by national courts on the basis of universal jurisdiction of perpetrators of war crimes committed abroad in internal conflicts in certain circumstances. These countries may soon be joined by a wealth of other countries which are in the process of adopting implementing legislation for the ICC statute. Some, such as Brazil,[180] Ecuador,[181] Greece,[182] Italy,[183] Sweden[184] and Switzerland, plan to include the principle of universal jurisdiction over the ICC crimes. These will reinforce the tangible trend taken by states to extend universal jurisdiction over war crimes committed in internal armed conflicts.

In conclusion, out of seventy-eight states studied, forty-two do not provide for universal jurisdiction for crimes committed in internal armed conflicts and only extend the principle of universal jurisdiction over grave breaches of the Geneva Conventions or extend universal jurisdiction over the offences which international treaties require states to prosecute. This group of states represents half of the countries studied, while only more than a third extend universal jurisdiction to both war crimes committed in internal and international armed conflicts. However, this minority of thirty-two states is not negligible and shows recent but tangible evidence that state practice is evolving in this area. We can also note that another four states have enacted draft ICC implementing legislation extending universal jurisdiction over war crimes committed in internal armed conflicts, bringing the number of states which have or will soon have universal jurisdiction over war crimes committed in internal armed conflicts to thirty-six(out of a total of seventy-eight states studied).[185] These results can be partly explained by the reluctance of states to provide for universal jurisdiction, especially in cases not clearly established by binding international instrument like war crimes in internal armed conflicts. Policy considerations also play a role, as many states clearly prefer not to get involved in the internal armed conflicts of other states. Furthermore, when states implement their obligations under the Geneva Conventions, it seems that they often amend the list of international crimes in their criminal codes, without necessarily providing for universal jurisdiction over these crimes in the general part of their criminal codes. Universal ratification of the Geneva Conventions is not accompanied by universal implementation of the grave breaches requirements in domestic criminal codes. A *fortiori* enforcement of individual responsibility for war crimes committed in internal armed conflicts may be even more random, as only thirty-two states provide for universal jurisdiction over these crimes.

Only a minority of states chose to implement 'pure universal jurisdiction'[186] whereby investigations or the issuance of an arrest warrant would be possible even if the alleged perpetrator is not present in the state territory. The majority of states seems to require the presence of the alleged offender or/and the consent of their Attorney-General before prosecutions of war criminals can be started.[187] This practice cannot be said to amount to an extensive and virtually uniform practice, but does reflect a certain amount of *opinio juris*. By giving their courts jurisdiction over war crimes committed in internal armed conflicts of other states, this group of states shows their belief either that universal jurisdiction over war crimes committed in internal conflicts is a principle already reflected in customary international law or that at the very minimum, there is no specific international norm prohibiting them from doing so.

2.2 Practice of international organisations and judicial institutions

2.2.1 The UN Security Council

This growing state practice is not, however, reinforced by consistent practice of the UN Security Council or other UN institutions. Since 1989 the Security Council has adopted many resolutions condemning serious violations of the laws of war committed in internal armed conflicts and calling for their authors to be held criminally responsible. In some circumstances, the Council has then called for the alleged perpetrators to be brought to justice without, however, specifying who should prosecute them.[188] In a few cases, the Security Council went further and specified who should prosecute them. In resolution 978 (27 February 1995), the Security Council urged:

> States to arrest and detain, in accordance with their national law and relevant standards of international law, pending prosecutions by the ICTR or by the appropriate national authorities, persons found within their territory against whom there is sufficient evidence that they were responsible for acts within the jurisdiction of the ICTR.

This resolution adopted after the Rwandan genocide is the closest the Council ever came to urging states to extend universal jurisdiction over war crimes committed in internal conflicts. In other circumstances, the Council called on the parties to the conflicts to bring the alleged perpetrators to justice.[189] In light of the failure of the parties to the Darfur conflict to bring perpetrators to justice, the Council called on all states to take measures to prevent alleged war criminals entering their territory, and to freeze the assets and economic resources of these alleged criminals. It stopped short, however, of calling on all states to prosecute these war criminals if found in their territory.[190] More recently, the Security Council adopted resolutions of a general character on the protection of civilians in armed conflicts where the Council emphasised 'the responsibility of states to end impunity and to prosecute those responsible for war crimes or serious violations of international humanitarian law'.[191] These few resolutions are evidence of *opinio juris* of states but this dictum does not per se enjoin states to extend universal jurisdiction over war crimes in internal armed conflicts and has not appeared in a consistent manner in the many resolutions adopted since 1989. It echoes the similar principle contained in the preamble to the Rome statute affirming the duty of states to prosecute without, however, explicitly clarifying if this duty applies to any state or just the territorial state.[192] In other words, this provision of the preamble does not explain whether the duty to prosecute those responsible for international crimes extends to crimes only committed in their territory or if it amounts to an obligation for states to prosecute alleged offenders on the basis of universal jurisdiction. The rejection of universal jurisdiction for the court itself during the debates in Rome militates against the latter interpretation.

The practice of the Security Council can be also assessed in light of the practice of other UN bodies. It is interesting to note that the Commission of Experts established pursuant to UN Security Council resolution 780 (1992) took the view that 'the only offences committed in internal armed conflict for which universal jurisdiction exists are crimes against humanity and genocide for which it applies irrespective of the conflicts' classification'.[193] This position can be opposed to the position taken by the UN Commission on Human Rights in a recently adopted resolution on the human rights situation in Sierra Leone. The Commission recalled:

> All factions and forces in Sierra Leone that in any armed conflict, including an armed conflict not of an international character, the taking of hostages, wilful killing and torture or inhuman treatment of persons taking no active part in the hostilities constitute grave breaches of international humanitarian law, and that all countries are under the obligation to search for persons alleged to have committed, or to have ordered to be committed, such grave breaches and to bring such persons, regardless of their nationality, before their own courts.[194]

The UN Secretary-General has also consistently called for the end of impunity in internal armed conflicts. The closest he went to affirming universal jurisdiction over war criminals was in a 2004 report on the protection of civilians in armed conflicts where he stated:

> The states on whose territory such crimes are being committed bear the foremost responsibility, but in the absence of timely and appropriate action by a state, the responsibility to respond falls to the international community.[195]

2.2.2 The ICJ and the *DRC v. Belgium* case

One may also turn to decisions from courts and tribunals, such as the International Court of Justice (ICJ) in order to determine the state of the law.[196] The right of states to prosecute war crimes committed in internal armed conflicts under universal jurisdiction was put under a spot light when the Democratic Republic of Congo (DRC) challenged the legality of an arrest warrant against its Minister of Foreign Affairs issued on 11 April 2000 by a Belgian investigating judge.[197] The Minister was charged with grave breaches of the Geneva Conventions and of the Additional Protocols and crimes against humanity on the basis of the 1993 Belgian law.[198] The DRC claimed that the universal jurisdiction that the Belgian state attributes to itself constituted a violation of the principle that a state may not exercise its authority in the territory of another state and of the principle of sovereign equality among all UN member states.[199] Secondly, it claimed that Belgium, by issuing this arrest warrant, had violated the immunity due to a minister of foreign affairs in office. In its final submissions, however, the DRC referred only to the second ground. The court decided only to address the issue whether Belgium violated the immunities of a minister of foreign affairs by issuing the arrest warrant.[200] The question whether there is a right in international law to extend universal jurisdiction over war crimes committed in internal conflicts was therefore left unanswered by the court.[201]

Judges could not agree on a common position on universal jurisdiction but relevant passages on this issue can be found in the opinions of various judges. Ten judges commented on the issue of universal jurisdiction in their separate or dissenting opinions. Most judges seem to recognise the admissibility of universal jurisdiction, but its conditions of applicability vary greatly between judges.[202] Of particular interest is the joint separate opinion of Judges Higgins, Kooijmans and Buergenthal. Their separate opinion is a carefully balanced discussion of universal jurisdiction, reaching albeit indecisive conclusions. They take the view that, save for the Belgian legislation, pure universal jurisdiction (i.e. the classical assertion of a universal jurisdiction over particular offences committed elsewhere by persons having no relationship or connection with the forum state) is not reflected in national legislation.[203] Many national cases and the majority of international conventions require the presence of the offender in its territory before a state can exercise universal jurisdiction.[204] The first conclusion therefore reached by these three judges is that there is no customary international norm allowing states to exercise jurisdiction on the basis of pure universal jurisdiction.[205] However, state practice does not point to the unlawfulness of such conduct. In their words, 'national legislation and case law is neutral as to the exercise of universal jurisdiction'.[206] They then note 'certain indications that a universal criminal jurisdiction for certain international crimes is clearly not regarded as unlawful'.[207] They conclude that there is no rule of international law, which makes the use of universal jurisdiction *in absentia* illegal[208] and that they believe a state choosing to do so should put in place some safeguards.[209] The last point made by these learned judges is that this universal criminal jurisdiction can only be exercised over those crimes 'regarded as the most heinous by the international community'.[210] It is disappointing, however, that their list of crimes over which such jurisdiction could be extended does not specifically include war crimes committed in internal armed conflicts.[211] Is this a simple oversight? Or does this silence reflect their uncertainty as to the right to extend universal jurisdiction over war crimes committed in internal armed conflicts?

If the principle of universal jurisdiction was not touched upon by the court itself, the limitations of its applicability were discussed at length. As far as the issue of immunity is concerned, the court found that a minister of foreign affairs enjoys inviolability and full immunity from criminal jurisdiction throughout the duration in office.[212] According to the court, there is no exception in customary international law to this rule, even where the Minister of Foreign Affairs is suspected of having committed war crimes or crimes against humanity. The court believes therefore that the circulation of the arrest warrant failed to respect the immunity of an incumbent minister of foreign affairs and in so doing, Belgium violated its international obligations towards the DRC. The court recalls that this immunity is not synonymous with impunity as the territorial state can always try foreign ministers or this state may choose to waive his immunity. Alternatively, an international tribunal may try such perpetrators. Lastly, once the minister ceases to hold office, the court believes that he could be tried by another court of another state in respect of acts committed prior or subsequent to the period in office as well as in respect of acts committed in a private capacity during the period in office.[213] The court stops short of establishing if war crimes or crimes against humanity committed while in office can be considered as private or official acts.[214]

These findings might be criticised for a number of reasons.[215] As pointed out by Professor Cassese,[216] the court did not draw a distinction between two categories of immunities, the functional or *ratione materiae* immunity on the one hand, and the personal immunity, on the other. Notwithstanding the position of the ICJ on this issue, the state of international law today recognises that a minister of foreign affairs or a head of state enjoys both functional and personal immunities while he is in office. The functional immunities are subject to exceptions, however, when the person commits international crimes.[217] The personal immunity the person enjoys will prevent any investigation or prosecution of these crimes while he is in office. However, once the person leaves office, he becomes liable to prosecution for international crimes committed before or during his time in office. He will go on enjoying functional immunity with respect to his official conduct, but the immunity he enjoys is not applicable to international crimes. The unlimited personal immunity that acting heads of state or ministers of foreign affairs[218] enjoy while in office will therefore prevent any attempt by a third state to stop a campaign of crimes against humanity or war crimes committed by such individuals. Foreign courts will have to wait for the end of the term of office of high-level politicians and for thousands of victims to be created, before foreign courts are able to participate in the fight against impunity. The ICJ together with the majority of the doctrine today make the law on immunities prevail over international criminal justice.[219]

Even more problematic is the statement by the court that only acts performed before and after the time in office as well as acts performed 'in a private capacity' during the time in office will not be covered by immunity and will be open to prosecution after the minister of foreign affairs' term in office. It is difficult not to imply from this statement that acts performed in an official capacity will never be questioned. Can acts of genocide or campaigns of war crimes really be ordered 'in a private capacity'? In the majority of cases international crimes will fall within the category of 'official acts', not subject to any prosecutions by courts of third states, contributing therefore to the impunity of heads of states and ministers of foreign affairs. This finding, actual or implied, of the ICJ judgment is at odds with the state of international law, as highlighted by recent national cases together with the position that states have always taken since the Second World War, according to which functional immunity cannot excuse international crimes. The position of the ICJ is disappointing, as it failed to analyse this clear trend, and more importantly it is damaging for international criminal justice.

This position will also lead to a two-speed justice. On the one hand, there are low-ranking individuals over whom universal jurisdiction can be extended under certain circumstances, on the other, high-ranking individuals can shield behind functional immunity. Similarly, on the one hand, the official capacity of a perpetrator does not bar jurisdiction by international courts and tribunals, but will on the other hand be operative before national courts, thereby creating two distinct regimes. The majority of the doctrine does not recognise, before national courts, an exception to personal immunities of heads of state in office, which would 'intolerably undermine international relations'.[220] On the other hand, it is admitted that such personal immunity is not applicable to proceedings before international tribunals.[221] What is the rationale behind the principle that personal and functional immunities cannot be opposed before international tribunals? Surely since the end of the First World War, the gravity of the crimes has called for the prosecution of those who have committed international crimes, regardless of their functions or positions and for dispensing with the sacrosanct immunities of heads of state in these circumstances. This rule is recognised in customary international law to be an exception to the practice of immunity for heads of state and other high officials.[222] The same rationale ought to apply when a domestic court wants to indict a head of state or high officials for such crimes as genocide, crimes against humanity and war crimes committed on a large scale.[223]

2.2.3 The *Lomé Accord Amnesty* decision of the Special Court for Sierra Leone

Also relevant to the issue whether universal jurisdiction extends over war crimes committed in internal armed conflict is the recent decision of the Appeals Chamber of the Special Court for Sierra Leone on the Lomé accord. Judges were asked to decide whether the Lomé accord, granting all rebel combatants immunity from prosecution in respect of their conduct during the armed conflicts since March 1991, prevented the court exercising its jurisdiction over the accused. Among various arguments,[224] the Appeals Chamber of the Special Court held the view that, when jurisdiction over certain crimes is universal, a state cannot deprive another state of its right to prosecute the offenders under universal jurisdiction by granting an amnesty to these offenders.[225] The Appeals Chamber then took the view that the international nature of the crimes contained in Articles 2–4 of its statute grants to any state the right to exercise universal jurisdiction over such offences. According to the Special Court, amnesties cannot cover crimes under international law that are the subject of universal jurisdiction.[226] These far-reaching statements are undermined, however, by the fact that the Chamber does not provide any authority or other arguments to support these findings. Particularly interesting would have been a discussion on this issue or any supporting authority which could reinforce the finding that war crimes committed in internal armed conflicts attract universal jurisdiction.[227] Furthermore, the Chamber first warns that 'not every activity that is seen as an international crime is susceptible to universal jurisdiction'[228] but then comes dangerously close to the oversimplification according to which international criminality and universal jurisdiction are necessarily conterminous.[229] What could have been ground-breaking statements on the state of customary international law today appear rather unpersuasive.

The practice of the UN Security Council and the recent judgment of the ICJ in the *Arrest Warrant* case demonstrate the relative uncertainty surrounding the existence in customary international law of a definite right allowing states to extend universal jurisdiction over war crimes committed in internal conflicts as well the limitations attached thereto.[230] The recently adopted Princeton principles on universal jurisdiction[231] illustrate this remark. The participants in the Princeton project chose to define universal jurisdiction as:

> Criminal jurisdiction based solely on the nature of the crime without regard to where the crime was committed, the nationality of the alleged or convicted perpetrator, the nationality of the victim or any other connection to the state exercising such jurisdiction.[232]

It is interesting to note first that, according to principle 1, universal jurisdiction can be exercised by national courts provided that the person is present before such body, and secondly that the category of serious crimes under international law over which universal jurisdiction can be extended does not include war crimes committed in internal conflicts.[233]

The Institute of International Law has also recently looked at the issue of universal jurisdiction.[234] The rapporteur, C. Tomushat, took the view that even if serious violations of the laws of war committed in internal armed conflicts amount to war crimes, this was not 'tantamount to saying that universal jurisdiction exists with regard to such crimes'.[235] Opinions were split among members of the commission and the draft resolution reflects this by denying the application of universal jurisdiction to war crimes committed in internal armed conflicts.[236] The resolution of the Institute of International Law adopted at its Krakow session in 2005[237] is differently crafted from the draft. The Institute takes the view that:

> Universal jurisdiction may be exercised over international crimes identified by international law as falling within that jurisdiction in matters such

as genocide, crimes against humanity, grave breaches of the 1949 Geneva Conventions for the protection of war victims or other serious violations of international humanitarian law committed in international or non-international armed conflict.[238]

Universal jurisdiction can therefore be extended over war crimes committed in internal armed conflicts if either treaty law or customary international law reflects this right. The Institute stops short of making a finding for each of these crimes, as to whether international law, as it stands today, allows for a right to extend jurisdiction over them. Interestingly, however, the Institute takes the view that the exercise of universal jurisdiction requires the presence of the alleged offender apart from acts of investigations and requests for extradition.[239] Similarly, the Institute resolution stresses the primacy of the jurisdiction of states having a significant link with the crime, the offender or the victim, over states wishing to extend universal jurisdiction over international crimes. The latter should even ask the territorial state or the offender's state of nationality before it takes it upon itself to try the offender.[240] The careful and rather restrictive approach taken by the ICJ, the Institute of International Law or the Princeton project can be opposed to the view of the International Committee of the Red Cross (ICRC) in its research on customary humanitarian law. The latter has found that a right to extend universal jurisdiction over war crimes committed in internal armed conflicts exists in customary international law.[241]

2.3 The exercise by domestic courts of universal jurisdiction over war crimes committed in internal armed conflicts

The domestic legislation of only a minority of states contains provisions allowing for the prosecution of individuals, who are alleged perpetrators of war crimes committed in an internal conflict of a third state. For the past ten years, however, there has been an increasing use of these provisions leading to the prosecutions of war criminals by third states on the basis of universal jurisdiction. This recent state practice is now analysed to assess the effectiveness of national enforcement of individual responsibility for war crimes committed in internal armed conflicts.[242]

2.3.1 Austria

As examined earlier, the Austrian Penal Code does not contain any provision on war crimes. Section 64(1) subparagraph 6 of the Austrian

Penal Code, however, provides for the application of Austrian law to punishable acts committed abroad, if Austria is specifically obliged by international law to prosecute these actions. This covers grave breaches of the Geneva Conventions, but neither war crimes in internal conflicts, nor genocide, as the Genocide Convention does not oblige third states to prosecute alleged perpetrators.

In 1993, however, charges of genocide, murder and arson, were brought against Dusko C., a Bosnian Serb accused of having committed atrocities in Kucice in central Bosnia-Herzegovina. Both the district court and the court of appeal found that they lacked jurisdiction, the alleged crimes having been committed by a foreigner in a foreign state.[243] The prosecutor appealed to the Austrian supreme court. The supreme court recognised the jurisdiction of Austrian courts on the basis of Article 65(1) subparagraph 2 of the Austrian penal code.[244] According to this article, Austrian criminal law may apply in respect of offences committed abroad, so long as the acts are also punishable in the place where they are committed, and provided the offender, if a foreigner, is present in Austria and cannot be extradited to another state due to reasons other than the nature and characteristics of the offence. The court accepted the arguments of the prosecution. First the double-criminality requirement was satisfied and secondly, because of the ongoing conflict extradition to Bosnia was not possible as no communication was possible between the two judicial institutions.

The court went on to consider whether the Genocide Convention could provide a basis for jurisdiction. The court interpreted Article 6 of the Genocide Convention as obliging states parties to extradite a suspected génocidaire to the state where the crimes had been committed, in the absence of an International Criminal Court. This obligation, in the view of the supreme court, is not absolute if the state where the alleged conduct has been committed, does not have a stable judiciary enabling a fair trial, as was the case in Bosnia in 1994. It follows from the object and purpose of the convention that Austrian courts in this case can exercise jurisdiction on the basis of the Genocide Convention.

Furthermore, notwithstanding the fact that there is no provision implementing the Geneva Conventions in the Austrian penal code, the supreme court stressed that the provisions of the Geneva Conventions and Protocols were applicable to the conflict in Bosnia.[245] Dusko C. was tried by the district court of Salzburg in May 1995 and found not guilty due to lack of evidence.[246] The five witnesses from Bosnia were not able to recognise the accused on confrontation.

This trial shows the difficulties encountered by national courts in securing evidence when exercising universal jurisdiction. However, this trial and the interpretation given to national and international law by the supreme court of Austria is quite remarkable and proves that problems of jurisdiction can be solved if the willingness to combat impunity is present.

2.3.2 Belgium

Belgian courts have been active in investigating and arresting suspected war criminals who took refuge in Belgium.[247] In 1995, Belgian authorities arrested four Rwandese citizens on charges of war crimes and issued international arrest warrants against three others on the basis of the war crimes law 1993.[248] At the request of the ICTR, Belgian courts deferred proceedings against them and transferred at least four Rwandese suspects to Arusha.[249] In other cases, Belgian courts confirmed their competence to try violations of the laws of war committed in internal armed conflicts such as in Rwanda.[250] The trial of four Rwandese began on 17 April 2001 in Brussels. They were found guilty of war crimes (violations of common Article 3 and Protocol II) and sentenced respectively to twenty, twenty-five and twelve years' imprisonment.[251] Belgium has been at the forefront of investigations and prosecutions of non-Belgians, who have committed violations of the laws of war against non-Belgians in armed conflicts outside Belgium.[252] However, the ICJ judgment of 14 February 2002 had unexpected consequences on other cases pending before Belgian courts.[253] First in the Ndombasi case, the Brussels court of appeal ruled that the proceedings against him were inadmissible from the start, as he was not in Belgian territory, a requirement set forth in Article 12 of the Belgian Code of Criminal Procedure.[254] Secondly in the case of Ariel Sharon, the Brussels court of appeal ordered, on similar grounds, the interruption of the proceedings against Ariel Sharon, as he could not be found in Belgian territory when proceedings started.[255] The court took the view that the exercise of universal jurisdiction *in absentia* is contrary to international law and the principle of sovereign equality of states,[256] effectively tolling the bell for universal jurisdiction in Belgium. Following further politically motivated complaints, which prompted intense international political pressure on Belgium, mainly from the USA, the Belgian Parliament came to rescind the war crimes law 1993 and adopted a new legislation dated 8 August 2003. This new legislation, amending both the criminal code and the code of criminal procedure,[257] represents the abandonment of absolute universal jurisdiction, beyond what international law required, in favour of a universal jurisdiction limited to what is strictly required under international law.[258] Article 12*bis* of the code of criminal procedure provides for the principle *aut dedere, aut judicare*, over certain international crimes without requiring the presence of the accused in Belgian territory. Belgian courts, however, will only have jurisdiction over crimes that Belgium has a duty to prosecute on the basis of international conventions or an international customary rule. Victims will not be able to start proceedings, which might only proceed if the federal prosecutor so decides.[259] If grave breaches of the 1949 Geneva Conventions could be prosecuted under this heading, one will have to prove that states are under a customary law obligation to prosecute war crimes committed in internal armed conflicts. If such a customary norm might be proven for the crime of genocide or a crime against humanity, it seems unlikely that in those circumstances, Belgian courts might instruct cases of war crimes committed in internal armed conflicts on the basis of universal jurisdiction.

Furthermore, Belgian courts will have jurisdiction over international crimes on the basis of two classical bases of jurisdiction: active and passive personality. On the basis of Article 6 of the code of criminal procedure, any Belgian citizen or any person residing in Belgium, at the time of the crime or at the beginning of investigation, who is suspected of having committed war crimes can be tried before Belgian courts. On the basis of Article 10, if the victim of war crimes is a Belgian national or has resided in Belgium for at least three years before the commission of the crime, Belgian courts will have jurisdiction over the alleged offender for a war crime committed in internal armed conflicts. Investigations might be able to start even if the alleged offender is not present in Belgian territory. Such actions, however, might not be triggered by the victims but only by the federal prosecutor, who decides to start an investigation. His decision is not subject to appeal.[260] Prosecutions of war crimes committed in internal armed conflicts might not therefore easily take place in Belgium on the basis of universal jurisdiction. Such crimes can only be prosecuted in Belgium if the victim or the author of the crime is a Belgian national or has resided in Belgium for more than three years. The Belgian Parliament has most certainly managed to stop the flood of politically motivated claims before Belgian courts, but at the same time has hindered greatly the access to judicial redress for a great number of victims of war crimes committed in internal armed conflicts.

It is interesting to note that, already in April 2005, the Belgian court of cassation ruled that the exclusion of refugees from the 5 August 2003 legislation, which necessitates that the victim be Belgian or in Belgian territory for at least three years, is contrary to the 1951 Convention on the Status of Refugees, which provides that refugees should enjoy the same treatment as nationals in matters pertaining to access to the courts.[261] Cases, where the victims of war crimes committed in internal armed conflicts also have the status of refugees in Belgium, might therefore be prosecuted before Belgian courts. Similarly, cases where the victims are Belgian nationals can still be tried before Belgian courts. The trial of Bernard Ntuyahanga is planned to start in Brussels on 19 April 2007 for his participation in the murders of the ten Belgian blue helmets in April 1994 in Rwanda together with the death of the Rwandese prime minister Agathe Uwililgiymana.

2.3.3 Denmark

Prosecutions were successfully brought against Refik S., a Bosnian Muslim, for having caused severe grievous bodily harm to detainees of the Croatian prison camp of Dretelj in Bosnia during the summer of 1993.[262] Some of these acts resulted in the death of three detainees and severe injuries and ill-treatment of twenty others. He was found guilty on fourteen charges relating to sections 245 and 246 of the Danish Penal Code and Articles 129, 130 and 146, 147 respectively of the Third and the Fourth 1949 Geneva Conventions. He was sentenced to eight years' imprisonment.[263] The court did not examine the character of the armed conflict in Bosnia at the time the offence was committed but decided to apply the grave breaches provisions of the Geneva Conventions. This factor might imply that the court believed the conditions of the grave breaches provisions to be met, assuming therefore the international character of the conflict.[264] Whatever the nature of the armed conflict at that time in Bosnia, this case is the first domestic prosecution in the world since 1949 to be based on the grave breaches provisions of the Geneva Conventions.[265]

2.3.4 France

Victims of the Yugoslav and Rwandese conflicts have used French jurisdiction in an attempt to bring perpetrators of war crimes, crimes against humanity and genocide to justice. For a long time, their actions have been unsuccessful. In the case of three Bosnian plaintiffs as well as in a number of cases brought by Rwandese refugees, the French courts

found no basis in French law for extending jurisdiction over genocide and crimes against humanity committed by non-nationals, against
foreigners and outside French territory.[266]

In the case of the Bosnian plaintiffs, the examining magistrate found
French courts competent to investigate charges of torture, on the basis
of the 1984 UN Convention on Torture, as well as war crimes, on the
basis of the 1949 Geneva Conventions.[267] The Paris court of appeal as
well as the court of cassation reversed, however, the conclusions reached
by the examining magistrate. The court of appeal believed that the 1984
Torture Convention does not create an unconditional obligation for
states to track down the author of alleged acts of torture. Jurisdiction
will only be established if the presence of the authors in French territory
could be proved. Similarly, the court took the view that in the absence of
implementing legislation, the 1949 Geneva Conventions lacked direct
effect in French law.[268] The court of cassation concurred with the court
of appeal,[269] and further argued that the 1995 law implementing
Security Council resolution 827 gives French courts jurisdiction to
prosecute war criminals, if the authors' presence in France is proven.
The plaintiffs were unable to prove that the suspected perpetrators were
in French territory and there was therefore no basis for jurisdiction
of the French courts. These judgments show the usual conservatism of
French jurisdictions which demand the presence in French territory of
the suspected criminals before commencing any investigation and
believe that the Geneva Conventions, even if ratified by France, lack
direct effect in the French legal system and do not create universal
jurisdiction for domestic courts.

A number of actions started by Rwandese refugees met a similar fate,
as the court of appeal of Paris consistently refused to admit jurisdiction
over genocide or war crimes committed against Rwandese in Rwanda.[270]
In the case *Radio Television les Milles Collines(RTLM)*, an incorporated
society, Reporters sans frontières (RSF) filed criminal complaints
against the leadership of RTLM, who actively encouraged the genocide
in Rwanda and lived in Paris at that time. Both the examining magistrate
and the court of appeal of Paris rejected the complaint as inadmissible
because RSF had not suffered any direct injury resulting from the
violations of the 1984 Torture Convention.[271]

The complaint filed by the plaintiffs, Dupaquier J. F, E. Kalinda et al.,
against the Rwandan priest, W. Munyeshyaka, is the only successful
prosecution carried out by French jurisdictions of a Rwandan refugee
for having participated in the genocide in Rwanda. The examining

magistrate declared that he had jurisdiction but only for acts of torture. The court of appeal of Nîmes reversed that decision, as jurisdiction should be established, according to the court, only on the basis of the most serious offence, i.e. genocide, and French courts do not have universal jurisdiction over genocide. The court of cassation reversed this surprising reasoning on 6 January 1998. The highest court found French jurisdiction competent to prosecute the Rwandan priest for genocide, crimes against humanity and war crimes committed in Rwanda on the basis of the 1996 French law implementing the Security Council resolution 955, which allows perpetrators of such offences who are present in France to be prosecuted.

The latter case remains the exception in the French judicial landscape.[272] Prosecutions of war criminals can only be conducted in France on the basis of the 1995 and 1996 laws and if the authors are present in French territory.[273] In practice, perpetrators of war crimes committed elsewhere than in ex-Yugoslavia and Rwanda, cannot be prosecuted by French courts.[274]

2.3.5 Germany

The German Penal Code provides for universal jurisdiction over certain crimes, such as genocide (Article 6.1) or other offences if they are made punishable by the terms of an international treaty binding on Germany (Article 6.9). At least six criminal investigations or prosecutions of persons charged with crimes committed in the former Yugoslavia have been conducted in Germany in the past ten years on the basis of these provisions. First, the Bavarian high court indicted Dusko T. for genocide but proceedings were interrupted and the defendant transferred to The Hague, at the request of the tribunal. In this case, the German supreme court took the view that some additional connection between the defendant and Germany was required in order for German courts to extend their jurisdictions over acts committed abroad by non-Germans.[275] The mere temporary presence of the suspect in German territory would not be a sufficient basis for prosecution in Germany. This requirement was justified by the necessity to ensure that the principle of non-interference in other states' domestic affairs is not infringed.

Secondly, the supreme court of Bavaria tried Novislav D. for complicity in genocide and for the murder of fourteen Muslim men in Eastern Bosnia in June 1992.[276] He was found guilty of fourteen cases of abetting murder and one case of attempted murder. He was not found responsible for the murder itself but his presence among the murderers was seen as abetting murder. He was found not guilty of genocide as he lacked the necessary *mens rea* of genocide. In this case, the basis of the court's jurisdiction was Article 6.9 of the German penal code, which obliges Germany to prosecute offences committed by non-nationals abroad, if Germany has an international obligation to do so.[277] The court found that Germany's duty to prosecute stemmed from Articles 146 and 147 of the Geneva Conventions. The court examined the character of the armed conflict and concluded that it was an international armed conflict at the time the offence was committed.[278] Furthermore, the victims were found to be protected persons under the meaning of the Geneva Conventions, making this case the first trial in Germany of a war criminal for grave breaches of the Geneva Conventions since 1949. Lastly, the link to Germany was established as the defendant was domiciled in Germany and Germany was not acting in its own interests, but was representing the whole community of states.

Thirdly, in the *Jorgic* case, the Dusseldorf high court found the defendant guilty on eleven counts of genocide and thirty counts of murder for having been actively involved in the elimination and expulsion of the Muslim population of the Bosnian region of Doboj in the summer of 1992.[279] Jurisdiction was based on Article 6.1 of the German penal code, genocide, and the court found that the defendant had the requisite intent to destroy in whole or in part, a national, racial, religious or ethnically distinct group. With regard to the other charges of murder and assault, jurisdiction was based on Article 6.9, grave breaches of the Geneva Conventions.[280] The link between Germany and the defendant was established, as Jorgic lived in Germany between 1969 and 1992 and was married to a German national. The defendant was sentenced to life imprisonment.[281]

Lastly, at least three other cases were investigated in Germany by the federal prosecutor of Karlsruhe against Maksim S. for genocide, rape and torture of Bosnian Muslims, and by a prosecutor in Munich against Djuradjd K. on suspicion of murder and crimes against humanity.[282] The Dusseldorf high court found a Bosnian Serb guilty of grave breaches of the Geneva Convention on the basis of Article 6.9 of the criminal code.[283] These investigations and trials show that the willingness to combat impunity and imaginative interpretation of national provisions have rendered possible swift and effective trials of Bosnian refugees in Germany for genocide and war crimes. It is sometimes difficult for national courts to gather all the necessary factual evidence, such as in the *Djajic* case, where the defendant was found not guilty of genocide because of lack of evidence of the necessary *mens rea*. These trials also show that there is a potential for divergence in case law between national courts and the ICTY, on issues such as the character of the armed conflict in Bosnia. The various German courts found the conflict in Bosnia at the time of the offence to be of an international character. It remains unclear if such trials could have gone ahead if the courts had found the conflict to be of an internal character.[284] With the adoption of a code of crimes against international law, prosecutions of war crimes committed in internal conflicts will be made possible, as it includes the principle of universal jurisdiction without requiring the existence of a link with Germany, though the first good opportunity to apply the code of crime against international law was refused by a federal prosecutor.[285]

2.3.6 The Netherlands

The criminal law in wartime act 1952 provides for the universal jurisdiction of Dutch courts over all violations of the laws and customs of war when they are committed in international or internal conflicts. Article 1.2 of the Act seems to imply, however, that Dutch courts will only have jurisdiction if the Netherlands is involved in the conflict where the acts have been committed. On 11 November 1997, the Dutch supreme court was asked to interpret the provisions of this Act in order to find out if Dutch courts could exercise jurisdiction over Darko K., a Bosnian Serb, who was accused of having killed two Muslims, attempting to rape two sisters and threatening or transferring other Muslims to a concentration camp in Bosnia in 1992.[286] The supreme court found that the wartime criminal law Act must be read in accordance with the government's intention to comply fully with its treaty obligations.[287] The court further asserted that Dutch criminal law is applicable to everyone who commits a serious violation of the laws of war outside the European territory of the Kingdom of the Netherlands, irrespective of whether the Netherlands was involved in the conflict. The supreme court confirmed therefore the jurisdiction of Dutch courts to try Darko K. for violations of common Article 3 of the Geneva Conventions on the basis of universal criminal jurisdiction and decided that military chambers should be competent to hear this case. The Dutch military court, acting as an appeal chamber, held that the conflict constituted an internal armed conflict and that the defendant could be found guilty of serious violations of common Article 3.[288] This decision from the supreme court confirms beyond any doubt that Dutch courts can extend universal criminal jurisdiction over serious violations of the laws of war independently of whether they were committed in internal or international conflicts. The recent international crimes Act 2003 confirms the jurisdiction of Dutch courts on the basis of universal jurisdiction over offences contained in the ICC statute if the suspect is present in the Netherlands.[289]

Interestingly, Dutch courts recently reaffirmed their jurisdiction over war crimes committed during a foreign armed conflict which took place between 1978 and 1982. The Hague district court convicted two Afghan asylum seekers for torture as violations of the laws and customs of war, for having taken part in the torture and mistreatment of Afghan civilians during the Afghan war of 1978–1982. They were sentenced to twelve and nine years' imprisonment, respectively. The Hague district court found that the conflict in Afghanistan amounted to an internal armed conflict and that it had jurisdiction over the alleged offenders on the basis of Dutch law read together with the 1949 Geneva Conventions. It took the view that, even if common Article 3 was not part of the grave breaches regime, nothing in the Geneva Conventions prevented the Netherlands from criminalising violations of common Article 3 and extending universal jurisdiction over them.[290] The court seems to have taken the view that by the end of the 1970s there was a right in international law (stemming out of the Geneva Conventions), or at least the absence of a prohibition, to extend universal jurisdiction over war crimes committed in internal armed conflicts.

2.3.7 Switzerland

In the past ten years Swiss jurisdictions have carried out a number of investigations of suspected war criminals, handed over suspects to the ICTR and pursued at least two cases before their own military courts. By a judgment dated 8 July 1996, the Swiss military court of cassation complied with a request by the ICTR for transfer to its jurisdiction of A.M, a Rwandese citizen, having found that the defendant could have been prosecuted in Switzerland on the basis of Article 2.9 of the military penal code for breaches of Articles 108–14 of this code.[291]

By a judgment dated 18 April 1997, the divisional military tribunal in Lausanne found it had jurisdiction to prosecute, on the basis of Article 2.9 of the military penal code, a Bosnian Serb accused of having breached Article 109 of that code (violations of the Third and Fourth Geneva Conventions).[292] This tribunal qualified the conflict in Bosnia at the time of the commission of the offence, as an international conflict but confirmed that in any event it was competent to deal with the case under Article 109 of the military penal code, whatever the nature of the armed conflict. The defendant was accused of beating and injuring civilian detainees at the Serbian-run detention camps of Omarska and Keraterm in Bosnia during the summer of 1992, but argued that he was in Austria and Germany at the time of the offences. The tribunal acquitted the defendant on the grounds that the confused evidence and testimonies at the trial were insufficient to establish his presence in the camps at the time of the crimes.[293] This decision is the first to be delivered by a Swiss military tribunal pursuant to the exercise of universal jurisdiction over war crimes. It illustrates, however, the difficulties of foreign domestic courts in obtaining the necessary evidence and proof to establish the guilt of the accused. The geographical and temporal distance between the foreign tribunal and the time and place of the offence, as well as the reluctance of surviving witnesses to testify, often makes the prosecution's work extremely difficult.[294]

In April 1999, the military tribunal of Lausanne prosecuted a Rwandan refugee, previously a mayor of a community in the Gitarama province of Rwanda, for crimes against humanity, war crimes and genocide. The defence contested the jurisdiction of Swiss courts over genocide and crimes against humanity solely on the basis of customary international law. The tribunal found that Swiss courts lacked jurisdiction over crimes against humanity and genocide, as there were no provisions in Swiss law for jurisdiction over these crimes or equivalent crimes in domestic law. The tribunal based its jurisdiction on Article 109 of the military penal code and took the view that an internal armed conflict was taking place in Rwanda at the time of the offences in the sense of both common Article 3 and Protocol II. The link between the accused, as a civilian agent of the state, and the armed forces and between the armed conflict and the crimes he was charged with was found to be established. The tribunal went to Rwanda and visited the crime scene. They heard about twenty-five witnesses during three weeks of trial. The defendant was found guilty of violations of the laws and customs of war and sentenced to life imprisonment.[295] This sentence was later reduced to fourteen years' imprisonment by the military appeal court.[296]

2.4 Conclusion

This section has assessed how far customary law today reflects the assumption that there is a customary law right for states to extend universal jurisdiction over war crimes committed in internal armed conflicts. Only two minor international instruments extend the principle of universal jurisdiction over war crimes committed in internal conflicts. Only more than a third of the states studied here (thirty-two out of seventy-eight) have domestic provisions enabling their courts to extend universal jurisdiction over war crimes committed in foreign internal conflicts, by non-nationals against non-nationals.[297] This significant practice is gaining momentum, as an increasing number of states parties to the ICC statute are adopting domestic legislation extending universal jurisdiction over war crimes committed in internal armed conflicts. However, this practice is not reinforced by the practice of the UN institutions. Security Council resolutions from 1970 to this day do not clearly affirm the right of states to extend universal jurisdiction over war crimes committed in internal conflicts. In the light of the preamble to the ICC statute, some UN Security Council resolutions affirm the responsibility of states to prosecute those responsible for war crimes, without specifying which states are under such an obligation: only the territorial states or any UN members through universal jurisdiction? The ICJ ruling in the *Warrant Arrest* case also weakened the status in international law of universal jurisdiction over war crimes committed in internal conflicts. The substantial immunities, both functional and personal, granted to heads of state and ministers of foreign affairs, according to the ICJ, render prosecutions of such people by third states less likely than ever before.

Finally, thirty-two states have some legislation providing for universal jurisdiction over war crimes committed in internal conflicts, but national prosecutions were carried out by only a few European states. Out of the review of national cases presented above, only three countries, Belgium, Switzerland and the Netherlands, successfully prosecuted individuals for war crimes committed in internal armed conflicts. In other instances, individuals were tried for genocide, grave breaches of the Geneva Conventions or for torture under the 1984 Torture Convention. Universal jurisdiction for grave breaches or the crime of torture, being enshrined in statutory norms, it will then be included in most national implementing legislation. This, in turn, will allow national prosecutions of these crimes to take place much more easily than for war crimes committed in internal armed conflict. The ICC implementing legislation adopted by a growing number of states will allow more prosecutions for war crimes in internal armed conflicts in the future, if offenders are found in the territory of these states.

Overall, this practice reflects a good amount of *opinio juris* but may not yet be qualified as extensive or virtually uniform practice, giving rise to a customary law norm. The principle by which every state would have a right enshrined in customary law to extend their jurisdiction over war crimes committed in any internal armed conflict is in the process of progressive development. Its crystallisation will depend, among other factors, on whether when implementing the ICC statute, a larger number of states choose to extend universal jurisdiction over these offences. States effectively prosecuting war criminals on the basis of universal jurisdiction or amending their national legislation to allow such cases to take place, cannot base their jurisdiction on non-existing conventional and customary norms. They must therefore either believe that customary law already gives them a right to do so, or that, in international law there is at least no prohibition to do so. Extending universal jurisdiction over war crimes in internal armed conflicts is not seen as a violation of the principle of non-interference in internal affairs of states, and the right to do so is about to crystallise in customary international law. The following extract, though concerning crimes against humanity, summarises well the state of customary law today relative to universal jurisdiction for war crimes committed in internal armed conflicts:

> While no general rule of positive international law can as yet be asserted which gives to states the right to punish foreign nationals for crimes against humanity in the same way as they are, for instance, entitled to punish acts of piracy, there are clear indications pointing to the gradual evolution of a significant principle of international law to that effect.[298]

Two subsidiary conclusions can also be drawn. First, if it is difficult today to affirm the existence of a customary norm establishing a right to extend universal jurisdiction over war crimes in internal conflicts, it is *a fortiori* impossible to agree with the statement that customary law today would reflect an obligation that states extend universal jurisdiction (under the principle *aut judicare, aut dedere*) over war crimes committed in internal armed conflicts. Some writers, as well as some ICTY Trial Chambers, have taken that view.[299] This does not seem to be supported by state practice at the moment. Secondly, this research indicates that the right to extend universal jurisdiction over war crimes may not include the option for states to initiate investigations and issue arrest warrants if the suspected perpetrator is not present in their territory. Only a few states have implemented 'pure universal jurisdiction' so far[300] and the general trend adopted by state practice seems to require at least the presence of the perpetrator in the territory before states may apply universal jurisdiction. The contours of this 'right in the making' remain blurred.

3. Prosecutions of war criminals by the domestic courts of war-torn countries

War crimes prosecutions may take place in the territory of states where the crimes were committed. These prosecutions, based mainly on territoriality or sometimes on the active personality principle, can be subject to political manipulations and their independence and impartiality are often put into question. In Africa, prosecutions by national courts following internal armed conflicts remain exceptional.[301] However, in the past decade, some national courts managed to conduct independent trials at the end of hostilities[302] while others received logistical and financial help from the international community to rebuild their judicial system and prosecute perpetrators for war crimes committed in internal armed conflicts.[303]

3.1 Bosnia-Herzegovina

Prosecutions by local courts in Bosnia are the fruit of the Rome Agreement. On the basis of the Rome Agreement on Sarajevo of 18 February 1996:

> Persons, other than those already indicted by the International Tribunal, may be arrested and detained for serious violations of international humanitarian law only pursuant to a previously issued order, warrant or indictment that has been reviewed and deemed consistent with international legal standards by the International Tribunal. Procedures will be developed for expeditious decision by the Tribunal and will be effective immediately upon such action.[304]

This agreement is also known as 'the Rules of the Road' and has become a sort of filter for national war crimes prosecutions in Bosnia-Herzegovina. The indictment of a person suspected of having committed war crimes is only possible once the ICTY Prosecutor's office has reviewed the case and approved the prosecutions. Local authorities submit their files to the office of the ICTY Prosecutor which then determines whether the evidence is sufficient by international standards to justify either the arrest or indictment of a suspect or the continued detention of a prisoner.[305] The ICTY Prosecutor may also decide whether to take steps to indict the persons and to request national courts to defer the case to the Tribunal. This review of national cases helps to enforce international legal standards at the national level and prevent 'show trials' or politically and ethnically motivated trials being set up.

Domestic trials concerned Bosnian Serbs, Muslims and Croats and illustrate the possibilities open to national courts of prosecuting their own citizens for war crimes after the end of hostilities. In some instances, defendants were found guilty of war crimes against the civilian population, on the basis of Article 142 of the Bosnian criminal code (genocide), Article 141, or war crimes against prisoners of war (Article 144). In these cases, the court found the accused guilty of violations of the third or fourth 1949 Geneva Conventions, as well as violations of additional Protocol I or the Hague regulations, committed during an international conflict in Bosnia-Herzegovina.[306] It is notable that prosecutions not only took place in the Federation of Bosnia-Herzegovina but also in Republika Srpska. The Modrica municipal court found a member of the Croatian armed forces (HVO) guilty of war crimes against the civilian population under Article 142(1) of the criminal code of the Republika Srpska for having ill-treated and killed four inmates in a detention centre.[307]

Local prosecutions also led in a certain number of cases to acquittals due to lack of evidence, inconsistent witness statements or other procedural difficulties.[308] In the case of Ibrahim D., neither the magistrate's court in Sarajevo nor the supreme court of the Federation took into account the potential responsibility of the offender for command responsibility.[309] The defendant himself recognised that he was familiar with certain illegalities but unfortunately neither court took into account the relevant case law of the ICTY and investigated his obligations to prevent or punish those violations of the laws of war committed by his subordinates.

Commentators have taken the view that 'the general lack of judicial independence and the politicisation of the courts and prosecutorial services have meant that even cases approved by the ICTY for prosecution under the Rules of the Road have not moved forward'.[310] From 1996 to 2004, it is reported that 'only about 50 war crimes suspects were prosecuted in Bosnia and Herzegovina' which is less than 10 per cent of those prosecutions, which were approved by the ICTY Prosecutor's office.[311] A number of reasons are advanced to explain this low number of prosecutions,[312] for example, the lack of co-operation between the police forces of the two Bosnian entities, the absence of an effective witness protection scheme and the absence of co-ordination between the fifteen cantonal or district prosecutors' offices throughout the country.[313]

The need for the ICTY to accomplish its mandate in the most timely manner has turned the spotlight back on national jurisdictions. At present, the Tribunal focuses on prosecutions of the highest-ranking political, military, paramilitary and civilian leaders and will refer some of the other cases to the courts of Bosnia-Herzegovina.[314] The aim is to have intermediary-level accused prosecuted by a special chamber within the state court of Bosnia-Herzegovina with jurisdiction over war crimes.[315] This chamber for war crimes within the state court was set up in early 2005 and has primary jurisdiction over all national war crimes' prosecutions.[316] It is staffed by national and international judges[317] and assisted by a special prosecutor for war crimes. The special prosecutor will also oversee the third tier of the judicial structure envisaged, i.e. prosecutions of low-ranking perpetrators to be tried by the local courts.[318] The special chamber within the state court hears some of the cases approved under the Rules of the Road agreement together with cases transferred by the ICTY to the special chamber under rule 11*bis* of the ICTY rules of procedure and evidence.[319] As of 1 December 2006, the ICTY has transferred the cases of nine accused persons to the special war crimes chamber.[320] The ICTY has refused to transfer the prosecutions of four other accused to Bosnia-Herzegovina.[321] Before a case can be transferred, a referral bench must satisfy itself that the accused will receive a fair trial and that the death penalty will not be imposed or carried out. It will examine the proposed state's willingness and capacity to accept the case of the accused. In doing so, it must consider the substantive law that might be applicable to the accused. In the *Mejakić* case, the Appeals Chamber was satisfied that there were appropriate provisions in the Socialist Federal Republic of Yugoslavia (SFRY) criminal code applicable at the time the offence was committed to address most, if not all, of the criminal acts alleged in the indictment.[322] The transposition of the ICTY indictment into a local indictment before the special war crimes chamber may not be an easy task. The 2003 criminal code of Bosnia-Herzegovina contains concepts such as crimes against humanity and the various modes of liability appearing in the ICTY statute. However, this criminal code can apply retroactively to events that took place in the 1990s only to the extent that it is more favourable to the accused than the criminal code of the SFRY of 1977. The latter does not seem to include the concept of crimes against humanity or to incriminate acts of persecution. Similarly, it seems doubtful that the doctrines of joint criminal enterprise and command responsibility, as understood by the ICTY case law, can be found in the 1977 criminal code and used against the defendants. This will create important differences of treatment, leading potentially to discrepancies in penalties imposed, between an accused tried by the ICTY and one tried by the special war crimes chamber in Sarajevo.

National jurisdictions in Bosnia have not been able to rise to the challenges of a vast number of potential war crimes prosecutions. International funding and expertise, presently engaged in the special war crimes chamber, is needed to build a more effective and impartial judicial system in Bosnia-Herzegovina capable of trying intermediary-level and low-ranking accused.[323] Scores of police and military officers suspected of participating in the atrocities still hold public jobs. The UN Mission in Bosnia-Herzegovina has developed a screening system of Bosnian police officers which has lead to the dismissal of police officers who allegedly committed major or persistent violations of the laws of war or human rights during the conflict. Commentators have reported that about 200 currently serving police officials had been identified as having questionable wartime backgrounds that warrant further investigation.[324] In Bosnia, this regime of non-prosecutorial sanctions for war crimes participates in the fight against impunity together with local courts and the special war crime chamber.

3.2 Cambodia

Efforts to bring leaders of the Khmer Rouge to justice for genocide, war crimes and crimes against humanity culminated in the adoption on 10 August 2001 of a Cambodian law establishing extraordinary chambers in the courts of Cambodia for the prosecution of crimes committed during the period of Democratic Kampuchea.[325] The UN insisted on the inclusion of international standards of fairness and independence as a prerequisite for the participation of the international community. In February 2002, however, the UN halted negotiations with the Cambodian authorities claiming that the independence and impartiality of this Khmer Rouge tribunal could not be guaranteed.[326] Negotiations resumed in December 2002 and ended on 6 June 2003 with the signature of the Agreement between the UN and the Royal Government of Cambodia concerning the prosecution under Cambodian law of crimes committed during the period of Democratic Kampuchea.[327]

On 27 October 2004, the law on the establishment of extraordinary chambers in the courts of Cambodia for the prosecution of crimes committed during the period of Democratic Cambodia was promulgated in order to bring into conformity the 2001 law establishing extraordinary chambers with the 2003 Agreement signed between the UN and Cambodia. The 2004 law provides for the establishment of extraordinary chambers having jurisdiction over senior leaders of Democratic Kampuchea and those who were most responsible for international and domestic crimes committed in Cambodia between April 1975 and January 1979.[328] The crimes falling within the jurisdiction of these chambers include genocide, grave breaches of the 1949 Geneva Conventions, the destruction of cultural property as defined in the 1954 Hague Convention, offences against internationally protected persons under the 1961 Vienna Convention on Diplomatic Relations and crimes against humanity as defined in the ICTR statute.[329] One may note that only grave breaches of the 1949 Geneva Conventions fall within the jurisdiction of the special chambers. Jurisdiction over serious violations of common Article 3 or other war crimes committed in internal armed conflicts has not been extended to the extraordinary chambers. Cambodia was engaged in quashing some internal uprisings, as well as being in armed hostilities with three of its neighbours from 1975 and many serious violations of the laws of war were committed against Cambodian civilians.[330] This omission could be seen as a rejection of the principle according to which such crimes amounted to war crimes in the middle of the 1970s.[331]

This law establishes a trial chamber, composed of three Cambodian judges and two international judges and a supreme court chamber composed of four Cambodian and three international judges. Convictions can only be made by unanimity or qualified majority, requiring therefore at least one international judge to agree with the Cambodian judges. The preponderance of national judges over international judges is in contrast with other hybrid systems but leaves the door potentially open for political interference and intimidation. There are to be two co-prosecutors, one Cambodian and one international. These chambers will be funded jointly by the Government of Cambodia and the UN through voluntary contributions of member states.

Between 1975 and 1979, 1.7 million people died and justice is long overdue in Cambodia. Pol Pot and his major accomplices have lived in Cambodia for more than twenty years with total impunity and many died before reaching any courtroom. This internationalised domestic tribunal, the fruit of prolonged negotiations between the UN and the Government of Cambodia, is to be welcomed even if non-governmental organisations and the Secretary-General of the UN have expressed doubts as to the extraordinary chambers' ability 'to meet international standards of procedural fairness and judicial independence and impartiality'.[332]

3.3 Croatia

After the hostilities had ended, Croatia also conducted trials mainly of Serb nationals, members of the Yugoslav Army, as well as Bosnian Serbs and Croatian nationals. They were found guilty of war crimes against the civilian population, against prisoners of war or of genocide[333] committed on Croatian territory, on the basis of the Croatian criminal code.[334] For example, the Split district court passed sentences on thirty-nine Serbs or Bosnian Serbs, twenty-seven of them in absentia, for attacking civilian populations and civilian targets and ill-treating and killing civilians and military detainees in Croatian territory.[335] The court cited many articles of the Geneva Conventions including common Article 3 and additional Protocol II, without, however, ever mentioning the character of the armed conflict. Similarly, the district court of Zadar, found nineteen accused, mostly members of the Yugoslav army, guilty of war crimes against the civilian population for having violated the Hague regulations of 1907, Article 3 of the 1949 Geneva Conventions and Articles 13 and 14 of Additional Protocol II, during the armed clashes between the former Yugoslavia Army and the armed forces of the Republic of Croatia. These attacks resulted in 'the death of 30 civilians and caused huge material damage on over 120 objects of the utmost cultural and economic importance'.[336]

Croatian courts also extended their jurisdiction over war crimes committed abroad by Croatian nationals. On 30 July 2002, for example, the Karlovac tribunal sentenced to twenty years' imprisonment a Muslim leader, Fikret A., for war crimes against civilians and prisoners of war committed in Bosnia-Herzegovina. At the end of the conflict, he fled to Croatia and being a Croatian national he could not be extradited to a foreign country.[337]

Despite some Croatian public opinion opposition, even a former general of the Croatian army, Mirko N., has been arrested for war crimes committed against Serb civilians in October 1991 in the Gospic region of Croatia. The Gospic five case was finally brought to an end on 24 March

2003 when the Rijeka county court found three of them, including the general Mirko N., guilty of war crimes. The other two indictees were acquitted of all charges due to lack of evidence.[338]

Other cases led to some acquittals[339] or to very lenient sentences. This was the case for three Croatian, former military policemen, who received a one year sentence for illegal arrests and torture leading to the deaths of an unknown number of Croatian Serb civilians. Explaining this sentence, the judge of the Bjelovar county court said in this case the offenders were 'Homeland defenders who committed crimes during war circumstances'.[340] This has led some commentators to say that 'proceedings were partly conducted unfairly and sometimes even in a virtual travesty of justice'.[341]

In the case of Croatia, the judicial system was not destroyed by the armed conflict and is rather well equipped to carry out war crimes prosecutions.[342] These trials show the relative feasibility and expediency of domestic trials when they are conducted in the territory where the war crimes have been committed.[343] Partiality in prosecuting mostly non-Croats or leniency towards members of the Croatian army remains a risk.[344] Commentators have identified the following shortcomings in Croatian war crimes prosecutions: the bias of the judiciary, the large number of trials held *in absentia*, the insufficient quality of indictments and the inappropriate treatment of witness, victim and plaintiff.[345] From 1991 to 2004, 4,774 persons were reported for war crimes, 1,675 were indicted, 778 convicted and 245 were acquitted.[346]

New challenges await the Croatian judicial system following the possible referral of cases by the ICTY to domestic courts in the states of the former Yugoslavia under rule 11*bis* of the ICTY rules of procedure and evidence.[347] Some problems arise from the fact that certain legal concepts, such as command responsibility contained in Article 7.3 of the ICTY statute were not, up to 2004, recognised in the Croatian substantive criminal law.[348] ICTY indictments must be translated into indictments which comply with Croatian criminal procedure. The ICTY will assess the capability of Croatia to hold fair trials and the independence and professionalism of its judiciary before any case can be transferred. The case of the Croatian generals, Rahim Ademi and Mirko Norac, is the first case to be referred back to Croatia by the ICTY.[349] The referral bench has to satisfy itself that an adequate legal framework exists which could criminalise the alleged behaviour of the accused and that, if found guilty, an appropriate punishment could be applied based on the offences currently charged before the Tribunal.[350] Concerning the discrepancies between the two bodies of law, the referral bench took the view that 'it should not exclude referral for the reason only that there may well be found to be a limited difference between the law applied by the Tribunal and the Croatian Court'.[351] It found that local courts had a few alternatives for determining the law applicable to the accused and that there were appropriate provisions to address most, if not all, of the accused's alleged criminal acts in the present indictment.[352]

3.4 East Timor

In resolution 1272 of 25 October 1999, the Security Council expressed 'its concern at reports indicating that systematic, widespread and flagrant violations of international humanitarian law and human rights law have been committed in East Timor'. It stressed further that 'persons committing such violations bear individual responsibility'. On the basis of chapter VII of the UN Charter, the Security Council by this same resolution created a UN Transitional Administration in East Timor (UNTAET) 'which will be endowed with overall responsibility for the administration of East Timor and will be empowered to exercise all legislative and executive authority, including the administration of justice'.[353]

Carrying out this mandate, the Transitional Administration in East Timor issued a number of regulations on the organisation of the courts in East Timor.[354] Regulation UNTAET/REG/2000/11 creates eight district courts in East Timor with jurisdiction over different geographical regions. Furthermore, the district court of Dili is given exclusive jurisdiction over the following serious criminal offences: genocide, war crimes, crimes against humanity, murder, sexual offences and torture.[355] Special panels of this district court of Dili, composed of one East Timorese judge and two international judges, have jurisdiction throughout the entire territory of East Timor to try perpetrators for the given crimes if committed between 1 January 1999 and 25 October 1999.[356]

Alongside some offences taken directly from the East Timor penal code such as murder or sexual offences, the special panels with jurisdiction over serious criminal offences will be able to try individuals for genocide, crimes against humanity and war crimes committed both in international or internal armed conflicts. The UNTAET Administration recognises that whatever the nature of the conflict, serious violations of human rights and humanitarian law amount to international crimes deserving specific treatment. Sections 4, 5 and 6 of regulation 2000/15 of the UNTAET are an exact copy of Articles 6, 7 and 8 of the statute of the International Criminal Court.[357] This reinforces the belief that the list of war crimes in internal armed conflict appearing in the ICC statute reflects customary international law.[358]

Faced with a totally destroyed judicial system, the UN Administration in East Timor had to rebuild courtroom facilities, appoint and train prosecutors and judges.[359] The serious crimes panels exercise both territorial and 'universal jurisdiction'. According to UNTAET regulation 2000/25, universal jurisdiction means 'jurisdiction irrespective of whether the serious criminal offence at issue was committed within the territory of East Timor; of whether the serious criminal offence was committed by an East Timorese citizen or of whether the victim of the serious criminal offence was an East Timorese citizen.'[360] This choice seems to have been guided by a willingness to give these special panels the opportunity of prosecuting conspiracy to commit genocide committed outside East Timor territory, for example, prosecuting Indonesian citizens and not only citizens of East Timor and lastly prosecuting individuals who might have committed a crime against UN personnel, i.e. non-East Timorese citizens.

Notwithstanding the lack of financial resources and international expertise, the right to be tried without undue delay has been relatively respected.[361] As of 1 October 2002, the serious crime unit has indicted 117 persons for crimes committed during the violent break-up with Indonesia and the special panels have completed 25 trials.[362] By 2003, the special panels had dealt with thirty-four cases, three of which had been finalised.[363]

During the first years of work, it is interesting to note that convictions were entered mainly for murder or other violations of the Indonesian criminal code. There was a shift in 2002 when the majority of people detained were charged for crimes against humanity.[364] By March 2003, 170 accused had been indicted, of whom 145 had been charged with crimes against humanity.[365] However, 98 out of these 170 people indicted, among them those bearing the greatest responsibility, are believed to be at large in Indonesia.[366] Co-operation of Indonesian authorities in surrendering suspects, witnesses or evidence has not been forthcoming.[367] So far, no prosecutions for war crimes have been carried out. The Prosecutor's office chose to charge people with murder instead, avoiding thereby the need to establish the existence of an armed conflict.[368] Under-staffing, limited resources and poor management have hampered the work of the serious crime unit and the special panels.[369] Due to lack of donor support, the serious crime unit was expected to finish all investigations by December 2004 and trials were due to stop in 2005, leaving the vast majority of serious crimes unpunished.[370]

3.5 Ethiopia

In Ethiopia, the transitional government created in 1992 a Special Prosecutor's Office to investigate and prosecute any person who committed an offence by abusing his position in the party, the government or mass organisations under the Dergue regime. Proceedings were opened in December 1994 to try members of the Dergue regime for genocide, war crimes and crimes against humanity. Alleged offenders are being tried for the killings of identified victims, enforced disappearances of others and for the forced relocation policy which caused the death of 100,000 persons. In May 2001, the Special Prosecutor estimated that proceedings were to finish in 2004, with 6,180 cases registered, 1,181 sentences already pronounced and 2,200 perpetrators still awaiting trial. Even if criticised for the length of the procedures, the lack of qualified personnel and the absence of some of the main leaders of the Dergue regime found guilty *in absentia*, the Ethiopian judicial system has carried out a surprising number of prosecutions in the quasi-ignorance of the international community.[371]

3.6 Indonesia

Following the violence in East Timor during 1999, Indonesia assured the Security Council of its commitment to bring those involved to justice in Indonesia.[372] Some prosecutions have been carried out by the Indonesian Ad Hoc Human Rights Tribunal in Jakarta.[373] This tribunal has jurisdiction over Indonesian citizens who would have committed genocide or crimes against humanity outside Indonesia. However, the Government of Indonesia restricted the jurisdiction of this tribunal to three out of thirteen districts of East Timor and for conduct committed only during the months of April and September 1999, omitting many atrocities committed in the other ten months of 1999 and in the other ten districts.[374] This ad hoc human rights tribunal has not been granted jurisdiction over war crimes.[375]

The judgments issued by this ad hoc human rights tribunal have led to many acquittals of persons bearing the greatest responsibility for international crimes.[376] This tribunal has been widely criticised for its unwillingness and inability to carry out properly prosecutions of senior members of the Indonesian military and police forces.[377] The Security Council did not consider creating an ad hoc international tribunal for East Timor but adopted instead a two-pronged approach to deal with massive human rights violations that took place in East Timor in 1999. However, many persons bearing the greatest responsibility are beyond the reach of the special panels in Dili and the ad hoc human rights tribunal in Jakarta seems to refuse to convict any members of the Indonesian armed or police forces for events committed in East Timor in 1999.[378] On the occasion of the last verdict reached by the ad hoc human rights tribunal on 5 August 2003, the European Union took the view that 'the trials have failed to deliver justice and did not result in a substantiated account of violence . . . These deficiencies in the process have jeopardised the credibility of the verdicts which were disproportionate to the seriousness of the crimes committed.'[379] The choice made by the UN of domestic prosecutions by two states has created 'an incomplete and one sided response to justice'.[380]

3.7 Iraq

The latest experiment in internationalised criminal justice has been the creation of the Iraqi special tribunal by the coalition provisional authority of Iraq on 10 December 2003.[381] This tribunal, often described as 'an instrument of victor's justice'[382] or the 'US justice with an Iraqi face',[383] is a judicial entity independent from the main Iraqi judicial system. It has concurrent jurisdiction with national courts but primacy over international crimes. Just as with the extraordinary chambers of Cambodia or the special war crimes court of Bosnia-Herzegovina, the special tribunal is a national institution which has some international aspects.[384] First, the tribunal has jurisdiction over Iraqi nationals or residents of Iraq for crimes committed between 17 July 1968 and 1 May 2003 in Iraqi territory or elsewhere, such as crimes committed in relation to the Iran–Iraq and the Iraq–Kuwait armed conflicts.[385] Secondly, the tribunal has jurisdiction over individuals who have allegedly committed genocide, crimes against humanity, war crimes in international and internal armed conflicts and a handful of crimes under Iraqi law.[386] The international crimes are taken almost verbatim from the ICC statute,[387] raising doubts in some cases about their retroactive application to events that took place up to thirty-five years ago. The list of war crimes applicable in internal armed conflicts is similar to Article 8 of the ICC statute. This could be seen as a statement that these crimes amounted to war crimes at the time of their commission. On the other hand, it is difficult to find sufficient state practice supporting the view that this conduct could be prosecuted as war crimes back in the 1960s. Even if common Article 3 had attained the status of customary norm in the 1970s, the international criminality of serious violations of common Article 3 was not yet recognised in customary international law.[388] This led some commentators to question the soundness of including international crimes, such as crimes against humanity and war crimes in internal armed conflicts, within the subject matter jurisdiction of the special tribunal.[389]

The third international aspect of the special tribunal is the opportunity for the Governing Council to appoint non-Iraqi judges and foreign advisors.[390] However, by the time of the first hearing in July 2004, all the members of the judiciary were Iraqi nationals.[391] Despite major security challenges, the special tribunal conducted the first trial of Saddam Hussein and seven co-accused between October 2005 and July 2006, charging them with the death of 148 Shiites in the village of Dujail during the 1980s. On 5 November 2006, Saddam Hussein was sentenced to death by hanging for murder, torture, and forced expulsions in connection with the deaths of 148 Iraqis. Another trial of Saddam Hussein and six co-accused started on 21 August 2006 for crimes committed during the military offensives in Kurdistan in 1988, often referred to as the 'Anfal' campaign, which left 180,000 people dead according to the Prosecutor. The financial and technical support of the coalition in Iraq has made the creation of this special tribunal possible, which is fully functioning despite great security risks and numerous criticisms raised over its ability to conduct fair trials and respect the rights of the accused.[392] It has also been criticised for its inability 'to render an accurate or comprehensive collective memory' and predictions are that 'it will provide a skewed historical account that will undoubtedly short-change as many alleged victims and nations as Nuremberg did'.[393]

3.8 Kosovo[394]

As in East Timor, the UN transitional administration is empowered to exercise legislative and executive authority and to take responsibility for the administration of justice in Kosovo.[395] The original idea to create a

Kosovo war and ethnic crimes court was abandoned in September 2000.[396] Instead, the administration chose to use the structure of the old system but at the same time try to establish a judiciary that would reflect the various ethnic communities and could become 'an ethnically and politically independent and impartial judicial system that enjoyed the confidence of the population'.[397] To a majority of Albanians, Serbs, Bosniacs, Roma and Turkish-appointed judges and prosecutors, a small number of international judges were appointed to sit on mixed panels to be principally in charge of sensitive cases such as war crimes, genocide, murder or drug-trafficking.[398] One interesting aspect of these prosecutions is that any of the parties may at any stage in the criminal proceedings petition the Department of Judicial Affairs for an international judge or prosecutor to be assigned to the case and/or a change of venue where 'this is considered necessary to ensure the independence and impartiality of the judiciary or the proper administration of justice'.[399] The law applicable to the special panels as well as other courts in Kosovo are the regulations promulgated by the Special Representative of the Secretary-General and the law in force in Kosovo on 22 March 1989.[400] War crimes prosecutions are therefore based on the criminal code of Yugoslavia and by the end of June 2002, seventeen war crimes trials had taken place in Kosovo.[401] During the first two years, many trials which had led to convictions for war crimes by a panel of local judges were overturned on appeal by a panel formed of a majority of international judges of the supreme court. The international judges, if present on the trial panel, were being out-voted by local judges resulting in Serbian defendants being found guilty. Furthermore, local prosecutors were 'overcharging' Serbian defendants.[402] The most recurrent reasons advanced by the supreme court when quashing first trial cases were the insufficient establishment of facts, the failure to call defence witnesses or the incorrect assessment of the evidence.[403] All these factors led the United Nations Interim Administration Mission in Kosovo (UNMIK) to issue new regulations in order to ensure majority international control over voting, with three professional judges, including a minimum of two international judges, together with two lay judges for war crimes cases. In August 2001, the first international prosecutor was appointed to the supreme court, bringing the total of international prosecutors to six.

The quality of district and supreme courts' decisions has improved over the years and some decisions are particularly noteworthy for their use of the ICTY case law and relevant customary international law. Of particular interest is the decision of the Mitrovica district court in the *Miroslav Vuković* case of 25 October 2002.[404] The court found the ICTY case law persuasive and adopted the same definition of an armed conflict. It found that an internal armed conflict existed in the municipality in question between September 1998 and May 1999 between the Kosovo Liberation Army (KLA) and the armed forces of the Former Republic of Yugoslavia (FRY). It also found that the victims were all civilians taking no active part in hostilities and that the nexus between the acts of the accused and the armed conflict was established. The accused was found guilty of war crimes pursuant to Article 142 of the criminal code of the SFRY, as encompassed by Article 147 of the Fourth Geneva Conventions, Article 4.2 of Protocol II and paragraph 1)a) of common Article 3.[405] Also noteworthy was the conduct of the trial of four Albanian members of the KLA indicted for war crimes. Various protests and demonstrations took place in support of the defendants. Their indictment and then trial created immense public interest. The district court of Pristina held public hearings between February and July 2003 and found that an internal armed conflict existed at the relevant time between the KLA and military and security forces of the SFRY, that each of the offences had a nexus with the armed conflict and that the victims of the offences were entitled to protection under common Article 3 and Protocol II. The district court also found the concept of command responsibility to be applicable in internal armed conflicts through international customary law.

Commentators took the view that such cases provide evidence that the UNMIK Department of Justice can provide sufficient logistical and financial support to enable high-profile trials to take place.[406] Despite steps in the right direction, breaches of due process and fair trial norms happened on a regular basis in the judicial criminal system of Kosovo. Some courts failed to reason their decisions on detention and punishment properly and to ensure that trials were heard without undue delay.[407] Shortage of personel and resources compared to the ICTY resources is often blamed for some of these shortcomings.[408] However, the elimination of bias in domestic war crimes trials in Kosovo has been assured by the presence of international judges and prosecutors and has led to important war crimes trials taking place domestically.

3.9 Russia

Despite the clear application of both Protocol II and common Article 3 to at least parts of the armed conflict that has been taking place in

Chechnya since 1999, the Russian Government seems to treat war crimes committed by Russian federal troops as domestic crimes, which can be amnestied under the resolution on amnesty for persons who committed socially dangerous acts in the course of the antiterrorist operation in the North Caucasus.[409] Very few prosecutions of Russian soldiers are reported. The case against Colonel Yuri Budanov in the North Caucasian district military court of Rostov-on-Don ended on 31 December 2002 with an acquittal. Budanov was found to be temporarily insane when he raped and killed an eighteen-year-old Chechen girl in 2000.[410]

4. Conclusion: domestic v. foreign prosecutions

It could be argued that territorial jurisdiction is always best. Othman takes the view that 'to have lasting effect, justice has to be locally ingrained'.[411] Access to evidence and witnesses, knowledge of local custom and the geography of the country, access by local people to the proceedings as well as the impact of local justice on reconciliation and on the reconstruction of a lasting peace are among the most obvious advantages of domestic prosecutions by war-torn countries. Furthermore, local prosecutions are certainly less costly than criminal justice administered internationally. However, mixed tribunals are not always suitable. The review of domestic prosecutions highlighted above shows that there is a real risk of bias and political interference in domestic prosecutions in war-torn countries. In some instances, such as in Indonesia, with the ad hoc human rights tribunal in Jakarta or in Sudan, with the special criminal court for the events in Darfur,[412] there is no real political willingness to carry out genuine and effective prosecutions of the main perpetrators of major atrocities. Furthermore, in many instances, the judicial system of countries after a sustained internal armed conflict is in tatters and war crimes prosecutions could not take place without external finance and the technical assistance of the international community. The examples of Bosnia, Sierra Leone, Cambodia, East Timor, Iraq or Kosovo are living proof that without international funds and expertise, it would not be possible for domestic courts to carry out fair and impartial trials of war criminals.

The multiplication of these hybrid or internationalised criminal chambers or tribunals has taken various forms. In some instances, they are born out of an international agreement between the UN and the local government, such as in Cambodia or Sierra Leone.[413] In other cases, the

UN in charge of rebuilding the justice systems of Kosovo or East Timor did set up, within the domestic judicial system, internationalised courts dealing with war crimes and human rights violations. In the last decade, the UN has been particularly active in helping to re-build domestic justice capacities through the creation of these hybrid tribunals. They all have in common the fact that they prosecute individuals for international crimes alongside domestic crimes and that their composition is of a mixed nature, trials being administered by international and national judges. Their seat is always in the state where the crimes have been committed and they are created as a taylor-made response to the particularities of the judicial system in place.[414] Their functioning depends on the existence of sufficient financial funds together with the necessary political support of the international community. It is sad to admit that, without some sort of international involvement in the judicial system of war-torn countries, fair and independent prosecutions of war crimes remain a rare phenomenon.[415]

Is the use of the courts of other states by victims – sometimes called the decentralised prosecution of war criminals through national courts[416] – a viable alternative to the enforcement of individual responsibility by local jurisdictions of war-torn countries? Prosecutions by the domestic courts of other states will always represent a welcome alternative in the absence of prosecutions in the states where the crimes were committed, as well as a necessary complement to prosecutions by international courts. Prosecutions by domestic courts of other states on the basis of universal jurisdiction appear today as an indispensable tool for the enforcement of individual responsibility for war crimes committed in internal conflicts, even if some have faced insurmountable problems of proof. Access to evidence and witnesses as well as the collaboration of the authorities of the states where the crimes have been committed, can be difficult. The temporal and geographical distances between the domestic courts of a third state and the place and time of the suspected criminal conduct, make the work of the prosecution hazardous and can lead to an acquittal of the suspected criminal for lack of evidence. Furthermore, such prosecutions can be costly for the state carrying them out. Prosecution by the domestic courts of third states is a necessary complement to national and international prosecutions, but it leaves the door open to potentially conflicting case law or at least an absence of uniformity as to the penalties and the treatment of each accused. Similarly, there is no real uniformity of treatment and penalties between individuals tried by the ICTY, for example, and those tried back home by the special chamber of the state court of Bosnia. This maybe is the price to pay if we really want to see as many war criminals as possible in courtrooms.

Decentralised prosecutions of war criminals also suffer from the inherent limitations of the principle of universal jurisdiction. The likelihood of prosecutions on the basis of universal jurisdiction is usually dependant on the presence of the alleged offender in the country, which is willing to extend its jurisdiction over him. The abandonment of 'pure universal jurisdiction' by Belgium, for example, goes to the heart of universal jurisdiction and the fight against impunity. Requiring the presence of the alleged offender in the territory of third states can be seen as the most rational use of the national judicial system as well as the best way to limit the flood of politically motivated claims. However, this procedural requirement will hinder the effectiveness of the entire concept of universal jurisdiction. In practice, no investigation can be started or arrest warrant issued before the alleged offender is present. If he is present for a short visit in that country, investigations might not have time to lead to an arrest warrant being served and the alleged offender will leave the country and evade justice. It will limit the travel abilities of alleged offenders and allow countries, which have chosen to extend universal jurisdiction over war criminals not to become a safe heaven for war criminals. However, this form of universal jurisdiction, chosen by a majority of states, will not stop highly mobile criminals and will not allow states to participate meaningfully in the greater fight against impunity.[417]

Furthermore, diplomatic immunities, granted to acting heads of state and ministers of foreign affairs, will also hinder the effectiveness of universal jurisdiction. The conclusions reached on this issue by the ICJ in *DRC v. Belgium* weaken the principle of universal jurisdiction and its potential use by domestic courts of third states. Belgium has changed its legislation and has severely limited the potential use by war crimes victims of the principle of universal jurisdiction before Belgian courts. Universal jurisdiction is not, however, dead. As seen in this chapter, Germany has given itself the means to be able to prosecute under universal jurisdiction war crimes committed in internal armed conflicts in the absence of prosecutions by the territorial states. Similarly, the 2005 decision of the Spanish constitutional court preserves the opportunity for Spanish courts to investigate, even without the presence of the alleged offender in Spain, and try individuals for war crimes committed in internal armed conflicts on the basis of universal jurisdiction.[418]

The absence of a clearly established customary right to extend universal jurisdiction over war crimes committed in internal armed conflicts coupled with the fact that only thirty-two states have included this principle in their criminal codes might lead to a limited number of third-state prosecutions for war crimes committed in internal armed conflicts. Domestically at least, it might be easier for victims of such crimes to rely on the 1984 Torture Convention, as it clearly includes the principle of universal jurisdiction.[419] Recent prosecutions in the Netherlands, France or Spain have shown that national domestic courts more readily extend universal jurisdiction over the crime of torture rather than over war crimes committed in internal armed conflicts.[420]

Notes

1. There are some exceptions to this bleak picture: prosecutions took place or are ongoing in countries which have just emerged from internal armed conflict, such as Ethiopia, Rwanda, Bosnia, Croatia and Kosovo, see section 3 of this chapter for more details.
2. See on these points, M. Morris, 'International guidelines against impunity: facilitating accountability' (1996) 59 *Law and contemporary problems* 29–39; G. Blewitt, 'The necessity for enforcement of international humanitarian law' (1995) *American Society of International Law Proceedings* 298–300.
3. L. Reydams, 'Universal jurisdiction over atrocities in Rwanda: theory and practice' (1996) 1 *European journal of crime, criminal law and criminal justice* 18. See also, C. Joyner, 'Arresting impunity: the case for universal jurisdiction in bringing war criminals to accountability' (1996) 59 *Law and contemporary problems* who affirms at 165: 'international condemnation of war crimes as offences of global concern implies the right of all states to prosecute all offenders, just as the world legal order previously permitted every state to prosecute pirates and slave traders'. See also Y. Dinstein, 'The universality principle and war crimes' in M. N. Schmitt (ed.), *International law studies: the law of military operations, lieber amicorum Professor J. Grunawalt* (Newport, Rhode Island: Naval War College, 1998) who affirms at p. 21: 'once violations of the laws of war qualify as war crimes, all come under the sway of the universality principle'. See also, Bassiouni and Wise, *Aut dedere, aut judicare: the duty to extradite or prosecute in international law* (Dordrecht: Martinus Nijhoff, 1995) p. 8 where they affirm: 'an international offence is conduct on the part of individuals which multilateral treaty obliges to suppress through criminal sanctions'. See also, M. Kamminga, 'Lessons learned from the exercise of universal jurisdiction in respect of gross human rights offences' (2001) 23 *Human rights quarterly* 947–48.

4. In general, see I. Brownlie, *Principles of public international law* (Oxford: Oxford University Press, 1996) p. 300 and Akehurst, 'Jurisdiction in international law' (1972–73) 46 *BYIL* 216.

5. One may also note that the US military tribunal at Nuremberg affirmed in the *re List and others case*: 'An international crime is . . . an act universally recognised as criminal, which is considered a grave matter of international concern and for some valid reason cannot be left within the exclusive jurisdiction of the State that would have control over it under ordinary circumstances.' It immediately added, however: 'The inherent nature of a war crime is ordinarily itself sufficient justi-fication for jurisdiction to attach in the courts of the belligerent into whose hands the alleged criminal has fallen.' Reported in United Nations War Crimes Commission, *Law Reports of Trials of War Criminals*, vol. 8 (London: Stationery Office, 1949) p. 54.

6. *Furundžija* trial, para. 156.

7. Lord Slynn, see [1998] 3 *WLR* 1456 at 1471F–1465G.

8. *R. v. Bartle and the Commissioner of Police for the Metropolis and others ex parte Pinochet*, opinion of the Lords of Appeal, judgment, 24 March 1999 (1999) 38 *ILM* 660. Lord Browne-Wilkinson seems to share the same view when he affirmed: 'I have no doubt that long before the Torture Convention of 1984 torture was an international crime in the highest sense. But there was no tribunal or court to punish international crimes of torture. Local courts could take jurisdiction.' *Ibid.*, 589–90.

9. A district court judge recently reaffirmed that English courts have no jurisdiction over non-statutory offences committed abroad. Crimes under customary international law are not incorporated into English criminal law. See case No. 8, *R. v. Bow Street Magistrates' Court*, 15 October 2003 [2003] EWHC 2730 (Admin), reported in (2003) *BYIL* 493.

10. Lord Browne-Wilkinson affirmed in this respect: 'The torture convention was agreed not in order to create an international crime which had not previously existed, but to provide an international system under which the international criminal - the torturer - could find no safe heaven', *ibid.*, 590.

11. Lord Millet, *ibid.*, 650. It is interesting to note that Lord Millet believes that for a crime prohibited by international law to attract universal jurisdiction, two criteria need to be satisfied: first the crime must be contrary to a peremptory norm of international law so as to infringe a *jus cogens* norm. Secondly, it must be so serious and on such a scale that it can justly be regarded as an attack on the international legal order. *Ibid.*, 649–50.

12. See Meron who declared: 'the question of what actions constitute crimes must be distinguished from the question of jurisdiction to try those crimes', T. Meron, 'International criminalisation of internal atrocities' (1995) 89 *AJIL* 561. See also G. Draper, 'The modern pattern of war criminality' (1976) 6 *Israel yearbook of human rights* 22 and C. Greenwood, 'International humanitarian law and the *Tadić*

case' (1996) 7 *EJIL* 277 and 279. Similarly, Dinstein takes the view that 'the universality principle does not apply in an automatic fashion to all international offences, although there seems to be a presumption today in favour of such application', Dinstein, 'The universality principle and war crimes' 21. See also V. Zakane, 'La compétence universelle des états dans le droit international contemporain' (2000) 8 *African yearbook of international law* 201. See finally, Carnegie when he affirms: 'The general argument that any crime under international law must be a crime of universal jurisdiction is an untenable one', in Carnegie, 'Jurisdiction over violations of the laws and customs of war' (1963) *BYIL* 421.

13. American Law Institute, *Restatement of the law (third), the foreign relations law of the USA* (1987) point IV, Jurisdiction and judgments, introductory note.

14. See Harvard Research in International Law, 'Draft convention on jurisdiction with respect to crime' (1935) 29 *AJIL* 435 (hereafter referred to as the Harvard Research project).

15. Dinstein 'The universality principle and war crimes' 17. Furthermore, the Permanent Court of International Justice (PCIJ) in the *Lotus* case seemed to emphasise that on the question of jurisdiction, international law 'left states a wide measure of discretion which is only limited in certain cases by prohibitive rules', see *Lotus Case*, merits (*France v. Turkey*) *PCIJ Reports*, Series A, No. 10, 1927, pp. 18–19.

16. These principles were first highlighted by the Harvard Research in International Law in 1935, 'Jurisdiction with respect to crime' 435. On these points, see in general, Jennings and Watts (eds.), *Oppenheim's international law* (London, New York: Longman, 9th edn, 1992) p. 456; C. Blakesley, 'Extraterritorial jurisdiction' in Bassiouni (ed.), *International criminal law*, vol. II (Ardsley, New York: Transnational Publishers, 1999) 2nd edn, pp. 33–105 and P. Gaeta, 'National prosecution of international crimes: international rules on ground of jurisdiction' in *Studi di diritto internazionale in onore di Gaetano Arango-Ruiz*, (Naples: Editoriale Scientifica, 2004) vol. 3, pp. 1923–43.

17. O. Schachter, 'International law in theory and practice, general course in public international law' (1982) 78 *Recueil des cours* 262.

18. On the definition of the concept of universal jurisdiction, see in particular, R. O'Keefe, 'Universal jurisdiction: clarifying the basic concept' (2004) 2 *JICJ* 735–60.

19. Universal jurisdiction is usually seen as a permissible right to extend jurisdiction. Meron took the view that: 'indeed, the true meaning of universal jurisdiction is that international law permits any state to apply its laws to certain offences even in the absence of territorial, nationality or other accepted contacts with the offender or the victim', Meron, 'International criminalisation of internal atrocities' 554. See also, Cassese when he affirms: 'Under customary international law, universal jurisdiction may only be triggered if those other states fail to act, or else have legal systems so inept or corrupt that they are unlikely to do justice. Universality only operates then as a default jurisdiction.' A. Cassese, 'Is the bell tolling for

universality? A plea for a sensible notion of universal jurisdiction' (2003) 1 *JICJ* 589 at 593.

20. See in general, W. B. Cowles, 'Universality of jurisdiction over war crimes' (1945) 33 *California law review* 177–218; Carnegie, 'Jurisdiction over violations of the laws and customs of war' 421; K. C. Randall, 'Universal jurisdiction under international law' (1998) 66 *Texas law review* 785–841, Dinstein, 'The universality principle and war crimes' 17–37; M. Henzelin, *Le principe de l'universalité en droit pénal international. Droit et obligation pour les états de poursuivre et juger selon le principe de l'universalité* (Basle, Geneva, Brussels: Helbing & Lichtenhahn, Faculté de droit de Genève, Bruylant); L. Reydams, *Universal jurisdiction: international and municipal legal perspectives* (Oxford: Oxford University Press, 2003); S. Macedo (ed.), *Universal jurisdiction, national courts and the prosecution of serious crimes under international law* (Philadelphia: University of Pennsylvania Press, 2004); S. Becker, 'Universal jurisdiction: how universal is it? A study of competing theories' (2002/2003) XII *Palestine yearbook of international law* 49–76; M. Kamminga, 'Lessons learned from the exercise of universal jurisdiction in respect of gross human rights offences' (2001) 23 *Human rights quarterly* 940–74; E. Kwakwa, 'The Cairo-Arusha principles on universal jurisdiction in respect of gross human rights offences: developing the frontiers of the principle of universal jurisdiction' (2002) 10 *African yearbook of international law* 407–23; G. Abi-Saab, 'The proper role of universal jurisdiction' (2003)1 *JICJ* 596–602; C. Kress, 'Universal jurisdiction over international crimes and the Institut de droit international' (2006) 4 *JICJ* 561–85, who comments on the Krakow resolution of the Institute of International Law on universal criminal jurisdiction with regard to the crime of genocide, crimes against humanity and war crimes, available online on www.idi-iil.org.

21. For a thorough analysis of the doctrine on the principle of universal jurisdiction, see L. Reydams, 'Universal jurisdiction', pp. 28–42.

22. Dinstein, 'The universality principle and war crimes', p. 22. See also Cowles, 'Universality of jurisdiction over war crimes' 217–18; M. Morris, 'Universal jurisdiction in a divided world' (2001) 35 *New England law review* 337; V. Zakane, 'La compétence universelle des états dans le droit international contemporain' (2000) 8 *African yearbook of international law* 183–222; M. Henzelin, 'La compétence pénale universelle, une question non résolue par l'arrêt Yerodia' (2002) *RGDIP* 819–53; Kamminga 'Lessons learned from the exercise of universal jurisdiction' 943–44; R. Wolfrum, 'Prosecution of international crimes by international and national criminal courts: concurring jurisdiciton' in *Studi di diritto internazionale in onore di Gaetano Arango-Ruiz* (Naples: Editoriale Scientifica, 2004) vol. 3, pp. 2200–1.

23. Such principle is now recognised in treaty law, see Article 105 of the 1982 UN Convention on the Law of the Sea. On the issue of piracy and universal jurisdiction, see the excellent article by E. Kontorovich, 'The piracy analogy: modern

universal jurisdiction's hollow foundation' (2004) 45 *Harvard international law journal* 183–237.

24. See Randall, 'Universal jurisdiction under international law' 792–93 and Becker, 'Universal jurisdiction: how universal is it?' 54–61, which takes the view that 'the justification for the theory of universal jurisdiction thus lies in the fact that without such jurisdiction, no country could prosecute the offender' 59. For a different view, see Kontorovich, 'The piracy analogy: modern universal jurisdiction's hollow foundations' 190, who takes the view that 'ships that pirates attacked were registered in a particular nation and thus were within the nation's flag jurisdiction; ... Thus the locus of piracy did not render standard jurisdictional rules inapplicable.'

25. See Randall, 'Universal jurisdiction under international law' 795. Kontorovich takes the view that pirates were not universally condemned because of the heinous nature of piracy but rather for the 'failure to comply with the formalities of licensing', Kontorovich, 'The piracy analogy: modern universal jurisdiction's hollow foundations' 210–23.

26. This crime is now also part of treaty law, see Article 110 of the 1982 UN Convention on the Law of the Sea, as well as the Convention to Suppress Slave Trade and Slavery of 1926 and the supplementary Convention of the Abolition of Slavery, the Slave Trade and Institutions or Practices Similar to Slavery of 1956. See Randall, 'Universal jurisdiction under international law' 798–800 as well as Blakesley, 'Extraterritorial jurisdiction', p. 31.

27. See Article 4 of the 1970 Hague Convention for the Suppression of Unlawful Seizure of Aircraft, 860 *UNTS* 105; Article 5 of the 1971 Montreal Convention for the Suppression of Unlawful Acts against the Safety of Civil Aviation, 974 *UNTS* 177.

28. See Article 3 of the 1973 Convention on the Prevention and Punishment of Crimes Against Internationally Protected Persons, including Diplomatic Agents, 1035 *UNTS* 167.

29. See Article 5 of the International Convention for the Suppression and Punishment of the Crime of Apartheid of 1973, 1015 *UNTS* 243.

30. See Article 5 of the 1979 International Convention against the Taking of Hostages, 1316 *UNTS* 21931.

31. See Article 8 of the 1980 Convention on the Physical Protection of Nuclear Material, 1456 *UNTS* 24631.

32. See Article 5 of the 1984 UN Convention against Torture and other Cruel Inhuman or Degrading Treatment or Punishment (New York, 10 December 1984, 1465 *UNTS* 85).

33. See Article 6 of the 1988 Convention for the Suppression of Unlawful Acts against the Safety of Maritime Navigation, 1678 *UNTS* 29004.

34. See Article 4 of the 1988 UN Convention against Illicit Traffic in Narcotic Drugs and Psychotropic Substances (Vienna, 20 December 1988, UN.Doc.E/CONF.82/15).

35. See Article 15 of the 2000 UN Convention against Transnational Organised Crime, www.uncjin.org/documents/conventions/dcatoc/final_documents_2.

36. See Article 9 of the 1989 International Convention against the Recruitment, Use, Financing and Training of Mercenaries (New York, 15 December 1989, UN.Doc.A/Res/44/34).

37. See Article 9 of the 1929 International Convention for the Suppression of Counterfeiting Currency (Geneva, April 1929, 112 *LNTS* 371).

38. See Article 5 of the 1998 European Convention for the Protection of the Environment through Criminal Law (Strasbourg, 4 November 1998, *ETS* No. 172).

39. See Article 10 of the 1994 Convention on the Safety of UN and Associated Personnel (New York, 9 December 1994, UN.Doc.A/49/742).

40. See Article 42 of the 2003 UN Convention against Corruption, www.unodc.org/pdf/crime/convention_corruption/signing/convention-e.pdf.

41. See Dinstein, 'The universality principle and war crimes', pp. 23–26.

42. For more details on this principle, see Bassiouni and Wise, *Aut dedere, aut judicare: the duty to extradite or prosecute in international law*, pp. 3–20.

43. In this respect, see the definition used by the Princeton project on universal jurisdiction, *Princeton principles on universal jurisdiction*, 23 July 2001, available online on www.princeton.edu/~lapa/unive_jur.pdf (hereafter referred to as 'the Princeton principles'). C. Tomushat stated: 'It can rightly be said that the pivotal element of universal jurisdiction is nothing else than the nature of the crime.' Tomushat, 'Universal criminal jurisdiction with respect to the crime of genocide, crimes against humanity and war crimes', *Institute of International Law yearbook*, vol. 71 (Paris: Pedone, 2005) part 1, p. 225.

44. This exercise has often been coined prescriptive 'universal jurisdiction *in absentia*'. See O'Keefe, 'Universal jurisdiction' 754–60. The Princeton principles declare that a state can initiate proceedings, request extradition and conduct an investigation even if the suspect is not present on the territory of the prosecuting state. Principle 1(2) requires only that the suspect is present on the territory before a judicial body can exercise universal jurisdiction.

45. The Harvard draft convention on jurisdiction with respect to crime declared in its Article 10 that the principle of universality would be actionable 'on the sole basis of the presence of the alien within the territory of the state assuming jurisdiction' (Harvard Research project, 573). A recent research into the universality principle also affirmed that 'the only connection between the crime and the prosecuting state that may be required is the physical presence of the alleged offender within the jurisdiction of that state'. See Commission on International Human Rights Law and Practice, International Law Association, *Final Report on the exercise of universal jurisdiction in respect of gross human rights offences* (2000) Report of the 69th conference of the International Law Association 403–31. See also Becker, 'Universal jurisdiction: how universal it is?' 51–54. It is interesting to note that the 2005 resolution of the Institute of International Law provides for states to be able to

investigate crimes and request extradition without necessarily requiring the presence of the offender in their territory. Paragraph 3b) of the resolution reads: 'Apart from acts of investigation and requests for extradition, the exercise of universal jurisdiction requires the presence of the alleged offender in the territory of the prosecuting states', available online on www.idi-iil.org.

46. In support of this view, see in particular, the dissenting opinion of Judge Van den Wyngaert, in *Case concerning the arrest warrant of 11 April 2000 (Congo v. Belgium)* [2002] *ICJ Reports* 121, reprinted in 41 *ILM* 536, 636 and 637.

47. This is not the view advanced by Judges Higgins, Kooijmans and Buergenthal in their joint separate opinion in the *Case concerning the Arrest Warrant of 11 April 2000*. In para. 41 of their opinion, they affirmed that 'by the loose use of language the latter has come to be referred to as "universal jurisdiction", though it is really an obligatory territorial jurisdiction over persons, albeit in relation to acts committed elsewhere'.

48. For more detail, see chapter 3, section 1 of this book.

49. The Geneva Conventions of 1864, 1906 and 1929 are either silent on the repression of violations of these conventions (1864) or simply call for states to promulgate penal provisions for the repression of some breaches of these conventions (1929). Very few states followed this injunction and the Hague Conventions of 1899 and 1907 provide only for the responsibility of states for the breaches of the conventions. See J. Pictet (and others), *Commentary to Convention I* (Geneva: ICRC, 1952) pp. 351–57. It is interesting to note that the Oxford manual of the Institute of International Law on the laws of war on land in 1880 provided: 'if any of the foregoing rules be violated, the offending parties should be punished, after a judiciary hearing, *by the belligerent in whose hands they are*' (emphasis added), cited in Cowles, 'Universality of jurisdiction over war crimes' 205.

50. Traditional titles of jurisdiction were relied upon; no claim to universal jurisdiction can be found. Articles 228 and 229 of the Versailles Treaty recognised the 'right of the Allied and Associated Powers to bring before military tribunals Germans accused of having committed acts in violation of the laws and customs of war'. See chapter 3, section 1.1 for more detail.

51. The report of the Commission is printed in (1920) 14 *AJIL* 95 at 121.

52. See Article 6 of the draft legislation produced by the 1927 conference for the unification of penal law, and Article 10 of the Harvard draft convention with respect to crime. On these points, see Amnesty International, *Universal jurisdiction: the duty of states to enact and enforce legislation* (latest amended version September 2002) pp. 7–10, accessible online at http://web.amnesty.org/web/web.nsf/pages/legal-memorandum. Similarly, the 1931 resolution of the Institute of International Law at its Cambridge session, provides for universal jurisdiction over certain international crimes, but fails to include war crimes in this list.

53. See also Cowles, 'Universality of jurisdiction over war crimes' 204–6, as well as Randall, 'Universal jurisdiction under international law' 803.

54. *Judgment of the International Military Tribunal for the trial of German major war criminals*, Nuremberg, 30 September–1 October 1946 (London: Stationery Office, 1946) p. 38. This statement can be put in perspective with the position taken by the Tokyo tribunal two years later, where it affirmed: 'In the result, the members of the Tribunal, being otherwise wholly without power in respect of the trial of the accused, have been empowered by the documents, which constituted the Tribunal and appointed them as members, to try the accused.' International Military Tribunal for the Far East, Tokyo, judgment 12 November 1948, section 'Jurisdiction of the tribunal'.

55. Draper, 'The modern pattern of war criminality' 22. Carnegie seems to concur with this view, see Carnegie, 'Jurisdiction over violations of the laws and customs of war' 414–15. For an opposite interpretation, see Dinstein, 'The universality principle and war crimes' 27.

56. It is possible to argue that the right of belligerents to try war criminals, whom they hold under custody, amounts to a variation of universal jurisdiction. It is possible to imagine that, in an armed conflict with many belligerents, a war criminal might fall into the hands of a belligerent state, which is neither the victim's territorial state, nor his nationality state, nor the author of the crime's nationality state. There is no doubt that the application of universal jurisdiction over war crimes is a form of jurisdiction that has evolved from the principle that belligerents can try enemies that have fallen into their hands. The right to prosecute alleged offenders has been extended from belligerents only to any state that has the person in custody.

57. Carnegie stated: 'it is submitted that no explanation of jurisdiction over war crimes exclusively on the basis of territoriality or the nationality principle is tenable; and the clearly passive personality principle may be legitimately applied in such cases under the rules of customary international law'; Carnegie, 'Jurisdiction over violations of the laws and customs of war' 420.

58. The *List* trial is reported in United Nations War Crimes Commission, *Law reports of trials of war criminals*, vol. 6 (London: Stationery Office, 1947), p. 37, cited in Carnegie, 'Jurisdiction over violations of the laws and customs of war' 416.

59. United Nations War Crimes Commission, *Law reports of trials of war criminals*, vol. 8 (London: Stationery Office, 1947) p. 54. As far as the universality principle is concerned, Carnegie concluded in 1963: 'it would seem therefore that in the developing process of international law, major war crimes may be well on their way to becoming crimes of universal jurisdiction'. Carnegie, 'Jurisdiction over violations of the laws and customs of war' 423; he comments further: 'the evidence for the exercise of this kind of jurisdiction in state practice is not as clear as that for the exercise of passive personality jurisdiction'.

60. Cowles, 'Universality of jurisdiction over war crimes' (1945) 33 *California law review* at 217, see also 207–16. He later affirmed in 1945: 'all civilised states have a

very real interest in the punishment of war crimes'. See also Dinstein, 'The universality principle and war crimes' 19–20.

61. United Nations War Crimes Commission, *Law reports of trials of war criminals*, vol. 15 (London: Stationery Office, 1949), foreword p. X.

62. Randall, 'Universal jurisdiction under international law' 805. He comments at 807 that the 'IMT's judgment and records actually evidence little or no explicit reliance on universal jurisdiction'.

63. *Ibid.*, 807–10.

64. United Nations War Crimes Commission, *Law reports of trials of war criminals*, vol. 1 (London: Stationery Office, 1947), p. 42.

65. The statement of the UN Secretary-General in 1949 illustrates the dubious customary law status of universal jurisdiction in 1945: 'it is . . . possible and perhaps . . . probable that the Nuremberg Tribunal considered the crimes under the Charter to be, as international crimes, subject to the jurisdiction of every State'. *The charter and judgment of the Nuremberg Tribunal: history and analysis*, UN.Doc.Appendix II, A/CN.4/5 (3 March 1949).

66. For details of the *Eichmann* trial and universal jurisdiction, see Randall, 'Universal jurisdiction under international law' 810–15. Universal jurisdiction was not the only basis of jurisdiction cited by the courts in these two trials. They relied on the protective principle as well as the passive personality principle together with universal jurisdiction.

67. Most authors today agree with this conclusion, see for example, Jennings and Watts (eds.), *Oppenheim's international law* (London and NY: Longman, 9th edn, 1992) vol. 1, p. 470; The American Law Institute, *1 Restatement of the law, the foreign relations law of the US*, 1987, para. 404. See also Meron, 'International criminalisation of internal atrocities' 572–73; F. Karlshoven, *The law of warfare, a summary of its recent history and trends in development* (Leiden, Geneva: Sijthoff, Henry Dunant Institute, 1973) p. 119 and R. Baxter, 'The municipal and international law basis of jurisdiction over war crimes' (1951) 28 *BYIL* 392.

68. See *Final record of the diplomatic conference of Geneva of 1949* (Berne, 1951) vol. II–B, pp. 114–18 and R. van Elst, 'Implementing universal jurisdiction over grave breaches of the Geneva Conventions' (2000) *Leiden journal of international law* 815.

69. J. Pictet (and others), *Commentary to Convention I* (Geneva: ICRC, 1952) pp. 365–66.

70. See M. Henzelin, 'La compétence pénale universelle: une question non résolue par l'arrêt Yerodia' (2002) *RGDIP* 846–52. This author notes that Judges Higgins, Kooijmans and Buergenthal took the view that the universality principle under the 1949 Geneva Conventions comes into being only if the alleged offender is present in the territory of the state in question. The Geneva Conventions, however, do not limit the possibility of states asking for the extradition of alleged offenders. Such demand could be made in furtherance of

the general obligation under the Geneva Conventions by states to ensure respect for the conventions. For a contrary view, see Reydams, *Universal juris-diction*, p. 55.

71. See below section 2.3 in this chapter for more detail. See also R. Maison, 'Les premiers cas d'application des dispositions pénales des Conventions de Genève par les juridictions internes' (1995) 6 *EJIL* 260.

72. For more details see section 2.1 in this chapter.

73. See Articles 49, 50, 129 and 146 of the four Geneva Conventions respectively.

74. For a different interpretation, see Meron, 'International criminalisation of internal atrocities' 569 and 576.

75. See Article 9 of the 1997 Convention on Landmines, Articles 14.1 and 14.2 of the 1996 Protocol II and Article 7 of the Chemical Weapons Convention.

76. See Article 16.1 of the Second Protocol to the Hague Convention of 1954 for the Protection of Cultural Property in the Event of Armed Conflict, 26 March 1999, UNESCO Doc.HC/1999/7 (1999) 38 *ILM* 769–82.

77. See Article 14 of the 1994 Convention on the Safety of the UN and Associated Personnel, (1995) *ILM* 484–93. This article provides: 'the state party in whose territory the alleged offender is present shall, if it does not extradite that person, submit, without exception whatsoever and without undue delay, the case to its competent authorities for the purpose of prosecution'.

78. Dinstein, 'The universality principle and war crimes' 27.

79. One might note, however, that the Rwandese Government expressed its opposition to the creation of the ICTR (but for other reasons) and also that China abstained during the vote on the setting up of the ICTR.

80. On the negotiations during the Rome conference, see E. La Haye, 'The jurisdiction of the International Criminal Court: controversies over the pre-conditions for the exercise of its jurisdiction' (1999) 46 *Netherlands international law review* 1–25.

81. This proposal was first presented at the last preparatory committee before the conference on 23 March 1998. See Article 9 further option of the draft statute for the ICC, UN.Doc.A/CONF.183.2/Add.1.

82. UN.Doc.A/AC.249/1998/DP.2, p. 2.

83. Extract from the German address on jurisdiction to the Committee of the Whole, 19 June 1998 (on file with the author).

84. During the first discussion on jurisdiction, the German proposal received explicit support from twelve out of fifty-four states who spoke on 19 June 1998: Belgium, Denmark, Jordan, the Czech Republic, Ukraine, Greece, the Netherlands, New Zealand, Italy, Portugal, and the Ivory Coast. Later on, the discussion papers of the Committee of the Whole dropped that option (see UN.Doc.A/CONF.183/C.1/L.53 and L.59). During the debate on jurisdiction of 9 July 1998, twenty-three states expressed their dismay that universal jurisdiction no longer appeared to be a feasible option for the jurisdiction of the court.

85. See Article 12 of the ICC statute and section 2 of chapter 6 for more details.

86. For more details, see B. Graefarth, 'Universal criminal jurisdiction and an International Criminal Court' (1990) *EJIL* 67.

87. On this point, see the remarks made by L. Arbour, 'Will the ICC have an impact on universal jurisdiction?' (2003) 1 *JICJ* 585–88. She takes the view that the preamble to the ICC statute should be seen as a 'call for the fullest exercise by states of their own international criminal jurisdiction and that includes of course, not only their permissive universal jurisdiction, but also their compulsory one' at 587.

88. See O. Triffterer (ed.), *Commentary on the Rome statute of the International Criminal Court, observers' notes, article by article* (Baden-Baden: Nomos Verlagsgesellschaft, 1999) p. 13 and T. Slade and R. Clark, 'Preamble and final clauses' in R. Lee (ed.), *The International Criminal Court, the making of the Rome statute, issues, negotiations, results* (The Hague, London, Boston: Kluwer Law International, 1999) pp. 421–50 at p. 427.

89. In the absence of more specific references, the documents presented in this section are either available online on www.icrc.org or on file with the author.

90. Some of these states took the view that their existing domestic law was adequate to provide effective criminal sanctions for any violations of the Geneva Convention. Others have ratified these instruments but never adopted any implementing legislation.

91. According to Articles 5 and 6 of the criminal law of **China**, China exercises criminal jurisdiction over war crimes committed in a third country only if they are committed by Chinese citizens or by foreigners who commit such crimes against Chinese citizens. See International Society for Military Law and the Law of War, *Collection of the national reports related to the questionnaire on investigation and prosecution of violations of the law of armed conflict*, XIV International Congress, Athens (10–15 May 1997) p. 55 (referred to hereafter as '*The questionnaire*').

92. See **Iran**'s answer to *The questionnaire, ibid.*, p. 57.

93. The **Senegalese** code of criminal procedure does not provide for the principle of universal jurisdiction and does not contain any general clause enabling local courts to extend their jurisdiction if such jurisdiction is provided for in an international treaty. See Reydams, *Universal jurisdiction*, pp. 180–82. The recent case against H. Habré showed that an international treaty such as the 1984 Torture Convention could not be relied upon by national courts in the absence of national implementing legislation (judgment of the court of appeals of Dakar, 4 July 2000). The 1949 Geneva Conventions and protocols do not seem to have been implemented nationally and no prosecution of war criminals could therefore be possible in Senegal on the basis of universal jurisdiction.

94. To this author's best knowledge, none of these states has implemented any of the obligations under the grave breaches regime of the Geneva Conventions. Their criminal legislation does not seem to provide for universal jurisdiction over war crimes.

95. The **Romanian** criminal code requires the offences either to be committed on Romanian territory or by Romanian citizens. See the Romanian answer to *The questionnaire*, p. 59.

96. See the War Crimes Act 1996 and the Expanded War Crimes Act 1997, para. 2401 b) of chapter 118 of the **US** Code.

97. See section 3 of the 1973 **Bangladeshi** Act to provide for the detention, prosecution and punishment of persons for genocide, crimes against humanity, war crimes and other crimes under international law.

98. See the 1994 Convention on the Safety of UN and Associated Personnel and the Second Protocol to the 1954 Hague Convention. The Rome statute does not oblige states to punish these offences but its preamble recalls the duty of states to prosecute international crimes.

99. These common law countries have all enacted a 'Geneva Conventions Act' which provides for prosecution on the basis of universal jurisdiction for grave breaches only. It is interesting to note that the Irish Geneva Conventions Act 1962 provides for the prosecution by Irish courts of minor breaches of the Geneva Conventions, but only if the breach is committed in Ireland or by a citizen of **Ireland** abroad. This does not seem to have been changed by the Geneva Conventions Amendment Act 1998, published in *Irish current law statutes*, 1998. For more details see (1999) 2 *YbIHL* 380.

100. Article 15(3) of the criminal code of **Armenia** extends the jurisdiction of Armenian courts over actions of foreign citizens abroad if they have committed a crime 'provided in an international treaty of the Republic of Armenia'. This translation is, however, rather unclear: is it the criminality of the conduct or universal jurisdiction, which needs to be provided by the international treaty? In the latter case, war crimes in internal armed conflicts would not be covered by universal jurisdiction.

101. Austrian legislation does not provide specifically for the prosecution of war crimes committed in internal armed conflict. Section 64(1) subpara. 6 of the **Austrian** penal code provides for the application of Austrian law to punishable acts committed abroad if Austria is specifically obliged by international law to prosecute these actions. This would cover grave breaches but would not extend to most war crimes committed in internal armed conflicts. See the Austrian answer to *The questionnaire*, p. 51. However, mention must also be made of section 65 (1) subpara. 2 which provides for the jurisdiction of Austrian courts 'if the offender, though he was a foreigner at the time when he committed the offence is found in Austria and if, due to reasons different from the nature and characteristics of the offence, is not extradited to a foreign state.' Admittedly, war crimes committed in internal armed conflicts could be prosecuted in Austria under this heading. For more details, see Reydams, *Universal jurisdiction*, pp. 91–101.

102. Article 7 of the 1993 **Belgium** Loi relative à la repression des violations graves du droit international humanitaire (*Moniteur belge* of 5 August 1993 pp. 17751–55) was the first of this kind to extend universal jurisdiction over war crimes

committed in internal armed conflicts. This legislation has, however, been abrogated by the 5 August 2003 legislation (*Moniteur belge* of 7 August 2003) and substantial limitations have been placed on the exercise of universal jurisdiction in Belgium. Belgian courts will be able to prosecute certain international crimes on the basis of universal jurisdiction under Article 12*bis* of the code of criminal procedure, but it is unlikely to be able to do so for war crimes committed in internal armed conflicts. For more details, see the section below dealing with national prosecutions in Belgium.

103. Article 7 of the **Brazilian** criminal code provides for the application of domestic law for crimes committed abroad and over which Brazil is obliged to prosecute on the basis of an international treaty. See the Brazilian answer to *The questionnaire*, p. 53.

104. Article 1.7 of the **Bolivian** criminal code provides that national courts will have jurisdiction to try those crimes which were committed abroad, independently of the nationality of the person presumed responsible and that of the victim, when the state through international treaties or conventions has pledged to punish them. See Amnesty International, '*The UK: the Pinochet case: universal jurisdiction and the absence of immunity for crimes against humanity*' (January 1999) Amnesty International document: EUR45/01/99, p. 11 (hereafter referred to as 'the *Amnesty International document*').

105. Article 12(1)c) of the 2003 criminal code of **Bosnia-Herzegovina** provides for the application of the criminal code to anyone who, outside Bosnia, commits 'a criminal offence which Bosnia and Herzegovina is bound to punish according to the provisions of international law and international treaties or intergovernmental agreements'. Domestic judges could take the view that international law provides states with an additional basis, universal jurisdiction, over certain crimes and could therefore rely on the later provision to try an alleged offender who committed a war crime in an internal armed conflict abroad. Jurisdiction of local courts over war crimes committed in internal armed conflicts might also be based on Article 12(4) and (5) of the criminal code, but this provision is not directed in particular to international crimes.

106. Chapter 3, section 19 of the **Czech** criminal code is entitled 'universal jurisdiction' and provides for the application of Czech law to foreign nationals who commit certain crimes abroad which are defined in the code including genocide, use of forbidden weapons, unpermitted conduct of war, plunder or cruelty in war. These provisions, however, apply in 'time of war or in combat'. It is unclear whether this formulation can include internal armed conflicts.

107. See Article 18(6) of the 2000 **Ecuadorian** code of criminal procedure. However, once the ICC implementing legislation is adopted in Ecuador, local courts will have universal jurisdiction over international crimes, independently of the place of commission of the crimes (Articles 1(e) and 2 of the draft legislation, draft available online on www.iccnow.org).

108. See article 9 of the criminal code of **El Salvador**, see *Amnesty International document*, p. 12.

109. Article 8 of the **Greek** criminal code provides for universal jurisdiction to 'apply for crimes committed abroad for which international treaties ratified by Greece, provide for the application of the Greek penal laws', see *The questionnaire*, p. 57.

110. See Article 5.5 of the criminal code of **Guatemala**, *Amnesty International document*, p. 12.

111. See chapter 1, section 4(c) of the 1978 criminal code of **Hungary**, which provides that Hungarian law shall be applied to acts committed by non-Hungarians abroad, if they are 'crimes against humanity (chapter XI) or any other crime, the prosecution of which is prescribed by an international treaty'. Universal jurisdiction is therefore provided for war crimes (title II of chapter XI of the criminal code) but chapter XI of the criminal code does not seem to extend to war crimes committed in internal armed conflicts as it applies to events 'in an operational or occupied area'.

112. See Article 5.5 of the **Honduran** criminal code, *Amnesty International document*, p. 12.

113. Article 16 of the Israeli penal code provides that 'Israeli penal law shall apply to foreign offences which Israel, by multilateral international conventions has undertaken to punish even if they are committed by a person who is not an Israeli national or resident of Israel regardless of where they were committed'. Israel could on this basis extend universal jurisdiction over grave breaches of the Geneva Conventions but not over the vast majority of war crimes committed in internal armed conflicts. See Reydams, *Universal jurisdiction*, pp. 158–60.

114. The draft amendment of the 1968 code of military justice of **Lebanon** provides for the inclusion of a new Article 146 which defines war crimes as all the grave breaches of the Geneva Conventions and Protocol I. Article 150 of this code provides for the exercise by national courts of universal jurisdiction over them.

115. Article 7.4 of the 1998 criminal code of **Kazakhstan** provides that the criminal code can apply in instances of crimes committed by foreigners abroad when it is provided for by an international treaty to which Kazakhstan is a party.

116. Like the criminal code of Armenia, Article 12 of the criminal code of **Moldova** provides for the jurisdiction of national courts over conduct committed by foreigners abroad if 'les crimes sont prévus par les traités internationaux auxquels la République de Moldavie est partie'. Moldova is not yet a party to the ICC statute.

117. See Article 6 of the **Mexican** criminal code, *Amnesty International document*, p. 12.

118. See Article 10 of the criminal code of **Panama**, *ibid.*, p. 13.

119. See Article 8, title 1, of the **Paraguayan** criminal code.

120. See Article 2 of the **Peruvian** criminal code, *Amnesty International document*, p. 13.

121. Article 12 of the 1996 criminal code of the **Russian Federation** provides for Russian courts to have jurisdiction over persons who have committed an offence

outside Russia 'if the crime runs counter to the interests of the Russian Federation and in cases provided for by international agreements of the Russian Federation'.

122. For **Turkey**, see its answers to *The questionnaire*, p. 61.

123. See Article 10.7 of the **Uruguayan** criminal code, *Amnesty International document*, p. 13.

124. Article 2, chapter 2 of the **Vietnamese** criminal code of 1985 provides for the possible prosecution of foreigners in cases stipulated by international instruments binding on Vietnam.

125. The Act of 25 July 1998 on military offences and penalties of **Yemen** provides in its Article 5 for the application of universal jurisdiction over war crimes committed in 'time of war'. It is unclear, however, whether this expression includes internal armed conflicts.

126. Article 12.3 of the 1999 criminal code of **Azerbaijan** provides for the jurisdiction of national courts over war crimes, crimes against humanity and other crimes committed by foreigners abroad. War crimes in the Azeri criminal code are violations of the norms of international humanitarian law in time of armed conflicts.

127. Article 6 of the 1999 criminal code of **Belarus** provides for the jurisdiction of national courts over war crimes, as defined in Articles 134–37 of the code, even if committed by foreigners abroad. These articles cover war crimes committed both in international and internal conflicts.

128. Article 24 of the law dated 8 May 2003 'portant répression du crime de génocide, des crimes contre l'humanité et des crimes de guerre' of **Burundi** provides for the jurisdiction of local courts over persons, who are not resident in Burundi or who are not in the territory of Burundi if they are suspected of having committed war crimes in internal armed conflicts.

129. Article 16(6) of the 2000 criminal code of **Colombia** extends the jurisdiction of local courts over foreign offenders found in Colombian territory if certain conditions are met, such as the refusal of any extradition request by the Colombian Government.

130. Article 7 of the 1970 penal code (as amended in 2002) provides for universal jurisdiction over a certain number of offences such as piracy or genocide, together with violations of international humanitarian law, as defined in international treaties to which **Costa Rica** is a party or in the criminal code. Article 378 of the criminal code sets out the penalties for war crimes committed in armed conflicts and Costa Rica ratified the ICC statute in 2001.

131. Article 14(1) of the **Croatian** penal code provides for the criminal code to be applied to anyone who commits outside its territory 'a criminal offence which the Republic of Croatia is bound to punish according to the provisions of international law and international treaties or intergovernmental agreements'. However, the 4 November 2003 law on application of the ICC statute and on the

prosecution of criminal acts against international law or war and humanitarian law contains an Article 10 which extends universal jurisdiction over alleged offenders found or extradited to Croatia and who are not prosecuted by the ICC or other states.

132. Article 8(1)(6) of the **Danish** criminal code establishes universal jurisdiction for war crimes under certain conditions: first that another state must have requested the extradition of the person in question, secondly that extradition must have been denied by Denmark and thirdly, that the alleged behaviour be a crime under Danish law. Denmark can prosecute war crimes committed in internal armed conflict but this will be subject to the above-mentioned conditions. See the Danish answer to *The questionnaire*, p. 56 and Reydams, *Universal jurisdiction*, pp. 126–28. This clause, often called the *aut dedere, aut judicare* clause, is similar to the Austrian criminal code. Without being specifically mentioned in the criminal code, war crimes in internal armed conflicts could be prosecuted under this heading.

133. See Loi modifiant et complétant certaines dispositions du code pénal, du code de l'organisation et de la compétence judicaire, du code pénal militaire et du code de justice militaire en application du statut de la Cour pénale internationale of September 2005. Article 4 of the penal code extends universal jurisdiction over war crimes as defined in the ICC statute if the alleged offender is present in the **DRC** territory when the authorities decide to open the investigations.

134. Section 8 of the criminal code of **Estonia** provides that 'regardless of the law of the place of commission of an act, the penal law of Estonia shall apply to an act committed outside the territory of Estonia if the punishability of the act arises from an international agreement binding on Estonia'. Even if the list of war crimes contained in the criminal code is applicable in 'war time' (leaving it therefore unclear whether these provisions could be seen to apply to internal armed conflicts), Estonia has been a party to the ICC statute since 2002. National courts will therefore be able to prosecute individuals who have allegedly committed war crimes in internal armed conflicts.

135. Article 17(1) of the 1957 criminal code of **Ethiopia** provides for the jurisdiction of Ethiopian courts over 'any person who has committed in a foreign country an offence against international law or an international offence specified in Ethiopian legislation, or an international treaty or a convention to which Ethiopia has adhered'. The Ethiopian criminal code contains a long list of war crimes applicable in time of war, armed conflict or occupation. Ethiopia is not yet a party to the ICC statute.

136. **French** jurisdictions cannot prosecute all war crimes committed in internal armed conflicts. They have jurisdiction to do so only over individuals who might have committed these crimes in Rwanda or in the ex-Yugoslavia, if the authors are found in French territory. See Article 2, chapter 1 of Loi 95–1, 2 January 1995 as well as Article 2 of Loi 96–432, 22 May 1996.

137. See chapter 1 section 7 of the criminal code of **Finland**, which extends the jurisdiction of Finnish courts over 'offences committed outside Finland where the punishability of the act is based on an international agreement binding on Finland or on another statute or regulation internationally binding on Finland (international offence)'. Section 1 of the Decree on the application of chapter 1, section 7 of the penal code of 16 August 1996 lists the offences, which should be considered as international crimes for the purposes of chapter 1, section 7 of the criminal code. Paragraph 2 includes serious war crimes which must be 'considered a grave breach of the Geneva Conventions ... as well as the Protocol relating to the protection of victims of non-international armed conflicts'. See also Finland's answer to *The questionnaire*, p. 57.

138. **Georgia's** criminal code provides for the repression of war crimes in international and internal conflicts. Article 5.3 of this code applies to foreign nationals for crimes committed abroad if 'criminal responsibility for the crime is provided by an international treaty of Georgia'. This formulation seems to include therefore any treaty, such as the ICC treaty, which provides for the criminal responsibility of individuals for war crimes in internal armed conflicts. Georgia has been a party to the ICC statute since 2003.

139. Article 8 of **Lithuania's** criminal code is entitled criminal responsibility for crimes under international agreements and provides that persons who have committed war crimes, as defined in the Lithuanian code, shall be liable under Lithuanian criminal laws, irrespective of their nationality, residence and place of commission of the crime.

140. Article 3 of the **Dutch** war crimes Act of 1952 provides for universal jurisdiction over violations of the laws of armed conflicts, including in time of civil war. However, the supreme court has recently found that an article of this Act requiring the Netherlands to be involved in the conflict for the Dutch court to be able to exercise jurisdiction, is unclear and will need to be amended. See the Dutch answers to *The questionnaire*, p. 59. See also the Dutch ICC implementing legislation below.

141. The newly amended criminal code of **Niger** provides for the prosecution of war crimes in Article 208.3 of the code and Article 208.8 gives jurisdiction to the national courts independently of the situs of the crimes.

142. See section 9, No. 5 and section 11 of the Military Penal Act, which give universal jurisdiction to **Norwegian** courts for violations of the Geneva Conventions and Additional Protocols. See the Norwegian answer to *The questionnaire*, p. 58.

143. The Law No. 31/2004 of 22 July 2004 adapting **Portuguese** criminal legislation to the statute of the ICC specifying conduct constituting crimes against international humanitarian law, 17th amendment of the criminal code provides in its chapter 1, Article 5, for the jurisdiction of local courts for war crimes committed abroad provided that the agent is to be found in Portugal and cannot be extradited or if it has been decided not to hand him over to the ICC.

144. The 1998 **Congolese** Act portant définition et répression du génocide, des crimes de guerre et des crimes contre l'humanité renders criminal the violations of the laws of war committed in internal conflicts and applies (Article 10) to any person who might have ordered or committed any of these crimes.

145. Chapter 2 section 3 of the **Swedish** criminal code gives Swedish Courts jurisdiction over crimes against international law, including war crimes. War crimes are defined in chapter 22 section 6 of the code and include war crimes committed in internal armed conflicts. See the Swedish answer to *The questionnaire*, p. 61.

146. The **Slovenian** criminal code applies to war crimes committed in internal armed conflicts and Article 123 (2) provides for the application of the criminal code to any 'foreign citizen who has, in a foreign country, committed a criminal offence against a third country or any of its citizens and has been apprehended in or extradited to the Republic of Slovenia, provided that the offence concerned is punishable by a prison sentence of at least three years according to the present code'.

147. Section 23.4, a)–g) of the judicial authority Act 6/1985 extends the scope of jurisdiction of the Spanish courts for the prosecution of acts perpetrated by foreigners abroad which under international treaties or agreements should be prosecuted in **Spain**. Among these crimes, commentators include all the serious and simple violations of the Geneva Conventions and Protocols as defined in sections 608–14 of the 1995 criminal code. See the Spanish answer to *The questionnaire*, p. 56, as well as M. P. Gonzalez, 'La répression des crimes de guerre et des crimes contre l'humanité dans le système juridique espagnol' in F. Lattanzi (ed), *Crimini di guerra et giurisdizione nazionale* ((Baden-Baden, Fagnagno Alto: Nomas Verlagsgesellschaft, Il Sirente, 1998) p. 151. See also the recent development in Spanish case law in relation to universal jurisdiction over charges of torture or terrorism in (2001/2002) 8 *Spanish yearbook of international law* 17–52; (2003) 9 *Spanish yearbook of international law* 255–61; (2000) 3 *YbIHL* 587–94 and H. Ascencio, 'The Spanish Constitutional Tribunal's decision in Guatemalan generals: unconditional universality is back' (2006) *4 JICJ* 586–94.

148. Article 6*bis* of the **Swiss** criminal code reads: 'the present code applies to any person who commits abroad a crime that the Confederation pursuant to an international treaty is obliged to prosecute.' This is completed by Article 2.9 of the military criminal code which extends the application of the code to 'breaches of international law in times of armed conflict committed by civilians or members of the armed forces other than the Swiss army forces, irrespective of whether committed in Switzerland or abroad', therefore implementing the principle of universal jurisdiction. The list of war crimes is included in Articles 108–14 of this Swiss criminal code. See A. Ziegler, 'Domestic prosecution and international co-operation with regard to violations of international humanitarian law: the case of Switzerland' (1997) 5 *Revue suisse de droit international et européen* 569 and M. Sassoli, 'Le génocide rwandais, la justice militaire suisse et le droit international' (2002) 2 *Revue suisse de droit*

international et européen 151–77. On 19 December 2003, the military penal code was amended by introducing subpara. 1*bis* to Article 9. It provides that the military penal code is applicable to aliens who have committed war crimes abroad and who are located in Switzerland, have a close link with Switzerland and are not extradited or surrendered to the ICC. See (2004) 86 *IRRC* 286–87.

149. Article 15 of the Criminal Code of **Tajikistan** provides that foreign nationals shall be liable under the criminal code for crimes committed outside the Tadjik borders if 'they have committed a crime provided for by the rules of international law recognised by the Republic of Tadjikistan or by international treaties and agreements or they have committed a crime of extreme gravity or a grave crime against the citizens of Tajikistan or the interests of the Republic of Tajikistan'. This provision would therefore extend to war crimes committed in internal armed conflicts.

150. No information on the scope of the domestic criminal code and the possible use of universal jurisdiction over war crimes could be found for states, which render criminal violations of the laws of war in internal armed conflicts, like Mozambique, Rwanda, Nicaragua, Jordan, Luxembourg and Poland.

151. I.e. common Article 3, Additional Protocol II and the ICC statute.

152. There are two exceptions to this statement. Violations of the 1994 Convention on the Safety of UN and Associated Personnel and the Second Protocol to the 1954 Hague Convention amount to war crimes in internal armed conflicts and these instruments explicitly provide for universal jurisdiction.

153. See section 2 of chapter 4.

154. The preamble affirms further: 'most serious crimes of concern to the international community as a whole must not go unpunished and their effective prosecution must be ensured by taking measures at the national level and by enhancing international co-operation'.

155. See section 8.1.c) of the International Crimes and ICC Act 2000 of **New Zealand**.

156. See section 13 of the NZ Act.

157. J. Hay, 'Implementing the Rome Statute: a pragmatic approach from a small common law jurisdiction' in *Acts of the Berlin conference on the Rome Statute, what's next: domestic and foreign approaches to the implementation of international criminal law in national law* (Berlin: Reader & International Criminal Law Society, 2000) p. 21.

158. New Zealand courts will therefore be able to try individuals for war crimes in internal conflicts committed after 1 October 2000, the date of the entry into force of the Act, i.e. before the entry into force of the ICC statute itself. On the basis of section 8.1a), New Zealand courts will be able to prosecute individuals for genocide and crimes against humanity on or after the commencement of the Act, or on or after the applicable date if these would have been offences under New Zealand law in force at the time the act occurred, had it occurred in New Zealand. The applicable date for genocide is 28 March 1979, the date

New Zealand's ratification of the Genocide Convention took effect. For crimes against humanity, the applicable date is 1 January 1991, the date from which the ICTY has jurisdiction. See Hay, *ibid.*, p. 24.

159. The **Australian** Act can be found online on http://scaleplus.law.gov.au. The offences applicable in internal armed conflicts appearing in Article 8.2.c) and e) of the statute are all included in the Australian Criminal Code.

160. See section 268.117 of the International Criminal Court Act 2002 (amendment of the Criminal Code Act 1995) read together with section 15.4 of the Criminal Code.

161. Commenting on this issue, Reydams takes the view that the Australian International Criminal Court Act is silent on the issue of a prerequisite of presence of an offender but the act 'contains no indication of an intent to enforce the law *in absentia*'. Reydams, *Universal jurisdiction*, pp. 88–92.

162. See sections 268.121 and 122 of the Australian International Criminal Court Act 2002. Section 268.121(3) provides that a person may be arrested, charged, remanded in custody or released on bail in connection with an offence under the Act before the necessary consent has been given by the Attorney-General.

163. See part II, section 8(1)(c) of the International Criminal Court Act 2006 of **Trinidad and Tobago**.

164. Section 8 of the **Canadian** Crimes against Humanity and War Crimes Act 2000.

165. Section 9(3) also requires the Attorney-General's written consent before a prosecution can proceed.

166. Section 6.4 of the Act provides that crimes contained in the ICC statute are, as of 17 July 1998, crimes according to customary international law and may be crimes according to customary international law before that date. This Act was also designed to strengthen the foundation of Canadian prosecutions for international crimes after the *Finta* ruling. See D. Robinson, 'Implementing international crimes: the Canadian approach' in *Acts of the Berlin conference on the Rome statute, what's next: domestic and foreign approaches to the implementation of international criminal law in national law* (Berlin: Reader & International Criminal Law Society, 2000) p. 26.

167. Chapter 2, Article 4(3) of the **South African** International Criminal Court Act 2002, Government Gazette, vol. 445, 18 July 2002, No. 23642.

168. It may be noted that the national director must also give his written consent before prosecution can proceed, see section 4(3) of the SA Bill.

169. See the Ley de cooperacion con la CPI en materia de lucha contra el genocidio, crimines de guerra y crimines de lesa humanidad (No. 18.026) of **Uruguay** of 4 October 2006. See also Ley de Implementacion del Estatuto de Roma de la Corte Penal Internacional (ley 26.200) of **Argentina** of 13 December 2006, both available online on www.iccnow.org.

170. See the **German** Act to introduce the code of crimes against international law of 26 June 2002, available online on www.iuscrim.mpg.de/forsch/online_pub.html as well as attached explanations and commentary.

171. Article 3 of the Act to introduce the code of crimes against international law reproducing section 153(f)(2) of the code of criminal procedure.

172. In this respect, see the commentary of Reydams, Reydams, *Universal jurisdiction*, pp. 144–46.

173. See section 2, paragraph 1a) of the **Dutch** Act of 19 June 2003 containing rules concerning serious violations of international humanitarian law (international crimes Act). Available online on www.icrc.org. For a commentary on this legislation, see M. Boot-Matthijssen and R. van Elst, 'Key provisions of the international crimes Act 2003' (2004) 35 *Netherlands yearbook of international law*, 279–86.

174. See section 52 of the **UK** International Criminal Court Act 2001.

175. House of Lords, *Hansard* text for 15 January 2001 (210115–03) column 929. The UK Government believed that it will not be a safe haven for perpetrators of international crimes committed in a foreign country, as the Act removes the dual criminality requirement in the case of ICC crimes. Even if the perpetrators would not be liable for prosecution in the UK, the UK will be able to extradite them. See also the criticism voiced by some members of the House of Lords during the second reading of the Bill in the Lords. Lord Lester of Herne Hill affirmed: 'there can be little justification for refusing UK courts full and universal jurisdiction over ICC crimes committed by non-nationals', House of Lords, *Hansard* text for 15 January 2001 (210115–03) column 938.

176. It remains unclear if the perpetrator has to have the legal status of resident in order to be considered as a UK resident.

177. The written consent of the Attorney-General is also necessary before any prosecution can begin. See sections 53(3) and 60(3) of the UK Act.

178. There have been a number of attempts before English courts to have arrest warrants issued against individuals for torture or grave breaches, while they were present in English territory. However, for reasons of diplomatic immunity (for a head of state, Robert Mugabe, and for a minister of defence, the *Mofaz* case), magistrates kept on refusing to issue arrest warrants, thereby allowing the UK to be a safe haven for torturers or other international war criminals. See (2004) *ICLQ* 769–74.

179. See Article 8 of the 2005 International Crimes Bill of **Kenya** (available online on www.iccnow.org). It is interesting to note that Kenyan courts will also have jurisdiction over a person who was a citizen of a state that was engaged in an armed conflict against Kenya (Article 8.b)ii), in furtherance of the principle established in international law according to which offenders of the laws of war can always be tried by the courts of the belligerent states into whose hands they have fallen.

180. The **Brazilian** Bill implementing the ICC statute provides local courts with the possibility of exercising universal jurisdiction over these international crimes when the offender enters Brazilian territory, see (2003) 6 *YbIHL* 458–59.

181. Articles 1(3) and 2 of the draft legislation on crimes against humanity of **Ecuador** provide for the extension of universal jurisdiction over international crimes, as defined in the ICC statute (available online on www.iccnow.org).

182. See P. Dascalopoulou-Livida, 'The implementation of the ICC statute in **Greece**: some thoughts' in C. Kress and F. Lattanzi (eds.), *The Rome statute and domestic legal orders*, vol. I (Baden-Baden, Ripa di Fagnano Alto: Nomos Verlagsgessellschaft, Il Sirente, 2000) p. 113. Universal jurisdiction is already provided for all the crimes contained in the ICTY and ICTR statutes irrespective of the law of the place where they were committed. (see *ibid.*, p. 118).

183. A national inter-ministerial commission for the implementation of international humanitarian law was created in Italy, see P. Benvenuti, 'Italy, implementation of the ICC statute in national legislation, constitutional aspects', in *ibid.*, p. 113, especially pp. 135–37. The draft Bill No. 2724 implements the crimes of the ICC statute into the **Italian** legal order and Article 15.3 provides for the jurisdiction of Italian courts in the absence of any third states or the ICC wanting to exercise jurisdiction over war criminals. This draft legislation is available online on www.iccnow.org.

184. The draft **Swedish** Act on international crimes contains the principle of universal jurisdiction over the ICC crimes, reported in (2002) 5 *YbIHL* 599.

185. These countries are Italy, Sweden, Brazil and Ecuador.

186. This is the case of Burundi, Trinidad and Tobago, Spain or New Zealand.

187. These procedural requirements do not change the nature of the jurisdiction, which remains universal jurisdiction as defined in the beginning of this section.

188. For the conflict in the former Yugoslavia, see, for example, SC resolutions 819 (16 April 1993) and 913 (22 April 1994). After the creation of the ICTY, it was, however, clear that the Council implied that the Tribunal should prosecute the alleged offenders. This attitude has now changed as the ICTY has to complete its prosecutions by 2010. The Security Council recalled therefore the duty of the countries of the former Yugoslavia to investigate those accused not tried by the ICTY, see resolution 1503 (28 August 2003). For Rwanda, see SC resolution 935 (1 July 1994). For Somalia, see SC resolutions 794 (3 December 1992), 814 (26 March 1993), 837 (6 June 1993) and 865 (22 September 1993). For Angola, see SC resolutions 1064 (11 July 1996), 1075 (11 October 1996) and 1087 (11 December 1996), the latter calling for the 'Angolan parties to give greater attention to investigating alleged human rights violations and punishing those found guilty by due process of law'. For Burundi, see SC resolutions 1072 (30 August 1996), 1577 (1 December 2004), 1602 (31 May 2005), 1606 (20 June 2005). For the RDC, see SC resolutions 1234 (9 April 1999), 1291 and 1304 (16 June 2000), 1341 (22 February 2001) 1468 (20 March 2003), 1592 (30 March 2005), 1635 (28 October 2005). In resolution 1592, the Security Council called on the Government of the RDC to bring perpetrators to justice. For Afghanistan, see SC resolutions 1193 (28 August 1998) and 1214 (8 December 1998). For

Georgia, see SC resolution 1339 (31 January 2001). For Sierra Leone, see SC resolution 1315 (14 August 2002). For East Timor, see SC resolutions 1264 (15 September 1999), 1272 (25 October 1999) and 1319 (20 September 2000). For the Ivory Coast, see SC resolution 1479 (13 May 2003). In relation to the situation in Sudan, see for example, SC resolutions 1556 (30 July 2004), 1574 (19 November 2004) and 1591 (29 March 2005).

189. In SC resolutions 1009 (10 August 1995) and 1019 (9 November 1995), the Council demanded that the Government of the Republic of Croatia bring to justice those responsible for serious violations of international humanitarian and human rights law. In SC resolution 1199 (23 September 1998), the Council underlined the 'need for the authorities of the FRY to bring to justice those members of the security forces who have been involved in the mistreatment of civilians and the destruction of property'. In these two cases however, Croatia and the FRY would not be prosecuting war criminals on the basis of universal jurisdiction but rather on the basis of the territoriality or passive personality principles. In SC resolution 1231 (11 March 1999) for Sierra Leone, the Council 'urged the appropriate authorities to investigate all allegations of such violations with a view to bringing the perpetrators to justice'. In relation to the situation in Sudan, the Security Council called on all parties and in particular the Sudanese Government to investigate and bring to justice those responsible, see for example, SC resolutions 1556 (30 July 2004) and 1564 (18 September 2004). The General Assembly took a similar view in its resolutions A/Res/56/175 (28 February 2002); A/Res/57/230 (27 February 2003). In relation to the situation in the DRC, the General Assembly recalled the obligation on the Congolese Government to bring those responsible to justice, see A/Res/59/207 (20 December 2004), A/Res/59/196 (11 March 2004) or A/Res/56/173 (27 February 2002).

190. See SC resolution 1591 (29 March 2005).

191. SC resolutions 1265 (17 September 1999), 1366 (30 August 2001) and 1379 (20 November 2001). See also SC resolutions 1314 (11 August 2000), 1325 (31 October 2000) which affirm the responsibility of 'all states to put an end to impunity and prosecute those responsible for genocide, war crimes and crimes against humanity' or 1612 (26 July 2005).

192. The preamble to the ICC statute recalls that 'it is the duty of every state to exercise its criminal jurisdiction over those responsible for international crimes.'

193. Final Report of the Commission of Experts, UN.Doc.S/1994/674, para. 42.

194. UN Commission on Human Rights resolution 1999/1 (6 April 1999). The Commission recognised in this extract the application of universal jurisdiction over war crimes committed in internal armed conflicts. It is surprising, however, that it chose to qualify them as 'grave breaches'.

195. Report of the UN Secretary-General S/2004/431 (28 May 2004), para. 39.

196. Article 38 of the ICJ statute provides that judicial decisions can be subsidiary sources of law.

197. See the *Arrest Warrant of 11 April 2000 (Democratic Republic of Congo v. Belgium)*, judgment [2002] *IJC Reports* 3 (hereafter referred to as the *Arrest Warrant judgment*).

198. Article 7 of the 1993 Belgian law provides that 'the Belgian courts shall have jurisdiction in respect of the offences provided for in the present law wheresoever they may have been committed'.

199. See para. 17 of the *Arrest Warrant judgment*.

200. For a criticism of this approach, see in particular paras. 2–18 of the separate opinion of Judges Higgins, Kooijmans and Buergenthal [2002] *ICJ Reports* 63–90 as well as the dissenting opinion of Judge Van Den Wyngaert [2002] *ICJ Reports* 137–87. Judge Oda on the contrary believed that 'the Court has shown wisdom in refraining from taking a definitive stance in this respect' [2002] *ICJ Reports* 46–53, para. 12.

201. See paras. 46 and 55 of the *Arrest Warrant* judgment.

202. Judge Van den Wyngaert is the only one to favour universal jurisdiction even if the offender is not present on the territory (*in absentia*). Other judges restrict its application to the crime of piracy or other specific international conventions (Judges Guillaume, Rezek and Ranjeva), while Judges Higgins, Kooijmans and Buergenthal accept the application of universal jurisdiction *in absentia* under certain conditions.

203. See paras. 20–21 of their separate opinion. In relation to national legislation, it is not quite true that the only legislation providing for universal jurisdiction *in absentia* is the Belgian one. At the time of writing, Belgium has repealed its legislation, but similar legislation implementing the ICC statute can be found in Germany, New Zealand and Australia. Furthermore, the latest ruling by the Spanish supreme court also reflects the possibility for Spanish courts to exercise universal jurisdiction *in absentia*. See H. Ascencio, 'The Spanish Constitutional Tribunal's decision in Guatemalan generals: unconditional universality is back' (2006) 4 *JICJ* 586–94.

204. See paras. 22–41 of their separate opinion. They qualify this practice (requiring the presence of the offender) not of universal jurisdiction, but of an obligatory territorial jurisdiction over persons, albeit in relation to acts committed elsewhere (para. 41).

205. See paras. 44–45.

206. Para. 45.

207. Paras. 46–52.

208. Para. 58 reads: 'there is no rule of international law which makes illegal co-operative overt acts designed to secure their presence within a state wishing to exercise jurisdiction'. In other words, it is not unlawful for Belgium to issue an arrest warrant in order to secure the presence of the offender on Belgian territory.

209. See para. 59. According to them, a state contemplating such use should offer to the national state of the prospective accused person the opportunity to act upon

the charges concerned itself. Such action should be undertaken by a prosecutor acting in full independence and consideration must be given to the special circumstances that require the exercise of such jurisdiction.

210. Para. 60 of their separate opinion.

211. See paras. 61–65.

212. See para. 54.

213. See para. 61.

214. Some judges decided to answer this issue. Judges Higgins, Kooijmans and Buergenthal take a clear view on this issue in para. 85 of their separate opinion. 'That immunity prevails only as long as the Minister is in office and continues to shield him or her after that time only for "official acts". It is now increasingly claimed in the literature . . . that serious international crimes cannot be regarded as official acts.'

215. See, in particular, the separate opinion of Judges Higgins, Kooijmans and Buergenthal as well as the dissenting opinion of Judge Van Den Wyngaert. Among the many commentaries written about this decision, see C. Wickremasinghe, 'Arrest warrant of 11 April 2000 (RDC v. Belgium), preliminary objections and merits, judgment of 14 February 2002' (2003) ICLQ 775–81; P. Sands, 'What is the ICJ for?' (2002) Revue belge de droit international 537–45; J. P. Cot, 'Eloge de l'indécision: la cour et la compétence universelle' (2002) Revue belge de droit international 546–53; J. Salmon, 'Libres propos sur l'arrêt de la CIJ du 14 février 2002 dans l'affaire relative au mandat d'arrêt du 11 avril 2000' (2002) Revue belge de droit international 512–17; A. Winants, 'The Yerodia ruling of the ICJ and the 1993/99 Belgian law on universal jurisdiction' (2003) 16 Leiden journal of international law 491–509; Kamto, 'Une troublante immunité totale du ministre des affaires étrangères' (2002) Revue belge de droit international 518–30; J. Wouters and L. De Smet, 'The ICJ's judgment in the case concerning the arrest warrant of 11 April 2000: some critical observations' (2001) 4 YbIHL 373–88; C. Bassiouni, 'Universal jurisdiction unrevisited: the International Court of Justice decision in case concerning the Arrest warrant of 11 April 2000' (2002/2003) XII Palestine yearbook of international law 27–48; D. Robinson, 'The impact of the human rights accountability movement on the international law of immunities' (2002) Canadian yearbook of international law 151–91.

216. See A. Cassese, 'When may senior state officials be tried for international crimes? Some comments on the Congo v. Belgium case' (2002) 13 EJIL 853–75.

217. In support of this finding, see Cassese, 'When may senior state officials be tried for international crimes?' 864–74; S. Wirth, 'Immunity for core crimes: the ICJ's judgment in the Congo v. Belgium case' (2002) 13 EJIL 877–93; Kamto, 'Une troublante immunité totale du ministre des affaires etrangères' 518–30; Wouters and De Smet, 'The ICJ's statement in the case concerning the Arrest warrant of 11 April 2000' 379–82 and S. Zappala, 'Do heads of state in office enjoy immunity from jurisdiction for international crimes? The Ghaddafi case before the French cour de cassation' (2001) 12 EJIL 595–612.

218. The judgment has also been criticised for equating the immunity of ministers of foreign affairs with the immunity of heads of state and for the lack of state practice and *opinio juris* highlighted by the court in finding the existence of this customary norm. See Wirth, 'Immunity for core crimes?' 879 and 889; Kamto, 'Une troublante immunité totale du ministre des affaires etrangères' 519–23. Kamto believes that the court went beyond its functions by creating the law, because there is no clear rule concerning the immunity of ministers of foreign affairs in international law. See also Wouters and De Smet, 'The ICJ's statement in the case concerning the *Arrest warrant of 11 April 2000*' 376–78.

219. The majority of the doctrine believes that lifting the personal immunity of heads of state for international crimes would seriously destabilise international relations. See Zappala, 'Do heads of state in office enjoy immunity of jurisdiction for international crimes?' 600, 605, 607.

220. Zappala, 'Do heads of state in office enjoy immunity of jurisdiction for international crimes' 600.

221. The Special Court for Sierra Leone recalled recently that immunities of heads of state cannot be opposed to international courts or tribunals. *Prosecutor v. Charles Ghankay Taylor*, case No. SCSL–2003–01–I, decision on immunity from jurisdiction (31 May 2004), in particular paras. 50–53.

222. V. Klingberg argues that this rule is not opposable to treaty-based international courts and that nationals of third states should not be tried by international courts such as the ICC or the Special Court for Sierra Leone. The exception to the regime of immunities would only be applicable before truly international institutions established under chapter VII of the UN, such as the ICTY and ICTR. The Versailles Treaty, however, provided for the prosecution of the German Kaiser before military courts of the belligerents. No international tribunal would have been set up for this trial and the function of the Kaiser would not have been a bar to his trial by domestic military tribunal. The exception to the laws on immunities ought not to be applicable only before truly international criminal tribunals. See V. Klingberg, '(Former) heads of state before international(ised) criminal courts: the case of *Charles Taylor* before the Special Court for Sierra Leone' (2003) 46 *German yearbook of international law* 537–64.

223. Obviously, some safeguards against politically motivated prosecutions have to be put in place. The 2003 new Belgian legislation has done so.

224. For a criticism of this decision, see A. Cassese, 'The Special Court and international law, the decision concerning the *Lomé agreement amnesty*' (2004) *JICJ* 1130–40.

225. *Prosecutor v. Morris Kallon & Brima Bassy Kamara*, case No. SCSL–2004–15–AR72(E), decision on challenge to jurisdiction: *Lomé accord amnesty* (13 March 2004) para. 67.

226. *Ibid.*, para. 71.

227. For a criticism of the decision on this point, see S. Meisenberg, 'Legality of amnesties in international humanitarian law, the *Lomé amnesty* decision of the Special Court for Sierra Leone' (2004) 86 *IRRC* 837–51.

228. *Prosecutor v. Morris Kallon & Brima Bassy Kamara*, case No. SCSL–2004–15–AR72(E), decision on challenge to jurisdiction: *Lomé accord amnesty* (13 March 2004) para. 68.

229. *Ibid.*, paras. 69–70. In para. 70, the Chamber states: 'one consequence of the nature of grave international crimes against humanity is that states, can under international law, exercise universal jurisdiction over such crimes.'

230. For sake of completeness, one might also note that an ICTY Trial Chamber has briefly touched upon the issue of universal jurisdiction. See *Prosecutor v. Milutinovic et al.*, decision on motion challenging jurisdiction, case No. IT–99–37–PT (6 May 2003) and in particular the separate opinion of Judge Robinson attached to this decision.

231. *Princeton principles on universal jurisdiction*, 23 July 2001, available online on www.princeton.edu/~lapa/unive_jur.pdf. See the commentary to the Princeton principles in S. Macedo (ed.), *Universal jurisdiction, national courts and the prosecution of serious crimes under international law* (Philadelphia: University of Pennsylvania Press, 2004) pp. 18–35.

232. See principle 1, *ibid.*

233. The commentary attached to the principles includes war crimes within the category of serious international crimes but defines them as grave breaches of the Geneva Conventions and Protocol I.

234. For a commentary on this resolution, see C. Kress, 'Universal jurisdiction over international crimes and the Institut de droit international' (2006) 4 *JICJ* 561–85.

235. C. Tomushat, 'Universal jurisdiction with respect to the crime of genocide, crimes against humanity and war crimes', *Yearbook of the Institute of International Law*, vol. 71, part 1 (Paris: Pedone, 2005) pp. 252–53.

236. The draft contained the following paragraph: 'To date, there is no sufficient evidence showing that war crimes committed in non-international armed conflict partake of the regime of universal jurisdiction', *Yearbook of the Institute of International Law* vol. 71, part 1 (Paris: Pedone, 2005) p. 387.

237. Available online on www.idi-iil.org.

238. Para. 1.a) of the resolution adopted 26 August 2005.

239. Para. 1.b) of the resolution.

240. See paras. 1.c) and d) of the resolution.

241. See rule 157 in J. M. Henckaerts and L. Doswald-Beck, *Customary international humanitarian law*, vol. I (Cambridge: Cambridge University Press, 2005) pp. 604–7.

242. This section will offer an overview of criminal prosecutions but will not study civil suits. Civil suits can be a complementary means of enforcing responsibility and in some cases a much more effective way of establishing responsibility and obtaining compensation for the victims. See in particular, the extensive case law

under the Alien Tort Act in the USA. See A. Eckert, '*Kadic v. Karadic*: whose international law?' (1996) 25 *Denver journal of international law and policy* 173 or the recent case of *Mehnovic v. Vuckovic*, US district court of the Northern District of Georgia, 29 April 2002 reported in (2002) 84 *IRRC* 711.

243. See A. Marschik, 'The politics of prosecution: European national approaches to war crimes' in T. McCormack and G. Simpson (eds.), *The law of war crimes* (The Hague, London, Boston: Kluwer Law International, 1997), pp. 77–82; *Universal jurisdiction in Europe: criminal prosecutions in Europe since 1990 for war crimes, crimes against humanity, torture and genocide*, published by the NGO Redress, p. 16 (hereafter referred to as 'Redress research paper') and Reydams, *Universal jurisdiction*, pp. 99–101.

244. Beschluss des oberste Gerichsthof, Os 99/94, 13 July 1994.

245. Marschik, 'The politics of prosecution', p. 80.

246. *Ibid.*, p. 81. It can be asked why the prosecutor in this case did not rely on section 64(1) subpara. 6 of the criminal code in conjunction with the Geneva Conventions to try the accused successfully. Reydams explained that the prosecutor was not allowed to choose a lesser charge (grave breach in comparison to genocide) if he believes that there is sufficient evidence to secure a conviction. See Reydams, *Universal jurisdiction*, p. 101.

247. For a detailed account of the activities undertaken by victims in Belgium or by the Belgian authority, see Reydams, *Universal jurisdiction*, pp. 109–12 as well as D. Vandermeersch, 'Prosecuting international crimes in Belgium' (2005) 3 *JICJ* 400–21.

248. See L. Reydams, 'Universal jurisdiction over atrocities in Rwanda, theory and practice' (1996) 1 *European journal of crime, criminal law and criminal justice* 35.

249. See court of cassation, second chamber, judgment of 15 May 1996 (1996) *Revue de droit pénal et de criminologie* 906; as well as court of cassation, vacation chamber, judgment of 9 July 1996 (1996) 89 *Revue du droit des étrangers* 372.

250. See the judgment of the Brussels court of appeal of 17 May 1995, chambre de mise en accusation, 17 May 1995 (1995) *Journal des tribunaux* 542, judgment later confirmed by the court of cassation, second chamber, 31 May 1995 (1996) *Revue de droit pénal et de criminologie* 198. See also the judgment of the Brussels tribunal, chambre du conseil, 22 July 1996, considering that there is a *prima facie* case against a Rwandese suspected of participation in the genocide and ordering the case to be submitted to the 'chambre des mises en accusation' (on file with the author).

251. Judgment of the cour d'assises of Brussels, 8 June 2001. The Belgium court of cassation confirmed this appeal court judgment on 9 January 2002, see (2002) 84 *IRRC* 709–10.

252. Reydams takes the view, however, that, after an effective and quick investigation of the four Butare indictees, it took the Belgian authorities almost five years to commit the suspects for trial. See Reydams, *Universal jurisdiction*, p. 111.

253. For a summary of the numerous (about thirty) complaints founded on the 1993 Belgian legislation against various heads of state or governments, see (2001) 4 *YbIHL* 453–59.

254. Chambre de mise en accusation of Brussels, 16 April 2002, reported by Reydams, *Universal jurisdiction*, p. 116. It is surprising, to say the least, that the court did not consider international law or the 1993 War Crimes Law and that, after issuing a request for the suspect's extradition, a municipal court decides that Belgian courts have no jurisdiction if the suspect is not voluntarily present in Belgium.

255. Chambre de mise en accusation of Brussels, 26 June 2002, reported by Reydams, *Universal jurisdiction*, p. 117; see also (2003) *Revue belge de droit international* 629–31.

256. Reydams, *Universal jurisdiction*, p. 117.

257. The list of war crimes is now contained in Article 136*quarter* of the criminal code; the basis of jurisdiction is included in the law of 17 April 1878 containing the introductory title of the code of criminal procedure (both texts can be consulted online on www.icrc.org).

258. For an excellent commentary to this new legislation, see P. D'Argent, 'L'expérience belge de la compétence universelle: beaucoup de bruit pour rien?' (2004) *RGDIP* 597–631. See also, S. Ratner, 'Belgium's war crimes statute: a postmortem' (2003) 97 *AJIL* 888–97; E. David, 'Universal jurisdiction in Belgian law' (2002/2003) XII *Palestine yearbook of international law* 77–116; (2002) 5 *YbIHL* 445–51 and (2003) 6 *YbIHL* 464–68.

259. Article 12*bis* also provides for situations where investigations might not need to proceed if the complaint is clearly unfounded or if the case would be better treated by the courts of a third state or the international criminal court.

260. In a similar way to Article 12*bis*, Article 10 provides for situations where investigations might not need to proceed (see above). This sole ability for the federal prosecutor to start such an investigation has been challenged before Belgium's administrative jurisdiction and procedure court, which has ordered the amendment of the existing law, see (2005) 87 *IRRC* 590.

261. (2005) 87 *IRRC* 590–91.

262. *The prosecution v. Refik S*, third chamber of the eastern division of the Danish high court, judgment of 25 November 1994 (on file with the author). Summary of the judgment can be found in (1998) 1 *YbIHL* 431; see also the 'Redress research paper', p. 22. His prosecution was not based on the domestic *aut dedere, aut judicare* clause, but on section 8(1)(5), which provides for universal jurisdiction over treaty offences, such as the grave breaches of the Geneva Conventions.

263. The defendant appealed to the supreme court of Denmark on the grounds that the facts, which formed the basis of the charges, were not serious enough to fall within the definition of grave breaches of the Geneva Conventions. The supreme court disagreed and confirmed the verdict in September 1995.

264. See R. Maison, 'Les premiers cas d'application des dispositions pénales des Conventions de Genève par les juridictions internes' 260. The ICTY in the *Tadić jurisdiction* decision cited this judgment and interpreted it as an example of domestic prosecution applying the grave breaches provisions, regardless of whether the conflict was internal or international. See *Tadić jurisdiction* decision, para. 83. See also, S. Boelaert-Suominen, 'Grave breaches, universal jurisdiction and internal armed conflicts: is customary law moving towards a uniform enforcement mechanism for all armed conflicts?' (2000) *Journal of conflict, peace and security* 95, and the 'Redress research paper', p. 22.

265. Investigations also commenced in 2001on the alleged participation of an Iraqi refugee living in Denmark for war crimes committed in the late 1980s in Iraq. See (2001) *YbIHL* 491 and (2002) *YbIHL* 483. In 2002, Denmark established a special International Crimes Office, responsible for investigating alleged incidents of crimes against humanity, genocide and war crimes committed outside Denmark, see (2002) *YbIHL* 481.

266. The Genocide Convention was set aside because it provides only for territorial jurisdiction or for an international tribunal but not for universal jurisdiction of domestic courts. The examining magistrate rejected the jurisdiction of French courts over crimes against humanity as he found that the customary rules on crimes against humanity are not explicit enough to create universal jurisdiction for domestic courts. See B. Stern commentary (1999) 93 *AJIL* 526.

267. Tribunal de grande instance of Paris, ordonnance du 6 Mai 1994, Examining Magistrate Getti (on file with the author). See also R. Maison, 'Les premiers cas d'application des dispositions pénales des Conventions de Genève par les juridictions internes' 264.

268. The court of appeal found that the Geneva Conventions are too general in character to be able to create rules directly on jurisdiction in criminal matters. See the Paris court of appeal, judgment of 24 November 1994 (on file with the author). For a critical commentary of this judgment, see C. Lomblois, 'De la compassion territoriale' (Spring 1995) *Revue de sciences criminelles et de droit pénal comparé* 399, as well as B. Stern, 'La compétence universelle en France: le cas des crimes commis en ex-Yougoslavie et au Rwanda' (1997) 40 *German yearbook of international law* 280–99.

269. *In re Javor*, cour de cassation, criminal chamber, Judgment of 26 March 1996, 132 *Bulletin criminel* 379. See case note by Stern (1999) 93 *AJIL* 525.

270. See the ordonnances d'incompetence given by the tribunal de grande instance of Paris, 23 February 1995 in the cases of *Kalinda C., Rubagumya C et al. v. X* as well as *Dupaquier J. F. and E v. X*. See B. Stern, 'La compétence universelle en France' 294.

271. See tribunal de grande instance de Paris, ordonnance, 9 February 1995 and court of appeal of Paris, 6 November 1995 (on file with the author). See L. Reydams 'Universal jurisdiction over atrocities in Rwanda, theory and practice' 43.

272. Some proceedings based on the Torture Convention have been more successful. In June 1999, investigations on the basis of the 1984 Torture Convention were started in France against Ely Ould Dha, for torture committed in Mauritania. In April 2000, the plaintiff managed to escape the country and took refuge in Mauritania.

273. The presence in France of the suspected criminals does not automatically trigger investigations or prosecutions by French courts. The opportunity to allow investigations to take place remains a political decision. The attempt by a Non-governmental Organisation (NGO) to start investigations before French courts against Laurent Désiré Kabila in November 1999 was rejected by the investigating magistrate on the grounds, among others, that Mr Kabila had been invited by the French authorities. See (2000) 19 *La nouvelle lettre de la FIDH* 9.

274. Similarly, immunities of acting heads of state is also respected by French courts and prevented any proceedings against M. Khadafi for terrorism, see F. Poirat, 'Immunité de juridiction pénale du chef d'Etat étranger en exercise et règle coutumière devant le juge judiciaire' (2001) *RDGIP* 473–91 and (2002) *AFDI* 755–57.

275. Decision of the Bundesgerichtshof in the case of *D. Tadić*, 13 February 1994. See the 'Redress research paper', p. 29 as well as the *Amnesty International report*, p. 16.

276. *Public prosecutor v. Djajic*, 23 May 1997, No. 20/96, (1998) *Neue Juristische Wochenschrift* 392, see also (1998) 92 *AJIL* 528.

277. As far as the link between the defendant and Germany is concerned, the Bavarian high court took the view that the nature of the crimes and the international efforts to stop the violations in Bosnia-Herzegovina were strong grounds for establishing a connection to Germany. See the 'Redress research paper', p. 29.

278. The JNA official withdrawal from Bosnia in May 1992 was seen by the court as only modifying the outside perception of the conflict. The Serb forces were seen by the court as an 'outside force' making the conflict an international one, see (1998) 92 *AJIL* 531.

279. *Public prosecutor v. Jorgic*, Oberlandesgericht Dusseldorf, 26 September 1997. See the 'Redress research paper', p. 29 as well as (1999) 2 *YbIHL* 366.

280. Here again, the court found the conflict to be of an international character and it qualified the victims as protected persons under the Geneva Conventions.

281. This judgment was later on confirmed by the German federal court of justice, Bundesgerichtshof, judgment of 30 April 1999, 3 StR 215/98 F. An appeal by the accused before the federal constitutional court was also rejected, Bundesverfassungsgericht, decision of the fourth chamber of the second senate, 12 December 2000, 2 BvR 1290/99.

282. See the *Amnesty International Report*, p. 16 as well as (2001) 4 *YbIHL* 527–29.

283. *Sokolović* case, higher regional court at Dusselforf, judgment of 29 November 1999. Oberlandesgericht Dusselforf, Urteil vom 29 November 1999, 2 StE 7/07. For a commentary of this case, see (1999) 2 *YbIHL* 368.

284. This question has been left unresolved by the federal court of justice when it reaffirmed the finding of the Dusseldorf high court that the conflict in Yugoslavia was an international armed conflict. See Bundesgerichthof, decision of the third criminal senate of 21 February 2001, 3 StR 372/00, available online on www.icrc.org.

285. Recently, the code of crimes against international law found one of its first applications, when victims of crimes committed in Uzbekistan filed a complaint before German courts against the former minister of internal affairs of Uzbekistan for acts of torture and crimes against humanity. The suspect was present in Germany to receive medical treatment. However, the federal pro-secutor refused to open official proceedings based on universal jurisdiction and the suspect left Germany. See S. Zappala, 'The German federal prosecutor's decision not to prosecute a former Uzbek minister' (2006) 4 *JICJ* 602–22.

286. Supreme court of the Netherlands, 11 November 1997, criminal division, No. 3717 Besch (decision on appeal in cassation against a decision of the court of appeal of Arnhem military division of 19 March 1997) (1998) 1 *YbIHL* 600. Decisions also available online on www.icrc.org.

287. The supreme court relied on the government's explanatory memorandum at the time of the adoption of the Act before the Dutch Parliament.

288. The supreme court did not disagree with the qualification made by the court of appeal but left the issue open. See also S. Boelaert-Suominen, 'Grave breaches, universal jurisdiction and internal armed conflicts' 94.

289. See section 2 of the international crimes Act 2003.

290. See G. Mettraux, 'Dutch courts' universal jurisdiction over violations of com-mon Article 3 qua war crimes' (2006) 4 *JICJ* 362–71.

291. Military court of cassation, 8 July 1996, *Re A. M*, unpublished (on file with the author). The transfer to Arusha of the person indicted by the ICTR was upheld by the federal court on 28 April 1997.

292. Tribunal militaire de division I, 18 April 1997, Lausanne, unpublished (on file with the author). For a commentary, see A. Ziegler (1998) 92 *AJIL* 78.

293. The tribunal affirmed in its judgment: 'si l'identité de l'accusé comme étant G. ne fait pas de doutes, les témoins tout en étant de bonne foi, confondent l'accusé avec une autre personne nommée Karlica, qu'ils pensent reconnaitre en l'accusé ... Les éléments contradictoires en possession du tribunal ne lui ont pas permis d'acquérir la conviction que l'accusé était à Prijedor, Kozarac, Omarska et Keraterm entre le 27 mai et la fin du mois de juillet 1992.'

294. On these points, see the case note by A. Ziegler (1998) 92 *AJIL* 82.

295. *Le temps*, Swiss newspaper, editions of 10–13 April and 1 May 1999; for more details see the 'Redress research paper', p. 42. See also the Swiss army website for a summary of the judgment on www.vbs.admin.ch.

296. See the judgment of 26 May 2000 of the Swiss military court of appeal 1 A (2000) 82 *IRRC* 826. This judgment was later confirmed by the Swiss tribunal militaire de cassation on 27 April 2001. For a commentary of these judgments, see B. H. Oxman and L. Reydams, 'Niyonteze v. *Public Prosecutor*' (2002) 96 *AJIL* 231 as well as Reydams, *Universal jurisdiction*, pp. 196–200 and M. Sassoli, 'Le génocide rwandais, la justice militaire suisse et le droit international' (2002) 2 *Revue suisse de droit international et européen* 151–77.

297. Four other states have enacted draft ICC implementing legislation extending the principle of universal jurisdiction to war crimes committed in internal armed conflict. The real figure will therefore soon be thirty-six states out of seventy-eight, almost half of the countries studied.

298. Jennings and Watts (eds.), *Oppenheim's international law* (London, New York: Longman, 9th edn., 1992) vol. I, p. 998. This extract was also cited by Judges Higgins, Kooijmans and Buergenthal in their separate opinion (para. 52) in the *Arrest warrant* case.

299. See the dissenting opinion of Judge Abi-Saab, in the *Tadić jurisdiction* decision, as well as para. 202 of the *Čelebići* trial judgment when the Trial Chamber affirms: 'In his Separate Opinion, however, Judge Abi-Saab opined that "a strong case can be made for the application of Article 2, even when the incriminated act takes place in an internal conflict". The majority of the Appeals Chamber did indeed recognise that a change in the customary law scope of the "grave breaches regime" in this direction may be occurring. This Trial Chamber is also of the view that the possibility that customary law has developed the provisions of the Geneva Conventions since 1949 to constitute an extension of the system of "grave breaches" to internal armed conflicts should be recognised.' On this issue, see also S. Boelaert-Suominen, 'Grave breaches, universal jurisdiction and internal armed conflicts' 63.

300. The possible use of universal jurisdiction *in absentia* has been chosen only by a handful of countries, such as New Zealand, Australia, Trinidad and Tobago and Spain.

301. The international community has not helped countries such as Angola, Liberia or the DRC to carry out impartial prosecutions for war crimes. For the situation of total impunity in the DRC, see the SG reports, S/2001/970 (6 October 2001) paras. 45–53 and S/2002/169 (15 February 2002) paras. 80–84. For an overview of the situation in Angola, see J. Doria, 'Angola: a case study in the challenges of achieving peace and the question of amnesty or prosecutions of war crimes in a mixed armed conflict' (2002) 5 *YbIHL* 3–60.

302. Hungary, for example, has recently looked into the events of the 1956 revolution. The constitutional court found that common Article 3 of the Geneva Conventions was applicable during the 1956 revolution. For more details, see (2000) 3 *YbIHL* 518–19. Similarly, local courts in Columbia carry out national prosecutions. On 1 December 1998 a special committee was established to promote investigations into cases concerning violations of human rights and

humanitarian law. A number of prosecutions took place but defendants are found guilty of municipal offences, such as kidnapping or murder and not of war crimes per se. See (2000) 3 *YbIHL* 458–61. For attempts to re-establish a judiciary and hold trials in Somalia, see M. Kelly, 'Transitional justice in peace operations: shaping the twilight zone in Somalia and East Timor' (2001) 4 *YbIHL* 213–51.

303. This section will look into national prosecutions for war crimes only. In some instances, such as Rwanda, local courts have conducted trials of individuals for genocide and crimes against humanity. See the Organic law No. 16/2004 establishing the organisation, competence and functioning of the *Gacaca* courts charged with prosecuting and trying the perpetrators of the crime of genocide and other crimes against humanity, committed between October 1, 1990 and December 31, 1994, see (2005) 87 *IRRC* 222 and (2001) 4 *YbIHL* 610–12.

304. *Rome Agreement on Sarajevo*, 18 February 1996, available online on www. nato.int/ifor/general/d960218b.htm.

305. 1,400 files containing allegations against more than 5,000 suspects have been submitted to the Rules of the Road unit of the ICTY; for further details, see J. Manuell and A. Kontic, 'Transitional justice: the prosecution of war crimes in Bosnia and Herzegovina under the Rules of the Road' (2002) 4 *YbIHL* 331–43 at 335.

306. See the trial of Ilic D. by the cantonal court in Tuzla, No. K: 177/96, 31 October 1997. Ilic D. was found guilty of war crimes against the civilian population and war crimes against prisoners of war, for having taken part many times in the ill-treatment of detained civilians and beating of detained prisoners of war in the camp of Batković in Bosnia-Herzegovina. He was sentenced to seven years' imprisonment. This judgment was later confirmed by the supreme court of the federation of Bosnia-Herzegovina, decision No. Kz-612/97, 19 May 1998. A commentary on these decisions is also available in (1999) 2 *YbIHL* 341.

See also the trial of Ibrahim D. by the cantonal court in Sarajevo, No. K-162/97, 6 October 1998. Ibrahim D. was found guilty of war crimes against the civilian population, for killing, torture, beating and other mistreatment of civilians detainees in 'concentration camps' in violation of Articles 75, 76 and 77 of Additional Protocol I. He was sentenced to ten years' imprisonment. The court found that 'the war in Bosnia and Herzegovina constituted an act of aggression by the Yugoslav Army of SR Yugoslavia/Serbia and Montenegro' and therefore amounted to an international conflict calling for the application of the Geneva Conventions.

See also the case of Zuhdija R. and Mustafa O. who were found guilty of violations of common Article 3 and Article 13 of the Third Geneva Conventions and sentenced to twelve years' imprisonment for war crimes under Article 144 of the criminal code. Bihac cantonal court, decision No. K7/97-RZ, 27 May 1997 reported in (1999) 2 *YbIHL* 340.

See also the two judgments of the supreme court of the federation of Bosnia-Herzegovina, in the case of Milan. H., Kz 422/97, 2 June 1998 and Borislav H., Kz 297/97, 29 July 1997 (on file with the author).

See also the Golubovic case which took place in the cantonal court of Mostar. On 25 July 2000, this court convicted three Bosnian policemen of war crimes against the civilian population for having killed four members of the Golubovic family. They were sentenced to twelve and nine years' imprisonment. See (2001) 4 *YbIHL* 460–61.

The Travnik county court also found Hanefija P. guilty of war crimes committed against civilians and sentenced him to fifteen years' imprisonment on 6 July 2001. See (2001) 4 *YbIHL* 462.

See also the various judgments in the G. Vasic case by the Sarajevo cantonal court. He was ultimately convicted for war crimes committed against civilians and prisoners of war and sentenced to four and a half years in jail. See (2001) 4 *YbIHL* 464.

307. Ferid H., Modrica municipal court, decision No. K-43/97, 23 October 1997, reported in (1999) 2 *YbIHL* 343.

308. See, for example, the acquittal of Miodrag A. by the magistrate's court of Sarajevo, 17 March 1999, case No. K-18/98, reported in (2000) 3 *YbIHL* 432. See also the case of Momir C. acquitted by the Sarajevo cantonal court, 18 October 2000 reported in (2001) 4 *YbIHL* 461–62; the case of three former soldiers of the Bosnian army acquitted by the Mostar cantonal court on 23 March 2001, reported in (2001) 4 *YbIHL* 462; the case of Miroslav P. acquitted by the cantonal court of Sarajevo on 26 September 2000, reported in (2001) 4 *YbIHL* 464 and the case of Valtko B. acquitted by the Sarajvo cantonal court on 17 January 2002, reported in (2001) 4 *YbIHL* 465.

309. Judgment of the magistrate's court in Sarajevo of 27 March 2000, case No. K-121/99 and appeals judgment of the supreme court of the federation of Bosnia-Herzegovina of 7 November 2000, case No. Kz.286/00 reported in (2000) 3 *YbIHL* 433–35.

310. G. Naarden, 'Non-prosecutorial sanctions for grave violations of international humanitarian law: wartime conduct of Bosnian police officials' (2003) 97 *AJIL* 342–52.

311. Manuell and Kontic, 'Transitional justice' 339.

312. Manuell and Kontic cite the political and ethnic tensions that still exist and the fact that victims and witnesses fear giving evidence in criminal proceedings in the absence of a witness protection scheme, see Manuell and Kontic, 'Transitional justice' 339. Naarden believes that Bosnian courts are ill-suited to cope with the huge number of cases. Naarden, 'Non-prosecutorial sanctions for grave violations of international humanitarian law' 344.

313. Manuell and Kontic, 'Transitional justice' 339–41.

314. See Security Council resolution 1329, 30 November 2000 as well as the address by Judge Claude Jorda to the UN Security Council, ICTY press release, 26 July 2002, JDH/P.I.S/690-e, available online on www.un.org/icty.

315. The state court is made up of three sections: one for war crimes, one for organised crimes and the last one dealing with administrative issues.
316. For more details, see Manuell and Kontic, 'Transitional justice' 341–43.
317. Each bench is composed of three judges, the presiding judge is Bosnian and the other two are international.
318. The prosecutor should also carry out the legal review function that has been performed by the Rules of the Road unit of the ICTY Prosecutor. See Manuell and Kontic, 'Transitional justice' 442.
319. Information on the special chamber of the state court is available online on www.sudbih.gov.ba/?jezik=E.
320. See, for example, *Prosecutor v. Rasević & Todović*, decision on referral of case under rule 11*bis*, case No. IT-97-25/1-PT (8 July 2005). See also in the same case the second decision of the referral bench dated 31 May 2006. The first decision of the referral bench was confirmed on appeal on 23 February 2006. An appeal by Todović to be sent to Serbia-Montenegro instead of Bosnia-Herzegovina was rejected by the Appeals Chamber. See *Prosecutor v. Rasević & Todović*, decision on Savo Todović's appeals against decisions on referral under rule 11*bis*, case No. IT-97-25/1-Ar 11*bis* and Ar11*bis*.2 (4 September 2006). The second case which has been transferred to Bosnia-Herzegovina is the case of *Prosecutor v. Mejakić et al.*, decision on joint defence appeal against decision on referral under rule 11*bis*, case No. IT-02-65-AR11*bis*.1 (7 April 2006). Four defendants were transferred to Bosnia in this case: Z. Mejakić, M. Gruban, D. Fustar and D. Knezević. On 14 November 2006, the special war crimes chamber gave its first judgment on an accused person transferred by the ICTY (see ICTY pres release JP/MOW/1126). Randovan Stanković was sentenced to sixteen years' imprisonment for rape and other crimes against humanity.
321. See *Prosecutor v. Stanković*, decision on referral of case under rule 11*bis*, case No. IT-96-23/2-PT (17 May 2005), granting the referral of the case to Bosnia-Herzegovina. This decision was reversed by the Appeals Chamber in its decision on rule 11*bis* referral, case No. IT-96-23/2-AR11*bis*.1 (1 September 2005). The case against Dragomir Milosevic was not transferred to Bosnia-Herzegovina; see decision on referral of case under rule 11*bis*, case No. IT-98-29/1-PT (8 July 2005). See also the refusals by the Appeals Chamber to refer the cases of *Prosecutor v. Gojko Janković*, decision on rule 11*bis* referral, case No. IT-96-23/2-AR11*bis*.2 (15 November 2005) and *Prosecutor v. Pasko Ljubičic*, decision on appeal against decision on referral under rule 11*bis*, case No. IT-00-41-AR11*bis*.1 (4 July 2006).
322. See the *Mejakić* Appeals Chamber decision referred to above, paras. 60–61.
323. The ICTY President considers the courts in Bosnia are still facing significant difficulties due to lack of co-operation between the two entities and the political pressure on judges and prosecutors, see *ibid.*, p. 4.
324. For more details, see Naarden, 'Non-prosecutorial sanctions for grave violations of international humanitarian law' 347.

325. For more details, see D. Mundis, 'New mechanisms for the enforcement of international humanitarian law' (2001) 95 *AJIL* 939–42; S. Linton, 'New approaches to international justice in Cambodia and East Timor' (2002) 84 *IRRC* 83–119; Cryer, *Prosecuting international crimes* (Cambridge: Cambridge University Press, 2005) pp. 65–69; C. Etcheson, 'Designing justice for Cambodia's Khmer rouge' in J. Carey, W. Dunlap and J. Pritchard (eds.), *International humanitarian law: prospects* (Ardsley: Transnational Publishers, 2006) pp. 191–209.

326. See the interesting article of T. Fawthrop, 'Who un-washes its hands of Khmer trial', *The Straits Times* (21 February 2002).

327. See UN.Doc.A/Res/57/228B (22 May 2003). For a detailed study of these chambers, see R. S. Taylor 'Better later than never: Cambodia's joint tribunal' in J. Stromseth, *Accountability for atrocities, national and international responses* (Ardsley, New York: Transnational Publishers, 2003) pp. 237–70; S. Williams, 'The Cambodian extraordinary chambers – a dangerous precedent for international justice?' (2004) 53 *ICLQ* 227–45; D. Boyle, 'Establishing the responsibility of the Khmer Rouge leadership for international crimes' (2002) 5 *YbIHL* 167–218; L. Keller, 'UNTAC in Cambodia – from occupation, civil war and genocide to peace' (2005) 9 *Max Planck yearbook of United Nations law* 127–78 and D. Kemper Donovan, 'Joint UN-Cambodia efforts to establish a Khmer Rouge tribunal' (2003) 44 *Harvard international law journal* 551–76. See also the symposium on 'Cambodian extraordinary chambers – justice at long last' published in (2006) 4 *JICJ* 283–430.

328. The Cambodian Government and the other countries in the region did not wish to place their conduct before or after those dates under judicial scrutiny.

329. These chambers will also have jurisdiction over crimes under Cambodian law, such as murder, torture and religious persecutions as defined under the 1956 Cambodian penal code.

330. See Williams, 'The Cambodian extraordinary chambers' 240. It can be argued that a state of civil war can be more clearly established during the reign of Lon Nol between 1970 and 1975. This period has been excluded from the temporal jurisdiction of the extraordinary chambers.

331. See Report of the group of experts for Cambodia pursuant to General Assembly resolution 52/125, 18 February 1999, UN.Doc.A/53/850 (16 March 1999), para. 75 and D. Boyle, 'Establishing the responsibility of the Khmer Rouge leadership for international crimes' 196.

332. Williams, 'The Cambodian extraordinary chambers' 245. See also Amnesty International, *Cambodia: Amnesty International's preliminary views and concerns about the draft agreement for the establishment of the Khmer Rouge special tribunal*, 21 March 2003 (ASA23/003/2003).

333. See the trial of Milos H. by the district court in Osijek, K-64/97-53, 25 June 1997. Milos H., a Serbian national, citizen of Croatia, was found guilty of genocide against the Croat people of the region of Branjina in Croatia, for

having looted Croatian properties, forced Croats to sign papers handing over their properties, put Croats into forced labour, committed mistreatment and torture of civil detainees and forced Croats to leave their houses and resettle in the free Republic of Croatia. He was sentenced to five years' imprisonment.

334. In some instances, some people were only charged for simple murder. See the trial of the district court of Zagreb of three HV soldiers for murdering nine members of a Bosniak family. Two of them were acquitted and the third one, who lives in Bosnia-Herzegovina, was found guilty in *abstentia*. The latter being also a Bosnian national cannot be extradited to Croatia and the crimes remain unpunished. See Bakovic, Topic and Majic, No. II-K-192/94, 15 November 1999, district court of Zagreb, reported in (2000) 3 *YbIHL* 463–65.

335. See Split district court, K15/95, 26 May 1997, unpublished (on file with author). The thirty-nine accused were sentenced to sentences from five to twenty years' imprisonment.

336. See the district court of Zadar, K74/96, judgment of 24 April 1997. The court sentenced the nineteen accused, many of them in *abstentia*, to sentences from ten to twenty years' imprisonment.

337. Reported in (2001) 4 *YbIHL* 488 and (2002) 5 *YbIHL* 478.

338. Reported in (2003) 6 *YbIHL* 485. See also (2001) 4 *YbIHL* 485–86.

339. See, for example, the acquittal of five Croatian Serbs by the court of Osijek, reported in (2000) 3 *YbIHL* 465; the acquittal of four Croatian police officers of war crimes charges by the court of Bjelovar in December 2001, reported in (2001) 4 *YbIHL* 484. See also the acquittal of eight former military police officers from Croatia by the Split county court on charges of killing and torturing Serb prisoners, reported in (2002) 5 *YbIHL* 476–77.

340. Bjelovar county court, 25 January 2002, reported in (2002) 5 *YbIHL* 475–76.

341. I. Josipovic, 'Responsibility for war crimes before national courts in Croatia' (2006) 88 *IRRC* 145–68 at 150.

342. The 2003 Act on application of the statute of the ICC and the prosecution of criminal offences against international laws of war and international humanitarian law, contains certain measures aimed at improving the efficiency of national proceedings with the creation of a special state attorney for war crimes and a special department for war crimes within the police service. See Josipovic, 'Responsibility for war crimes before national courts in Croatia' 160–61.

343. For examples of other prosecutions that have taken place in Croatia, see also (1999) 2 *YbIHL* 354 and (2001) 4 *YbIHL* 484–87.

344. See also the work carried out by the Centre of Peace, Non-violence and Human Rights on war crimes trials in Croatia: *Monitoring of war crimes trials: annual report 2005*, Centre for Peace, Non-violence and Human Rights, Osijek, 2005 and *Background report: domestic war crimes trial 2004*, OSCE, 26 April 2005.

345. See the excellent analysis by Josipovic, 'Responsibility for war crimes before national courts in Croatia' 150–54.

346. Josipovic, 'Responsibility for war crimes before national courts in Croatia' 152.

347. Under rule 11*bis*, a bench of three judges can refer a case to the authorities of a state, i) in whose territory the crime was committed, ii) in which the accused was arrested or iii) having jurisdiction and being willing and adequately prepared to accept such a case. The bench needs to be satisfied that the accused will receive a fair trial and that the death penalty will not be imposed or carried out. It shall take into account the gravity of the crime and the level of responsibility of the accused.

348. In 2004, ICC implementing legislation was adopted in Croatia, integrating therefore command responsibility within the criminal code, but this provision cannot apply retroactively. See Josipovic, 'Responsibility for war crimes before national courts in Croatia' 146–54.

349. See *Prosecutor v. R. Ademi & M. Norać*, decision for referral to the authorities of the Republic of Croatia pursuant to rule 11*bis*, case No. IT-04-78-PT (14 September 2005).

350. *Ibid.*, para. 32.

351. *Ibid.*, para. 46.

352. *Ibid.*, para. 46. For a discussion on command responsibility, see in particular paras. 38–35.

353. SC resolution 1272 (25 October 1999).

354. See especially UN.Doc.UNTAET/REG/2000/11, /15, and /25.

355. UN.Doc.UNTAET/REG/2000/11 (6 March 2000).

356. See SG report on the UNTAET, UN.Doc.S/2001/42. For more details, see M. Othman, 'East Timor: a critique of the model of accountability for serious human rights and international humanitarian law violations' (2003) 72 *Nordic journal of international law* 449–82; M. Othman, 'The framework of prosecutions and the court system in East Timor' in K. Ambos and M. Othman (eds.), *New approaches in international criminal justice: Kosovo, East Timor, Sierra Leone and Cambodia* (Freiburg: Max Planck Institute for International Law, 2003) pp. 85–112; L. A. Dickinson, 'The dance of complementarity: relationships among domestic, international and transnational accountability mechanisms in East Timor and Indonesia' in J. Stromseth (ed.), *Accountability for atrocities, national and international responses* (Ardsley, New York: Transnational Publishers, 2003) pp. 319–74; S. de Bertodano, 'Current developments in internationalised courts' (2003) 1 *JICJ* 226–44 at 230.

357. One may notice that the only difference between these two texts, is the absence in the East Timor text of the definition of crimes against humanity of Article 7.2a) of the ICC statute. A possible explanation for the absence of the definition of 'an attack against a civilian population' in the East Timor regulation could be the doubtful customary value of this definition in the ICC statute.

358. It is also interesting that the drafters of this regulation, by including both grave breaches of the Geneva Conventions alongside the war crimes applicable in internal armed conflict, did not prejudge the nature of the armed conflict which took place in East Timor.

359. See D. Mundis, 'New mechanisms for the enforcement of international humanitarian law' 942–45; H. Strohmeyer, 'Collapse and reconstruction of a judicial system: the UN missions in Kosovo and East Timor' (2001) 95 *AJIL* 46 and S. Chesterman, 'Justice under international administration: Kosovo, East Timor and Afghanistan' (2001) 12 *Finnish yearbook of international law* 143–64.

360. See section 2.2 of the Regulation 2000/15 of UNTAET, UN.Doc.UNTAET/REG/ 2000/15.

361. See the thorough analysis made by Othman, 'East Timor: a critique of the model of accountability' 468. A list of cases and their summaries are available online on www.jsmp.minihub.org/Trialsnew.htm.

362. See the latest SG report, S/2002/432 (17 April 2002) pp. 6 and 12.

363. (2003) 6 *YbIHL* 487.

364. For a commentary on the first cases, see S. Linton, 'Prosecuting atrocities at the district court of Dili' (2001) 2 *Melbourne journal of international law* 414.

365. Othman, 'East Timor: a critique of the model of accountability' 466–67.

366. See Othman, 'East Timor: a critique of the model of accountability' 472.

367. *Ibid.*, 472. Othman takes the view that 'throughout this process, there has been a glaring absence of reciprocal co-operation from Indonesia'.

368. The special panel has, however, considered the question whether there was an armed conflict in East Timor in 1999. In the *P. V. Jone Marques and others* trial, the panel found that the crimes against humanity committed in East Timor were linked to an armed conflict.

369. See C. L. Sriram, 'Globalising justice: from universal jurisdiction to mixed tribunals' (2004) 22/1 *Netherlands quarterly of human rights* 20–25; Cryer, *Prosecuting international crimes*, p. 70 and de Bertodano, 'Current developments in internationalised courts' 231.

370. See http://hrw.org/english/docs/2005/01/13/eastti9825.htm.

371. For more details, see S. H. Deming, 'War crimes and international criminal law' (1995) 28 *Akron law review* 421; D. Turns, 'War crimes without war? The applicability of international humanitarian law to atrocities in non-international conflicts' (1995) 7 *African journal of international and comparative law* 808; D. Haile, 'Accountability for crimes of the past and the challenges of criminal prosecutions. The case of Ethiopia' (2000) 15 *Leuven law series*; see also (2001) 4 *YbIHL* 499 on this issue.

372. Letter dated 27 November 2000 from the permanent mission of Indonesia to the President of the Security Council, UN.Doc.S/2000/1125, para. 27.

373. See the decree of the President (No. 90/2001) regarding amendment of the presidential decree (No. 53/2001) on the formation of an ad hoc tribunal for

human rights violations at the central Jakarta court, 1 August 2001, *State Gazette of the Republic of Indonesia* No. 111/2001.

374. See SG report S/2002/432 (17 April 2002) p. 6, para. 37; Othman, 'East Timor: a critique of the model of accountability' 473–80 and Othman, 'The framework of prosecutions and the court system in East Timor' 100–9 and O. Olsen, 'Investigation of serious crimes in East Timor' in K. Ambos and M. Othman (eds.), *New approaches in international criminal justice: Kosovo, East Timor, Sierra Leone and Cambodia* (Freiburg: Max Planck Institute for International Law, 2003) pp. 113–30.

375. The commission to investigate human rights abuses in East Timor was to investigate violations of human rights in East Timor before the creation of the ad hoc tribunal and found that the violence that erupted in East Timor was the result of a systematic campaign of violence and was not an internal armed conflict. See (2000) 3 *YbIHL* 523.

376. Twelve of the eighteen defendants were acquitted. See the acquittal of the former chief of police of East Timor and two district administrators, reported in Othman 'East Timor: a critique of the model of accountability' 475–76. As of the end of 2002, eighteen persons had been indicted. For a summary of some cases, see (2002) 5 *YbIHL* 517–19. See also, de Bertodano, 'Current developments in internalised courts' 234–36.

377. Othman, 'East Timor: a critique of the model of accountability' 476–79. See the thorough analysis of the first three cases by S. Linton, 'Unravelling the first three trials at Indonesia's ad hoc court for human rights violations in East Timor' (2004) 17 *Leiden journal of international law* 303–61. See also Dickinson, 'The dance of complementarity' pp. 344–43 and (2002) 5 *YbIHL* 518–19.

378. Othman, 'The framework of prosecutions and the court system in East Timor' p. 107.

379. Declaration by the EU Presidency on ad hoc human rights tribunal for crimes committed in East Timor, press release 11928/03, 6 August 2003. See also the press release dated 21 August 2002, 11524/02.

380. Othman, 'The framework of prosecutions and the court system in East Timor' p. 112.

381. The statute of the Iraqi special tribunal is reproduced in (2004) 43 *ILM* 231.

382. J. E. Alvarez, 'Trying Hussein: between hubris and hegemony' (2004) 2 *JICJ* 313–29.

383. H. Megally and P. van Zyl, 'US justice with an Iraqi face' *International Herald Tribune* (4 December 2003).

384. Some have taken the view that this tribunal is not sufficiently international to achieve the goals set for it. See M. Scharf, 'Is it international enough? A critique of the Iraqi Special Tribunal in light of the goals of international justice' (2004) 2 *JICJ* 330–37. See also M. Newton, 'The Iraqi high criminal court: controversy and contributions' (2006) 88 *IRRC* 399–425.

385. Article 1b) of the statute of the Iraqi special tribunal. One might note the very long temporal jurisdiction of the tribunal. It might be difficult to investigate and prosecute crimes committed more than thirty-five years ago. Furthermore, it is

unclear whether Iranian authorities or Kuwaiti authorities will co-operate with the special tribunal in facilitating the collection of evidence or the production of witnesses. The special tribunal will have no authority to request the production of documents from Iran or Kuwait.

386. See Articles 11–14 of the Iraqi special tribunal.

387. The definition of crimes against humanity is taken from Article 7 of the ICC statute. Only forced sterilisation and apartheid have been omitted.

388. It is argued in chapter 4 of this book that, at the time the ICTY issued the *Tadić* jurisdiction decision of 1995, it was premature for the tribunal to conclude that, in light of state practice up to 1991, serious violations of the laws of war committed in internal armed conflict attracted international responsibility.

389. See I. Bantekas, 'The Iraqi special tribunal for crimes against humanity' (2004) 54 *ICLQ* 237–53, 242. See also, Y. Shany, 'Does one size fit all? Reading the jurisdictional provisions of the new Iraqi special tribunal statute in the light of the statutes of the International Criminal Tribunals' (2004) 2 *JICJ* 338–46.

390. See Article 4(d) of the special tribunal statute, as well as Articles 6(b), 7(n) and 8(j).

391. See Bantekas, 'The Iraqi special tribunal for crimes against humanity' 247. The lack of qualified and impartial Iraqi judges as well as their lack of expertise in war crimes trials are also noted by the doctrine. See Scharf, 'Is it international enough' 332–33.

392. See the various editorial comments on the Iraqi tribunal published in (2004) 2 *JICJ* 313–52.

393. Alvarez, 'Trying Hussein' 321.

394. Some war crimes trials have also taken place in Montenegro, against Yugoslav nationals who have committed war crimes during the Bosnian war. See, for example, (2000) 3 *YbIHL* 496; (2002) 5 *YbIHL* 487. In Serbia, courts found individuals guilty of domestic crimes, see (2000) 4 *YbIHL* 494–95 or of war crimes, see (2002) 5 *YbIHL* 489–90 and (2003) 6 *YbIHL* 582.

395. See Strohmeyer, 'Collapse and reconstruction of a judicial system' 46; Mundis 'New mechanisms for the enforcement of international humanitarian law' 945–48 and S. Chesterman, 'Justice under international administration' 143–64.

396. See Mundis 'New mechanisms for the enforcement of international humanitarian law' 946 and SG report on the UN Interim Administration in Kosovo, UN.Doc.S/2000/538, para. 60.

397. Strohmeyer, 'Collapse and reconstruction of a judicial system' 53.

398. See the SG reports on the UN Interim Administration Mission in Kosovo, UN.Doc.S/2001/926, para. 49; S/2002/62, paras. 25–28.

399. UNMIK regulation UNMIK/REG/2000/64, 15 December 2000, available online on http://unmikonline.org/regulations.

400. See UNMIK regulations 1999/24, 12 December 1999 and 1999/59, 27 October 2000. The legislation in force after 22 March 1989 can be applied by domestic courts if they are found not to be discriminatory.

401. See *Kosovo's war crimes trials: a review (September 2002)*, OSCE Mission in Kosovo, Department of human rights and the rules of law, legal systems monitoring section, available online on www.osce.org/documents/mik/2002/09/857_en.pdf. The OSCE Mission in Kosovo gives a detailed description of the seventeen cases held up to June 2002 in Kosovo. Other summaries of judgments can be found in (2001) 4 *YbIHL* 507–14; (2000) 3 *YbIHL* 497–98; (2002) 5 *YbIHL* 491–501.

402. For more details, see (2001) 4 *YbIHL* 501–7 and *Kosovo's war crimes trials: a review* (September 2002) pp. 34–35.

403. See *Kosovo's war crimes trials: a review* (September 2002) pp. 48–49. Up to June 2002, the supreme court panels had reversed eight out of the eleven convictions it had reviewed in war crimes cases.

404. On 18 January 2001, the district court of Mitrovica found Miroslav V. guilty of genocide on the basis of Article 141 of the Yugoslav criminal code. This verdict was overruled by the supreme court of Kosovo on 31 August 2001 (supreme court of Kosovo A.156/2001). The case was sent back to the lower court for retrial. On 25 October 2002, the district court of Mitrovica gave its judgment. See (2002) 5 *YbIHL* 493–94.

405. See (2002) 5 *YbIHL* 494.

406. See the remarks of M. Hartmann in (2003) 6 *YbIHL* 601.

407. See the conclusions reached by the OSCE in *Kosovo, review of the criminal justice system 1999–2005, reforms and residual concerns*, OSCE, Department of human rights and rule of law, legal system monitoring section, March 2006, as well as Cryer, *Prosecuting international crimes*, p. 70.

408. See Hartmann in (2003) 6 *YbIHL* 601.

409. See (2000) 3 *YbIHL* 564–68.

410. See (2002) 5 *YbIHL* 589–90.

411. Othman, 'East Timor: a critique of the model of accountability' 471.

412. On 7 June 2005, the Sudanese Government established a special criminal court for the events in Darfur; a first conviction for serious human rights violations was made on 15 August 2005. However, investigations have been carried out in only a few cases of reported human rights violations and none of the cases so far seems to have addressed the major violations of humanitarian law that took place during the conflict in Darfur during 2003 and 2004. See UN.Doc.S/2005/523 (11 August 2005), S/2005/592 (19 September 2005) and S/2005/650 (14 October 2005), in particular paras. 17–22.

413. Similarly, the special court within the Bosnian state court is the product of negotiations between Bosnia-Herzegovina and the international community. The special tribunal in Iraq was created by a regulation issued by the coalition provisional authority in Iraq.

414. On these issues, see C. L. Sriram, 'Globalising justice: from universal jurisdiction to mixed tribunals' 7–32.

415. In Afghanistan, the UN is playing a substantially reduced role from that in Kosovo or East Timor. It is there to facilitate democratic transition rather than to lead or administer the country. The rule of law has not been a priority and there does not seem to be any serious judicial mechanism set up to deal with war crimes and crimes against humanity committed by the Talibans and other Afghan armed groups. See S. Chesterman, 'Justice under international administration: Kosovo, East Timor and Afghanistan' 143–64 and P. Danchin, 'Transitional justice in Afghanistan: confronting violations of international humanitarian and human rights law' (2001) 4 *YbIHL* 3–51.

416. See R. Wolfrum, 'The decentralised prosecution of international offences through national courts' (1994) 24 *Israel yearbook of human rights* 183–201.

417. On this point, see Abi-Saab, 'The proper role of universal jurisdiction' 601 and Henzelin, 'La competence pénale universelle, une question non résolue par l'arrêt Yerodia' 839–43.

418. See H. Ascencio, 'The Spanish constitutional tribunal's decision in Guatemalan generals: unconditional universality is back' (2006) 4 *JICJ* 586–94. Spain has investigated foreign individuals under its domestic legislation for genocide or torture but has not yet investigated war crimes in internal armed conflict.

419. States parties are even under an obligation to prosecute alleged offenders for the crime of torture, if they are found in their territory and are not extradited to another state. See Article 5.2 of the 1984 Convention against Torture and Other Cruel, Inhuman or Degrading Treatment, UN.GA.Res.39146 (10 December 1984).

420. See the prosecution of Sebastien N. by the Rotterdam district court on 7 April 2004, reported in (2004) *NILR* 439–43. For recent French prosecutions, see D. Turns, 'Certain criminal proceedings in France (*Republic of Congo v. France*) provisional measures order of 17 June 2003' (2004) *ICLQ* 747–52. For some Spanish genocide prosecutions, torture and terrorism, see (2000) 3 *YbIHL* 587–94.

6

International prosecutions of war criminals and internal armed conflicts

The international enforcement of individual criminal responsibility for violations of international law was first envisaged in 1915 by France, Great Britain and Russia following the massacre of more than one million Armenians.[1] These countries qualified the event as a 'crime against civilisation and humanity' for which the members of the Turkish Government should be held responsible.[2] In 1946, the prosecutions of Nazis war criminals were the first effective international enforcement of individual responsibility for violations of the laws of war and crimes against humanity committed in international armed conflicts. As far as internal armed conflicts are concerned, the international enforcement of individual responsibility for war crimes per se was neither envisaged in the 1949 Geneva Conventions nor in Protocol II of 1977. The failure to provide for individual criminal responsibility for war crimes in Protocol II explains why up to the 1990s, violations of the laws of war, when committed during an internal armed conflict, were prosecuted as domestic crimes and did not attract international responsibility.

The past decade saw the extension of international criminal responsibility from conduct committed in international conflicts to similar conduct committed in internal conflicts. Violations of the laws of war committed in internal conflicts have been recognised as amounting to war crimes for which individual responsibility must be enforced at a national or an international level. Before, international criminal law was simply not applicable in the sphere of internal armed conflicts. These achievements represent a quantum leap for the enforcement of individual responsibility for war crimes in internal conflicts.

Faced with massive violations of the laws of war during internal armed conflicts and growing impunity, the international community chose to place greater reliance on international criminal justice, with the creation of both the International Criminal Tribunal for the former

Yugoslovia (ICTY) and the International Criminal Tribunal for Rwanda (ICTR), culminating in the adoption of the statute for an International Criminal Court in 1998 and the creation of the Special Court for Sierra Leone. In the absence of any prosecutions by the states on whose territory war crimes have been committed, alleged perpetrators, or at least the ones most responsible for war crimes, could be prosecuted by international courts or tribunals. The ICTY and ICTR are current examples of international enforcement of such responsibility. However, both tribunals have a limited geographical and temporal scope of jurisdiction and are a creation of the UN Security Council. The ICC statute entered into force on 1 July 2002. The court could have a wide geographical scope, if a large number of states decide to ratify the statute, and may therefore be seen as the most viable solution both as a means of enforcing individual responsibility and as a powerful deterrent to future offenders.

This chapter will assess the role played by these international criminal institutions in the enforcement of individual criminal responsibility for war crimes committed in internal armed conflicts. First, the legacy of both International Criminal Tribunals will be studied, before highlighting the difficulties encountered by these institutions when enforcing individual criminal responsibility for war crimes in internal conflicts. Secondly, the statute of the ICC will be evaluated to find out whether the court could effectively enforce such responsibility. The viability and effectiveness of international enforcement compared to national enforcement of individual responsibility for war crimes will be ascertained.

1. The ad hoc International Criminal Tribunals as a means of enforcing individual responsibility for war crimes committed in internal armed conflicts

The ICTY[3] and ICTR[4] were set up under chapter VII of the UN Charter as subsidiary organs of the Security Council within the terms of Article 29 of the Charter[5] and have a limited jurisdiction in space and time. Both International Criminal Tribunals[6] and national courts have concurrent jurisdiction to try alleged war criminals, but the Tribunals have primacy to do so over national courts.[7] A natural consequence of the primacy of the tribunals is the power given to them to request national courts to interrupt any domestic proceedings and defer to their competence.[8] Furthermore, every UN member state is under a general obligation to co-operate with the Tribunals in the investigation and prosecution of persons suspected of war crimes.[9] These factors put them in a good position to enforce individual criminal responsibility in internal conflicts. The Special Court for Sierra Leone, however, has primacy over the national courts of Sierra Leone but this primacy does not extend to courts of third states. It lacks the power to request the surrender of an accused, the production of evidence or witnesses from any third state. This section will look first at the achievements of these institutions before studying the difficulties that they have encountered.[10]

1.1 The contributions of the International Criminal Tribunals in the enforcement of individual responsibility for war crimes

Both the ICTY and the ICTR have played a paramount role in the enforcement of individual criminal responsibility for war crimes committed in internal armed conflicts. The work of the Tribunals has clearly sent a signal to the international community that atrocities committed in internal armed conflicts engage the international responsibility of offenders. Such responsibility not only exists on paper but is successfully pursued by both Tribunals. Justice is seen to be done both in The Hague and Arusha and this should contribute directly to the effort of reconciliation in both countries. By 1 December 2006, proceedings are ongoing against sixty-four accused persons in The Hague[11] and eleven trials involving twenty-seven accused are in progress in Arusha. Several important political or high-ranking military figures have finally made their way to the ICTY such as Slobodan Milošević, I. Plavšić or the generals Krstić or Galić. The ICTY has concluded proceedings against ninety-seven persons of whom forty-five have been sentenced, five acquitted, thirty-six others either died or their indictment has been withdrawn and twelve were referred to national jurisdictions. In the ICTR, the great majority of the political leaders who allegedly fomented or carried out genocide are in custody in Arusha.[12] Proceedings are much slower than in the ICTY and in total, the ICTR has delivered twenty-two judgments involving twenty-eight accused. Between 1995 and 1999, the ICTR only delivered six judgments, involving seven accused. Between 1999 and 2003, the work pace almost doubled to nine judgments involving fourteen accused.[13]

Compared to the number of alleged war criminals present in the former Yugoslavia and Rwanda, both tribunals have prosecuted a very small number of individuals. They have concentrated their efforts on trying the most responsible individuals, both political and military leaders. In doing so, they transformed an embryonic field of law into a fully fledged discipline and are the very first international institutions to have enforced individual responsibility for war crimes committed in internal armed conflicts.

1.1.1 The definition of internal armed conflict in the case law of the Tribunals

The landmark decision of the ICTY, the *Tadić* decision on jurisdiction, was fundamental in the development of international criminal law. Notwithstanding the observation of the Commission of Experts for the former Yugoslavia,[14] Article 3 of the ICTY statute was interpreted by the majority of the Appeals Chamber to include serious violations of common Article 3 and any other serious violations of customary rules applicable in internal armed conflicts. As a result, compared with the ICTR statute or even the International Criminal Court (ICC), the ICTY statute is the instrument with potentially the widest subject matter jurisdiction in internal armed conflicts. The Appeals Chamber in the seminal *Tadić* decision on jurisdiction went on to define an internal armed conflict to exist 'whenever there is protracted armed violence between governmental authorities and organised armed groups or between such groups within a state'.[15] Since then, each Trial Chamber had to determine if the case at hand amounted to an armed conflict. As seen in chapter 1 of this book, to do so, they assessed on the one hand the organised nature of the rebel groups and on the other hand the duration or intensity of the armed violence between such groups or between governmental authorities and rebel groups. In assessing the duration or intensity of the conflict, Trial Chambers have looked at various factors such as the seriousness of attacks and their recurrence,[16] the spread of these armed clashes over territory and time,[17] whether various parties were able to operate from a territory under their control,[18] an increase in the number of government forces, the mobilisation of volunteers and the distribution of weapons among both parties to the conflict,[19] as well as whether the conflict had attracted the attention of the UN Security Council and whether any resolutions on that matter had been passed.[20] In order to assess the organisation of the parties to the conflict, Trial Chambers took into account such factors as the existence of headquarters, designated zones of operation and the ability to procure, transport and distribute arms.[21]

As seen in chapter 1, the recent trial judgment in the *Limaj* case details these criteria even further in order to determine whether the conflict between governmental forces and the Kosovo Liberation Army (KLA) in Kosovo in 1998 amounted to an internal armed conflict.[22] The case law of the ICTY on this issue is of fundamental importance in the field of internal armed conflicts. The paramount weakness of the concept of internal armed conflict is the difficulty of agreeing on a definition and deciding whether or not the case at hand amounts to an armed conflict. The case law of the ICTY provides plentiful criteria that will enable states or other tribunals to assess the character of the armed conflict they are facing.

The ICTR uses the same test as the ICTY to 'evaluate both the intensity and organisation of the parties to the conflict' for each of their cases.[23] This tribunal took the view that assessing whether the hostilities are of sufficient intensity 'does not depend on the subjective judgment of the parties to the conflicts', but rather on the objective level of violence taking place between the various armed groups.[24]

The Tribunals not only elaborated detailed criteria to distinguish an armed conflict from a situation of internal disturbances, but also created a test which enables courts to determine whether the internal armed conflict has been internationalised by a foreign intervention in this internal conflict.[25] The ICTY Appeals Chamber found that there are two ways by which an internal armed conflict may become international:

1. If another state intervenes in that conflict through its troops
2. If some of the participants in the internal armed conflict act on behalf of that state.[26]

If the participants to the armed conflict are not organised into a military structure, the Appeals Chamber takes the view that one needs to prove they acted upon specific instructions or directives from a state, before they can be seen as acting on behalf of a state and as a result internationalise the entire conflict.[27] If the participants in the internal armed conflict are organised into a military structure, the Appeals Chamber believes that one need only prove that the intervening state exercises an overall control of this rebel group.[28] If the overall control can be proven, this rebel group will be considered to act on behalf of the state and the foreign intervention will therefore render the entire conflict international. Overall control can be shown if the foreign state equips and finances the activities of the armed group as well as co-ordinates or helps in the general planning of its military activity.[29] This precedent of the ICTY Appeals Chamber was consistently upheld in successive trial judgments[30] and represents the most clearly articulated and relevant case which clarifies the circumstances in which an internal armed conflict becomes internationalised as a consequence of a foreign intervention.[31]

It is interesting to note that the ICTY Prosecutor maintained Article 2 charges and successfully established the international nature of the armed conflict in only seven cases out of eighteen.[32] In the other eleven cases[33], the Prosecutor only established the existence of an armed conflict. It shows that the Prosecutor tries to avoid having to prove the internationality of the conflict but he does not need to undertake this difficult task to prosecute war criminals successfully. The nature of the conflict becomes almost irrelevant in the way prosecutions for war crimes are conducted in the ICTY.[34]

1.1.2 The constitutive elements of war crimes in internal armed conflicts

Following the *Tadić* decision, the subsequent case law of both Tribunals has clarified the constitutive elements of war crimes when committed in internal armed conflicts. In order to be found guilty of war crimes, the alleged perpetrators must have committed a crime against persons protected by common Article 3 or Additional Protocol II.[35] The ICTY and ICTR Chambers have determined who falls within the category of victims of war crimes committed in internal armed conflicts by:

> Asking whether at the time of the alleged offence, the alleged victim of the proscribed acts was directly taking part in hostilities, being those hostilities in the context of which the alleged offences are said to have been committed. If the answer to that question is negative, the victim will enjoy the protection of the proscriptions contained in common Article 3.[36]

According to the Tribunals, a civilian will be considered to be 'directly taking part in hostilities' and will lose the protection of common Article 3 if he was involved in 'acts of war which by their nature or purpose were likely to cause actual harm to the personnel and equipment of the enemy armed forces'.[37]

The case law of the Tribunals, in particular of the ICTR, has also looked at the issue of who can be potential perpetrators of war crimes in internal conflicts.[38] The post-World War II cases support the imposition of individual criminal liability for war crimes on belligerent soldiers and civilians alike and the case law of both Tribunals confirms it. Up to 2001, the ICTR Trial Chambers took the view, however, that a civilian, in order to be found guilty of war crimes, needed to be 'mandated and expected as public officials or agents or persons otherwise holding public authority de facto representing the government to support or fulfil the war efforts'.[39] According to this view, to be found guilty of war crimes civilians needed therefore to be public officials or persons holding public authority. It excluded the possibility of finding guilty individuals who choose to help one of the belligerent parties without necessarily holding any public office. This case law can be seen as restricting the categories of perpetrators unnecessarily, rather than taking into account the limitations of war crimes by imposing the proof of a close relationship between the acts of the perpetrators and the armed conflict.[40] The ruling of this Trial Chamber was overturned by the Appeals Chamber in the *Akayesu* case when it declared:

> The Appeals Chamber is therefore of the opinion that international humanitarian law would be lessened and called into question if it were to be admitted that certain persons be exonerated from individual criminal responsibility for a violation of common Article 3 under the pretext that they did not belong to a specific category.[41]
>
> This nexus between violations and the armed conflict implies that, in most cases, the perpetrator of the crime will probably have a special relationship with one party to the conflict. However, such a special relationship is not a condition precedent to the application of common Article 3 and, hence of Article 4 of the statute. In the opinion of the Appeals Chamber, the Trial Chamber erred in requiring that a special relationship should be a separate condition for triggering criminal responsibility for a violation of Article 4 of the statute.[42]

The Appeals Chamber chose not to limit the categories of perpetrators of war crimes in internal armed conflicts but rather to put the emphasis on the link between the acts of the perpetrators and the armed conflict in order to distinguish between a domestic crime and a war crime. The majority of the doctrine and recent international case law require the acts of the perpetrator to be associated with the armed conflict rather than requiring the perpetrator himself to have a close relationship with one party to the armed conflict.

The third constitutive element of a war crime is the establishment of a nexus or a link between the conduct of the perpetrator and the armed conflict.[43] As seen in more detail in section 1.3 of chapter 3, the ICTY in particular has developed detailed criteria in order to establish that the crimes charged were committed in a time of armed conflict and that there was a nexus between the conduct of the perpetrator and the armed conflict. For a crime to amount to a war crime, it is essential to establish the existence of a geographical and temporal connection between the conduct of the accused and the armed conflict.[44] The ICTY Appeals Chamber in the *Kunarac* case summarises the criteria applied by the tribunal:

> 60. What ultimately distinguishes a war crime from a purely domestic offence is that a war crime is shaped by or dependent upon the environment – the armed conflict – in which it is committed. It need not have been planned or supported by some form of plan or policy. The armed conflict need not have been causal to the commission of the crime, but the existence of an armed conflict must, at a minimum, have played a substantial part in the perpetrator's ability to commit it, his decision to commit it, the manner in which it was committed or the purpose for which it was committed. Hence, it if can be established, as in the present case, that the perpetrator acted in furtherance of or under the guise of the armed conflict, it would be sufficient to conclude that his acts were closely related to the armed conflict . . .
>
> 61. In determining whether or not the act in question is sufficiently related to the armed conflict, the Trial Chamber may take into account, *inter alia* the following factors: the fact that the perpetrator is a combatant; the fact that the victim is non-combatant; the fact that the victim is a member of the opposing party; the fact that the act may be said to serve the ultimate goal of a military campaign; and the fact that the crime is committed as part of or in the context of the perpetrator's official duties.

The ICTR Trial Chambers seem to be more restrictive by requiring the acts of the perpetrator 'to be committed in conjunction with the armed conflict'[45] or the existence of a 'direct link between the crimes committed and the hostilities'.[46] Apparently more restrictive, these criteria in fact reflect the real nature of war crimes, especially when committed in an internal armed conflict. These criteria allow judges to distinguish between domestic crimes and war crimes. In applying these criteria, one has to be particularly vigilant when the accused is a non-combatant.[47] The ICTR Prosecutor has found it difficult to establish all the constitutive elements of war crimes. Trial Chambers concluded either that the accused did not fall within the category of perpetrators[48] or that the nexus between the acts of the accused and the armed conflict was not established.[49] Up to 2003, all accused were acquitted of war crimes by Trial Chambers.[50]

In the *Rutaganda* case, the Appeals Chamber reversed the acquittal of Rutaganda for war crimes. In finding that a nexus existed between the acts of the accused and the armed conflict, it took into account the following factors: the fact that the perpetrator participated in attacks against the civilian population alongside soldiers of the presidential guard, the fact that he exercised de facto influence and authority over a paramilitary group, which committed the massacres, and the fact that the victims were persons protected under common Article 3 and Protocol II.[51] Since then, ICTR Trial Chambers have found other accused guilty of war crimes committed during the Rwandese conflict.[52]

The case law of both Tribunals has been instrumental in defining the constitutive elements of war crimes when committed in internal armed conflicts. The detailed criteria developed shed light on the particularities of war crimes committed in internal armed conflicts and also represent useful benchmarks for domestic judges in charge of war crimes prosecutions.

1.1.3 List of war crimes in internal armed conflicts

In its seminal *Tadić* jurisdiction decision, the Appeals Chamber affirmed:

> Customary international law imposes criminal liability for serious violations of common Article 3, as supplemented by other general principles or rules on the protection of victims of internal armed conflicts, and for breaching certain fundamental principles and rules regarding means and methods of combat in civil strife.[53]

This finding led to the prosecution of a wide range of war crimes under Article 3 of the statute. The Appeals Chamber recently recalled:

> All the rules applicable to international armed conflicts do not automatically apply to an internal armed conflict and what may constitute a war crime in the context of an international armed conflict does not necessarily constitute a war crime if committed in an internal conflict.[54]

Each Trial Chamber has had to verify whether the conduct of the perpetrator was not only illegal in internal armed conflict but also attracted individual criminal responsibility under customary international law. The Appeals Chamber and the Trial Chambers of both the ICTY and ICTR have established the constitutive elements and convicted individuals for the following war crimes in internal armed conflicts:

- serious violations of common Article 3, in particular murder,[55] torture,[56] cruel treatment[57] and outrages upon personal dignity[58]
- serious violations of Additional Protocol II, in particular murder, cruel treatment, torture, outrages upon personal dignity in particular rape,[59] slavery,[60] pillage[61] and attacks against the civilian population[62]

- wanton destruction of cities, towns or villages, or devastation not
  justified by military necessity, recognised under Article 3b) of the
  ICTY statute and Article 23g) of the Hague regulations[63]
- attacks on civilian objects[64]
- seizure of, destruction or wilful damage done to institutions dedicated to religion, recognised under Article 3d) of the ICTY statute
  and Article 27 of the Hague regulations.[65]

1.1.4 Prosecuting war crimes

Once the existence of an armed conflict is proven and the criminality is
established for a particular conduct in customary law, the ICTY has
prosecuted alleged war criminals independently of the character of the
armed conflict in which the war crimes were committed. The forms of
direct participation contained in Article 7.1 of the ICTY statute have
been applied to alleged perpetrators regardless of whether they committed a war crime in internal or international armed conflict.
Individuals have been prosecuted for having planned, instigated,
ordered, committed or otherwise aided and abetted in the planning,
preparation or execution of war crimes.[66] Another form of liability, not
explicitly contained in these articles, was also applied to war crimes
committed in internal armed conflicts, in light of the absence of any
challenge made by the defence. This is the theory of common purpose or
joint criminal enterprise, which has been described as 'an understanding
or arrangement amounting to an agreement between two or more
persons that they will commit a crime'.[67]

Alleged war criminals have also been prosecuted before both tribunals
under Articles 7(3) or 6(3) of their respective statute for having failed to
prevent or punish the criminal acts of their subordinates, of which they
knew or had reason to know.[68] The defence in one case before the ICTY
challenged the applicability of this particular form of responsibility in
the context of internal armed conflicts.[69] The Appeals Chamber found
that this form of liability was applicable also in the context of internal
armed conflicts. It first took the view that command responsibility
would be applicable to violations of common Article 3 committed in
the course of an international armed conflict. 'It is difficult to see why
the concept would not equally apply to breaches of the same prohibitions when committed in the course of internal armed conflicts.'[70]
It then went on to study the relationship between command responsibility and responsible command, and took the view that whenever there
is an organised military force, it implies responsible command and that

in turn responsible command implies command responsibility.[71] 'Command responsibility is the most effective method by which international criminal law can enforce responsible command.'[72] Thus,

> If customary international law recognises that some war crimes can be committed by a member of an organised military force in the course of an internal armed conflict; it therefore also recognises that there can be command responsibility in respect of such crimes.[73]

Even in the absence of clear or unequivocal state practice and *opinio juris* in this respect, it does seem reasonable to take the view, as the Appeals Chamber stated, that:

> The basis of the commander's responsibility lies in his obligations as commander of troops making up an organised military force under his command, and not in the particular theatre in which the act was committed by a member of that military force.[74]

The Appeals Chamber found that this principle was reflected in customary international law but did not specify at what point this principle became applicable in internal armed conflict.[75] It would be safe to assume that this principle started to apply when violations of the laws of war committed in internal armed conflicts were deemed to attract international responsibility.

In the same way that the forms of liability applicable to war crimes committed in international conflicts were applied to war crimes committed in internal conflicts, the Tribunals developed and clarified issues such as cumulative charging, cumulative convictions and the permissibility of defences available to the defendants, such as superior orders, reprisal or duress independently of the character of the armed conflict.[76] There again, it seems difficult to refute the view that, once the concept of war crimes is found to be applicable in internal armed conflicts, the parameters of war criminality, which were created to regulate international armed conflicts, will extend to internal armed conflicts.

Both Tribunals have been fully functioning criminal tribunals for more than ten years and have produced the solid foundations of a new discipline, international criminal law and in particular the international criminal law applicable in internal armed conflicts. They have produced a wealth of decisions both on substantial law and issues of criminal procedure, ranging from the right to represent yourself in court, to the vagueness of the indictments or the meaning of the right to be tried without undue delay. Their work has been instrumental in triggering national prosecutions in countries such as in the former Yugoslavia and Rwanda[77] and their case law amounts to real benchmarks for any courts or tribunals prosecuting war crimes.[78] They prove that war crimes committed in internal armed conflicts can be successfully prosecuted by international tribunals after an internal armed conflict has ended. Notwithstanding these breakthroughs, the work of the Tribunals also reveals the limitations encountered by these institutions in enforcing individual criminal responsibility.

1.2 The limitations of the International Criminal Tribunals in the enforcement of individual responsibility for war crimes in internal armed conflicts

The work of both International Criminal Tribunals has revealed the difficulties that can arise when enforcing individual criminal responsibility for war crimes in internal armed conflicts. Some are of a legal nature while others are more practical difficulties that are encountered also when enforcing individual responsibility for war crimes committed in international conflicts.

1.2.1 The case law of the Tribunals: constructive interpretation or faithful determination of the content of customary international law?

The International Tribunals have transformed an embryonic field of law into a fully fledged discipline. The ICTY statute is particularly short and grants the tribunal jurisdiction over an illustrative list of serious violations of the laws of war contained in Article 3.[79] In doing so, the Security Council implied that other serious violations of the laws of war could fall within the tribunal's jurisdiction and that it would be for the judges to determine which of those were as well as establishing the constitutive elements of each offence prosecuted. A great deal of international criminal law applicable in internal armed conflicts in particular, is therefore the fruit of customary law interpretation by various Trial Chambers and the Appeals Chamber of the Tribunals.

The first issue, which needed resolution and whose outcome has varied slightly over the years, has been to determine the applicable law of the tribunal. Can the tribunal apply customary law alongside treaty law? In his report to the Security Council accompanying the draft statute of the tribunal, the UN Secretary-General stated that the tribunal was to apply 'rules of international humanitarian law which are beyond any doubt part of customary law so that the problem of adherence of some but not all States to specific conventions does not arise'.[80] This requirement has been interpreted differently by judges over the years. In its landmark *Tadić* decision on jurisdiction, the Appeals Chamber found that Article 3 of the statute was 'a general clause covering all violations of humanitarian law not falling under article 2 or covered by articles 4 or 5' of the statute.[81] Four conditions were laid out by the Appeals Chamber for a violation of international humanitarian law to be subject to Article 3 of the statute. The violation must constitute a serious infringement of a rule of international humanitarian law.[82] In turn, this rule must be reflected in customary law or treaty law. Lastly, the violation of this rule must entail, under customary international law or treaty law, the individual criminal responsibility of the author.[83] At the outset, it must be noted that treaty norms applicable in internal armed conflicts did not provide for individual criminal responsibility of the offenders at the time the offences were committed between 1991 and 1995. In order to fulfil the last condition spelled out by the Appeals Chamber in the *Tadić* jurisdiction decision, the criminality of serious violations of the laws of war in internal armed conflicts must therefore always be reflected in customary international law. It is not entirely clear how these conditions spelled out in paragraph 94 of the Appeals Chamber's decision can be reconciled with paragraph 143 of the same decision, where the Appeals Chamber takes the view that:

> The International Tribunal is authorised to apply in addition to customary international law, any treaty which: (i) was unquestionably binding on the parties at the time of the alleged offence; and (ii) was not in conflict with or derogated from peremptory norms of international law, as are most customary rules of international humanitarian law.

Can a Trial Chamber find an accused person guilty of a breach of a treaty norm, such as Article 13 of the Additional Protocol II, for example, when the said treaty is unquestionably binding on the parties at the time of the alleged offence, but does not provide for the individual criminal responsibility of the offender in case of breach in internal armed conflicts? As far as war crimes committed in internal armed conflicts are concerned, it therefore seems that Trial Chambers should always assure themselves that the serious violation in question entailed individual criminal responsibility in customary international law at the time of the commission of the offence, in order to respect the principle *nullum crimen sine lege*.

After 1995, Chambers have tended to follow the recommendations of the Secretary-General and have taken the view that the subject-matter jurisdiction of the Tribunal needed to be based on 'firm foundations of customary international law'.[84] In one instance, a Trial Chamber even refused to prosecute an accused for an offence contained in the indictment, but which was not reflected in customary international law.[85] These precedents were not, however, followed by a Trial Chamber in the *Galić* case,[86] when it found the accused guilty of the crime of terror and attacks against the civilian population, based on Additional Protocol I.[87] The Trial Chamber in this case refrained from finding that the crime of terror was reflected in customary international law, stating only that it was sufficient for the crime to be applicable between the parties through Additional Protocol I,[88] notwithstanding the fact that the Prosecutor did not plead that the conflict was of an international character.[89] The Appeals Chamber has recently given its appeal judgment on this case and once again looked at the issue of the law applicable. It declared in the *Galić* appeal judgment:

> While conventional law can form the basis for the International Tribunal's jurisdiction, provided that the above conditions are met, an analysis of the jurisprudence of the International Tribunal demonstrates that the Judges have consistently endeavoured to satisfy themselves that the crimes charged in the indictments before them were crimes under international law at the time of their commission and were sufficiently defined under that body of law.[90]

In the first part of this proposition, the Appeals Chamber makes reference to paragraph 143 of the *Tadić* jurisdiction decision, discussed above. It is, however, unclear how conventional law can form the basis of the offender's individual criminal responsibility in internal armed conflicts, when, at the time the offences were committed, this body of law did not provide for international responsibility of individuals in internal armed conflicts. If the Security Council wanted the Tribunal to apply agreements that had been negotiated between parties, such as the 22 May 1992 agreement in Bosnia-Herzegovina, it is unclear why the statute or the Secretary-General's report did not provide for it or at least envisage it. The above-cited statement confirms, however, that ICTY Chambers have entered 'convictions only where it is satisfied that the offence is proscribed under customary international law at the time of its commission'.[91]

Following the Secretary-General's report and the interpretation of Article 3 of the statute given by the Appeals Chamber in the *Tadić* jurisdiction decision, Trial Chambers have had to determine first whether the conduct in question was criminal in customary international law but needed also to determine the elements, both material and mental, of the said crime in customary international law. Determining the content of customary international law is a difficult exercise, which will come from the judges' assessment of the amount and strength of state practice and *opinio juris* on a particular issue at the time the offence was committed.[92] In the laws of armed conflict, the Appeals Chamber noted that 'it is difficult if not impossible to pinpoint the actual behaviour of troops in the field for the purpose of establishing whether they in fact comply with, or disregard certain standards of behaviour'.[93] It is no surprise therefore that the Tribunals have been treated as 'customary midwifes'.[94] The variability of opinions between judges of the same bench on the existence or absence of a particular customary norm and the variability between Trial Chambers' judgments on the elements of a crime, reflected in customary international law, illustrate the difficulty of the exercise. In the *Erdemovic* case, judges of the Appeals Chamber had divergent views on the status of duress in customary international law. The majority held the view that duress could not entirely exonerate an individual who has committed war crimes or crimes against humanity, while Judge Cassese believed that in international criminal law, duress can be relied upon by an accused person.[95] Recently, the majority of the Appeals Chamber concluded that customary international law imposed individual criminal liability for violations of the prohibition of terror against the civilian population from 1991.[96] After a careful analysis of the practice available, Judge Schomburg took the view that it was 'not possible to assert beyond any doubt that the crime was indeed part of customary international law at the time of *Galić*'s criminal conduct'.[97]

On the determination of the elements of certain crimes, various Trial Chambers looked into the content of customary international law and defined the offences in different ways. The constitutive elements of the crime of rape have varied, once defined as 'physical invasion of a sexual nature,'[98] it was also defined as 'a violation of sexual autonomy' or as 'a sexual penetration'.[99] Furthermore, the question whether the absence of consent was an element per se of the crime of rape was also solved in different ways by Trial Chambers[100] until the Appeals Chamber gave its own interpretation of customary law and settled the definition in 2002.[101] The constitutive elements of the crime of torture under customary law have also been defined differently by Trial Chambers as well as the Appeals Chamber. Some benches took the view that the definition of torture in Article 1(1) of the 1984 Torture Convention was representative of customary international law.[102] The Appeals Chamber adopted that definition in 2000[103] before preferring the definition given in the *Kunarac* case in 2002, which did not require that at least one of the persons involved in the torture process be a public official or have acted in a non-private capacity.[104]

Another rather fundamental change in the Tribunal's case law took place recently when, after more than ten years in existence, the Appeals Chamber took the view that the existence and international character of an armed conflict are both jurisdictional prerequisites as well as substantive elements of crimes prosecuted under Article 2 of the statute.[105] Up to the *Kordić* and *Natelitić* appeal judgments, the existence of an armed conflict and its character had been treated as jurisdictional prerequisites for the Tribunal to be able to exercise its jurisdiction under Articles 2 and 3 of the statute. In all the previous cases tried by the ICTY, the Prosecutor was not required to show that the accused needed to be aware of the factual circumstances that established the existence and the nature of the armed conflict. The Appeals Chamber explains neither the reason for such a shift in 2006, nor the potential consequences that this finding could have had on all the previous cases tried by the Tribunal. The difficulties and limitations in requiring proof that the accused had knowledge of the existence and nature of the armed conflict are further explained in section 3, chapter 3 of this book.

While it is possible that 'two judges, both acting reasonably, can come to different conclusions on the basis of the same evidence',[106] the paucity of state practice advanced by some Chambers[107] tends to show that custom is largely postulated rather than relying on demonstrated assertions.[108] A reasoned opinion firmly establishing the basis in customary law of all offences and forms of liability for which an accused is convicted, is a condition *sine qua non* for the respect of the principle *nullum crimen sine lege* and as a result an indispensable component of a right to receive a fair trial.[109] As Judge Schomburg affirmed:

> It would be detrimental not only to the Tribunal but also to the future development of international criminal law and international criminal jurisdiction if our jurisprudence gave the appearance of inventing crimes – thus highly politicising its function – where the conduct in question was not without any doubt penalised at the time when it took place.[110]

1.2.2 Issues of co-operation

A major practical difficulty for international prosecutions lies in securing suspected criminals as well as the necessary evidence to try them.[111]
The delays inherent in setting up both Tribunals have meant that the
evidence can deteriorate or be destroyed, witnesses can relocate or be
intimated and perpetrators can disappear.[112] Unlike the Nuremberg
Tribunal, the International Criminal Tribunals do not have control
over the territory where the crimes have been committed and at the
time they were set up did not have any suspected criminals in custody. In
practice, the tribunals have no power to arrest suspects or to force
accused persons to appear before them.[113] They have to rely on national
authorities to fulfil these functions. The effectiveness of the Tribunals
themselves therefore depends heavily on the co-operation of states to
arrest suspected criminals in their territory, and transfer them to the
Tribunals, along with any information, testimony or evidence they
may need.

Article 29(2) and Article 28(2) of the ICTY and ICTR statutes respectively, list the obligation of states to co-operate with any request for
assistance or an order by a Trial Chamber relative to:

– the identification and location of persons
– the taking of testimony and the production of evidence[114]
– the service of documents[115]
– the arrest or detention of persons
– the surrender or the transfer of the accused to the Tribunal.[116]

The Prosecutor of the ICTY has publicly indicted 161 individuals
and proceedings are ongoing against 64 persons with 6 accused remaining
at large.[117] Ten indicted criminals have been successfully transferred
from states such as Austria, Bosnia, Croatia, Germany and Serbia to the
ICTY.[118] In general, from 2000 onwards the Federation of Bosnia-
Herzegovina as well as Croatia,[119] have co-operated satisfactorily with
the ICTY.[120] However, some western states have been reluctant to send
witnesses from their military forces to the Tribunals[121] and both the
Republika Srpska[122] and the Government of Serbia are not co-operating
satisfactorily with the ICTY in the arrest of war criminals and the transfer
of information and evidence to the Tribunal with the notable exception of
the transfer by Yugoslavia of Slobodan Milošević.[123] Between 1993 and
1998, the ICTY had issued 205 arrest warrants and only 6 had been
executed by various states.[124] Particularly in the early years of the ICTY,

the Tribunal relied on NATO forces to execute arrests warrants in Bosnia and on foreign states to transfer indictees to the Tribunal, in the light of the unwillingness of national authorities in the Balkans to do so.[125] Recently, the Prosecutor reported, however, that the last successful operation to arrest a fugitive was conducted in July 2002 and that NATO and European Union Forces (EUFOR) in Bosnia-Herzegovina did not co-ordinate their efforts sufficiently to effect the capture and transfer of Karadzic.[126]

State co-operation with the ICTR has gradually improved. The Tribunal holds, as of 1 December 2006, fifty-seven detainees in custody and eighteen indicted persons are still at large. Ten persons were arrested in Cameroon, fourteen in Kenya, eight in Tanzania, six in Belgium, three in Zambia, two each in France, Benin, Congo, the Democratic Republic of the Congo (DRC), Mali, the Ivory Coast, Togo, Gabon, the Netherlands, South Africa and Switzerland, and one each in Angola, Namibia, Burkina Fasso, Denmark, Senegal, Italy, Uganda, the UK and the USA.[127] Other countries, however, such as the DRC,[128] where many perpetrators took refuge, or Rwanda and Uganda have hardly co-operated satisfactorily with the ICTR.[129] The absence of co-operation by states often results in investigations being halted or major war criminals staying at large. The travel restrictions imposed by Rwanda on ICTR witnesses, for example, brought many proceedings in Arusha to a halt.[130] The latest report from the ICTR President to the Security Council discusses the satisfactory co-operation from Rwanda which has facilitated a steady flow of witnesses from Kigali to Arusha and provided relevant documents to the court proceedings.[131]

In theory, because the ad hoc tribunals were created under chapter VII of the UN Charter, states' obligations to co-operate should take precedence over other international obligations.[132] Both Security Council resolutions creating the tribunals declare that all states shall co-operate fully with the tribunals and 'take any measures necessary under their domestic law to implement the provisions of the . . . resolution and the statute including the obligations of states to comply with requests for assistance or orders issued by a Trial Chamber'.[133] All UN member states are therefore under an obligation to provide the legal assistance that either Tribunal requests. In practice, the Tribunals have very little coercive means at their disposal to force recalcitrant states to co-operate. The rules of procedure and evidence provide for the consequences of non-compliance by states with a request for deferral, with a failure to execute a warrant and in other similar cases.[134] If, for instance, a state fails to file a response which satisfies the Trial Chamber that it has taken or is taking adequate steps to comply with the order, the Trial Chamber may request the President of the Tribunal to report the matter to the Security Council.[135] Such reports to the Security Council have been made in the cases of the most notorious indictees such as Radovan Karadžić and Ratko Mladić.[136] The Council has responded with statements insisting upon compliance addressed to the recalcitrant state or entity, warning of the possibility of further enforcement measures, but stopping short of taking any further action.[137] Faced with the recent lack of co-operation by Rwanda, the President of the ICTR as well as the Prosecutor sent letters to the Security Council complaining of Rwanda's lack of co-operation. Rwanda started to change its policy when the ICTR Prosecutor put a freeze on investigations of the Rwandan Patriotic Front's (RPF) activities during 1994, raising criticism that the ICTR might become a 'victor's tribunal'.[138]

Neither statute makes provision for circumstances in which a state may refuse to accede to an order from the Tribunal. The Appeals Chamber, in the *Blaškić* case, dismissed, for example, Croatia's claim that there is an absolute national security privilege.[139] It went on to affirm that states are subject to binding orders from the Tribunal for documentary evidence to be produced.[140] It found that the Tribunal lacked any direct enforcement power against states, but that it has an inherent power to make judicial findings and is empowered to report these to the Security Council, which may impose sanctions on recalcitrant states.[141]

Because of the often-met difficulty for international prosecutors to search freely locations in the former Yugoslavia or Rwanda and seize documents and other types of evidence,[142] both International Tribunals have relied heavily on witness testimonies as the main source of evidence in court. Witnesses can be vulnerable to external threat or pressure. They are asked to try to remember, years after the crimes took place, extremely traumatic events and have to travel to The Hague or Arusha to give their testimony.[143] Major contradictions between testimonies given by the same person in different trials at the ICTR are not a rare phenomenon.[144] The importance of securing the co-operation of the states concerned is even greater in the case of internal armed conflicts. If the state where the crimes were committed or the state where most perpetrators have sought refuge do not co-operate with the Tribunals, this may prevent prosecutions for war crimes and hamper the effectiveness of the international institution as a whole. The DRC's lack of co-operation and the restrictions imposed on witnesses travelling by the Rwandan Government illustrate this danger.

Co-operation between international tribunals and states, in particular the states where the offences were committed in case of internal armed conflicts, is the indispensable pre-requisite to the efficiency of the Tribunals[145] and to the international prosecution of war crimes committed in internal armed conflicts. During the ICTY's early years, Balkan States were largely non-co-operative and indicted persons took a long time to reach the ICTY detention unit.[146] The decisions, in 1997, by NATO and the Stabilisation Force in Bosnia and Herzegovina (SFOR) actively to search and arrest war criminals profoundly changed the dynamics and sent clear signals to indicted war criminals that they would not be able to retain their freedom much longer. Promise of financial aid has often been attached to the transfer of accused persons.[147] Transfers or 'voluntary' surrendering of the first indictees before the ICTY was often the result of considerable political pressure put on Croatia, for example, at the beginning of the life of the Tribunal.[148] Diplomatic and political pressures from influential states, the Presidents of the ICTY and the prosecutors slowly turned the tide of non-compliance. Since the death of F. Tudjman and the transfer of Slobodan Milošević, Balkan States can be said to co-operate in a largely satisfactory manner with the ICTY. This being said, a number of 'big fishes' remain at large. The continued absence of Mladić and Karadžić from the courtrooms in The Hague is a constant reminder that securing the custody of war criminals by international tribunals is heavily dependant on the co-operation of states. The rule 61 procedure,[149] the reports from the Presidents of the Tribunals to the Security Council of non-compliance by certain states, and the diplomatic pressure imposed on these states have had limited effect in forcing them to co-operate.[150] As commentators noted, 'in practice co-operation worked on the basis of voluntary compliance and was best achieved if it was tailored to the particular requirements of the state concerned'.[151] 'Where good faith is lacking, the absence of compulsory mechanisms to ensure the prompt enforcement of court orders for the production of relevant evidence remains an inherent weakness in the scheme of international justice.'[152]

1.2.3 The legacy of the international tribunals: failings and achievements

Critics of international criminal justice as rendered by the International Criminal Tribunals often cite the administrative weight of these institutions, the absence in custody of some major war criminals, the length of trials and pre-trial detention as well as the costs of these institutions. The

ICTY has even been caricaturised as being 'too costly, too inefficient and too ineffective'.[153]

The combined budget of both Tribunals reaches $250 million per year and represents more than 10 percent of the total annual UN regular budget.[154] Their total cost over seventeen or eighteen years of life will probably reach $2.5 billion.[155] Everybody would agree that these costs appear astronomical in comparison to the 200 or so individuals who will ultimately be tried by the Tribunals before 2010–2012. However, international criminal justice is always expensive and cannot be compared to domestic systems. The cost of investigating massive human rights violations over almost ten years of conflict in the Balkans, for example, the cost of running detention units and of paying for the defence of indicted persons are particularly high in international criminal justice.

The cost of these institutions[156] is also linked to the length of proceedings in both Tribunals. The *Rutaganda* trial is illustrative of the length that proceedings can take at the ICTR; Rutaganda was arrested in Zambia in 1995, transferred to Arusha in 1996 and the appeal judgment in his case was given on 26 May 2003. If seven years of proceedings remain an exception, even at the ICTR, pre-trial detentions and trials take up much more time than in domestic trials. The length of international trials can be explained: massive human rights violations are tried years after they took place; the investigation and gathering of evidence can prove to be a time-consuming and perilous exercise in the absence of co-operation by national authorities. Trials are conducted in two or three languages, and all documents also need to be translated into these languages. Lastly adequate preparation time needs to be allocated to the defence if the Tribunals are to assure all defendants receive a fair trial.[157] If these factors explain the time that international prosecutions take, they do not entirely answer the fact that they remain cumbersome and lengthy.

Both Tribunals have tackled this well-founded criticism and adopted various measures to fight delays and expedite trial and appeal proceedings.[158] Judges have amended their rules of procedure and evidence to provide for the creation of pre-trial and pre-appeal judges,[159] for the admission of more written evidence under rules 92*bis*, 92*ter* and 92*quater*[160] of the ICTY rule of procedure and evidence, in order to prevent witnesses coming back many times to repeat their testimonies at the tribunal and amendments have been adopted to allow judges to place limits upon the Prosecution's cases.[161] At the ICTY, a third Trial Chamber was created and in 2001 the Security Council accepted that a pool of *ad litem* judges be nominated, which has enabled six trials to be held simultaneously in the three courtrooms.[162] Finally, it might also be noted that, at least in the ICTY, if proper guarantees are provided, the provisional release of indicted persons has slowly become the norm in order to reduce the problems of long pre-trial detentions.[163]

Pressurised to finish their work as soon as possible by the international community, the Tribunals have also decided to focus their prosecutions on high-level accused, both political and military, and to send intermediary and low-level accused back to national courts. To date, the ICTY has transferred the case of twelve ICTY indicted persons: nine to Bosnia-Herzegovina, two to Croatia and one to the Republic of Serbia.[164] The high court of Bosnia has recently given its first judgment on a case referred back to it by the ICTY.[165] Following the ICTY's footsteps, the ICTR has also adopted a completion strategy and the ICTR Prosecutor envisages transferring seventeen cases to national jurisdiction.[166] Furthermore, the Prosecutor also plans the transfer of dossiers, requiring further investigations to national jurisdiction for trial. Case files in respect of thirty suspects have already been communicated to Rwanda and one to Belgium.[167] The transferred cases have the beneficial effect of bringing the administration of criminal justice back home, allowing effective national war crimes trials to take place in the country where atrocities have been committed and strengthening national judicial capabilities.[168] It might represent a remedy to the often-cited criticism that international justice is too remote from the place where crimes have been committed and that victims and local population have no direct or easy access to international courtrooms. The international community must, however, help Rwanda deal with the transferred cases and provide long-awaited financial and technical help for justice to be seen to be done in Rwanda. If no help is forthcoming, the transfer of cases will only appear as a cheap and easy substitute to lengthy and costly international trials, which the international community is no longer prepared to pay for.[169]

The two ad hoc tribunals have also failed to prevent the recurrence of war crimes in the same region. The ICTY did not deter potential offenders and did not manage to prevent the Srebrenica massacres or the events in Kosovo from 1998 to 2000.[170] This may, however, be asking too much of a new-born institution. Critics also denounce the inability of the ICTR to dispel 'the deep-seated animosity between the two segments of the Rwandan population'.[171] International criminal justice ought to make past enemies aware of the extreme criminality of their actions. The gravity of the crimes perpetrated in Rwanda in 1994 have to be internalised not only by Hutus extremists, still active from their bases in the DRC, but also by Rwandan society as a whole, in order to be able to talk about reconciliation or reconstruction of a post-genocidal society.[172] The fact that the majority of persons indicted by the ICTR continue to negate the extent of the massacres that took place in Rwanda in 1994 illustrates the failure of the Tribunal to launch a real transformation of values among the Rwandan society. The cost and length of the ICTR prosecutions cannot but be compared to the lack of legal and financial means at the disposal of the Rwanda Government to deal with almost 125,000 individuals in custody for genocide in Rwanda.[173] Justice needs 'to be brought home' by the International Tribunal for it to help achieve reconciliation.

Because international prosecutions by the two ad hoc tribunals are costly and lengthy, they will be reserved for a few and might not achieve all the goals for which they were established.[174] However, the International Criminal Tribunals are an indispensable piece of the international justice puzzle; they have shown that international justice is feasible and there can be an international criminal response to internal atrocities. They are now unavoidable players in the fight against impunity and participate in shedding light on the local history of massive human rights and humanitarian law violations.

2. The International Criminal Court as a means of enforcing individual criminal responsibility for war crimes committed in internal armed conflicts

The adoption of the statute for an International Criminal Court[175] was characterised by the UN Secretary-General as 'a gift of hope to future generations, and a giant step forward in the march towards universal human rights and the rule of law'.[176] Unlike both International Criminal Tribunals, the ICC cannot be blamed for being an ad hoc institution dealing with events *a posteriori* and potentially violating the principle *nullum crimen sine lege*. It only has jurisdiction over events which took place after 1 July 2002 and its subject-matter jurisdiction is said to reflect customary law at the time of its adoption.[177]

Can the ICC effectively end the spiral of impunity in internal armed conflicts? Is the ICC sufficiently well equipped to carry out prosecutions for crimes committed in internal armed conflicts when national authorities have decided not to act? The negotiators have succeeded in adopting a broad subject-matter jurisdiction for the court, but its dependence on states' co-operation makes it difficult to foresee how it will effectively prosecute war crimes committed in internal armed conflicts. Success will depend on factors, such as the establishment of the jurisdiction of the court and the co-operation of states in securing the custody of war criminals as well as the necessary evidence to try them. We will look first at the subject-matter jurisdiction of the court before clarifying the mechanism for the establishment of the jurisdiction of the court and the principles which guide the creation of the criminal institution.

Thirdly, it is necessary to study the relationship between the ICC and national courts and in particular the co-operation provisions embodied in the statute, in order to find out if overall this permanent institution can play an active role in the prosecution of individuals for war crimes committed in internal armed conflicts.

2.1 The jurisdiction ratione materiae of the International Criminal Court

As noted in chapter 4,[178] the ICC statute is the second instrument expressly to include a great number of war crimes committed in internal armed conflicts. The list of war crimes appearing in Article 8(2)(e) mirrors for a great part the list of war crimes applicable in international conflicts in Article 8(2)(b) but is much shorter.[179] It contains conducts forbidden by common Article 3, Protocol II and The Hague regulations. The court will not, however, be able to prosecute isolated occurrences of war crimes. The *chapeau* of Article 8 of the statute expressly restricts the jurisdiction of the court over war crimes 'in particular when committed as part of a plan or policy or as part of a large scale commission of such crimes'. This language may exclude war crimes committed during low-level armed conflicts, which do not reach the threshold imposed by Article 8.

Furthermore, this wide subject-matter jurisdiction is restricted in practice by a transitional provision adopted in order to secure the support of certain states during the last days of the Rome conference.[180] On becoming party to the statute, a state may declare that it does not accept the jurisdiction of the court with respect to war crimes when such crimes are alleged to have been committed by its nationals or in its territory.[181] This declaration is valid for a period of seven years after the entry into force of the statute for the state concerned. This article is intended to reduce the fears of states, which send a lot of servicemen abroad, that their soldiers would be tried by the ICC for war crimes. If states choose to opt out from the jurisdiction for war crimes, this transitional solution will create a de facto opt-out regime, which changes the nature of the jurisdiction and negates the concept of the automatic jurisdiction of the court over all core crimes. It may have devastating effects on the capacity of the ICC to prosecute war criminals in internal conflicts if a number of states decide to use this article.[182] Furthermore, this provision puts the states which become party to the statute at an advantage, compared to the states which decide not to accede to it. It creates an unequal situation whereby a state party has the option to exclude the court's jurisdiction for war crimes over its nationals and from situations which take place on its territory. At the other end of the spectrum, in the case of an armed conflict taking place in the territory of a non-state party and referred by the UN Security Council to the court, the non-state party will not be able to rely on this opt-out mechanism to exclude war crimes from the jurisdiction of the court. The same is valid for a non-state party which decides by declaration to accept the exercise of jurisdiction by the court in respect of certain crimes pursuant to Article 12.3 of the statute. Declarations pursuant to Article 12.4 of the statute were made by France and Columbia upon ratification. The court will not have the jurisdiction to try suspects for war crimes allegedly committed by their nationals or in their territory for a period of seven years after the entry into force of the statute for these countries. It is unclear whether this period is renewable. The next review conference, which should take place in 2009, will review that article and its method of application.

2.2 The establishment of the jurisdiction of the International Criminal Court

The adoption of a wide subject-matter jurisdiction for crimes committed in internal armed conflict contrasts sharply with the way the jurisdiction has been heavily circumscribed in other respects. The court is intended to exercise 'jurisdiction only over the most serious crimes of concern to the international community as a whole'[183] and to be 'complementary to national criminal jurisdictions'.[184] Acting in 'complementarity' with national jurisdictions means in practice that national courts will have priority over the ICC to carry out prosecutions. To achieve this goal, the statute has established some preconditions to the exercise of the court's jurisdiction as well as strict criteria of admissibility of a case. To assess the ICC's capacity to prosecute war crimes committed in internal armed conflicts effectively, it is necessary to look first at these preconditions before studying the mechanism by which a situation is brought to the attention of the court.

2.2.1 Preconditions for the exercise of the ICC jurisdiction

Article 12 of the statute lays down the preconditions for the exercise of the court's jurisdiction:

1. The Court may exercise its jurisdiction if one or more of the following states are parties to this statute or have accepted the jurisdiction of the Court in accordance with paragraph 3:
   a) The states on the territory of which the act or omission in question occurred or, if the crime was committed on board a vessel or aircraft, the state of registration of that vessel or aircraft;
   b) The state of which the person being investigated or prosecuted is a national.
2. If the acceptance of a state which is not a party to this statute is required under paragraph 2, that state may, by declaration lodged with the Registrar accept the exercise of jurisdiction by the Court with respect to the crime in question.

At the Rome conference, opinions were split between states who wanted to see the principle of universal jurisdiction extended to the court,[185] and those who wished to see that the consent of specific states be obtained before the court could exercise its jurisdiction.[186] The option finally adopted in Article 12 was not an option embodied in the draft statute and was in reality a last-minute compromise.[187] The regime of alternative consent, either by the territorial state or by the state of nationality of the accused, is applicable when a state refers a situation to the Prosecutor, or when the Prosecutor has started an investigation. It is not, however, applicable when a situation is referred to the Prosecutor by a decision of the Security Council under chapter VII of the UN Charter. This regime is not new; territoriality and active nationality are the two most common bases of jurisdiction recognised in international law and an inherent feature of statehood.[188] Instead of trying the person itself, the territorial state delegates that power to the ICC by ratifying the statute. In most cases, third states are not consulted, nor their agreement obtained, before a state exercises its jurisdiction over events which took place on its territory. In general, an individual, military or civilian, who enters the territory of a foreign state, is subject to that state's sovereign jurisdiction if the individual commits an offence in its territory. That state can either try this individual or extradite him to a third state (where, for example, he would have committed another wrongdoing). Article 12 of the ICC statute does not therefore infringe upon state sovereignty any more than universally accepted norms of international criminal law and extradition law.[189]

For internal armed conflicts, the consequences of this political compromise are far-reaching. In most internal armed conflicts, the territorial state will be the state of nationality of the accused. States with serious internal problems may well decline to become parties to the statute. Therefore, in cases where the territorial state was not party to the court before the armed conflict broke out, the preconditions contained in Article 12 will act as a bar to the exercise of the court's jurisdiction.

For the ICC to be able to prosecute war crimes committed in internal armed conflicts, one can envisage three situations: the Security Council can refer the situation to the court under chapter VII; the state where the internal conflict took place was party to the court before the beginning of the armed conflict; or, a decision from that country is taken at the end of hostilities to lodge a declaration of acceptance of the court's jurisdiction with the registrar.[190] It seems that the conditions contained in Article 12 dilute the jurisdiction to such an extent, that the court could only exercise its jurisdiction over a minority of internal armed conflicts. A state, which stays outside the framework of the court, will not need to worry about it having jurisdiction over war crimes which occur on its soil.[191] If a majority of states decide not to ratify the statute, war crimes committed in internal armed conflicts will remain unpunished in most cases where consent from the territorial state cannot be obtained. One may also note that in internal conflicts, there will be a lack of reciprocity between belligerents. The jurisdiction of the court will depend exclusively on the attitude of the governmental side in an internal armed conflict. The universality of the treaty will therefore be of the utmost importance for the court to play an effective role in preventing the occurrence of such crimes and in punishing the criminals in internal armed conflicts.

Practice during the first four years of the court's life has revealed that, surprisingly, the preconditions to the exercise of the court's jurisdiction were not factors that prevented the court from investigating war crimes committed in internal armed conflicts. First, as of 1 January 2007, the ICC statute has 139 signatories and 104 states parties. Of these 104 states parties, 3 states facing long-lasting internal armed conflicts have already referred these situations to the court pursuant to Articles 13(1) and 14 of the statute.[192] A fourth case of internal armed conflict was referred to the court by the Security Council pursuant to resolution 1593 on 31 March 2005.[193] With the exception of crimes allegedly committed by nationals of twenty-five states parties in the conflict in Iraq, the office of the ICC Prosecutor has only examined or investigated situations of internal armed conflicts.[194]

2.2.2 The exercise of jurisdiction by the court

Once the preconditions for the exercise of its jurisdiction are fulfilled, three distinct entities can trigger the jurisdiction of the court. According to Article 13 of the statute, a situation in which one or more of the crimes contained in Article 5 appears to have been committed can be referred to the Prosecutor:

1. by a state party, or
2. by the Security Council acting under chapter VII of the UN Charter,[195] or
3. the Prosecutor in person can initiate an investigation in respect of a crime falling within the jurisdiction of the court.

These three possibilities will be analysed.

Any state party, the territorial state or any other state party, may refer a situation to the Prosecutor requesting an investigation in order to determine whether one or more specific persons should be charged with the commission of those crimes falling within the court's jurisdiction. The state party shall submit to the Prosecutor all supporting documentation available to it. The power by a state party other than the territorial state to refer a situation to the court may be particularly relevant in internal armed conflicts. Even if such referral does not give rise to prosecutions by the court, it may be seen as a public condemnation of such crimes and trigger national prosecutions either where the crimes were committed or elsewhere. The referrals so far have been made by three states which have referred situations taking place in their territory to the Prosecutor, pursuant to Articles 13(1) and 14 of the statute.[196]

Secondly, the Security Council acting under chapter VII can trigger the jurisdiction of the court. The Security Council will first have to establish that the situation amounts to a breach of the peace, an act of aggression or a threat to international peace and security and then that the referral to the ICC is a measure necessary to address the threat to the peace, for example. This may not be easy to establish in cases of internal armed conflicts. The commission of serious crimes may not be found to amount to a breach of or a threat to the peace. Furthermore, the affirmative vote of nine members of the Council and the absence of veto by any permanent members will be necessary before a situation is referred to the court. Political willingness to qualify the internal conflict in question as a threat to the peace and to refer the situation to the court may be lacking. This fear did not materialise in the case of the Sudan. The Security Council, acting under chapter VII, decided to refer the situation in the Darfur region of Sudan since 1 July 2002 to the Prosecutor of the ICC on 31 March 2005. The investigation into the Darfur situation started on 6 June 2005 and the Prosecutor has nearly completed investigations into several incidents that took place in 2003 and 2004. He is preparing to submit evidence to the Pre-Trial Chamber before the end of February 2007 and obtain the necessary arrest warrants in this case.[197]

Another obstacle to the establishment of the court's jurisdiction is the power granted to the Security Council to request the court to defer or to suspend investigation or prosecution for a period of twelve months.[198] Article 16 requires the affirmative vote of nine members of the Council and the absence of any veto by the permanent members for this measure. The advantage of the adopted formula is therefore to make such a request or renewal by the Security Council, an open process. Article 16 fails, however, to require the Council to take appropriate measures regarding the situation where one or more serious crimes have been committed. Does it mean that the Council could block the work of the court just by qualifying the situation of a breach of the peace without taking any other measure? The openness of the process under chapter VII should minimise this risk, which is nonetheless present.

In 2002, the Security Council gave itself a second means to prevent the court from exercising its jurisdiction by adopting resolution 1422.[199] The latter provides that 'if a case arises involving current or former officials or personnel from a contributing state not a party to the Rome statute over acts or omissions relating to United Nations established or authorised operation', the Security Council requests the court not to commence or proceed with the investigation or prosecution of any such case for a twelve-month period starting 1 July 2002, unless the Security Council decides otherwise. Personnel of UN peace-keeping missions or military operations authorised by the Security Council from a contributing state not party to the ICC will automatically fall outside the court's jurisdiction and therefore seem to be above the law. It is difficult to see how the conditions under Article 39 of the Charter were fulfilled for the Security Council to take this resolution under chapter VII and it is equally questionable how the Security Council can unilaterally amend a multilateral treaty such as the Rome statute.[200] Under strong US pressure, the Security Council renewed this resolution in 2003[201] but strong opposition from permanent and non-permanent members of the Security Council in 2004 has prevented a renewal ever since.

Thirdly, if states parties, or the Security Council are not taking the initiative to bring a situation to the court, the Prosecutor may initiate *proprio motu* an investigation into a situation where one or more crimes falling within the court's jurisdiction have been committed.[202] Article 15 provides that once 'the prosecutor concludes that there is a reasonable basis to proceed with an investigation, he shall submit to the pre-trial chamber a request for authorisation of an investigation'.[203] 'If the pre-trial chamber considers that there is a reasonable basis to proceed with an investigation, and that the case appears to fall within the jurisdiction of the court, it shall authorise the commencement of the investigation.'[204] If the Pre-Trial Chamber does not authorise an investigation, the Prosecutor can always present a subsequent request based on new facts or evidence regarding the same situation.[205] The Prosecutor will start investigations on the basis of information received from governmental and non-governmental organisations. These *proprio motu* powers are carefully restrained by the authorisation procedure of the Pre-Trial Chamber, as well as the principle of complementarity. They represent, however, a powerful weapon especially for crimes committed in internal conflicts, if the Security Council is unable to act or states parties are unwilling to refer a situation to the court. Even if the authorisation of an investigation is refused, the attempt by the Prosecutor to obtain it, may be seen as a strong indication that serious crimes may have been committed. This could be sufficient to trigger national prosecutions in the territorial state or elsewhere.

The difficulty of establishing the ICC jurisdiction may not enable the court to counter effectively the unwillingness, or the inability, of states to bring to justice the perpetrators of war crimes committed in internal armed conflicts.[206] Unlike the jurisdiction of both International Criminal Tribunals, the jurisdiction of the court is based only on the consent of states, either at the time of ratification or accession to the statute or on an ad hoc basis after the commission of these serious crimes. This makes the court particularly dependent on the willingness of states to give jurisdiction to the court and diminishes the court's potential effectiveness to prosecute war crimes in internal armed conflicts.

The only jurisdictional link, which could have enabled the court to prosecute effectively war crimes in internal armed conflicts, would have been to give it the same right as any member of the international community under the principle of universal jurisdiction. As seen in chapter 4, any state has a right to bring the perpetrators of genocide or war crimes to justice, independently and without the consent of the state of nationality of the accused, or the territorial state.

2.2.3 Issues of admissibility: the principle of complementarity[207]

Once the jurisdiction of the court is established, the case must also be deemed admissible before the court can exercise its jurisdiction over alleged perpetrators.[208] Article 17 of the statute establishes the rules governing the principle of complementarity, which is seen as the real cornerstone of the court.[209] In the ICC statute, complementarity has to be understood as leaving the primacy to exercise jurisdiction over genocide, crimes against humanity and war crimes to national jurisdictions. Complementarity will in effect act as a barrier to the exercise of the court's jurisdiction. The court will only be able to exercise jurisdiction over crimes where national jurisdictions may be 'unable or unwilling' to judge the perpetrators of such crimes.[210] Inability and unwillingness well describe the main reasons behind the lack of prosecutions by national authorities following an internal conflict, making the ICC, at least on paper, an institution well geared to enforce individual responsibility for war crimes in internal armed conflicts.

The court will be able to start an investigation when states parties are 'unable' to do so, have decided not to act, or when they have clearly been 'unwilling', i.e. acted inconsistently with an intent of bringing the person to justice.[211] In order to determine the inability of national jurisdictions to try the perpetrators of such crimes, the court will have to prove 'a total or substantial collapse or unavailability of national judicial systems'.[212] In order to establish unwillingness, judges will need to determine whether the proceedings undertaken at a national level were made 'for the purpose of shielding the person concerned from criminal responsibility, or if the proceedings were not conducted independently or impartially, or in a manner which is inconsistent with an intent to bring the person concerned to justice'.[213] Alternatively, the court will be able to prove unwillingness if there has been an 'unjustified delay in bringing the accused to justice'.

In short, the court will not exercise its jurisdiction and the case will be deemed inadmissible where the person has already been investigated or prosecuted by a state, or if the case has been investigated by a state which has decided not to prosecute the person. Alternatively, where such a person has already been tried for the same conduct, or where such a case is not of sufficient gravity to justify further action by the court,[214] the court will not be able to exercise its jurisdiction. In all other situations not falling within the four categories enumerated above, the case will be deemed admissible. The difficult question of amnesty laws, especially in cases of internal armed conflicts, was omitted as being too delicate during the preparatory committee sessions, and was not discussed further at the Rome conference. One can nonetheless imagine a national law granting amnesty to perpetrators of crimes against humanity or war crimes without investigating the responsibility for these atrocities. In the light of Article 17, this situation may be interpreted by the court as a case of genuine unwillingness to carry out investigations or prosecutions. The alleged perpetrators could therefore be tried by the ICC, even if they benefited from a full amnesty in their country. On the other hand, a situation may arise where responsibility had been investigated but the perpetrators were granted amnesty from punishment. If such a case were to be brought before the court, it might be declared inadmissible on the basis of Article 17(1)(b).[215] The issue of a case's admissibility may be a delicate matter for the court to decide, as it will be judging the quality of national prosecutions.[216]

Effective exercise of jurisdiction by a state will prevent the court from exercising its own jurisdiction.[217] The court is really meant to act as a safety net or a palliative to the deficiency of states. However, the principle of complementarity may well have an indirect but very positive effect. In order to avoid having the court prosecute their nationals for crimes which occurred in their territory, states may choose to implement the statute in their domestic legislation and to exercise jurisdiction over war crimes committed in internal armed conflicts. This could have the drawback of multiplying distinct definitions of the crimes and possibly create conflicting case law on the various constitutive elements of war crimes. On the other hand, a state which would want to assert jurisdiction over international crimes in order to prevent the ICC from doing so, will in all likelihood adopt national legislation implementing the list of crimes contained in the ICC statute and will also be naturally influenced by the elements of crimes adopted by the Assembly of the States Parties.

Three out of the five cases now in front of the court were referred by states parties pursuant to Articles 13(a) and 14 of the statute.[218] In each case, it is the territorial state, where the crimes have been committed, which decided to refer the situations to the court. It is open to debate whether such referrals can be reconciled with the principle of complementarity, as defined in Article 17 of the statute. In the case of Uganda at least, the government is not unable to carry out prosecutions of the Lord's Resistance Army's (LRA) alleged war criminals. Would these cases be seen as falling within the definition of 'unwillingness' by states to prosecute? It is also possible to think that by referring their own internal situations to the ICC Prosecutor, these states have waived their right to investigate and prosecute alleged criminals and also waive, as a consequence, any claim as to inadmissibility of the case on the basis of complementarity.[219]

2.3 Co-operation between national courts and the International Criminal Court[220]

Next to the pre-conditions, the triggering mechanism and the admissibility issues, there are other obstacles to the exercise of the court's jurisdiction. A practical difficulty for the court consists in securing suspects as well as the necessary evidence to try them. The issue of co-operation between national authorities and the ICC goes to the heart of an effective court. The court has no enforcement agencies at its disposal and therefore relies on national authorities to execute arrest warrants, to seize evidentiary material or to compel witnesses to give testimony. Unlike the co-operation obligation imposed by the statutes of both International Tribunals, states have negotiated the detailed mechanism of co-operation between the court and states parties in part nine of the statute. Part nine reflects a state-orientated approach and represents a compromise between the need to have an effective criminal court, on the one hand and states' concern for certain crucial issues, on the other hand. Most of the difficulties arising from this mechanism of co-operation are not particular to the enforcement of individual criminal responsibility for war crimes in internal armed conflicts but are obviously encountered by the court when enforcing responsibility for any of the other crimes of the statute. In order to assess the potential effectiveness of the ICC in prosecuting war crimes in internal armed conflicts, however, it is necessary to explain briefly the main features of co-operation embodied in the statute as well as the limits put on the obligation to co-operate.

2.3.1 The forms of co-operation between the states and the ICC

Article 86 provides for the general obligation of states parties 'to co-operate fully with the Court in its investigation and prosecution of crimes within the jurisdiction of the court'.[221] States, which are not party to the ICC statute, can be invited by the court 'to provide assistance on the basis of an ad hoc agreement, an agreement with such a state or any other basis'.[222] The obligation on states parties to co-operate is further defined in Articles 89 and 93(1), which provide for the arrest and surrender of persons to the court, as well as other forms of co-operation such as the service of documents, the protection of victims and witnesses or the execution of searches and seizures.

Upon receipt of a request by the court for the arrest and surrender of a person, states parties shall comply with such request. Compliance with it, however, should be in accordance with domestic procedural law.[223] In the case of competing requests between the ICC and another state party request, the requested state shall give priority to the ICC's request, if the court has already determined that the case is admissible.[224] A state-orientated approach has been adopted in other cases, where the requested state is free to decide which request to execute.[225] For example, in the case where the requested state is under an existing international obligation to extradite the person to the requesting state (non-party to the statute), it can determine whether to surrender the person to the ICC or to the requesting state.[226]

One may note that the regime of co-operation does not contain any specific rules dealing with the co-operation obligations of non-state entities such as armed groups involved in internal armed conflicts. If such groups are bound to respect the co-operation regime contained in part nine via the state party, are they also entitled to similar treatment to the states parties and can they rely on the various grounds for refusal to co-operate contained in the statute?

The regime of co-operation is further weakened by the absence of any coercive means to enforce co-operation and by the limits on the obligations to co-operate enshrined in the statute.

2.3.2 Consequences of failure to co-operate with the court

What are the consequences of states parties or states who have entered into an agreement with the court failing to fulfil their obligations? What can the ICC do to enforce compliance? On these issues, the statute is laconic to the point of reticence.[227] Article 85(5)(b) and (7) provide for the possibility for the court to make a finding of states' failure to co-operate and to refer the matter to the Assembly of States Parties, or where the Security Council referred the matter to the court, such finding can be referred to the Security Council. The statute does not provide any information about the consequences of a referral to the Security Council. The Security Council could possibly impose, under Article 40 of the UN Charter, temporary measures against the responsible state or even some coercive measure under Article 42.[228] If the matter is referred to the Assembly of States Parties, Article 112(1)(f) of the statute obliges the Assembly only to 'consider any question relating to non-co-operation'. The matter being substantive rather than procedural, any decision taken by the Assembly, if not attained by consensus, will have to be 'approved by a two-thirds majority of those present and voting, provided that an absolute majority of States parties constitutes the quorum for voting'.[229]

The absence of any coercive measures at the court's disposal is particularly worrying in cases of non-co-operation by a state party in internal armed conflicts. The court will find itself toothless if the state party where the internal conflict took place does not co-operate and the Security Council chooses not to take any coercive measures. Similarly, the difficult issue of co-operation between the court and armed groups involved in an internal conflict has not been dealt with in the statute. How is the court to enjoin armed groups involved in internal armed conflicts to co-operate and what can the court do if these groups do not co-operate?

The court may have to develop a strategic view on how it will foster co-operation with states parties and non-state entities and how it will address the issues of non-compliance.

2.3.3 Limits on the obligation to co-operate

Another aspect of the court's chronic weaknesses is illustrated by the various grounds for refusal to co-operate embodied in the statute. The statute does not contain any article entitled per se grounds for refusal to co-operate. However, the general co-operation obligation with the prosecution and investigation of crimes are subject to a number of exceptions detailed in part nine.

With respect to both surrender and other forms of co-operation, the first exception deals with conflicts between the court's request and national proceedings in the requested state.[230] In the case of an ongoing investigation or prosecution in the requested state over a crime different from that to which the request relates, this state may refuse the immediate execution of the request and postpone it for a period of time agreed upon with the court.[231] In the case of parallel national proceedings for the same conduct, the requested state can postpone the execution of the request as long as an admissibility ruling of the ICC is pending.[232]

In both cases envisaged, this exception does not amount to a ground for refusal to co-operate, but simply for postponing co-operation with the court.

A second limitation on co-operation was advanced by a number of common law countries and dealt with special evidentiary requirements in their legal system. Article 91(2)(c) provides that a request for co-operation shall contain such documents, statements or information as may be necessary to meet the requirements for the surrender process in the requested state. Similarly, Article 91(4) provides for consultation between the state party and the court, with the view of informing the court of any specific evidentiary requirement under the national law of the requested state. There again, a process of consultation and negotiation between the court and the requested state is aimed at easing co-operation between the two entities, but ultimately requires the court to respect specific national requirements.

The third ground of refusal, or limitation on the obligation to co-operate, applicable both for surrender and other forms of co-operation, is enshrined in Article 98. It concerns international immunities and other legal conflicts between the international obligations of the requested state towards the ICC, and towards another state under international law.[233] Article 98(1) bars the ICC from requesting a surrender or assistance that would require the requested state to act inconsistently with its obligation under international law with respect to the diplomatic immunity of a person or property of a third state, unless the court can first obtain the consent of the third state for the waiver of the immunity.[234] This article represents the clear submission of the ICC to the sovereignty of third states with respect to state or diplomatic immunities under international law. Furthermore, this provision does not seem easily reconcilable with the provisions contained in Article 27(2), which provides that 'immunities or special procedural rules which may attach to the official capacity of a person, whether under national or international law, shall not bar the Court from exercising its jurisdiction over such a person'. Could this article be relied upon by states parties to the ICC and non-parties alike?[235]

Article 98(2) addresses the issue of the obligation of the requested state towards the state of nationality of a person wanted by the ICC, which requires the consent of that state. The main concern of certain states was to respect the obligations of host states under status-of-forces agreements. Under these agreements, the forces of a sending state can remain under the jurisdiction of that state and not under the jurisdiction of the host state. Paragraph 2 ensures that, unless the ICC can first obtain the consent of the sending state, the court may not request the surrender of a national of that state from the host state. The requested state will therefore not need to fulfil its obligations of co-operation under the statute.[236]

Lastly, with respect to other forms of co-operation than surrender, grounds of refusal based on national law and essential national security interests are included in Article 93(3) and (4). The requested state may invoke, on the basis of Article 93(3), a conflicting 'existing fundamental legal principle of general application'. Such a fundamental principle can be constitutional in character and will trigger consultations between the court and the requested state. If the matter cannot be resolved by consultation, the court will have to modify its request as necessary.[237] The expression used in this article is of the vaguest form and meaning and may be open to abuse by states. Furthermore, Article 93(4) provides another ground for refusal to co-operate, by authorising a state party to deny a request of assistance by the court, if the request concerns the production of any documents or disclosure of evidence which relates to its national security. Article 72 provides for a detailed scheme of consultations and specific measures, whenever states consider their national security interests prejudiced by a disclosure of information to the court.[238] If no solution can be reached, because the state does not act 'in accordance with its obligation under the statute', the court can only determine that fact and refer the matter to the Assembly of States Parties. Ultimately, in cases covered by Articles 98, 93(3) and (4), the court itself has to accommodate concerns of states and can only inform the Assembly of States Parties, or the Security Council, if there is a failure by the state to fulfil its obligations under part nine of the statute.

These limitations on the obligations to co-operate with the court symbolise the state-orientated approach chosen by the drafters of the Rome statute. They also illustrate a certain reluctance of states to enforce effectively individual responsibility for war crimes at the international level. The statute does not contain all the traditional interstate grounds for refusal to co-operate, such as the non-extradition of nationals,[239] but the aspects highlighted here amount to serious weaknesses in the general system of co-operation of states parties with the ICC. Similarly, as noted above, no specific provision or mechanism in the statute regulates the co-operation of non-state entities, such as armed groups in internal armed conflicts, with the court. These weaknesses will certainly hinder the effectiveness of the institution itself in prosecuting war crimes in internal armed conflicts. Can we really expect

tainted governments, who might not have referred their internal situation, to assist the court effectively in its investigations and prosecutions
of war crimes committed in their territory?[240]

2.4. Conclusion and assessment of the first four years of the life of the International Criminal Court

Both the mechanism for establishing the jurisdiction of the court and
the co-operation regime suffer from a considerable number of imperfec-
tions and cast some doubt on the potential effectiveness of the future
ICC to prosecute war crimes committed in internal armed conflicts. As
observed in section 2.2, the application of universal jurisdiction, carefully constrained by the complementarity principle, by the primacy of
national jurisdictions, and by all the other checks and balances in the
statute,[241] was the only way the court could participate effectively in the
fight against impunity in internal armed conflicts. Article 124 weakens
even further the jurisdictional regime of the court together with Security
Council resolution 1422 of 12 July 2002.

Furthermore, the ICC may not be able to deal with large numbers of
investigations. The court may become more of a deterrent than a real
enforcement mechanism. The mere existence of the court and the
principle of complementarity will encourage states to retain domestic
control over prosecuting nationals charged with such crimes. As a direct
result of the existence of the court, a number of states have implemented
national legislation, including the crimes of genocide, crimes against
humanity or war crimes in internal conflicts. As seen in chapter 5, some
states also extended their jurisdiction over such crimes not only when
committed in their territory but also abroad. Since July 2002, the role of
the court in triggering national prosecutions, in order to avoid the court
prosecuting the case itself, is also to be noted.[242]

The first four years of life of the court have, however, proved the
pessimists wrong. The court is not sitting and silently watching war
crimes on a large scale or crimes against humanity being committed. The
office of the Prosecutor has been extremely active in investigating the
situations of Uganda and the DRC, referred directly by the territorial
states themselves as well as the situation in the Darfur region of Sudan
referred to the court by the UN Security Council. The Prosecutor also
analysed seven other potential situations in order to determine whether
to open investigations. Of these known cases, all but one,[243] concerned
alleged crimes committed in internal armed conflicts.

The situation in northern Uganda was referred to the court by the Ugandan Government in December 2003.[244] The decision to open investigations was taken by the Prosecutor in July 2004. Five arrest warrants were issued in July 2005 against members of the LRA, who are charged with crimes against humanity and war crimes, including murder, sexual enslavement, pillaging, rape and the forced enlistment of child soldiers. To date, none of the five members of the LRA has been arrested or surrendered to the court.[245] The Prosecutor conducted sixteen missions in Uganda for the purpose of interviewing witnesses and collecting materials in preparation for the confirmation of the indictments. Pre-Trial Chamber II issued requests for arrest and surrender of the five indictees to the Governments of Uganda, the DRC and the Sudan. Furthermore, Interpol issued red notices for the arrest of the five LRA commanders.[246] Co-operation by states parties as well as the Sudan is crucial in order to assure the transfer of these indictees to the court.

The DRC referred the situation in its country to the court in March 2004 and investigations began in June 2004.[247] The office of the Prosecutor conducted over sixty missions in the region in order to gather evidence and witness testimonies.[248] This led the Prosecutor to submit an application for an arrest warrant to be issued against Thomas Lubanga Dyilo, for having allegedly committed the war crimes of enlisting and conscripting children under the age of fifteen and using them to participate actively in hostilities. The arrest warrant was issued by Pre-Trial Chamber I on 10 February 2006 under seal and then unsealed on 17 March 2006. He was arrested and surrendered to the court by the authorities of the DRC on 17 March 2006, becoming the first ever indictee to be transferred to the ICC. Pre-Trial Chamber I held a hearing to confirm the charges against the accused on 9–28 November 2006. On 29 January 2007, Pre-Trial Chamber I confirmed the charges against the accused. The Chamber found that there was sufficient evidence to establish substantial grounds to believe that Thomas Lubanga Dyilo was criminally responsible as co-perpetrator for the war crimes of enlisting and conscripting children under the age of fifteen years into the FPLC, the military wing of the Union des Patriotes Congolais and using them to participate actively in hostilities in Ituri (DRC) from September 2002 to 13 August 2003. Pre-Trial Chamber I therefore referred the case for trial before a Trial Chamber. The Prosecutor has also been investigating various crimes by a number of armed groups in the Ituri region of the DRC and has opened a second case into crimes committed by another Ituri armed group.

Following the Security Council referral of 31 March 2005, the Prosecutor opened investigations into the Darfur situation on 6 June 2005.[249] The Office of the Prosecutor conducted more than 70 missions to 17 different countries, taking more than 100 formal witness statements and collecting over 8,800 documents. For security reasons, the Prosecutor was not able to conduct investigations in the Darfur region itself. On 14 December 2006, the Prosecutor informed the UN Security Council that he had nearly completed an investigation into a series of incidents that took place in Darfur in 2003 and 2004.[250] He will be putting evidence to the ICC judges and presumably wanting arrest warrants to be issued early in 2007.

The work conducted by the ICC in the first four years of its life calls for a series of remarks. First, the fulfillment of the pre-conditions to the court's jurisdiction contained in Article 12 of the statute did not represent an obstacle to the establishment of the court's jurisdiction. Secondly, the three trigger mechanisms have already been in action: three states parties have referred cases pursuant to Article 13(a); the Security Council has referred one situation to the court pursuant to Article 13(b) and the Prosecutor might initiate an investigation in respect of crimes committed in the territory of a state not party, who has lodged a declaration with the registrar accepting the court's jurisdiction pursuant to Article 12(3).[251] Thirdly, even if the Prosecutor adopted a policy of inviting voluntary referrals from states instead of triggering *proprio motu* cases, increasing therefore the likelihood of co-operation and support by the territorial states, state co-operation in providing evidence and in executing arrest warrants remains a very big challenge for the court. In the case of Thomas Lubanga Dyilo, the challenge was met as he was already detained in the DRC. In the case of the arrest warrants issued against LRA's commanders, the need for co-operation and support from states parties and non-states parties remains of critical importance. The court cannot really function without state co-operation: it can initiate investigations, gather evidence and take witness testimonies. However, it crucially needs the co-operation of the territorial state and the neighbouring states in order to access the place where the crimes were allegedly committed, obtain key evidence and arrest and transfer indictees to the court.[252] The President of the ICC recently affirmed: 'In establishing the ICC, states set up a system designed on two pillars. The Court itself is the judicial pillar. The enforcement pillar belongs to states.'[253]

Fourthly, in every situation under investigation so far, the Prosecutor had to investigate the alleged crimes while an internal armed conflict was ongoing. In the Darfur situations, security issues for the ICC staff and the potential witnesses prevented the Prosecutor from conducting investigations in the region itself. This has undoubtedly made investigations more difficult, lengthy and costly.[254] Furthermore, in the case of Uganda and the DRC, territorial states have referred their ongoing internal armed conflict situation to the court, somehow as a measure of last resort after a decade or more of armed conflict and as a way of escaping the international duty for states to prosecute individuals who would have committed international crimes, a duty reaffirmed in the preamble to the ICC statute.[255] Referring their internal armed conflict to the court is a way of breaking a political deadlock and avoiding taking the political and social risk of trying rebel forces at home.[256] ICC trials could rightly be seen as a depoliticised venue for justice, which would be perceived in the country itself as more independent and impartial than domestic justice.[257] It is unclear, however, whether the court's role to substitute itself for a state otherwise able to conduct judicial proceedings, was envisaged by the drafters of the Rome statute. Do the situations of Uganda and the DRC fall within the definition of complementarity and meet the conditions of admissibility of a case? Nothing seems to prevent states from voluntarily relinquishing jurisdiction in favour of the ICC. One commentator suggests that, if a state has voluntarily relinquished jurisdiction to the ICC and there is therefore no conflict of jurisdiction between the states and the court, the criteria set out in Article 17(2) and (3) would not apply.[258] In order to define more simply the role of the court in comparison to national jurisdictions and to make the court more politically acceptable, the Rome negotiators and most commentators have widely circulated the view that the court will only be able to exercise jurisdiction over crimes where national jurisdictions may be 'unable or unwilling' to judge the perpetrators of such crimes. A closer reading of Article 17(1) reveals, however, that there are four instances in which the court shall determine that a case is inadmissible. A case will be deemed inadmissible when the person has already been investigated or prosecuted by a state, or if the case has been investigated by a state which has decided not to prosecute the person. Alternatively, where such a person has already been tried for the same conduct, or where such a case is not of sufficient gravity to justify further action by the court, the case will also be inadmissible. As a result, if the situation under study does not fit into one of these four categories, the case must be deemed admissible. The definition of inability and unwillingness which then appear in paragraphs 2 and 3 of Article 17, are only relevant when a state has investigated or prosecuted a case (Article 17(1)(a) and (b)). In other words, inability and unwillingness do not represent the only criteria of admissibility of a case. In the case of a voluntary referral of the situation to the court by a state party, an instance not included in the list of Article 17(1), such situation must be deemed to fulfil the criteria of admissibility.[259]

Fifthly, the work of the ICC has had an impact on ongoing armed conflicts such as the armed conflict in northern Uganda.[260] The first five suspects of the LRA have not been surrendered to the court yet, but the issuing of the arrest warrants has had significant impact on the ground. According to the Prosecutor, crimes allegedly committed by the LRA in northern Uganda have decreased and the LRA was forced to leave south Sudan and move its headquarters next to the DRC border. The loss of the LRA's safe heaven in Sudan, has led the LRA to engage in negotiations and to stop hostilities in August 2006.[261] These are compelling signs that the ICC is able to play its role as a deterrent mechanism and ultimately to help achieve peace in the region.[262]

It is too early to assess the impact of the ICC and the long-term role the institution will be able to play in the fight against impunity. However, with a first trial to take place in 2007 and a few other situations under investigation, the ICC has met the challenge of establishing its credibility in the new international world order. Widespread ratification of the statute, as well as the adoption of national implementing legislation on co-operation with the court, should allow the court to meet its objectives of providing justice, deterring international crimes and participating in the establishment of lasting peace in war-torn countries.

Notes

1. Some authors argue that the very first 'international tribunal' which tried individuals for offences committed against civilians during internal disturbances is the International Military Commission established by the British forces in Crete in 1898. See L. Green, 'Criminal responsibility of individuals in non-international conflicts' (2002) 45 *German yearbook of international law* 86–88.
2. The Peace Treaty of Sèvres signed on 10 August 1920 provided that Turkey had to surrender the alleged perpetrators of genocide to the allied powers, who would designate the tribunal which shall try the accused persons, see Articles 226, 228 and 230 of the Sèvres Treaty. On the allied failed attempts to prosecute the alleged perpetrators of genocide against the Armenian people, see V. Dadrian, *The history of the Armenian genocide* (Providence, Oxford: Berghahn books, 1995) pp. 303–16.

3. For this section, see in particular, P. Rowe, 'War crimes and the former Yugoslavia, the legal difficulties' (1993) 32 *Revue de droit militaire et droit de la guerre* 317; F. Lattanzi, 'La répression pénale des crimes du droit international: des juridictions internes aux juridictions internationales' in *Law in humanitarian crises: how can international humanitarian law be made effective in armed conflicts?* (Luxembourg: Office for the official publications of the European Communities, vol. 1, 1995) p. 121; W. J. Fenrick, 'Some international law problems related to prosecutions before the International Criminal Tribunal for the Former Yugoslavia' (1995) 6 *Duke journal of comparative and international law* 103; P. Sob, 'The dynamics of International Criminal Tribunals' (1998) 67 *Nordic journal of international law* 139; D. Sarooshi, 'The powers of the UN International Criminal Tribunals' (1998) 2 *Max Planck yearbook of UN law* p. 141; J. O'Brien, 'The international tribunal for violations of international humanitarian law in the former Yugoslavia' (1993) 67 *AJIL* 639.

4. For this section, see O. Dubois, 'Rwanda's national criminal courts and the International Tribunal' (1997) 828 *IRRC* 717.

5. For the ICTY, see para. 28 of the SG report pursuant to para. 2 of SC resolution 808, UN.Doc.S/25704 (3 May 1993). For the ICTR, see para. 8 of the SG report pursuant to para. 5 of the SC resolution 955, UN.Doc.S/1995/134 (13 February 1995).

6. Hereafter referred to as 'International Tribunals' or 'Tribunals'.

7. See Article 9 of the ICTY statute, and Article 8 of the ICTR statute. However, both statutes provide for the principle *non bis in idem*. This principle provides that no person shall be tried before a national court for violations of international humanitarian law for which they have already been tried by one of the International Tribunals. Both Tribunals might try a case against a person already convicted by a national court, but only under certain conditions, see Article 9.2 of the ICTR statute and Article 10.2 of the ICTY statute. For an overview of the relationship between national courts and the ICTR, see F. Harhoff, 'Consonance or rivalry? Calibrating the efforts to prosecute war crimes in national and international tribunals' (1997) 7 *Duke journal of comparative and international law* 571.

8. See Article 9.2 for the ICTY and Article 8.2 for the ICTR.

9. This obligation is implicit in the general obligation of states to give effect to Security Council resolutions adopted under chapter VII of the UN Charter and is explicitly provided in para. 4 of SC resolution 827, for example.

10. By the end of 2006, the Special Court for Sierra Leone has not issued any judgment. It is therefore too early to assess the work of this international tribunal. However, important decisions issued so far by the Special Court are discussed in chapters 4 and 5 of this book.

11. Six of which are still at large.

12. Eighteen indictees are still at large.

13. See www.ictr.org.

14. The commission noted: 'it must be observed that the violations of the laws of war referred to in article 3 of the statute of the International Tribunal are offences when committed in international, but not in internal armed conflicts'. See final report of the Commission of Experts for the former Yugoslavia established pursuant to SC resolution 780 (1992), UN.Doc.S/1994/674 (5 May 1994) para. 54.

15. *Tadić* jurisdiction, para. 70.

16. See *Tadić* trial, para. 565, *Kordić* trial, para. 29, *Čelebići* trial, paras. 186–89.

17. See *Tadić* trial, paras. 566 and 568, *Kordić* trial, para. 30, *Kunarac* trial, para. 567, *Čelebići* trial, para. 186, *Stakić* trial, para. 572.

18. See *Čelebići* trial, para. 187.

19. See *Čelebići* trial, para. 188, *Milošević* rule 98*bis* decision, paras. 30–31.

20. See *Tadić* trial, para. 567 and *Čelebići* trial, para. 190.

21. See *Milošević* rule 98*bis* decision, paras. 23–24.

22. For more details, see chapter 1, section 1.2 of this book.

23. See *Akayesu* trial, paras. 619–26, *Kayishema* trial, para. 170, *Musema* trial, para. 250, *Rutaganda* trial, paras. 92–93, *Cyangugu* trial, para. 767 (judicial notice of the state of internal armed conflict had been taken in this case), *Semanza* trial, paras. 355 and 514, *Bagilishema* trial, paras. 99–101 or *Kamuhanda* trial, paras. 721–24. In Rwanda, the RPF told the ICRC that it considers itself bound by the Geneva Conventions and their Additional Protocols, see Report of the UN High Commissioner for Human Rights on his mission to Rwanda of 11–12 May 1994, Document E/C.N4/S-3/3, 19 May 1994.

24. See *Akayesu* trial, para. 603. For a commentary, see H. Speiker, 'The International Criminal Court and non-international armed conflicts' (2000) 13 *Leiden journal of international law* 408–9.

25. For a detailed account of the case of the ICTY, see section 2.3 of chapter 1.

26. *Tadić* appeal, para. 84.

27. *Tadić* appeal, para. 132.

28. *Tadić* appeal, para. 131.

29. *Tadić* appeal, para. 131.

30. See the trial judgments in *Aleksovski* (para. 46), *Blaskić* (paras. 94 and 122), *Naletilić* trial (paras. 283–88) and *Kordić* (para. 145) cases and the appeal judgments in *Čelebići* (para. 26), *Aleksovski* (paras. 120–26) and *Kordić* (paras. 299–313).

31. For a detailed study of the ICTY case law on these points, see section 2.3 of chapter 1.

32. These cases are the *Tadić, Blaškić, Aleksovski, Kordić, Naletilić/Martinović, Brdjanin* and *Čelibići* cases.

33. These cases are the *Krstić, Kvočka, Krnojelac, Kunarac, Erdemović, Furundžija, Galić, Kupreškić, Simić, Vasiljević, Stakić, Orić, Limaj, Hadžihasanović, Strugar, Blagojević, Halilović* and *Jelisić* cases.

34. Obviously, the list of crimes for which an individual can be prosecuted is not identical in internal and international conflict.

35. See, for example, *Tadić* trial, para. 615, *Akayesu* trial, para. 629, *Rutaganda* trial, paras. 99–101 and 438, *Musema* trial, paras. 276–81, *Kayishema-Ruzindana* trial, paras. 177–81.

36. *Tadić* trial, para. 615. See also *Akayesu* appeal, para. 438, which defines this category as 'persons who are not taking any active part in the hostilities'; *Naletilić* trial, para. 229; *Čelebići* appeal, para. 420; *Semanza* trial, para. 365 or *Musema* trial, para. 280.

37. *Musema* trial, para. 279.

38. See *Akayesu* appeal, paras. 432–45, *Akayesu* trial, paras. 630–34, 640–43, *Rutaganda* trial, paras. 96–98 and 439, *Musema* trial, paras. 264–75, *Kayishema-Ruzindana* trial, paras. 173–76 and 616–23.

39. *Akayesu* trial, paras. 630–34. This jurisprudence was upheld in the subsequent trial cases: *Rutaganda* trial (paras. 96–98), *Musema* trial (paras. 264–75) and *Kayishema/Ruzindana* trial (paras. 173–76). For a commentary and critique to the *Akayesu* judgment, see D. M. Amann, 'Prosecutor v. Akayesu, Case ICTR-96-4-T, 2 September 1998' (1999) 93 *AJIL* 195–99 at 199.

40. Some authors disagree with this view. R. Arnold believes that one needs to prove the link between the perpetrator and one party to the armed conflict, rather than only a link between the acts of the perpetrator and the armed conflict. A civilian needs to be linked to a party to the conflict if he is to be found responsible for war crime. See R. Arnold, 'The liability of civilians under international humanitarian law's war crimes provisions' (2002) 5 *YbIHL* 344–59.

41. *Akayesu* appeal, para. 443.

42. *Ibid.*, para. 444.

43. See *Tadić* jurisdiction, para. 70, *Kunarac* appeal, paras. 57–59, *Akayesu* appeal, paras. 437–38, 444, *Akayesu* trial, paras. 642–44, *Kayishema-Ruzindana* trial, paras. 188, 602–23, *Musema* trial, paras. 259–60 and 974–75, *Rutaganda* trial, paras. 104–05 and 440–44.

44. See also the recent discussion on this topic in the *Stakić* appeal, paras. 340–49.

45. *Akayesu* trial, para. 643.

46. *Kayishema/Ruzindana* trial, paras. 603 and 623.

47. The ICTR Appeals Chamber in the *Rutaganda* case recalled the necessity of considering a whole number of factors when determining the relationship between the offence and an armed conflict and warned that 'particular care is needed when the accused is a non-combatant'. *Rutaganda* appeal, para. 570.

48. See, for example, *Akayesu* trial, paras. 599–644, *Kayishema* trial, paras. 616 and 623.

49. See *Rutaganda* trial, paras. 86–107; *Kamuhanda* trial, para. 737–44. The Trial Chamber in this case took the view that the 'prosecution has not shown sufficiently how and in what capacity the accused supported the government effort against the RPF. No convincing evidence has been presented to demonstrate that the accused, either in a private capacity or in his role as a civil servant, worked

with the military, actively supported the war effort or that the accused's actions were closely related to the hostilities or committed in conjunction with the armed conflict', *ibid.*, para. 741; *Kayishema* trial, paras. 185–89, 599–602 and 623; *Ntakirutimana* trial, para. 861.

50. Akayesu, Kayishema, Ruzindana, Musema, and Rutuganda have all been found not guilty for violations of Article 4 of the ICTR statute by Trial Chambers. On 26 May 2003, the ICTR Appeals Chamber reversed the acquittal of Rutaganda for violations of common Article 3 and Additional Protocol II. Just before this judgment, Trial Chamber III found that the nexus was established between the perpetrator and the accused in the *Semanza* case, see *Semanza* trial, paras. 516–22.

51. See *Rutaganda* appeal, para. 577, see also para. 579.

52. See *Semanza* trial, paras. 511–22; *Semanza* appeal, paras. 365–71 and *Cyangugu* trial, paras. 793 and 802.

53. *Tadić* jurisdiction decision, para. 134.

54. *Hadžihasanović* appeal decision on command responsibility, para. 12.

55. For the war crime of murder committed in internal armed conflict, see *Krstić* trial, paras. 484–89; *Tadić* trial, paras. 609–13; *Vasiljević* trial, para. 205; *Krnojelac* trial, para. 324; *Kupreškić* trial, paras. 560–61; *Jelisić* trial, para. 35; *Čelibići* trial, paras. 422 and 439; *Stakić* trial, paras. 584–87; *Rutaganda* trial, para. 79 (acquitted at trial but convicted for war crime on appeal, para. 584); *Semanza* trial, paras. 353, 535 and 551; *Blagojević* trial, para. 556 and *Strugar* trial, paras. 235–46.

56. For the war crime of torture committed in internal armed conflict, see *Furundžija* appeal, para. 11; *Kunarac* appeal, paras. 142–56; *Kvočka* appeal, para. 284; *Kunarac* trial, paras. 465–97; *Krnojelac* trial, paras. 177–88 and *Furundžija* trial, paras. 134–64.

57. For the war crime of cruel treatment committed in internal armed conflict, see *Tadić* trial, paras. 609–13 and *Strugar* trial, para. 261.

58. For the war crime of outrage upon personal dignity committed in internal armed conflict, see *Aleksovski* trial, paras. 47–57; *Kunarac* trial, paras. 498–514 and *Kunarac* appeal, paras. 161–66.

59. For the war crime of rape committed in internal armed conflict, see *Kunarac* trial, paras. 436–64; *Kunarac* appeal, paras. 127–33; *Furundžija* trial, paras. 165–89 and *Semanza* trial, para. 551.

60. For the war crime of slavery committed in internal armed conflict, see *Krnojelac* trial, para. 353. The Trial Chamber held in this case: 'the express prohibition of slavery in Additional Protocol II of 1977, which relates to internal armed conflict, confirms the conclusion that slavery is prohibited by customary international humanitarian law outside the context of a crime against humanity'.

61. For the war crime of pillage or plunder committed in internal armed conflict, see in particular *Čelibići* trial, para. 315 and *Hadžihasanović* trial, paras. 49–56.

62. For the war crime of attacks against the civilian population committed in internal armed conflict, see *Galić* trial, paras. 56–62; *Prosecutor v. Pavle Strugar, Miodrag*

Jokić and others, decision on interlocutory appeal, 22 November 2002, IT-01-42-AR72, para. 10 and *Strugar* trial, paras. 220–22.

63. For the war crime of wanton destruction of cities not justified by military necessity committed in internal armed conflicts, see *Hadžihasanović* trial, paras. 39–48; *Hadšihasanović* rule 98*bis* decision, paras. 95–107; *Strugar* trial, paras. 227–28 and 233 and *Orić* trial, paras. 579–89.

64. For the war crime of attacks on civilians objects committed in internal armed conflicts, see *Strugar* trial, paras. 223–26. The Trial Chamber in the *Strugar* case noted the absence of the prohibition of attacks against civilian objects in additional Protocol II but affirmed that such violation triggered individual criminal responsibility in customary international law nonetheless. (*Strugar* trial, para. 224)

65. For the war crime of seizure or destruction or wilful damage done to institutions dedicated to religion, see *Hadžihasanović* trial, paras. 57–64 and *Strugar* trial, paras. 229–33.

66. Forms of liability will not be studied in detail in this book. Many articles or books are dedicated to this particular subject; in relation to the case law of the ICTY/ICTR, see in particular, G. Mettraux, *International crimes and the ad hoc tribunals* (Oxford: Oxford University Press, 2005) pp. 269–95.

67. *Krnojelac* trial, para. 80. See also *Tadić* appeal, paras. 195–226; *Krnojelac* appeal, paras. 28–32 or *Vasiljević* appeal, paras. 96–98. For a critical analysis of this concept, see Mettraux, *International crimes and the ad hoc tribunals*, pp. 287–93.

68. For a detailed study of this principle under the case law of the tribunals, see Mettraux, *International crimes and the ad hoc tribunals*, pp. 296–310.

69. See the *Hadžihasanović* command responsibility appeal decision, paras. 11–31. For a commentary on this decision, see C. Greenwood, 'Command responsibility and the Hadžihasanović decision' (2004) 2 *JICJ* 598–605.

70. *Ibid.*, para. 13.

71. See *ibid.*, paras. 14–17.

72. *Ibid.*, para. 16.

73. *Ibid.*, para. 18.

74. *Ibid.*, para. 20.

75. The Chamber held that command responsibility was part of customary international law relating to international armed conflict before the adoption of Protocol I. *Ibid.*, para. 29.

76. For duress, necessity and superior orders see the *Erdemović* trial judgment. For the permissibility of cumulative charging and cumulative convictions, see *Čelibići*, *Kunarac* and *Musema* appeal jugments. On these points, see W. Fenrick, 'The development of the law of armed conflict through the jurisprudence of the ICTY' in M. Schmitt (ed.), *The law of military operations, lieber americorum Professor J. Grunawalt*, International Law Studies vol. 72 (Newport, Rhode Island: Naval War College, 1998) p. 77; S. Murphy, 'Progress and jurisprudence of the ICTY' (1999) 93 *AJIL* 57 and Mettraux, *International crimes and the ad hoc tribunals*, pp. 315–42.

77. In 1994, only forty lawyers remained in the country. Since 1997, national jurisdictions in Rwanda have dealt with 5,000–6,000 cases. See R. Sezibera, 'The only way to bring justice to Rwanda' published in the *Washington Post* on 7 April 2002.

78. On this last point, see R. Kolb, 'The jurisprudence of the Yugoslav and Rwandan criminal tribunals on their jurisdiction and on international crimes' (2000) *BYIL* 257 and T. Meron, 'Reflections on the prosecutions of war crimes by international tribunals' (2006) 100 *AJIL* 551–79.

79. Article 3 of the ICTY statute reads: 'The International Tribunal shall have the power to prosecute persons violating the laws or customs or war. Such violations shall include, but not be limited to: . . .'

80. Report of the Secretary-General pursuant to para. 2 of Security Council resolution 808 (3 May 1993) para. 34.

81. *Tadić* jurisdiction decision, para. 89.

82. This condition subsumed two requirements: (i) the violation must constitute an infringement of a rule of international humanitarian law and (ii) the violation must be serious. See *Tadić* jurisdiction decision, para. 94.

83. *Ibid.*, para. 94.

84. *Hadžihasanović* command responsibility appeal decision, para. 55.

85. See *Vasiljević* trial, paras. 193–204. The Trial Chamber found that the crime of violence to life and person was not 'defined with sufficient clarity under customary international law for its general nature, its criminal character and its approximate gravity to have been sufficiently foreseeable and accessible' (para. 201). The Trial Chamber was not satisfied that such offence gave rise to individual criminal responsibility under customary international law (para. 203).

86. Other Trial Chambers had hinted before that they could apply international agreements or conventions, see, for example, *Blaškić* trial, para. 169.

87. See *Galić* trial, paras. 63–138. For a commentary on this decision, see G. Mettraux, *International crimes and the ad hoc criminal tribunals*, pp. 7–10.

88. Article 51 of Additional Protocol I was applicable between the parties through an agreement signed under the auspices of the ICRC. Parties to the conflict in Bosnia-Herzegovina signed an agreement on 22 May 1992, which provided for some provisions of Additional Protocol I to be applicable between the parties and for the punishment of those responsible in case of violation.

89. In para. 22 of the *Galić* trial judgment, the Trial Chamber stated that it 'does not deem it necessary to decide on the qualification of the conflict in and around Sarajevo'. The indictment did not contain Article 2 charges on grave breaches and the Prosecutor did not plead that the conflict was international. With all due respect to the Trial Chamber's reasoning, the only conclusion that can be drawn from this, is that the armed conflict in and around Sarajevo was an internal armed conflict, for the purpose of this trial. It is crucial to determine in which type of conflict, international or non-international, the crimes were committed, in order to be able to determine the law applicable.

90. *Galić* appeal, para. 83.

91. *Blaškić* appeal, para. 141. See also *Ojdanić* appeal decision of 21 May 2003, para. 9, where the Appeals Chamber declared that: 'the Tribunal only has jurisdiction over a listed crime in the statute if that crime was recognised as such under customary international law at the time it was allegedly committed'. See also *Čelibići* appeal, para. 178 and *Hadžihasanović* command responsibility appeal decision, para. 55.

92. The task of the Tribunals is particularly tricky, as the state of customary law must be established at the time the offences took place. The Tribunals cannot rely on the many instances of state practice and *opinio juris* that were expressed during the negotiations of the ICC statute.

93. *Tadić* jurisdiction decision, para. 99.

94. See the insightful discussion of this issue by Mettraux, *International crimes and the ad hoc tribunals*, pp. 13–18.

95. See *Erdemović* appeal, paras. 46–55 and the dissenting opinion of Judge Cassese paras. 13–55.

96. *Galić* appeal, paras. 81–98.

97. Separate and partially dissenting opinion of Judge Schomburg, para. 4. In his view, the practice highlighted in the Appeals Chamber's judgment cannot be viewed as evidence of extensive and virtually uniform state practice; see paras. 8–22. Judge Schomburg notes also that the Appeals Chamber should have been more explicit in its view that customary law reflected the crime in question in both international and internal armed conflicts (para. 16). In his view, 'one cannot conscientiously base a conviction in criminal matters on a continuing trend of nations criminalising terror as a method of warfare' (footnote omitted, para. 21).

98. See *Akayesu* trial, para. 598 and *Čelibići* trial, para. 479.

99. See *Furundžija* trial, para. 185 and *Kunarac* trial, para. 460.

100. For the Kunarac Trial Chamber, the absence of consent is an element of the crime, while Trial Chambers in the Akayesu, Čelibići, Furundžija and Kvočka cases found that the act needed to be committed 'on a person under circumstances that are coercive' or 'by coercion or force or threat of force against the victim or a third person'. In all these examples, Trial Chambers set out to determine the content of customary law at the time of the commission of the offence.

101. See *Kunarac* appeal, paras. 127–33.

102. See *Furundžija* trial, para. 161 and *Čelibići* trial, para. 459.

103. *Furundžija* appeal, para. 111.

104. *Kunarac* appeal, paras. 145–48. The Appeals Chamber took the view that the first statement of the Chamber in Furundžija 'is tantamount to a statement that the definition of torture in the Torture Convention reflects customary international law as far as the obligation of States is concerned' but this must be 'distinguished from an assertion that this definition wholly reflects customary international law regarding the meaning of the crime of torture generally'. (see para. 148)

105. *Naletilić* appeal, para. 116 and *Kordić* appeal, para. 311.
106. *Tadić* appeal, para. 64, *Rutaganda* appeal, para. 22.
107. In the *Tadić* jurisdiction decision, the Appeals Chamber cited only four military manuals, two domestic criminal codes, two Security Council resolutions, and the case law of Nigerian rebels and members of the Federal Army taken to court for violations of international humanitarian law, before concluding that individual criminal responsibility for war crimes in internal armed conflicts was reflected in customary law (see chapter 4 in this book). As to the crime of outrages of human dignity, see in the *Aleksovski* trial judgment (paras. 47–57) the quasi-absence of any demonstration of the existence of a customary norm establishing the criminality of this conduct. In the *Blaškić* trial judgment, the Trial Chamber recalls that 'violations of Article 3 of the statute ... are by definition serious violations of international humanitarian law within the meaning of the statute. They are thus *likely* to incur individual criminal responsibility in accordance with article 7 of the statute' (para. 176, emphasis added). The Trial Chamber concludes that customary international law imposes criminal responsibility for serious violations of common Article 3 and determines the constitutive elements of the offences, whilst providing hardly any basis for such findings (paras. 179–87). See also *Kordić* trial, paras. 165–69 and *Prosecutor v. Pavle Strugar et al.*, case IT-01-42-AR72, decision on interlocutory appeal (22 November 2002), in which the Appeals Chamber affirms that customary international law establishes that attacks on civilians and unlawful attacks on civilian objects entail individual criminal responsibility, without citing any supportive materials for such findings.
108. A commentator has taken the view that 'the natural tendency of the Tribunals will be to postulate custom whenever possible in order to bypass the jurisdictional obstacle'. See R. Kolb, 'The jurisprudence of the Yugoslav and Rwandan criminal tribunals on their jurisdiction and on international crimes' (2000) *BYIL* 257, 262. This author believes that 'a real analysis of the elements of custom is in effect unimaginable within the compass of the task of the Tribunals' 263. See also, R. Kolb, 'The jurisprudence of the Yugoslav and Rwandan criminal tribunals on their jurisdiction and on international crimes 2000–2004' (2004) *BYIL* 269–97.
109. On these issues, see Mettraux, *International crimes and the ad hoc tribunals*, pp. 13–18. Mettraux rightly points out that 'a statement that a norm is customary is therefore only ever as good as the explanation referred to by the court in support of its finding to that effect' p. 15.
110. Separate and partially dissenting opinion of Judge Schomburg, *Galić* appeal, para. 21.
111. See in general, R. Cryer, *Prosecuting international crimes* (Cambridge: Cambridge University Press, 2005) pp. 132–42; R. Kerr, *The International Criminal Tribunal for the former Yugoslavia, an exercise in law, politics and diplomacy* (Oxford: Oxford University Press, 2004) pp. 115–74.
112. On the difficulties encountered by ICTY investigators, see for example, M. B. Harmon and F. Gaynor, 'Prosecuting massive crimes with primitive

tools: three difficulties encountered by prosecutors in international criminal proceedings' (2004) 2 *JICJ* 403–26, 405–8.

113. SFOR in Bosnia has been acting as an 'international police force' in gathering information and arresting war criminals. The study of the legal basis for multinational forces to arrest persons indicted by the Tribunals is, however, beyond the scope of this book. The inability of the Tribunals to secure the arrest of indicted persons has been and remains a crucial issue. See Harmon and Gaynor, 'Prosecuting massives crimes with primitive tools' 408–12.

114. See in particular, G. Sluiter, 'Obtaining evidence for the ICTY: an overview and assessment of domestic implementing legislation' (1998) *NILR* 87 and F. Hampson, 'The ICTY and the reluctant witness' (1998) 47 *ICLQ* 50.

115. See in particular, R.Wedgwood, 'The International Criminal Tribunal and sub-poenas for state documents' in Schmitt and Green (eds.), *The law of armed conflicts into the next millenium*, vol. 71 (Newport, Rhode Island: Naval War College, 1998) p. 483.

116. These obligations are further defined in the rules of procedure and evidence, for the ICTY, for example, see rules 8–10, 40 and 56.

117. As of 1 December 2006.

118. As of 1 December 2006, a further sixteen defendants surrendered to The Hague Tribunal and the remaining nineteen were arrested and detained by SFOR. For more details on arrests by national authorities, see Kerr, *The International Criminal Tribunal for the former Yugoslavia*, pp. 148–53.

119. See S. O'Shea, 'Interaction between international criminal tribunals and national legal systems' (1995–96) 28 *International law and politics* 393. Croatia co-operated more completely with the Tribunal after the death of the president F. Tudjman. In the thirteenth report of the ICTY to the Security Council, the Prosecutor qualified the co-operation of the Government of Croatia as 'swift and satisfactory', see thirteenth annual report of the ICTY to the Security Council, UN.Doc.S/2006/666 (21 August 2006) para. 77.

120. On the consequences on an international trial of the absence of co-operation by a state, see Harmon and Gaynor, 'Prosecuting massive crimes with primitive tools' 414–18.

121. The French Ministry of Defence has often refused to send their soldiers to give evidence or testify as witnesses in front of the ICTY. See Kerr, *The International Criminal Tribunal for the former Yugoslavia*, p. 129. In November 2006, French soldiers were allowed to testify before the ICTR under special and rather restrictive conditions.

122. Not one of the forty-eight publicly indicted war criminals residing in the territory of the Bosnian Serb entity has been transferred to the ICTY.

123. On 11 April 2002, the Federal Government of Yugoslavia passed the Law on co-operation of the FRY with the ICTY, announcing therefore a possible change

of policy. Ranko Češić was transferred to The Hague after being arrested by the Serb authorities on 17 June 2002. In the thirteenth annual report of the ICTY to the Security Council, the Prosecutor takes the view that the co-operation by the Government of Serbia 'is not complete, consistent or expeditious', UN.Doc.S/ 2006/666 (21 August 2006) para. 79. In the past years, no progress was made to arrest and transfer the six indicted persons still at large, all of whom have connections with Serbia. *Ibid.*, para. 79.

124. Reported by G. K. McDonald, 'Problems, obstacles and achievements of the ICTY' (2004) 2 *JICJ* 558–71, 563.

125. See Kerr, *The International Criminal Tribunal for the former Yugoslavia*, pp. 154–69.

126. Thirteenth annual report of the ICTY to the Security Council, UN.Doc.S/2006/ 666 (21 August 2006) para. 85.

127. As of 1 December 2006.

128. In February 2002, the ICTR Registrar asked the Government of the DRC to hand over sixty Rwandans believed to have planned the genocide. To date, two indictees have been transferred to Arusha.

129. For a case of failure to co-operate with the ICTR, see G. Sluiter, 'To co-operate or not to co-operate? The case of the failed transfer of Ntakirutimana to the Rwanda Tribunal' (1998) 11 *Leiden journal of international law* 383.

130. At regular intervals, the ICTR has also faced hostilities and lack of co-operation from both associations of victims in Rwanda or the Rwandan Government itself. The first rupture between the ICTR and the Rwandan Government took place in November 1999 when the Appeals Chamber attempted to free Barayagwiza for serious violations of his human rights prior to his arrival in the ICTR detention facilities. A few months later, the Appeals Chamber revisited and overturned its first ruling. See *Prosecutor v. Barayagwiza*, ICTR-97-19-AR72, decision (19 November 1999) and decision (Prosecutor's request for review or reconsideration) (31 March 2000).

131. See Eleventh annual report of the ICTR, UN.Doc.S/2006/658 (16 August 2006).

132. See Article 103 of the UN Charter. See O. Swaak-Goldman, 'Recent developments in international criminal law: trying to stay afloat between scylla and charybdis' (2005) 54 *ICLQ* 691–704. Also Article 25 of the UN Charter provides that all member and non-member states are legally bound to carry out decisions of the Security Council under chapter VII.

133. See SC resolutions 827 (25 May 1993) and 955 (8 November 1994).

134. See rules 7*bis*, 11, 13, 59 and 61 of the rules of procedure and evidence.

135. The rules are silent on what happens after the matter is brought to the attention of the Security Council. It might take action to force compliance, such as economic sanctions or military action.

136. See McDonald, 'Problems, obstacles and achievements of the ICTY' 562–67.

137. See for example, SC resolution 1120 (4 July 1997) on the failure of Croatia to co-operate fully with the ICTY or SC resolution 1207 (17 November 1998) on the

failure of the SFRY to execute arrest warrants. For a thorough study of this subject, see D. Mundis, 'Reporting non-compliance: rule 7*bis*' in R. May *et al.* (eds.), *Essays on ICTY procedure and evidence in honour of Gabrielle Kirk McDonald* (The Hague: Kluwer Law International, 2001) pp. 421–38; L. F. Damrosh, 'Criminal actions in national and international tribunals' (1997) 269 *Recueil des cours* 236; D. Orentlicher *et al.*, *Making justice work: the report of the Century Foundation* (New York: Century Foundation Press, 1998) p. 11; Hammon and Gaynor, 'Prosecuting massive crimes with primitive tools' 419–21 and G. K. McDonald, 'Problems, obstacles and achievements of the ICTY' 562–67. In his article, Judge McDonald took the view that reporting non-compliance to the Security Council 'has never truly worked because the Security Council has failed to respond in a meaningful way', 562.

138. See the excellent article by J. Maogoto, 'The International Criminal Tribunal for Rwanda: a paper umbrella in the rain? Initial pitfalls and brighter prospects' (2004) 73 *Nordic journal of international law* 187–221.

139. See the Appeals Chamber's judgment on the request of the Republic of Croatia for a review of the decision of Trial Chamber II of 18 July 1997 (29 October 1997) paras. 38 and 43.

140. *Ibid.*, para. 26.

141. See in the *Blaškić* case, judgment on the request of the Republic of Croatia for a review of the decision of Trial Chamber II of 18 July 1997 (29 October 1997) paras. 25–34.

142. Articles 18(2) and 17(2) of both statutes give the Prosecutor the power to 'question suspects, victims and witnesses, to collect evidence and to conduct on-site investigations' without the consent of the state concerned. This is not always easily carried out. In 1999, the Socialist Federal Republic of Yugoslavia (SFRY) refused to allow the ICTY prosecutor into Kosovo to investigate.

143. On these issues, see F. Harhoff, 'Legal and practical problems in the international prosecution of individuals' (2000) 69 *Nordic journal of international law* 53–61.

144. Another practical problem related to international trials is the protection afforded to protected witnesses. It is logistically difficult to bring anyone to testify without their domestic environment knowing that they testified before the international tribunal. Furthermore, the protection of these witnesses from reprisals after their return is almost impossible.

145. K. Oellers-Frahm, 'Co-operation; the indispensable prerequisite to the efficiency of International Criminal Tribunals' (1995) *ASIL Proceedings* p. 304.

146. In this respect, see L. Arbour, 'The crucial years' (2004) 2 *JICJ* 396–402.

147. It is well known that the day after Milošević was transferred to The Hague, $1.3 billion worth of aid was pledged to the SFRY. See Kerr, *The International Criminal Tribunal for the former Yugoslavia*, p. 125.

148. See Kerr, *The International Criminal Tribunal for the former Yugoslavia*, p. 123. The prospect of European Union membership has also been a powerful incentive for the Balkan States to co-operate with the ICTY.

149. If a state fails to execute a warrant of arrest, the Prosecutor can start a procedure under rule 61, in order to seek in open court a confirmation by the Trial Chamber that there are reasonable grounds for believing that the accused has committed all or any of the crimes charged in the indictment. If the Chamber is so satisfied, it will confirm the indictment and issue an international arrest warrant. Such a procedure has the advantage of publicly branding an accused as an 'international fugitive' and establishing a sort of 'public record of atrocities.' See Oellers-Frahm, *ibid.* and O'Shea, 'Interaction between international criminal tribunals and national legal systems' 395. This procedure has been used in six cases so far. These decisions appear in vol. 108 of the *International Law Reports.* See also G. K. McDonald, 'Problems, obstacles and achievements of the ICTY' 560–62.

150. At the end of 1999, former President McDonald wrote to the Security Council: 'As I have stressed repeatedly in reporting such non-compliance to the Security Council, the Tribunal is at the mercy of the international community for enforcement of its orders. The Tribunal lacks coercive mechanisms and must rely on the international community to give effect to its arrest warrants and other orders', reproduced in *ICTY Yearbook* 1999, 209–10.

151. Kerr, *The International Criminal Tribunal for the former Yugoslavia*, p. 128.

152. Hammon and Gaynor, 'Prosecuting massive crimes with primitive tools' 418.

153. R. Zacklin, 'The failings of ad hoc international tribunals' (2004) 2 *JICJ* 545. For a different view, see D. Wippman, 'The costs of international justice' (2006) 100 *AJIL* 861–87.

154. *Ibid.*, 543.

155. C. P. Romano, 'The price of international justice' (2005) 4 *Law and practice of international courts and tribunals* 281–328, 296.

156. The Special Court for Sierra Leone is financed through voluntary contributions rather than through the UN general or peacekeeping budget. This factor created some delays in setting up the court and might impact on its efficiency and life time. See Cryer, *Prosecuting international crimes*, p. 64.

157. On these issues, see A. Cassese, 'The ICTY: a living and vital reality' (2004) 2 *JICJ* 585–97.

158. The ICTY President reported to the General Assembly in October 2006 that a working group on speeding up appeals and trials had been created. Judges studied their respective reports and substantial amendments to the rules of procedure and evidence were made. See address of Judge Fausto Pocar, President of the ICTY to the UN General Assembly, ICTY press release No. MO/1121e annex (9 October 2006).

159. The pre-trial judge shall 'ensure that the proceedings are not unduly delayed and shall take any measure necessary to prepare for a fair and expeditious trial' (rule 65*ter*B). They will establish work plans which set deadlines on the parties to disclose materials, reach agreements on agreed facts and file their written briefs as early as possible. In April 2006, rules were also amended to allow for a pre-trial

judge to be one of the judges to sit on the trial. This judge takes increased measures to prepare the case for trial efficiently and encourages the Prosecutor to focus her case and to limit the presentation of her evidence. See address of Judge Fausto Pocar to the UN General Assembly, ICTY press release (9 October 2006).

160. The ICTY rule 92*bis* provides for the admission of written statements and transcripts in lieu or oral testimony when the testimony of that witness goes to proof of a matter other than the acts and conduct of the accused as charged in the indictment. Under the newly adopted rule 92*ter*, a Trial chamber can admit evidence from a witness that proves the acts and conduct of the accused as charged in the indictment, if the witness is present in court, available for cross-examination and if the witness attests that the written statement in question accurately reflects his declaration. On these issues, see S. Bourgon, 'Procedural problems hindering expeditious and fair justice' (2004) 2 *JICJ* 526–32.

161. Judges have amended rule 73*bis* to authorise Trial Chambers either to invite or direct the Prosecutor to select those counts in the indictment on which to proceed. There is a strong willingness on the part of the judges to place limits upon the Prosecutor's cases and to narrow the breadth and scope of her indictments. See address of Fausto Pocar, President of the ICTY to the General Assembly, press release (9 October 2006). The President also noted the strong opposition by the Prosecutor to this amendment.

162. More recently, Security Council resolution 1660 (28 February 2006) provides for the appointment of *ad litem* reserve judges to the three largest trials of multi-accused. This would prevent delays that could be caused by the inability of one judge to continue sitting on a case.

163. See rule 65 of the ICTY rules of procedure and evidence.

164. On 17 November 2006, the ICTY decided to transfer the case of Vladimir Kovacevic to the Republic of Serbia. It is the first time that an ICTY indicted person's case is referred to Serbia. See *Prosecutor v. Vladimir Kovacević*, case IT-01-42/2-I, decision on referral pursuant to rule 11*bis* (17 November 2006).

165. On 14 November 2006, the special war crimes chamber of the High Court of Bosnia gave its judgment in the case of Radovan Stankovic. Stankovic was the first ICTY indictee whose case was transferred to the national courts of Bosnia under rule 11*bis*. He was found guilty of crimes against humanity of rape and sentenced to sixteen years' imprisonment. See ICTY press release JP/MOW/1126e (14 November 2006).

166. These will be five persons actually detained in Arusha and twelve indictees still at large.

167. See letter dated 29 May 2006 from the ICTR President to the President of the Security Council, UN.Doc.S/2006/358 (1 June 2006) para. 39. Some concerns remain, however, as to whether Rwanda as well as other African countries can conduct fair and independent trials. Furthermore, the state to which the case is transferred needs to have the adequate national legislation to try the person for

the crimes for which he has been indicted by the ICTR. The ICTR Appeals Chamber confirmed the refusal to transfer Michel Bagaragaza to Norway on 30 August 2006, because its legislation did not cover the crime of genocide. See *Prosecutor v. Michel Bagaragaza*, ICTR-05-86-Ar11*bis*, decision on rule 11*bis* appeal (30 August 2006).

168. This is certainly the case for Bosnia-Herzegovina. In Rwanda, however, there does not seem to be anything in place in order to enhance the capabilities of the Rwandan justice system to provide a fair and impartial trial to these alleged criminals.

169. There will also be an obvious imbalance between the special war crimes chamber of the high court of Bosnia-Herzegovina, which is both financially and technically supported by the international community and Rwanda, if nothing is done to help the latter provide an impartial trial to these accused.

170. See. L. Johnson, 'Ten years: reflections on the drafting' (2004) 2 *JICJ* 378.

171. J. Maogoto, 'The ICTR: a paper umbrella in the rain? Initial pitfalls and brighter prospects' (2004) *Nordic journal of international law* 187–221, 196.

172. On these points, see Maogoto, *ibid.*, 196–207.

173. See Maogoto, *ibid.*, 203. In 1996, a special chamber to try the genocide cases was created in Rwanda, but by 2003 it has only been able to deal with about 5,000. Since 2003, the traditional *Gacaca* system has been adopted in order to deal with low-level accused. It might be the beginning of a solution in order to deal with the astronomical numbers of individuals jailed in Rwanda since 1994 and form the basis of a possible reconciliation within Rwandan society.

174. In this respect, International Criminal Tribunals should try only high-level perpetrators. War criminals, who receive sentences of less than ten years, might not have necessitated a costly international trial and national courts should undertake such trials.

175. UN.Doc.A/CONF.183/C.1/L.76/ Add.1. Hereafter referred to either as 'ICC' or 'the court'.

176. Statement of the UN Secretary-General Kofi Annan at the closing ceremony of the Rome conference (18 July 1998).

177. See on these points, H. von Hebel and D. Robinson, 'Crimes within the jurisdiction of the court' in R. Lee (ed.), *The International Criminal Court, the making of the Rome statute* (The Hague, Boston: Kluwer Law International, 1999) pp. 103–5.

178. See chapter 4 for a detailed study of the ICC jurisdiction.

179. Article 8.2.b) contains twenty-six offences whereas Article 8.2.e) has only twelve.

180. Certain states, including India, France and the USA, had expressed the wish to see the categories of crimes against humanity and of war crimes subject to an opt-in regime. See the US proposal for an opt-in protocol, UN.Doc.A/CONF.183/C.1/L.90.

181. Article 124 of the ICC statute.

182. This transitional provision does not specify any possibility for renewal. The article will be reviewed at the review conference, which should take place seven

years after the entry into force of the statute. If no renewal is possible, this provision should not, in the long term, damage in a durable way the jurisdiction of the court.

183. See the preamble to the ICC statute.

184. Article 1 of the ICC statute.

185. See section 1.2 of chapter 4 for more details.

186. For example, the USA tabled a proposal which required the cumulative consent of the territorial state and the state of nationality of the accused. This requirement can be traced back to Article 27 of the 1953 draft statute for an international criminal court elaborated by the 1953 Committee on International Criminal Jurisdiction (see GA Official Records, IX, Supp. 12 A/2645, 23–26, 1954). The Republic of Korea wanted the court to obtain consent from one or more of the interested states in order to exercise jurisdiction, i.e. the territorial state, the custodial state, the state of nationality of the accused or the state of nationality of the victim. For a detailed study of all proposals during the Rome conference, see E. La Haye, 'The jurisdiction of the ICC: controversies over the preconditions for exercising its jurisdiction' (1999) 46 *NILR* 1; S. A. Williams, 'The Rome statute on the ICC – universal jurisdiction or state consent to make or break the package deal' in M. Schmitt (ed.), *International law across the spectrum of conflict: essays in honour of Professor L. C. Green on the occasion of his eightieth birthday* (Newport, Rhode Island: Naval War College, 2000), vol. 75, pp. 539–63.

187. One of the reasons behind the USA's fierce opposition to the ICC is the adoption of Article 12 of the statute. The USA has been arguing since 1998 that this article extends the jurisdiction of the ICC over nationals of non-state parties. The literature on this issue is extensive, see for example, D. Scheffer, 'The United States and the ICC' (1999) 93 *AJIL* 12; R. Wedgwood, 'The ICC: an American view' (1999) 10 *EJIL* 93; La Haye 'The jurisdiction of the ICC' 1; L. A. Casey and D. B. Rivkin, 'The Rome statute's unlawful application to non-state parties' (2003) 44 *Virginia journal of international law* 63–89; F. Megret, 'Epilogue to an endless debate: the ICC's third party jurisdiction and the looming revolution of international law' (2001) 12 *EJIL* 247–68 or R. Alter, 'International criminal law: a bittersweet year for supporters and critics of the ICC' (2003) 37 *The international lawyer* 541–50.

188. As to the concept of nationality, see Z. Deen-Racsmany, 'The nationality of the offender and the jurisdiction of the International Criminal Court' (2001) 95 *AJIL* 606–23.

189. See Alter, 'International criminal law: a bittersweet year for supporters and critics of the ICC' 545.

190. This could be done pursuant to Article 12(3) of the statute. The Ivory Coast, a state not party to the statute, lodged a declaration of acceptance of the jurisdiction of the court pursuant to Article 12(3) of the statute in February 2005. On the

application of Article 12(3) in practice, see C. Stahn, M. El Zeidy and H. Olasolo, 'The ICC's ad hoc jurisdiction revisited' (2005) 99 *AJIL* 421–31; S. Freeland, 'How open should the door be? – Declarations by non-states parties under Article 12(3) of the Rome statute of the ICC' (2006) 75 *Nordic journal of international law* 211–41 and C. Stahn, 'Why some doors may be closed already: second thoughts on a case by case treatment of Article 12(3) declarations' (2006) 75 *Nordic journal of international law* 243–48.

191. There is one exception to this proposition: a state may find the court exercising its jurisdiction over a situation which took place on its soil, if such a situation has been referred to the court by the Security Council under chapter VII of the UN Charter. Such a referral requires the adoption of a chapter VII resolution with the positive vote of nine members of the Security Council and the absence of a veto.

192. In December 2003, Uganda referred the long-lasting internal armed conflict of northern Uganda to the court. In April 2004, the DRC referred the situation on its territory since July 2002 to the court. Lastly, in December 2004, the Government of the Republic of Central Africa referred the situation on its territory to the court.

193. See UN Security Council resolution 1593 (31 March 2005) in which the Council 'decides to refer the situation in Darfur since 1 July 2002 to the Prosecutor' of the ICC.

194. See the report of the ICC Prosecutor to the fifth session of the Assembly of States Parties on 23 November 2006, p. 5. Available online on www.icc-cpi.int.

195. Article 13 reads: 'The Court may exercise its jurisdiction with respect to a crime referred to in article 5 of the statute if:

– A situation in which one or more of such crimes appears to have been committed is referred to the prosecutor by a State Party;
– A situation in which one or more of such crimes appears to have been committed is referred to the prosecutor by the Security Council acting under chapter VII of the Charter of the United Nations;
– The prosecutor has initiated an investigation in respect of such a crime in accordance with article 15.'

196. In December 2003, Uganda referred the long-lasting internal armed conflict of northern Uganda to the court. In July 2004, the Prosecutor decided to open the investigations into the situation of northern Uganda. In April 2004, the DRC referred the situation on its territory since July 2002 to the court. The Prosecutor decided to open the investigations in the DRC in June 2004. Lastly, in December 2004, the Government of the Republic of Central Africa referred the situation on its territory to the court. The Prosecutor has not yet decided to open an investigation in this latter case.

197. See press release of the Office of the ICC Prosecutor, ICC-OTP-20061215-193 (14 December 2006), available online on www.icc-cpi.int/press/pressreleases/217.html.

198. Article 16 of the ICC statute. It is notable that the Rome conference managed to depart from the original proposal contained in Article 23.3 of the ICC draft of the International Law Commission which prevented any prosecution by the court if the Security Council was dealing with the situation qualified as a threat to or a breach of the peace or an act of aggression. See La Haye, 'The jurisdiction of the ICC' 12.

199. UN.Doc.S/RES/1422 (12 July 2002).

200. Views have been expressed that the Council acted beyond its power by changing the negotiated terms of a multilateral treaty through a Security Council resolution. See the declarations made by Canada and Switzerland during the tenth session of the Preparatory Commission for the ICC on 3 July 2002. The Canadian statement can be found in (2002) *Canadian yearbook of international law* 475–77.

201. See UN.Doc.S/RES/1487(12 June 2003).

202. About a third of states in Rome were against giving *proprio motu* power to the Prosecutor as it may become a political toy or be overburdened by political complaints. For more details, see La Haye, 'The jurisdiction of the ICC' 15.

203. Article 15(3).

204. Article 15(4).

205. Article 15(5).

206. For similar views, see in particular, H. Kaul and C. Kress, 'Jurisdiction and co-operation in the statute of the ICC: principles and compromises' (1998) 1 *YbIHL* 170; A. Cassese, 'The statute of the ICC: some preliminary reflections' (1999) 10 *EJIL* 161 and L. Condorelli, 'La Cour pénale internationale: un pas de géant, pourvu qu'il soit accompli . . .' (1999) 103 *RGDIP* 16.

207. On the issue of complementarity, see R. E. Fife, 'The International Criminal Court, whence it came, where it goes' (2000) *Nordic journal of international law* 63–85; M. Benzing, 'The complementarity regime of the ICC: international criminal justice between state sovereignty and the fight against impunity' (2003) 7 *Max Planck yearbook of United Nations law* 591–632; see W. Burke-White, 'Complementarity in practice: the ICC as part of a system of multi-level global governance in the DRC' (2005) 18 *Leiden journal of international law* 556–90 and X. Philippe, 'The principle of universal jurisdiction and complementarity: how do the two principles intermesh?'(2006) 88 *IRRC* 375–98.

208. Views on the doctrine are split as to whether the principle of complementarity also applies to referrals made by the Security Council. It is reasonable to think, however, that it will be for the court itself to determine the admissibility of a case for every situation brought to it. Articles 19 and 53(1)(b) of the statute clearly apply to referrals made by the Security Council. Article 53(1) requires the Prosecutor to have regard to the admissibility of a case when deciding whether to start investigating a case referred to the court by the Security Council. On this issue, see Benzing, 'The complementarity regime of the ICC' 625–28.

209. Many states stressed the primary obligation of all states to exercise their jurisdiction over relevant crimes and the absence of any role for the court when such

jurisdiction was exercised. See opening addresses of many states during the
Rome conference, 15–18 June 1998.

210. Article 17.

211. For a detailed analysis of these concepts, see Benzing, 'The complementarity
regime of the ICC' 601–20.

212. Article 17(3).

213. Article 17(2).

214. Article 17(1).

215. Article 17(1)(b) reads: '. . . a case is inadmissible where . . . the case has been
investigated by a state which has jurisdiction over it and the state has decided not
to prosecute the person concerned, unless the decision resulted from the unwillingness or inability of the state genuinely to prosecute'.

216. On the issue of amnesty, see J. Gavron, 'Amnesties in the light of developments
in international law and the establishment of the International Criminal
Court'(2002) 51 *ICLQ* 91–117.

217. One might also note that when the Prosecutor initiates an investigation pursuant
to Article 13(a) or (c), he shall notify states parties, as well as those states which
would normally exercise jurisdiction over the crimes. Within one month of
receipt of the notification, a state, which has investigated or is investigating
the crimes, may ask the Prosecutor to defer to the state's investigation. See
Article 18 of the statute for more details.

218. The cases are the situations referred to the court by Uganda, the Congo and the
African Central Republic. The situation in the Darfur region of Sudan was
referred to the court by the Security Council and the Ivory Coast, a state non-
party to the statute, lodged a declaration of acceptance of the jurisdiction of the
court pursuant to Article 12(3) of the statute in February 2005.

219. On this last point, see Benzing, 'The complementarity regime of the
ICC' 629–31. See also, D. Sarooshi, 'Prosecutorial policy and the ICC' (2004)
2 *JICJ* 940–43; C. Kress, 'Self-referrals and waivers of complementarity' (2004) 2
JICJ 944–48; P. Gaeta, 'Is the practice of self-referrals a sound start for the ICC?'
(2004) 2 *JICJ* 949–52.

220. This vast subject can only be covered very briefly here. For more details, see
B. Broomhall, *International justice and the ICC* (Oxford: Oxford University Press,
2003) pp. 155–60; P. Mochochoko, 'International co-operation and judicial assistance' in R. Lee (ed.), *The International Criminal Court, the making of the Rome
statute* (The Hague, Boston: Kluwer Law International, 1999) p. 305; H. P. Kaul and
C. Kress, 'Jurisdiction and co-operation in the statute of the ICC' 143; D. Rinoldi
and N. Parisi, 'International co-operation and judicial assistance between the ICC
and states parties' in F.Lattanzi and W.Schabas (eds.), *Essays on the Rome statute of
the ICC*, vol. I (Ripa di Fagnano Alto: Il Sirente,1999) p. 339; Cassese, 'The statute of
the ICC: some preliminary reflections' (1999) 10 *EJIL* 144; M. Arsanjani, 'The Rome
statute of the International Criminal Court' (1999) 93 *AJIL* 40.

221. Article 86.

222. Article 87(5)(a). On this issue, see Z. Wenqi, 'On co-operation by states not party to the ICC' (2006) 88 *IRRC* 87–110.

223. States are under an obligation to ensure that there are procedures available under their national law for all the forms of co-operation which are specified in Part IX (Article 88).

224. See Article 90(2).

225. For a criticism of these provisions, see Cassese, 'The statute of the ICC: some preliminary reflections' 166.

226. See Article 90(6). In that case, the statute cites some factors, such as the dates of the requests or the interests of the requesting state, to be taken into account by the requested state when it determines whether to surrender or extradite.

227. See Rinoldi and Parisi, 'International co-operation and judicial assistance between the ICC and states parties' p. 376. For a criticism of these provisions, see Cassese, 'The statute of the ICC: some preliminary reflections' 166.

228. On the relationship between the ICC and the Security Council and the potential role of the Security Council in strengthening the co-operation of states with the court, see M. Bergsmo, 'Occasional remarks on certain state concerns about the jurisdictional reach of the ICC, and their possible implications for the relationship between the court and the Security Council' (2000) 69 *Nordic journal of international law* 87–113 at 109–13; see also, Broomhall, *International justice and the ICC* pp. 160–61 and D. Sarooshi, 'The peace and justice paradox: the ICC and the UN Security Council' in McGoldrick, Rowe and Donnelly (eds.), *The permanent International Criminal Court, legal and policy issues* (Oxford, Portland Oregon: Hart Publishing, 2004) pp. 102–5.

229. See Article 112(7)(a). The Assembly of States Parties could adopt sanctions against a state, which fails to fulfil its obligations under part IX.

230. See for, example, Article 87(3)(c).

231. See Article 94(1).

232. See Article 95.

233. For more detail, see the excellent article of D. Akande, 'International law immunities and the ICC' (2004) 98 *AJIL* 407–33 as well as Broomhall, *International justice and the ICC* pp. 128–50.

234. The drafters wanted to take account here of the fact that the inviolability of a diplomatic premise for example may be an obstacle to executing a request both vis à vis a state party and a non-state party. See Kaul and Kress 'Jurisdiction and co-operation in the statute of the ICC' 164.

235. For a careful consideration of this problem, see Akande, 'International immunities and the ICC' 419–33.

236. For an interpretation of this article, see Kaul and Kress, 'Jurisdiction and co-operation in the statute of the ICC' 164.

237. Article 93(3).
238. See Article 72. For a commentary of this provision, see D. Pigaroff, 'Protection of national security information' in R. Lee (ed.), *The ICC, the making of the Rome statute* (The Hague, Boston: Kluwer Law International, 1999) p. 270.
239. For the difference between extradition and transfer, see Article 102.
240. On some of these issues, see Bergsmo, 'Occasional remarks on certain state concerns' 97.
241. See Article 15(3), whereby the prosecutor shall submit to the pre-trial chamber a request for authorisation of an investigation, when he initiates investigation *proprio motu*. See Article 17 for the grounds of admissibility as well as Articles 18 and 19 on challenges to the jurisdiction of the court or inadmissibility of a case.
242. The Office of the Prosecutor received information on alleged war crimes committed in Iraq by nationals of states parties but decided not to start investigations because in respect of each of these incidents, national proceedings had been initiated. See UN.Doc.A/61/217 (3 August 2006) para. 31.
243. The Prosecutor looked into the possibility of starting investigations of nationals of states parties having committed crimes of wilful killing and inhuman treatment in Iraq. He found that the situation did not appear to meet the required gravity threshold and that national proceedings had been initiated in respect of these incidents. See report of the ICC to the General Assembly, UN.Doc.A/61/217 (3 August 2006) para. 31.
244. For more information of the Ugandan referral, see P. Akhavan, The LRA's case: Uganda's submission of the first state referral to the ICC' (2005) 99 *AJIL* 403–20 and K. Apuuli, 'The ICC arrest warrants for the LRA leaders and peace prospects for Northern Uganda' (2006) 4 *JICJ* 179–87.
245. One of the five commanders of the LRA, Raska Lukwiya, has recently been confirmed dead after DNA testing.
246. These red notices are transmitted to Interpol central bureaus in 184 countries. The red notices are part of the Interpol global network of law enforcement agencies, created to assist in tracing and arresting wanted fugitives. See ICC Prosecutor press release (ICC-OTP-2006601-138) (1 June 2006).
247. On the referral from the DRC to the court, see W. Burke-White, 'Complementarity in practice: the ICC as part of a system of multi-level global governance in the DRC' (2005) 18 *Leiden journal of international law* 556–90.
248. On the situation in the DRC, see report of the ICC to the General Assembly, UN.Doc.A/61/217 (3 August 2006) paras. 18–20 and Office of the Prosecutor Press Release (ICC-OTP-20060302-126) (17 March 2006.)
249. On the issue of the financial burden linked to this referral by the Security Council, see W.M. Reisman, 'On paying the piper: financial responsibility for Security Council referrals to the ICC' (2005) 99 *AJIL* 615–18. See also R. Cryer, 'Sudan, resolution 1593 and international criminal justice' (2006) 19 *Leiden journal of international law* 195–222.

250. See Office of the ICC Prosecutor press release (ICC-OTP-20061215-193) (14 December 2006) as well as UN.Doc.A/61/217 (3 August 2006) paras. 23–29.

251. The Ivory Coast has lodged a declaration accepting the jurisdiction of the court in February 2005.

252. In this respect, it is very important that states adopt the necessary implementing legislation to comply with their obligation to co-operate under part nine of the statute. Similarly, states should ratify the agreement on privileges and immunities of the court, so that the latter could carry out its functions unimpeded on states' territories and could organise the travel of victims and witnesses to the court.

253. See the opening remarks of Judge Philippe Kirsch to the fifth session of the Assembly of States Parties (23 November 2006) p. 3 (available on the ICC's website).

254. In its report on the activities performed during the first three years (June 2003–June 2006) dated 12 September 2006, the Prosecutor wrote on p. 2: 'the second challenge faced by the Office was how to conduct investigations into situations of on-going violence. Two critical measures to meet the challenges presented by these exceptional logistical difficulties were to reduce the length and scope of the investigation. In the LRA case, the arrest warrant were requested after 10 months of investigation and in the Thomas Lubang Dyilo case the arrest warrant was requested after 18 months.'

255. Payam Akhavan, who advised the Ugandan Government in this matter, does not seem to share these considerations. He affirms that Uganda's decision to invoke the ICC was shaped by security considerations in the region. He stated: 'In pursuing this option, Uganda was not relinquishing a responsibility that it could discharge on its own. Nor was Uganda pursuing a narrow political agenda.' See Akhavan, 'The LRA's case' 404.

256. On some of these issues, see W. Burke-White, 'Complementarity in practice: the ICC as part of a system of multi-level global governance in the DRC' (2005) 18 *Leiden journal of international law* 556–90. See, in particular, the political benefits expected by the Congolese Government after the Congolese referral to the ICC, 563–68.

257. On this point, see Akhavan, 'The LRA's case' 410.

258. See Akhavan, 'The LRA's case' 413.

259. On this issue, see also M. Arsanjani and M. Reisman, 'The law-in-action of the ICC' (2005) 99 *AJIL* 386–402 and Burke-White, 'Complementarity in practice: the ICC as part of a system of multi-level global governance in the DRC' 556–90.

260. The referral to the court of the situation in Darfur did not, however, seem to have the same beneficial effect as in Uganda on the level of violence in the region.

261. See the Prosecutor's address to the fifth session of the Assembly of States Parties (23 November 2006) pp. 2–3 (available on the court's website).

262. See the opening remarks of Judge Philippe Kirsch to the fifth session of the Assembly of States Parties (23 November 2006) p. 2 (available on the court's website).

Concluding remarks

A remarkable revolution has taken place in the field of internal armed conflicts in the last fifteen years. Coming out of decades of torpor, the law regulating internal armed conflicts has evolved dramatically on a number of levels. As seen in chapter 1, the definition of internal armed conflicts has been developed and consolidated by international judicial institutions such as the International Criminal Tribunal for the former Yugoslavia (ICTY) and by state practice through the negotiations of the International Criminal Court (ICC) statute. Even if the precise determination of a state of internal armed conflict remains a difficult and controversial exercise, a consolidated definition of internal armed conflict has taken shape. Common Article 3 and customary law principles regulate internal armed conflicts defined as 'prolonged armed violence between governmental forces and organised armed groups or between such groups' within a state. Protocol II and its higher threshold of applicability[1] has lost importance, as most of Protocol II provisions are reflected in customary law and apply in this generic category of internal armed conflicts. This definition, however, does not settle all difficulties, since states can still claim that the violence in their countries does not reach that threshold. States enjoy a broad discretion in the regulation of internal disturbances and sporadic armed violence which fall below the established threshold.

Secondly, there has been the clear development of a solid body of customary law regulating internal armed conflicts. As shown in chapter 2, the core of Protocol II together with common Article 3 and rules prohibiting attacks against the civilian population and civilian objects, as well as the use of gas or other chemical weapons, are now customarily applicable in internal armed conflicts. As a result, the essence of the laws of war governing international conflicts is also operative in internal conflicts. The overlap between the two categories of conflict is not complete but the core principles applicable in international conflicts have been extended to internal conflicts.

Thirdly, the real breakthrough of the 1990s consists in the recognition in international law that the commission of serious violations of the laws of war in internal armed conflicts entails individual criminal responsibility.[2] Since 1993, four international judicial institutions have been given jurisdiction over war crimes committed in internal conflicts. Despite the paucity of state practice highlighted, the *Tadić* decision on jurisdiction has been the main catalyst in the evolution of the principle of war criminality in internal armed conflicts. Without it, the ICC statute and the statute for the Special Court for Sierra Leone would not provide these courts with jurisdiction over war crimes committed in internal armed conflicts. The survey of national legislation, criminal codes and military manuals undertaken in chapter 4 shows a recent but clear trend by states to treat serious violations of the laws of war committed in internal conflicts as war crimes. This practice, with over fifty-four states[3] known to have extended the concept of war crimes to internal conflicts in their domestic legislation, is not universal but certainly amounts to substantial or widespread state practice. Furthermore, the analysis of unilateral statements by states, the practice of international organisations and the entry into force of the ICC statute with 104 states parties, show that this practice is coupled with a strong belief by most states that the commission of serious violations of the laws of war creates individual criminal responsibility in international law.

Today, there is extensive evidence that this principle has crystallised in customary international law. It is argued, however, that in the early 1990s, customary law did not reflect a sufficiently extensive state practice accepted as law. It was therefore premature for the Appeals Chamber in the *Tadić* case to conclude that such a principle was established in customary law at the time the offences were committed. Ironically, most of the subsequent practice highlighted in this work such as the adoption of the ICC statute, the majority of national legislation and the unilateral statements by states, were made possible to a great extent only by virtue of the audacity of the ICTY Appeals Chamber in the *Tadić* case. Could this conclusion have an impact on the legality of the convictions for war crimes pronounced by the ICTY? In other words, has the Tribunal violated the principle of legality by finding individuals guilty of war crimes committed in internal armed conflicts during the early 1990s? Conventional law cannot form the basis of these convictions, as individual criminal responsibility was not provided in treaty law at the time of commission of the offence.[4] As these convictions are based only on customary international law, a strict interpretation of the state of customary law during the conflicts in the former Yugoslavia calls for an affirmative answer. One could agree with Judge Li that the Appeals Chamber findings in the *Tadić* case in 1995 amounted to 'an unwarranted assumption of legislative power'.[5] If the legal rigour of the *Tadić* finding can be put into question, morality was certainly calling for the international criminal responsibility of war criminals for serious violations of the laws of war committed in internal armed conflicts.[6] At the national level, the principle of legality would not be violated. Individuals could be found criminally responsible as these conducts were clearly prohibited and qualified as war crimes in the criminal codes of states forming part of the former Yugoslavia at the time of commission of the offence.[7] As to the conflict in Bosnia-Herzegovina in particular, the various belligerent groups entered into a number of agreements under the auspices of the International Committee of the Red Cross (ICRC) and rendered applicable most of the law regulating international armed conflicts, including the principle of individual criminal responsibility for war crimes.

The other manifestations of the revolution that took place in the law regulating internal armed conflicts, are a consequence of the recognition that serious violations of the laws of war amount to war crimes. This status allowed international and national tribunals to extend their jurisdiction over war crimes committed in internal armed conflicts. Three distinct forums are capable of prosecuting alleged war criminals. They complement each other and their concurrent jurisdiction makes it more likely that war crimes committed in internal conflicts will be prosecuted.

First, perpetrators of war crimes can be prosecuted by the state where the acts were committed, either by the state of their own nationality or by the state of nationality of the victims. In internal armed conflicts, these will frequently be one and the same, the state where the acts were committed or territorial state. Recent war crimes prosecutions by domestic courts of territorial states were assessed for Cambodia, Ethiopia, Croatia, Bosnia-Herzegovina, Indonesia, Iraq, Kosovo, Russia and East Timor.[8] Prosecutions by national courts of the states where the crimes were committed present clear advantages.[9] Evidence, witnesses and victims are usually at hand and bringing prosecutions will be critical for the re-establishment of peace and the rule of law in the country. Unfortunately, states emerging from an internal conflict are often either unwilling or unable to prosecute war crimes. In many instances, amnesties are granted or states simply do not have the substantive law, the resources, personnel or the infrastructure to bring complex, expensive and time-consuming war crimes prosecutions. East Timor and Kosovo are good illustrations of the collapse of a pre-existing judicial infrastructure, which could not have undertaken any independent prosecutions without UN expertise and financial backing.[10]

Secondly, an alternative to the failure of territorial states' domestic courts to prosecute war criminals consists in allowing prosecutions by the courts of third states on the basis of universal jurisdiction. The universal condemnation of war crimes committed in internal conflicts does not automatically mean that states have a right enshrined in international law to exercise universal jurisdiction over them. Chapter 5 concludes that, notwithstanding the thirty-two states' legislation extending universal jurisdiction over war crimes in internal conflicts, relatively few prosecutions have taken place.[11] They are mostly restricted to European states. There is no general rule reflected in customary law, which grants states the right to extend universal jurisdiction over war crimes committed in internal conflicts. This principle is in the process of progressive development. The principle of universal jurisdiction carries with it some inherent limitations that may explain the absence of a customary norm at present. Practical difficulties, such as getting access to the evidence and securing the co-operation of the states where the crimes have been committed, coupled with policy contingencies explain the fact that states still hesitate to extend universal jurisdiction over war crimes committed in internal conflicts. Policy considerations should not be underestimated, as many states clearly prefer not to get involved in the internal conflicts of other states. Successful prosecutions in Switzerland, France or Belgium have shown, however, that once national jurisdictions have gained expertise, decided to devote the necessary resources and can count on the assistance of the territorial state, perpetrators can be tried fairly and speedily by the courts of third states. These prosecutions also serve as a deterrent and signal clearly to war criminals that serious violations of the laws of war committed in internal armed conflicts amount to international crimes and may be prosecuted in a growing number of states.

Thirdly, in the absence of prosecutions by domestic courts, or in association with them, individual responsibility for war crimes can be enforced by international tribunals or the ICC.[12] As seen in chapter 6, both the ICTY and ICTR have contributed hugely to the development of the principle of individual criminal responsibility for war crimes in internal armed conflicts and to the restoration of the rules of law in the former Yugoslavia and Rwanda. The experience of both Tribunals has shown that the process of justice should be accessible and visible and that co-operation by states with the Tribunals remains an indispensable condition for the effective prosecutions of war criminals. It is also clear that the ICC and both Tribunals can only deal with a limited number of war criminals and should concentrate on 'big fishes', leaving the bulk of mid-level and low-level perpetrators to domestic courts.[13] The preamble to the ICC statute clearly places the obligation to prosecute international crimes on states first, the court being able to prosecute the most serious international crimes only if no prosecutions are brought at the national level.

Furthermore, it is possible to draw other subsidiary conclusions. First, national prosecutions by third states on the basis of universal jurisdiction or by domestic courts of the territorial states are a necessary complement to war crimes prosecutions by international tribunals. The former represents the most feasible method to enforce responsibility for war crimes in internal conflicts. International prosecutions by the ICTY and ICTR are restricted to events that took place in these two regions at particular times. The prosecutions to be undertaken by the ICC may be limited in numbers, as the co-operation regime contains many lacunae. However, the establishment of these International Tribunals and the role of the ICC as both a court of last resort and a deterrent cannot be underestimated, and should stimulate domestic prosecutions of these crimes.

Secondly, it is crucial that the international community continues to build up partnerships with states which have just emerged from an internal conflict in order to help them carry out impartial prosecutions of war crimes at home. The second part of the 1990s has seen a different engagement of the UN in this respect. The Special Court for Sierra Leone was established through an agreement between Sierra Leone and the UN. It is a good example of a hybrid or mixed institution, applying both international and national law and bringing prosecutions of war crimes with the financial help and expertise of the international community. Similarly, international funding and expertise helped rebuild the shattered judicial infrastructure of East Timor and Kosovo. To fight impunity effectively, however, it is essential that the international community and the UN engage with war-torn countries when and where weapons have fallen silent. The disengagement of the international community would only leave the door open to unfair prosecutions or to the granting of amnesty.

Thirdly, if the main bulk of substantive law applicable in international conflicts has come to regulate internal conflicts, there remain important differences in the jurisdictional regime between the two types of armed conflicts. The mandatory regime of *aut judicare, aut dedere* applicable to grave breaches of the Geneva Conventions and Protocol I is not applicable to war crimes committed in internal armed conflicts. Furthermore, the customary right for all states to extend universal jurisdiction over war crimes committed in international armed conflicts has not yet been extended to internal armed conflicts.

It is argued, however, that the recognition in international law that serious violations of the laws of war in internal armed conflicts amount to war crimes has been tremendously important. It has allowed the ICC to have jurisdiction over such crimes and created the impetus for states to reconsider their approach towards these violations and amend their own criminal legislation. Today, an important number of states have granted the status of war crimes to such violations within their domestic systems and some have even extended universal jurisdiction over them. Enforcement is still scarce but as Draper puts it 'the establishment of a legal norm may precede its regular enforcement, but the existence of such a norm is a value in itself'.[14] The existence of the principle of individual responsibility for war crimes committed in internal conflicts has therefore provided the foundations to build a culture of compliance with the law. However, it is only one tool in this greater endeavour, which must be consolidated and enforced in the twenty-first century.

Notes

1. Protocol II applies in 'an armed conflict which takes place in the territory of a high contracting party between its armed forces and dissident armed forces or other organised groups which, under responsible command, exercises such control over a part of its territory as to enable them to carry out sustained and concerted military operations and to implement this Protocol' (Article 1.1 of Protocol II).
2. This phenomenon is covered in chapter 4 of this book.
3. Out of ninety-nine states studied, fifty-four treat violations of the laws of war committed in internal armed conflicts as war crimes.
4. In the early 1990s, no international treaty applicable in internal armed conflicts provided for individual criminal responsibility for war crimes.
5. Judge Li dissenting opinion, *Tadić* jurisdiction decision, para. 13
6. Probably to avoid that type of situation, the Secretary-General, in his report to the SC accompanying the statute of the Tribunal, recalls that the Tribunal was to apply 'rules of international humanitarian law which are beyond any doubt part of customary law so that the problem of adherence of some but not all States to

specific conventions does not arise'. Report of the Secretary-General pursuant to para. 2 of Security Council resolution 808 (3 May 1993) para. 34.

7. See the criminal codes of Bosnia-Herzegovina, Croatia and the former Yugoslavia in chapter 4 of this book.

8. In the case of Cambodia, East Timor and Kosovo, prosecutions are brought with the technical and financial help of the international community.

9. On this point, see in particular, R. Wedgwood, 'National courts and the prosecution of war crimes' in G. MacDonald and O. Swaak-Goldman (eds.), *Substantive and procedural aspects of international criminal law: the experience of international and national courts* (The Hague: Kluwer Law International, 2000) vol. 1, pp. 393–413 and J. Charney, 'International criminal law and the role of domestic courts' (2001) 95 *AJIL* 120–24. See also the conclusions reached at the end of chapter 5.

10. See H. Strohmeyer, 'Collapse and reconstruction of a judicial system: the United Nations missions in Kosovo and East Timor' (2001) 95 *AJIL* 46.

11. War crime prosecutions have been rather rare but other prosecutions by territorial states for torture or for common crimes under national law might have taken place after the end of hostilities.

12. On the impartiality and independence of international tribunals, see UN.Doc.S/1994/1125 (4 October 1994) paras. 133–42.

13. Security Council resolution 1329 specifies that the ICTY mission was to try 'civilian, military and paramilitary leaders . . . in preference to minor actors'. UN.Doc.Res.1329 (30 November 2000). See also ICTY press releases of 14 June and 26 July 2002, available online on www.un.org/icty.

14. G. Draper, 'The Geneva Conventions of 1949' (1965–1) 114 *Recueil des cours* 100.

SELECT BIBLIOGRAPHY

Abi-Saab G., 'Non international armed conflicts', in UNESCO, *International dimensions of humanitarian law* (Dordrecht: Martinus Nijhoff, UNESCO, Henri Dunant Institute, 1988) pp. 217–39.

'The 1977 Protocols and general international law: some preliminary reflexions' in Delissen A. and Tanja G. (eds.), *Humanitarian law of armed conflicts, challenges ahead: essays in honour of Fritz Karlshoven* (Dordrecht: Martinus Nijhoff Publishers, 1991) pp. 115–26.

'The concept of war crimes' in Yee S. and Tieya W. (eds.), *International law in the post-cold war world: essays in memory of Li Haopei* (London: Routledge, 2001) pp. 99–118.

'The proper role of universal jurisdiction' (2003) 1 *JICJ* 596–602.

'Wars of national liberation and the laws of war' (1972) 3 *Annales d'études internationales* 96.

Abi-Saab R., 'Les conflits internes aujourd'hui' in Ghebali V. Y and Kappeler D. (eds.), *Les multiples aspects de relations internationales: études à la mémoire du professeur Jean Siotis* (Brussels: Bruylant, 1995) pp. 313–25.

L'article 3 commun aux Conventions de Genève (Geneva: Institute Henri Dunant, Pedone, 1986).

Abresch W., 'A human rights law of internal armed conflict: the European Court of Human Rights in Chechnya' (2005) 16 *EJIL* 741–67.

Acts of the Berlin Conference on the Rome Statute, what's next: domestic and foreign approaches to the implementation of international criminal law in national law (Berlin: Reader & International Criminal Law Society, 2000).

Adachi Samio, 'The Asian concept' in UNESCO, *International dimensions of humanitarian law* (Dordrecht: Henry Dunant Institute, UNESCO, Martinus Nijhoff, 1988) p. 13.

Akande D., 'International law immunities and the ICC' (2004) 98 *AJIL* 407–33.

Akehurst M., 'Jurisdiction in international law' (1972–73) 46 *BYIL* 216.

Akhavan P., 'Justice in the Hague, peace in the former Yugoslavia? A commentary on the UN War Crimes Tribunal' (1998) 20 *Human rights quarterly* 737.

'The International Criminal Tribunal for Rwanda: the politics and pragmatics of punishment' (1996) 90 *AJIL* 501.

'The LRA case: Uganda's submission of the first state referral to the International Criminal Court' (2005) 99 *AJIL* 403–20.

Aldrich G., 'Jurisdiction of the ICTY' (1996) 90 *AJIL* 64.

'The laws of war on land' (2000) 94 *AJIL* 61.

Alter R., 'International criminal law: a bittersweet year for supporters and critics of the ICC' (2003) 37 *The international lawyer* 541–50.

Alvarez E., 'Trying Hussein: between hubris and hegemony' (2004) 2 *JICJ* 313–29.

Amann D. M., '*Prosecutor v. Akayesu*, Case ICTR-96-4-T, 2 September 1998' (1999) 93 *AJIL* 195–99.

Ambos K., 'Impunity and international criminal law, a case study on Colombia, Peru, Bolivia, Chile and Argentina' (1997) 18 *Human rights law journal* 1.

Ambos K. and Othman M. (eds), *New approaches in international criminal justice: Kosovo, East Timor, Sierra Leone and Cambodia* (Freiburg: Edition iuscrim, 2003).

Andries A., van den Wijngaert C. and David E., 'Commentaire de la loi du 6 juin 1993 relative à la répression des infractions graves au droit international humanitaire' (1994) *Revue de droit pénal et de criminologie* 1114.

Apuuli K., 'The ICC arrest warrants for the LRA leaders and peace prospects for Northern Uganda' (2006) 4 *JICJ* 179–87.

Arbour L., 'The crucial years' (2004) 2 *JICJ* 396–402.

'Will the ICC have an impact on universal jurisdiction?' (2003) 1 *JICJ* 585–88.

Arnold R., 'The liability of civilians under international humanitarian law's war crimes provisions' (2002) 5 *YbIHL* 344–59.

Arsanjani M., 'The Rome statute of the International Criminal Court' (1999) 93 *AJIL* 40.

Arsanjani M. and Reisman M., 'The law-in-action of the ICC' (2005) 99 *AJIL* 386–402.

Ascencio H., 'The Spanish constitutional tribunal's decision in Guatemalan generals: unconditional universality is back' (2006) 4 *JICJ* 586–94.

Bantekas I., 'The Iraqi special tribunal for crimes against humanity' (2004) 54 *ICLQ* 237–53.

Bassiouni C., *Crimes against humanity in international law* (The Hague: Martinus Nijhoff Publishers, 1992).

'The normative framework of international humanitarian law: overlaps, gaps and ambiguities' (1998) 8 *Transnational law and contemporary problems* 199.

'Universal jurisdiction unrevisited: the International Court of Justice decision in case concerning the arrest warrant of 11 April 2000' (2002/2003) XII *The Palestine yearbook of international law* 27–48.

Bassiouni C. and Wise E., *Aut dedere, aut judicare – the duty to extradite or prosecute in international law* (Dordrecht: Martinus Nijhoff Publishers, 1995).

Baxter R., 'Multilateral treaties as evidence of customary international law' (1965–66) 41 *BYIL* 300.

'The municipal and international law basis of jurisdiction over war crimes' (1951) 28 *BYIL* 392.

Becker S., 'Universal jurisdiction: how universal it it? A study of competing theories' (2002/2003) XII *The Palestine yearbook of international law* 49–76.

Benvenuti P., 'Italy, Implementation of the ICC statute in national legislation, constitutional aspects' in Kress C. and Lattanzi F. (eds.), *The Rome statute and domestic legal orders* (Baden-Baden, Ripa di Fagnano Alto: Nomos Verlagsgessellschaft, Il Sirente, 2000) vol. I.

Benzing M., 'The complementarity regime of the ICC: international criminal justice between state sovereignty and the fight against impunity' (2003) 7 *Max Planck yearbook of United Nations law* 591–632.

Bergsmo M., 'Occasional remarks on certain state concerns about the jurisdictional reach of the ICC, and their possible implications for the relationship between the court and the Security Council' (2000) 69 *Nordic journal of international law* 87–113.

Besson M. and de Vezac P, 'Les sanctions des violations des conventions de Genève du 12 Août 1949' (1997) 3 *Droit et défense, revue générale du droit de la sécurité et de la défense* 4.

Bierzanek R., 'Quelques remarques sur l'applicabilité du droit international humanitaire des conflits armés aux conflits internes internationalisés' in Swinarski C. (ed.), *Studies and essays on international humanitarian law and Red Cross principles in honour of J. Pictet* (Geneva: ICRC, Martinus Njihoff Publishers, 1984) pp. 281–90.

Blakesley C., 'Extraterritorial jurisdiction', in Bassiouni C. (ed.), *International criminal law* (Ardsley, New York: Transnational Publishers, 1999) vol. II, 2nd edn, pp. 33–105.

Blewitt G., 'The necessity for enforcement of international humanitarian law' (1995) *American Society of International Law Proceedings* 298–300.

Boelaert-Suominen S., 'Grave breaches, universal jurisdiction and internal armed conflicts: is customary law moving towards a uniform enforcement mechanism for all armed conflicts?' (2000) *Journal of conflict, peace and security* 95.

Boisson de Chazournes L. and Condorelli L., 'Quelques remarques à propos de l'obligation des états de "respecter et faire respecter" le droit international humanitaire "en toutes circonstances"' in Zwinarski C. (ed.), *Etudes et essais sur le droit international humanitaire et sur les principes de la Croix-Rouge en l'honneur de Jean Pictet* (Geneva, Dordrecht: ICRC, Martinus Nijhoff Publishers, 1984).

Bond J. E., *The rules of riot: internal conflicts and the laws of war* (Princeton: Princeton University Press, 1974).

Boot-Matthijssen M. and van Elst R., 'Key provisions of the International Crimes Act 2003' (2004) 35 *Netherlands yearbook of international law* 251–96.

Borrowdale A., 'The future of the law of war: the place of the Additional Protocols of 1977 in customary international law' (1981) 14 *Comparative and international law journal of Southern Africa* 79–91.

Bosch W., *Judgment on Nuremberg, American attitudes toward the major German war-crime trials* (Chapel Hill: The University of California Press, 1970).

Bosnjak M. and Zagorac D., 'Slovenia' in Kress C., Lattanzi F., Bromhall B. and Santori (eds.), *The Rome statute and domestic legal orders, vol. II, constitutional issues, co-operation and enforcement* (Baden-Baden, Ripa di Fagnano Alto: Nomos Verlagsgessellschaft, Il Sirente, 2005) pp. 309–30.

Bothe M., 'Article 2 and Protocol II: case studies of Nigeria and El Salvador (1982) 31 *American University law review* 902.

'Conflits armés internes et droit international humanitaire' (1978) 82 *RGDIP* 82–102.

'War crimes' in Cassese A., Gaeta P. and Jones (eds.), *The Rome statute of the International Criminal Court: a commentary* (Oxford: Oxford University Press, 2002) vol. I.

Bourgon S., 'Procedural problems hindering expeditious and fair justice' (2004) 2 *JICJ* 526–32.

Boyle D., 'Establishing the responsibility of the Khmer Rouge leadership for international crimes' (2002) 5 *YbIHL* 167–218.

Bravo F., 'Méthodes de recherche de la coutume internationale dans la pratique des états' (1985) 192 *Recueil des cours* 237–316.

Brierly J., *The law of nations*, 6th edn, edited by Waldock H. (Oxford: Clarendon Press, 1963).

Broomhall B., *International justice and the ICC* (Oxford: Oxford University Press, 2003).

Brownlie I., *Principles of public international law* (Oxford: Oxford University Press, 1996).

Burgos H. 'The application of international humanitarian law as compared to human rights law in situations qualified as internal armed conflict' in Karlshoven F. and Sandoz Y. (eds.), *Implementation of international humanitarian law* (Dordrecht: Martinus Nijhoff Publishers, 1989).

Burke-White W., 'Complementarity in practice: the ICC as part of a system of multi-level global governance in the DRC' (2005) 18 *Leiden journal of international law* 556–90.

Carey J., Dunlap W. and Pritchard J. (eds.), *International humanitarian law: prospects* (Ardsley: Transnational Publishers, 2006).

Carnahan B., 'Lincoln, Lieber and the laws of war: the origins and limits of the principle of military necessity' (1998) 92 *AJIL* 213–31.

Carnegie A. R., 'Jurisdiction over violations of the laws and customs of war' (1963) *BYIL* 421.

Casey L. A. and Rivkin D. B., 'The Rome statute's unlawful application to non-state parties' (2003) 44 *Virginia journal of international law* 63–89.

Cassese A., 'The status of rebels under the 1977 Geneva Protocol on non-international armed conflicts' (1981) 30 *ICLQ* 423.

'Is the bell tolling for universality? A plea for a sensible notion of universal jurisdiction' (2003) 1 *JICJ* 589–95.

'La guerre civile et le droit international' (1986) 90 *RGDIP* 571–73.

'Reflections on international criminal justice' (1998) 61 *Modern law review* 1–10.

'The ICTY: a living and vital reality' (2004) 2 *JICJ* 585–97.

'The Special Court and international law, the decision concerning the Lomé agreement amnesty' (2004) *JICJ* 1130–40.

'The statute of the ICC: some preliminary reflections' (1999) 10 *EJIL* 161.

'When may senior state officials be tried for international crimes? Some comments on the *Congo. v. Belgium* case' (2002) 13 *EJIL* 853–75.

International criminal law (Oxford: Oxford University Press, 2003).

'The Spanish Civil War and the development of customary law concerning internal armed conflict' in A. Cassese (ed.), *Current problems of international law: essays on UN law and on the laws of armed conflict* (Milan: A. Giuffre, 1975) pp. 287–318.

Cassese A. (ed.), *The new humanitarian law of armed conflict, proceedings of the 1976 and 1977 conferences* (Naples: Ed. Scientifica, 1980).

Charney J., 'International criminal law and the role of domestic courts' (2001) 95 *AJIL* 120–24.

Chesterman S., 'Justice under international administration: Kosovo, East Timor and Afghanistan' (2001) 12 *Finnish yearbook of international law* 143–64.

Cho S., 'Applicability of international humanitarian law to internal armed conflicts', Ph.D. thesis, University of Cambridge (1996).

Ciobanu D., 'The concept and determination of the existence of armed conflicts not of an international character' (1975) 58 *Rivista di diritto internazionale* 48–79.

Commission on International Human Rights Law and Practice, International Law Association, *Final Report on the exercise of universal jurisdiction in respect of gross human rights offences* (2000) Report of the 69th conference of the International Association 403–31.

Condorelli L., 'La Cour pénale internationale: un pas de géant, pourvu qu'il soit accompli . . .' (1999) 103 *RGDIP* 16.

'War crimes and internal conflicts in the statute of the International Criminal Court', in Politi M. and Nesi G., *The Rome statute of the International Criminal Court, a challenge to impunity* (Aldershot: Ashgate, 2001) pp. 107–17.

Condorelli L. (ed.), *The United Nations and international humanitarian law* (Paris: Pedone, 1996).

Cot J. P., 'Eloge de l'indécision: la cour et la compétence universelle' (2002) *Revue belge de droit international* 546–53.

Cowles W. B., 'Universality of jurisdiction over war crimes' (1945) 33 *California law review* 177–218.

Cryer R., 'Sudan, resolution 1593 and international criminal justice' (2006) 19 *Leiden journal of international law* 195–222.

   Prosecuting international crimes, selectivity and the international criminal law regime (Cambridge: Cambridge University Press, 2005).

D'Argent P., 'L'expérience belge de la compétence universelle: beaucoup de bruit pour rien?' (2004) *RGDIP* 597–631.

Dadrian V., *The history of the Armenian genocide* (Providence, Oxford: Berghahn books, 1995).

Daillier P., 'La répression pénale en France des crimes de guerre et des crimes contre l'humanité en ex-Yugoslavie', in Lattanzi F. (ed.), *Dai tribunali penali internationazionali ad hoc a una corte permanente* (Naples: Ed. Scientifica, 1996).

Damrosh L. F., 'Criminal actions in national and international tribunals' (1997) 269 *Recueil des cours* 236.

Danchin P., 'Transitional justice in Afghanistan: confronting violations of international humanitarian and human rights law' (2001) 4 *YbIHL* 3–51.

Dascalopoulou-Livida P., 'The implementation of the ICC statute in Greece: some thoughts' in C. Kress and Lattanzi F. (eds.), *The Rome statute and domestic legal orders* (Baden-Baden, Ripa di Fagnano Alto: Nomos Verlagsgessellschaft, Il Sirente, 2000) vol. I, p. 113.

David E., 'La loi belge sur les crimes de guerre' (1995) *Revue belge de droit international* 668.

   'Le tribunal international pénal pour l'ex-Yougoslavie' (1992) *Revue belge de droit international* 565.

   'Universal jurisdiction in Belgian law' (2002/2003) XII *The Palestine yearbook of international law* 77–116.

   Précis de droit des conflits armés (Brussels: Bruylant, 1994).

Davidson E., *The Trials of the Germans, an account of the twenty-two defendants before the IMT at Nuremberg* (New York: the Macmillan Company, 1966).

de Bertodano S., 'Current developments in internationalised courts' (2003) 1 *JICJ* 226–44.

De Hemptinne J., 'La poursuite et le jugement des hauts responsables politiques et militaires par le Tribunal pénal international pour l'ex-Yougoslavie' (1997) *Revue de droit pénal et de criminologie* 988.

De Vattel E., *The law of nations* (London: Newbery, Richardson, Crowder, Caslon, Longman, Law, Fuller, Coote & Kearsly, 1760).

Deen-Racsmany Z., 'The nationality of the offender and the jurisdiction of the International Criminal Court' (2001) 95 *AJIL* 606–23.

Delissen A. and Tanja G. (eds.), *Humanitarian law of armed conflicts, challenges ahead: essays in honour of Fritz Karlshoven* (Dordrecht: Martinus Nijhoff, 1991).

Deming S. H., 'War crimes and international criminal law' (1995) 28 *Akron law review* 421.

Dhokalia R. P., 'Civil wars and international law' (1971) 11 *Indian journal of international law* 225.

Dickinson L. A., 'The dance of complementarity: relationships among domestic, international and transnational accountability mechanisms in East Timor and Indonesia' in Stromseth J. (ed.), *Accountability for atrocities, national and international responses* (Ardsley, New York: Transnational Publishers, 2003) pp. 319–74.

Dinstein Y., 'The distinctions between war crimes and crimes against peace' in Dinstein Y. and Tabory M. (eds.), *War crimes in international law* (The Hague, Boston: Martinus Nijhoff, 1996).

   'The universality principle and war crimes' in Schmitt M. N. (ed.), *International law studies: the law of military operations, lieber amicorum Professor J. Grunawalt* (Newport, Rhode Island: Naval War College, 1998) pp. 17–37.

   War, aggression and self-defence (Cambridge: Cambridge University Press, 4th edn, 2005).

Dinstein Y. and Tabory M. (eds.), *War crimes in international law* (The Hague, Boston: Martinus Nijhoff, 1996).

Dörmann K., *Elements of war crimes under the Rome statute of the International Criminal Court, sources and commentary* (Cambridge: Cambridge University Press, 2002).

Doria J., 'Angola: a case study in the challenges of achieving peace and the question of amnesty or prosecutions of war crimes in a mixed armed conflict' (2002) 5 *YbIHL* 3–60.

Doswald-Beck L., 'New protocol on blinding laser weapons (1996) *IRRC* 272–98.

Draper G., 'The Geneva Conventions of 1949' (1965–I) 114 *Recueil des cours* 100.

   'The modern pattern of war criminality' (1976) 6 *Israel yearbook of human rights* 22.

   'Humanitarian law and internal armed conflicts' (1983) 13 *Georgian journal of international and comparative law* 253–77.

Dubois O., 'Rwanda's national criminal courts and the International Tribunal' (1997) 828 *IRRC* 717.

Dupuy R. J. and A. Leonetti, 'La notion de conflit armé à caractère non international', in Cassese A. (ed.), *The new humanitarian law of armed conflict* (Naples: Editoriale Scientifica, 1979) pp. 258–76.

Eide, Rosas and Meron T., 'Combating lawlessness in gray zone conflicts through minimum humanitarian standards' (1995) 89 *AJIL* 215.

Elagab O. Y., 'The Special Court for Sierra Leone: some constraints' (2004) 8 *International journal of human rights* 249–73.

Elder D., 'The historical background of common Article 3 of the Geneva Convention of 1949' (1979) 11 *Case Western Reserve journal of international law* 37–69.

Emmanuelli C., 'Les forces des Nations Unies et le droit international humanitaire' in Condorelli L. (ed.), *The United Nations and international humanitarian law* (Paris: Pedone, 1996) pp. 345–70.

Engelschion T. S., 'Prosecution of war crimes and violations of human rights in Ethiopia' (1994) 8 *Yearbook of African law* 50.

Etcheson C., 'Designing justice for Cambodia's Khmer rouge' in Carey J., Dunlap W. and Pritchard J. (eds.), *International humanitarian law: prospects* (Ardsley: Transnational Publishers, 2006) pp. 191–209.

Falk R., *The international law of civil war* (Baltimore: John Hopkins Press, 1971).

Farer T., 'The humanitarian laws of war in civil strife: towards a definition of international armed conflict' (1971) 7 *Revue belge du droit international* 20–55.

Fawthrop T., 'Who un-washes its hands of Khmer trial? *The Straits Times* (21 February 2002).

Fenrick W., 'The development of the law of armed conflict through the jurisprudence of the ICTY' in Schmitt M. (ed.), *The law of military operations, lieber americorum Professor J. Grunawalt*, International Law Studies vol. 72 (Newport, Rhode Island: Naval War College, 1998) p. 77.

'Some international law problems related to prosecutions before the International Criminal Tribunal for the Former Yugoslavia' (1995) 6 *Duke journal of comparative and international law* 103.

Ferdinandusse W. N., *Direct application of international criminal law in national courts* (The Hague: Asser Institute, 2006).

Fife R. E., 'The International Criminal Court, whence it came, where it goes' (2000) *Nordic journal of international law* 63–85.

Fleck D., 'The protocols additional to the Geneva conventions and customary international law' (1990) 29 *Revue de droit pénal militaire* 497–505.

Fleck D. (ed.), *The handbook of humanitarian law in armed conflicts* (Oxford: Oxford University Press, 1995).

Forsythe D., 'Legal management of internal war: the 1977 Protocol on non-international armed conflicts' (1978) 72 *AJIL* 275.

'Human rights and internal conflicts: trends and recent developments' (1982) 12 *California western international law journal* 301.

Fox G., 'International law and civil wars' (1994) 26 *International law and politics* 633–54.

Freeland S., 'How open should the door be? – Declarations by non-states parties under Article 12(3) of the Rome statute of the ICC' (2006) 75 *Nordic journal of international law* 211–41.

Freeman M. Harris *et al.*, 'Bringing war criminals to justice: obligations, options, recommendations' in Orentlicher D. *et al.* (ed.), *Making justice work: the report of the Century Foundation* (New York: Century Foundation Press, 1998) pp. 27–32.

Gaeta P., 'National prosecution of international crimes: international rules on grounds of jurisdiction' in *Studi di diritto internazionale in onore di Gaetano Arango-Ruiz* (Naples: Editoriale Scientifica, 2004) vol. 3, pp. 1923–43.

Gavron J., 'Amnesties in the light of developments in international law and the establishment of the International Criminal Court' (2002) 51 *ICLQ* 91–117.

Ghebali V. Y. and Kappeler D. (eds.), *Les multiples aspects de relations internationales: études à la mémoire du professeur Jean Siotis* (Brussels: Bruylant, 1995).

Gilbert J., 'UK approach to implementation of ICC crimes', *Acts of the Berlin conference on 'the Rome Statute, what's next: domestic and foreign approaches to the implementation of international criminal law in national law'* (Berlin: Reader and International Criminal Law Society, 2000) p. 6.

Ginsburgs G. and Kudriavtsev V. (eds.), *The Nuremberg trial and international law* (Dordrecht: Martinus Nijhoff Publishers, 1990).

Goldstone R., 'Justice as a tool for peace-making: truth commissions and international criminal tribunals' (1996) 28 *International law and politics* 486–87.

Gonzalez M. P., 'La répression des crimes de guerre et des crimes contre l'humanité dans le système juridique espagnol' in Lattanzi F. (ed.), *Crimini di guerra et giurisdizione nazionale* (Baden-Baden, Fagnagno Alto: Nomas Verlagsgesellschaft, Il Sirente, 1998) p. 151.

Graditsky T., 'La responsabilité pénale individuelle pour violation du droit international humanitaire applicable en situation de conflit armé non international' (1998) 829 *IRRC* 40.

Graefarth B., 'Universal criminal jurisdiction and an International Criminal Court' (1990) *EJIL* 67.

Gray C., 'Bosnia and Herzegovina: civil war or inter-state conflict? Characterization and consequences' (1996) 67 *BYIL* 171.

Green L. 'The law of armed conflict and the enforcement of international criminal law' (1984) *Canadian yearbook of international law* 3–25.

'Criminal responsibility of individuals in non-international armed conflicts' (2002) 45 *German yearbook of international law* 82–114.

'What is–why is there– the law of war?' in Schmitt M. and Green L. (eds.), *The law of armed conflicts into the next millennium* (Newport, Rhode Island: Naval War College, 1998) vol. 71, pp. 141–83.

'Enforcement of the law in international and non-international conflicts, the way ahead' (1996) 24 *Denver journal of international law and policy* 285–320.

The contemporary law of armed conflicts (Manchester, New York: Manchester University Press, 1993).

Greenwood C., 'Command responsibility and the *Hadžihasanović* decision' (2004) 2 *JICJ* 598–605.

'Historical development and legal basis' in Fleck D. (ed.), *The handbook of humanitarian law in armed conflicts* (Oxford: Oxford University Press, 1995).

'International humanitarian law and the *Tadić* case' (1996) 7 *EJIL* 280.

'The law of weaponry at the start of the new millennium' in Schmitt M. and Green L. (eds.), *The law of armed conflicts into the next millennium* (Newport, Rhode Island: Naval War College, 1998) vol. 71, pp. 185–231.

Greppi E., 'The evolution of individual criminal responsibility under international law' (1999) 835 *IRRC* 531.

Grotius H., *De jure belli ac pacis libri tres (1625)* vol. II, chap. XX, section XL (Carnegie, Classics of international law, F. Kelsey trans., 1925).

Haile D., 'Accountability for crimes of the past and the challenges of criminal prosecutions. The case of Ethiopia' (2000) 15 *Leuven law series.*

Hampson F., 'The ICTY and the reluctant witness' (1998) 47 *ICLQ* 50.

Harhoff F., 'Consonance or rivalry? Calibrating the efforts to prosecute war crimes in national and international tribunals' (1997) 7 *Duke journal of comparative and international law* 571.

'Legal and practical problems in the international prosecution of individuals' (2000) 69 *Nordic journal of international law* 53–61.

Harmon M. B. and Gaynor F., 'Prosecuting massive crimes with primitive tools: three difficulties encountered by prosecutors in international criminal proceedings' (2004) 2 *JICJ* 403–26.

Harvard Research in International Law, 'Draft convention on jurisdiction with respect to crime' (1935) 29 *AJIL* 435.

Henckaerts J. M., 'Study on customary international humanitarian law: a contribution to the understanding and respect for the rule of law in armed conflict' (2005) 87 *IRRC* 175–212.

Henckaerts J. M. and Doswald-Beck L., *Customary international humanitarian law* (Cambridge: Cambridge University Press, 2005).

Henzelin M., 'La compétence pénale universelle, une question non résolue par l'arrêt Yerodia' (2002) *RGDIP* 819–53.

Le principe de l'universalité en droit pénal international. Droit et obligation pour les etats de poursuivre et juger selon le principe de l'universalité (Basle, Geneva, Brussels: Helbing & Lichtenhahn, Faculté de droit de Genève, Bruylant).

Herby P., 'First session of the review conference of states parties to the 1980 UN Convention on Certain Conventional Weapons (CCW)' (1996) 312 *IRRC* 361.

Hoffman M. H., 'The customary law of non-international armed conflict: evidence from the US civil war' (1990) *IRRC* 322–43.

Hosoya C., Ando N., Omuma Y. and Minear R. (eds.), *The Tokyo war crimes trial, an international symposium* (New York, Tokyo: Kodansha International Ltd, 1986).

Institute of International Law, 'Wiesbaden session 1975' (1975) 56 *Annuaire de l'Institut de Droit International.*

International Committee of the Red Cross, *Annual report* (1956) (Geneva: ICRC, 1957).

Annual report (1962) (Geneva: ICRC, 1963).

Annual report (1983) (Geneva: ICRC, 1984).

Annual report (1987) (Geneva: ICRC, 1988).

Annual report (1989) (Geneva: ICRC, 1990).

Annual report (1992) (Geneva: ICRC, 1993).

Jallow H. B., 'The Legal Framework of the Special Court for Sierra Leone' in Ambos K. and Othman M. (eds.), *New approaches in international criminal justice: Kosovo, East Timor, Sierra Leone and Cambodia* (Freiburg: Edition iuscrim, 2003) pp. 149–71.

Jennings R. and Watts A. (eds.), *Oppenheim's international law* (London, New York: Longman, 9th edn, 1992).

Johnson L., 'Ten years: reflections on the drafting' (2004) 2 *JICJ* 378.

Josipovic I., 'Responsibility for war crimes before national courts in Croatia' (2006) 88 *IRRC* 145–68.

Joyner C., 'Arresting impunity: the case for universal jurisdiction in bringing war criminals to accountability' (1996) 59 *Law and contemporary problems* 165.

Judgment of the International Military Tribunal for the Trial of German Major War Criminals, Nuremberg, 30 September–1 October 1946 (London: Stationery Office, 1946).

Kammerhofer J., 'Uncertainty in the formal sources of international law: customary international law and some of its problems' (2004) 15 *EJIL* 523–53.

Kamminga M., 'Lessons learned from the exercise of universal jurisdiction in respect of gross human rights offences' (2001) 23 *Human rights quarterly* 940–74.

Kamto M., 'Une troublante immunité totale du ministre des affaires étrangères' (2002) *Revue belge de droit international* 518–30.

Karlshoven F., 'Applicability of customary international law in non-international armed conflicts' in A. Cassese (ed.), *Current problems of international law: essays on UN law and on the laws of armed conflict* (Milan: Giuffre, 1975) p. 276.

Constraints on the waging of war (Geneva: ICRC, 1991).

The law of warfare, a summary of its recent history and trends in development (Leiden, Geneva: Sijthoff, Henry Dunant Institute, 1973).

Karlshoven F. and Sandoz Y. (eds.), *Implementation of international humanitarian law* (Dordrecht: Martinus Nijhoff Publishers, 1989).

Kaul H. and C. Kress, 'Jurisdiction and co-operation in the statute of the ICC: principles and compromises' (1998) 1 *YbIHL* 143.

Keen M. H., *The laws of war in the late middle Ages* (London: Routledge and K. Paul, 1965).

Keller L., 'UNTAC in Cambodia – from occupation, civil war and genocide to peace' (2005) 9 *Max Planck yearbook of United Nations law* 127–78.

Kelly M., 'Transitional justice in peace operations: shaping the twilight zone in Somalia and East Timor' (2001) 4 *YbIHL* 213–51.

Kemper Donovan D., 'Joint UN–Cambodia efforts to establish a Khmer Rouge tribunal' (2003) 44 *Harvard international law journal* 551–76.

Kerr R., *The International Criminal Tribunal for the former Yugoslavia, an exercise in law, politics and diplomacy* (Oxford: Oxford University Press, 2004).

Kessler B., 'The duty to ensure respect under common Article 1 of the Geneva Conventions: its implications on international and non-international armed conflicts' (2001) 44 *German yearbook of international law* 498–516.

Klingberg V., '(Former) heads of state before international(ised) criminal courts: the case of Charles Taylor before the Special Court for Sierra Leone' (2003) 46 *German yearbook of international law* 537–64.

Kolb R., *Ius in bello, Le droit international des conflit armés, Précis* (Basle: Helbing & Lichtenham, 2003).

   'Selected problems in the theory of customary international law' (2003) *NILR* 119–50.

   'The jurisprudence of the Yugoslav and Rwandan Criminal Tribunals on their jurisdiction and on international crimes' (2000) *BYIL* 257.

   'The jurisprudence of the Yugoslav and Rwandan Criminal Tribunals on their jurisdiction and on international crimes 2000–2004' (2004) *BYIL* 269–97.

   'The relationship between international law and human rights: a brief history of the 1948 Universal Declaration of Human Rights and the 1949 Geneva Conventions' (1998) *IRRC* 409.

Kolb R., Porretto G. and Vité S., *L'application du droit international humanitaire et des droits de l'homme aux organisations internationale, Forces de paix et administrations civiles transitoires* (Brussels: Bruylant, 2005) pp. 175–93.

Kontorovich E., 'The piracy analogy: modern universal jurisdiction's hollow foundation' (2004) 45 *Harvard international law journal* 183–237.

Kress C., 'Universal jurisdiction over international crimes and the Institut de droit international' (2006) 4 *JICJ* 561–85.

'War crimes committed in non-international armed conflict and the emerging system of international criminal justice' (2000) 30 *Israel yearbook on human rights* 103–78.

Kress C., Lattanzi F., Bromhall B. and Santori (eds.), *The Rome statute and domestic legal orders, vol. II, constitutional issues, co-operation and enforcement* (Baden-Baden, Ripa di Fagnano Alto: Nomos Verlagsgesellschaft, Il Sirente, 2005).

Kwakwa E., 'The Cairo–Arusha principles on universal jurisdiction in respect of gross human rights offences: developing the frontiers of the principle of universal jurisdiction' (2002) 10 *African yearbook of international law* 407–23.

The international law of armed conflict: personal and material fields of application (Dordrecht: Kluwer, 1992).

La Haye E., 'The elaboration of elements for war crimes' in Lattanzi F. and Schabas W. (eds.), *Essays on the Rome statute of the International Criminal Court* (Ripa di Fagnano Alto: Il Sirente, 2004) vol. II, pp. 305–31.

'The jurisdiction of the International Criminal Court: controversies over the pre-conditions for the exercise of its jurisdiction' (1999) 46 *Netherlands international law review* 1–25.

La Haye E. *et al.*, 'War crimes' in R. Lee (ed.), *The International Criminal Court: elements of crimes and rules of procedure and evidence* (Ardsley, New York: Transnational Publishers, 2001).

Lachs M., *War crimes, an attempt to define the issues* (London: Stevens, 1945).

Lattanzi F., 'La répression pénale des crimes du droit international: des juridictions internes aux juridictions internationales' in *Law in humanitarian crises: how can international humanitarian law be made effective in armed conflicts?* (Luxembourg: Office for the official publications of the European Communities, vol. 1, 1995).

Lattanzi F. (ed.), *Dai tribunali penali internationazionali ad hoc a una corte permanente* (Naples: Ed. Scientifica, 1996).

Lattanzi F. and Schabas W. (eds.), *Essays on the Rome statute of the International Criminal Court* (Ripa di Fagnano Alto: Il Sirente, 2004), vol. II.

Lauterpacht H., 'The law of nations and the punishment of war crimes' (1944) *BYIL* 58–95.

Recognition in international law (Cambridge: Cambridge University Press, 1947).

Lee R. (ed.), *The International Criminal Court: the making of the Rome statute issues, negotiations and results* (The Hague: Kluwer Law International, 1999).

Levie H., 'War crimes' in Schmitt M. (ed.), *The law of military operations: lieber amicorum Jack Grunawalt* (Newport, Rhode Island: Naval War College, 1998) pp. 95–112.

Linton S., 'New approaches to international justice in Cambodia and East Timor' (2002) 84 *IRRC* 83–119.

'Prosecuting atrocities at the district court of Dili' (2001) 2 *Melbourne journal of international law* 414.

'Unravelling the first three trials at Indonesia's ad hoc court for human rights violations in East Timor' (2004) 17 *Leiden journal of international law* 303–61.

Lomblois C., 'De la compassion territoriale' (1995) *Revue de sciences criminelles et de droit pénal comparé* 399.

Luard E. (ed.), *The international regulation of civil wars* (London: Thames and Hudson, 1972).

Macedo S. (ed.), *Universal jurisdiction, national courts and the prosecution of serious crimes under international law* (Philadelphia: University of Pennsylvania Press, 2004).

Maison R., 'Les premiers cas d'application des dispositions pénales des Conventions de Genève par les juridictions internes' (1995) 6 *EJIL* 260.

Manuell J. and Kontic A., 'Transitional justice: the prosecution of war crimes in Bosnia and Herzegovina under the rules of the road' (2002) 4 *YbIHL* 331–43.

Maogoto J., 'The ICTR: a paper umbrella in the rain? Initial pitfalls and brighter prospects' (2004) *Nordic journal of international law* 187–221.

War crimes and realpolitik, international justice from World War I to the twenty-first century (London: Lynne Rienner Publishers, 2004).

Maresca L., 'Second review conference of the Convention on Certain Conventional Weapons' (2002) 845 *IRRC* 255.

Marschik A., 'The politics of prosecution: European national approaches to war crimes' in McCormack T. and Simpson G. (eds.), *The law of war crimes* (The Hague, London, Boston: Kluwer Law International, 1997) pp. 77–82.

Maslen S. and Herby P., 'An international ban on anti-personnel mines, history and negotiation of the Ottawa treaty' (1998) *IRRC* 693–713.

Masse M., 'Ex-Yugouslavie, Rwanda: une compétence virtuelle des juridictions française' (1997) *Revue de sciences criminelles* 893.

Matheson M. J., 'Humanitarian law conference, remarks of Michael J. Matheson' (1987) 2 *American University Journal of international law and policy*.

May R. *et al.* (eds.), *Essays on ICTY procedure and evidence in honour of Gabrielle Kirk McDonald* (The Hague: Kluwer Law International, 2001).

McCormack T., 'Selective reaction to atrocity: war crimes and the development of international criminal law' (1997) 60 *Albany law review* 681–731.

McCormack T. and Simpson G. (eds.), *The law of war crimes* (The Hague, London, Boston: Kluwer Law International, 1997).

McDonald A., 'Sierra Leone's shoestring Special Court' (2002) *IRRC* 121.

MacDonald G. K., 'Problems, obstacles and achievements of the ICTY' (2004) 2 *JICJ* 558–71.

MacDonald G. and Swaak-Goldman O. (eds.), *Substantive and procedural aspects of international criminal law: the experience of international and national courts* (The Hague: Kluwer Law International, 2000), vol. 1.

McGoldrick D., Rowe P. and Donnelly E. (eds.), *The Permanent International Criminal Court, legal and policy issues* (Oxford and Portland, Oregon: Hart Publishing, 2004).

Megally H. and van Zyl P., 'US justice with an Iraqi face' *International Herald Tribune* (4 December 2003).

Megret F., 'Epilogue to an endless debate: the ICC's third party jurisdiction and the looming revolution of international law' (2001) 12 *EJIL* 247–68.

Meisenberg S., 'Legality of amnesties in international humanitarian law: the Lomé amnesty decision of the Special Court for Sierra Leone' (2004) 86 *IRRC* 837–51.

Meron T., 'Classification of armed conflict in the former Yugoslavia: Nicaragua's fallout' (1998) 92 *AJIL* 240.

'Crimes and accountability in Shakespeare' (1998) 92 *AJIL* 1–40.

'Francis Lieber's code and principles of humanity' (1997) 36 *Columbia journal of transnational law* 271–81.

'International criminalisation of internal atrocities' (1995) 89 *AJIL* 561.

'Reflections on the prosecutions of war crimes by international tribunals' (2006) 100 *AJIL* 551–79.

'The continuing role of custom in the formation of international humanitarian law' (1996) 90 *AJIL* 242.

'The Geneva Conventions as customary law' (1987) 81 *AJIL* 359.

'War crimes in Yugoslavia and the development of international law' (1994) 88 *AJIL* 78.

Henry's wars and Shakespeare's laws: perspectives on the law of war in the later Middle Ages (Oxford: Clarendon Press, 1993).

Human rights and humanitarian norms as customary law (Oxford: Clarendon Press, 1989).

Mettraux G., 'Dutch courts' universal jurisdiction over violations of common Article 3 qua war crimes' (2006) 4 *JICJ* 362–71.

'US courts-martial and the armed conflict in the Philippines (1899–1902): their contribution to national case law on war crimes' (2003) 1 *JICJ* 135.

International crimes and the ad hoc Tribunals (Oxford: Oxford University Press, 2005).

Meyrowitz H., 'Le droit de la guerre dans le conflit vietnamien' (1967) *AFDI* 156.

Minear R. H., *Victors' justice, the Tokyo war crimes trial* (Princeton: Princeton University Press, 1971).

Mochochoko P., 'International co-operation and judicial assistance' in Lee R. (ed.), *The International Criminal Court, the making of the Rome statute* (The Hague, Boston: Kluwer Law International, 1999) p. 305.

Moir L., 'The historical development of the application of humanitarian law in non-international armed conflict to 1949' (1998) 47 *ICLQ* 337–61.

    The law of internal armed conflict (Cambridge: Cambridge University Press, 2002).

Möller A., *International law in peace and war* (Copenhagen: Levin & Munksgaard, 1935).

Momtaz D., 'Le droit international humanitaire applicable aux conflits armés non internationaux' (2001) 292 *Recueil des cours* 49–55.

    'War crimes in non-international armed conflicts under the statute of the International Criminal Court' (1999) 2 *YbIHL* p. 177.

Moore J., *Law and civil war in the modern world* (Baltimore: John Hopkins University Press, 1974).

Morris M., 'International guidelines against impunity: facilitating accountability' (1996) 59 *Law and contemporary problems* 29–39.

    'Universal jurisdiction in a divided world' (2001) 35 *New England law review* 337.

Mubiala M., 'Le tribunal international pour le Rwanda' (1995) 7 *African journal of international and comparative law* 610.

Mundis D., 'New mechanisms for the enforcement of international humanitarian law' (2001) 95 *AJIL* 939–42.

    'Reporting non-compliance: rule 7*bis*', in May R. *et al.* (eds.), *Essays on ICTY procedure and evidence in honour of Gabrielle Kirk McDonald* (The Hague: Kluwer Law International, 2001) pp. 421–38.

Murphy S., 'Progress and jurisprudence of the ICTY' (1999) 93 *AJIL* 57.

Myren R., 'Applying international laws of war to non-international armed conflicts: past attempts and future strategies' (1990) 37 *NILR* 367.

Naarden G., 'Non-prosecutorial sanctions for grave violations of international humanitarian law: wartime conduct of Bosnian police officials' (2003) 97 *AJIL* 342–52.

Newton M., 'The Iraqi high criminal court: controversy and contributions' (2006) 88 *IRRC* 399–425.

Nwogugu E. I. V., 'The Nigerian civil war: a case study in the law of war' (1974) 14 *Indian journal of international law* 13–53.

O'Brien J., 'The international tribunal for violations of international humanitarian law in the former Yugoslavia' (1993) 67 *AJIL* 639.

O'Donnell D., 'Trends in the application of international humanitarian law by UN human rights mechanisms' (1998) *IRRC* 481.

O'Keefe R., 'Universal jurisdiction: clarifying the basic concept' (2004) 2 *JICJ* 735–60.

O'Shea S., 'Interaction between international criminal tribunals and national legal systems' (1995–96) 28 *International law and politics* 393.

Oellers-Frahm K., 'Co-operation; the indispensable prerequisite to the efficiency of International Criminal Tribunals' (1995) ASIL proceedings p. 304.

Olsen O., 'Investigation of serious crimes in East Timor' in Ambos K. and Othman M. (eds.), *New approaches in international criminal justice: Kosovo, East Timor, Sierra Leone and Cambodia* (Freiburg: Max Planck Institute for International Law, 2003) pp. 113–30.

Olson L., 'Provoking the dragon on the patio. Matters of transitional justice: penal repression vs. amnesties' (2006) 88 *IRRC* 275–94.

Oppenheim L. and Lauterpacht H., *International law – a treatise* (London: Longman, Green and Co., 1952).

Orentlicher D. *et al.*, *Making justice work: the report of the Century Foundation* (New York: Century Foundation Press, 1998).

Osiel M., 'Why prosecute? Critics of punishment of mass atrocities' (2000) 22 *Human rights quarterly* 118.

Othman M., 'East Timor: a critique of the model of accountability for serious human rights and international humanitarian law violations' (2003) 72 *Nordic journal of international law* 449–82.

'The framework of prosecutions and the court system in East Timor', in Ambos K. and Othman M. (eds.), *New approaches in international criminal justice: Kosovo, East Timor, Sierra Leone and Cambodia* (Freiburg: Max Planck Institute for International Law, 2003) pp. 85–112.

Pack M., 'Developments at the Special Court for Sierra Leone' (2005) 4 *Law and practice of international courts and tribunals* 171–92.

Padelford N., 'International law and the Spanish Civil War' (1937) 31 *AJIL* 226–43.

Paust J., 'Applicability of international criminal laws to events in the former Yugoslavia' (1994) 9 *American University journal of international law and policy* 499.

Pazartzis P., 'Tribunaux pénaux internationalisés: une nouvelle approche de la justice pénale (inter)nationale?' (2003) *AFDI* 641–61.

Pellet A., 'Le Tribunal criminel international pour l'ex-Yougoslavie: poudre aux yeux ou avancée décisive?' (1995) *RGDIP* 7.

Perna L., 'Written and customary provisions relating to the conduct of hostilities and treatment of victims of armed conflicts in ancient India' (1989) *IRRC* 340.

The formation of the treaty law of non-international armed conflicts (Leiden, Boston: Martinus Nijhoff Publishers, 2006).

Philippe X., 'The principle of universal jurisdiction and complementarity: how do the two principles intermesh?'(2006) 88 *IRRC* 375–98.

Phillipson C., *The international law and custom of ancient Greece and Rome* (London: Macmillan and Co., 1911).

Pictet J., *The Geneva Conventions of 12 August 1949 – commentary to Convention I* (Geneva: ICRC, 1952).

The Geneva Conventions of 12 August 1949 – commentary on the IV Geneva Convention relative to the protection of civilian persons in times of war (Geneva: ICRC, 1958).

Commentary on the Geneva Conventions of 12 August 1949 (Geneva: ICRC, 1960).

Pigaroff D., 'Protection of national security information', in Lee R. (ed.), *The ICC, the making of the Rome statute* (The Hague, Boston: Kluwer Law International, 1999) p. 270.

Pinto R., 'Les règles du droit international concernant la guerre civile' (1965/I) 114 *Recueil des cours* 482.

Plattner D., 'The penal repression of violations of international humanitarian law applicable in non-international armed conflicts' (1990) 30 *IRRC* 424.

Politi M. and Nesi G., *The Rome statute of the International Criminal Court, a challenge to impunity* (Aldershot: Ashgate, 2001).

Poirat F., 'Immunité de juridiction pénale du chef d'etat étranger en exercise et règle coutumière devant le juge judiciaire' (2001) *RDGIP* 473–91.

Provost R., *International human rights and humanitarian law* (Cambridge: Cambridge University Press, 2002).

Queguinner J. F., 'Dix ans après la création du Tribunal pénal international pour l'ex-Yougoslavie: évaluation de l'apport de sa jurisprudence au droit international humanitaire' (2003) 85 *IRRC* 279–81.

Quénivet N., 'The Moscow hostage crisis in the light of the armed conflict in Chechnya' (2001) *YbIHL* 348–72.

Randall K. C, 'Universal jurisdiction under international law' (1998) 66 *Texas law review* 785–841.

Ratner S., 'Belgium's war crimes statute: a postmortem' (2003) 97 *AJIL* 888–97.

Ratner S. and Abrams J., *Accountability for human rights atrocities in international law* (Oxford: Oxford University Press, 1997).

Reidy A., 'The approach of the European Commission and Court of Human Rights to international humanitarian law' (1998) *IRRC* 513.

Reisman W. M., 'On paying the piper: financial responsibility for Security Council referrals to the ICC' (2005) 99 *AJIL* 615–18.

Reverdin O., 'Le Général Guillaume-Henri Dufour, précurseur d'Henri Dunant' in Swinarski C. (ed.), *Studies and essays on international humanitarian law and Red Cross principles in honour of J. Pictet* (Geneva : ICRC, Martinus Njihoff Publishers, 1984) pp. 951–58.

Reydams L., 'Universal jurisdiction over atrocities in Rwanda' (1996) 1 *European journal of crime, criminal law and criminal justice* 18–47.

Universal jurisdiction: international and municipal legal perspectives (Oxford: Oxford University Press, 2003).

Rinoldi D. and Parisi N., 'International co-operation and judicial assistance between the ICC and states parties' in Lattanzi F. and Schabas W. (eds.), *Essays on the Rome statute of the ICC* (Ripa di Fagnano Alto: Il Sirente, 1999) vol. I, p. 339.

Roberts A., 'Traditional and modern approaches to customary international law: a reconciliation' (2001) 95 *AJIL* 757–91.

Roberts A. and Guelf R. (eds.), *Documents on the laws of war* (Oxford: Clarendon Press, 1989).

Robertson A., 'Humanitarian law and human rights' in Swinarski C. (ed.), *Studies and essays on international humanitarian law and Red Cross principles, in honour of J. Pictet* (Geneva : ICRC, Martinus Njihoff Publishers, 1984) p. 793.

Robinson D., 'Implementing international crimes: the Canadian approach' in *Acts of the Berlin Conference on 'the Rome Statute, what's next: domestic and foreign approaches to the implementation of international criminal law in national law'* (Berlin: Reader & International Criminal Law Society, 2000) p. 26.

'The impact of the human rights accountability movement on the international law of immunities' (2002) *Canadian yearbook of international law* 151–91.

Robinson D. and H. v. Hebel, 'War crimes in internal armed conflicts: article 8 of the ICC Statute' (1999) 2 *YbIHL* 193.

Roht-Arriaza N. and Gibson L., 'The developing jurisprudence on amnesty' (1998) 20 *Human rights quarterly* 865.

Röling B., 'Aspects of the criminal responsibility for violations of the laws of war' in Cassese A. (ed.), *The new humanitarian law of armed conflicts* (Naples: Editoriale Scientifica, 1979) pp. 199–231.

'Criminal responsibility for violations of the laws of war' (1976) 12 *Revue belge de droit international* 13.

Romano C. P., 'The price of international justice' (2005) 4 *Law and practice of international courts and tribunals* 281–328, 296.

Rosensweig L. and Blank, 'The laws of war in Shakespeare: international vs. internal armed conflict' (1997–1998) 30 *International law and politics* 251–90.

Rowe P., 'Liability for war crimes during a non-international armed conflict' (1996) *Military law and laws of war review* 152.

'The International Criminal Tribunal for Yugoslavia: the decision of the Appeals Chamber on the interlocutory appeal on jurisdiction in the *Tadić* case' (1996) 45 *ICLQ* 691.

'War crimes and the former Yugoslavia, the legal difficulties' (1993) 32 *Revue de droit militaire et droit de la guerre* 317.

Rupesinghe K., *Civil wars, civil peace, an introduction to conflict resolution* (London: Pluto Press, 1998).

Salmon J., 'Libres propos sur l'arrêt de la CIJ du 14 février 2002 dans l'affaire relative au mandat d'arrêt du 11 avril 2000' (2002) *Revue belge de droit international* 512–17.

Sandoz Y., 'Implementing international humanitarian law' in UNESCO, *International dimensions of humanitarian law* (Dordrecht: Henry Dunant Institute, UNESCO, Martinus Nijhoff, 1988) pp. 259–82.

'Penal aspects of international humanitarian law' in Bassiouni C. (ed.), *International criminal law* (Dobbs Ferry: International Publishers, 1986) vol. I, pp. 209–32.

Sandoz Y., Swinarski C. and Zimmermann R. (eds.), *Commentary on the Additional Protocols of 1977 to the Geneva Conventions of 1949* (Geneva: ICRC, Martinus Nijhoff, 1987).

Sands P., 'What is the ICJ for?' (2002) *Revue belge de droit international* 537–45.

Sarooshi D., 'The peace and justice paradox: the ICC and the UN Security Council' in McGoldrick D., Rowe P. and Donnelly E. (eds.), *The permanent international criminal court, legal and policy issues* (Oxford and Portland Oregon: Hart Publishing, 2004) p. 102.

'The powers of the UN International Criminal Tribunals' (1998) 2 *Max Planck yearbook of UN law* p. 141.

Sassoli M., 'La première décision de la chambre d'appel du Tribunal Pénal International pour l'ex-Yougoslavie' (1996) 100 *RGDIP* 129.

'Le génocide rwandais, la justice militaire suisse et le droit international' (2002) 2 *Revue suisse de droit international et européen* 151–77.

Sassoli M. and Bouvier A. (eds.), *How does law protect in war?* (Geneva: ICRC, 1999).

Schachter O., 'International law in theory and practice, general course in public international law' (1982) 78 *Recueil des cours* 262.

Scharf M., 'Is it international enough? A critique of the Iraqi Special Tribunal in light of the goals of international justice' (2004) 2 *JICJ* 330–37.

'The letter of the law: the scope of international legal obligation to prosecute human rights crime' (1996) 59 *Law and contemporary problems* 41.

Scheffer D., 'The United States and the ICC' (1999) 93 *AJIL* 12.

Schindler D., 'Le droit international humanitaire et les conflits armés internationalisés' (1982) *IRRC* 263.

'The different types of armed conflict according to the Geneva Conventions and Protocols' (1979) 163 *Recueil des cours* 151.

Schindler D. and Toman J. (eds.), *The laws of armed conflict. A collection of conventions, resolutions and other documents* (Dordrecht: Martinus Nijhoff, 1996).

Schlögel A., 'Civil war' (1970) 108 *IRRC* 123–34.

Schmitt M. N. (ed.), *International law studies: the law of military operations, lieber amicorum Professor J. Grunawalt* (Newport, Rhode Island: Naval War College, 1998).

Schmitt M. and Green L. (eds.), *The law of armed conflicts into the next millennium* (Newport, Rhode Island: Naval War College, 1998).

Sezibera R., 'The only way to bring justice to Rwanda' *Washington Post*, 7 April 2002.

Shany Y., 'Does one size fit all? Reading the jurisdictional provisions of the new Iraqi Special Tribunal statute in the light of the statutes of the International Criminal Tribunals' (2004) 2 *JICJ* 338–46.

Shaw M., *International Law*, 3rd edn (Cambridge: Cambridge University Press, 1997).

Shraga D. and Zacklin R., 'The International Criminal Tribunal for Rwanda' (1996) 7 *EJIL* 501.

Siotis, *Le droit de la guerre et les conflits armés d'un caractère non international* (Paris: Librairie de droit et de jurisprudence, 1958).

SIPRI Yearbook, armaments, disarmament and international security (Oxford: Oxford University Press, 2005 and 2006).

Slade T. and Clark R., 'Preamble and final clauses' in Lee R. (ed.), *The International Criminal Court, the making of the Rome statute, issues, negotiations, results* (The Hague, London, Boston: Kluwer Law International, 1999) pp. 421–50.

Sluiter G., 'Obtaining evidence for the ICTY: an overview and assessment of domestic implementing legislation' (1998) *NILR* 87.

'To co-operate or not to co-operate? The case of the failed transfer of Ntakirutimana to the Rwanda Tribunal' (1998) 11 *Leiden journal of international law* 383.

Smith B., *Reaching judgment at Nuremberg* (London: Andre Deutsch Ltd, 1977).

Sob P., 'The dynamics of International Criminal Tribunals' (1998) 67 *Nordic journal of international law* 139.

Spieker H., 'The International Criminal Court and non-international armed conflicts' (2000) 13 *Leiden journal of international law* 395–425.

'Twenty-five years after the adoption of additional Protocol II: breakthrough or failure of humanitarian legal protection?' (2001) 4 *YbIHL* 129–66.

Sriram C. L., 'Globalising justice: from universal jurisdiction to mixed tribunals' (2004) 22/1 *Netherlands quarterly of human rights* 20–25.

Stafford N. K., 'A model war crimes court: Sierra Leone' (2003) 10 *ILSA Journal of international and comparative law* 117–42.

Stahn C., 'Why some doors may be closed already: second thoughts on a case-by-case treatment of Article 12(3) declarations' (2006) 75 *Nordic journal of international law* 243–48.

Stahn C., El Zeidy M. and Olasolo H., 'The ICC's ad hoc jurisdiction revisited' (2005) 99 *AJIL* 421–31.

Stern B., 'La compétence universelle en France: le cas des crimes commis en ex-Yougoslavie et au Rwanda' (1997) 40 *German yearbook of international law* 280–99.

Stewart James, 'Towards a single definition of armed conflict in international humanitarian law: a critique of internationalized armed conflict' (2003) 85 *IRRC* 313–49.

Strohmeyer H., 'Collapse and reconstruction of a judicial system: the United Nations missions in Kosovo and East Timor' (2001) 95 *AJIL* 46.

Stromseth J. (ed.), *Accountability for atrocities, national and international responses* (Ardsley, New York: Transnational Publishers, 2003).

Sun Tzu, *The art of war* (Oxford: Clarendon Press, 1963).

Sunga L., 'The first indictments of the ICTR' (1997) 18 *Human rights law journal* 329.

Swaak-Goldman O., 'Recent developments in international criminal law: trying to stay afloat between Scylla and Charybdis' (2005) 54 *ICLQ* 691–704.

Swinarski C. (ed.), *Studies and essays on international humanitarian law and Red Cross principles in honour of J. Pictet* (Geneva: ICRC, Martinus Njihoff Publishers, 1984).

Taubenfeld H. J., 'The applicability of the laws of war in civil war' in Moore J. (ed.), *Law and civil war in the modern world* (Baltimore: John Hopkins University Press, 1974) pp. 499–517.

Taylor R. S., 'Better later than never: Cambodia's joint tribunal' in Stromseth J., *Accountability for atrocities, national and international responses* (Ardsley, New York: Transnational Publishers, 2003) pp. 237–70.

The manual of the law of armed conflict, UK Ministry of Defence (Oxford: Oxford University Press, 2004).

Ticehurst R., 'The Martens Clause and the laws of armed conflict' (1997) *IRRC* 125–34.

Tomushat C., 'Universal jurisdiction with respect to the crime of genocide, crimes against humanity and war crimes', *Yearbook of the Institute of International Law* (Paris: Pedone, 2005) vol. 71, part1, pp. 252–53.

Triffterer O. (ed.), *Commentary on the Rome statute of the International Criminal Court, observers' notes, article by article* (Baden-Baden: Nomos Verlagsgesellschaft, 1999).

Turns D., 'At the vanishing point of international humanitarian law: methods and means of warfare in non-international armed conflicts' (2002) 45 *German yearbook of international law* 115–48 at 122–26.

'Certain criminal proceedings in France (*Republic of Congo v. France*) provisional measures order of 17 June 2003' (2004) *ICLQ* 747–52.

'War crimes without war? The applicability of international humanitarian law to atrocities in non-international conflicts' (1995) 7 *African journal of international and comparative law* 808.

Tusa A., *The Nuremberg trial* (New York: Cooper Square Press, 2003).

Umozurike U. O., 'The application of international humanitarian law to civil conflicts' (1992) 4 *African journal of international and comparative law* 500.

United Nations War Crimes Commission, *Law reports of trials of war criminals*, vol. 1 (London: HMSO, 1947).

The history of the UN War Crimes Commission and the development of the laws of war (London: HMSO, 1948).

Law reports of trials of war criminals, vol. 8 (London: HMSO, 1949).

Law reports of trials of war criminals, vol. 15 (London: HMSO, 1949).

Van der Stoel M., Report on the situation of human rights in Iraq, Special Rapporteur of the Commission on Human Rights, UN.Doc.E/CN./1992/31 (18 February 1992).

Van Elst R., 'Implementing universal jurisdiction over grave breaches of the Geneva Conventions' (2000) *Leiden journal of international law* 815.

Veuthey M., 'Les conflits armés de caractère non international et le droit humanitaire' in Cassese A. (ed.), *Current problems of international law: essays on UN law and on the laws of armed conflict*, (Milan: Giuffre, 1975) p. 246.

Von Clausewitz C., *On war* (Princeton N. J.: Princeton University Press, 1989).

Von Hebel H. and Robinson D., 'Crimes within the jurisdiction of the court' in Lee R. (ed.), *The International Criminal Court, the making of the Rome statute, issues, negotiations, results* (The Hague: Kluwer Law International, 1999) pp. 79–141.

Weckel P., 'L'institution d'un tribunal international pour la répression des crimes de droit humanitaire en Yougoslavie' (1993) 39 *AFDI* 232.

Wedgwood R., 'National courts and the prosecution of war crimes' in MacDonald G. and Swaak-Goldman O., (eds.), *Substantive and procedural aspects of international criminal law: the experience of international and national courts* (The Hague: Kluwer Law International, 2000) vol. 1, pp. 393–413.

'The ICC: an American view' (1999) 10 *EJIL* 93.

'The International Criminal Tribunal and subpoenas for state documents' in Schmitt M. and Green L. (eds.), *The law of armed conflicts into the next millenium*, vol. 71 (Newport, Rhode Island: Naval War College, 1998).

Wehberg H., 'La guerre civile et le droit international' (1938/I) 63 *Recueil des cours* 63.

Wells D., *War crimes and the laws of war,* 2nd edn (Lanham: University Press of America, 1991).

Wenqi Z., 'On co-operation by states not party to the ICC' (2006) 88 *IRRC* 87–110.

Weyembergh A., 'La notion de conflit armé, le droit international humanitaire et les forces des Nations Unies en Somalie' (1999) *Revue de droit pénal et de criminologie* 177–201.

Wheaton H., *Elements of international law*, 8th edn edited by R. Dana (London: Sampson Low, Son & Co., 1866).

Wickremasinghe C., 'Arrest warrant of 11 April 2000 (*RDC v. Belgium*), preliminary objections and merits, judgment of 14 February 2002' (2003) *ICLQ* 775–81.

Wieviorka A. (ed.), *Les procès de Nuremberg et de Tokyo* (Brussels: Editions Complexe, 1996).

Williams S. A., 'The Rome statute on the ICC – universal jurisdiction or state consent to make or break the package deal' in Schmitt M. (ed.), *International law across the spectrum of conflict: essays in honour of Professor L.C. Green on the occasion of his eightieth birthday* (Newport, Rhode Island: Naval War College, 2000) vol. 75, pp. 539–63.

Williams S., 'The Cambodian extraordinary chambers – a dangerous precedent for international justice?' (2004) 53 *ICLQ* 227–45.

Winants A., 'The Yerodia ruling of the ICJ and the 1993/99 Belgian law on universal jurisdiction' (2003) 16 *Leiden journal of international law* 491–509.

Wippman D., 'The costs of international justice' (2006) 100 *AJIL* 861–87.

Wirth S., 'Immunity for core crimes: the ICJ's judgment in the *Congo v. Belgium case*' (2002) 13 *EJIL* 877–93.

Wolfke K., *Custom in present international law* (Dordrecht, Boston: Martinus Nijhoff, 1993).

Wolfrum R., 'Prosecution of international crimes by international and national criminal courts: concurring jurisdiction' in *Studi di diritto internazionale in onore di Gaetano Arango-Ruiz* (Naples: Editoriale Scientifica, 2004) vol. 3, pp. 2200–1.

'The decentralised prosecution of international offences through national courts' (1994) 24 *Israel yearbook of human rights* 183–201.

Woolsey T., *Introduction to the study of international law*, 4th edn (London: Sampson Low, Marston, Low & Searle, 1875).

Wouters J. and De Smet L., 'The ICJ's judgment in the case concerning the arrest warrant of 11 April 2000: some critical observations' (2001) 4 *YbIHL* 373–88.

Yee S. and Tieya W. (eds.), *International law in the post-cold war world: essays in memory of Li Haopei* (London: Routledge, 2001).

Zacklin R., 'The failings of ad hoc international tribunals' (2004) 2 *JICJ* 545.

Zakane V., 'La compétence universelle des états dans le droit international contemporain' (2000) 8 *African yearbook of international law* 183–222.

Zappala S., 'Do heads of state in office enjoy immunity from jurisdiction for international crimes? The Ghaddafi case before the French cour de cassation' (2001) 12 *EJIL* 595–612.

'The German Federal Prosecutor's decision not to prosecute a former Uzbek minister' (2006) 4 *JICJ* 602–22.

Zegveld L., 'The Inter-American Commission on Human Rights and international humanitarian law: a comment on the *Tablada* case' (1998) *IRRC* 505.

Accountability of armed opposition groups in international law (Cambridge: Cambridge University Press, 2002).

Zemanek K., 'The legal foundations of the international system' (1997) 226 *Recueil des cours* 157–67.

Ziegler A., 'Domestic prosecution and international co-operation with regard to violations of international humanitarian law: the case of Switzerland' (1997) 5 *Revue suisse de droit international et droit européen* 561–85.

Zwinarski C. (ed.), *Etudes et essais sur le droit international humanitaire et sur les principes de la Croix-Rouge en l'honneur de Jean Pictet* (Geneva, Dordrecht: ICRC, Martinus Nijhoff Publishers, 1984).

INDEX